Contents

About the Guide

This third edition of the *Time Out Rome Guide* has been revised and rewritten by a team of experts who live and work in Rome. It is one in a series of 17 city guides that includes London, Paris, Prague, Budapest, New York, San Francisco and Sydney. The *Time Out Rome Guide* gives you a complete picture of Rome, from the architectural glories and major tourist sites, to the most obscure *osteria* to the hippest bar. What's more, you'll get the lowdown on everything from the food served up at Roman banquets to the precise time of day to drink *cappuccino*, from the Vatican's new craze for technology to hotel rooms for sadomasochists. Most guides linger on Rome's extraordinary past; the *Time Out Guide* goes further, continuing into its thriving and constantly surprising present.

CHECKED AND CORRECT

As far as possible, all the information in this guide was checked and correct at the time of writing. However, Roman owners and managers can be highly erratic in their answers to questions about opening times, the dates of exhibitions, admission fees, and even their address and phone number: you have been warned. Wherever you're going, it's always a good idea to phone before setting out,

and even then the information you receive is not always reliable.

In particular, we have tried to include information on access for travellers with disabilities, but once again it's wise to phone first to check that your needs can be met.

PRICES

The prices listed throughout this guide should be taken as guidelines. However, low inflation and a steady exchange rate that favours pound- and dollar-wielding visitors mean that the unpleasant surprises common a few years ago should now be a thing of the past. If prices and services somewhere vary greatly from those we have quoted, ask if there's a good reason. If not, go elsewhere and then please let us know. We try to give the best and most up-to-date advice, so we always want to hear if you've been overcharged or badly treated.

CREDIT CARDS

Throughout the guide, the following abbreviations have been used for credit cards: **AmEx** American Express; **DC** Diners' Club; **EC** Eurocheque card; **MC** Mastercard/Access; **V** Visa/Barclaycard.

BOLD

Within any chapter, we may mention people, places or events that are listed elsewhere in the guide. In these cases we have highlighted the person, place or event by printing it in **bold**. This means you can find it in the index and locate its full listing.

RIGHT TO REPLY

It should be stressed that in all cases the information we give is impartial. No organisation or enterprise had been included in this guide because its owner or manager has advertised in our publications. We hope you enjoy the *Time Out Rome Guide* but if you disagree with any of our reviews, let us know. Your comments on places you have visited are always welcome and will be taken into account when we compile future editions of the guide. For this purpose, you will find a reader's reply card at the back of the book.

There's an on-line version of this guide, as well as all the weekly events listings information for Rome and other international cities at:
http://www.timeout.co.uk

Edited and designed by
Time Out Guides Limited
Universal House
251 Tottenham Court Road
London W1P OAB
Tel + 44 (0)171 813 3000
Fax + 44 (0)171 813 6001
E-mail net@timeout.co.uk
http://www.timeout.co.uk

Editorial
Managing Editor Peter Fiennes
Editor Anne Hanley
Copy Editor Ian Cunningham
Researcher Fulvia Angelini
Indexer Jacqueline Brind

Design
Art Director John Oakey
Art Editor Paul Tansley
Designer Mandy Martin
Picture Editor Catherine Hardcastle
Picture Researcher Michaela Freeman

Advertising
Group Advertisement Director Lesley Gill
Sales Director Mark Phillips
Advertisement Sales (Rome) Margherita Tedone

Administration
Publisher Tony Elliott
Managing Director Mike Hardwick
Financial Director Kevin Ellis
Marketing Director Gillian Auld
Production Manager Mark Lamond
Accountant Catherine Bowen

Features in this Guide were written and researched by:

Introduction Michael Dibdin. **History** Ferdie McDonald, *Extracting the Urine* Anne Hanley, *Myths of the Decline and Fall, The Feats of Santa Francesca* Robert Adams, *Party Lines* Sarah Delaney. **Rome Today** Andrew Gumbel, *Rome by Numbers* Anne Hanley. **Architecture** Paul Duncan, Ros Belford. **Rome by Season** Anne Hanley, William Ward. **Sightseeing** Anne Hanley, William Ward, Ros Belford, *The Ghetto* Lee Marshall, *The Magnificent Seven* Peter Douglas, Charles Lambert, *Tales of the City* Peter Douglas, *A Rome with a View, The Green, Green Parts of Rome* Peter Douglas, Charles Lambert. **Ancient Sites** Jane Shaw, Ros Belford, *Getting into Locked Sites* Anne Hanley. **Churches** Robert Adams, Sam Cole, Sarah Delaney. **Museums & Galleries** Charles Lambert, Jane Shaw, *Artemisia* Anne Hanley. **The Vatican City** Philippa Hitchen, William Ward. **Accommodation** Fiona Benson, Jane Shaw. **Restaurants** Lee Marshall. **Snacks** Lee Marshall, *Eating In* Anne Hanley. **Wine Bars** Lee Marshall. **Cafés & Bars** Sarah Delaney, *How to Handle the Roman Bar* Lee Marshall. **Pubs** Lee Marshall, *Bar Humbug* Peter Douglas. **Ice Cream** Lee Marshall. **Shopping** Charles Lambert, Peter Douglas. **Services** Charles Lambert, Peter Douglas. **Children** Sarah Delaney, Lee Marshall. **Film** Lee Marshall. **Gay Rome** Peter Douglas, Charles Lambert. **Lesbian Rome** Christine Eade. **Media** Andrew Gumbel. **Music: Classical & Opera** Robert Adams. **Music: Rock, Roots & Jazz** Mike Cooper. **Nightlife** Kier Fraser. **Sport & Fitness** Tom Wright. **Theatre & Dance** Linda Bordoni. **Trips Out of Town** Lee Marshall, Sam Cole, Charles Lambert, *Car-free Jaunts, This Sporting Life* Anne Hanley. **Directory: Essential Information** Jane Shaw, Sam Cole. **Getting Around** Peter Douglas, Sam Cole. **Women's Rome** Christine Eade. **Living & Working in Rome** Jane Shaw, Peter Douglas, Anne Hanley.

The Editor would like to thank Shirley Herbert, Fulvia Angelini and the staff of Hotel Celio for all their help.

Maps by Mapworld

Photography by Francesca Yorke except for: pages 33, 209 **Anthony Cullen**. The picture on page 96 was supplied by the featured establishment.

Introduction

Actually, I am probably the last person who should be writing this introduction, since what I like doing in Rome is something which requires no guide book – that is, nothing. Doing nothing *alla romana* is not a question of idleness or indolence. On the contrary, it is extremely demanding and rewarding activity which the Romans have raised to the level of an art form. At its best, it involves experiences which will sound random and meaningless to anyone else, but which you will remember for the rest of your life.

Nevertheless, Rome notoriously contains a large number of obligatory tourist sites to which sooner or later you will have to pay your respects. Unless you are in the enviable position of being able to stay for a month, this means that two trips will be necessary. The first will be taken up with battling the crowds and the one-way system to the Vatican Museums, wondering what Saint Peter's has got to recommend it beyond sheer size, and trying to work out if that vestigial foundation in the Forum is the Temple of Mars or Jupiter – to say nothing of discovering that the church or museum you've spent an hour getting to is *chiuso per restauro* and has been for longer than it took to build it in the first place.

The pay-off for all this cultural earnestness comes with the second visit, when you can start the serious business of doing nothing. In fact, you should start several weeks before arrival, by getting as fit as you would if planning an Alpine walking tour. Unless you are a racing driver and/or own a tank, don't even think about driving in Rome. Public transport tends to be chaotic, crowded and largely incomprehensible even to the locals. The only way to do nothing is on foot. Bring a pair of comfortable, thick-soled shoes and be prepared to walk ten miles a day, and not just on the flat. Remember the famous Seven Hills of Rome? They're still there.

The first stage is to set off early in the morning and then get lost. Getting lost in Rome is surprisingly easy. More difficult is the second stage, which is to notice *everything*, from the tree growing out of a wall to the couple arguing across the street and the secret garden just visible through that doorway. Sooner or later you'll blunder into Piazza Navona or Campo dei Fiori or over to Trastevere, which is infinitely more satisfying than seeking them out, and in the meantime you'll have seen a hundred people and places and things which you'll never forget or ever be able to find again.

Next comes lunch, a Roman ritual which makes a pontifical high mass look like a drop-in prayer meeting. This may consist of five courses at a restaurant or – my favourite – a selection of goodies you've bought during your earlier peregrina-

tions, eaten *all'aperto* somewhere green and peaceful like the Aventine. Either way, you'll need a siesta back at the hotel to sleep it off, after which it's time to head out again. Doing nothing in the evening should be a slightly less strenuous reprise of the morning version, involving much sipping, nibbling and, above all, people-watching.

For in the last resort Rome is not about architecture or history, it's about the Romans. As Fran Lebowitz put it: 'One only needs to spend a few hours there to realise that Fellini was making documentaries.' But remember that people-watching is not just a spectator sport. For every person you watch, ten will be watching you. Dress and act accordingly, and get into the spirit of things.

Remember also that the city's true name is Roma, which inverts neatly to form *amor* – appropriately enough, since people tend to love or hate the place. There is a case to be made for either view, as any native will be happy to explain to you. Like all great lovers, Rome can be moody or capricious, not to say bloody impossible. Peevish comparisons with better organised and less demanding cities ('Why can't you be more like Florence?') will only make things worse. Try to be patient and indulgent, to relax and keep a sense of humour. Rome will reward you as no other city can, by making you feel as all her visitors have for over two thousand years: that you are the first person to really understand and appreciate her, the only one truly worthy of her infinite charms. *Michael Dibdin, author of the Aurelio Zen series.*

BALL🎈ON

SILK
COTTON
CASHMERE

In Context

Key Events

Romulus & Remus

*= *Traditional dates*
*753 BC Romulus kills Remus and founds Rome.
*750 BC Rape of the Sabine Women.
*611 BC Tarquin elected king. The Forum is drained.
*509 BC The Tarquins are ousted after one of them rapes Lucretia.
*507-6 BC Roman Republic founded. The Latins and Etruscans declare war.
*499 BC Thanks to Castor and Pollux, Romans beat Latins at Battle of Lake Regillus.
*494 BC Plebeians revolt. Tribunate founded.
*450 BC Roman Law codified into the Twelve Tables.
434 BC War against the Etruscans.
390 BC Gauls sack Rome.
264-146 BC Punic Wars against Carthage. In 146 Carthage is destroyed.
212 BC Rome conquers Sicily.
200-168 BC Rome conquers Greece. Greek gods introduced to Rome.
186 BC 1,000 men and women executed for immoral acts during the Bacchanalia.
100 BC Birth of Julius Caesar.
92-89 BC Social Wars against former Italian allies who want independence.
70 BC Pompey and Crassus elected consuls.
60-50 BC Julius Caesar, Pompey and Crassus form the first triumvirate.
55 BC Caesar invades Britain.
51-50 BC Caesar conquers Gaul and crosses the Rubicon.
48 BC Caesar defeats Pompey and meets Cleopatra.
45 BC Caesar declared *imperator* (emperor).
44 BC Caesar assassinated by Brutus and Cassius.
43-32 BC Second triumvirate: Octavian, Mark Antony and Lepidus.

Pax Romana

31 BC Battle of Actium. Antony and Cleopatra defeated and Octavian becomes sole ruler.
14 AD Death of Augustus. Tiberius becomes emperor.
37 Caligula accedes.
41 Caligula assassinated. Claudius accedes.
64 Nero clears Rome's slums by setting fire to the city.
67 Saints Peter and Paul are martyred.
80 Colosseum completed.
106 Trajan conquers Dacia.
125 Pantheon rebuilt to designs by Hadrian.
164-180 Great Plague kills thousands throughout Empire.
270 Series of military disasters culminates in loss of Dacia to the Goths.
284-305 Empire divided by Diocletian into East and West.

A New Religion

296 Severe persecution of Christians.
313 Constantine proclaims Edict of Milan, tolerating Christianity.
382 Severe persecution of pagans.
410 Alaric the Goth sacks Rome.
475-6 Byzantium becomes seat of empire. Goths rule Rome.
567 Lombards overrun much of Italy.
778 Charlemagne defeats the last Lombard King of Italy.

800 Pope Leo III crowns Charlemagne Holy Roman Emperor.
1084 Holy Roman Emperor Henry IV sacks Rome. Robert Guiscard and the Normans, ostensibly supporting the Pope, sack Rome in revenge and make a killing.
1097 First Crusade begins.
1300 First Holy Year. Thousands of pilgrims flock to Rome – the tourist industry has begun.
1309 Pope Clement V moves the papacy to Avignon.
1347 Cola di Rienzo's republic.
1417 End of Great Schism in the Papacy.

The Renaissance

1494 Charles VIII of France invades Italy.
1508 Michelangelo begins the Sistine ceiling.
1527 Sack of Rome.
1556 Roman Jews confined to the Ghetto.
1563 Council of Trent launches the Counter-Reformation.
1585 Sixtus V begins to change the layout of Rome.
1626 The new Saint Peter's is consecrated.
1689 Death of Queen Christina of Sweden.
1721 Bonnie Prince Charlie born in Rome.
1773 Jesuits expelled from Rome.
1798 French abduct the Pope and declare Rome a republic.
1806 End of Holy Roman Empire.
1808 Napoleon annexes Rome as free city in French Empire.
1821 Death of Keats in Rome.
1849-66 French troops rule Rome.

A Capital Again

1870 Italian army enters Rome and the city is made capital of a united Italy.
1922 Mussolini marches on Rome.
1929 Lateran Treaty creates the Vatican State.
1944 Rome liberated. King Vittorio Emanuele III abdicates.
1946 A national referendum makes Italy a republic. King Umberto II goes into exile.
1957 European Common Market Treaty signed in Rome.
1959 Fellini's *La Dolce Vita* released.
1960 Olympic Games held in Rome.
1962 Second Vatican Council promulgates major reforms.
1978 Red Brigade assassinate Prime Minister Aldo Moro.
1981 John Paul II shot and wounded in Saint Peter's Square.
1990 World Cup held in Italy.
May-July 1992 Anti-Mafia magistrates Giovanni Falcone and Paolo Borsellino killed in ambushes in Palermo.
15 Jan 1993 Cosa Nostra boss of bosses Salvatore Riina arrested in Palermo after 24 years on the run.
17 Feb 1993 *Tangentopoli* investigations begin in Milan: hundreds of MPs and industrialists become embroiled in the nationwide anti-corruption sweep.
Summer 1993 Bombs planted by the Sicilian Mafia explode in Rome, Florence and Milan, killing 11 people and injuring dozens more.
6 Dec 1993 Francesco Rutelli narrowly beats former fascist Gianfranco Fini to become Rome's first Green mayor.
27 Mar 1994 Media tycoon Silvio Berlusconi comes to power at head of right-wing coalition. Internal bickering brings down government after just seven months.
26 Sept 1995 Seven-times premier Giulio Andreotti goes on trial for collusion with the Mafia.
21 Apr 1996 Left-wing coalition led by Romano Prodi wins general election.

Romulus & Remus

After a rape, a fratricide and the intervention of a benevolent wolf, Rome is founded.

Rome sucks... the first citizens with their adoptive mother.

Out of their legends Roman historians created a self-glorifying chronicle, complete with exact dates, for the foundation of the city and its earliest rulers. According to them, Rome was founded by Romulus, on 21 April 753 BC, a date still celebrated as the city's official 'birthday' (*see chapter* **Rome by Season**).

The twins Romulus and Remus were the result of a rape by the god of war, Mars, of a local princess called Rhea Silvia. Cast adrift as babies on the Tiber and washed up in the marshy area below the Palatine Hill, they were suckled by a she-wolf until found by a shepherd. In time, Romulus rose to be leader of his tribe, quarrelled with and killed his brother, founded the city and, deciding his community was short on females, abducted all the women of the neighbouring Sabine tribe.

The true origins of Rome are lost, but traces of ninth-century BC huts have been excavated on the Palatine – proof that there was a primitive village there at least. The first historically documented king of Rome was the Etruscan, Tarquinius Priscus, who reigned from 616 BC. It was probably Etruscans who drained the marshy area between the seven hills to create the **Forum**, hub of the city's political, economic and religious life.

According to Roman historians, in 509 BC the son of King Tarquinius Superbus raped Lucretia, the wife of a Roman, Collatinus. The next day, before killing herself, she told her husband and his friend Brutus what had happened, and in revenge they led a Roman rebellion against the Tarquins. The Etruscan dynasty was expelled and the Roman Republic was founded, with Brutus and Collatinus as the first *Consuls* or chief magistrates.

This is doubtless a romanticised account of what happened, but in time Etruscan influence over the region did wane and authority passed to Rome's magistrates. Chief among them were the two annually elected Consuls, guided by a council of elders called the *Senate*. The number of people who could participate in the political life of the Republic was limited to a few ancient families or clans who formed the Patrician class. Only they could vote, be appointed to the Senate or hold the more important public and religious offices.

The lower classes, or Plebeians, struggled for a greater say in their own affairs. In 494 BC, the office of *Tribune of the Plebs* was created to represent their interests, and by 367 BC a Plebeian could hold the office of Consul. The class system, however, was maintained – rich or successful Plebeians were simply designated Patricians.

Whatever their political differences, the Romans of the Republic were united by a belief in their right to conquer other tribes. Their superb military organisation, and an agile policy of divide-and-rule in making alliances, allowed them to pick off the neighbouring peoples of central and southern Italy, and bring the other Latin communities – including the Etruscans – under Roman control. To ensure the spread of Roman power, new cities were established in the conquered territories, and the Romans created the infrastructure necessary to support their conquests. The first great Roman road, the Via Appia, was begun in 312 BC, and shortly afterwards work started on the Aqua Appia, the first great aqueduct to bring fresh water to the city. The port of Ostia, founded at the mouth of the Tiber in 380 BC, expanded rapidly, and a stream of barges plied the river, bringing corn, wine, oil and building materials to the city.

Rome's expansion brought her into conflict with two equally powerful peoples, the Carthaginians of North Africa and Spain, and the Greeks, who had colonised southern Italy and Sicily. The latter were expelled from mainland Italy in 272 BC, but the Punic Wars against the Carthaginians lasted almost 120 years, and Rome was more than once in danger of annihilation. In 219 BC Hannibal made his historic crossing of the Alps, gaining control of much of Italy, but was too cautious to press home his advantage with an assault on Rome. Carthage was finally destroyed in 146 BC, leaving Rome in control of the western Mediterranean.

In the early days of the Republic most Romans, rich or poor, had been farmers, tending to their own land or livestock in the surrounding countryside. Wars like those against Carthage, however, had required huge standing armies. At the same time, much of the land in Italy had been been laid waste, either by Hannibal or the Roman armies. Wealthy Romans bought huge estates at knockdown prices, while landless peasants flocked to the capital. By the end of the second century BC, the Romans were a race of soldiers, engineers, administrators and merchants, supported by tribute in the form of money and goods from defeated enemies and the slave labour of prisoners taken in battle. Keeping the mass of the Roman poor contented required the exaction of still more tribute from the conquered territories. A parasitic relationship was thus established, in which all classes in Rome lived off the rest of the Empire.

The political situation in the first century BC became more and more anarchic. Vast armies were required to fight distant wars on the boundaries of the Empire, and soldiers came to owe more loyalty to their general, who rewarded them with the fruits of conquest, than to the government back in Rome. The result was a succession of civil wars between rival generals, making a mockery of the old Roman system of government.

Caesar and Pompey, the two greatest generals of the mid-first century, tried to bury their differences in a three-man *Triumvirate* with Crassus, but in 50 BC Caesar, then Governor of Gaul, defied the Senate by bringing his army into Italy ('crossing the Rubicon', the river that marked the Italian border). All opposition was swept aside, and for the last six years of his life Caesar ruled Rome as a dictator. But the Republican spirit was not quite dead, and in 44 BC he was assassinated. Ironically, his death did not lead to the restoration of the Republic, but to a power struggle between Mark Antony and Caesar's nephew, Octavian, which escalated into a full-blown civil war.

PAX ROMANA

Eventually, Octavian defeated Mark Antony and Cleopatra at the Battle of Actium in 31 BC. The Empire now stretched from Gaul and Spain in the west to Egypt and Asia Minor in the east, and to hold it together a single central power was needed. Naturally Octavian felt the person to embody that power was himself, and took the name Augustus, implying that he enjoyed the favour of the gods, acting under good auspices.

Extracting the Urine

When it came to filling the coffers of Imperial Rome, no emperor could beat Vespasian (69-79 AD), a rough-and-ready soldier who fought his way to the top and hung on there. In his relatively short reign, he achieved two major objectives: consolidating the *pax romana* and starting an impressive building programme.

An ascetic man with an eye not on self-enrichment but the glorification of Rome (his personal life was a model of frugality), Vespasian rescinded tax exemptions and freely imposed new levies. In some cases this caused riots (as proconsul in Africa in 63 he was pelted with turnips); in others, bewilderment. Vespasian's son Titus couldn't fathom why he would stoop to imposing a tax on the contents of the city's public lavatories. Little did he know that urine was an essential element in cleansing and thickening wool, a fact which had not escaped his shrewd father.

Handing Titus a coin from the tax office, a smug Vespasian asked, 'Does it smell?' Titus replied that it didn't. 'That's strange,' said Vespasian, 'considering it's come straight from the urinals.'

Popular as Vespasian became, popular history remembers him chiefly for his municipal avarice. Rome's famously reeking *pissoirs*, which blighted the city streets until the early 1990s, were fondly known as *vespasiani*.

Julius Caesar, *emperor and god.*

To give greater authority to his assumption of absolute power, Augustus encouraged the cult of his uncle, Julius Caesar, as a god, building a temple to him in the Forum. The **Ara Pacis**, decorated with a frieze showing Augustus and his family, was a reminder that it was he who had brought peace to the Roman world Later in his reign, statues of Augustus sprang up all over the Empire and he was more than happy to be worshiped as a god himself.

Augustus lived on the Palatine Hill in a relatively modest house, but later emperors indulged their apparently limitless wealth and power to the full, building a series of palaces across the Palatine. The last member of Augustus' family to inherit the Empire was the megalomaniac Nero, who built himself the most enormous palace Rome had ever seen, the *Domus Aurea* or 'golden house'. Extending from the Palatine across the valley occupied by the **Colosseum**, it boasted walls clad in gold and mother-of-pearl, ceilings of pure ivory, an artificial lake and a park full of exotic beasts.

When Nero died in 68 AD, leaving no heir, the Empire was up for grabs, and generals converged from all over the Empire to claim the throne. The eventual winner of this power struggle was a bluff soldier called Vespasian, founder of the Flavian dynasty (*see* **Extracting the Urine**).

GREEKS BEARING GIFTS

Over the next hundred years, Rome enjoyed an era of unparalleled stability and the Empire reached its greatest extent during the reign of Trajan (98-117). Thereafter it was a matter of protecting the existing boundaries and making sure civil war did not threaten the Empire from within.

Peace throughout the Mediterranean encouraged trade and brought even greater prosperity to

Rome. At the same time, however, as Roman citizenship was extended to many people born in the provinces, the power and influence of the capital and its inhabitants declined. Many talented imperial officials, generals and even emperors were Greeks, North Africans or Spaniards. Trajan and Hadrian, for example, were both born in Spain.

To keep this increasingly disparate mass of people content, emperors relied on the policy neatly summed up in the poet Juvenal's phrase 'bread and circuses'. From the first century AD a regular hand-out of grain was given to poor families, ostensibly to maintain a supply of fit young men for the army, but also to ensure that unrest in the city was kept to a minimum. Such a degree of generosity to the poor of Rome, however, necessitated still further exploitation of the outlying provinces of the Empire. Even in years of famine, Spain and Egypt were required to send grain to Rome.

Rome was now the most populous metropolis the world had ever seen. At the time of Augustus the population was about one million, but by the reign of Trajan a century later, it had risen to 1,500,000. No other city even approached this size until the nineteenth century. It was superbly equipped in its public areas, with eight bridges across the Tiber, magnificent major buildings and 18 large squares.

As well as food hand-outs, the other means used to keep more than a million fairly idle souls quiet and loyal to their emperor was the staging of lavish public entertainments. The most famous venue for public spectacles was the Colosseum, built by the emperors Vespasian and Domitian and completed in 96 AD. The appetite of the Roman crowd for blood was almost unappeasable, and sometimes hundreds of people and animals were massacred in the arena in a single day.

The golden age of Rome ended with the death of Marcus Aurelius in 180 AD. Defending the eastern provinces and fortifying the borders along the Danube and the Rhine placed a huge strain on the imperial purse and on the manpower of the legions. At the same time, the traditionally exploitative relationship between the Roman state and its distant provinces meant that the latter were unable to defend themselves against attack.

The threat from barbarian invaders and civil wars became so serious that during the third century Aurelius was obliged to fortify Rome itself with a massive protective wall. The **Aurelian Wall**, graced by Saint Paul and later reinforced by medieval popes, still surrounds the old city. It is a splendid monument to the engineering skills of the ancient Romans, but it gives a rather misleading picture of Imperial Rome. In its heyday, the city needed no defences. Its protection lay in the vastness of its Empire and the guaranteed security of the *pax romana*.

A New Religion

The Empire crumbles, barbarians bay at the city gates, and Rome turns to Christ.

The end of the third century AD was a turning point in the history of Rome. Radical decisions taken by two powerful emperors, Diocletian (286-305) and Constantine (306-337), ensured that the city's days as head of a great Empire were numbered. Diocletian established new capital cities at Mediolanum (Milan) and Nicomedia (in present-day Turkey) and divided the Empire into four sectors, sharing power with a second 'Augustus', Maximian, and two 'Caesars', Constantius and Galerius. The priorities of the Empire were now to defend the Rhine and Danube borders against invading Germanic tribes, and the eastern provinces from the Persians. Rome was abandoned to look after itself.

The reign of Diocletian is also remembered for the systematic persecution of the Christians by the Roman authorities. Christian communities had been established in Rome very soon after the death

*The oft-rebuilt **San Paolo fuori le Mura**.*

of Christ, and centred around clandestine meeting-houses called *tituli* (*see chapter* **Churches**). Christianity, though, was just one of a number of mystical cults that had spread from the Middle East through the Roman Empire. Its followers were probably fewer than the devotees of Mithraism, a Persian religion open only to men. Christianity, with its promise of personal salvation in the afterlife, had a broader base, especially among the oppressed classes – slaves, freedmen and women. Moreover, within two decades of the persecutions of Diocletian, Emperor Constantine first tolerated, then recognised Christianity as the official religion of the Roman Empire.

BORN AGAIN

When Constantius, Constantine's father and commander of the western provinces, died at York in 306, his army acclaimed young Constantine as 'Augustus' in his place. The early part of his reign was taken up with campaigns against rival emperors, the most powerful being Maxentius, who commanded Italy and North Africa.

The decisive battle was fought just to the north of Rome at the Milvian Bridge (Ponte Milvio) in 312. Before the battle a flaming cross is said to have appeared in the sky, with the words 'by this sign shall you conquer' written on it in Greek. According to legend, Constantine's Gaulish cavalry swept Maxentius' superior forces into the Tiber. The following year, in the Edict of Milan, Constantine decreed that Christianity should be tolerated throughout the Empire. Later in his reign, when he had gained control of the eastern Empire and started to build his great new capital city at Byzantium (Constantinople), it became the official religion of the state.

Christianity was much stronger in the east than in the west, and its effect on Roman life was at first limited, with Christianity simply co-existing with the other religions. Constantine's reign saw the building of three great basilicas, but these were situated on the outskirts of the city. Saint Peter's and Saint Paul's without the Walls (**San Paolo fuori le Mura**) were built over existing shrines, while the Bishop of Rome was given land by the Laterani family to build a basilica beside the Aurelian Wall – today's **San Giovanni in Laterano**. To give the city credibility as a centre of the up-and-coming religion, fragments alleged

Myths of the Decline and Fall

As every schoolboy used to know, with the fall of the Western Empire in 476 AD ancient history came to an end, the lights went out, and Ages were Dark until the Renaissance.

But was the decline and fall so abrupt? Rome itself testifies to another version of events.

For the ancient Roman in the street, a basilica was a great, rectangular, flat-roofed assembly hall; the great Christian basilicas – built and embroidered upon from the fourth century until well into the Renaissance – stress a continuity with that classical tradition and a strong sense of being Roman. The superb mosaics of **Santa Pudenziana** (*see chapter* **Churches**) are worthy of an Imperial palace, and the colonnaded sanctuary of **San Lorenzo fuori le Mura** (*see chapter* **Churches**) could well have graced any pagan temple, yet both are fifth century works.

Despite the pillaging and decay, much of the ancient city survived well into the sixth and seventh centuries. The Byzantine usurper Phocas was still aware of the symbolic importance of the Roman Forum (*see chaper* **Ancient Sites**)

when he erected his famous column there, near the Via Sacra, in 608 AD. Even in his day, Romans met and did business in all the old places. Trajan's Forum, which remained almost intact into the seventh century, continued to host sporadic literary meetings; the city walls were in use and regularly repaired; the great baths were still frequented; and there was an official responsible for the upkeep of the Imperial buildings on the Palatine (the *curator palati*) as late as 687.

During the long years of decline, Rome clung tenaciously to these symbols of its past. Meanwhile, the civilised world continued to draw on the city's cultural wealth. Conventional wisdom places the birthplace of Renaissance art in Florence, and maintains that it all started with the painter Giotto. Yet that master's revolutionary naturalism arguably owes much more to the classical statues he studied during his stay in Rome, and to the glorious mosaics being made there, than to the stiff, iconic tradition handed down to him by his Tuscan teacher Cimabue.

to be of the 'True Cross' were brought from the Holy Land by Constantine's mother, Saint Helena. The relics are still preserved in the church of **Santa Croce in Gerusalemme** (*see chapter* **Churches**). Meanwhile, life in fourth-century Rome went on much as before. The departure of part of the imperial court to the east was a heavy blow to a city accustomed to considering itself the *caput mundi*, or capital of the world, but the old pagan holidays were still observed, games were staged, and bread was doled out to the poor.

The Roman world, however, was beginning to fall apart. Constantine learned nothing from the conflicts created by Diocletian's division of power, and on his death left the Empire to be split between his three sons. From this point on, the Western Empire and the Byzantine Empire were two separate entities, united for the last time under Theodosius in the late fourth century. Byzantium would stand for another thousand years, while Rome's glorious palaces, temples, aqueducts, statues and fountains would be destroyed by successive waves of Germanic invaders.

The first great shock came in 410, when Alaric's Visigoths marched into Italy and sacked Rome. Even more significant was the conquest of North Africa by the Vandals in 435, cutting Rome off from its main source of grain. In 455 the Vandals too sacked Rome, removing everything of value that they could carry. After this, the Western

Empire survived in name alone. The great aqueducts supplying water to Rome ceased to function, while much of the Italian countryside was laid waste. The emperors in Rome were the puppets of the assorted Germanic invaders who controlled the Italian peninsula.

The last emperor, Romulus, was given the diminutive nickname Augustulus, because he was such a feeble shadow of the Empire's founder. In 476 he was deposed by the German chieftain Odoacer, who gave himself the title King of Italy. He was in turn deposed by Theodoric the Ostrogoth, who invaded Italy with the support of the Eastern Empire and established a court in Ravenna which ruled with surprising stability for the next thirty years.

In the sixth century much of Italy was reconquered by the Eastern Empire. But then, around 570, yet another Germanic tribe swept in. The Lombards over-ran much of the centre of the peninsula, but when they threatened to besiege Rome they met their match in Pope Gregory the Great (590-604), who bought them off with tribute. Gregory was a tireless organiser, overseeing the running of the estates acquired by the church throughout western Europe, encouraging the establishment of new monasteries and convents, and sending missionaries as far afield as Britain.

He also did a great deal to build up the prestige of the papacy. Until then Rome had been merely one

Enjoy a cloistered experience at **San Giovanni in Laterano**.

of the centres of the early Church, the others – Byzantium, Jerusalem, Antioch and Alexandria – all being in the east. Disputes were sometimes referred to the Bishop of Rome, but many Christians, particularly in the eastern Churches, did not acknowledge him to have any overall primacy. The collapse of all secular government in the west, above all in Italy, meant that the papacy emerged almost by default as the sole centre of authority, a political leader as well as head of the Roman Church.

BADLANDS

The Dark Ages must have been particularly galling for the inhabitants of Rome, living among the magnificent ruins of a vanished golden age. There was no fresh water, as the aqueducts cut during the invasions of the fifth century had never been repaired. People took most of their water from the Tiber and disease was rife. Formerly built-up areas reverted to grazing land or were planted as vegetable gardens by monks, who owned much of the land. Fear of invasion meant that the countryside around the city was practically deserted.

As the city shrank, the ancient ruins became convenient quarries for builders. Marble and other limestone was burned to make cement, most of which was used to repair the city's fortifications. Rome saw more wars, invasions, sieges and disturbances in the Middle Ages than it had ever witnessed under the Republic and Empire.

For several centuries the city still owed nominal allegiance to the emperor in Byzantium and his representative in Italy, the *exarch*, whose court

was at Ravenna. His troops were normally too busy defending their own cities in north-east Italy to be much help to Rome. The city did have a military commander, a *dux*, and a *comune* (city council) that met, as the *Comune di Roma* still does today, on the Capitoline Hill, but the papacy also had its parallel courts and administration. In the end the power of the Church prevailed. In time, this was to cause a permanent rift with Byzantium and the eastern Orthodox Church.

A NEW EMPIRE

During the Dark Ages the Roman Church set out on a nostalgic effort to re-establish something akin to the old Empire. When the Lombards seized Ravenna in 751 and threatened to do the same to Rome, Pope Stephen II seized the initiative and enlisted Pepin, King of the Franks, as defender of the Church. The alliance of the papacy with the Franks was sealed by the victories of Pepin's son, Charlemagne, over the Lombards, and his subsequent crowning as Holy Roman Emperor in Saint Peter's on Christmas Day 800.

Rome appeared to have recovered much of its long-lost power and prestige. It had an Emperor to protect it, blessed by the Pope, who in return was rewarded by the gift of large areas of land in central Italy. As things turned out, this arrangement caused nothing but trouble for the next 500 years,

Drum-like **Castel Sant'Angelo** *was once the papal bolthole.*

as popes, emperors and other monarchs vied to determine whose power was greatest. The Roman nobles took sides in these endless disputes, seizing every occasion to promote members of their own families to the papacy and frequently reducing the city to a state of anarchy. At regular intervals one faction or another would idealistically declare Rome to be a Republic once more, though this never had any real effect.

The prestige of the papacy reached a low ebb in the tenth century when the Frankish Empire collapsed and the papal crown was passed around a series of dissipated Roman nobles. One of these, John XII (955-964), was obliged to call on the Saxon King Otto for assistance, crowned him Holy Roman Emperor, and immediately thought better of it. He began to plot against Otto, who rushed to Rome and commanded the clergy and people never again to elect a Pope without the consent of himself or his successors.

In the second half of the eleventh century, Pope Gregory VII (1073-1085) set up the College of Cardinals, giving them sole authority to elect all future popes. He also insisted that no bishop or abbot could be invested by a lay ruler such as a king or emperor, which led to a cataclysmic struggle for power with the Emperor Henry IV.

In 1084 the Emperor entered Rome, bringing with him a new candidate to replace Gregory VII, who had taken refuge in the **Castel Sant'Angelo**. At this point a Norman army arrived to rescue the Pope, but unfortunately they also took the opportunity to sack the city, burning and looting many churches. Gregory left the city a broken man and died the following year.

Despite never-ending conflict between rival factions, usually headed by the powerful Colonna and Orsini families, the twelfth and thirteenth centuries were a period of great architectural innovation in Rome. The creative spirit of the Middle Ages is preserved in beautiful cloisters like those of **San Giovanni** and **San Lorenzo fuori le Mura**, and in many Romanesque churches with graceful brick bell-towers and floors of fine mosaic (*see chapters* **Architecture** *and* **Churches**).

Rome's prestige, however, suffered a severe blow in 1309, when the French overruled the College of Cardinals and imposed their own candidate as pope, who promptly removed the papacy to Avignon. A pope returned to Rome in 1378, but the situation became farcical, with three sides competing for the papal throne.

Stability was only restored in 1417, when Oddo Colonna was elected Pope Martin V at the Council of Constance, marking the end of the Great Schism. He eventually returned to Rome in 1420, and found the city and the surrounding Papal States in a ruinous condition.

The Feats of Santa Francesca

In the early years of Christianity, Rome did an impressive line in martyrs and saintly popes. During the late Middle Ages and the Renaissance, when the rest of Italy was hopping on the beatification bandwagon, the Eternal City managed only one first-class saint: Santa Francesca Romana (1384-1440).

Prone merely to weird visions of snakes and necrophilia, Francesca cannot really rival the extremes of near-contemporaries such as the wacky Saint Catherine of Siena, who as a penance used to eat the scabs and drink the pus of the terminally ill. There is, however, something touchingly Roman about the way Francesca managed to combine mysticism, the founding of a major religious order, bringing up her six children and waiting hand and foot on a demanding husband.

Married off at 13, Francesca devoted her spare time to looking after Rome's poor in a period of almost uninterrupted famine. In 1425 she founded a society of devout women under the rule of Saint Benedict, in the great medieval complex of Tor de' Specchi, opposite the **Capitoline**. But Francesca's 'nuns' did not take the traditional vows, and could doff the habit whenever they felt like it.

This anomaly saved the order from the anticlerical ravages of Napoleon when he descended on Rome in the late eighteenth century. Unable to figure out whether it qualified for persecution, Napoleon decided to leave well alone, making Tor de' Specchi the only religious house in Rome, and one of the very few in Europe, which can boast an uninterrupted tradition of monastic life.

Francesca Romana is now the patron saint of motorists, perhaps because of the running dialogue she reputedly kept up with her guardian angel – an early form of life insurance.

Tor de' Specchi is open to the public once a year on March 9, Francesca's feast day. The fine frescoes of her visions (including the snake obsession) are well worth seeing. Don't miss out on the *unguento di Santa Francesca*, an alarming black cure-all paste made on the yoghurt principle, its mould culture developed by the good lady herself.

Renaissance Rome

The vain, hedonistic and corrupt society which gave rise to some of the world's greatest art.

With the reign of Pope Martin V (1417-1431) some semblance of dignity was restored to the office of Vicar of Christ on Earth. Martin's reign finally resolved the perennial uncertainty as to who ruled the city, and henceforth the city councillors would be nominees of the Pope. At the same time, the popes chose to make the Vatican their principal residence, as it offered greater security than their traditional seat in the Lateran Palace.

Successive popes took advantage of this new sense of authority and Rome became an international city once more. Meanwhile, the renewed prestige of the papacy enabled it to draw funds from all over Catholic Europe in the form of tithes and taxes. The papacy also developed the money-spinning idea of the Holy Year, first instituted in 1300 and repeated in 1423, 1450 and 1475. Such measures enabled the church to finance the lavish artistic patronage of Renaissance Rome.

Nicholas V (1447-55) is remembered as the pope who brought the spirit of the Renaissance to Rome. A lover of philosophy, science and the arts, he founded the **Vatican Library** and had many ancient Greek texts translated into Latin. He also made plans for the rebuilding of **Saint Peter's**, the structure of which was found to be perilously unstable. The Venetian Pope Paul II (1464-71) built the city's first great Renaissance palazzo, the massive **Palazzo Venezia**, and his successor, Sixtus IV, invited leading artists from Tuscany and Umbria – Botticelli, Perugino, Ghirlandaio and Pinturicchio – to fresco the walls of his new **Sistine Chapel** in the Vatican.

Since the papacy had become such a fat prize, the great families of Italy redoubled their efforts to secure it, and always had younger sons groomed and ready as potential popes. The French and Spanish kings, too, usually had their own candidates. Consequently, Renaissance Popes are not associated with any great spirituality. Sixtus IV and his successors Innocent VIII and Alexander VI (the infamous Rodrigo Borgia) devoted far more of their energies to politics and war than to spiritual matters, and papal armies were continually in the field, carving out an ever-increasing area of central Italy for themselves.

AMBITION AND COMEUPPANCE

The epitome of the worldly Renaissance pope, Julius II (1503-13), made the idea of a strong papal state a reality, at the same time reviving the dream of restoring Rome to its former greatness as the spiritual capital of the world. He started the magnificent collection of classical sculpture which is the nucleus of today's Vatican Museums, and invited the greatest architects, sculptors and painters of his day to Rome. Chief among them were Bramante, Michelangelo and Raphael. Julius' rule was not as enlightened as he liked to think, but he did issue a bull forbidding simony (the buying or selling of church offices) in the election of

*Pope Julius II enjoyed living it up at **Villa Farnesina**, in Trastevere.*

the pope. In his own financial dealings, he depended on the advice and loans of the fabulously wealthy Sienese banker Agostino Chigi, whose beautiful villa beside the Tiber, now known as the **Villa Farnesina**, still gives a vivid impression of the luxurious lifestyle of the papal court.

Julius' successors, however, were less successful. Some were simply *bon viveurs*, like Giovanni de' Medici who, on being made Pope Leo X in 1513, said to his brother, 'God has given us the papacy. Let us enjoy it.' Enjoy it he did. A great patron of the arts, his other passions were hunting, music, theatre and throwing spectacular dinner parties. He plunged the papacy into debt, spending huge sums on French hounds, Icelandic falcons, and banquets of nightingale pies, peacock's tongues and lampreys cooked in Cretan wine.

Future popes had to face two great threats to the *status quo* of Catholic Europe: the protests of Martin Luther against the Catholic Church – and against Roman extravagance in particular – and the growing rivalry between Francis I of France and Charles V of Spain.

The year 1523 saw the death of Adrian VI, a Flemish protégé of Charles V. He was succeeded by Clement VII, formerly Giulio de' Medici, who rather unwisely backed France against the all-powerful King of Spain. By now, the great Catholic monarchs of France and Spain were establishing themselves as the dominant powers in Europe. Charles captured the Duchy of Milan in 1525 and threatened to take over the whole of Italy in retaliation for the Pope's disloyalty. In 1527 a large, ill-disciplined imperial army, many of whom were Germans with Lutheran condemnations of Rome ringing in their ears, took and sacked the city. The looters were chiefly interested in gold and ready money but they also destroyed churches and thousands of houses, burned or stole countless precious relics and works of art, looted tombs, and killed indiscriminately. The dead lay unburied in the streets, sometimes for months.

Porta del Popolo, *gateway to the north.*

The Pope held out for seven months in Castel Sant'Angelo but eventually slunk away in disguise. He returned the following year and eventually crowned Charles as Holy Roman Emperor in Bologna. In return, Charles grudgingly confirmed Clement VII's sovereignty over the Papal States.

THE COUNTER-REFORMATION

The Sack of Rome put an end to the Renaissance popes' dream of making Rome a great political power. The prime concerns now were to rebuild the city and carry out the Counter-Reformation, the Catholic Church's response to Protestantism.

The first great Counter-Reformation Pope was Alessandro Farnese, Paul III (1534-49), a child of the Renaissance who had led a riotous youth and produced four illegitimate children. He realised that if Catholicism was to hold its own against austere Protestantism, lavish ecclesiastical lifestyles had to be restrained. Paul summoned the Council of Trent to define the Catholic faith, and encouraged new religious groups such as the Jesuits over the older, discredited orders. The Society of Jesus was founded by the Spaniard Ignatius of Loyola and approved in 1540. From their mother church in Rome, the **Gesù** (*see chapter* **Churches**), the Jesuits led the fight against heresy and set out to convert the world.

Pope Paul IV (1555-59) was the next major reformer of the Church, a firm believer in the Inquisition, the burning of heretics and homosexuals, and the strictest censorship. He expelled all Jews from the Papal States, except those in Rome itself, whom he confined to the **Ghetto** (*see chapter* **Sightseeing**).

By the end of the sixteenth century, the authority of the papacy was on the wane outside Rome and the papal treasury was increasingly dependent on loans. Nevertheless, in the following century different popes continued to spend money as if the Vatican treasury were inexhaustible. But the inevitable result was to draw off wealth from other parts of society, and the economy of the Papal States became chronically depressed.

When Paul V (1605-21) placed an *interdict* – a kind of mass excommunication – on the Venetians, the wealthy republic took not the slightest notice. With little military or economic power to back up his threat, the Pope was forced to concede that the ability of the Church to interfere in the business of other states was now very limited.

However, two centuries of papal opulence had turned Rome into a spectacular city. Squalor and poverty were still the norm for most of its people: the streets of **Trastevere** and the **Monti** district (the old Roman Suburra) were filthy and dangerous, and the city's Jewish population had been enclosed since 1556 in the even more insanitary conditions of the Ghetto. Yet from dirty, unpaved

Party Lines

Any excuse would do to throw a party in Renaissance Rome, from the election of a pope or the canonization of a saint, to the safe return of a papal legate. After all, Rome was *caput mundi*, and the Vatican the hub of world power. What better way to make friends and – much more importantly – influence people than to mount an extravaganza of frantic festivities and show them just what Rome was capable of?

Once the invites were sent out, Rome would be transformed with massive backdrops, roaring bonfires, horse races, firework displays, and multi-coloured processions, with rolling contraptions compared to which modern fairground floats pale into insignificance.

Rome's party period got off the ground with the Jubilee Holy Year of 1500, but it was not until the seventeenth century that the city became *festa* capital of Europe. Highly respected architects and artists such as Gian Lorenzo Bernini and Pietro da Cortona were drafted in to create the elaborate pyrotechnic machines and catafalques.

With little more than wooden carts, soggy paper and hefty ropes, party planners and skilled artisans were able to create storms, floods, thunder, earthquakes and lightning, complete with sound effects. In 1662, when the French Dauphin was born, Bernini transformed Piazza di Spagna into a mountain, using papier mâché rocks, trees, angels and clouds. Firework dolphins appeared from a fountain and exploded into a mass of sparks.

Artists and architects used these showcases of the ephemeral to drum up ideas for more durable projects. **Bernini's Elephant** at Piazza della Minerva, for example, was inspired by his catafalque for the birth of the Spanish Infanta in 1650.

For Rome's humbler inhabitants, on the other hand, these extravaganzas were only too fleeting. As the last firework fizzled out, and the papier mâché went up in flames, a more desolate backdrop would emerge: the misery, poverty and disease of the workaday papal city.

---

alleys you could emerge into a glorious open space with fountains playing, like the **Piazza Navona**.

At least the city was now at peace. The rich no longer shut themselves up in fortress-like palazzi, but built delightful villas in landscaped parks, such as **Villa Borghese** and **Villa Pamphili**. Rome had many attractions, in spite of the waning prestige of the popes. There was a resurgence of interest in the classical past, and the city discovered the joys of tourism. Rome was about to be invaded again.

CARNIVAL FUN

That Rome produced little great art or architecture in the eighteenth century was due in part to the poor state of papal finances. The two great Roman sites that date from this period, the **Spanish Steps** and the **Fontana di Trevi** are really a late flowering of the earlier Roman Baroque. The few building projects that were undertaken were for the benefit of tourists, notably Giuseppe Valadier's splendid park on the **Pincio** and the neo-classical facelift he gave to **Piazza del Popolo**.

Although on the surface Rome was a cultured city, there were many customs that reeked of medieval superstition. Writers like Smollett, Gibbon and Goethe, forgetting the full brutality of ancient Rome, all remarked on the contrast between the sophistication of that vanished civilisation and the barbarism lurking beneath the surface of papal Rome. There were, for example, the

sinister black-hooded priests of **San Giovanni Decollato** (*see chapter* **Churches**), whose duty was to give the last rites to condemned prisoners. And some of the executions were still carried out by *martello*, in which the condemned man was beaten about the temples with a hammer before having his throat cut and his stomach ripped open. This savage method used until the 1820s.

Executions were traditionally staged in the Piazza del Popolo, and were often timed to coincide with the Carnival, a period of frantic merry-making before the beginning of Lent. For a few days Via del Corso resembled a masked ball, as bands played and people showered each other with confetti, flour, water and more dangerous missiles. The centrepiece was the traditional race of riderless horses along the Corso. They had heavy balls filled with spikes dangling at their sides to spur them on as they ran.

Rome was a city of spectacle for much of the rest of the year, too (*see* **Party Lines** *above*), even though most Romans were cynical about their spiritual leaders. During the summer, Piazza Navona was flooded by blocking the outlets of the fountains, and the nobility drove around the piazza in their carriages while street urchins frolicked in the water, begging for coins. The only time the city fell quiet was in late summer, when everyone who could left the city for their villas in the Alban Hills to escape the stifling heat and the threat of malaria.

A Capital Again

The creation of Italy and its entry into the modern world.

In 1798 everything changed. French troops under Napoleon occupied the city, and Rome became a Republic once more. Pope Pius VI, a feeble old man, was exiled from the city and died in France.

Like most of the attempts to restore the Roman Republic, this one was short-lived. The next pope, Pius VII, elected in Venice, signed a *Concordat* with Napoleon in 1801, allowing him to return to Rome. The papacy was expelled once again when French troops returned in 1808, but Romans were not keen to be conscripted into Napoleon's armies. When the Pope finally reclaimed Rome after the fall of Napoleon in 1814, the noble families and many of the people welcomed his return.

The patchwork of duchies, principalities and kingdoms that had existed in Italy before Napoleon's invasions was restored after 1815. The Papal States were also handed back to Pius VII. Nevertheless, the brief taste of liberty under the French helped inspire a movement for unification, modernisation and independence from the domination of foreign rulers, such as Austria in the north and the Bourbon Kingdom of the Two Sicilies in the south.

The *Risorgimento* was the movement for the unification of the country, but in itself it was very diverse. Its supporters ranged from liberals who believed in unification for economic reasons, to conservatives who looked to the papacy itself to unify Italy. Initially, the most prominent were the idealistic republicans of the *Giovane Italia* (Young Italy) movement headed by Giuseppe Mazzini. They were flanked by more extreme groups and secret societies such as the *Carbonari*.

Two reactionary popes, Leo XII (1823-29) and Gregory XVI (1831-46), used a network of police spies and censorship to put down opposition of any kind. Most of the unrest in the Papal States was in the north; in Rome life went on much as before. Travellers continued to visit: Dickens and Lord Macaulay both visited Rome, and were horrified at the repressive regime of the papacy.

The election of a new pope in 1846 aroused great optimism. Pius IX had a liberal reputation and immediately announced an amnesty for over 400 political prisoners. However, the spate of revolutions that spread through Europe in 1848 radically altered his attitude. In November that year his chief minister was assassinated and Pius fled in panic to Naples. In his absence a popular assembly declared Rome a Republic. Seizing the chance to make his dream reality, Guiseppe Mazzini

rushed to the city, where he was chosen as one of a triumvirate of rulers. Meanwhile, another idealist arrived in Rome to defend the Republic, accompanied by 500 followers. Giuseppe Garibaldi was a former sailor who had fought in various wars of liberation in South America.

Ironically, Republican France, with Napoleon I's nephew Louis Napoleon as President, decided it was her duty to restore the Pope to Italy. Louis Napoleon's motivation was simple: he wished to counter the power of Austria within Italy. A French force marched on Rome, but was repelled by the *Garibaldini*, or followers of Garibaldi – a ragbag mixture of former papal troops, young volunteers and enthusiastic citizens. When reinforcements arrived, the French attacked again, mounting their assault from the gardens of **Villa Pamphili**. For the whole of June 1849, the defenders fought from their positions on the **Gianicolo**, but the end of the Republic was inevitable.

For the next 20 years, while the rest of Italy was being united under King Vittorio Emanuele of Piedmont, a garrison of French troops protected Pope Pius from invasion. Garibaldi protested vainly to the politicians of the new state – it was, he said, a question of *Roma o Morte* ('Rome or death') – but the Kingdom of Italy, established in 1860, was not prepared to take on the might of Napoleon III's France. Meanwhile, the policies of the formerly liberal Pius IX were becoming increasingly reactionary. In 1869 he convened the first Vatican Council in order to set down the Catholic Church's response to the upheavals of the industrial age. It did so with intransigence, making the doctrine of papal infallibility part of the official dogma of the Church for the first time.

The **Vittoriale**, *with reclining Bruce Forsyth.*

*Garibaldi rises above it all in **Gianicolo**.*

MODERNISATION AT LAST

Even though it was still under papal rule, Rome had been chosen as the capital of the newly unified kingdom. In 1870, with the defeat of Napoleon III in the Franco-Prussian war, the French withdrew from Rome, and Italian troops occupied the city. Pius IX withdrew into the Vatican, refusing to hand over the keys of the **Quirinale**, the future residence of the Italian royal family. Troops arriving in the city had to break in.

There followed the most rapid period of change Rome had experienced since the fall of the Empire. The new capital needed government buildings and housing for the civil servants who worked in them. Church properties were confiscated and for a time government officials worked in converted monasteries and convents. Two aristocratic palazzi were adapted to house the Italian parliament. **Palazzo di Montecitorio** became the Chamber of Deputies, and **Palazzo Madama** the Senate.

The city's great building boom lasted for over 30 years. Via Nazionale and Via Cavour linked the old city with the new Stazione Termini in the east, and Corso Vittorio Emanuele was driven through the historic centre. The new ministries were often massive piles quite out of keeping with their surroundings, a notable example being the monstrous **Vittoriale**, the marble monument to **Vittorio Emanuele**, erected in Piazza Venezia.

Rome was little affected by World War I, but following the war social unrest broke out, with the fear of socialism giving rise to fascism. Benito

Mussolini was a radical journalist who became alienated from the far left and shifted to the extreme right. Like so many before him, he turned to ancient Rome to find an emblem to embody his idea of a totalitarian state: *fasces* were the bundles of rods tied round an axe carried by the Roman *Lictors* (marshals) as they walked in front of the city's *Consuls*. In 1922 Mussolini sent his black-shirt squads on their 'March on Rome', demanding, and winning, full power in the government. He had been prepared to back out at the first sign of real resistance by the constitutional parties, and himself made the 'March' by train.

Mussolini's ambition was to transform the country into a dynamic society. Among other things, he wanted to put Italians in uniform and stop them eating pasta, which he thought made them lazy and un-warlike. His ideas for changing the face of Rome were equally far-fetched. He planned to rebuild Rome in gleaming marble, with *fora*, obelisks, and heroic statues proclaiming the *Duce* (Leader) as a modern Augustus at the head of a new Roman Empire. The most prominent surviving monument to his megalomania is the suburb of **EUR**, planned to house an international exhibition of fascism.

Fascist Italy was incredibly ineffectual, and when put to the test in World War II, it rapidly foundered. Mussolini was ousted from power in 1943, and the citizens of Rome had no difficulty in changing their allegiance from the Axis to the Allies. During the period of German occupation that followed, Italian partisans showed themselves capable of acts of courage that had never been displayed in the cause of fascism. Rome was declared an open city – the *Roma Città Aperta* of Rossellini's great film – meaning that the Germans agreed not to defend it, pitching their defence south of the city around Frascati. While other Italian cities and towns were pounded by shells and bombs, Rome suffered only one serious bombing raid during the whole war.

After the war Italy voted to become a Republic and Rome quickly adapted to the new political structures. *Partitocrazia* – government by a group of political parties sharing power and dividing up lucrative government jobs and contracts between them – suited the Roman approach to life well. The political unrest of the 1970s affected Rome less than it did Milan or Turin, and the Romans simply swam with the political tide, voting in their first Communist mayor in 1976.

The city has benefited greatly from Italy's post-war economic boom. It has spread radially along its major arterial roads. The problem of the city authorities since the war has been how to preserve the old city and yet encourage development. Rome's main industry is still being itself, whether as capital of Italy or historical relic, and the city continues to thrive, trading as it has done for the last 1,500 years on its unforgettable past.

Rome Today

New political order – or business as usual?

Infra dig ... Rome's past unearthed.

Today's Rome suffers from a strange inferiority complex towards its own history. The physical evidence of past greatness is all around, in the ancient monuments, the churches, the squares, the fountains and the great palaces of popes and emperors. What has *modern* Rome got to offer, apart from endless sprawling suburbs, traffic and surly post office workers? A vague feeling of inadequacy and restlessness pervades the whole city. When Rome became capital of Italy in 1870 it, and the papacy it housed, were no more than a political irrelevance in a provincial backwater. Despite more than a century of tawdry growth, the city is still struggling to find a role it can be proud of.

Modern Romans react to their city in much the same way that petulant adolescents react to their parents. They are difficult, vain and disrespectful. They fill squares with cars and rubbish and let buildings grow grimy and rotten. They strut the streets as though they had built them themselves, and create huge obstacles for anyone else who tries to butt in. Above all, they are indifferent. *Menefreghismo*, not giving a damn, is the disease that stalks Rome.

At times the past seems like a trap that constricts the Romans' desperate yearning for freedom. That helps explain why they drive like

Rome by Numbers

Resident population (1991 census)	2,775,250
Female	1,449,660
Male	1,325,590
Aged over 65	14.5% of total
Romans who consider themselves 'deeply religious'	10.6%
Romans who consider themselves 'not religious at all'	19.1%
Restaurants (1997)	c.3,600
Bars (1997)	c.6,500
Hotel beds in Rome (1995)	84,425
Total tourists in hotels (1996)	5,727,042
Tourists expected for the 2000 Jubilee Holy Year	35,000,000
Rubbish produced daily per tourist	600g
Number of cars on Rome's roads	2,000,000
Bus and tram passengers daily	2,200,000
Metro passengers daily	800,000

Distance travelled yearly by Rome's 157 trams	5,000,000km
Buses on streets in rush hour	1,950
Bus inspectors	120
People caught without tickets on buses (daily average)	589
Average speed of buses	13.5km per hour
Murders reported (1995)	105
Rapes reported (1995)	132
Bouncing cheques reported (1995)	73,092
Plant species found in urban area	1,200
Land vertebrates found in urban area	144
Reptile species	14
Bird species	101
Mammal species	23

Sources Istat, Confesercenti, Roma 2004 Olympic Bid Committee, ATAC, Cotral, EPT, Università Cattolica.

lunatics even though there's nothing much to do when they get to where they are going; why they are constantly chasing the latest fad, even though it invariably looks very much like last year's; why they are always jostling for position, looking for a leg-up or a discount, in a frenzied race to appear smarter and more streetwise than their neighbour.

And yet there is a strange fondness in the relationship between Rome and its past. Old buildings are not pickled in nostalgia; they are part of the surroundings and accepted as such. Kids kick footballs around the pillars of the Pantheon, women walk on cobblestones in high heels, and drivers barrel down narrow alleys, squeezing their cars into the tiniest of parking places. Romans use their city as a backdrop against which to play out their lives with great passion and drama. Why have a simple wedding when you can line the street leading up to the church with olive trees and illuminate it with coloured spotlights? Why have a straightforward argument when you can ham it up for the benefit of the neighbours? Romans know that every piazza and every church cloister looks like a stage, and when these venues are not being co-opted for real plays and concerts, the city folk improvise their own melodramas.

The cast is huge: aging would-be writers; jaded tourists who forgot to leave; women with rasping voices, outlandish jewellery and leathery skin; Filipina maids; secret Freemasons; whistle-blowing demonstrators; film directors good and bad; Brazilian transvestites; beggars; pickpockets; illegal immigrants selling flowers or cooking pasta in restaurants; ancient film stars re-visiting their old haunts on the Via Veneto.

And where does the government fit into all this? A wind of change has been blowing through the city hall on the Capitoline Hill since 1993, when the old political order collapsed and one of the country's most prominent Greens, Francesco Rutelli, won the mayor's seat by a whisker against the neofascist leader Gianfranco Fini. The changes have been palpable. Church façades blackened over centuries are suddenly clean. The opera house, once run with legendary extravagance but little talent, is under new management. Parking regulations have been revolutionised, new tram-lines have been laid and there are ambitious plans to bring the city's notoriously lumbering bus system under control. More is in store as the city gears up for the millennium. Billions of lire in investment are promised; major projects include a third Metro line and new facilities for both the city centre and the suburbs. And yet one detects warning signs of the bad habits of the old Rome. One of the millennial proposals is for 50 new churches. Who needs them in a singularly faithless city with more churches than it knows what to do with?

Can Rome ever truly reform its corrupt and decadent soul? Gore Vidal once said that Rome was the best place from which to watch the end of the world. The attempts to avert Rome's terminal decline are laudable, but the city's infuriating, enigmatic and restless soul is still very much alive.

Political Animals

Whatever happened to Italy's revolution? Back in the heady days of the early nineties, it seemed that the entire political and business establishment was being frogmarched off to jail as the dizzying structure of kickbacks and bribery that had propped up an entire ruling class came crashing down. There were promises of sea-changes in politics, in the justice system, in the economy — everywhere, in fact, that had been held back for half a century by the dictates of Cold War geopolitics and the dead hand of the Christian Democrat Party.

Alas, it was not to be. Although plenty of prominent figures went to jail *before* their trials, usually for a week or two, only a handful have actually ended up behind bars for a prescribed term. The magistrates who so spectacularly captured the *zeitgeist*, and prosecuted all those sleaze-buckets responsible for bringing the country to the brink of ruin, suddenly found themselves the victims of a vicious backlash.

Politically, there were high hopes of a fresh start when Silvio Berlusconi and his motley coalition of free-marketeers, northern separatists and neo-fascists took power in 1994. But they were rapidly torn apart by their own contradictions, and the system has since reverted to its normal pattern of factional bickering and policy paralysis. The electoral system does not work, parliament is too divided to function properly, and even the left — which was kept out of government for 50 years — has been unable to do anything but maintain a festering status quo since coming to power in the 1996 elections. One of its electoral pledges was to institute far-reaching constitutional reform, but the logic of the system has worked inexorably against the overhaul it so badly needs. A parliamentary committee called the *bicamerale* broke up in June 1997 with nothing but a string of awkward compromises and petty betrayals to show for its work. If reform ever looked like changing anything in this country, they'd abolish it.

Architecture

From Baroque to Brutalist, Rome's got it all.

The **Pantheon**, *perfectly preserved.*

'The beauty of Rome lies in what is in ruins,' wrote a visitor to the city in 1444. You can see what he meant if you look at the relics of Republican- and Imperial-era buildings strewn around the **Forum, Palatine** and **Imperial Fora**. Decaying ruins are wonderfully evocative, but they can also be fiendishly tricky to interpret. (*See chapter* **Directory: Architectural Terms**.) So it's fortunate that there are still some superbly preserved structures such as the **Colosseum, Pantheon, Trajan's Markets** and **Trajan's Column**, to give an idea of just how splendid the ancient city really was.

Major buildings expressed all the glamour and sophistication of ancient Rome. In imitation of ancient Greece, important façades followed the system or Orders: different proportions, based on the width of the columns. There were Greek orders: Doric, plain and sturdy; Ionic, more slender and ornate; and Corinthian, the most delicate and ornate of all. The **Colosseum** is a good example

of how the Orders were used: hefty and rooted Doric at the bottom to 'support' the construction; lighter, more elegant Ionic in the middle to provide a suitable visual link between the bottom; and the delicate, decorative Corinthian top layer. Further embellishment was often provided by statues, reliefs and, in some cases, painted façades.

Whole genres of building were based on Greek models. Temples were usually colonnaded: either rectangular like the temples of Saturn or Portunus, or circular like the temples of Vesta and **Hercules Victor**. Other common buildings included Greek-style theatres and their Roman relative, the amphitheatre, an elliptical structure designed for blood sports. It seems, however, that the Romans did develop some forms of building themselves: the first known basilicas are found in Rome, as are the first baths with heated and running water.

The commonest stone around Rome was soft, volcanic *tufa*. This was clearly not an ideal building material, and as early as the third century BC a form of concrete had been developed, made of *pozzolana* (a volcanic ash), lime and *tufa* rubble. As this wasn't exactly aesthetically pleasing, later buildings were faced with thin veneers of coloured marble or travertine (a calcareous limestone). Without concrete, constructing the Pantheon would have been impossible. The huge hemispherical dome is the largest example of a cast-concrete construction made before the twentieth century. Other feats of cast-concrete engineering include the **Baths of Diocletian** and the **Baths of Caracalla**. Look at the ruined domes of the latter: you can see the layers of brick, concrete and marble and get an idea of how the building was put together. Brick, the other fundamental Roman building material, was used to face buildings, to lend internal support to concrete walls, and as a material in its own right. The most impressive example is **Trajan's Markets**, with its numerous layers, domes, nooks and crannies. (*See chapter* **Ancient Sites**.)

Early Christian Rome

There are traces of the early Christians everywhere in Rome – and they are not confined to the dank **Catacombs** and grisly reliquaries of martyrs. Scores of early churches survive, although often the original building is hidden beneath later accretions and decoration. But the tell-tale signs are there if you know what to look for.

Early Christian basilical churches are the ghosts of ancient Roman basilicas. Churches founded in the fourth and fifth centuries such as **San Paolo fuori le Mura**, **San Giovanni in Laterano**, **Santi Quattro Coronati**, **Santa Maria in Trastevere**, **San Pietro in Vincoli** and **Santa Sabina** are the most tangible connection we have with the interiors of ancient civic Rome. Go into any of them and imagine them shorn of their later decoration. The construction is generally simple and stately. Most are rectangular, with a flat roof and a colonnade separating a tall nave from lower aisles. Natural light enters the nave from high windows, while the aisles are lit from the ground-floor windows. Behind the altar, opposite the entrance, is an apse topped by a conch.

Santa Sabina on the Aventine has survived virtually intact and still evokes the taste for classical forms that survived long after the demise of pagan Rome. Built between 422 and 432 AD, and stripped of later accretions in 1936, it even retains the original selenite windows.

The fortunes of the Catholic church are reflected in the architecture. When it was poor, as in the fifth century, buildings were plain and functional; when it was rich, in periods such as the eighth and twelfth centuries, churches were adorned with brilliant polychromatic mosaics. The most magnificent to have survived are in **Santa Maria Maggiore**, **Santa Prassede** and **Santa Maria in Trastevere**. Many churches have exquisitely carved pulpits, walled choirs and Paschal candlesticks decorated with glass and gilding, and inlaid marble floors. Examples include **Santa Maria in Cosmedin**, **San Clemente** and **Santa Sabina**.

Very occasionally circular churches were built, perhaps inspired by Roman tombs like Hadrian's mausoleum (now the **Castel Sant'Angelo**) and the **Mausoleum of Augustus**. The dazzling mosaic-caked **Santa Costanza** was probably built in the fourth century as a mausoleum for the daughters of Emperor Constantine, while its contemporary, **Santo Stefano Rotondo**, was a seat of the cult of proto-martyr Saint Stephen. Its shape may derive from its occupying the site of an earlier circular building which could have been part of

Bramante's **Tempietto**, *emulating the spirit of antiquity.*

the Roman market, the **Macellum Magnum**. Equally, it might have been inspired by the design of the church of the Holy Sepulchre in Jerusalem (*see chapter* **Churches**).

As for civic architecture, this was a period in which the main families of Rome were in an almost constant battle for power. Consequently most felt it necessary to live in fortresses with lookout towers. The **Torre delle Milizie**, behind Trajan's Markets, and the **Torre degli Anguillara**, in Trastevere, are good examples.

The Renaissance

In the late fourteenth century, while a huge revolution in art, architecture and thought was taking place in Tuscany, Rome was a crumbling, dirty, medieval city. Only in the fifteenth century, when the popes began to bring the threads of the great revival in art, literature and humanistic thought to Rome, was the Tuscan influence felt.

In 1445 the Florentine architect Filarete created Rome's first significant Renaissance work: the magnificent central bronze doors of **Saint Peter's**. However, it was only in the reign of Pope Nicholas V (1447-55) that the Renaissance really began to flourish. Nicholas decided that the Church had to be reconciled with secular culture and that Rome should become worthy of its glorious past. Much of the city as he found it was in a state of collapse, its streets filled with cattle, sheep and goat-herds. Nicholas was a highly educated man who knew the architectural theorist Leon Battista Alberti and other key protagonists of the early Renaissance. His motivation, however, was more evangelistic than humanistic. If Rome was to take on the role as the focus of Christianity, it had to look the part. Nicholas believed that faith would be strengthened if people were surrounded by 'majestic buildings, lasting memorials, witnesses to their faith planted on earth as if by the hand of God'. Following consultations with Alberti, Nicholas began to rebuild Saint Peter's itself, which at the time was in imminent danger of collapse. Meanwhile, those with lucrative church connections built fabulous palaces: in 1508 papal banker Agostino Chigi commissioned a lavish villa, now the **Villa Farnesina**, and in 1515 work started on **Palazzo Farnese** for Cardinal Alessandro Farnese.

The Roman Renaissance gathered momentum under Pope Pius II (1458-64), a cultured Tuscan steeped in classical literature and an acclaimed orator and poet, who forbade the destruction of ancient buildings. Under Pope Sixtus IV (1471-84), roads were paved and widened, churches such as **Santa Maria della Pace** and **Santa Maria del Popolo** were rebuilt, the **Ponte Sisto** was begun and the **Sistine Chapel** was built and decorated

by some of the foremost artists of the time, among them Ghirlandaio, Pinturicchio and Signorelli.

Donato Bramante came to Rome in 1499 and in 1502 built the **Tempietto** to mark the spot traditionally thought to be that of Saint Peter's execution. A domed cylinder surrounded by a Tuscan Doric colonnade, it came closer than any other building to the spirit of antiquity. Miniature in scale but exquisitely proportioned, with perfectly detailed capitals, entablatures and dome, it is a masterly evocation of the majesty of ancient Rome – which was precisely what the Renaissance sought to emulate.

Rome's Renaissance reached its peak with Julius II (1503-13), who made Bramante his principal architect, and commissioned Michelangelo to sculpt his tomb and fresco the ceiling of the **Sistine Chapel** and Raphael to decorate the *stanze* in the **Vatican Palace**. Not satisfied with the restoration of Saint Peter's initiated by his predecessors, Julius decided to scrap the old building and start again. The job was given to Bramante, and in 1506 the foundation stone for the new Saint Peter's was laid.

Bramante's design for Saint Peter's was based on a Greek cross. Work proceeded apace, but following the master's death in 1514 there was a long delay. In 1547 Michelangelo took over, keeping to the centralised design, but increasing the scale tremendously. After his death in 1564, it was left to Giacomo del Duca to erect the dome during the papacy of Sixtus V (1585-90), an obsessive town-planner responsible for the layout of much of modern Rome. However, the effect of the centralised design was subsequently wrecked by Paul V (1605-21), who commissioned Carlo Maderno to lengthen the nave in line with the new ideals of the Counter-Reformation.

The Baroque

This period was characterised by the austere reforms of the Council of Trent (1545-63), designed to counter the ideas of Luther's reformation, and by the establishment of heavy-handed new orders such as the Jesuits and Oratarians. Consequently, the earliest churches of the period, among them the **Chiesa Nuova**, were plain and were provided with long naves suitable for processions. The **Gesù**, with its wide nave and barrel-vaulted ceiling, was deemed ideal for the preaching purposes of the Jesuits, as the preacher was clearly visible to the congregation.

As the Counter-Reformation gathered pace, great cycles of decoration preaching the mysteries of the faith (such as the *Cappella Sistina* of **Santa Maria Maggiore**) or inspiring the onlooker to identify with the sufferings of the martyrs (as in the blood-thirsty frescoes adorning the walls of **Santo Stefano Rotondo**) began to appear and, on their

*The world's largest free-standing concrete dome at the **Palazzo dello Sport**.*

heels, an increasingly exuberant and theatrical style of art and architecture, known as the Baroque.

It is largely the endlessly inventive confections of the Baroque which make Rome what it is today, creating a magnificent backdrop for everyday life and a dramatic setting for earlier monuments. The Baroque is found not only in the city's churches, but also in its villas, fountains, squares and palaces and their painted, sculpted and gilded adornments.

Architects like Giacomo della Porta (1532/3-1602), who worked on **Sant'Andrea della Valle**, and Domenico Fontana (1543-1607), who worked at **Santa Maria Maggiore** and the church of **San Carlo alle Quattro Fontane**, set the scene in which the real shapers of the Baroque grew up. These were the architects Gian Lorenzo Bernini (1598-1680), poet, playwright, sculptor and painter; Francesco Borromini (1598-1667), an eccentric genius with a passion for archaeology; and Pietro da Cortona (1598-1669), master of architecture, painting and theology. All of them worked on the **Palazzo Barberini**.

Bernini virtually made the Baroque his own with his imaginative use of coloured marbles, bronze and stucco, his combination of sensuality and mysticism and the inspired sense of movement and immediacy that he gave to his sculpture. For more than 20 years he was the artistic dictator of Rome, and was jealously guarded by his Barberini patrons. He carried out much of the decoration of the interior of Saint Peter's for Pope Urban VIII Barberini (there are Barberini 'bees' all over the *baldacchino*) and dominated all the arts to the extent that he caused the relative neglect of Borromini, Rome's other great genius.

Bernini said that quarrelsome, neurotic Borromini 'had been sent to destroy architecture'. Indeed, for centuries Borromini was vilified as a wild revolutionary. Now he is recognised as one of the great masters of the period and perhaps the greatest of all in the invention of plans and the creation of spatial effects. The most startling examples of his work are **San Carlo alle Quattro Fontane** and **Sant'Ivo alla Sapienza**, both of which break all the conventional rules of architecture. Perhaps because of his temperament (he eventually committed suicide), he never attained anything like the public acclaim awarded to Bernini, but his patrons allowed him a freedom to evolve his own ideas which he might not have enjoyed had he worked for popes such as Urban VIII or Alexander VII.

Like Bernini, Pietro da Cortona created some of his greatest works for the Barberini popes. He was principally a painter, and his most significant contribution to architecture was his three-dimensional treatment of the wall. At **Santa Maria della Pace** he combined opposing convex forms which, curving sharply at the ends, are almost flat in the middle. The result is almost theatrical. Squeezed into a tiny piazza, the church resembles a stage set.

The hallmarks of the buildings by Bernini, Borromini and da Cortona are the preference for curves, complex forms, massive scale, dramatic effects of light and shadow, and movement and counter-movement – spirals, ovals, and curves moving in opposite directions. Interiors were adorned with an undiluted richness emanating from coloured marbles and gilded stucco. In statues and paintings, saints and martyrs were depicted in hideous misery or orgasmic ecstasy.

Sometimes architecture, painting and sculpture were combined, most successfully in the Cornaro chapel in **Santa Maria della Vittoria** and the *baldacchino* in **Saint Peter's** by Bernini.

None of this would have been possible without the patronage of the popes and their families and of the various religious orders. The popes were responsible for the decoration of Saint Peter's (Urban VIII, 1623-44); the colonnade in front of it (Alexander VII, 1655-67); the layout of the **Piazza Navona** and the redecoration of **San Giovanni in Laterano** (Innocent X, 1644-55). Their cardinal-nephews inspired a great many lesser building schemes: redecoration or restoration of existing churches, and private villas, gardens, palaces and picture galleries.

The religious orders were no less profligate. The great churches of the period were the initial testing ground – none more so than the **Gesù** which, although built during the Counter-Reformation, wasn't completed until well into the Baroque period. It was originally intended to have bare interior walls and only in the 1640s did it begin to acquire the alarming profusion of decoration, illusion and ornament that you see today. Other churches decorated by the orders in high-Baroque style include **Sant'Ignazio**, **Sant'Andrea della Valle** and the **Chiesa Nuova**.

In the eighteenth century the Baroque gained something of a Rococo gloss with Francesco de Sanctis' **Spanish Steps**, Filippo Raguzzini's pretty Ospedale di San Gallicano (in Trastevere), Nicola Salvi's **Fontana di Trevi** and Fernando Fuga's hallucinatory Palazzo della Consulta on **Piazza del Quirinale**. In the nineteenth century, little happened until 1870, when Rome became the capital of a united Italy, triggering a new phase of urban development. The best examples include the neo-classical **Piazza Vittorio Emanuele**, the flamboyant **Palazzo delle Esposizioni** and the imperious, jingoistic **Vittorio Emanuele** monument in Piazza Venezia.

Twentieth-Century Rome

The architectural triumphs of twentieth-century Rome are largely confined to the Fascist era. **Stazione Termini** is a strident and impressive example. Begun just before World War II, its wide, overhanging entrance portal, repeated arches and huge foyer are still stunning nearly half a century after their completion. Other Fascist buildings are dotted around the periphery of the city. On the north side of the Tiber is the **Foro Italico**, a magnificent sports complex – though it is doubtful whether its builders intended the huge statues of naked male athletes to be quite as homo-erotic as they are. The best collection of buildings from the period are found at **EUR**, a surreal, clinical example of 1930s town planning, where buildings such

The swooping ceiling at **Stazione Termini**.

as the **Palazzo della Civiltà del Lavoro** and the **Museo della Civiltà Romana** look as though they were designed to feature in de Chirico cityscapes. The **Palazzo dello Sport**, built by Pier Luigi Nervi and Marcello Piacentini for the 1960 Olympic Games, has a reinforced concrete dome which, with a diameter of 100 metres, took from the Pantheon the record for the world's largest free-standing concrete dome.

There are few other modern buildings in central Rome but there would have been scores if Mussolini had got his way. Talking to the city council, he said: 'In five years, Rome must appear wonderful to the whole world: immense, orderly and powerful, as she was in the days of the first empire of Augustus. The approaches to the Theatre of Marcellus, the Campidoglio and the Pantheon must be cleared of everything that has grown up round them during the centuries of decadence. Within five years the hill of the Pantheon must be visible through an avenue leading from Piazza Colonna.' Fortunately the war distracted and then removed him before he was able to wreak too much havoc.

You only have to look at the Via dei Fori Imperiali that links the **Colosseum** with the **Piazza Venezia** to see the result of Mussolini's unenlightened attempts to 'improve' the city. The road bludgeoned its way across the ruins of the ancient *fora*, covering and in some cases obliterating them. There have long been plans to remove the road and turn the area between the Colosseum and the Piazza Venezia into a huge archaeological park, but nothing has been done.

From the 1950s to the 1970s, Rome, in common with other European cities, received its share of functional apartment and office blocks. In recent years building projects have been considerably more positive in conception. The great postmodernist Paolo Portoghesi's visionary **mosque** was recently opened near the Catacombs of Priscilla, and work is currently in progress on an ambitious new municipal **auditorium** near the Olympic Village, designed by Renzo Piano and due for completion before the millennium.

Rome by Season

Whether you're here in the height of summer or the depths of winter, chances are there's a party going on somewhere.

Ancient Rome had over 150 public holidays a year, which probably contributed significantly to its demise. Today there are only ten – well within the EU average – though the debate on reintroducing one or two of them rumbles on.

Romans are fond of their breaks, often extending them by taking a few extra days off between the end of their official holiday and the following weekend, a practice known as *il ponte* (the bridge). At the faintest hint of sun, festive citizens in their tens of thousands will brave hours of exhaust fumes at a motorway tollbooth for a glimpse of sea or mountain – plus a bacchanalian feast in some rustic spot to help forget the woes of city life.

Different districts of Rome celebrate their particular patron saint with anything from a bit of limp bunting on the front of a church, to a week of all-in parading and feasting. For really special events, makeshift stages are erected in squares and occupied far into the night by lusty crooners of Roman love songs.

Some workers have their own saints' days. Don't phone the Rome bus company on May 26: it's the feast of San Filippo Neri, patron saint of public transport.

If today's celebrations fail to match up to the baroque extravaganzas of the past (*see* chapter **Renaissance Rome: Party Lines**) they can still be charming, and at times very impressive, especially when the Roman passion for fireworks is allowed free rein.

All public holidays are marked here with an asterisk. Additional information is obtainable from tourist offices.

Spring

Festa di San Giuseppe
Around Trionfale. Metro Ottaviano/bus to Piazza Risorgimento. **Date** 19 Mar.
Although no longer an official public holiday, the feast of Saint Joseph, legal father of Jesus, retains a wide following. Only carpenters and woodworkers still get the day off. Until quite recently, the air would be thick with the smell of batter biscuits called *bigné* (found all over Italy, but under a different name in each place) being fried on every street corner. Nowadays this tradition is maintained only in the *quartiere* Trionfale, in north-west Rome.

Roma City Marathon
Via dei Fori Imperiali. Metro Colosseo/bus to Piazza Venezia. **Information** 30 18 30 22/30 18 33 02/30 18 30 16. **Date** 3rd Sun in March.

Rome's annual marathon may not have reached the standard of London or New York, but its reputation is growing and it's starting to attract big-name runners. A city-to-sea half-marathon is held three weeks before the big event.

Festa di Primavera – Mostra delle Azalee
Trinità dei Monti, Piazza di Spagna. Metro Spagna/bus to Via del Tritone or Piazza San Silvestro. **Dates** end Mar-early Apr.
Spring arrives early in Rome, bringing with it masses of flowers. When the azaleas come out, some 3,000 huge vases of them are arranged on the Spanish Steps, displacing the resident army of tourists and their putative Roman escorts.

Settimana Santa & Pasqua
Vatican: *Metro Ottaviano/bus Piazza Risorgimento.* **Colosseum/Palatine:** *Metro Colosseo/bus or tram to Colosseum.* **Information** 69 82. **Dates** Mar, Apr.
Rome's tourist season starts with the Pope's big moment. On the Saturday before *Domenica delle Palme* (Palm Sunday) the city is flooded with tour groups from all over the world, here to attend the open-air mass in Saint Peter's Square. During the *Settimana Santa* (Holy Week) that follows, Rome offers Christendom's nearest equivalent to the collective fervour of Mecca, with non-stop services, rituals and chants in the city's 610 places of Catholic worship. Specific information on events and times is best obtained from street posters. Events culminate in the Pope's night-time mass at the Colosseum on Good Friday.
On *Pasquetta* (Easter Monday) the city empties again, as the Romans traditionally leave the city for their first picnic *fuori le porte* (outside the city gates) and eat *porchetta* (Roman roast pork) and *torta pasqualina* (a cheese bread served with salami and hard-boiled eggs). *See also* chapter **The Vatican City.**

Concerti al Pincio
Piazzale Napoleone I. Metro Flaminio/bus to Piazza del Popolo or Piazzale Flaminio. **Information** 48 89 91.
Date every Sunday morning Apr-July.
Brass bands lend a martial air to the Sunday morning parade of Romans and their children on the Pincio hill by the Villa Borghese gardens.

Natale di Roma
Campidoglio: Bus to Piazza Venezia.
Giardino degli Aranci/Viale Aventino: *Metro Circo Massimo.* **Information** 48 89 91. **Date** 21 Apr.
It may seem odd that a city should have a birthday, but not to the Romans, whose city was 'born' in 753 BC (*see* chapter **History: Romulus & Remus**). The spectacular main birthday celebrations take place at the Campidoglio and the Giardino degli Aranci on the Aventine Hill. The City Hall and all the other palazzi on the hill are covered with *fiaccole romane* (shallow, long-burning candles) to extraordinary effect, and enormous quantities of fireworks are let off.

Festa della Liberazione*
Piazza Venezia: *Bus to Piazza Venezia.*
Mausoleo delle Fosse Ardeatine: *Via Ardeatine, 174.* **Information** 51 46 742. **Date** 25 April.

The liberation of Italy by the Allies in World War II is celebrated in a relatively subdued fashion. The main ceremony is attended by the President at the Mausoleum of the Ardeatine Caves, where the Nazis murdered 335 Romans in 1944. The head of state also lays a wreath on the Tomb of the Unknown Soldier on the **Vittorio Emanuele Monument** in Piazza Venezia, one of the few occasions when this urban white elephant is used.

Concorso Ippico Internazionale di Piazza di Siena

Villa Borghese. Metro Flaminio or Spagna/train to Piazzale Flaminio/bus or tram to Piazzale Flaminio or Via Vittorio Veneto. **Information** 32 79 939. **Dates** end of Apr-beginning of May.

The international show-jumping event at the Piazza di Siena Hippodrome in the Villa Borghese is one of the few truly jet-set occasions that Rome still has to offer. With international horses and riders competing in the Mediterranean equivalent of Ascot, it's as smart and as self-consciously *all'inglese* as can be imagined.

Primo Maggio*

Piazza San Giovanni. Metro San Giovanni/bus or tram to San Giovanni or Piazzale Appio. **Information** 84 76 514. **Date** 1 May.

The main event of May Day in Rome is the big free rock concert outside the basilica of San Giovanni, sponsored by the union federation CGIL-CSIL-UIL. It starts mid-afternoon and goes on well into the night, and features top Italian bands plus a sprinkling of left-leaning international names.

Campionato Internazionale di Tennis (Italian Open)

Foro Italico, Viale dei Gladiatori. Bus to Lungotevere Maresciallo Cadorna. **Information** 32 33 807. **Dates** 1-15 May.

Italy's annual tennis championships are one of the first big events in the European tennis season. They are played on the clay courts at Mussolini's **Foro Italico** sports complex. *See also chapter* **Sport & Fitness**.

Mostra dell'Antiquariato

Via de' Coronari. Bus to Corso del Rinascimento, Corso Vittorio Emanuele or Lungotevere Tor di Nona. **Information** 48 89 91. **Dates** mid-end May; mid-end Oct.

Via de' Coronari is the centre of Rome's antiques trade (*see chapter* **Sightseeing**: *centro storico*). During the 20-day antiques fairs, the shops stay open until late, creating an open-house atmosphere and allowing you to browse to your heart's content.

Fiera Internazionale di Roma (Rome International Trade Fair)

Ente Autonomo Fiera di Roma, Via Cristoforo Colombo, 281, 00147 Rome (51 38 141/fax 51 38 1415). Metro San Paolo/bus to Piazza Navigatori. **Dates** 26 May-early June. **Admission** L4,000-6,000.

Rome is not a major industrial city compared with, say, Milan. However, of the 20 or so annual fairs at the Fiera di Roma site, this one is the most important, and a chance to check out what Italians call *il Made in Italy*.

Fiera d'Arte di Via Margutta

Via Margutta. Metro Spagna/bus to Piazza del Popolo or Piazzale Flaminio. **Information** 81 23 340. **Dates** end of May; end of Oct.

If Via Veneto was where the *Dolce Vita* set hung out at night, Via Margutta was where they did their serious daubing. Few active painters still live here, but the street is still chock-full of art galleries. The high points of their year are the two art fairs, each lasting four days, with paintings ranging from the so-so to the downright terrible cramming every available inch of wall space.

Ceramic Christs vie for space with Old English Sheepdogs at one of Rome's street fairs.

Summer

Festa delle Forze Armate (Armed Forces Day)

Via dei Fori Imperiali. Metro Colosseo/bus to Via dei Fori Imperiali or Piazza Venezia. **Information** 48 89 91. **Date** 2 June.

Today's military parades down Via dei Fori Imperiali are somewhat muted compared with the extravagant shows put on by Mussolini. Proceedings are limited to a fly-past and a wreath-laying ceremony on the Tomb of the Unknown Soldier in the Piazza Venezia.

Estate Romana

Various locations. **Information** 48 89 91. **Dates** June-Aug.

After several years in the doldrums, the Estate Romana (Rome Summer) has once again become a major date in the Roman calendar, bringing an embarrassing choice of music and film to a city which for much of the time is too empty to absorb fully the wealth of events available. *Piazze, palazzi,* parks and courtyards come alive to the sound of local jazz and rock bands, and films are shown on makeshift screens late into the night.

Festa di San Giovanni

San Giovanni in Laterano. Metro San Giovanni/bus or tram to Piazza San Giovanni or Piazzale Appio. **Information** 69 82. **Date** 23 June.

Another saint's day that has lost its resonance, except in San Giovanni, where singing, dancing and games go on all night in the streets. It's *de rigueur* to eat *lumache in umido* (stewed snails) and *porchetta* (roast pork). The religious highlight is the candlelit procession, usually with the Pope as star, leading into the basilica of San Giovanni in Laterano.

Tevere Expo

Tiber Embankment. Bus to Lungotevere Castello or Lungotevere Tor di Nona. **Information** 68 69 068/fax 68 75 947. **Dates** 23 June-31 July.

A full-scale handicrafts fair along the banks of the Tiber, between Ponte Sant'Angelo and Ponte Cavour, with the main entrance by Castel Sant'Angelo. It's open during the day, but is most spectacular at night. There are also entertainers, sports, bars and bands.

San Pietro e San Paolo*

San Paolo fuori le Mura. Metro San Paolo/bus to Piazzale San Paolo and Via Ostiense. **Information** 54 10 341. **Date** 29 June.

The two founders of Catholicism share the honours as twin patron saints of Rome, and each are duly honoured with religious celebrations in their respective basilicas, Saint Peter's and San Paolo fuori le Mura. Outside San Paolo there is also an all-night street fair along the Via Ostiense.

Teatro dell'Opera Summer Season

Teatro dell'Opera, Via Firenze, 72. **Information** 48 17 003/fax 48 81 253). **Dates** July to mid-Aug.

This open-air opera and ballet season tends to be shunted around as venue after venue runs into bureaucratic hitches. In 1997 it was divided between the Baths of Caracalla, the delightful open-air theatre of the National Dance Academy on the Aventine, and the Olimpico soccer stadium. Generally dominated by classic favourites.

RomaEuropa Festival

Metro Castro Pretorio/bus to Via XX Settembre. **Information** 47 42 286. **Dates** July-Oct.

This ambitious pan-European arts festival presents the very best of the participating countries' avant-garde cultural offerings, and is attracting more countries every year. The programmes, however, tend to be dominated by established, officially-sponsored modern-art groups. The worthy tone of

*Brass bands play in the **Pincio** gardens.*

the event limits its potential as a showcase for new talent. *See also chapter* **Theatre & Dance.**

Palio Madama Margherita

Castelmadama. By car: A24 to Castelmadama/train to Avezzano from Termini/bus COTRAL from Metro Rebibbia. **Information** 07 74 44 078/07 74 44 82 10. **Dates** 10, 11 July.

While not quite as spectacular as its more famous Siena counterpart, this horse race and parade in sixteenth-century costumes around a small town near Tivoli (*see chapter* **Trips Out of Town**) saves you a much longer journey. The race is held in honour of the town's sixteenth-century ruler, Margaret of Parma, also remembered in Rome's **Palazzo Madama**.

Roma Alta Moda

Piazza di Spagna. Metro Spagna/bus to Piazza San Silvestro. **Information** 48 28 933. **Dates** mid-July.

Rome's fashion community has long been overshadowed by the trendy goings-on in Milan, but it strikes back with *Alta Moda*. The Piazza di Spagna and several major hotels host sneak-preview evening fashion shows, complete with the usual supermodels, of the following year's *haute couture* collections by Roman designers and Italy's other top labels.

Festa di Noantri

Viale Trastevere. Bus to Viale Trastevere. **Information** 48 89 91. **Dates** mid two weeks of July.

Roughly translatable as 'a knees-up for us plebs', and theoretically in honour of the Madonna del Carmine, with whose procession the events begin, La Festa di Noantri is one of the last surviving glimmers of Trastevere's once-proud working-class culture. For two weeks the busiest section of Viale Trastevere and some of the surrounding streets are blocked off to traffic and filled with market stalls, open into the small hours. A spectacular firework display rounds off the closing night.

Festa delle Catene

Chiesa di San Pietro in Vincoli, Piazza di San Pietro in Vincoli. Metro Cavour/bus to Via Cavour. **Information** 69 82. **Date** 1 Aug.

Chains alleged to be those in which Saint Peter was dragged to his execution are solemnly displayed in a special mass at the delightful church of Saint Peter in Chains (*see chapter* **Churches**).

Festa della Madonna della Neve

Basilica di Santa Maria Maggiore. Metro Cavour or Termini/bus to Piazza dell'Esquilino or Termini. **Information** 48 31 95. **Date** Aug 5.

For Romans sweating it out through a sticky August, snow is an enticing thought. Perhaps that's why the legend of the snowfall over the Esquiline Hill on 5th August 352AD still has such resonance. A deluge of rose petals flutters down on mass-goers in a special service in Santa Maria Maggiore.

Ferragosto – la Festa dell'Assunta*

Date 15 Aug.

The Feast of the Assumption is the high point of summer; even those who remain in Rome in August go away for this long weekend, and practically everything is closed. The very few restaurants that do stay open serve the traditional Ferragosto dish of *pollo con i peperoni*: chicken with peppers.

Autumn

Ognissanti*/ Giornata dei Defunti

Cimitero Il Verano, Piazzale il Verano. Bus or tram to Piazzale Verano. **Information** 49 15 11; 69 82. **Dates** 1, 2 Nov.

Otherwise known as *Tutti Santi*, All Saints' Day is followed by *La Commemorazioni dei Defunti* (or *Tutti i Morti*), when the Pope often celebrates Mass at the vast city cemetery of Il Verano. It is traditional for people to take flowers to the graves of their families.

Winter

Settimana dei Beni Culturali

Various locations. **Information** 58 99 359. **Dates** 1st or 2nd week Dec.

All museums, public monuments and excavation sites are open to the public without charge for a week. Save money and visit many museums and sites that are generally closed.

Immacolata Concezione*

Piazza di Spagna: *Metro Spagna/bus to Piazza San Silvestro or via del Tritone.* **Santa Maria Maggiore:**

Metro Cavour or Termini/bus to Piazza dell'Esquilino or Termini. **Information** 69 82. **Date** 8 Dec.

The statue of the Madonna in Piazza di Spagna is the focal point of this feast day, when, with the Pope looking on, the fire brigade runs a ladder run up Mary's column, and a lucky fireman gets to place a wreath over her outstretched arm. (In times past, it was the Pope himself who scaled the ladder.) At the base of the column, locals and city dignitaries deposit immense quantities of flowers. Later in the day, the Pope continues on to Santa Maria Maggiore to say mass.

Natale* and Santa Stefano*

Dates 25 and 26 Dec.

Oddly enough, the world centre of Catholicism is no great shakes at Christmas. The traditional northern trappings of Yuletide consumerism, with Babbo Natale (Father Christmas) very much in evidence, have asserted themselves strongly in recent years, with extra-long opening hours, Sunday shopping bonanzas and some very tacky street decorations. A walk among the frantic throng on Via del Corso on the weekend before Christmas could put you off present-buying for life. All this is a recent import: until recently, it was Epiphany that really counted. For a taste of something approaching a traditional Roman Christmas, you can seek tickets to the papal midnight mass in Saint Peter's (from the Vatican's Prefettura, 69 88 30 17, but get your order in months ahead), or visit the many cribs in the centre's churches. Saint Peter's Square boasts an immense Christmas tree, along with the biggest crib of them all.

San Silvestro/Capo d'Anno

Dates 31 Dec, 1 Jan.

New Year's Eve is a night to stay inside, and not only because most restaurants are shut: the firework mayhem which builds to a crescendo in the few minutes before midnight (there's no Big Ben here, and watches tend to be unsynchronised) is an unforgettable experience from your hotel window, but reminiscent of the worst days of Beirut if you happen to be caught up in it at street level. Best experienced in popular areas such as Testaccio or San Lorenzo, but there are hazards here too: some older residents still honour the tradition of chucking unwanted consumer durables off the balcony.

Epifania - La Befana*

Piazza Navona. Bus to Corso Vittorio Emanuele or Corso Rinascimento. **Date** 6 Jan.

As a reflection of the Romans' pagan spirit, the Feast of the Epiphany is generally better known by the name of the mythological character they are celebrating, *La Befana*, or the old witch. According to legend, this Mother Christmas only brought presents to good children, while the others got pieces of coal. Today, all Roman *bambini* get their presents anyway, and the coal comes in the form of a sickly black sweet. Between mid-December and 6th January, **Piazza Navona** is filled with market stalls, selling sweets and other cheap tat. The climax is reached on the night between the 5th and 6th of January.

Carnevale

Date the week before Lent (usually late Feb/early Mar).

In the Middle Ages, this pagan farewell to winter revelling before the rigours of Lent was celebrated in lurid abandon outside the city walls on **Monte Testaccio**. Anxious to keep a check on their libidinous subjects, the Renaissance popes brought the ceremony back within the walls to the Via Lata, renaming it Via del Corso in honour of the Carnival processions subsequently held along it. Primary school children dressed up as the favourite Disney character of the moment parade with their proud parents by day, while older children shower the streets with confetti and shaving foam by night. For adults, it's party time on *Martedi Grasso* (Shrove Tuesday) and over the previous weekend.

Sightseeing

Rome by Area

Centro storico

Arco di Costantino (Arch of Constantine) p65; Biblioteca Centrale per i Ragazzi (Children's Library) p183; Campo de' Fiori p41; Campo Marzio (Campus Martius) p35; Chiesa Nuova/Santa Maria in Vallicella p84; Il Gesù (p84); Sant'Agnese in Agone p85; Sant'Andrea della Valle p85; Santi Cosma e Damiano p82; Sant'Ivo alla Sapienza p85; San Luigi dei Francesi p80; Santa Maria in Campitelli p85; Santa Maria in Cosmedin (Bocca della Verità) p82; Santa Maria della Pace p82; San Nicola in Carcere p78. Circo Massimo (Circus Maximus) p66; Cloaca Maxima p71; Colosseo (Colosseum) p66; Fontana del Moro p41; Fontana dei Quattro Fiumi p41; Fontana delle Tartarughe p43; Foro Romano (Roman Forum) p68; Galleria Spada p91; Ghetto p44; Musei Capitolini (Capitoline Museums) p95; Museo d'Arte Ebraica (Museum of Jewish Art) p96; Museo Napoleonico p96; Palatino (Palatine) p46; Palazzo Borghese p43; Palazzo della Cancelleria p43; Palazzo Cenci p43; Palazzo Farnese p43; Palazzo Madama p44; Palazzo Massimo alle Colonne p44; Palazzo Pamphili p46; Palazzo Senatorio p45; Piazza del Campidoglio (Capitol) p45; Piazza Farnese p45; Piazza Navona p45; Piazza Venezia p46; Ponte Rotto p71; Portico d'Ottavia (Portico of Octavia) p71; Teatro di Marcello (Theatre of Marcellus) p75; Tempio di Fortuna Virilis (Temple of Portunus) p75; Tempio di Vesta (Temple of Hercules Victor) p75.

Tridente

Accademia di San Luca p88; Ara Pacis p52. All Saints p247; Sant'Ignazio di Loyola p85; San Lorenzo in Lucina p78; Santa Maria del Popolo p84; Santa Maria Sopra Minerva p83; Santa Maria in Via p82. Colonna di Marco Aurelio (Column of Marcus Aurelius) p66; Fontana di Trevi (Trevi Fountain) p54; Galleria Colonna p89; Galleria Doria Pamphili p89; Keats-Shelley Memorial House p98; Mausoleo di Augusto (Mausoleum of Augustus) p70; Obelisco con l'Elefante (Bernini's Elephant) 52; Palazzo Chigi p46; Palazzo Montecitorio p54; Palazzo Ruspoli p88; Pantheon p71; Piazza Augusto Imperatore p52; Piazza Colonna p46; Piazza di Pietra p48; Piazza del Popolo p54; Piazza di San Silvestro p48; Piazza di Spagna p54; Pincio p54; Scalinata di Trinità dei Monti (Spanish Steps) p54; Tempio di Adriano (Temple of Hadrian) p73; Via del Babuino p52; Via Condotti p52; Via del Corso p46; Via Margutta p52; Via di Ripetta p52.

Via Veneto & Quirinale

Sant'Andrea al Quirinale p85; San Carlo alle Quattro Fontane p85; Santa Maria della Vittoria p85; Santi Vincenzo e Anastasio p82. Fontana dell'Acqua Felice p56; Fontana delle Api p56; Fontana del Tritone p56; Galleria Borghese p97; Galleria Comunale d'Arte Moderna e Contemporanea p88; Museo Nazionale delle

Paste Alimentari p99; Palazzo Barberini p98;
Palazzo delle Esposizioni p88; Palazzo del
Quirinale p56; Piazza Barberini p55; Piazza del
Quirinale p56; Piazza di Siena p56; Quattro
Fontane p56; Via Veneto p54; Villa Borghese p56.

Trastevere

Santa Cecilia p76; San Francesco a Ripa p85;
Santa Maria in Trastevere p83; San Pietro in
Montorio p84; Tempietto di Bramante p84;
Fontana Paola p58; Galleria Nazionale d'Arte
Antica (Palazzo Corsini) p89; Gianicolo p58; Isola
Tiberina (Tiber Island) p58; Museo del Folklore
p96; Palazzo Corsini p58; Piazza di Santa Maria in
Trastevere p58; Porta Portese p56; Porta San
Pancrazio p56; Orto Botanico p58; Villa Farnesina
p59.

Monti & Esquilino

Santa Croce in Gerusalemme p81; San Giovanni
in Laterano (Saint John Lateran) p78; Santa
Maria Maggiore p79; San Martino ai Monti p78;
San Pietro in Vincoli (Saint Peter in Chains)
p82; Santa Prassede p83; Santa Pudenziana p83.
Colle Oppio p60; Colonna di Traiano (Trajan's
Column) p68; Domus Aurea (Nero's Golden
House) p60; Fontana delle Naiadi p60; Fori
Imperiali (Imperial Fora) p66; Piazza del
Cinquecento p60; Piazza della Repubblica p60;
Piazza Vittorio Emanuele p60; Mercati Traiani
(Trajan's Market) p75; Museo Nazionale d'Arte
Orientale p93; Museo Nazionale Romano p93;
Museo Nazionale degli Strumenti Musicali p98;
Museo Storico della Liberazione di Roma p97;
Teatro dell'Opera p199; Terme di Diocleziano
(Baths of Diocletian) p66; Torre delle Milizie p59;
Via Panisperna p60; Villa Aldobrandini p60.

Aventino, Celio & Testaccio

Antiquarium Comunale p91; San Clemente p78;
Santi Giovanni e Paolo p78; San Gregorio Magno
p85; Santa Maria in Domenica p83; Santi Quattro
Coronati p81; Santa Sabina p81. L'Emporio
(Emporium) p66; Food and Agricultural Agency
p60; Mattatoio p61; Monte Testaccio p71; Museo di
Via Ostiense p93; Parco Savello p61; Piazza dei
Cavalieri di Malta p61; Piramide di Gaio Cestio
(Pyramid of Caius Cestius) p73; Porta San Paolo
p62; Protestant Cemetery p62; Terme di Caracalla
(Baths of Caracalla) p66; Villa Celimontana p60.

EUR

Museo dell'Alto Medioevo p95; Museo della
Civiltà Romana p96; Museo Nazionale delle Arti e
Tradizioni Popolari p97; Museo Preistorico ed
Etnografico L. Pigorini p93; Palazzo della Civiltà
del Lavoro p62; Palazzo dello Sport p62.

Other Areas

North

Castel Sant'Angelo p94; La Moschea (Mosque)
p247; Sant'Agnese Fuori le Mura p82; Santa
Costanza p82. Foro Italico p62; Galleria Comunale
d'Arte Moderna e Contemporanea ex-
Stabilmento Peroni p91; Galleria Nazionale d'Arte
Moderna e Contemporanea p91; Giardino
Zoologico (Zoo) p183; Museo delle Anime dei
Defunti p98; Museo Nazionale di Villa Giulia p93;
Museo Storico dell'Arma dei Carabinieri p99;
Museo Storico Nazionale dell'Arte Sanitaria p99.

South

San Lorenzo Fuori le Mura p82; San Paolo Fuori
le Mura (Saint Paul Without the Walls) p79.

Sightseeing

A first trip to Rome is rather like a hot bath – immerse yourself gradually.

Over 2,000 years of history, much of it at the centre of the Western stage, has left Rome with more magnificent piazzas, palaces, churches, ancient sites and monuments than any other European city. Yet far from being a sterile open-air museum, it is one of Europe's most vivacious capitals, and its accumulated glories now form the backdrop for the chaotic exuberance of everyday life.

For an essential first impression, forget the tourist trail and seat yourself at a table outside any central café. Watch passing nuns deftly consuming fast-melting ice creams, dyed-and-pierced students loitering with no courses to go to and Daddy's BMW parked round the corner, politicians screaming past in dark-blue Alfa-Romeos, and trendy seminarians with their DMs protruding ostentatiously from below hitched-up cassocks. Breathe in car fumes mixed with a hint of anarchy as Rome rushes compulsively by.

This done, you can proceed to outdoor sights, and there are enough of these to keep you busy for weeks. Each square contains a fountain or palace of interest and beauty, each narrow street some ancient hidden courtyard. When you've absorbed a place by day, return in the evening. Many sites are floodlit by night and even those which aren't look spectacular in a blend of moonlight and the soft glow from street lamps. Then, finally, it's time to begin with the museums, galleries, _palazzi_ and churches which are – and which contain – Rome's seemingly inexhaustible artistic treasures.

This chapter provides a thumbnail sketch of each of Rome's areas and gives information on some of their most outstanding sights. Details of **Ancient Sites**, **Churches**, **Museums & Galleries** and **The Vatican** are provided in specific chapters.

The _centro storico_

The tightly-knit web of narrow streets and piazzas on the right bank of the river Tiber forms the core of Rome's _centro storico_ (historic centre). By day it teems with small shops, markets, craft workshops and restaurants; by night it buzzes with clubs, bars and more restaurants.

There are sharp social and economic contrasts here. In ancient cobbled streets off Via dei Banchi Vecchi and Via del Governo Vecchio, dingy motorcycle repair shops spill out onto pavements shared

There's nothing like a dome: **St Peter's.**

with chic lunchtime cafés, and exclusive boutiques stand cheek-by-jowl with grubby-looking junk shops. The inhabitants are also a mixed bunch: ever-higher rates have not yet succeeded in pushing all the centre's poor out to dismal suburbs, and down-at-heel pensioners still shuffle among the fur-coated occupants of smart apartments carved out of patrician _palazzi_.

In ancient times, much of the area on either side of the present-day Corso Vittorio Emanuele was relatively thinly populated, and a large section of it to the north was kept empty as the Campus Martius, the training ground reserved for games and exercises to keep Romans ready for war. The main centre of population in ancient Rome was to the south-east, around the Forum. The area now referred to as the _centro storico_ was built up from the Dark Ages onwards, under papal rule, and became the centre of Rome.

The inhabitants of the _centro_ have been making a living out of tourists for centuries. Via de' Coronari is now home to some of the old centre's showiest antiques shops, but it started out in the fifteenth century as the Via Recta, or straight

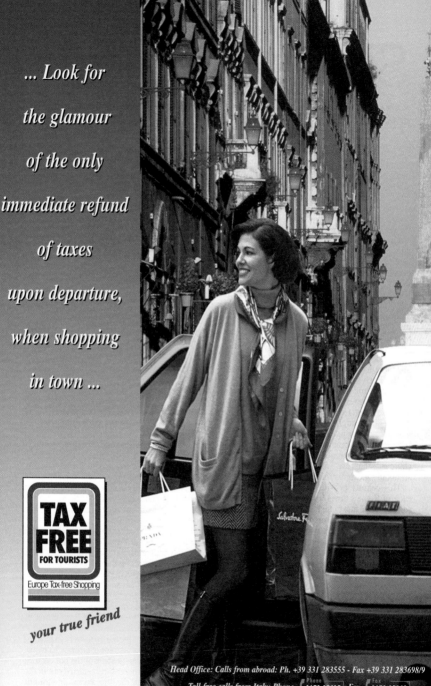

... *Look for*
the glamour
of the only
immediate refund
of taxes
upon departure,
when shopping
in town ...

Campo de' Fiori, *for overpriced veg by day, sparkling wine bars by night. See page 41.*

street, designed to ferry pilgrims to the Vatican quickly, with their money-bags intact. However, within a few years rosary-makers (*coronari*), ancestors of modern souvenir-sellers, had taken over the street and were making a killing out of the passing trade.

By the time of the high Renaissance, there were over two dozen banks, hundreds of hotels and numerous courtesans in the area, servicing the financial deals and physical needs of visiting ecclesiastics, pilgrims and businessmen. Survivors of the era include the sixteenth-century Banco di Santo Spirito, originally the papal mint; and a fifteenth century inn, the Osteria dell'Orso on Via dell'Orso which during the Renaissance was inhabited mainly by upmarket courtesans.

In the 1880s, the Corso Vittorio Emanuele, linking Stazione Termini with the Vatican, was driven through the district, carving a gracious, though now heavily trafficked and grimy, course past historic churches and *palazzi*. It is plied by the infamous 64 bus, main means of transport between central Rome and the **Vatican**, and also much loved by petty thieves and frotteurs, attracted by the wallets, handbags and scantily-clad backsides of unwary tourists.

One of the pleasantest aspects of the *centro storico* is that there is no sense of its being a museum city preserved for tourists and academics. Corso Vittorio is a thundering office-lined thoroughfare; Via de' Coronari carries on its brisk antiques trade, barely deigning to notice passing tourists; the myriad shops on Via del Governo Vecchio pitch their

Frotteurs get their kicks on **Route 64**.

wares to residents as much as visitors. Even picturesque Via Giulia, with its abundance of art galleries and high, ivy-dripping walls, is predominantly a haphazard ante-chamber and moped-park for the high school at its far end.

The *centro*'s squares, too, may have venerable histories and architecture but they share the area's endearingly self-deprecating character, forming magnificent sets for the happenings of everyday life. **Piazza Venezia** is a traffic roundabout of breathtaking proportions, daunting even for locals as they dice with death to cross on foot. For pedestrian activity, pride of place has to go to the great theatre of Baroque Rome, **Piazza Navona**. Despite its gracious sweep, Bernini fountains and pavement cafés, its denizens range from soothsayers, caricature artists, buskers and suburban

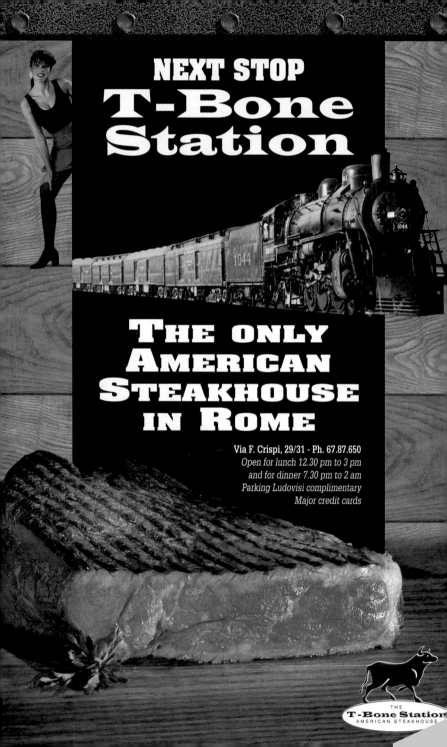

NEXT STOP
T-Bone Station

THE ONLY AMERICAN STEAKHOUSE IN ROME

Via F. Crispi, 29/31 - Ph. 67.87.650
Open for lunch 12.30 pm to 3 pm
and for dinner 7.30 pm to 2 am
Parking Ludovisi complimentary
Major credit cards

THE
T-Bone Station
AMERICAN STEAKHOUSE

smoothies to tourists, nuns, businessmen, ladies of leisure and anyone who simply wants a gossip.

Between the **Campo de' Fiori** and Via Giulia is solemn, operatic **Piazza Farnese**, with its twin fountains. Overlooking them is **Palazzo Farnese**, designed by Michelangelo and now home to the French Embassy. Just off Piazza Navona, in little Piazza Pasquino, stands the patron of the city's scandalmongers, a severely truncated classical statue lodged against one wall of a car-packed triangle. Placed here in 1501, it is known as Pasquino, supposedly after a tailor who had his shop in the piazza and did work for the Vatican, becoming famous for regaling his mates with insider gossip. He left some of his best stories and lampoons pinned to the statue, and when other people joined in it became the Renaissance equivalent of *Private Eye*. Scurrilous and libellous verses, called *pasquinate* and usually targeted at the aristocratic and ecclesiastical establishment, were attached to the statue anonymously to be read by all. In papal Rome, this was just about the only channel of free speech. In time, Pasquino gained correspondents, as the lampoons he carried were 'answered' by others, and he engaged in dialogues with other 'talking statues' such as Madame Lucrezia (on Piazza Venezia), Luigi Abate (next to **Sant'Andrea della Valle**) and Marforio (in the Palazzo Nuovo courtyard of the **Capitoline Museums**).

The streets in the area between Corso Vittorio and Via Arenula converge on the Campo de'Fiori. All have medieval names referring to the trades

The inescapable **Colosseum**. *See page 66.*

Visit the **Protestant Cemetery** *and fall in love with death. See page 62.*

practised in them: Baullari (trunk-makers), Chiavari (key-makers), Cappellari (hatters), Giubonnari (jacket-makers), Barbieri (barbers) – all evidence of the medieval practice of obliging like-skilled craftsmen to set up shop in the same street. Even after 500 years, Via de' Giubbonari has kept the faith, with central Rome's highest concentration of clothes shops. Via de' Cappellari, on the other hand, has shifted emphasis but not character: its medieval buildings open up as workshops on the ground floors, and carpenters and furniture restorers work in the street. Despite the prices, the quality of the goods and services on offer is low: the smarter shops on Via Giulia and Via Monserrato offer better quality.

At night, the whole area on either side of Corso Vittorio is chaotic with obsessive to-ing and fro-ing between pizzerias, trattorias, gelaterias and bars. The most popular area for nightlife stretches from Piazza Navona towards the river, and is known as *il triangolo della Pace* after the eternally fashionable Bar della Pace on Via della Pace. Smartly dressed Romans gather to drink, meet or pose in and around the bars along these narrow cobbled streets. Others get bottles of beer from cheap bars and hang out on the fringes.

The most historically significant part of the *centro* lies beyond the Capitoline. It was here that Rome had its birthplace in the **Roman Forum** and the **Palatine**, and it's here that you will find the monument which for centuries has been the city's best-recognised landmark: the **Colosseum**.

The Sights

Campo de' Fiori

Bus to Corso Vittorio Emanuele or Via Arenula/tram to Via Arenula.

Home to Rome's most picturesque – though most costly – food market in the mornings, Campo de' Fiori is an amiable piazza, surrounded by houses with chafed walls, warped shutters and pigeons nesting on their sills. The Campo has been a focus of Roman life since the fifteenth century. Lucrezia Borgia was born nearby, her brother was murdered down the road, and Caravaggio played a game of tennis on the piazza, then murdered his opponent for having the temerity to beat him. The cowled statue in the centre is of Giordano Bruno, burned at the stake on the spot (*dove il rogo arse* – where the pyre burned, as the inscription says) in 1600 for reaching the conclusion that philosophy and magic were superior to religion. The market begins around 6am and packs up in the early afternoon, when people flow into the Campo's restaurants for lunch. Afternoons are quiet and slow, with things beginning to pick up around 6pm, when the ever-popular **Vineria** wine bar (*see chapter* **Eating & Drinking**) opens up. By 10pm the restaurants are full again, and by midnight the Vineria crowd has expanded to fill the entire square.

Fontana dei Quattro Fiumi and Fontana del Moro

Piazza Navona. Bus to Corso Vittorio Emanuele or Corso del Rinascimento.

At the centre of the **Piazza Navona**, the 'Fountain of the Four Rivers', finished in 1651, is one of the most extravagant masterpieces designed – though only partly sculpted – by Bernini. Its main figures represent the rivers Ganges, Nile, Danube and Plate, surrounded by geographically appropriate flora and fauna. The figure of the Nile is veiled, as its source was unknown, though for centuries the story went that Bernini designed it that way so the river god appeared to be recoiling in horror from the façade of **Sant'Agnese in Agone** which was designed by his great rival Borromini. In

*Join every other visitor to Rome at the **Piazza di Spagna**. See page 54.*

fotografia Uberto Gasche - art Indiveri

SILK
COTTON
CASHMERE

R O M E   M I L A N   L O N D O N*   M A D R I D

BALLOON - Show room Piazza di Spagna, 35 Rome
Franchising and Distribution Ph. +39-6-24403801 Fax +39-6-24403841
* Next opening Spring 1998

Phwooar...look at the apse on that. See **Architectural Terms,** *page 264.*

fact, the church was built after the fountain was finished. The obelisk in its centre came from the ancient Circus of Maxentius on the Via Appia Antica. The less spectacular Fontana del Moro is at the southern end of the piazza. The central figure (called the Moor, although he looks more like a portly sea god wrestling with a dolphin) was the only part designed by Bernini himself.

Fontana delle Tartarughe
Piazza Mattei, The Ghetto. Bus to Largo di Torre Argentina.
One of Rome's most delicate fountains lies in the maze of streets that make up the old **Ghetto.** Four elegant boys cavort around its base, helping some tortoises struggle up to the waters above them. According to legend, Giacomo della Porta and Taddeo Landini built the fountain in a single night for the Duke of Mattei. The Duke, the story goes, had just lost all his money and consequently his fiancée, and wanted to prove to her father that he could still achieve great things. The tortoises, possibly by Bernini, were added in the following century.

Palazzo Borghese
Largo della Fontanella Borghese. Bus to Lungotevere Marzio.
This huge building, known as the 'harpsichord' because of its curvaceous walls and keyboard-shaped raised terrace, was designed in the mid-sixteenth century, probably by Vignola, the architect of the **Gesù,** and bought by Cardinal Camillo Borghese, later Pope Paul V, in 1605. Its most flamboyant inhabitant was Pauline Bonaparte, sister of Napoleon, who was reluctantly married to a listless Borghese prince, Camillo. She hated the house, complaining that it was cold, damp, looked like an art gallery and had no bathroom. Part of the palace is now used as a carpet showroom, so you should be able to have a wander inside. The rest is the Spanish Embassy. Try to get into the courtyard, or at least peer over the automatic gates, to see the fantastic gardens with their statuary, hanging plants and inevitable cats.

Palazzo della Cancelleria
Piazza della Cancelleria. Bus to Corso Vittorio Emanuele. **Closed to the public.**
One of the most refined examples of Renaissance architecture in Rome, the Palazzo della Cancelleria was built,

possibly by Bramante, between 1483 and 1513 for Raffaele Riario. He was the great-nephew of Pope Sixtus IV, who made him a cardinal at the age of 17, though Raffaele didn't allow his ecclesiastical duties to cramp his style. He is said to have raised a third of the cost of this palace with the proceeds of a single night's gambling. He also got involved in some anti-Medici plotting, and in retaliation the palace was confiscated for the Church when Giovanni de' Medici became Pope Leo X in 1513. It later became the Papal Chancellery and is still Vatican property, given over to papal offices. The fourth-century church of San Lorenzo in Damaso was incorporated into one side of the building.

Palazzo Cenci
Vicolo dei Cenci. Bus to Via Arenula or Lungotevere dei Cenci. **Closed to the public.**
Hidden in the middle of the Ghetto, this unassuming palazzo was home to the Cenci family, who attained notoriety in 1598 when Beatrice Cenci, her mother and two brothers were arrested for hiring thugs to murder her father. Popular opinion came to her defence, however, when it was revealed that the father had forced Beatrice to commit incest. Despite all this, the Pope condemned her to death and she was beheaded outside **Castel Sant'Angelo** in 1599. Shelley used the story in The Cenci, a play which was banned in London until 1886, on account of the subject matter.

Palazzo Farnese
Piazza Farnese (68 74 834). Bus to Corso Vittorio Emanuele.
The Palazzo has housed the French Embassy since the 1870s and is not generally open to the public, though guided tours can sometimes be arranged by appointment (preference is given to art historians). Often considered the finest Renaissance palace in Rome, this huge building was begun for Cardinal Alessandro Farnese (later Pope Paul III) in 1514 by Antonio da Sangallo the Younger. He died before it was completed and in 1546 Michelangelo took over. He was responsible for most of the upper storeys and the grand cornice along the roof. After his death the building was completed by Giacomo della Porta. The interior contains some superb frescoes by Annibale Carracci.

The Ghetto

Rome's Jews occupy a unique place in the history of the Diaspora. They have managed to maintain an uninterrupted presence in the city for over 2,000 years, making this Europe's longest-surviving Jewish community and one which enjoyed a surprising degree of security, even at times (such as in the years immediately following the Black Death) when waves of anti-semitism were sweeping the rest of Europe. Some Italian Jews even applied a rather fanciful Hebrew eymology to *Italia*, deriving from it *I Tal Ya* – island of the dew of God.

It may seem odd that the city which was the great centre of power for the Christian Church should have represented such a safe haven, but security came at a price. The popes took on the double role of protectors (seeking to curb outbreaks of popular violence against Jews) and oppressors, bringing the Jews under their direct jurisdiction and making sure they paid for the privilege. The first documented tax on Roman Jews dates back to 1310, and set the pattern for the tradition of blackmail which characterised the Church's relations with the Jewish community until the nineteenth century. Payment exempted Jews from having to take part in the humiliating Carnival games, where they were liable to be packed into barrels and rolled from the top of **Mount Testaccio**.

The historic memory of this exploitation was revived in September 1943, when the German occupiers demanded 50kg of gold from the Jewish community, to be produced within 36 hours. After an appeal to which both Jews and non-Jews responded, the target was reached, but this time the blackmail did not bring security. On 16 October over a thousand Jews, most of them women and children, were rounded up and deported in cattle trucks to Auschwitz. In all, a quarter of Rome's Jews died in the concentration camps, a proportion that would certainly have been higher had it not been for the help given by wide sections of Roman society, including the Catholic priesthood.

Rome's Jews had originally settled in Trastevere, but by the thirteenth century they had started to cross the river into the area which later became the Jewish Ghetto: three cramped hectares in one corner of the *centro storico*, immediately to the north of the Tiber island. Its chief landmark today is the imposing modern synagogue, begun in 1874. The synagogue incorporates the **Museo di Arte Ebraica**, a small museum of Roman Jewish life and ritual, containing the few objects which survived the Nazi occupation.

The Ghetto (the word is Venetian in origin) was definitively walled off in 1556 after the bull *Cum nimis absurdam*, issued by the anti-semitic Pope Paul IV, ordered a physical separation between the Jewish and Christian parts of the city. Many Jews actually welcomed the protection which walls and curfews afforded, despite the fact that they were also obliged periodically to attend mass in churches, where they were lectured on their sinfulness. However, overcrowding, the loss of property rights and trade restrictions imposed on the community all took their toll, and the Ghetto went into a long, painful decline between the sixteenth and eighteenth centuries.

By the time of Italian unification in 1870, conditions for the more than 5,000 people who lived there were desperately squalid. The new government ordered that the walls be destroyed and large sections of the district rebuilt.

The Via Portico d'Ottavia, with its anarchic hotchpotch of ancient, medieval and Renaissance architecture, used to mark the Ghetto's boundary. Nowadays, this is still the centre of Jewish life in the city, even though many of the old people you'll see sitting around chatting during the evening have come in from the suburbs. It's also a good place to sample that unique hybrid which is Roman Jewish cookery. Restaurants like **Da Giggetto** (*see chapter* **Restaurants**) specialise in such delicacies as artichokes fried Jewish-style, while at one end of the street, in a tiny unmarked corner shop, an all-female bakery turns out a *torta di ricotta e visciole* – a ricotta and damson tart – which has achieved legendary status among Roman gourmets.

Palazzo Madama

Corso del Rinascimento (67 061). Bus to Corso del Rinascimento. **Open** first Sat of every month; free guided tours in Italian 10am-6pm.

Home of the Italian Senate since 1871, this palazzo was built by the Medici family as their Rome residence in the sixteenth century. Its rather twee façade, with a frieze of cherubs and bunches of fruit, was added 100 years later. The *Madama* of its name was Margaret of Parma (1522-86), the illegitimate daughter of Emperor Charles V, who came to live here in the 1560s before moving to the Netherlands, where she instigated some of the bloodiest excesses of the religious wars.

Palazzo Massimo alle Colonne

Corso Vittorio Emanuele, 141 (68 64 032). Bus to Corso Vittorio Emanuele. **Open** March 16 only; times vary.

The Massimo were one of the oldest aristocratic families in the city, claiming to trace their descent from ancient Rome. In 1797, Napoleon asked a member of the family if they were real-

Piazza Venezia, *with the plug-ugly* **Vittoriale** *in front,* **Palazzo Venezia** *to the right. See p46.*

ly descended from Fabius Maximus, the opponent of Hannibal, and received the haughty reply that they could not prove it, as 'the story has only been told in our family for 1,200 years'. When their palace was built in the 1530s by Baldassare Peruzzi, its unique design – curved walls with a portico built into the bend – aroused suitable admiration. The interior is only open to the public on one day each year, March 16, in commemoration of the day in 1583 when a young Massimo was allegedly raised from the dead by the benevolent Counter-Reformation saint Philip Neri. At the rear of the palace is the Piazza de' Massimi, dominated by an ancient column originally from Domitian's Theatre, which stood close by.

Piazza del Campidoglio (The Capitoline)

Bus to Piazza Venezia.
Michelangelo designed this elegant piazza for Pope Paul III in the 1530s. It took about 100 years to complete, but although some of his ideas were modified along the way, it is still much as he envisaged it. It stands on top of the Capitoline, politically the most important of ancient Rome's seven hills and site of the three major temples – to Jupiter, symbolic father of the city; Minerva, goddess of

wisdom; and Juno Moneta, a vigilant goddess who was expected to sound the alarm in times of danger. The temple of Juno, the site of which is now occupied by the church of Santa Maria in Aracoeli, housed the sacred Capitoline geese in commemoration of the gaggle that supposedly raised the alarm when the Gauls attacked Rome in 390 BC. The best approach to the Campidoglio is via a refined ramp of steps called the *cordonata*, also by Michelangelo, that sweeps up from the Via del Teatro di Marcello. At the top, the steps are flanked by two giant Roman statues of mythical twins Castor and Pollux, placed here in 1583. The palace facing you from the top of the steps is the Palazzo Senatorio, Rome's city hall, completed by Giacomo della Porta and Girolamo Rainaldi to a design by Michelangelo. To the left is the **Palazzo Nuovo** and to the right the **Palazzo dei Conservatori**, which together make up the **Capitoline Museums**. For four centuries, the pedestal in the middle of the square supported a magnificent second-century equestrian statue of the Emperor Marcus Aurelius, placed here by Michelangelo. The statue you see today is a faithful computer-generated copy; the original, after years of restoration, is now behind glass in the ground floor of the Palazzo Nuovo.

Piazza Farnese

Bus to Corso Vittorio Emanuele.
Serene, elegant and dominated by the refined façade of Michelangelo's **Palazzo Farnese**, the piazza is a world away from the bustle of adjacent Campo de' Fiori. It's uncluttered save for the two fountains created in the seventeenth century out of granite bath tubs from the **Baths of Caracalla** and topped with lilies – the Farnese emblem. The area is most evocative at night when the palace is lit up and chandeliers inside are switched on to reveal ceilings with sumptuous frescoes.

Piazza Navona

Bus to Corso Vittorio Emanuele or Corso Rinascimento.
This tremendous, theatrical oval, dominated by the gleaming marble composition of Bernini's **Fontana dei Quattro Fiumi**, is the hub of the *centro storico*. The piazza owes its

shape to an ancient stadium, built here in 86 AD by the Emperor Domitian, which was the scene of at least one martyrdom (Saint Agatha was thrown to her death for refusing to marry), as well as sporting events. Just to the north of the piazza, you can still see some remains of the original arena, sunk below the level of Corso Rinascimento. The piazza acquired its current form in the mid-seventeenth century. Its western side is dominated by Borromini's façade for the church of **Sant'Agnese in Agone** and the adjacent Palazzo Pamphili, built for Pope Innocent X in 1644-50.

Piazza Venezia

Bus to Piazza Venezia.

Piazza Venezia is dominated by the glacial **Vittoriale**, a piece of nationalistic kitsch which outdoes anything dreamed up by the ancients. Built on a scale unmatched even by Saint Peter's, this vast pile, entirely out of proportion with anything around it, was constructed between 1885 and 1911 to honour the first king of united Italy. Featuring an equestrian statue of Vittorio Emanuele, who sports a moustache three metres long, it is also the home of the eternal flame, Italy's memorial to the unknown soldier, guarded by soldiers day and night. As for the piazza, six main roads converge here, making it a dizzying roundabout. The west side is formed by the **Palazzo Venezia**, now a museum containing little of interest and hosting occasional exhibitions of very varying standards (*see chapter* **Museums & Galleries**). The palace, one of the first Renaissance buildings in Rome, was built in the late fifteenth century for the Venetian Pope Paul II. Centuries later, Mussolini established his headquarters here, delivering regular orations to the crowds from the balcony overlooking the piazza, where pedestrians were prevented from standing still by security-obsessed guards.

The *Tridente*

Via del Corso shoots down from **Piazza del Popolo** to **Piazza Venezia**, jammed with traffic and hemmed in by clothes shops, shoe shops and banks. It forms the central prong of three streets (the others are Via del Babuino and Via di Ripetta) known, for reasons which will be obvious when you see them on a map, as *Il Tridente*, the 'trident' of Rome. At weekends bus-loads of teenagers from the suburbs swarm to this grid of narrow streets to strut amongst *jeanserie*, while during the week well-heeled Romans browse in Armani, Gucci and Bulgari and crowds of Japanese visitors queue patiently to enter the Prada fashion pagoda.

Via del Corso is the last urban stretch of the ancient Via Flaminia, which linked Rome with the north Adriatic coast. Over the past 2,000 years it has been successively a processional route for Roman legions, a country lane, a track for Carnival races and, from the late nineteenth century, a showcase street for the capital.

The street's liveliest period began in the mid-fifteenth century, when Pope Paul II began to fret over the debauched goings-on at the pre-Lenten Carnival celebrations in **Testaccio**. He decided to transfer all the races and processions to somewhere within the city walls where he and his troops could keep an eye on things. The obvious spot was the Via Flaminia – then known simply

The Magnificent Seven

Even nth-generation Romans muddle up the seven hills of the ancient city. Just for the record, they are (in anti-clockwise order): the Capitoline, the Palatine, the Aventine, the Caelium, the Esquiline, the Viminal and the Quirinal. It's easy to get confused, since the development of the modern city has incorporated a number of sizeable geological blips into the urban sprawl.

Perhaps the most unusual of these is **Monte Testaccio**. Now sheltering a buzzing night scene at its foot, this fifty-metre-high hill is composed entirely of the shards of over 50 million *amphorae* (earthenware jars), making it probably the oldest rubbish tip in the world.

To the ancient Romans the topography of the city would have been very different. The hills were higher and the valleys deeper. They would also be surprised to see that the Vaelium, a hill that once stood between the Esquiline and the Forum, has disappeared. In his desperation to see the Colosseum from the windows of **Palazzo Venezia**, Mussolini not only demolished the homes of some 2,000 people, but also flattened the hill itself, moving 300,000 cubic metres of earth in order to do so.

as the Via Lata, or wide street – at the end of which he had his new **Palazzo Venezia** built. He had the street paved (using funds raised by a tax on prostitutes) and renamed it *Il Corso* (the Avenue). For over four centuries Romans flocked there at Carnival time to be entertained by such edifying spectacles as races between press-ganged Jews, hunchbacks, prostitutes, and horses with hot pitch up their *recta* to make them run faster. These grotesqueries only stopped after Italian unification in the 1870s, when the new national government set up shop half-way along the Via del Corso. The cheap shops and eateries which lined the street were shut down and replaced by pompous neoclassical offices for banks and insurance companies. This set the tone for what remains the country's political heart: the Chamber of Deputies in **Palazzo Montecitorio**, situated in the piazza of the same name, and Palazzo Chigi, the prime minister's office in Piazza Colonna.

*Augustus' Egyptian obelisk in **Piazza del Popolo**. See page 54.*

Legends of Machiavellian wheeler-dealing cling to each restaurant and bar in the vicinity of the parliament building. Older MPs can be distinguished by their shapeless green Tyrolean swing coats, which inexplicably never went out of fashion in Roman political circles. Younger ones tend to look like somebody's secretary. More impressive are the ministers' chauffeurs in their sharp suits, mirror shades and identical haircuts, lined up outside Palazzo Chigi during cabinet meetings.

There have been changes in the *Tridente*'s other squares, too. The symmetrically elegant **Piazza del Popolo** was once the papacy's favourite place for executions; now, virtually traffic free, it's a popular meeting point. And though Federico Fellini no longer graces the **Canova** bar, his spirit hovers over it and its equally famous rival across the way, **Rosati** (*see chapter* **Eating & Drinking**).

To the west of the Corso is the charmingly Rococo **Piazza Sant'Ignazio** with its severe Jesuit church, while in the Piazza di Pietra the columns of the **Temple of Hadrian** can be seen embedded in the walls of Rome's singularly inactive stock exchange. Further over still lies **Piazza della Rotonda**, home to the **Pantheon** and adorned with a central fountain whose steps provide an ever-popular hang-out for hippies, punks and other counter-culture varieties. All seem oblivious to the well-heeled tourists paying over the odds for coffee. Piazza San Silvestro, to the east, has been reduced to a noisy bus terminus. It's a short walk from here to the **Fontana di Trevi**.

The most famous piazza in the area, the **Piazza di Spagna**, was at the centre of what eighteenth-century Romans called *er ghetto de l'inglesi* (the English ghetto), despite having its fair share of Grand Tourists from all over Europe (to Romans, all foreigners were English, and all were equally fleeceable). The whole area was given over to sheep and ruins until Pope Sixtus V (1585-90) subjected it to a touch of his favourite hobby: town-planning. Nowadays, the piazza has lost little of its charm, despite the fact that since its metro stop was opened in the early 1980s it has become a favourite hang-out for suburban youths, who fill the square and the **Spanish Steps** above it, importuning foreign females. A vast branch of McDonald's, the opening of which was fiercely

---

Tales of the City

Of the many Anglo-Saxon writers who have made pilgrimages to Rome, the American novelist Henry James (1843-1916) must rank among the most assiduous. From *Daisy Miller* (1878) to *The Portrait of a Lady* (1881) and *The Golden Bowl* (1904), the city provided the setting for many of his tales, especially those which explore his favourite theme of innocent Americans being duped by wily Europeans. If you wish to follow in James's footsteps, here are some hints for a two-day visit as ambitious as the master's ... and considerably faster-paced than his fiction.

After booking comfortable rooms on Via del Corso you should exhaust yourself on your first day by visiting the **Forum**, the **Pantheon**, **Saint Peter's**, **Castel Sant'Angelo**, the **Appian Way** and 'all the piazzas'. The fact that the statue of **Marcus Aurelius** on the **Capitoline** is a computer-generated copy of the original shouldn't stop you from getting off on those massive bronze thighs. 'Here at last was a *man*!' sighed Henry to a friend – so unlike 'that poor sexless old Pope'.

Next morning, if you want to get away from it all – and rest those aching feet – hire a horse and canter off into what's left of the 'purple Campagna' surrounding the city. Back in town, sip afternoon tea with your loaded ex-pat chums in their swish apartments in **Palazzo Barberini** or on the Via Gregoriana. Later on, if you fancy eyeing up the local talent, forget about today's flirt-spots at the **Spanish Steps** and the **Fontana di Trevi**; go Jamesian and circle the **Pincio** and the **Villa Borghese** in your carriage. Beware of sightseeing at night, however. Daisy Miller's nocturnal visit to the **Colosseum** leads to a nasty dose of *malaria perniciosa* and an early grave 'beneath the cypresses and the thick spring flowers' of the **Protestant Cemetery**.

It is in the Cemetery that some of the more unusual reminders of James' life and work are found. Look out for the tomb of Julia Newberry, the flirtatious and short-lived American girl who inspired Daisy. The cemetery also contains the mortal remains of Constance Fenimore Woolson, who nurtured an unrequited love for the confirmed bachelor and ultimately threw herself out of a window in Venice.

It is also the last resting place of sculptor Hendrick Andersen, who resides in the showiest grave in the cemetery, a tomb of his own design. James was 56 when he met this 'lovable youth'. His infatuation lasted the rest of his life, even though the younger artist's fixation with 'unsaleable nakedness' and his megalomaniacal designs for colossal fountains and proto-fascist new towns brought the ageing novelist to the brink of despair.

Marcus Aurelius, *now a computer-generated copy, is still a mighty sight. See page 45.*

The **Fontana di Trevi**, *drowning in an ocean of tat. See page 54.*

contested by local designers headed by Valentino, feeds the flirting and flitting hordes.

The grid of streets below the Piazza di Spagna is home to the latest creations of Valentino and the like, with Via Condotti still unchallenged as the city's chief shopping thoroughfare. The Spagna district also holds relics of the Rome of original Grand Tourists such as Keats, Shelley, Byron, Goethe and the Brownings. You can still have a coffee at **Caffè Greco**, whose clients have included Casanova and mad King Ludwig of Bavaria, or a cuppa at **Babington's Tea Rooms**, set up by two Victorian spinsters, or visit the house where Keats died of consumption and a broken heart (*see chapter* **Museums & Galleries**). For a price, you can sleep in the **Hotel d'Inghilterra** where the rooms still resemble those of a London gentlemen's club (*see chapter* **Accommodation**).

Leading out of Piazza di Spagna to the north-west is Via del Babuino, once home to artists and composers such as Poussin and Wagner and now lined with serious antique and interior design shops. The street is named after a statue which was considered so ugly it was named 'the baboon'. It's close to the incongruously neo-gothic All Saint's Church, designed by the English architect GE Street and looking for all the world like a stray from an English village – an impression confirmed by the tea and biscuits served in the garden behind on sunny Sundays.

Tucked in beside Via del Babuino is Via Margutta, synonymous with the bohemian art boom of the 1950s and 1960s and with Rome's great mythologist Federico Fellini, who lived here until his death in 1993.

The third arm of the *Tridente*, Via di Ripetta, has a quite different feel. It's lined with art-book shops, art-supply shops and bars full of students from the nearby art college. Halfway down the street is the emphatic Piazza Augusto Imperatore, built by Mussolini around the rather neglected family funeral-mound of the Emperor Augustus, with the intention of having himself buried there with the Caesars. Above, encased in glass, is the magnificent **Ara Pacis**, erected by Augustus to celebrate peace in the Mediterranean after his conquest of Gaul and Spain. Beyond the square are two fine churches: San Girolamo degli Illirici, serving Rome's Croatian community, and San Rocco, built for local innkeepers and Tiber boatmen by Alexander VI (1492-1503).

The Sights

Bernini's Elephant (Obelisco con l'Elefante 'Il Pulcino della Minerva')
Piazza della Minerva. Bus to Largo di Torre Argentina.
This cuddly marble elephant, with its wrinkled bottom and benign expression, has stood in Piazza della Minerva since 1667. It was designed by Bernini as a tribute to Pope

A Rome with a View

If claustrophobic bustle and chaos are detracting from your appreciation of the glories of historic Rome, rise above them. With the exception of turn-of-the-century bleach-white monuments like the **Vittoriale** and the Law Courts, the city's unique terracotta skyline has been wonderfully preserved.

The best way to see it is from any one of the following vantage points, all of which reveal unfamiliar aspects of such familiar landmarks as the Colosseum and the Pantheon, and show the topsy-turvy streets of the city as it has grown along the winding Tiber, over the seven hills and far away.

The Aventine, Quirinal, Pincio and Gianicolo offer spectacular views, particularly during the late afternoon, when the sun lights up the ochre of the city's façades. Dawns and sunsets can be spectacular, especially in summer. An explanatory plaque atop the Gianicolo will help you to pick out monuments below.

Alternatively, move indoors to take a Tosca-like climb to the top of **Castel Sant'Angelo**, from which you can see the **Castelli Romani**, or wind up the claustrophobically narrow steps in the shell of Saint Peter's dome. Top spots have also been nabbed by some of Rome's most exclusive hotels. Dress up and splash out for the luxurious view offered by the rooftop terrace of the **Hassler Villa Medici** or the bar and restaurant in the **Hotel Eden** (*see chapter* **Accommodation**).

Alexander VII; elephants were both a symbol of wisdom and a model of sexual abstinence. They were believed to be monogamous and to mate only once every five years, which, the Church felt, was the way things should be. The sixth-century BC Egyptian obelisk it carries on its back came from an ancient temple dedicated to the goddess Isis.

Fontana di Trevi

Piazza di Trevi. Metro Barberini/bus to Piazza San Silvestro.
This is known the world over as the fountain where Anita Ekberg cooled off in *La Dolce Vita*. Although it's tucked away in a tiny piazza, it's almost impossible to miss, as the alleys which approach it are glutted with souvenir shops and takeaway pizzerias and full of the sound of water. Permanently surrounded by crowds, the fountain's creamy travertine gleams beneath powerful torrents of water and constant camera flashes. The attention is justified: it's a magnificent Rococo extravaganza of rearing sea horses, conch-blowing tritons, craggy rocks and flimsy trees, cavorting below the wall of the Palazzo Poli. The fountain, designed by Nicolò Salvi for Pope Clement XII, was finished in 1762, though the canal that feeds it has been here since Roman times. Would-be Ekbergs should think twice before plunging in: not only are they likely to be arrested, but the water contains unpalatable quantities of bleach.

Palazzo di Montecitorio

Piazza di Montecitorio (67 601). Open first Sun of every month; free guided tours in Italian 10am-6pm. Weekdays: guided group visits by appointment only. *Closed* Aug.
Since 1871 this has been the Chamber of Deputies, which is why police and barricades sometimes prevent you from getting anywhere near its elegantly curving façade. The building was designed by Bernini in 1650 for Pope Innocent X, and although much of it has been greatly altered since, the clock tower, columns and window sills of rough-hewn stone are his originals.

Piazza del Popolo

Metro Flaminio/train or bus to Piazzale Flaminio.
For centuries Piazza del Popolo was the first glimpse most travellers got of Rome, for it lies directly inside the city's northern gate, the Porta del Popolo. If Grand Tourists were unlucky enough to arrive during Carnival time, they were likely to witness condemned criminals being tortured for the entertainment of the populace. The piazza was given its present oval form by neo-classical architect Giuseppe Valadier in the early nineteenth century. The obelisk in the centre was taken from Egypt by Augustus and stood in the **Circus Maximus** until 1589, when it was moved to its present site by Pope Sixtus V. It appears to stand at the apex of a perfect triangle formed by Via di Ripetta, Via del Corso and Via del Babuino, although this is an illusion. The churches on either side of Via del Corso, Santa Maria dei Miracoli and Santa Maria di Monte Santo, appear to be twins but are actually different sizes. Carlo Rainaldi, who designed them in the 1660s, made them and the adjacent street angles appear symmetrical by giving one an oval dome, and the other a round one. The Piazza's greatest monument, though, is the church of **Santa Maria del Popolo**, begun in 1472. In the piazza itself are the fashionable cafés **Rosati** and **Canova**.

Piazza di Spagna

Metro Spagna/bus to Piazza San Silvestro.
Piazza di Spagna has been a compulsory stop for visitors to Rome since the eighteenth century, when a host of poets and musicians stayed in the vicinity. The square takes its name from the Spanish Embassy, which has been here for several centuries, but it's better known for the recently renovated **Spanish Steps**, the elegant double staircase built in the 1720s that cascades down from the church of the Trinità dei Monti. At Christmas a crib is erected half-way up; in spring, the steps are adorned with huge tubs of azaleas for the fashion shows that take place there (*see chapter* **Rome by Season**). At the foot of the stairs is a delightful boat-shaped fountain, designed in 1627 by Gianlorenzo Bernini or his less famous father Pietro, and ingeniously sunk below ground level to compensate for the low pressure of the delicious Acqua Vergine which feeds it.

Pincio

Piazza del Pincio. Metro Flaminio/train or bus to Piazzale Flaminio.
Overlooking the **Piazza del Popolo** is one of the oldest gardens in Rome. The Pinci family began the first gardens here in the fourth century, though the present layout was designed by Valadier in 1814. The garden is best known for its view of the Vatican at sunset, with the dome of Saint Peter's silhouetted in gold. There are also particularly good views of the Gianicolo and the **Fontana Paola**. Don't miss the squat dome of the Pantheon, and the statue on top of the **Column of Marcus Aurelius** in the Piazza Colonna. The paved area behind the viewpoint is popular with cyclists (bikes can be hired nearby) and roller skaters. To the southeast is the Casino Valadier, with an exorbitantly expensive restaurant and tea-room but a stupendous view.

Via Veneto and the Quirinale

Rome's most famous modern street – officially Via *Vittorio* Veneto – cuts through the heart of the palace and gardens of the Villa Ludovisi, built and laid out in 1662. It was one of the largest among the princely villas that dotted Rome until the Piedmontese influx after 1870, when most were

Bernini's **Fontana di Tritone**, *see page 56.*

Chewing the fat on Via Veneto.

sold off by aristocratic owners to the new breed of building speculators. Fortunately for Rome, the **Villa Borghese**, just to the north, was taken over by the state and is still a public park.

In 1885 Prince Buoncompagni Ludovisi (whose two surnames have been given to major roads in the area) sold off his glorious estate and with the proceeds built a massive palazzo in part of the grounds. Crippled by running costs and the tax bill on the sale of the land, he sold it to Margherita, widow of King Umberto I. The renamed Villa Margherita, half-way down Via Veneto, is now the American Embassy.

The area was swiftly built up, immediately acquiring the reputation for luxury that it retained right up to the late 1960s. The area on the hill, known as the *quartiere Ludovisi*, largely consists of late nineteenth-century palazzi and villas; the lower part, which extends as far as Via XX Settembre and **Piazza Barberini**, was mostly rebuilt during the fascist era, when Via Barberini and Via Bissolati were relentlessly bulldozed through the urban fabric. The two streets are now the heart of Rome's airline and travel business, while the *quartiere Ludovisi* is synonymous with the upper end of the finance, media and service industries.

Via Veneto itself is lined with major hotels and the headquarters of publishers, banks and insurance companies. With its impersonal expense-account restaurants and unenticing glass-fronted cafés, the broad sweep of Via Veneto could be a street in any northern-European business district.

The worldwide reputation it acquired in the 1950s was largely due to the enormous American presence at **Cinecittà** (*see chapter* **Film**). Fellini's 1959 film *La Dolce Vita*, starring the late and much lamented Marcello Mastroianni, consecrated the scene and coined the term *paparazzo* – the surname of a character in the film, modelled on the legendary photographer Tadzio Secchiaroli.

The road is occasionally closed to traffic in a doomed attempt to lend it a more festive air, but there is little *vita* on Via Veneto, apart from visitors in droves. The local tourist industry obligingly resurrects the corpse for them. What they get are bimbos on the doorsteps of wildly expensive night-clubs, enticing them in for atrocious floor-shows, terrible food and sleazy company.

At the foot of Via Veneto is Piazza Barberini, overlooked by the huge **Palazzo Barberini** (*see chapter* **Museums & Galleries**), with Bernini's **Fontana del Tritone** as its centrepiece. In ancient times, the site was occupied by the Flora Circus, where erotic dances would mark the coming of spring.

From Piazza Barberini, Via delle Quattro Fontane shoots to the top of the Quirinal hill, where it bisects the equally straight Via del Quirinale. From the crossroads here there are extraordinary views of the obelisks at Trinità dei Monti and **Santa Maria Maggiore** (*see chapter* **Churches**). The finest point of the Quirinal is the polygonal **Piazza del Quirinale** at the far end of the street, from where the view over the city is spectacular, particularly at sunset.

The Sights

Fontana dell'Acqua Felice

Piazza San Bernardo. Metro Repubblica/bus to Piazza Repubblica or Via XX Settembre.

The Acqua Felice was designed by Domenico Fontana in the form of a triumphal arch and was completed in 1589. It was one of the many urban improvements commissioned by Pope Sixtus V, and provided the neighbourhood with clean water from an ancient aqueduct. The statue of Moses in the central niche, by Leonardo Sormani, has been roundly condemned as an atrocity ever since it was unveiled in 1586.

Fontana del Tritone and Fontana delle Api

Piazza Barberini. Metro Barberini/bus to Piazza Barberini.

Like many Bernini figures, this cheerful Triton, stranded at a hellish traffic junction, has a well-developed abdomen. Completed in 1642, he sits, his two fish-tail legs tucked beneath him, on a shell supported by four dolphins, and blows water through a conch in his mouth. The bees on the coat of arms were a symbol of the Barberini, the family of Bernini's great patron, Pope Urban VIII. Bees feature again on another Bernini fountain, the Fontana delle Api (Fountain of the Bees), across the piazza at the foot of Via Veneto. This time they're trying to crawl out of the water.

Piazza del Quirinale

Bus to Piazza Venezia or Via Nazionale.

One of the centres of official Rome, this rather lifeless expanse is dominated by the huge, orange **Palazzo del Quirinale**, the lofty public rooms and beautiful formal gardens of which can be visited free of charge on the second and fourth Sunday of the month (closed Aug; tel 46 991). Begun in 1574 as the Pope's summer palace, it was the main home of the kings of Italy from 1870 to 1946 and is now the official residence of the President. At the centre of the piazza is an obelisk originally from the **Mausoleum of Augustus**. The square is dominated by disproportionately large Roman statues of Castor and Pollux, each five and a half metres tall, atop a fountain which was moved here in the early 1800s after – legend has it – many centuries of use as a cattle trough in the Roman Forum.

Quattro Fontane

Bus to Piazza Barberini or Via Nazionale.

At the fume-filled crossroads between Via delle Quattro Fontane and Via XX Settembre, these four charming Baroque fountains date from 1593 and represent four gods. The river god accompanied by the she-wolf is obviously the Tiber, though it is unclear whether the other male figure is meant to represent the Nile or the Aniene. The females are probably Juno (with duck) and Diana.

Villa Borghese

Metro Flaminio Spagna/train to Piazzale Flaminio/bus to Piazzale Flaminio or Via Vittorio Veneto, Viale delle Belle Arti, Via Pinciana/tram to Viale delle Belle Arti.

The park and gardens around the Casino Borghese (part of the **Galleria Borghese**) were laid out in the seventeenth century for the pleasure of Cardinal Scipione Borghese, sybaritic nephew of Pope Paul V. A lavish patron of the arts, he amassed the measureless collection of art, sculpture and antiquities, now once again on show in the Casino after an unforgivable 14-year closure from 1983 to 1997 for restoration. The garden was a kind of Baroque fun park, with trick fountains which sprayed unwitting passers-by, automata and erotic paintings. Today the park is used for jogging, dog-walking, outdoor parties, picnics and cruising. Wandering around is a great way to recuperate from an overdose of sightseeing and carbon monoxide, though culture vultures can continue to swot it out in the Etruscan museum in nearby **Villa Giulia** and the **Galleria Nazionale d'Arte Moderna e Contemporanea**. The park also houses the **Dei Piccoli** children's cinema and Rome's **Zoo**. Other sights worth looking out for include the Piazza di Siena, an elegantly-shaped arena used for opera and show-jumping among other things, several imitation ancient temples, a lake and a fake medieval castle. There is also a good view of the *Moro Torto* section of the **Aurelian Wall** from the bridge between the Pincio and Villa Borghese.

Trastevere

There's been a small colony on the west bank of the Tiber (*trans Tiberim*, hence Trastevere) since the foundation of Rome, reached by a ford where the Ponte Palatino now crosses from Piazza Bocca della Verità. During the Empire Trastevere was sufficiently important to be included within the **Aurelian Wall**, the main gates of which still exist (now called Porta Portese and Porta San Pancrazio). The area consisted mainly of vegetable gardens, orchards and hunting woodlands belonging to noble families, most famously the Caesars (Cleopatra is thought to have stayed in the area).

After the fall of the Empire, Trastevere was gradually colonised by Syrian and Jewish trading communities, and the remains of an early synagogue can still be seen in Vicolo dell'Atleta. In the early Middle Ages the Jews moved across the Tiber to the **Ghetto** and in time Trastevere became the main working-class district of the papal capital.

During the two centuries prior to Italian unification, and for a while afterwards, there was a strong tradition of violent rivalry between the *bulli trasteverini* (Trastevere toughs) and the *Monticiani* (the boys from **Monti**). The gangs, their leaders, and their stone-throwing battles, knife-fights and frequent fatalities became enshrined in popular lore, a prototype *West Side Story* duly written down by dialect poet Giuseppe Gioacchino Belli (1791-1863) and illustrated by Hogarth-meets-Goya cartoonist Bartolomeo Pinelli (1781-1835). The 200-odd sonnets by the former (whose top-hatted statue now graces Piazza Belli, the taxi-rank at the beginning of Viale Trastevere) are still a useful way to make sense of the character and philosophy of the modern-day Roman. Despite the fact that Trastevere strove hard to prove itself a separate city, the good-humoured cynicism, proud independence and fun-loving vulgarity which set it apart have now come to be regarded as quintessentially Roman traits.

Nowadays, Trastevere contends with **Testaccio** across the river for the title of *er core de Roma* – the heart of Rome – and Trastevere is still putting up a good fight. Although many of its apartments have fallen into the hands of American artists and other

The world's first shopping mall: **Trajan's Market**. *See p76.*

assorted foreigners, the boisterous character of the locals is still in evidence: old ladies sit outside their kitchen doors commenting on passers-by as they shell the peas; neighbours shout to one another across the street from high windows; and Trastevere remains an area where it is difficult to do anything without everyone knowing about it.

Great steps have been taken recently to curb Trastevere's chronic traffic problem, much to the annoyance of locals who have found one-way streets springing up in the most unexpected places. In the evening, a tiny electric bus now plies the district, which is off-limits to all but residents' cars. Roman frequenters of the district's restaurants, pizzerias and arthouse cinemas seem undaunted by this new arrangement, and locals have even more room to spill out onto their streets for a walk and a gossip on warm nights.

Trastevere is divided into two sharply different sectors by the traffic-snarled avenue of the same name. South of the *viale* is a quiet, evocative enclave where you will find the highest concentration of locals. The warren of lanes around the church of **Santa Cecilia** is a good place to wander aimlessly, watching local craftsmen at work. This area faces onto the *isola tiberina*, or Tiber Island. Connected to the mainland by two bridges, both Roman in origin, the island is peopled during the day by pyjama-clad patients from its venerable Fatebenefratelli (Do-Good Brothers) hospital. To the north of the *viale* lies the true tourist mecca: all streets seem to lead to the stunning **Piazza di Santa Maria in Trastevere.** This still manages to preserve an aura of ancient calm, despite the impromptu football matches played against the walls of its church and the fiendish mandolin-strummers who serenade the diners at its two over-priced restaurants.

In some streets in this area, notably Vicolo del Cinque and Via della Scala, it seems that every ground-floor space is either a restaurant, a 'piano bar', or a herbal bookshop with tea-room attached. When the bustle gets too much, escape it with a stroll along the Via della Lungara. Widened and repaved by Pope Julius II to mirror his Via Giulia on the other bank of the Tiber, it contains some of Rome's finest palazzi, including the Raphael-frescoed **Villa Farnesina**, the magnificent loggia of which has been restored recently, and the **Palazzo Corsini** which backs onto the beautiful **Orto Botanico** (Botanical Gardens). Not to mention the notorious Regina Coeli, a medieval prison still – though not for long, if current plans to close it down are ever carried through. The prisoners' relatives and friends cheerfully mill around outside, and on summer nights you can occasionally hear the sounds of inmates partying.

Above the prison, the **Gianicolo** offers a chance for prisoners' spouses to shout messages down to their locked-up loved-ones during exercise hour. Reached by the tortuous Via Garibaldi, which passes by the dramatic baroque **Fontana Paola**,

the view from the Gianicolo is Rome's most spectacular (*see* **A Rome with a View** *page 52*). The spreading pine tree and statue-dotted gardens are dominated by an enormous equestrian statue of Giuseppe Garibaldi, close to which a cannon is fired every day at noon.

The Sights

Casa della Fornarina
Via di Santa Dorotea, 20 (58 18 284). Bus to Lungotevere Sanzio or Piazza Sonnino.
This unassuming house is believed to have been that of Margherita, *La Fornarina* (the Baker's Girl), Raphael's model and lover for many years. Universally considered a fallen woman for her very publicly untoward conduct with the artist, poor Margherita was rejected by Raphael on his deathbed as he sought to atone for his life of sin and debauchery. According to local lore, Margherita took refuge in the convent of Sant'Apollonia in the Piazza Santa Margherita, just around the corner from her home.

Fontana Paola
Via Giuseppe Garibaldi, Gianicolo. Bus to Gianicolo (Trastevere night service).
This huge fountain on the Gianicolo hill was intended, like the **Fontana dell'Acqua Felice**, to resemble a triumphal arch. The columns used came from the original Saint Peter's basilica. The fountain was designed in 1612 by Flaminio Ponzio and Giovanni Fontana for Pope Paul V, from whom it takes its name. Its original purpose was to reopen an ancient aqueduct, built by Emperor Trajan to bring water from Lake Bracciano.

Gianicolo
Bus to Gianicolo (Trastevere night service).
The Janiculum, as it was called in ancient Rome, offers the best view of the city (*see* **A Rome with a View** *page 52*). In 1849 the Gianicolo was the scene of one of the fiercest battles in the struggle for Italian unity, when Giuseppe Garibaldi, leader of the unification forces, and his makeshift army defended the Roman Republic against French troops sent to restore papal rule. His is the equestrian statue in the middle of the square, while the busts that line the road up are those of the thousand martyrs of the *Risorgimento*. Carrying on past the equestrian statue of Garibaldi's equally heroic wife Anita, you reach a curious lighthouse, the gift of Italian emigrants in Argentina. The view from here takes in the ochre shades of medieval and baroque Rome. At the Vatican end of the walk, opposite the Ospedale del Bambino Gesù, you overlook Saint Peter's and the Castel Sant'Angelo.

Orto Botanico
Via Corsini (68 64 193). Bus to Lungotevere Farnesina or Piazza Sonnino. **Open** 9am-6.30pm Mon-Sat.
Admission L4,000.
Established in 1883, when some of the grounds of the **Palazzo Corsini** were donated to Rome University, the Orto Botanico contains some 7,000 species in wondrous green exuberance barely held in check: here there is none of the sterile order which can render botanical gardens so cold. Plants tumble over steps and into fountains and fishponds, creating verdant hidden corners disturbed only by frolicking children parked here by Trastevere mums.

Piazza di Santa Maria in Trastevere
Bus to Piazza Sonnino.
This is the heart and soul of the neighbourhood, a traffic-free cobbled square. Overlooking the fountain, built by Carlo Fontana in 1692, are the fantastic thirteenth-century mosaics on the façade of **Santa Maria in Trastevere**, one of the oldest churches in Rome. Legend has it that a miraculous well of

oil sprung from this spot and flowed to the Tiber all day when Christ was born. A small street leading out of the piazza, **Via della Fonte dell'Olio** (Oil Well Street), commemorates this.

Villa Farnesina

Via della Lungara, 230 (68 80 17 67). Bus to Lungotevere Farnesina or Piazza Sonnino. **Open** 9am-1pm Mon-Sat. **Admission** L6,000.

This pretty villa was built in 1508-11 by Baldassare Peruzzi as a pleasure palace and holiday home for the rich papal banker and party-giver Agostino Chigi. It has been owned and named after the powerful Farnese family since 1577, when the Chigis went bankrupt. Chigi was one of Raphael's main patrons and in its day the villa was stuffed with great works of art, though many were later sold to pay off debts. Luckily it has retained its frescoes, by Raphael, Peruzzi, Sodoma, Sebastiano del Piombo and Raphael's assistants Giulio Romano, Francesco Penni and Giovanni da Udine. Up the white-panelled stairs is the Salone delle Prospettive, painted by Peruzzi with views of sixteenth-century Rome. Next to this is Agostino Chigi's bedroom, with a life-sized fresco of the *Marriage of Alexander the Great and Roxanne* by Sodoma. As with most of Sodoma's paintings, this is a rather sordid number showing the couple being relieved of their clothes by vicious little cherubs.

Monti and Esquilino

Stretching from the **Fori Imperiali** to **Stazione Termini** and Rome's main University campus, these two *rioni* (districts) are criss-crossed by some of the city's busiest and least interesting streets and dominated by more than their fair share of dismal bureaucratic *palazzi*. This said, there are isolated unmissable sights, such as **Trajan's Markets** and the **Baths of Diocletian**, not to mention a great market and the nearest thing Rome has to a multi-cultural zone.

A single *rione* until 1874, Monti and Esquilino were ancient Rome's most exclusive suburbs, their green heights dotted with patrician villas and temples. Paradoxically, they overlooked one of the city's worst slums: the grimy, thronging Suburra area in the marshy swamp between the Quirinal, Viminal and Esquiline hills.

Barbarian invasions forced Rome's élite down from their hilltop residences to the relative safety of what is now the *centro storico*, close to the river Tiber. The hill areas went into decline and, despite being well within the **Aurelian Wall**, remained almost uninhabited until the Middle Ages, when Monti became the battleground of numerous bullish families: the Conti, the Frangipani, the Annibali, the Caetani and the Capocci, who are remembered in the names of local streets. Each of these clans constructed their own fortress, with its own *torre* (tower). At the end of the thirteenth century, when anarchy reached its peak, there were some 200 towers in Rome; of the dozen that remain, more than half are to be found here, including the Torre delle Milizie behind **Trajan's Markets**.

In the sixteenth century Sixtus V, the great town planner of Counter-Reformation Rome, definitively reincorporated the area into the city. He ordered the building of the great Via Felice, which stretch-

es (today changing names several times along its length) from the top of the **Spanish Steps** in the north to **Santa Croce in Gerusalemme** in the south, a dead-straight 3.5km sweep. Until the building of Via Nazionale and Via Cavour 300 years later, the whole *rione* developed around this axis. However, as late as 1850, 70 per cent of Monti and Esquilino was still farmland or classical ruins.

Italian unification brought dramatic changes to the area. As well as being split into two separate *rioni*, Monti and Esquilino became a hub of the newly-formed state. Architect Quintino Sella designed a ministerial and administrative district focusing on the semi-circular, arcaded **Piazza della Repubblica**, from which Via Nazionale descends to the old centre. The arrival of the railway at **Termini** in the 1860s had already attracted a rush of frenzied speculators who snapped up most of the surrounding land. A decade later, when Rome became the capital of unified Italy, they made an even bigger killing. The ancient ruins dotting the area were swept away and a whole new city-within-a-city was built, in the grid mode favoured by the ruling Turinese, covering nearly 300 hectares.

Apart from the **Baths of Diocletian** and the multi-storey Roman shopping mall at **Trajan's Markets**, or the stunning early churches (**San Pietro in Vincoli, Santa Prassede** and **San Martino ai Monti** – *see chapter* **Churches**) which dot the Esquiline, today's Monti and Esquilino have comparatively little to interest the culture-hungry tourist. But there are isolated attractions which make a stopover there an interesting alternative to the rest of Rome.

The ancient Suburra slum now has a real life of its own. Here you'll find Via dei Serpenti, the workaday, villagey high street that connects dreary Via Nazionale with drearier Via Cavour; Piazza degli Zingari, site of a medieval gypsy encampment; and Via dei Capocci, which has long been a centre of prostitution. Via del Boschetto is packed with restaurants; Via di San Martino ai Monti has more than its fair share of pubs.

The area between Termini and **Piazza Vittorio Emanuele** is as close as Rome gets to an ethnic zone. Shops selling food and goods from all over the world are frequented mostly by natives of the countries in question, in what during the daytime can be a refreshing escape from the overwhelmingly Roman atmosphere of the Piazza Vittorio market. At night, however, the area is dead to the world.

If you've had your fill of the picturesque and need a shot of the Kafkaesque, take a look at such monolithic examples of Italian public architecture as the Ministry of the Interior on Piazza del Viminale, the Bank of Italy headquarters at Palazzo Koch on Via Nazionale, the **Teatro dell'Opera** in Via Firenze, and the Sisde secret police headquarters on Via Lanza. Or wander down undulating Via Panisperna, past the lab where in 1934 Enrico Fermi and Ettore Majorana first split the atom.

Other highlights include the massive basilica of **San Giovanni in Laterano**, immediately recognizable by the host of gigantic statue-saints partying atop its façade, and the scant, usually locked, remains of Nero's Domus Aurea (Golden House) in the Colle Oppio park, which is frequented at night by Rome's far-right youth and a sprinkling of its braver gays. The whole area has never really recovered from the concerted planning assault of a century ago. But there are compensations, in the form of two smallish parks, one in Via Piacenza, and the other the endearing hanging garden of **Villa Aldobrandini**.

The Sights

Piazza dei Cinquecento and Stazione Termini

Metro Termini/bus to Piazza della Repubblica.
Piazza dei Cinquecento has recently undergone a major facelift and now provides a fitting setting for Stazione Termini, one of the most remarkable modern public structures in Italy. Architect Angiolo Mazzoni produced a triumph of undulating horizontal geometry, complete with tubular towers of metaphysical grace straight out of a De Chirico painting. Building began in 1938 but was interrupted by the war, and the station was not inaugurated until 1950.

Piazza della Repubblica

Metro Termini/bus to Piazza della Repubblica.
Better known to Roman citizens as Piazza Esedra, this heavily-trafficked roundabout is the traditional starting point for major demonstrations and a favourite hang-out for the motley overflow who frequent Stazione Termini. The Fontana delle Naiadi at its centre was unveiled in 1911, but the nudity of the art-nouveau nymphs languishing seductively around it so shocked clerical circles that it was boarded up again for several years.

Piazza Vittorio Emanuele

Metro Termini/bus to Piazza Vittorio Emanuele.
The neighbourhood around the Piazza was designed to be one of Rome's smartest when it was built at the turn of the century. For a while the area was perilously close to becoming a slum, but it's been given a new lease of life by recent refurbishments and new arrivals, who flocked to take advantage of the cheap rents and transformed it into a lively multi-ethnic area. The revamped gardens inside the Piazza Vittorio Emanuele market offer a cool place to rest in the shade of palm trees. As you do, have a go at breaking the still-encoded recipe for making gold on the *Porta Magica*, the curious door which is all that remains of the Villa Palombara.

Villa Aldobrandini

Via Mazzarino, 11. Metro Cavour/bus to Via Nazionale.
Open 7am-dusk daily.
The villa itself was built in the sixteenth century for the Dukes of Urbino and later bought by the Aldobrandini Pope Clement VIII. It is now state property and closed to the public, but the gardens remain open. Reached through a little gate off Via Mazzarino, they are formally laid out, with neat gravel paths and well-tended lawns. During renovation the gardens were raised about 30m above street level, so weary tourists can sit and enjoy splendid views over the city.

Aventino, Celio and Testaccio

The exclusive, leafy Aventine hill boasts Rome's highest property prices and hosts an independent passport-issuing state in the headquarters of the Knights of Malta in the square of the same name (**Piazza dei Cavalieri di Malta**). Two delightful parks offer spectacular views, particularly at sundown, and the churches are an added bonus: the glorious fifth-century **Santa Sabina**, and Santa Prisca, which stands over Rome's best-restored mithraic shrine.

There are still elderly people on the Aventine and its sister hill San Saba, just across the busy Viale Aventino, who remember farmers herding their sheep and goats into the piazzas here of an evening before taking them off to market the next morning. And, until the unappetising debris left by a sudden influx of Latin American transvestite prostitutes made it a health hazard, old ladies could until very recently be seen picking *rughetta* (rocket) for salads amid the grass at the foot of the **Aurelian Wall**.

For a taste of what large swathes of Rome must have been like as the Barbarians swept in and sent the locals fleeing to what is now the *centro storico*, you need to head for the wilder areas of the Celio. Approached by the steep, winding street opposite the sprawling white marble cuboids of the UN's Food and Agricultural Agency, originally built to house Mussolini's Colonies Ministry, the Celio is lush and unkempt, containing a massive ramshackle structure in which Mother Teresa of Calcutta's nuns feed the poor and grow broad beans, and the immense false-fronted church of **San Gregorio Magno**, with its picturesquely overgrown vegetable garden. It was from here that Saint Augustine was dispatched, in the sixth century, to convert the pagan hordes of far-off Britain.

An arcaded street leads past the church of **Santi Giovanni e Paolo**, built over a street of Roman houses, to the **Villa Celimontana** park. The grid of narrow streets on the hill's lower slopes are full of trattorias. They also contain three ancient churches: **San Clemente**, **Santi Quattro Coronati** and Santo Stefano Rotondo.

Further south, though still within the Wall, is the wedge-shaped **Testaccio** district. This is one of the few areas of central Rome where a sense of community is strongly felt, and where the line between courtyard and street is blurred enough to allow old ladies to pop into the local *alimentari* in their dressing-gown and slippers. Elsa Morante chose this as the setting for her sprawling Marxist novel *La Storia* (*History*). The best place to begin is the morning market in Piazza Testaccio, a beautiful square, shaded by plane trees, containing one of Rome's best-stocked and liveliest food markets. Once a desperately poor area, Testaccio has reaped the benefits of post-war prosperity without losing either its character or its original residents, few of whom give more than a scornful passing glance to the health-food shops and other trappings of gentrification. Most of the apartment blocks are still publicly owned, and let at controlled rates. Writers at the turn of the century deplored the conditions here: a quarter of all families slept in the kitchen, and tenants were forced to brave the suspended walkways (*ballatoi*) which connected the various apartments on each floor. For a glimpse of these *ballatoi*, venture into the courtyard of the block at Piazza Testaccio, 20.

You'll meet few visitors in Testaccio by day, the only recognized tourist destinations being the **Protestant Cemetery**, the **Pyramid of Caius Cestius** and the somewhat more obscure **Monte Testaccio** and **Emporium**. By night, however, the area is inundated with non-residents, who flock to the cheap pizzerias, the multi-cultural social centre **Villaggio Globale** (*see chapter* **Music: Rock, Roots & Jazz**) and, most of all, the myriad clubs burrowed into the flanks of Monte Testaccio (*see chapter* **Nightlife**).

The Sights

Il Mattatoio

Piazza Giustiniani. Bus to Via Marmorata or Lungotevere Testaccio.
With its Doric arches and bizarre statuary, the Mattatoio, the municipal slaughterhouse, was considered Europe's most

state-of-the-art building of its type when it was completed in 1891. It managed to support an eightfold increase in the city's population, and provided Testaccio's residents with work (not to mention noise and smells) until it was finally pensioned off in 1975. Since then, constant bickering between politicians, architects and town planners over what to do with the structure has caused complete stasis. In the absence of an overall plan, bits are used as a car pound, an old people's club, stables for carriages, facilities for the Testaccio music school, and the venue of the **Villaggio Globale**.

Parco Savello

Via di Santa Sabina, Aventino. Metro Circo Massimo/bus to Piazzale Ugo La Malfa. **Open** dawn to dusk daily.
Inside the walls of the Savello family's twelfth-century castle is a pretty garden full of orange trees and massive terracotta pots containing dark green plants. Close by on the Via di Valle Murcia are the city rose gardens, which are especially sweet-smelling – but also very crowded – in late spring and early summer.

Piazza dei Cavalieri di Malta

Lungotevere Aventino. Metro Circo Massimo.
Designed by the great fantasist Piranesi in the eighteenth century, this diminutive square with its mysterious reliefs and orderly cypress trees looks like the set for some surrealist drama. It takes its name from the Knights of Malta, whose priory is at number 3. If you look through the little hole in the priory doorway, you'll see one of Piranesi's most spectacular illusions. At the end of a neat avenue of trees sits the dome of Saint Peter's, apparently only a few metres away. This is probably the only keyhole in the world through which you can see three sovereign states: Italy, the Vatican, and the aristocratic, theocratic Knights of Malta itself, an independent state with its own head of state, number plates (starting SMOM) and passports.

The Green, Green Parts of Rome

Pounding Rome's pavements, dodging its traffic and breathing its air can be a wearying experience even for the most determined tourist, so when exhaustion sets in, it's comforting to know that you're in one of Europe's greenest cities.

For large expanses of verdure, the **Villa Borghese** is closest to the city centre, but the trek to the immense **Villa Pamphili** or to the gloriously leafy **Villa Ada** is only slightly longer and far more rewarding if you're looking for a retreat from crowds.

Rome also has smaller corners of greenery that are on, rather than off, the beaten track. During the sleepy hours after lunch, try some of the following natural escapes from traffic and the tourist hordes, most of which offer peace, quiet, somnolent cats and a tinkling fountain or two.

If you're in Trastevere, drop in on the city's **Orto Botanico** (Botanical Gardens). They may not be Kew, but their shady palm-lined paths provide some pleasant surprises, such as a herb garden and a scent-and-touch garden for the sight-impaired. Alternatively, try the Gianicolo hill (good for views) or the **Villa Sciarra** with

its roses rambling over Roman remains.

After trailing down Via Nazionale or up Via Quattro Novembre from Trajan's Markets, take a breather in the quiet garden of **Villa Aldobrandini**. Not far away in Via Piacenza, between the Quirinal and the Palazzo delle Esposizioni, a shaded terrace offers a small but picturesque haven.

The Colosseum area is also flanked by a number of smaller parks, such as the Colle Oppio and the rather more get-away-from-it-all Villa Celimontana. On the neighbouring Aventine hill, the church of **Santa Sabina** is sandwiched between two of Rome's most charming garden terraces, with blossom-laden trees and views of the city's skyline. In spring, you can also take a breather in the Roseto Comunale, the council rose gardens, as you wind down from the Aventine towards the Circus Maximus.

Finally, if you're staying near the station, don't forget that the chaos of the **Piazza Vittorio Emanuele** market has a reasonably relaxing public garden at its heart. (*See also chapter* **Children**.)

Protestant Cemetery

Via Caio Cestio 6, Testaccio. Metro Piramide/bus or tram to Via Marmorata or Porta San Paolo. **Open** *Oct-Mar,* 9am-5pm Tue-Sun; *Apr-Sept,* 9am-6pm Tue-Sun.
Admission free (donation expected).

'It might make one in love with death to know that one should be buried in so sweet a place.' So Shelley described the burial place of his friend Keats in the preface to his poem *Adonais,* little knowing that he too would be taking up permanent residence there, after a fatal boating accident, just a year later. Miraculously, given that only a wall divides it from the chaos of Piazza di Porta San Paolo, it remains a haven of peace. The inhabitants of the cemetery are not limited to Protestants: there are Russian Orthodox, Chinese, Buddhist and even atheist tombs as well. To get in, ring the bell. A detailed map is available at the entrance which will help you discover the graves of celebrities such as Goethe's son Julius, Joseph Severn, faithful companion to Keats, and Antonio Gramsci, founder of the Italian Communist Party, who was imprisoned under Mussolini.

EUR

Italian fascism managed to be simultaneously monstrous and absurd, but its delusions of grandeur helped produce some of the most interesting European architecture and town planning this century. In the early 1930s Giuseppe Bottai, Mussolini's Governor of Rome and the leading arbiter of fascist taste, had the bright idea of expanding landbound Rome towards the sea, some 20km away. He combined this with the notion of a Universal Exhibition, pencilled in for 1942 and intended to combine permanent cultural exhibition spaces with a monument to fascism.

Popular fascist architect Marcello Piacentini was charged with co-ordinating the vastly ambitious project, but in the event few of the original designs were ever built. The planning committee became so bogged down in argument that little had been achieved when the outbreak of World War II forced work to be suspended.

During the latter war years the exhibition site was inhabited in turns by the occupying German army, the Allied forces, and Italian refugees. After the war, work was resumed, but with a very different spirit. The site was renamed EUR – *Esposizione Universale Romana* – and relieved of its fascist content.

When Viale Cristoforo Colombo and the Metro were completed, thereby connecting EUR with central Rome, the area finally came to life, and many of Italy's best architects – Giovanni Muzio, Mario de Renzi, Ludovico Quaroni and partners Luigi Figini and Gino Pollini – left their mark on it. Many consider the results to be the archetype of bombastic modernism, but they are certainly not easily forgotten: fascist-inspired buildings such as Guerrini's **Palazzo della Civiltà del Lavoro,** popularly known as *il Colosseo Quadrato* – the square Colosseum – and Arnaldo Foschini's toytown church of Santi Pietro e Pablo can be seen alongside post-war palazzi like Adalberto Libera's highly original Palazzo dei Congressi and Studio BBPR's superbly functional Post Office.

The 1960 Olympic Games offered another stimulus for filling out the area. The masterpiece is Nervi and Piacenti's flying saucer-like **Palazzo dello Sport,** hovering over EUR's artificial lake and now most often used for major rock concerts and political conventions. The area contains several other useful attractions, such as the **LUNEUR Park** funfair, the **Piscina delle Rose** swimming pool and several museums (*see chapters* **Museums & Galleries, Children** *and* **Sport & Fitness**).

Most Romans never visit EUR except on business or to go to a concert. At night, however, and especially in summer, it becomes the playground of fun-loving, suntanned, wealthy brats. Rome's desire to be a little bit of California finds its most eloquent expression in EUR's relatively unsnarled, tree-lined boulevards, and there's a definite whiff of rich-kid, good-time culture in the air.

Other Districts

Northern Suburbs

FLAMINIA

The dead-straight Via Flaminia shoots north from **Piazza del Popolo,** crossing the river at the ancient Ponte Milvio, where Constantine is supposed to have had his battle-winning vision of Christ (*see chapter* **History**). On the way, the road passes through another affluent residential area, which is also full of sports facilities: on the east bank, the **Stadio Flaminio** and **Palazzetto dello Sport,** and on the west the **Foro Italico,** site of the Olympic football stadium, swimming pool and tennis courts (*see chapter* **Sport & Fitness**).

MONTEVERDE

Climbing the steep hills behind Trastevere is Monteverde Vecchio, a leafy, well-heeled, left-leaning suburb. Further west is Monteverde Nuovo, a charmless, more downmarket and mainly post-war addition.

NOMENTANA

Via Nomentana is the main road leading out of Rome to the east, crossed at right-angles by the once-majestic Viale Regina Margherita and Viale Regina Elena, which connect Parioli to San Lorenzo. It's flanked on either side by another fairly middle-class residential area. To the south-east, the area around the Via Tiburtina is rather more low-rent.

PARIOLI

North of the Villa Borghese, this is one of the dearest but also one of the dullest residential areas of the city, built between the late nineteenth century and the 1930s on the hilltop estates of some of Baroque Rome's finest private villas. When

Palazzo della Civiltà del Lavoro, *EUR's square Colosseum.*

Romans refer to *pariolini*, they have in mind the sort of wholesome youths who feel naked without a designer jacket, jeans pressed by the family's *filipina* maid, a cellphone and a four-wheel-drive.

PRATI

A more modest version of Parioli, again largely built in the nineteenth century, on the flat meadowland (*prati*) behind **Castel Sant'Angelo**, bordering on the Vatican. A (potentially expensive) wander for lunch or retail therapy down its main shopping street, Via Cola di Rienzo, is a good antidote to a surfeit of culture. Otherwise, its main features are the Trionfale flower market, the endless military barracks lining Viale delle Milizie, some quiet, tree-lined residential streets close to the river, and the headquarters of the RAI, the Italian state broadcaster.

Southern Suburbs

OSTIENSE/GARBATELLA

This region lies south of Testaccio and is a similarly interesting area of late nineteenth- and early twentieth-century workers' housing: many of the residential blocks are outstanding pieces of architecture. Despite a degree of urban blight, it retains a strong community feel.

SAN GIOVANNI

San Giovanni is a nineteenth-century area just inside the city walls, built around the ancient basilica of Rome's official cathedral, **San Giovanni in Laterano**. It's a busy shopping area, surrounded by swathes of monotonous apartment blocks.

SAN LORENZO

Badly built, densely populated, and still showing wounds from World War II, San Lorenzo is scarred like an alley cat. It is also one of Rome's liveliest neighbourhoods, full of packed bars and restaurants, artists, graffiti, and cultural diversity. The area has a history of rebellion. It was designed in the 1880s as a working class ghetto with few public services or amenities, and soon developed into Rome's most radical district, led by anarchist workers. The street battles of the 1920s between the *squadracci fascisti* and the *sanlorenzini* form part of Italian left-wing legend.

Tours

The tours run by the commercial bus companies listed here are all of the traditional, coach-and-guide variety and can be booked from most hotels.

110 Tourist Bus

Operated by the city transport authority ATAC, the 110 provides a three-hour tour of the city, beginning at Termini and taking in virtually all the major sites. The driver gives brief explanations in several languages, and there's a free multilingual brochure. There are five stops on the route. It costs L15,000 and leaves Piazza dei Cinquecento at 3.30pm every day

from April to October (Sat and Sun only, Nov-Mar). Tickets from the ATAC desk in Piazza dei Cinquecento from 3pm.

American Express

Piazza di Spagna, 38 (67 641). Metro Spagna. **Open** 9am-5.30pm Mon-Fri; 9am-12.30pm Sat (9am-3pm Sat, Apr-Sept). **Credit** AmEx.
As well as coach tours of the main Roman sites and to Tivoli (L55,000), Pompeii, Naples and Capri (L160,000-180,000), AmEx organises three- to four-hour walking tours of the city, given in English, costing L40,000-56,000.

Appian Line

Piazza Esquilino, 6 (48 78 61). Metro Termini/bus to Piazza Esquilino. **Open** 6.30am-8pm daily. **Credit** AmEx, DC, EC, MC, V.
As well as selling travel tickets, this agency organises daily bus tours of Rome (L40-58,000) and excursions further afield, to destinations such as Naples and Pompeii (L135,000). Don't bother booking the Rome trips – just turn up 15 minutes before the tour leaves. Coaches leave at 9am and 4pm, Mon-Fri.

Green Line Tours

Via Farini, 5a (48 27 480). Metro Termini/bus or tram to Termini or Piazza Esquilino. **Open** 6.30am-9pm daily. **Credit** AmEx, DC, V.
Coach tours in Rome and day trips outside town. A three-hour tour costs around L45,000; day trips L180,000.

Horse-drawn Carriages

If you're an unashamed tourist you'll find plenty of old-fashioned carriages ready to take you for a ride around town. They carry up to five people and can be hired for an hour, half a day or a day. The price should be around L80,000 for an hour, and you should agree on it before setting off – it's often worth haggling to get the rate down. Just make sure that the price is per hour and not per person. Drivers accept cash only. Carriages can be hired in the Piazza di Spagna, Piazza Navona, Saint Peter's Square, Via Veneto and Villa Borghese.

Walking Tours

La Repubblica's Thursday listings supplement *Trovaroma* lists (under *Roma Verde*) organised walking and cycling tours in and around Rome – usually in Italian only. Especially good are trips organised by **Ruota Libera** (82 72 410) and **Bikermania** (0775 85 56 90). Specialised agencies include:

Enjoy Rome

Via Varese, 39 (44 51 843). Metro/bus to Termini.
This friendly English-speaking agency organises daily walking and cycle tours for small groups of Rome's major sites. L30,000 (L26,000 for under-26s).

Scala Reale Archeological Itineraries

Via Varese, 52 (44 70 08 98). Metro/bus to Termini.
Founded by an American and his Italian wife, Scala Reale offers walking, bicycle and moped tours around the city, as well as trips further afield. Groups are small, commentaries detailed.

Secret Walks in Rome

Via Medaglia d'Oro, 127 (39 72 87 28).
Anglophone actors and residents lead daily walks around the less well-known sights of Rome. There's a membership fee of L3,000 and walks cost L20,000 each, with a 20% discount for students. Accompanied children under 12 go free.

Ancient Sites

The skeleton of the old city lies just beneath the skin of the new.

The ancient sites of Rome have been treated in a rather cavalier fashion. Some have later buildings on top, inside or next to them, and most have been used at some time or other as a handy source of building materials. Some are still present, well hidden under a tangle of weeds and shrubs, while others have disappeared completely, discernible only in the outlines they have handed down to modern streets and buildings. Still others, thankfully, are well preserved, well restored and on view.

The most concentrated and fully excavated cluster lies in the area bound by the **Capitoline**, **Palatine**, **Esquiline** and **Quirinal** hills. This was the official heart of the ancient city, where the fates of nations were decided, military triumphs celebrated, and citizens entertained by the death of gladiators and the mass slaughter of wild animals. There were also taverns, a dole office, brothels and markets, including the world's first shopping mall, in the multi-storey **Trajan's Markets**. Here too was the most desirable residential area in Rome, the Palatine Hill, where – if the ancient historians are to be believed – the sexual excesses of emperors, empresses, politicians and poets were matched by only by the passion with which they plotted against and poisoned one another. *See also chapters* **Architecture**, **Sightseeing** *and* **Museums & Galleries**.

Ara Pacis Augustae

Via di Ripetta (67 10 3569). Bus to Piazza Augusto Imperatore. **Open** 9am-sunset Tue-Sat; 9am-1pm Sun. **Admission** L3,750.

Inside a modern glass pavilion above the Tiber is a reconstruction of the Ara Pacis, or altar of peace, one of the most artistically distinguished monuments of ancient Rome. It was inaugurated in 9 BC to celebrate the wealth and security that Augustus' victories in Spain and Gaul had brought to the Empire. Originally located near Piazza San Lorenzo in Lucina, the altar was rebuilt on this site earlier this century, from ancient fragments amassed through a fiendishly difficult excavation over many years and a trawl through various Italian and French museums. The altar itself sits in an enclosure carved inside and out with delicately realistic reliefs. The lower band is decorated with a relief of swirling acanthus leaves and swans with outstretched wings. The upper band shows a procession, thought to depict the ceremonies surrounding the dedication of the altar. With the help of a booklet on sale at the entrance, you can put faces to the names of Augustus and his family.

Arch of Constantine *(Arco di Constantino)*

Piazza del Colosseo. Metro Colosseo/bus to Piazza del Colosseo.

Constantine's triumphal arch was one of the last great Roman monuments, erected in 315 AD, shortly before he

abandoned the city for Byzantium. Although it appears magnificent enough at first glance, a close look reveals its splendours to be shallow – most of the carvings and statues were simply scavenged from other monuments around the city.

Aurelian Wall *(Mura Aureliane)* and Museo delle Mura

Via di Porta San Sebastiano (70 47 52 84). Bus to Piazza Numa Pompilio, then a long walk, or to Via delle Mura Latine. **Open** 9am-7pm Tue-Sun. **Admission** L3,750

The ancient wall still forms a near-complete circle around central Rome. Large fragments of the original wall remain, while other sections were rebuilt in the Middle Ages. It was first built around 270 AD by Emperor Aurelian, at a time when Rome's power was waning and formidable defences were required. Among the best-preserved parts of the ancient construction today are the *Muro Torto* (crooked wall) section between the **Pincio** and **Villa Borghese**; the Porta Ostiense,

Getting into Locked Sites

The immense frustration of arriving at that ancient monument you've always wanted to visit, only to find it firmly locked and open only by application to the infamous Ripartizione X of the city council's heritage office, can be avoided with a little forethought.

Once you have ascertained that prior permission is necessary (see individual listings in this book), send a fax detailing the monuments you wish to see, and the dates you will be in Rome, to the number 67 10 31 18. The fax should read:

All'attenzione della Ripartizione X

Il sottoscritto (La sottoscritta if you're a woman) [your name], *che sara' in visita a Roma dal* [starting date of holiday] *al* [finishing date of holiday] *chiede l'autorizzazione a visitare* [list of requested sites]. *Potra' essere contattato (contattata* if you're a woman] *a Roma al seguente indirizzo:* [name and phone number of your accommodation in Rome].

In fede, [signature].

At least a week after sending the fax, and at least a week before you wish to visit the site, phone 67 10 38 19 to settle a time for your appointment. There are people at this number who, if pushed, will admit to speaking English.

renamed Porta San Paolo in honour of Saint Paul, who walked through it on the way to his execution; and the area around the Porta San Giovanni. Best preserved of any of the gates is the Porta San Sebastiano, originally Aurelian's splendid Porta Appia at the head of the **Via Appia Antica**, which now houses a museum dedicated to the history of the walls, the Museo delle Mura. Although the museum is of limited interest, it allows access to a walkway along the walls.

Baths of Caracalla (*Terme di Caracalla*)

Viale delle Terme di Caracalla, 52 (57 58 626). Metro Circo Massimo/bus to Viale Aventino. **Open** 9am-1pm Mon, Sun; 9am-two hours before sunset Tue-Sat. **Admission** L8,000.

These high-vaulted ruins, surrounded by trees and grass, are pleasantly peaceful today, though they were anything but tranquil in their heyday, when they were full of Romans sweating it out in baths and gyms. You can get some idea of the splendour of the baths from the fragments of mosaic and statuary littering the ground, though the more impressive finds are to be seen in the Vatican's **Pio Cristiano Museum**. The baths were built at the beginning of the third century AD, the fifth to be built in Rome, and the largest up to that time (though the later **Baths of Diocletian** were even bigger). The two large rooms down the sides were gymnasia. After exercising, the Romans cleansed themselves in saunas and a series of baths. The baths were usually open from midday until sunset, and were opulent social centres where people came to relax after work. The complex also contained a library (still identifiable on one side of the baths), a garden, shops and stalls.

Baths of Diocletian (*Terme di Diocleziano*)

Via Enrico de Nicola, 79; Via Romita (48 80 530). Metro Repubblica or Termini/bus to Piazza della Repubblica.

Diocletian's baths, built between 298-306 AD, were the largest in Rome, covering over a hectare and able to accommodate 3,000 people at a time. Remaining fragments of the immense structure can now be seen in the church of Santa Maria degli Angeli (the *tepidarium* and part of the central hall), the church of San Bernardo alle Terme (a circular hall) and in the gardens and buildings of the **Museo Nazionale Romano**. Some sculptures have been left behind in the Baths' *Aula Ottagona* (Octagonal Hall) in Via Romita, once home to Rome's planetarium, and now open free of charge. By the millennium, some of the Baths will be reopened as the epigraphic museum, containing writing from ancient Roman walls, while the rest will remain a storehouse and restoration centre.

Circus Maximus (*Circo Massimo*)

Via del Circo Massimo. Metro Circo Massimo/bus or tram to Viale Aventino.

Ancient Rome's major chariot-racing venue is now ringed by several lanes of traffic, but with a bit of imagination it's still possible to visualise the flat base of the long, grassy basis as the racetrack, and the sloping sides as the stadium stands. At the southern end there are remains of the original seating, although the tower there is medieval. This was the oldest and largest of Rome's ancient arenas, and chariot races were held here from at least the fourth century BC onwards. It was rebuilt by Julius Caesar, and by the days of the Empire could hold as many as 300,000 people. The circus was also used for mock sea battles (when the arena was flooded with millions of gallons of water), the ever-popular fights with wild animals and the occasional large-scale execution.

Colosseum (*Colosseo*)

Piazza del Colosseo. Metro Colosseo/bus to Piazza del Colosseo. **Open** 9am-two hours before sunset Mon, Tue, Thur-Sat; 9am-1pm Wed, Sun. **Admission** L8,000; ground floor free.

It seems that nothing can be filmed in the city without the producer showing a few seconds of the traffic speeding past this massive building, which now looks like a partly eaten giant cake. It's also one of the most interesting ancient ruins in Rome, as its internal structure was exposed as it decayed. It was built in 72 AD by Vespasian on the newly-drained site of an artificial lake in the grounds of Nero's Domus Aurea, or Golden House. Favourite shows involved gladiators: slaves or prisoners fighting each other (not to mention all sorts of wild animals) with swords, nets and tridents. Several bloody deaths were guaranteed at every performance.

If you climb to the top of the Colosseum and look down to the centre of the building, you can see a maze of passages, originally underground, through which the animals were funnelled on their way into the arena. You can also see the scale of the building – it held 55,000 people and the emperor had his own box at the south end of the stadium. The cross at the edge of the arena was erected in honour of the many Christians believed to have been fed to the lions here. However, gladiatorial combats were banned in the early fifth century, and the Colosseum fell into disuse a century later, after wild animal fights stopped pulling in the crowds. The Colosseum is currently undergoing a massive, though slow-moving, facelift, scheduled for completion by 2000.

Column of Marcus Aurelius (*Colonna di Marco Aurelio*)

Piazza Colonna. Bus to Via del Corso.

This 30-metre-high column was built between 180 and 196 AD to commemorate the victories of that most intellectual of Roman emperors, Marcus Aurelius. Author of the famous *Meditations*, he died while campaigning in 180. The reliefs on the column, modelled on the earlier ones on Trajan's Column in the **Imperial Fora**, are vivid illustrations of Roman army life. A statue of Marcus Aurelius on top of the column was replaced by one of Saint Paul in 1589.

Emporium

Lungotevere Testaccio. Bus or tram to Piazza dell'Emporio. **Normally closed to the public.**

From the second century BC, the bank just south of Ponte Sublicio (built in 1919) was Rome's Emporium, the remains of which can still be seen from the bridge. Excavated in the 1970s, this was the ancient wharf area from which steps led up to the Porticus Emilia, a huge covered warehouse 60m wide and almost half a kilometre long. Behind the Porticus were the *horrea*, or grain warehouses, built under Tiberius to help control the imperial grain monopoly. The whole area is open to the public on very few random days a year, usually around the feast of Testaccio's patron saint, Santa Maria in Liberatrice, in early June.

Imperial Fora (*Fori Imperiali*)

Via dei Fori Imperiali. Metro Colosseo/bus to Colosseum. **Admission** by permission only (*see* **Getting into Locked Sites** *page 65*).

The area consists of five separate *fora*, each built by a different emperor. Not only had the previous Forum become too small to cope with the legal, social and commercial life of the city, but building a new Forum was also a convenient way of combining philanthropy with propaganda. All but one was built to celebrate a major military triumph. Now sliced across by multi-laned **Via dei Fori Imperiali** (a brainwave of Mussolini), all that remains of the *fora* today are a few columns, the odd wall and fragments of masonry, though archaeologists are hard at work trying to unearth more.

The earliest of the Imperial Fora was begun by Julius Caesar in 51 BC after he had conquered Gaul. Augustus built his in 31 BC after he had avenged Caesar's death. In the 'Temple of Peace' of the Forum of Vespasian, built in 71 AD, the treasures

*Once you've raced round it on a Vespa, you can explore the **Colosseum**.*

The Roman Forum

In the earliest days of the Republic the Foro Romano, or Roman Forum, was much like any Italian piazza today: an open space where people would shop, gossip, catch up on the latest news and perhaps visit a temple. In the second century BC, by which time Rome was the capital of an empire which included Greece, Sicily and Carthage, it was decided that the city needed a more dignified centre. The food stalls were moved out and law courts and offices were built. In time this new centre was also deemed too small, and emperors began to build the new **Fori Imperiali**. Nevertheless, the Roman Forum remained the symbolic heart of the Empire. and emperors continued to renovate and embellish it until the fourth century AD.

What we see now consists of little more than the layouts of floors and a few columns, but with a bit of imagination a tour around the Forum can give an accurate impression of what ancient Rome looked like. Before entering, look down over the Forum from behind the **Piazza del Campidoglio** for a view of its overall layout. Its central thoroughfare, the Via Sacra, runs almost directly through the middle. As you go into the Forum from the main entrance, you come to the ruins of the Basilica Amelia on the right. This was a large hall originally built for business and moneylending in 179 BC, though the remains are mainly from later periods. Look out for the bronze coins fused into the floor. The brick building beside it is a 1930s reconstruction of the Curia (senate house).

Standing out to the left of the Curia is the best-preserved monument in this part of the Forum: the massive Arch of Septimius Severus, built in 203 AD to celebrate victory over the Parthians. Near here was the Golden Milestone (Millarium Aureum), from which all distances were measured.

To the left of the Arch of Septimius are the remains of Caesar's rostra, a platform from which speeches and demonstrations of power were made, and from where Mark Antony supposedly asked the Roman populace to lend him their ears. To its

looted from the Temple of Jerusalem were displayed. This event was commemorated in the reliefs on the **Arch of Titus** in the **Roman Forum**. A Temple to Minerva was the main feature of the Forum of Nerva, dated 98 AD. Part of its original frieze survives. The most ambitious of all the fora was the Forum of Trajan, built in 113 AD after the Emperor Trajan had annexed Dacia – roughly present-day Romania. The story of his campaign against the Dacians is told in the beautifully carved reliefs spiralling up the only great surviving remnant of his Forum, **Trajan's Column**. The column is 38m high, and there are over a hundred scenes carved up its sides. Originally they were painted and would have been easily visible from galleries on the nearby buildings. They are difficult to see today, but there are replicas in the **Museo della Civiltà Romana** which make it easier to appreciate the extraordinary detail. The statue of Saint Peter on top of the column was added by Pope Sixtus V in 1587 to replace the original one of Trajan. Overlooking the site is **Trajan's Markets**.

left, in turn, are the eight columns that formed part of the Temple of Saturn, built in the fifth century BC. The state treasury was housed underneath it. Also clearly visible from here is the Column of Phocas, erected in 608 AD by Pope Boniface IV to thank the Byzantine Emperor for giving him the Pantheon as a church. Visible on the other side of the Via Sacra are the foundations of the Basilica Giulia, built by Julius Caesar in 55 BC and once a major –and by all accounts very noisy – law court. Ancient board games are carved into the steps.

Further into the Forum, on the right, are three elegant columns that formed part of the Temple of Castor and Pollux, the saviours of Rome. According to legend, these twin giants and their horses appeared to the Romans during a battle in 499 BC and helped the Republic to victory.

Beyond the Temple are the remains of the round Temple of Vesta and, within its garden (the Atrium Vestae), the rectangular House of the Vestal Virgins. On the other side of the Via Sacra are the columns of the Temple of Antonius and Faustina, built to honour a second-century emperor and his wife and, since the eleventh century, part of the church of San Lorenzo in Miranda. The oldest graves ever unearthed in Rome were found here; the bodies are now housed in the nearby Antiquarium Forense. The circular building on the right of the temple is the Temple of Romulus, dating from the fourth century AD. It has nothing to do with the co-founder of Rome: this Romulus was a son of the Emperor Maxentius, who died in 309. The bronze door of his temple is still locked with the original key.

Looming above these temples are three giant vaults that were part of the Basilica of Maxentius (also known as the Basilica of Constantine), begun in 306 AD and studied by Michelangelo and Bramante when they were designing Saint Peter's.

The southern exit of the Forum lies beyond the Arch of Titus, built in 81 AD to celebrate the sacking of Jerusalem; the event is depicted in the elaborate relic panels (you can just make out the sacred seven-branched candelabra). A path to the right of the Arch leads to the Palatine hill.

Entrance *Largo Romolo e Romo, Via dei Fori Imperiali (69 90 110). Metro Colosseo/bus to Via dei Fori Imperiali or Piazza Venezia.* **Open** *Apr-Sept* 9am-6pm Mon-Sat, 9am-1pm Sun; *Oct-Mar* 9am-sunset Mon-Sat, 9am-1pm Sun. **Admission** L12,000 (includes **Palatine**); no charge for under-18s and EU citizens over 60 with ID.

Mamertine Prison (*Carcere Mamertino*)

Clivo Argentario, 1, near Via di San Pietro in Carcere (67 92 902). Bus to Piazza Venezia. **Open** *Oct-Mar* 9am-noon, 2-5pm daily; *Apr-Sept* 9am-noon, 2.30-6pm daily. **Admission** donation expected.

Anyone who was thought to threaten the security of the Roman state was thrown into this dank, dark and oppressive little prison. In those days, the only way down to the lower level (built in the fourth century BC) was through a hole in the floor above, and the numberless prisoners who starved to death here were then tossed into the **Cloaca Maxima**, the city's main sewer. Today you can get in (and out) via a steep narrow staircase. There is a Christian altar in the prison because of a legend that Saint Peter was imprisoned here; the spring that bubbles up at the altar's side is said to be one he created miraculously to baptise other prisoners and two of his guards. Before you linger too long, please note the place closes for lunch.

The Via Appia Antica

Begun in the late fourth century BC by the statesman, lawmaker and sometime official censor Appius Claudius Caecus, the Via Appia Antica is one of the oldest Roman roads. Eventually it reached as far as Brindisi on the Adriatic coast, making it the Romans' main route to their eastern provinces. In addition, because of a fifth-century BC law banning burials within the city, the road became lined with the tombs and mausoleums of Rome's important families.

It is now a favoured retreat for lovers, ensconced in parked cars with steamed-up windows, and popular with men visiting the handful of elderly prostitutes who sit by their braziers at the Raccordo Anulare end.

However, it is the tombs of the ancient families and three sets of **Catacombs** that attract the bulk of the road's visitors. Near the Porta di San Sebastiano, built by Aurelian when he walled the city during the fourth century AD, is the austere church of Domine Quo Vadis? Its main claim to fame lies just inside the door – the imprints of two long flat feet are supposed to have been left by Christ when he appeared to Saint Peter, who was running away from Rome and crucifixion. Christ told him he was going back to Rome to be crucified again and Peter was thus shamed into returning himself. The painting on the left hand side of the altar depicts his martyrdom.

A memorial to a more recent act of barbarity stands beyond the Catacombs of Domitilla. This is the Fosse Ardeatine, formerly a quarry, where 335 Italians were shot by the Nazis in 1944 as a reprisal for a resistance attack. They now lie here in an underground mausoleum.

Beyond the Catacomb of San Sebastiano are three of the road's most famous ancient sites. At the junction with Vicolo della Basilica are the overgrown remains of the fourth-century Tomb of Romulus, the same beloved son of the Emperor Maxentius commemorated in the Temple of Romulus in the **Roman Forum**. The red brick walls behind it are the ruins of the

Circus of Maxentius, built by Romulus' father for chariot racing.

On top of a hill to the south is a squat brick cylinder that is the Tomb of Cecilia Metella, from the first century BC. Cecilia had merely married into the wealthy Metella family, who nevertheless gave her this unusually lavish tomb. During the fourteenth century the Caetani family, relatives of Pope Boniface VIII, turned the tomb into a fortress, adding the crenellations around its top, and proceeded to extract tolls from passers-by.

After the tomb comes a long stretch of road that in parts still retains the original round slabs used by the Romans. The tombs that line it are picturesquely overgrown and have been attracting artists since at least the eighteenth century.

Much further on, about half-way between the crossings with Via Erode Attico and Via Del Casal Rotondo, is the site of the second century AD Villa of the Quintilli. Beyond this point the road is quieter and the landscape wilder, with fragments of aqueduct standing in the fields. Any turning to the left will take you eventually to Via Appia Nuova, the main route back to the centre of Rome.

Getting There The Via Appia Antica is most easily approached from the far end. Take the Metro to Colli Albani, then the 660 bus, which will drop you in front of the Tomb of Cecilia Metella. Bus 218 from San Giovanni in Laterano will drop you off by Domine Quo Vadis? Alternatively, take a walk or bike ride there on Sunday, when the whole length of the road from Porta San Sebastiano is closed to traffic. A special shuttle bus service is planned for the year 2000.

Mausoleum of Augustus (*Mausoleo di Augusto*)

Piazza Augusto Imperatore or Via di Ripetta. Bus to Piazza Augusto Imperatore. **Open** by permission only (*see* **Getting into Locked Sites** *page 65*).

It's hard to believe that this forlorn-looking brick cylinder was one of the most important monuments of ancient Rome. It was originally covered with marble pillars and statues, all of which have long since been looted. Two obelisks that stood on either side of the main entrance are now in the Piazza del Quirinale and the Piazza dell'Esquilino. It was built in honour of Augustus, who had brought peace to the city and its Empire, and was begun in 28 BC. The first person buried there was Augustus' nephew Marcellus, also commemorated in the **Theatre of Marcellus**, his favourite son-in-law and probable successor, who died young in 23 BC. Augustus himself was laid to rest in the central chamber on his death in 14 AD, and many more of the early Caesars later joined him. In the Middle Ages the mausoleum was used as a fortress and later as a concert hall, but Mussolini had it restored, perhaps because he thought it a fitting place for his own corpse. He also planted the cedars and built the fascist-classical style square that now surrounds the tomb.

Monte Testaccio

Via Zabaglia, 24. Metro Piramide/bus or tram to Via Marmorata or Piazza San Paolo. **Open** by permission only (*see* **Getting into Locked Sites** *page 65*).

Also known as the *Monte dei Cocci* – the hill of shards – Monte Testaccio is just that: although it's covered by soil and scrubby plants, underneath it's nothing but a pile of broken *amphorae*, ancient earthenware jars, flung here between 140 and 255 AD. The vast majority came from the Roman province of Betica (Andalusia) and contained olive oil. In the Middle Ages, Monte Testaccio and the area below it were famous as the site of the Carnival celebrations, in which the horse races and religious pageants of the nobility vied wth the less refined sports of the people. Pigs, bulls and wild boar would be packed into carts at the top of the hill and sent careering down; any survivors of the impact were finished off at the bottom by men with spears. Now clubs and restaurants have been built into the base of the hill, and some afford glimpses of the *amphora* mound beyond.

Pantheon

Piazza della Rotonda (68 30 02 30). Bus to Largo Argentina or Via del Corso. **Open** 9am-6.30pm Mon-Sat; 9am-1pm Sun. **Admission** free.

The Pantheon is the best preserved of the remains of ancient Rome. It was built by Hadrian in 119-128 AD as a temple to the 12 most important classical deities, though the inscription on the pediment records an earlier Pantheon, built 100 years previously by Augustus' General Marcus Agrippa – which confused historians for centuries. Its fine state of preservation is due to the building's conversion to a Christian church in 608, when it was presented to the Pope by the Byzantine Emperor Phocas. The Pantheon has nevertheless suffered over the years – notably when the bronze cladding was

stripped from the roof in 667, and when Pope Urban VIII allowed Bernini to remove the remaining bronze from the beams in the portico to melt down for his *baldacchino* in **Saint Peter's** in the 1620s. The simplicity of the Pantheon's exterior is largely unchanged, and it still retains its original Roman bronze doors.

The key to its extraordinary harmony is its dimensions. The radius of the interior dome is exactly equal to its height, so it could potentially accommodate a perfect circle. At the centre of the dome is a circular hole nine metres in diameter, the *oculus*, which is the only source of light and a symbolic link between the temple and the heavens. The building is still officially a church, but it's easy to overlook this, in spite of all the paraphernalia added over the years and all the tombs of eminent Italians, including Raphael and the first king of united Italy, Vittorio Emanuele. Until the eighteenth century the portico was used as a market, and if you look at the columns you can see notches in the stonework which were used as supports for the stalls.

Ponte Rotto and the Cloaca Maxima

Views from Ponte Palatino, Isola Tiberina and Lungotevere Pierleoni. Bus to Piazza Sonnino, Piazza di Monte Savello, Lungotevere Pierleoni, Lungotevere Ripa.

The 'broken bridge' was the first stone bridge in Rome (142 BC). It partially fell down at least twice before finally collapsing in 1598. Near its west side, the tunnel in the embankment is the gaping mouth of the **Cloaca Maxima**, the city's 'great sewer', first built under the Tarquins (Rome's Etruscan kings) in the sixth century BC to drain the area round the Forum, and given its final form in the first century BC.

Portico of Octavia (*Portico d'Ottavia*)

Via del Portico d'Ottavia. Bus to Piazza di Monte Savello or Via del Teatro di Marcello.

These remains have been nonchalantly built around and into over the centuries, and are now held together by rusting braces forming the porch of the church of **Sant'Angelo in Pescheria**. They originally formed the entrance to a massive colonnaded square containing shops, libraries and tem-

A Roman ruin for a ruined Roman: **Pyramid of Gaius Cestius**. *See page 73.*

*The circular church of San Teodoro, gripping the **Palatine** hillside.*

ples. Emperor Augustus rebuilt the portico in the first century BC and dedicated it to his sister Octavia. The isolated columns outside belong to a later (213 AD) restoration by Septimius Severus. For centuries the portico also formed part of Rome's main fish market, hence the name of the church.

Pyramid of Gaius Cestius (*Piramide di Caio Cestio*)

Piazza di Porta San Paolo. Metro Piramide/train to Ostiense/bus or tram to Piazza di Porta San Paolo. **Open** by permission only (*see* **Getting into Locked Sites** *page 65*).

Standing out from the brick **Aurelian Wall** is a miniature Egyptian pyramid. It was built by an obscure first-century BC magistrate and *tribune* who was so impressed by the tombs of the pharaohs that he decided he wanted one of his own. He did not build it with quite as much technical care as the Egyptians used on their pyramids (it's made of brick and simply clad in marble) but nevertheless it has survived remarkably well since Cestius was buried here in 12 BC.

Temple of Hadrian (*Tempio di Adriano*)

Piazza di Pietra. Bus to Via del Corso.

Along the south side of the otherwise unremarkable Piazza di Pietra are eleven 15-metre-high Corinthian columns, now embedded in the grimy wall of Rome's highly inactive stock

The Palatine

The Beverly Hills of ancient Rome, the Palatine hill was where the movers and shakers of both Republic and Empire built their palaces. The choice of location was understandable: the Palatine overlooks the Roman Forum, yet is a comfortable distance from disturbances and riff-raff down in the valley.

Admission to the Palatine is included in the ticket to the **Roman Forum** (and vice versa), but be warned: staff shortages mean that parts of the area, such as the Domus Livia, are often closed without warning.

If you enter the Palatine from the Forum you pass the Farnese gardens on the right, laid out in the sixteenth century and one of the oldest botanical gardens in Europe, full of orange trees, burbling fountains and box hedges. Like many of the great buildings of Rome, the gardens were created for a member of a papal family, Cardinal Alessandro Farnese, who used them for lavish garden parties. The pavilion at the top of the hill is seventeenth-century, with a good view over the Forum. Underneath the gardens, behind the pavilion, is the Cryptoporticus, a long semi-subterranean tunnel built by Nero, either for hot-weather promenades or as a secret route between the Palatine buildings and his palace, the Domus Aurea (Golden House), across the valley on the Oppian hill. Lit only by slits in the walls, the Cryptoporticus is welcomingly cool in summer, and at one end there are mouldy remnants of a stucco ceiling-frieze and mosaics on the floor.

South of the gardens are the remains of the imperial palaces built by Domitian at the end of the first century AD, which became the principal residence of the emperors for the next three centuries. The nearest section, the Domus Flavia, contained the public rooms. According to the biographer Suetonius, Domitian was so terrified of assassination that he had the walls faced with shiny selenite so he could see any-

body creeping up behind him. Sadly for him, this did not prevent his eventual murder. You can see the foundations of a strange room, with what looks like a maze in the middle, which was the courtyard. Next to this was the dining room, where parts of the marble floor have survived, though it's usually covered for protection. The brick oval in the middle was probably a fountain.

Next door is the emperor's private residence, the Domus Augustana. The oval building close by may have been a garden or a mini-stadium for Domitian's private entertainment. To the south lie the remains of the comparatively small palace and baths of Septimius Severus, some of the best-preserved buildings in the area. Unfortunately they are almost permanently closed to visitors.

Back towards the Farnese gardens is the Domus Livia, named after Augustus' wife. The wall paintings here date from the late Republic and include *trompe l'œil* marble panels and scenes from mythology.

Entrance *Largo Romolo e Romo, Via dei Fori Imperiali (69 90 110). Metro Colosseo/bus to Via dei Fori Imperiali or Piazza Venezia.* **Open** *Apr-Sept* 9am-6pm Mon-Sat, 9am-1pm Sun; *Oct-Mar* 9am-sunset Mon-Sat, 9am-1pm Sun. **Admission** L12,000 (includes **Roman Forum**); no charge for under-18s and EU citizens over 60 with ID.

The Catacombs

Miles of underground galleries lined with burial chambers were dug into the volvanic rock beneath the soil of ancient Rome. The reason for this was simple: burial within the walls of Rome was forbidden, and tombs built above ground like those that line the **Via Appia Antica** were very expensive. Most of the Catacombs date from the fourth century BC to the first century AD. Many of the tombs are pagan, among them the Columbarium (literally, the dovecote) of Pomponius Hylas, in the Parco degli Scipione; a few are Jewish. The most famous, however, are those of the Christians, who were able to bury their dead and carry out ceremonies in the Catacombs, unmolested by their pagan persecutors.

The standard form of burial was in a niche carved in the rock. The body, wrapped in linen and often embalmed, was laid in the niche, which was then sealed with tiles or slabs of marble. The grander, arched niches tend to be the graves of martyrs or other important believers, while some wealthy families had their own crypts where they could all be buried together. Frescoes on the walls often illustrate the indomitability of faith. Popular symbols include representations of Christ as a fish or a shepherd, while a lamb or a sheep represents humanity. Human figures with their arms raised as if acknowledging applause are actually praying in the manner of the early Christians.

When Christianity became Rome's official religion, the Catacombs took on a special significance because they contained the bones of many saints and martyrs, among them Saint Sebastian, Saint Agnes and Saint Cecilia. The Catacombs of Saint Sebastian may also have been used to house the relics of Saint Peter and Saint Paul during the third century, when worship at their shrines was still strictly forbidden.

Like so many of Rome's ancient monuments, the Catacombs tended to be forgotten for long periods, then rediscovered. In the ninth century huge quantities of bones were dug up and reburied in Saint Peter's and elsewhere, but most of these vast underground cities of the dead lay undisturbed until the extent of them became apparent in the sixteenth century. Catacombs can be found all over suburban Rome and about 300km of them are known. The most frequently visited are the Catacombs of San Callisto, San Sebastiano and Domitilla along the **Via Appia Antica**. More atmospheric, however, are the Catacombs of Priscilla outside the Villa Ada,

where you are shown around by nuns who live in the convent above. Priscilla belonged to a noble Roman family who converted to Christianity and opened up a catacomb beneath their house. It eventually held around 40,000 corpses and is about 50m deep. Highlights of the visit include the Greek chapel, painted with very early frescoes of bibilical stories. All catacombs close at 5pm in winter.

Catacombs of San Callisto *Via Appia Antica, 110 (51 36 725). Metro Colli Albani then bus to Via Appia Antica.* **Open** 9.30am-noon, 2.30-5.30pm Mon-Wed, Fri, Sun. **Admission** L8,000.

Catacombs of Domitilla *Via delle Sette Chiesa, 282 (51 10 342). Bus to Via delle Sette Chiese.* **Open** 8.30am-noon, 2.30-5.30pm Mon, Wed-Sun. **Admission** L8,000.

Catacombs of Priscilla *Via Salaria, 430 (86 20 62 72). Bus to Via Salaria.* **Open** 8.30am-noon, 2.30-5pm Tue, Sun. **Admission** L8,000.

Catacombs of San Sebastiano *Via Appia Antica, 136 (78 87 035). Metro Colli Albani then bus to Via Appia Antica.* **Open** 9am-noon, 2.30-5.30pm, Mon-Wed, Fri, Sun. **Admission** L8,000.

Columbarium of Pomponius Hylas *Via di Porta Latina, 10. Metro Circo Massimo.* **Open** by permission only (*see* **Getting into Locked Sites** *page 65*).

exchange (Borsa). These originally formed part of a temple built to honour Emperor Hadrian by his adopted son, Antoninus Pius, in 145 AD.

Temples of Hercules Victor and Portunus (*Tempio di Vesta e Tempio di Fortuna Virilis*)

Piazza della Bocca della Verità. Bus to Piazza Bocca della Verità.

Like the **Pantheon**, both of these diminutive Republican-era temples owe their exceptional state of preservation to their conversion into churches during the Middle Ages. The round one, which looks like an English folly, was built in the first century BC and dedicated to Hercules. Early archaeologists were confused by its round shape, similar to the Temple of Vesta in the **Roman Forum** and mistakenly dubbed it the Temple of Vesta. It's still best known by this name in Rome. The second temple, similarly perfect in form, is a century older and was dedicated to Portunus, the god of harbours, as this was the port area of ancient Rome. This was also misattributed as being dedicated to 'manly fortune'. Both temples were deconsecrated and declared ancient monuments in the 1920s on the orders of Mussolini.

Theatre of Marcellus (*Teatro di Marcello*)

Via del Teatro di Marcello. Bus to Via del Teatro di Marcello. **Open** by permission only (*see* **Getting into Locked Sites** *page 65*).

If you haven't time to seek formal permission to enter, don't give up: the Theatre is visible from outside. It's one of the strangest and most impressive sights in Rome – the façade of a Renaissance palace grafted on to an ancient, crumbling circular theatre. Julius Caesar began the massive theatre to rival Pompey's building in the Campus Martius, but it was finished in 11 BC by Augustus, who named it after his favourite nephew (*see above* **Mausoleum of Augustus**). At one time the theatre was connected to the adjacent

Portico of Octavia and originally had three tiers in different styles (Ionic, Doric and Corinthian), but the top one has collapsed. After the theatre was abandoned in the fourth century AD it had various uses, including that of fortress, before Baldassare Peruzzi built a palace for the Savelli family on top of the crumbling remains in the sixteenth century. This palace has now been converted into luxurious and hugely expensive apartments. To the north of the theatre are three columns that were part of the Temple of Apollo, built in 433 BC.

Trajan's Markets (*Mercati Traiani*)

Via IV Novembre, 94 (67 90 048). Bus to Via Nazionale. **Open** 9am-7pm Tue-Sat; 9am-1pm Sun. **Admission** L3,750; L2,500 students, *free* last Sunday of month and for EC citizens under 18 and over 60.

This market building was built on the orders of Trajan in the first decade of the second century. It was designed by Apollodorus of Damascus (whom Hadrian later had killed on suspicion of treachery) and is the ancient Roman equivalent of a shopping mall. The most distinctive feature is a multi-storey brick crescent or *hemicycle*, which gives access into Trajan's Forum in the **Imperial Fora**. At the back of the crescent is a large hall which may have been used for the distribution of the corn dole – an early form of social security. In total there were five levels to the building, containing about 150 small shops. These were probably organised into areas – the ground floor for wine and oil, first floor for fruit and flowers, and so on. Although the shops are all empty, they are mostly intact, and you can still see some of the ridges into which shutters were dropped at closing time.

Attached to the market are several medieval buildings, including the Torre delle Milizie (military tower), part of a fortress built by Pope Gregory IX in the thirteenth century, which for many years was erroneously believed to be the one from which Nero watched Rome burn after he'd supposedly set fire to it.

*The world conquered, the Romans got down to some serious shopping at **Trajan's Markets**.*

Churches

The sheer number of churches in Rome is enough to bring most visitors to their knees.

There are more than 400 churches in the *centro storico* alone – excessive even for the capital of the Roman Catholic Church and one of the birthplaces of western Christianity. Rome has hundreds of exquisite and fascinating churches, as across the centuries popes, princes and aristocrats commissioned artists and architects to build, rebuild, adorn, fresco and paint their city's places of worship. The motive was not wholly philanthropic. For many, it was a cynical means of assuring a place in Heaven, securing temporal power and increasing the popularity of the Church authorities. Whatever the reasons, the results of all this apparent beneficence form some of Rome's most spectacular sights.

What follows is a selection of the most interesting churches in Rome. Most are open every day from 8.30 or 9am until noon or 1pm, and again from 4 to 7pm. However, opening hours can be changed at short notice, especially at the smaller churches, where there may not be anyone available to unlock the doors at the stipulated time.

Churches are places of worship, so visitors are asked to respect certain dress codes. These are rigorously enforced, especially in the big basilicas. Very short shorts and bare shoulders are not allowed, so carry a shawl or long-sleeved shirt when you're sightseeing. You may also consider carrying binoculars and a torch to see into all the distant, badly-lit corners. Have a ready supply of coins (L100, 200 and 500) for feeding the meters that light up the most interesting chapels. Although you may be admitted to churches during services, you will be expected not to take photographs, talk loudly or wander around.

Inevitably, some churches will be undergoing restoration work, both inside and out. Because of the complexities of the tasks involved, this work often takes far longer than expected, so, while you're likely to find some spectacularly gleaming façades and sparkling frescoes on your tour of Roman churches, you will also find others shrouded in scaffolding.

For the basilica of Saint Peter's and the chapels within the Vatican, *see chapter* **The Vatican City**.

From Pagan to Christian

The new cult of Christianity appeared in Rome a decade or so after the death of Christ, some years before Peter and Paul visited the city. The early Christians met secretly in private houses, or in community centres known as *tituli* (titles) and named after their owners. Christians were considered politically dangerous because they refused to accept the supremacy of Roman law or the deification of emperors, and they suffered persecution of varying degrees of intensity, depending on the whims of any given ruler. The first churches were often named after early martyrs, who were put to death in imaginatively grisly ways during the religion's first three centuries. In 312-3, Emperor Constantine adopted Christianity as the new state religion and began an extensive programme of church building, often on the sites of *tituli* or over the graves of the martyrs.

Over the centuries, new churches have been built over many of these simple places of worship, but some have survived beneath their more extravagant successors and can still be visited today.

Santa Cecilia in Trastevere

Piazza di Santa Cecilia (58 99 289). Bus to Viale Trastevere. **Open** *main church* 10am-noon, 4-6pm, daily; *Cavallini frescoes* 10-11.30am Tue, Thur; 11am-noon Sun. **Admission** *Excavations* L2,000; *Cavallini frescoes* donation expected.

This pretty church stands on the site of a fifth-century building which was founded over a Roman house, the bath and store rooms of which can still be visited. According to legend, it was the home of Valerio, a Roman patrician who was so impressed (if not frustrated) by his Christian wife Cecilia's maintaining her vow of chastity that he too converted. Valerio was martyred for his pains, and Cecilia was arrested while attempting to bury his body. Her martyrdom was something of a botched job – following a failed attempt to suffocate her in the hot steam baths of her house, her persecutors tried to behead her with three strokes of an axe (the maximum permitted). She took several days to die, which, according to one legend, she spent singing. In any event, she became the patron saint of music. In 1599 her tomb was opened, revealing her still-undecayed body. It rapidly disintegrated, but not before a sketch had been made, on which Stefano Maderna based the astonishingly delicate sculpture which lies below the high altar.

Make sure your visit to this church coincides with the very short opening times in which you can see a small remaining fragment of what must have been one of the world's greatest frescoes. Pietro Cavallini's late thirteenth century *Last Judgement* is high up in the gallery and miraculously survived the rebuilding of the church. While still working within a Byzantine-style framework, Cavallini floods the seated

*The peaceful gardens of **Santa Cecilia** complement the beauty of the church.*

apostles with a totally new kind of light (note the depth of the faces) – the same light that was to reappear in Giotto's work and which has led some scholars to believe that Cavallini, and not Giotto, was responsible for the Saint Francis fresco cycle in Assisi. (*See* **Myths of the Decline & Fall** *in chapter* **History – A New Religion**.)

San Clemente

Via San Giovanni in Laterano (70 45 10 18). Metro Colosseo/bus to Colosseo or Via Labicana.
Open 9am-12.30pm, 3.30-6pm, daily *Oct-Mar;* 9am-12.30pm, 3.30-6.30pm, daily *Apr-Sept.* **Admission** *Excavations* L2,000.

San Clemente is one of the most intriguing of all Rome's buildings: three layers of history one on top of the other, with a narrow first-century alley you can still walk down. The existing basilica is a smaller twelfth-century copy of its fourth-century predecessor, which in turn was built over a early Christian *titulus*, or community centre. The original church was burnt down when the Normans sacked Rome in 1084, but the *schola cantorum*, a walled marble choir, survived, and was moved upstairs to the new church, where it still stands. However, the most striking feature is a vivid medieval mosaic in the apse, showing the vine of life spiralling around delightful pastoral scenes. Peasants tending their flocks and crops are interspersed with saints and prophets, and the whole mosaic centres on the crucified Christ. Also worth seeing is the chapel of Saint Catherine, with frescoes by Masolino (possibly helped by Masaccio) which have recently been restored.

Steps lead down from the sacristy to the fourth-century basilica, the layout of which is obscured by a series of walls built to support the church above. Some rapidly fading frescoes illustrate episodes from Saint Clement's miracle-packed life. They are difficult to interpret, but the guide on sale in the sacristy helps. At the end of the underground basilica, past the strange twentieth-century Slavic memorial to the inventor of Cyrillic script, the 'apostle of the Slavs' Saint Cyril (whose long-lost burial site is here), a stairway leads down to the remains of the second-century apartment block or *insula*, where the cult of the god Mithras was celebrated. Mithraism, Christianity's main rival in the late Empire, was a complex, mystical religion of Persian origin. It had several parallels with Christianity, including initiation and communion rituals. With the rise of Christianity, belief in Mithraism petered out, and in 395 it was outlawed. Three rooms have been excavated: the ante-room, with benches and a stucco ceiling; the sanctuary, with an altar depicting Mithras killing a bull; and a school room. On the other side of the lane are the ground-floor rooms of the Roman house, used by early Christians as a meeting place.

Santi Giovanni e Paolo

Piazza Santi Giovanni e Paolo, 13 (70 05 236). Metro Colosseo/bus or tram to Via di San Gregorio. **Open** 9.30-11.30am, 3.30-6pm, daily.

Along the side of the church, in Via di Clivo di Scauro, you can still make out three Roman buildings. One of the buildings was used as an early Christian meeting house, the *Titulus Pammachius*, before being unified with the other two and converted into a basilica around 398. The restoration of the original *titulus*, containing early Christian and pagan frescoes and martyrs' tombs, is now complete, but to view the tombs, you must phone the number given above in advance. The present-day church façade has been restored to its original medieval appearance, but the interior was kitted out in the eighteenth century, and seems more like a luxury banqueting hall than a church, with creamy stucco work and extravagant chandeliers. Ask the sacristan for permission to view the remains of the thirteenth-century frescoes and the impressive Temple of Claudius. The latter once dominated the Celian hill, and is now hidden under the church monastery and the bell tower.

San Lorenzo in Lucina

Piazza San Lorenzo in Lucina, 16a (68 71 494). Bus to Via del Corso or Piazza Augusto Imperatore. **Open** 8am-noon, 5-8pm, daily.

This twelfth-century church was built on the site of an early Christian place of worship which in turn is believed to stand on the site of an ancient well sacred to Juno. Its exterior incorporates some Roman columns, and the seventeenth-century interior contains a wealth of treasures, including Bernini portrait busts in the Fonseca Chapel, a kitsch seventeenth-century *Crucifixion* by Guido Reni, and a monument to French artist Nicholas Poussin, who died in Rome in 1665. There is also an ancient grill, reputed to be the one on which the martyr Saint Lawrence was roasted to death.

San Martino ai Monti

Viale del Monte Oppio, 28 (48 63 126). Metro Cavour or Vittorio Emanuele/bus to Piazza Esquilino. **Open** 7am-noon, 4.30-6.30pm, daily *Oct-Mar;* 7am-noon, 4.30-7pm, daily *Apr-Sept.*

The main reason to visit is to see the third-century *titulus* underneath this ninth-century church. It's a spooky and rarely visited place, littered with bits of sculpture, decaying mosaics and frescoes. The church above the *titulus* is chiefly remarkable for two frescoes: one showing **San Giovanni in Laterano** as it was before Borromini's changes (far left, by Dughet), and the other portraying the original Saint Peter's basilica (far right, by Gagliardi).

San Nicola in Carcere

Via del Teatro di Marcello, 46 (68 69 972). Bus to Via del Teatro di Marcello. **Open** 7.30am-noon, 4-7pm, Mon-Sat, 10am-1pm Sun *mid Sept-end July.*

This church was built in the eleventh century within the ruins of three Republican-era temples. These were dedicated to the two-faced god, Janus, to the goddess Juno, and to Spes (Hope). They overlooked the city's fruit and vegetable market, the Forum Holitarium, whose columns you can still see embedded in the wall.

Constantine & the Basilica Form

Constantine's Edict of Milan in 313 allowed Christianity to come out into the open, but many Romans, including the Senate, were still pagan. To avoid problems, the earliest official places of worship were built on the edges of the city. Only **San Giovanni in Laterano** and **Santa Croce** were allowed to be built within the city walls.

The new buildings were simple and designed to be inconspicuous on the outside. Their form derived from secular Roman basilicas or meeting halls, with one important difference: the side-apse was moved to the far end to form the sanctuary. All decoration was confined to the interior, hidden from the prying gaze of the uninitiated, and was often splendid in the extreme. The design of the pagan temple, with a façade as the backdrop to ritual sacrifice, was turned inside out. The marble columns now ran the length of the nave, with the worshipers inside.

San Giovanni in Laterano

Piazza di San Giovanni in Laterano, 4 (69 88 64 33). Metro San Giovanni/bus or tram to Piazza San Giovanni. **Open** *Cloister* 7am-6pm Mon-Fri, 7am-7pm Sat-Sun *Oct-Mar;* 7am-7pm daily *Apr-Sept. Museum* 9am-5pm Mon-Fri *Oct-Mar;* 9am-6pm Mon-Fri *Apr-Sept.* **Admission** *Cloister and museum* L4,000.

Nuff respect ... **San Giovanni in Laterano** *demands decorum from visitors.*

Constantine himself built San Giovanni, around 313, on the site of an imperial palace. This is still technically the cathedral of Rome. Little remains of the original basilica, as it has burnt down twice and been much restored and rebuilt over the years. San Giovanni's problem was that it was in an under-populated area of the city which was almost impossible to defend. The impressive façade, surmounted by 15 huge statues, dates from the latest of these rebuildings and was designed by Alessandro Gallei in 1735. The interior was last transformed in 1646 by Borromini, who encased the original columns in pillars and stucco. The enormous bronze doors in the main entrance came originally from the Senate House in the Forum. A thirteenth-century mosaic in the apse survived the modernisation, as did a fragment of fresco attributed to Giotto (behind the first column on the right); it shows Pope Boniface VIII announcing the first Holy Year in 1300. Another survivor is the gothic altar canopy or *baldacchino* at the head of the nave, holding the heads of Saints Paul and Peter. More attractive are the thirteenth-century cloisters: their twisted columns, studded with multicoloured mosaics, were the work of the Vassalletto family.

The north façade was added in 1586 by Domenico Fontana. To the right of this is the octagonal baptistry, founded by Constantine and rebuilt in 432 and 1637. Restored after a bomb exploded nearby in summer 1993, it holds some fine fifth- and seventh-century mosaics. On the eastern side of Piazza San Giovanni are the remaining sections of the former papal residence, the Lateran Palace, the recently-restored (but, sadly, inaccessible to the public) Sancta Sanctorum, the Pope's former private chapel, and the Scala Santa, or Holy Staircase. These 28 steps (protected by wooden boards) were once the ceremonial steps of the old palace, but are traditionally believed to be those Christ climbed on his way to trial at Pontius Pilate's house in Jerusalem. They were supposedly brought to Rome by Constantine's mother, Saint Helena (*see below* **Relics**). Devout pilgrims ascend the steps on their knees, particularly on Good Friday. In 1510, Martin Luther gave this a go, but half-way up the steps he decided that relics were a theological irrelevance and walked back down again.

Santa Maria Maggiore

Piazza di Santa Maria Maggiore (48 31 95). Metro Cavour/bus to Piazza Esquilino. **Open** 7am-7pm daily.
Behind this blowsy Baroque façade is one of the most striking basilica-form churches in Rome. A flat-roofed nave shoots between two aisles to a triumphal arch and apse. Thirteenth-century mosaics in the apse by Jacopo Torriti show Mary, dressed as a Byzantine Empress, being crowned Queen of Heaven by Christ. She is also depicted in fifth-century mosaics on the triumphal arch. The ceiling in the main nave is said to have been made from the first shipment of gold extracted from the Americas by Ferdinand and Isabella of Spain, and was presented to the church by the Borgia Pope, Alexander VI.

In the sixteenth and seventeenth centuries, two incredibly flamboyant chapels were added. The first was the Capella Sistina, designed by Domenico Fontana for Sixtus V (1585-90), and elaborately decorated with multi-coloured marble, gilt and precious stones. Sixtus had ancient buildings ransacked for materials, and employed virtually every sculptor then working in the city. Directly opposite is the Cappella Paolina, a large and even gaudier Greek-cross chapel, designed by Flaminio Ponzio in 1611 for Paul V, to house an icon of the Madonna. The chapel also contains a relief by Maderno showing Pope Liberius tracing the plan of the basilica, after a dream in which the Virgin instructed him to build a church on the spot where snow would fall the next morning. The snow fell on 5 August 352, and the anniversary of this miracle is commemorated every year, when thousands of flower petals are released from the roof of the church.

San Paolo fuori le Mura

Via Ostiense, 186, Ostiense (54 10 341). Metro San Paolo/bus to Piazzale San Paolo. **Open** 7.30am-6.45pm Mon-Sat; 7am-6.45pm Sun.
Constantine founded San Paolo to commemorate the martyrdom of Saint Paul at nearby Tre Fontane – named after three fountains that sprang up as his severed head bounced three times. The church has been destroyed, rebuilt and restored several times, and the present building is only 150

Caravaggio

If you're looking for a theme for your Roman pavement-pounding, try following the works of the roguish genius Michelangelo Merisi – better known as Caravaggio (1573-1610), whose psychological realism and spiritually-charged lighting techniques were to influence painting profoundly for centuries to come.

An artist with a temper who flouted convention and authority, Caravaggio swaggered about Via della Scrofa brandishing a sword and spent a fair amount of time in jail for using it, and other weapons, to good effect. He fled from Rome in 1606 after killing a man in the Campo Marzio, beginning an odyssey as a fugitive that took him to Naples, Malta and Sicily before he died alone in Tuscany in 1610 at the age of 36.

To get an idea of why church authorities loved to hate him, start at the **Church of Sant'Agostino**, where the *Madonna of the Pilgrims* shows one of the most natural and grace-filled Virgin and Child scenes ever painted … together with surrounding pilgrims so dirty and scruffy that the commissioning church refused to accep the picture. Around the corner, in the church of **San Luigi dei Francesi** (see listing below), go to the last chapel on the left and take a look at the dark trio of paintings depicting the life of Saint Matthew. Pop some coins into the light machine and behold! – divine rays touch Saint Matthew as Christ calls him to follow. In the church of **Santa Maria del Popolo**, the *Crucifixion of Saint Peter* and the *Conversion of Saint Paul*, are packed with concentrated interior energy.

Despite being charged by the conventionally pious with vulgarizing the sacred, Caravaggio kept churning out masterpieces, and wily private collectors were always ready to pick up scandalous rejects at bargain basement prices. The **Galleria Borghese** boasts six Caravaggios, including the self-portrait *Sick Bacchus* and a singularly untriumphant David displaying the silent scream of the beheaded Goliath. The **Doria Pamphili Gallery** is home to *Mary Magdalene*, *Rest during the Flight into Egypt* and *Saint John the Baptist*. The Pinocoteca at the **Vatican Museums** holds the important *Entombment*, the **Palazzo Barberini** has a *Narcissus* and a *Judith and Holofernes*, and the **Capitoline Museums** boast another *Saint John the Baptist* and *Fortune Teller*.

Church of Sant'Agostino *Via della Scrofa, 80 (68 80 19 62). Bus to Corso Rinascimento.* **Open** 8am-noon, 4.30-7.30pm, daily.
San Luigi dei Francesi *Via Santa Giovanna d'Arco (68 80 36 29). Bus to Corso Rinascimento.* **Open** 8am-12.30pm, 3.30-7pm, Mon-Wed, Fri-Sat; 8am-12.30pm Thur, Sun).

years old, though a few details and a wonderful cloister survive from its ancient beginnings. The greatest damage to the basilica occurred in a fire in 1823, although subsequent restorers also contributed to the destruction of the older building. Surviving features include eleventh-century doors decorated with biblical scenes; the elegant thirteenth-century *ciborio* over the altar by Arnolfo di Cambio; and a strange twelfth-century Easter candlestick featuring human-, lion-, and goat-headed beasts spewing the vine of life from their mouths.

The cloister is a good example of *Cosmatesque* work (*see below* **Mosaics & Cosmati**), its twisted columns inlaid with mosaic and supporting an elaborate arcade of different coloured marble and sculpted reliefs. In the sacristy there are several canvases and four frescoed portraits, the remnants of a series of papal portraits that once lined the nave. The modern church has carried on this tradition, replacing the originals with mosaic portraits of all the popes from Peter to the present incumbent. There are only eight spaces left, after which, apparently, the world will end.

Santi Quattro Coronati

Via dei Santi Quattro Coronati, 20 (70 47 54 27). Metro Colosseo/bus or tram to Via Labicana. **Open** 9.30am-noon, 4.30-6pm, Mon-Sat; 9.30-10.30am, 4.30-6pm, Sun.
The basilica dates from the fourteenth century but, like **San Clemente** down the road, it was burnt down by the Normans in 1084. It was rebuilt as a fortified monastery, with the church itself reduced to half its original size. The early basilica form is still discernible, and the columns which once ran along the aisles are embedded in the walls of the innermost courtyard. There is also a beautiful cloister, dating from about 1220. In the oratory next to the church (ring the bell and ask the nuns for the key – it will cost you L1,000 to turn the light on) is an entertaining fresco cycle depicting the Donation of Constantine and painted in the thirteenth century as a defence of the popes' temporal power. A pox-ridden Constantine is cured by Pope Sylvester and, in gratitude, crowns him with a tiara and gives him a cap which symbolises the Pope's spiritual and earthly power. Finally, just to make sure there was no doubt about Sylvester's capacity for heroics, he resuscitates a bull killed as a sacrifice, and frees the Romans from a dragon.

Santa Sabina

Piazza Pietro d'Illiria, 1 (57 43 573). Metro Circo Massimo/bus to Piazzale Ugo La Malfa. **Open** 7am-12.30pm, 3.30-7pm, daily.
As well as grand, patriarchal churches, a series of more modest parish churches was built on the basilica plan in the fifth century. One of the best examples is Santa Sabina, brutally 'restored' in 1936 to what was considered its original appearance. Built over an earlier *titulus*, it has a high nave with towering, elegant columns supporting an arcade. The floor is original, as are the wooden doors carved with scenes from the New Testament, including one of the earliest renderings of the crucifixion. There is also a pleasant, simple cloister. If it is closed, ask the sacristan to let you in.

Relics

The cult of the martyrs developed from the Roman Church's desire to keep alive the historical memory of its suffering under the persecutions, both as a form of popular devotion and as propaganda in the struggle for primacy over the older Churches of the East.

Quite distinct from this tradition was the roaring trade in relics from the Holy Land started by Saint Helena, Constantine's mother, and which continued up to the Crusades. She set off with a shopping list and came back with everything she wanted – many of her finds are still in the church she founded in Rome, **Santa Croce in Gerusalemme**. It was this type of relic-on-demand (the surviving bits of True Cross would cover a football pitch) that was to give the whole practice such a bad name in years to come.

Santi Bonifacio e Alessio

Piazza di Sant'Alessio, 23 (57 43 446). Metro Circo Massimo/bus to Piazzale Ugo La Malfa. **Open** 8.30am-12.30pm, 3-5pm, daily *Oct-Mar*; 8.30am-12.30pm, 3.30-6.30pm, daily *Apr-Sept.*
Inside this church is an eighteenth-century chapel incorporating part of a wooden staircase. The early Christian saint Alexis fled to the Holy Land to escape an arranged marriage, and returned years later disguised as a beggar. Unrecognised, he asked his father for hospitality and lived under the staircase for the next 17 years, only revealing his identity on his death bed. A chapel should perhaps also be dedicated to his fiancée who faithfully awaited his return.

Santa Croce in Gerusalemme

Piazza di Santa Croce in Gerusalemme, 12 (70 14 769). Bus or tram to Piazza di Porta Maggiore. **Open** 6am-12.30pm, 3.30-6.30pm, daily *Oct-Mar*; 6am-12.30pm, 3.30-7.30pm, daily *Apr-Sept.*
Founded by Saint Helena in 320, this church began its life as a hall in her palace. The outline of the original building can be clearly seen from the grounds of the Museo Nazionale degli Strumenti Musicali (*see chapter* **Museums & Galleries**). It was built to house the relics of Christ's cross, which are now behind glass in a dull, fascist-style chapel dating from the 1930s. As well as three pieces of the cross and a nail, there are two thorns from Christ's crown, a section of the good thief's cross and the finger of Saint Thomas –

Fine frescoes at **Santi Quattro Coronati**.

allegedly the very one which the doubting saint stuck into Christ's wound. Bagfulls of soil from Calvary are under the tiles in the charming lower chapel, which is decorated with fifteenth-century mosaics.

Santa Maria in Via

Via Santa Maria in Via (67 96 760). Metro Barberini/bus to Piazza San Silvestro or Via del Corso. **Open** 7am-12.30pm, 4-7.30pm, daily.

The ornate Baroque façade, completed in 1681 by Carlo Rainaldi, a pupil of Bernini, hides a little chapel containing a thirteenth-century well whose water supposedly has the power to cure the sick. When mass is not being held, an old lady sells water from the well at L1,000 a shot.

San Pietro in Vincoli

Piazza di San Pietro in Vincoli, 4a (48 82 865). Metro Colosseo or Cavour/bus to Via Cavour. **Open** 7am-12.30pm, 3.30-6pm, daily *Oct-Mar*; 7am-12.30pm, 3.30-7pm, daily *Apr-Sept.*

Dominating the tomb of Pope Julius II is Michelangelo's imposing *Moses*. However, the church is more revered by Catholics for containing the chains believed to have shackled Saint Peter, both in Jerusalem and in the **Mamertine Prison** (*see chapter* **Ancient Sites**). There are several relics of Peter in Rome – footprints in the church of Santa Francesca Romana (see **The Feats of Santa Francesca** *page 12*), a head print, where he butted the ground as he was thrown into the Mamertine Prison, and his head itself in **San Giovanni in Laterano** – but the chains are the most venerated of all, displayed here in a glass case over the altar. They are paraded around the city every 1st August.

Santi Vincenzo ed Anastasio

Vicolo dei Modelli, 73 (67 83 098). Metro Barberini/bus to San Silvestro. **Open** 7am-noon, 4-7pm, daily.

Your chance to stand in the presence of the livers, spleens and pancreases of every Pope from Sixtus V (1585-1590) to Leo XIII (1878-1903). After each Pope's death his innards were bottled, labelled and deposited here – but you can't see them.

Mosaics & Cosmati

The art of mosaic originated in Asia, and was mainly used by the Ancient Greeks and Romans to create elaborate pavements from pieces of marble and coloured stone. The Christians adapted the technique to extend glittering mosaics onto the walls and vaults of their early churches. They mostly used glass pieces *(tesserae)*, outlined in gold leaf and placed to reflect light, and create infinite variations of colour. The changing styles in mosaics can be traced in the churches listed here.

The Cosmati family revolutionised the art of mosaic in the twelfth century, by reusing bits and pieces from ancient buildings and sawing up columns into round disks to create inlaid marble floors, thrones, tombs, fonts and other church fittings. Called *Cosmatesque*, this work can be found in churches all over the city.

Sant'Agnese fuori le Mura & Santa Costanza

Via Nomentana, 349 (86 10 840). Bus to Via Nomentana. **Open** *Sant'Agnese* 8am-noon, 4-7.30pm, daily. *Santa Costanza* 9am-noon Mon; 9am-noon, 4-6pm, Tue-Sat; noon-6pm Sun.

The circular mausoleum of Santa Costanza was built for Constantine's daughters, Constance and Helen, and is decorated with the world's earliest surviving Christian mosaics. They don't look very Christian – simple pastoral scenes with a spiralling vine encircling figures joyfully collecting and treading grapes – but historians insist the wine being made represents Christ's blood. In the adjoining church of Sant'Agnese, also dating from Constantine's time, there is a seventh-century apse mosaic showing a stilted figure of Saint Agnes standing on the flames of her martyrdom, flanked by two popes. Like the mosaics of **San Lorenzo**, there is little of the classical tradition here. Try to persuade the sacristan to let you tour the Catacombs, which he is reluctant to do for groups of fewer than four.

Santi Cosma e Damiano

Via dei Fori Imperiali, 1 (69 91 540). Metro Colosseo/bus to Via dei Fori Imperiali. **Open** 8am-1pm, 4-7pm, daily.

This small church on the fringe of the Forum incorporates the pagan Temple of Romulus. It has a wonderful sixth-century mosaic in the apse, representing the Second Coming, with the figure of Christ appearing huge against a blue setting as he descends a staircase of clouds to earth. This massive style was the last phase in the development of late Roman mosaic, just before the Byzantine conquest brought to an end a tradition which began the self-consciously classical mosaics of **Santa Pudenziana**.

San Lorenzo fuori le Mura

Piazzale del Verano, 3 (49 15 11). Metro Policlinico/bus or tram to Piazzale del Verano. **Open** 3.30-6pm Mon-Fri, 3.30-6.30pm Sat-Sun, *Oct-Mar;* 6.30am-noon, 3.30-6.30pm, daily *Apr-Sept.*

This basilica on the ancient Via Tiburtina was donated by Constantine to house the roasted remains of Saint Lawrence. Rebuilt in the fifth century by Pope Pegasus, it was then united with a neighbouring church, using the Pegasus church as the chancel. **San Lorenzo**, **San Giovanni in Laterano**, **Saint Peter's**, **San Paolo fuori le Mura** and **Santa Maria Maggiore** make up the five patriarchal basilicas of Rome. The figures in the sixth-century mosaics inside the triumphal arch in San Lorenzo reflect the influence of Byzantine culture in this period. They are flat, stiff and outlined in black, floating motionlessly against the gold ground. There is little modelling or play of light and shade, and the colouring is not as subtle as in the earlier mosaics. This is partly due to the Greek-inspired use of marble, instead of the glass *tesserae* normally favoured by the Romans.

Santa Maria in Cosmedin

Piazza della Bocca della Verità, 18 (67 81 419). Bus to Piazza della Bocca della Verità. **Open** 9am-noon, 3-6pm, daily.

Santa Maria in Cosmedin was originally built in the sixth century next to a temple dedicated to Hercules Victor (*see chapter* **Ancient Sites**). It was enlarged in the ninth century, and given a beautiful campanile in the twelfth. Between the eleventh and thirteenth centuries, much of the decoration was replaced with Cosmati work: the spiralling floor, the throne, the choir, the thirteenth-century *baldacchino* over the ultimate example of recycling, a Roman bath tub used as an altar.

On Sunday mornings at 10.30 a Byzantine rite mass is sung in the church. If you want to prove a point, stick your hand into the mouth of **La Bocca della Verità** (the 'Mouth of Truth') a worn stone face under the portico that was probably an ancient drain cover, and which is said to bite the hands of liars. According to legend it was much used by husbands to test the faithfulness of their wives. The scene in *Roman Holiday* where Gregory Peck ad-libs getting his hand bitten, eliciting an unscripted shriek of genuine alarm from Audrey Hepburn, is one of the most delightful moments in cinema.

Seconds later there was blood everywhere ... a thrill-seeker at **Santa Maria in Cosmedin**.

Santa Maria in Domenica

Piazza della Navicella, 12 (70 05 19). Bus to Via della Navicella. **Open** *9am-noon, 3.30-6pm, daily Oct-Mar; 9am-noon, 3.30-7pm, daily Apr-Sept.*
Santa Maria dates from the ninth century; the sixteenth-century portico and ceiling were added by Pope Leo X. In the apse, behind the modern altar, is one of the most charming mosaics in Rome. Commissioned in the ninth century by Pope Paschal I, it shows the Virgin and Child surrounded by a crowd of saints. The Pope kneels at their feet with the square halo of the living. Over their heads, the apostles are apparently skipping through a flower-filled meadow, with Christ in the centre.

Santa Maria in Trastevere

Piazza Santa Maria in Trastevere (58 14 802). Bus to Viale Trastevere. **Open** *7.30-12.30pm, 4-7pm, daily.*
The first church of Santa Maria was begun in 337 by Pope Julius I, and was the first of many Roman churches dedicated to the Virgin. The present church is twelfth-century and has some wonderful mosaics. Those on the façade show Mary breast-feeding Christ, and ten women with crowns and lanterns on a gold background. Their significance is uncertain, as they have been altered over the years, but they may represent the parable of the wise and foolish virgins. Inside, there are wonderful thirteenth-century mosaics by the nearly-forgotten Pietro Cavallini, whose relaxed, realistic figures represent the re-emergence of a Roman style after long years of the hegemony of Byzantine models.

Santa Prassede

Via Santa Prassede, 9a (48 82 456). Metro Cavour or Vittorio Emanuele/bus to Piazza Esquilino. **Open** *7.30am-noon, 4-6.30pm, daily.*
This church is a scaled-down copy of the old Saint Peter's (*see chapter* **The Vatican City**), a ninth-century attempt to recreate an early Christian basilica. Unfortunately, as the uneven brickwork shows, the Romans had lost the knack. The home-grown mosaic artists were no better, so Pope Paschal I decided to import mosaic workers from Byzantium

to decorate the church. The results are exotic and rich, and what they lack in subtle modelling they make up for in glorious colours, flowing drapery and fluid body movements.

Santa Pudenziana

Via Urbana, 160 (48 14 622). Metro Cavour/bus to Piazza Esquilino. **Open** *8am-noon, 3-6pm, daily.*
The mosaic on the apse of Santa Pudenziana dates from the fourth century (though it was brutally restored in the sixteenth) and is a remarkable example of the continuity between pagan and Christian art, depicting Christ and the apostles as wealthy Romans wearing togas, against a glorious Turner-esque sunset. Were it not for Christ's halo and symbols of the four evangelists in the sky, this could be mistaken for a portrait of senators.

Renaissance

Renaissance art and architecture arrived in Rome in the mid-fifteenth century, when Pope Nicholas V and his successors commissioned the greatest artists of the day to create a city fit to be the capital of Christendom.

Santa Maria sopra Minerva

Piazza della Minerva, 42 or Via Beato Angelico, 35 (67 93 926). Bus to Largo di Torre Argentina. **Open** *7am-noon, 4-7pm, daily.*
Santa Maria is a gothic church built on the site of an ancient temple of Minerva, but the best of its art works are Renaissance. On the right of the transept is the superb Carafa chapel, with late fifteenth-century frescoes by Filippino Lippi (1457-1504), commissioned by Cardinal Oliviero Carafa in honour of Saint Thomas Aquinas. Carafa took Renaissance self-assurance to extremes: the altar painting shows him being presented to the Virgin, as Gabriel informs her she's going to give birth to Christ. The tomb of the Carafa Pope Paul IV (1555-59) is also in the chapel. He was one of the

prime movers of the Counter-Reformation (*see below* **The Baroque**), mainly remembered for persecuting the Jews and ordering Daniele da Volterra to paint loincloths on the nudes of Michelangelo's *Last Judgement*. A bronze loincloth was also ordered to cover Christ's genitals on a work by Michelangelo here in Santa Maria. The statue was finished by Pietro Urbano and depicts an heroic Christ holding up a flimsy cross. A much better, early Renaissance work is the *Madonna and Child* by Fra Angelico, which is in the chapel on the left side of the altar, close to his own tomb.

Santa Maria della Pace

Vicolo del Arco della Pace, 5 (68 61 156). Bus to Corso Rinascimento. **Open** 10am-noon, 4-6pm, Tue-Sat; 9-11am Sun.
As the front door is usually locked, you're likely to enter this church via a simple, beautifully harmonious cloister by Bramante, his first work after arriving in Rome in the early 1500s. The church itself was built in 1482 for Pope Sixtus IV, while the Baroque façade was added by Pietro da Cortona in 1656. The church's most famous artwork, Raphael's *Sibyls*, painted in 1514 for Agostino Chigi, the playboy banker and first owner of the **Villa Farnesina** (*see chapter* **Sightseeing**), is just inside the door.

Santa Maria del Popolo

Piazza del Popolo, 12 (36 10 836). Metro Flaminio/bus to Piazzale Flaminio. **Open** 7am-noon, 4-7pm, Mon-Sat; 8am-1.30pm, 4.30-7.30pm, Sun.
According to legend, Santa Maria del Popolo occupies the site of a garden in which Nero's nurse and mistress secretly buried his corpse. A thousand years later the site was still believed to be haunted by demons, and in 1099, Pope Paschal II built a chapel there. Almost four centuries later Pope Sixtus IV rebuilt the chapel as a church, financing it by taxing foreign churches and selling ecclesiastical jobs.

In the apse are Rome's first stained-glass windows, created by French artist Guillaume de Marcillat in 1509. The apse itself was designed by Bramante, the Chigi Chapel by Raphael, and the choir ceiling and two of the chapels in the right aisle (first and third) were exquisitely frescoed by Pinturicchio, the Borgias' favourite artist. Most intriguing is the Chigi Chapel, designed by Raphael for Agostino Chigi. The mosaics in the dome depict God creating the sun and the seven planets, and Agostino's personal horoscope: with binoculars, you can just about make out a crab, a bull, a lion and a pair of scales. The chapel was completed by Bernini who, on the orders of Agostino's descendant, Pope Alexander VII, added the two theatrical statues of Daniel and Habbakuk. The church's greatest possessions are the two masterpieces by Caravaggio in the Cerasi Chapel, his paintings of Saint Peter and Saint Paul (*see* **Caravaggio** *page 80*).

Tempietto di Bramante, San Pietro in Montorio

Piazza San Pietro in Montorio, 2 (58 13 940). Bus to Porta San Pancrazio. **Open** 8am-noon, 4-7pm, daily.
In the courtyard alongside San Pietro in Montorio, on the alleged site of Saint Peter's crucifixion, is a perfectly proportioned round temple by Bramante. Built in 1502, it was one of the most influential of all Renaissance buildings, the first modern building designed to follow exactly the proportions of the classical orders (in this case, Doric – *see chapter* **Architecture**). The church itself contains a chapel by Vasari, Sebastiano del Piombo's *Flagellation*, and works by Bernini and his followers.

The Baroque

During the Renaissance, churches were freely decorated with nudes, classical motifs and pagan symbols. The challenge of Protestantism, however, drove the Catholic church into a period of defen-

sive internal reform, known as the Counter-Reformation, which was characterised by an austere, intense faith epitomised by new religious orders such as the Jesuits (*see also chapter* **History**: **Renaissance Rome**). In future, it was decreed, church decoration was to eschew any pagan references, and its purpose would be to inspire awe and humility.

Early Counter-Reformation churches were quite sparsely decorated. However, as Catholicism regained its confidence, so did art. Baroque churches were the most sumptuous religious fantasies yet seen. The mid-seventeenth century was dominated by Gian Lorenzo Bernini (1598-1680) and Francesco Borromini (1598-1667). Bernini was confident, brilliant, a master of all the arts, and enjoyed the favour of five successive popes; his saints are sensual, and his church designs showy, delighting in intellectual and visual tricks. Borromini was altogether a nervier, spikier character. He started out as a mason, and his work is characterised by its sculptural quality and a complex and innovative use of geometric forms.

La Chiesa Nuova/Santa Maria in Vallicella

Piazza della Chiesa Nuova (68 75 289). Bus to Corso Vittorio Emanuele. **Open** 8am-noon, 4.30-7pm, daily.
Filippo Neri was a Florentine businessman who gave up his career to live and work among the poor in Rome. He was a personable character who danced on altars and played practical jokes on priests, and became one of the most popular figures in the city. He founded the Oratorian Order to continue his work. Work began on the Chiesa Nuova, the order's headquarters, in 1575 with funds raised by his followers. Neri wanted a large and simple building, but after his death the whitewashed walls were covered with exuberant frescoes and multi-coloured marbles. Ceiling frescoes and the gloriously delicate stucco work are by Pietro da Cortona. Rubens contributed three altar paintings in 1606-8. The result is one of the most satisfying church interiors in Rome. Singing was an important part of Oratorian services, and oratory as a musical form developed out of the order's musical services. Next to the church, Borromini designed the fine Oratorio dei Filippini, which is still used for concerts.

Il Gesù

Piazza del Gesù (67 86 341). Bus to Largo di Torre Argentina or Piazza Venezia. **Open** 6am-12.30pm, 4.30-7.15pm, daily *Oct-Mar*; 6am-12.30pm, 4-7.30pm, daily *Apr-Sept.*
The huge Gesù is the main church of the Jesuits, the order founded by Basque soldier Ignatius Loyola in the 1530s. Realising the power of appealing directly to the emotions, he devised a series of 'spiritual exercises' aimed at training devotees to experience the agony and ecstasy of the saints. The Gesù itself was designed to involve the congregation as closely as possible in the proceedings, with a nave unobstructed by aisles so the view of the main altar wasn't blocked. Work started in 1568, and the façade (recently sandblasted clean) by Giacomo della Porta was added in 1575. His design was repeated *ad nauseam* from one end of the country to the other for decades afterwards. A large, bright fresco by Il Baciccia (under restoration) decorates the gilded ceiling of the nave, which seems to dissolve on either side as stucco figures by Antonio Raggi, and other painted images are sucked up into the dazzling light of the heavens. The fig-

ures falling back to earth are presumably Protestants. On the left is perhaps the most spectacular Baroque achievement, the chapel of Saint'Ignazio by Andrea Pozzo (1696-1700), adorned with gold, silver and coloured marble. It includes what was long believed to be the biggest lump of lapis lazuli in the world. In fact, it's covered concrete. Outside the church, at Piazza del Gesù, 45, you can visit the rooms of Saint Ignatius, which contain a wonderful painted corridor by Pozzo, with *trompe l'œil* special effects, and mementoes of the saint, including his death mask.

Sant'Agnese in Agone

Piazza Navona (67 94 435). Bus to Corso Vittorio Emanuele or Corso Rinascimento. **Open** 5-6.30pm Mon-Sat; 10am-1pm Sun.

The grandest building on Piazza Navona, Sant'Agnese was started by Carlo and Girolamo Rainaldi for Pope Innocent X in 1652. It was intended to be their masterpiece of Baroque, but they then quarrelled with the Pope, and Borromini was appointed in their place. He revised the design considerably, and added the concave façade that is one of his greatest achievements. The *trompe l'œil* interior is typically Borromini, with pillars distributed irregularly to create the illusion that the apses are the same size.

Sant'Andrea al Quirinale

Via del Quirinale, 29 (47 44 801). Metro Repubblica/bus to Via Nazionale. **Open** 8am-noon, 4-7pm, Wed-Mon *Sept-July*; 8am-noon Wed-Mon *Aug*.

This oval church, decorated in pink marble, is a typically theatrical Bernini production, finished in 1670 and cleverly designed to create a sense of grandeur in a small space. Inside, every surface is lavishly decorated, but pride of place must go to a plaster Saint Andrew floating through a broken pediment on his way to Heaven.

Sant'Andrea della Valle

Piazza Sant'Andrea della Valle/Corso Vittorio Emanuele (68 61 339). Bus to Corso Vittorio Emanuele. **Open** 7.30am-noon, 4.30-7.30pm, daily.

Sant'Andrea was originally designed by Giacomo della Porta for the Theatine order in 1524, but the church's façade and dizzyingly frescoed dome both date from about a century later, when the Church was in a far more flamboyant frame of mind. Lanfranco nearly died while painting the dome fresco – supposedly because his rival Domenichino had sabotaged the scaffolding on which he was working. Puccini set the opening act of his opera *Tosca* in the first chapel on the left inside the church.

San Carlo alle Quattro Fontane

Via del Quirinale, 23 (48 83 261). Metro Repubblica/bus to Via Nazionale. **Open** 9.30am-12.30pm, 4-6pm, Mon-Fri; 9am-1pm Sat.

This was Borromini's first solo commission (1634-1641), an ingenious building for a cramped site. The most remarkable feature is the oval dome. The geometrical coffers in its decoration decrease in size towards the lantern to give the illusion of additional height, and the illumination, through hidden windows, make it appear to be floating in mid-air.

San Francesco a Ripa

Piazza San Francesco d'Assisi, 88 (58 19 020). Bus to Viale Trastevere. **Open** 7am-noon, 4-7pm, daily.

In a quiet corner of Trastevere, this seventeenth-century church stands on the site of the hospice where Saint Francis of Assisi stayed when he visited Rome in 1219. The original church was built by Rodolfo Anguillara, one of his richer followers, in the thirteenth century. The church was entirely rebuilt in the 1680s, and now the rather standard Baroque interior rings to the guitar-strumming of a thriving parish church. It should be visited for Bernini's sculpture of the *Beata Ludovica Albertoni* (1674), showing the aristocratic Franciscan nun dying in one of those agonised, sexually ambiguous ecstasies.

San Gregorio Magno

Piazza di San Gregorio (70 08 227). Metro Circo Massimo/bus or tram to Via di San Gregorio. **Open** 9am-12.30pm, 3.30-6.30pm, daily.

Although it is now essentially a Baroque building, finished by Giovanni Battista Soria in 1633, this church is most famous as the starting point for Saint Augustine's mission in the sixth century to convert England to Christianity. It was originally the family home of one of the most remarkable popes, Saint Gregory the Great, who converted the site into a monastery in 575. In the chapel to the right of the altar is a sculpted marble chair, dating from the first century BC, which is reputed to have been used by Gregory as his papal throne. Also here is the tomb of Tudor diplomat Sir Edward Carne, who came to Rome several times to persuade the Pope to annul the marriage of Henry VIII and Catherine of Aragon, so he could marry Anne Boleyn.

Sant'Ignazio di Loyola

Piazza Sant'Ignazio (67 94 406). Bus to Via del Corso. **Open** 7.30am-12.30pm, 4.15-7.15pm, daily.

Sant'Ignazio was built to commemorate the canonisation of Saint Ignatius in 1626. *Trompe l'œil* columns soar above the nave, and architraves by Andrea Pozzo open to a cloudy Heaven into which figures are ascending. Trickery was also involved in creating the dome. The Dominican monks next door to the church claimed that a real dome would rob them of light, so, rather than tussle with seventeenth-century town planners, Pozzo simply painted a dome on the inside of the roof. The result is pretty convincing if you stand on the disc embedded in the nave's floor. Walk away, and the illusion collapses.

Sant'Ivo alla Sapienza

Corso Rinascimento, 40. Bus to Corso Rinascimento. **Open** 10am-noon Sun.

Perhaps Borromini's most imaginative geometrical design, with a concave façade countered by the convex bulk of the dome, which terminates in a bizarre corkscrew spire. The interior is based on a six-pointed star, but the opposition of convex and concave surfaces continues in the floor plan, on the walls and up into the dome.

Santa Maria della Vittoria

Via XX Settembre, 17 (48 26 190). Metro Repubblica/bus to Via XX Settembre. **Open** 7.30am-noon, 4.30-7pm, daily *Sept-mid-July*; 7am-10.30am, 5-7pm, daily *mid-July-end Aug*

This modest-looking Baroque church, its interior cosily candle-lit and lovingly adorned with marble and gilt, holds one of Bernini's most famous works. *The Ecstasy of Saint Teresa*, in the Cornaro chapel, shows the Spanish mystic floating on a cloud in a supposedly spiritual trance after a teasing, androgynous angel has pierced her with a burning arrow. The result is more than a little ambiguous: as a former president of France commented, 'If that is divine love, I know all about it'. When the chapel is seen as a whole, with the heavens painted in the dome, the light filters through a hidden window, reflecting gilded rays and bathing Teresa in a heavenly glow. She is surrounded by a row of witnesses – members of the Cornaro family sitting in a balcony and earnestly discussing the spectacle.

Santa Maria in Campitelli

Piazza di Campitelli (68 80 39 78). Bus to Via del Teatro di Marcello. **Open** 7am-noon, 4-7pm, daily.

This church was commissioned in 1656 to house the medieval icon of the Madonna del Portico, to which the population had prayed (successfully) for a prompt release from a bout of the plague. Carlo Rainaldi completed his masterpiece in 1667: a solemn, austere exercise in mass and light. Notice the complexity of the floor plan: Greek cross plus (hidden) dome plus apse, with a series of side chapels to provide movement in and out. Inside are some fine Baroque paintings and a spectacularly over-the-top gilt altar tabernacle by Giovanni Antonio de Rossi.

Museums & Galleries

Rome's treasure-houses offer a taste of everything from Baroque art to pasta.

Until not that many years ago, visitors to the artistic treasures of Rome were likely to be greeted by scaffolding and closed doors as they ran a dispiriting gamut of eccentric opening hours, wildcat strikes and apparently endless restoration programmes. Recently, however, things have taken a definite turn for the better, and the days when substantial quantities of Rome's art remained tantalisingly out of reach are now largely over.

The causes of the improvement include a Green-led city council with cultural heritage and international public relations high on its agenda; a left-wing cultural heritage minister with an unquenchable determination to bring Italy's museums into the twentieth century; and a general public which has begun to shrug off the lethargy brought on by decades of misrule and now expects something better from its administrators.

In 1993 a 'non-stop' law was introduced, obliging museums to be open continuously from 9am to 7pm, Tuesday to Sunday, and on two Mondays each month. Museums run by the Comune di Roma now comply with this, and have promised to keep some key collections open until midnight during the summer. Others, however, may still use the excuse of staff shortages to stick to the old mornings-only schedule. The opening hours listed here were correct at the time of writing, but you should be prepared for changes.

The other major problem to affect some of Rome's most important museums was that of long-term restoration work. A huge push by the city council has led to the reopening of several long-closed venues such as the **Antiquarium Comunale**, the **Museo Napoleonico** and, above all, the revamped **Galleria Borghese**, now part of the newly-coined *Parco dei Musei* (Park of

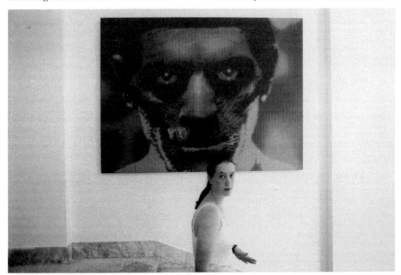

*Keep an eye on the **Galleria Nazionale d'Arte Moderna e Contemporanea**. See page 91.*

The Famous Five

Three of the artists below are particularly associated with Rome; the fourth is an unexpected fish out of water. The fifth has only one, unfinished work in Rome, but then he is Leonardo, and any single work represents a significant proportion of his surviving *œuvre*. The list of venues given is not exhaustive, but it should help you find some of the best works by each artist.

Bernini (1598-1680)

You're never far from a Bernini façade, but don't let that distract you from his sculpture. For this there's nowhere better than the **Galleria Borghese**, where the freshly restored marble will knock you off your feet; follow that with his ecstatic women in the churches **Santa Maria della Vittoria** (*above*) and **San Francesco a Ripa**. The **Fontana dei Quattro Fiumi** in Piazza Navona and the **Fontana del Tritone** fountain in Piazza Barberini show that he could also do justice to heavier male forms.

Michelangelo (1475-1564)

Of course, it has to be the **Sistine Chapel**, followed by a glimpse of his *Pietà* in **Saint Peter's**. *Moses* is in the church of **San Pietro in Vincoli**, *Christ* in **Santa Maria sopra Minerva**. For a taste of Michelangelo's architectural genius, take in the **Piazza del Campidoglio**, which remains essentially as he designed it, and **Palazzo Farnese**.

Raphael (1483-1520)

Drop into the Vatican **Pinacoteca** for his last work, *The Transfiguration*. **Villa Farnesina** has his *Triumph of Galatea* and the **Galleria Borghese** a *Deposition*. You could also visit **Palazzo Barberini** to take in the disputed portrait of Raphael's supposed mistress, *La Fornarina*.

Rubens (1577-1640)

The Flemish master beat Italian contemporaries Caravaggio and Reni in adopting the fluid lines, constant movement and dramatic foreshortenings of the new Baroque style. Rubens paid only one brief but artistically crucial visit to Rome as a young man, but his work was eagerly acquired by the great papal families of the period. **Galleria Nazionale d'Arte Antica** has a remarkably full-blooded Saint Sebastian, while **Galleria Spada** contains a portrait of an otherwise unremembered cardinal. Other paintings can be seen in the **Galleria dell'Accademia di San Luca**, the **Capitoline Museums** (a delightful *Romulus and Remus with She-Wolf*), and **Galleria Colonna** (*The Assumption of the Virgin* and *Jacob and Esau*). **Galleria Borghese** contains a fine *Deposition*, painted in Rome during Rubens' visit in 1605. But the artist's greatest contribution to the city can be seen in the **Chiesa Nuova** (*see chapter* **Churches**), where three extraordinary works hang above and beside the main altar.

Leonardo (1452-1519)

His unfinished *Saint Jerome* is in the Vatican **Pinacoteca**. The intensely detailed parts that he worked on most contrast dramatically with the areas of bare or nearly-bare canvas.

Museums) – a recognition of the fact that Villa Borghese is at the hub of some of the city's most important museums.

The most significant ancient collections are in the **Vatican Museums** (*see chapter* **The Vatican City**), the **Capitoline Museums**, the **Museo Nazionale Romano** and the **Museo Nazionale di Villa Giulia**. The city is also crammed with Renaissance and Baroque paintings, best seen in **Palazzo Barberini**, **Galleria Borghese** and **Galleria Doria Pamphili**.

The Vatican and Capitoline are the oldest public museums in the world, and many other important collections (particularly of paintings and sculptures) are still to be seen in the historic palazzi of the rich patrons who originally amassed them. Although there is a certain pleasure in seeing spectacular works of art in opulent surroundings, the standard of exhibition is often less than sophisticated. You will encounter old-fashioned and ineffective display techniques, with even some of the most famous paintings virtually invisible – either hung too high or atrociously lit. Museums have miles of display cases full of unexplained exhibits, and if artefacts are labelled it is nearly always in Italian only. Things are improving, especially in new and recently restored museums, but don't expect hands-on, interactive displays.

Ticket offices normally stop issuing tickets half an hour before the museum closes. Entrance to all state museums is free to EC citizens under 18 and over 60. Those with student ID can also take advantage of frequent discounts. Many sites – mainly ancient monuments, but also some museums – have restricted access (*see* **Rome for the Disabled** *in chapter* **Directory**).

Public Galleries

The **Palazzo delle Esposizioni** continues almost single-handedly to offer a rich programme of art, cinema, music, theatre and exhibitions, while the **Galleria Comunale di Arte Moderna** puts on shows by less well-known contemporary artists. So too does the Stabilimento Peroni, worth a visit for the building itself, recently reopened as part of the **Galleria Comunale d'Arte Moderna e Contemporanea**.

Accademia Valentino

Piazza Mignanelli, 23a (67 92 292). Metro Spagna/bus to Piazza San Silvestro. **Open** 9am-7pm Tue-Sun. **Admission** L12,000.

This palazzo, lovingly restored by international designer Valentino, has become a fixture on the Roman art scene since its inauguration a few years ago. Its adventurous and imaginative programming suggests that Valentino's motive is not merely self-promotion.
No wheelchair access.

Galleria Comunale d'Arte Moderna e Contemporanea

Via F. Crispi, 24 (47 42 848). Metro Barberini/bus to Via Barberini. **Open** 9am-6.30pm Tue-Sat; 9am-1pm Sun. **Admission** L10,000.

Unlike its national counterpart (*see below*) this city-run gallery concentrates on smaller shows, with the emphasis on one-person exhibitions and retrospectives. The permanent collection contains works by such figures as Rodin, De Pisis, Morandi, Guttuso, Afro and Capogrossi.
Wheelchair access.

Galleria Comunale d'Arte Moderna e Contemporanea (formerly Stabilimento Peroni)

Via Alessandria (47 42 848). Bus to Piazza Fiume. **Open** exhibition times vary. **Admission** depends on exhibition.

Apart from being a fascinating example of industrial archaeology, this refurbished ex-brewery looks set to become a valuable addition to the capital's public galleries and a sign of the council's interest in new art. Opened in summer 1997 with rotating shows by 120 young Roman artists, the space promises to inject some new blood into an often stagnant local scene.
No wheelchair access.

Palazzo delle Esposizioni

Via Nazionale, 194 (48 85 465). Metro Repubblica/bus to Via Nazionale. **Open** 10am-9pm Mon, Wed-Sun. **Admission** L12,000.

Dating from the late nineteenth century, the Palazzo was one of the city's first purpose-built exhibition halls. After years of neglect and restoration, it reopened in 1990 to become Rome's most prominent cultural centre, holding exhibitions, film screenings, conferences and many other events. The complex incorporates a car park, bookshop, design shop, bar and rooftop restaurant, as well as the *Centro di Ricerca e Documentazione Arti Visive*, an archive covering aspects of contemporary Italian and international art; phone ahead if you want to visit.
Wheelchair access from Via Piacenza.

Palazzo Ruspoli

Via del Corso, 418 (68 30 73 44). Bus to Piazza San Silvestro. **Open** exhibition times vary. **Admission** depends on exhibition.

The palace of one of Rome's old noble families is now used for major touring exhibitions of art, photography, archaeology and history. It stays open late into the evening at least one or two nights a week. The basement rooms (entrance on Via Fontanella Borghese) are often used for photographic exhibitions and admission is sometimes free.
No wheelchair access.

Permanent collections

Most art collections in Rome were created by the great papal families during the Renaissance and Baroque periods, and the range of art on show is often stamped with very personal tastes: there are relatively few works earlier than 1300 or later than 1800. However, there are some genuine masterpieces in all the main collections.

Galleria dell'Accademia di San Luca

Piazza dell'Accademia, 77 (67 98 850). Metro Barberini/bus to Piazza San Silvestro. **Open** 10am-12.30pm Mon, Wed, Fri and last Sun of each month. **Closed** July and Aug. **Admission** L4,000.

This august institution was founded in 1577 to train artists in the grand Renaissance style. The highlight of the collection is a fragment of a Raphael fresco, though there are also works by Titian, Rubens, Reni and Van Dyck, as well as fascinating self-portraits by the few women members of the Academy, who included Lavinia Fontana (*see* **Artemisia** *page 89*) and Angelica Kauffman. Note the curious elliptical staircase near the entrance, a typically original structure by Borromini.
No wheelchair access.

Galleria Colonna

Via della Pilotta, 17 (67 94 362). Bus to Piazza Venezia.
Open 9am-1pm Sat. **Closed** Aug. **Admission** L10,000.
It's well worth making the effort one Saturday morning to see this lavish six-roomed gallery (completed in 1703), which forms part of the family-owned Palazzo Colonna. All the rooms are opulently decorated. The Great Hall has a dramatic frescoed ceiling depicting the Apotheosis of Marcantonio Colonna. The next room is the Hall of the Desks, so called because of two lavish writing desks, one decorated with *pietra dura* and bronze statuettes, the other covered with carved ivory. The ceiling is a fantasy of evil cherubs, endangered maidens and threatening Turks by Sebastiano Ricci. Other highlights include the wonderfully sensuous *Venus and Cupid* by Bronzino, the nightmarish *Temptation of Saint Anthony* by a follower of Hieronymus Bosch, and the finest picture in the collection, Annibale Carracci's appropriately earthy *The Bean-Eater*, a familiar face to those who buy their art in Woolworths and a welcome contrast to all the religious art on display.
No wheelchair access.

Galleria Doria Pamphili

Piazza del Collegio Romano, 2 (67 97 323). Bus to Piazza Venezia. **Open** 10am-5pm Mon-Wed, Fri-Sun. **Closed** 15-30 August. **Admission** *museum* L12,000; *private apartments* L5,000.
One of Rome's finest private art collections, this is housed in a rambling palace owned by the Doria Pamphili family, a pillar of Rome's papal aristocracy now headed by two half-British siblings. For many years the collection was crammed onto the walls of four corridors (*braccio*); it has now spilled into the fifteenth-century wing of the palace. Among the works on show are a portrait by Raphael of two gentlemen, Correggio's unfinished *Allegory of Virtue*, and two Titians, *Religion Succoured by Spain* and a self-possessed *Salome* holding the head of John the Baptist. Caravaggio is represented by the early *Rest during the Flight into Egypt* and a penitent *Mary Magdalene*. Two Guercino paintings stand out: *Hermione Finding the Body of Tancredi* and the martyred *Saint Agnes* as she fails to catch light at the stake. After

so many angelic, smiling cherubs, Guido Reni's squabbling brats in Braccio 2 is something of a relief. The suite of rooms that leads off this corridor houses a number of works by Dutch and Flemish artists, including Brueghels Jan and Pieter the Elder. The collection's greatest jewel is probably the extraordinary portrait by Velázquez of the Pamphili pope Innocent X, displayed in a separate room, alongside a Bernini bust of the same pontiff. Landscapes by the Carracci, Lorrain, Salvator Rosa and others are found in Braccio 4.
For an additional L5,000 there is a guided tour of the private apartments, in Italian only, although cursory notes in each room pick out some of the highlights in English. There are important works of art here too, including a delicate *Annunciation* by Filippo Lippi, and Sebastiano del Piombo's portrait of the great Genoese admiral and patriarch Andrea Doria, as Neptune. In the Smoking Room, decorated for an English Doria Pamphili wife last century, a Victorian fireplace and fat leather armchairs echo the mood of a gentleman's club. The spectacular eighteenth-century ballroom leads into the Yellow Room, with its Gobelin tapestries, and to a series of elegant rooms beyond. The chapel has a *trompe l'œil* painted ceiling.
Wheelchair access with assistance.

Galleria Nazionale d'Arte Antica (Palazzo Corsini)

Via della Lungara, 10, Trastevere (68 80 23 23). Bus to Lungotevere della Farnesina or Piazza Sonnino. **Open** 9am-7pm Tue-Fri; 9am-2pm Sat; 9am-1pm Sun, public holidays. **Admission** L8,000.
This palace, the work of Ferdinando Fuga, incorporated the earlier Palazzo Riario, the Roman residence of seventeenth-century socialite and Catholic convert Queen Christina after her flight from Sweden. A plaque marks the room in which she died in 1689. Today the palace houses some of the National Art Collection, the more important part being in the **Palazzo Barberini**. The original palace grounds behind the building are now Rome's botanical garden, the **Orto Botanico**. The galleries are beautifully painted with frescoes and *trompe l'œils* and specialise in paintings from the sixteenth and seventeenth centuries. There are the usual

Artemisia

When Artemisia Gentileschi (1593-c1651) burst onto Rome's art scene in the early 1600s, there was no such thing as a 'woman artist' – only a brush-wielding female freak. Not surprisingly, given the climate of her times, she gained her fame not for her powerful, Caravaggio-esque works, but for a messy and very public rape trial. For several months in 1612, Rome was treated to almost daily instalments of intimate details about Artemisia's alleged deflowering by her artist father's associate Agostino Tassi. Tassi ended up in jail for a brief spell, and Artemisia was left with an enduring reputation as used merchandise – as well as a penchant for startling depictions of a calm, determined Judith gorily severing the head of a prostrate Holofernes.

While the Capodimonte gallery in Naples, where she lived from the 1630s until her death,

houses the largest collection of Artemisia's works, her famous *Madonna and Child* (1609) and *Saint Cecilia Playing a Lute* (1610) can be seen in the **Galleria Spada**. *Judith* (1610) is on display in the **Pinacoteca** (*see chapter* **The Vatican City**). A major film of her life was premiered at the Venice Film Festival in late 1997.

Just to prove that Artemisia wasn't the only 'freak' at work in sixteenth- and seventeenth-century Italy, the Spada contains further evidence of the many female artists neglected by a still male-dominated world of art history. Among these are *Cleopatra* (complete with eccentric headgear) by Lavinia Fontana (1552-1614). More works by this Bolognese painter can be seen at the **Galleria dell'Accademia di San Luca** (*Self-Portrait with Spinnet*), the church of **Santa Sabina** (*Vision of Saint Hyacinthe*) and the **Borghese Gallery** (*Minerva at her Toilet*).

scores of Holy Families, and Madonnas and Children (the most memorable a *Madonna* by Van Dyck). Other works include a sensual pair of Annunciations by Guercino; two Saint Sebastians, one by Rubens, the other by Annibale Carracci; Caravaggio's resolutely unadorned *Narcissus;* and a triptych by Fra Angelico. The works by Guido Reni also stand out, notably the melancholy *Salome*.
Wheelchair access with assistance.

Galleria Nazionale d'Arte Moderna e Contemporanea

Viale delle Belle Arti, 131 (32 29 81). Bus/tram to Viale delle Belle Arti. **Open** 9am-7pm Tue-Sat; 9am-1pm Sun, public holidays. **Admission** L8,000.
Italy's national collection of modern art, housed in a massive, purpose-built neo-classical palace dating from 1912, covers the nineteenth and twentieth centuries. Compared to that of the Renaissance and Baroque, Italian art of this period is relatively unknown outside Italy. When you've seen what's on display here, you may understand why. The nineteenth-century collection contains works by the *macchiaioli*, who, like the pointillists, used tiny spots of colour to create paintings that look like hazy photographs. The twentieth-century component is stronger, with a host of works by such artists as De' Chirico, Carrà, Sironi, Casorati, Marini and others, as well as representatives of modern movements such as *Arte povera* and the *Transavanguardia*. There's also an interesting assortment of works by international artists, among them Klimt, Kandinsky, Cézanne and Henry Moore. The museum holds major temporary exhibitions and has a well-stocked shop.
No wheelchair access.

Galleria Spada

Palazzo Spada, Piazza Capo di Ferro, 3 (68 61 158). Bus to Largo di Torre Argentina. **Open** 9am-7pm Tue-Sat; 9am-1.30pm Sun. **Admission** L8,000.
One of Rome's prettiest palaces, built for Cardinal Girolamo Capo di Ferro in 1540, Palazzo Spada was acquired by Cardinal Bernardino Spada in 1632. Its most famous feature is Borromini's ingenious *trompe l'œil* colonnade in the garden, which is 9m long but appears much longer. Today, the palace houses the offices of the Italian Council of State, as well as the art collection of Cardinal Spada, and is continually guarded by *carabinieri*. Since the collection is in its original setting on the lavishly decorated walls of the palace, some of the works are too high or too badly lit to be seen satisfactorily, though it is possible to make out most of the major paintings. Spada's portrait of his patron Reni is on show in Room 1. More portraits follow in Room 2, including Titian's wonderful, albeit unfinished *Musician,* while Room 3 contains massive, gloomy paintings such as Guercino's *Death of Dido* and Jan Breughel the Elder's very un-Roman *Landscape with Windmill.* Look out for the unidentified gilded statue of *Chronos* tucking into the inner thigh of his own child. Room 4 has two powerful works by Artemisia Gentileschi, *Saint Cecilia playing a Lute* and *Madonna and Child (see* **Artemisia** *page 89)* and *Martyrdom of a Saint* by Domenichino.
No wheelchair access.

Museo di Palazzo Venezia

Via del Plebiscito, 118 (67 98 865). Bus to Piazza Venezia. **Open** 9am-1.30pm Tue-Sat; 9am-1pm Sun. **Admission** L8,000.
The main theme of this underrated collection is medieval decorative art, and there are some true delights to be found. A beautiful thirteenth-century Byzantine enamel of *Christ*

Borromini's colonnade at **Galleria Spada**.

Pantokrator hides among the church furnishings in Room 5, and there are some wonderful pre-Renaissance religious paintings in Room 6. Look out for a disconcertingly jolly *Crucifixion* among the usual Madonnas, children and angstridden saints. You will also find great carved chests, tapestries, silver and ceramic work, and eighteenth-century porcelain including some Meissen. Bernini is represented by some terracotta rough studies, including those for the **Fontana del Tritone** and one for the angels on Ponte Sant'Angelo (built to link Castel Sant'Angelo with the *centro storico*), while an impressive fresco of a gold zodiac and extraordinary *trompe l'œil* columns, believed to be by Mantegna, can be seen in Room 4. The huge *Sala del Mappamondo*, so called because of an early map of the world kept there in the sixteenth century, was Mussolini's office. *Il Duce* habitually left the lights on all night so passers-by would think he was working.
Wheelchair access with assistance.

The Ancients

Not surprisingly, Rome has impressive collections of its own ancient art (often copies from Greek originals), as well as artefacts from Egypt, Greece, Assyria and other civilisations. Much of this was plunder brought to Rome by pillaging victorious armies; other works were collected in succeeding centuries by equally voracious popes and patrician families. As ever, not all the collections are particularly well displayed, and few give as much explanation of what you're looking at as you might like.

Antiquarium Comunale

Via del Parco del Celio, 22 (70 01 569). Metro Circo Massimo or Colosseo. **Open** 9am-7pm Tue-Sat; 9am-1pm Sun. **Admission** L3,750.
There's something charmingly provincial about this quiet museum in a villa on the Celio hill. Like any local museum, it houses the ancient finds of the area; this being Rome, however, the collection is rather better than you would find elsewhere. Much of what's on show came to light when the city was being extended at the turn of the last century. The pick of the finds was nabbed by the major national collections, but this little museum has hung on to a wonderful range of domestic artefacts, tools and kitchen equipment, which look surprisingly similar to modern equivalents. Perhaps the most touching exhibit is a jointed doll, a sort of ancient (small busted) Barbie. It was found in the tomb of a young girl who died shortly before she was due to be married and is exquisitely carved, even detailing the complicated hairstyle fashionable in the second century AD.
No wheelchair access.

Museo Barracco di Scultura Antica

Piazza dei Baullari, 1 or Corso Vittorio Emanuele, 168 (68 80 68 48). Bus to Corso Vittorio Emanuele. **Open** 9am-7pm Tue-Sat; 9am-1pm Sun. **Admission** L3,750; L10,000 for special exhibitions.
This small collection of mainly pre-Roman art was amassed by Senator Giovanni Barracco during the first half of this century. His interests ran the whole gamut of ancient art, and there are some extraordinary Assyrian reliefs, Attic vases, Egyptian hieroglyphs, sphinxes and bas-reliefs, and Babylonian stone lions, as well as Roman and Etruscan exhibits and some superb Greek sculptures. Don't miss the copy in Room VII of *Wounded Bitch* by Lysippus.
No wheelchair access.

Museo Nazionale d'Arte Orientale

Via Merulana, 248 (48 74 415). Bus to Via Merulana.
Open 9am-1pm 2nd and 4th Mon of month, Wed, Fri-Sun; 9am-7pm Tue, Thur. **Admission** L8,000.
For a break from unrelenting Roman artefacts, try this impressive collection of oriental art in its recently restored home, a somewhat gloomy palazzo near Santa Maria Maggiore. All the exhibits are well displayed and sympathetically lit, although the labels are fairly basic. Information sheets at the beginning of the exhibitions are in Italian and border on the esoteric. The museum is arranged geographically and roughly chronologically. First are ancient artefacts from the Near East – pottery, gold, votive offerings – some dating back to the third millennium. Then come the eleventh- to eighteenth-century painted fans from Tibet, sacred sculptures and some modern-looking Chinese pottery from the fifteenth century. Perhaps the most unusual exhibits, reliefs from the Swat culture, come from Italian-funded excavations in north-east Pakistan.
Wheelchair access.

Museo Nazionale Romano

Viale Enrico de Nicola, 79 or Piazza dei Cinquecento (48 80 530). Metro/bus to Termini. **Open** 9am-2pm Tue-Sat; 9am-1pm Sun. **Admission** L12,000.
Long housed in the Baths of Diocletian, this spectacular state collection of ancient art is currently being rearranged and re-located, not without some confusion. The airy and recently restored **Palazzo Massimo alle Colonne** (*see chapter* **Sightseeing**), which was originally scheduled to open for the 1990 World Cup, is now home to part of the collection and promises to be one of the best museums in Rome when it's finished. Exhibits are well displayed and explained in both Italian and English, with printed information sheets in each room. At present you can see some sculpture, including wonderful portrait busts of the emperors and their families, an interesting exhibition of Roman currency, some fragments of mosaic, and one of the museum's greatest treasures: an extraordinary Greek relief from about 460 BC, showing the birth of Aphrodite and known as the Ludovisi Throne, whose authenticity, however, has recently been questioned by art guru Federico Zeri.
Fragments of ancient statuary are still on display in and around the courtyard of the museum's original home. Designed by Michelangelo in the 1560s, this courtyard formed the cloister of a convent attached to the church of **Santa Maria degli Angeli** and was built in the ruins of the fourth-century AD Baths of Diocletian, the largest baths ever seen in ancient Rome. The Octagonal Hall (Via Romita, 10am-7pm, admission free), originally the south-western corner of the Baths, now contains some important sculptures, including the Lyceum Apollo and the Aphrodite of Cyrene. Palazzo Massimo is due to be completed by the end of 1997, after which only a small collection of wall inscriptions will be housed in the Baths. The rest will be used as a restoration centre and storage space.
Wheelchair access to Palazzo Massimo and with assistance at Viale Enrico de Nicola, 79.

Museo Nazionale di Villa Giulia

Piazzale di Villa Giulia, 9 (32 26 571). Bus/tram to Viale delle Belle Arti. **Open** 9am-7pm Tue-Sat; 9am-2pm Sun. **Admission** L8,000.
The palace was built for pleasure-loving Pope Julius III in the mid-sixteenth century. Extensive gardens and pavilions were laid out by Vignola and Vasari, while Ammannati and Michelangelo both had a hand in the creation of the fountains. The villa was transformed into a museum in 1889, and houses an exhaustive collection of Etruscan art and artefacts, much of it inadequately labelled. The Etruscans lived in Tuscany, Umbria and Lazio from the eighth century BC until their high-

ly-developed civilisation was destroyed in a series of devastating wars with the Romans in the first century BC. Most of the exhibits in the collection, amassed from major finds all over the region, came from tombs: scarcely any Etruscan buildings have survived, as the Romans wrecked the lot. From the evidence available, it appears that the Etruscans were an elegant, sophisticated, life-loving bunch (*see chapters* **History** *and* **Trips out of Town**). The most recent addition to the museum is a terracotta relief, dating from the fifth century BC, from the pediment of a temple from the port of Pyrgi. In its life-size depiction of episodes from the Theban cycle, this reveals the Greek presence in Etruscan art of the period.
In the garden is a reconstruction of an Etruscan temple. Now restored, it mirrors the Etruscan love of detail: everything is covered in elaborate decoration. The red, black and white pottery in the villa shows scenes of dancing, hunting and more intimate pleasures. The Faliscan crater, an urn dating from the fourth century BC, depicts Dawn rising in her chariot, and the Chigi vase features hunting tales from the sixth century BC. Even the jewellery is covered with carved animals, as are the hundreds of miniature vases, pieces of furniture, domestic implements and models of buildings made to accompany the dead to their eternal life. The sixth-century BC terracotta Sarcofago degli Sposi, presumably made as a tomb for a husband and wife, is adorned with a sculpture of the happy couple reclining on its lid.
Look out for the frescoes in the colonnaded loggia, as well as the sunken *nymphaeum* (water garden) opposite the museum entrance, decorated with mosaics, fountains and statues, where the Santa Cecilia academy presents breathtaking summer concerts (*see chapter* **Music: Classical & Opera**).
Wheelchair access with assistance.

Museo Preistorico ed Etnografico L. Pigorini

Piazza Guglielmo Marconi, 14, EUR (54 95 21). Metro Magliana/bus to Piazza Guglielmo Marconi. **Open** 9am-2pm Mon-Sat; 9am-1pm Sun. **Admission** L8,000.
This museum displays prehistoric Italian artefacts and ethnological material from various world cultures. The lobby contains a reconstruction of the Guattari cave, with a genuine Neanderthal skull. On the first floor the ethnological collection houses a predictable range of spears, pottery, jewellery, head dresses, masks, a few textiles and a couple of shrunken heads. The second floor has archaeological finds from digs all over Italy, including mammoth tusks and teeth and some human bones. More recent finds include decorated shells and bones, arrow heads and reconstructed tombs. The museum also organises frequent one-off exhibitions on ethnological themes.
Wheelchair access.

Museo di Via Ostiense

Via R. Persichetti, 3 (57 43 193). Metro Piramide. **Open** 9am-1pm Tue-Sat. **Admission** L4,000.
This small but characteristic museum is dauntingly placed in the middle of the frantic traffic roundabout at the beginning of the road that leads to Ostia and just opposite the station for **Ostia Antica**. A visit can be usefully combined with one to the actual excavations of the ancient city (*see chapter* **Trips out of Town**). The ancient gatehouse contains artefacts and prints describing the story of the historic roadway of Via Ostiense, as well as two large-scale models of the city of Ostia and the Port of Trajan.
No wheelchair access.

Find out what ruined Rome at **Museo della Civiltà Romana**. *See page 96.*

History

While none of these museums provides a comprehensive overview of the history of Rome, each of them, with varying degrees of success, gives a picture of particular aspects.

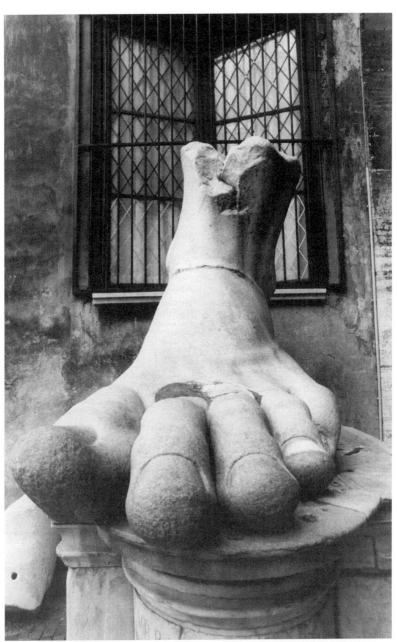

Constantine keeps a toehold in the **Capitoline Museums**.

The Capitoline Museums

Standing on opposite sides of Michelangelo's **Piazza del Campidoglio** and housed in the twin palaces of Palazzo Nuovo and Palazzo dei Conservatori, the Capitoline Museums are the oldest public museums in the world. The collection they house was started in 1471, when Pope Sixtus IV presented the Roman people with a group of classical sculptures. Until the creation of the **Vatican Museums**, Sixtus' successors continued to enrich the collection with examples of ancient art, most of it sculpture, and, at a later date, some important Renaissance and post-Renaissance paintings. The entire collection was finally made available to all in 1734, by Pope Clement XII.

The Palazzo Nuovo (on your left as you come up Michelangelo's gently sloping ramp) houses one of Europe's most significant groups of ancient sculpture, including the Hall of Philosophers, which is lined with Roman copies of busts of Greek politicians and philosophers. There are two rooms of Roman busts, providing a good indication of contemporary fashions and hairstyles; the most spectacular are those of women in the Emperor's room. They date from the Flavian period (first century AD) and show that pasta-spiral hair-dos were most definitely the new look for the new millennium. Not all the subjects, though, are patrician. In the main gallery a drunken old woman clutches an urn of wine, while the Dove Room contains statues of children, including one of a little girl protecting a bird from a snake. The dove mosaic came from Hadrian's villa at Tivoli.

As was the fashion at the time, there are several Roman copies of Greek works, including the Capitoline Venus. This was based on Praxiteles' Venus of Cnodis, which was considered so erotic by the fourth-century BC inhabitants of Kos that one desperate citizen was caught *in flagrante delicto* with it. The most remarkable work in the collection, however, is the extraordinarily moving *Dying Gaul*, probably based on a third-century BC Greek original.

On the ground floor stands the gilded equestrian bronze of Emperor Marcus Aurelius, deposed by pollution from the plinth outside, which now holds a replica.

Across the square you enter the Palazzo dei Conservatori. The courtyard contains what is left of a colossal statue of Constantine (the rest was made of wood) which originally stood in the Basilica of Maxentius (*see* **The Roman Forum** *in chapter* **Ancient Sites**). Among the highlights of the exhibits in this part of the museum is the much-reproduced She-Wolf. This one is a fifth-century BC Etruscan bronze; the suckling twins were added during the Renaissance by, according to tradition, Antonio del Pollaiolo. The first-century BC bronze of a boy removing a thorn from his foot, known as the *Spinario*, is probably an original Greek work.

The Pinacoteca Capitolina contains a number of significant works. Although the most striking is Caravaggio's sensual *Saint John the Baptist*, painted in 1596, don't let it overshadow paintings by artists such as Rubens, Titian, Veronese, Van Dyck, Dossi and Domenichino.

Musei Capitolini

Piazza del Campidoglio, 1 (67 10 20 71). Bus to Piazza Venezia. **Open** *9am-7pm Tue-Sun.* **Admission** *L10,000; L5,000 students; under-18s, over-60s free. No wheelchair access.*

Castel Sant'Angelo

Lungotevere Castello, 50 (68 75 036). Bus to Via della Conciliazione or Piazza Cavour. **Open** *9am-8pm Mon-Wed, Sun; 9am-11.30pm Thur-Sat.* **Closed** *2nd and 4th Tue of each month.* **Admission** *L8,000.*

Begun by the Emperor Hadrian in 135 AD as his own mausoleum, Castel Sant'Angelo has since functioned as a fortress and a prison as well as a papal residence. The passageway connecting it to the Vatican is still visible, a reminder of the days when petrified popes, threatened by invading forces, scampered from Saint Peter's to the relative safety of the castle. Although it now plays host to temporary art shows (displays of stolen paintings and artefacts recovered by the police are regular choices), the real pleasure of a visit to Castel Sant'Angelo lies in being able to wander around it freely, from Hadrian's original ramp-like entrance to the upper terraces, with their superb views of the city and beyond. In between, there is much to see: the lavish Renaissance salons, decorated with spectacular frescoes and *trompe l'œils;* the chapel in the *Cortile di Onore* designed by Michelangelo for Leo X; and, half-way up an easily-missed staircase, Clement VII's surprisingly tiny personal bathroom, painted by Giulio Romano. *No wheelchair access.*

Museo dell'Alto Medioevo

Viale Lincoln, 3, EUR (59 25 806). Bus to Piazza Guglielmo Marconi. **Open** *9am-2pm Tue-Sat; 9am-1pm Sun.* **Admission** *L4,000.*

This museum concentrates on the decorative arts of the period between the fall of the Roman Empire and the Renaissance. Exhibits of intricately carved gold and silver decorated swords, buckles and horse tackle have survived, along with more mundane objects: jewellery made of painted ceramic beads, and the metal frames of what may be Europe's earliest folding chairs. Church masonry carved with Celtic designs, and fragments of rich embroidery from the robes of medieval priests are also worth checking out. *No wheelchair acccess.*

Museo di Arte Ebraica

*Comunità Israelitica, Lungotevere dei Cenci (68 40 061).
Bus to Via Arenula or Piazza di Monte Savello.* **Open**
9am-4.30pm Mon-Thur; 9.30am-2pm Fri; 9am-12.30pm
Sun. **Closed** Sat and Jewish holidays. **Admission** L8,000.

As well as luxurious crowns, Torah mantles and silver-
ware, the museum presents vivid reminders of the persecution suffered by Rome's Jewish community at various
times during its 2,000-year history. Copies of sixteenth-
century papal edicts banning Jews from an ever-growing
list of activities are a disturbing foretaste of the horrors
forced upon them by the Nazis, which in turn are commemorated by stark photographs and heart-rending relics
from the concentration camps. In 1982, a terrorist bomb
killed a small child outside the synagogue; since then there
has been a permanent police guard outside and heavy security within. Admission includes a visit to the synagogue,
built in the 1870s.
No wheelchair access.

Museo della Civiltà Romana

*Piazza Giovanni Agnelli, 10, EUR (59 26 041). Metro
Magliana/bus to Piazza Guglielmo Marconi.* **Open** 9am-
7pm, Tue-Sat; 9am-1pm Sun. **Admission** L5,000.

The exhibits here date from 1937, when Mussolini mounted
a massive celebration to mark the bi-millennium of Augustus
becoming the first emperor. Any parallels between Augustus'
reign and his own were, of course, coincidental. The building
– vast blank walls and massive straight columns – is fascist-
classical at its most grandiloquent. Parts of the museum are
closed, but there should be enough of this rather clinical collection of models and reconstructions of archaeological finds
for you to get the gist of life as lived in ancient Rome.

Models detail the construction of ancient Rome's main buildings and there is a fascinating cutaway model of the
Colosseum's maze of tunnels and lifts. There are also full-
scale casts of the reliefs on the Column of Trajan in the
Imperial Fora which enable you to examine their intricate
details more easily than when standing next to the real thing.
The centrepiece is a giant model of Rome in the fourth cen-

tury AD, showing the famous buildings in their original
state. All in all, this outwardly daunting museum manages
to put into context the fragments and artefacts found in the
miles of glass cases all over Rome.
Wheelchair access.

Museo del Folklore e dei Poeti Romaneschi

*Piazza Sant'Egidio, 1b, Trastevere (58 16 563). Bus to
Viale Trastevere.* **Open** 9am-7pm Tue-Sat; 9am-1pm Sun.
Admission L3,750.

The folklore museum, currently undergoing restoration but
scheduled to open by the end of 1997, is housed in a
seventeenth-century convent that formerly belonged to an
order of Carmelite nuns. It contains an entertaining collection of period paintings and prints, along with a series of
waxwork tableaux relating to the life, work, pastimes and
superstitions of the man in the street in eighteenth- and nineteenth-century Italy. Don't miss the riotous nativity scene
set in the busy back streets of Naples.
No wheelchair access.

Museo Napoleonico

*Via Zanardelli, 1 or Piazza Ponte Umberto, 1 (68 80 62
86). Bus to Corso Rinascimento.* **Open** 9am-7pm Tue-Sat;
9am-1pm Sun. **Admission** L3,750.

Although Napoleon spent only a short time in Rome, other
members of his family, including his mother Letizia and
sister Pauline, settled here. This collection of art and memorabilia relating (sometimes tenuously) to the family was
left to the city in 1927 by Napoleon's last descendants, the
Counts Primoli. The museum has recently been restored
and redecorated in keeping with an aristocratic palazzo of
the early nineteenth century. You will find portraits of family members, including one by David of Napoleon's sister
Carlotta, alongside uniforms and clothes and some of
Canova's studies for the infamous sculpture of Pauline (now
on show at the **Galleria Borghese**), including a cast of
her right breast.
Wheelchair access.

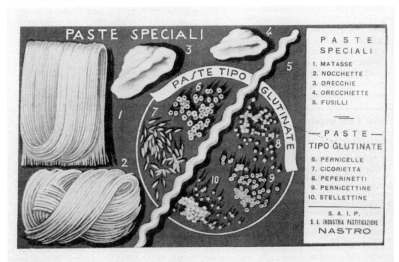

A paean to pasta... the **Museo Nazionale delle Paste Alimentari**. *See page 99.*

Galleria Borghese

In December 1983 a piece of plaster fell from the ceiling of the pleasure palace that houses the Borghese collection. For the next 14 years the building lay dormant in a cocoon of scaffolding. Now at last, with every inch of its internal and external decorations returned to their original splendour and all its sculptures restored, the gallery is open for business again.

Designed in 1613 by Flemish architect Jan van Santen, *Il Casino*, as the palace was known, was built to house the art collection of Cardinal Scipione Borghese, an aesthete, bon viveur, and one of Bernini's greatest patrons. Rooms 2-5 contain some spectacular works by the great architect-sculptor, made early in his career but already showing his genius: look how Pluto's hand presses into Proserpine's marble thigh in *The Rape of Proserpine*. Room 3 houses perhaps Bernini's

most famous work, *Apollo and Daphne*, showing the nymph fleeing the sun god, her desperate attempt at flight hampered as she turns into a laurel tree. Another sculptural highlight, dating from 1804, is Canova's sculpture of Pauline, sister of Napoleon and wife of Prince Camillo Borghese (*see* **Palazzo Borghese** *in chapter* **Sightseeing**). She is portrayed as a seductive, topless Venus, and Borghese thought the work so provocative he forbade even the artist to see it. (Asked by a shocked friend how she could bear to pose naked, Pauline is said to have replied: 'The studio was heated'.)

The Galleria contains several important pieces of classical sculpture, many of them Roman copies of Greek originals. Among the most renowned are a series of busts of the emperors, a Roman copy of a Greek dancing faun, and a copy of a sleeping hermaphrodite, displayed with his/her back to the onlooker so the breasts and genitals are invisible. The imposing salon has fourth-century floor mosaics showing gladiators fighting wild animals.

Room 8 is mainly devoted to six major works by Caravaggio, including his *David Holding Aloft the Head of Goliath*, his luscious *Boy with a Basket of Fruit* and an uncanny *Madonna of the Serpent*. His *Sick Bacchus* is believed to be a self-portrait. Other major works are on the first floor, and include Titian's recently restored *Sacred and Profane Love*, *The Deposition* by Raphael and several major works by Correggio, including *Danae*, commissioned as sixteenth-century soft porn for Charles V of Spain.

Because so many of the masterpieces on display are fragile, the number of visitors to the Galleria is limited to no more than 300 on the ground floor and 90 on the first floor at any one time. Visits must therefore be booked beforehand (*see below*).

Galleria Borghese

Piazzale Scipione Borghese, 5 (information 85 48 577, bookings 84 24 16 07, 9.30am-6pm Mon-Fri). Metro Spagna/bus or tram to Via Veneto. **Open** 9am-7pm Tue-Sun. **Admission** L10,000 + L2,000 booking fee. *Limited wheelchair access.*

Museo Nazionale delle Arti e Tradizioni Popolari

Piazza Guglielmo Marconi, 8, EUR (59 26 148). Metro Magliana/bus to Piazza Guglielmo Marconi. **Open** 9am-2pm Mon-Sat; 9am-1pm Sun. **Admission** L4,000.

This is an enormous and entertaining collection dedicated to Italian folk art and rural tradition. One room is full of elaborately decorated carts and horse tack and a bizarre collection of votive offerings left to local saints. Most of these are painted wooden panels showing horrible diseases, or wax models of affected bits of anatomy (lungs, a breast and a brain). Malevolent-looking puppets fill one room; another displays costumes and carnival artefacts; and there's an exquisite collection of traditional jewellery,

with photographs showing how it was worn. Other collections cover traditional crafts and musical instruments. *No wheelchair access.*

Museo Storico della Liberazione di Roma

Via Tasso, 145 (70 03 866). Metro San Giovanni/bus to Piazza San Giovanni in Laterano. **Open** 4-7pm Tue, Thur, Fri; 9.30am-12.30pm Sat, Sun. **Admission** free.

Prisoners of the Nazis were brought to this grim building for interrogation during the occupation of Rome in 1943-44. The museum commemorates those prisoners: resistance fighters; passive victims taken in reprisal; and members of the Nazis' many proscribed groups, among them Jews, homosexuals and Communists. The walls are covered with photographs and

Palazzo Barberini

Maderno, Bernini and Borromini all contributed to the design of this palace, built for one of the Barberini popes between 1627 and 1633. Borromini's handiwork can be seen in the characteristically curving secondary staircase on the right, while Bernini was responsible for the main staircase. The most famous feature of the interior is the *Gran Salone*, dramatically frescoed by Pietro da Cortona in 1633-39 with depictions of *The Triumph of Divine Providence*.

The art collection is arranged chronologically in frescoed rooms. Highlights include Filippo Lippi's *Madonna* (with possibly the ugliest Christ-child ever painted) in Room II and an enigmatic portrait of a courtesan, *La Fornarina*, traditionally (though probably wrongly) believed to represent Raphael's mistress (*see* **Casa della Fornarina** *in chapter* **Sightseeing**). In Room V, there's a *Holy Family* by Andrea del Sarto, and a portrait of Erasmus by Flemish artist Quentin Metsys is in Room VI. There are more great pieces in Room VIII, including *The Nativity* and *The Baptism of Christ* by El Greco, Tintoretto's dramatic *Christ and the Woman taken in Adultery* and Titian's *Venus and Adonis*. Room XI has two Caravaggios, one of Judith rather gingerly cutting off Holofernes' head. Other important paintings

include a Holbein portrait, *Henry VIII Dressed for his Wedding to Anne of Cleves* (it's been suggested that this may be a copy), Bronzino's forceful portrait of Stefano Colonna, Guido Reni's portrait of incest-victim Beatrice Cenci (*see* **Palazzo Cenci** *in chapter* **Sightseeing**). A Bernini bust of Pope Urban VIII – who commissioned the palace – can be found in Room XVIII. Work by Raphael's best-known follower, Sodoma (the nickname was accurate), includes *Rape of the Sabine Women*, with predictably compliant subjects, and *The Mystic Marriage of Saint Catherine*. On the second floor the collection continues with later paintings: Venetian scenes by Canaletto and a self-portrait by Artemisia Gentileschi (*see* **Artemisia** *page 89*).

Visitors also have access to a suite of small private rooms, exquisitely painted and furnished for Princess Cornelia Costanza Barberini in the eighteenth century. She was the last of the Barberinis, and the name died out when she married into the Colonna family. These rooms also house some Barberini family clothes and furniture.

Palazzo Barberini
Via delle Quattro Fontane, 13 (48 14 591). Metro Barberini/bus to Piazza Barberini. **Open** 9am-2pm Tue-Sat, 9am-1pm Sun. **Admission** L8,000. *No wheelchair access.*

---

biographies of some who passed through on their way to die, and several of the cells have been preserved as they were, complete with prisoners' farewell messages to their families. It's a moving and a chilling place, which you won't forget in a hurry. *Wheelchair access.*

Music & Literature

Keats-Shelley Memorial House
Piazza di Spagna, 26 (67 84 235). Metro Spagna. **Open** *summer* 9am-1pm, 3-6pm Mon-Fri; *winter* 9am-1pm, 2.30-5.30pm Mon-Fri. **Admission** L5,000.
The house at the bottom of the Spanish Steps where the 25-year-old John Keats died of tuberculosis in 1821 is crammed with mementoes of Keats, Shelley and Byron. A lock of Keats' hair and his death mask, a minuscule urn holding tiny pieces of Shelley's charred skeleton, copies of documents and letters, and a massive library make this an enthusiast's paradise. Devotees of the Romantics should also make the pilgrimage to the **Protestant Cemetery** in Testaccio, where both Keats and Shelley are buried.
No wheelchair access.

Museo Nazionale degli Strumenti Musicali
Piazza Santa Croce in Gerusalemme, 9a (70 14 796). Metro San Giovanni/bus to Piazza Santa Croce in Gerusalemme. **Open** 9am-2pm Tue-Sat. **Admission** L4,000.
In the first half of this century, opera singer Evan Gorga collected more than 800 rare and beautiful musical instruments.

Taken by the state as compensation when Gorga went bankrupt, the collection forms a comprehensive overview of the history of European music since ancient times. The instruments of the Renaissance and Baroque periods dominate; look out for the exquisite, triple-stringed Barberini harp, a seventeenth-century harpsichord and elegantly curving lutes and viols.
No wheelchair access.

The Gruesome & the Bizarre

If you've had enough of frescoes, friezes and fine art, try one of these museums. They may not have set out to be particularly entertaining, but all contain strange displays and exhibits that you won't see elsewhere.

Museo delle Anime dei Defunti
Chiesa del Sacro Cuore del Suffragio, Lungotevere Prati, 12 (68 80 65 17). Bus to Piazza Cavour. **Open** 9-11am, 5-7pm daily. **Admission** free.
This macabre collection contains the hand- and finger-prints left on the prayer books and clothes of the living by dead loved ones, reminding their survivors to say mass to release their souls from Purgatory into Heaven. Begun just over a century ago, the collection is intended to convince the sceptical of life after death. A startling exhibit is the incandescent hand-print of a nun, Clara Scholers, on the habit of fellow-sister Margherita Hahrendorf, left in Westphalia in

1696. Another dead soul apparently left hand-scorched bank notes outside a church where he wanted his mass to be said. *No wheelchair access.*

Museo delle Cere

Piazza dei Santi Apostoli, 67 (67 96 482). Bus to Piazza Venezia. **Open** *Oct-Mar* 9am-8pm daily; *Apr-Sept* 9am-9pm daily. **Admission** L7,000.

Most of the models in this shabby, old-fashioned wax museum are incredibly un-lifelike. They are arranged to show real and less-real scenes from history, including an unlikely tableau in which Leonardo paints the Mona Lisa beneath the gaze of Machiavelli and the Medicis. In another, Pope John XXIII appears to be acting as a game show host but is in fact naming a new cardinal. Bizarre figures line the walls, all with the same repressed smirks on their faces, except for a hyper-ventilating Sleeping Beauty. The requisite chamber of horrors has a garrotte, a gas chamber and an electric chair. *Wheelchair access.*

Museo Nazionale delle Paste Alimentari

Piazza Scanderbeg, 117 (69 91 119). Bus to Via del Tritone. **Open** *summer* 9.30am-12.30pm, 4-7pm Mon-Fri; 9.30am-6.30pm Sat; *winter* as above except 9.30am-12.30pm Sat. **Admission** L12,000.

This grandly named tribute to pasta is one of the best-organised museums in Rome. Visitors are each issued with a portable CD player with commentary in Italian, English, French, German or Japanese to talk them through the collection of pasta-making equipment, prints and photographs of famous, and not so famous, people enjoying pasta, and art

inspired by Italy's national dish. You'll hear more than is strictly necessary on the techniques of pasta making, and some of the displays (particularly a series of eighteenth-century prints, which seem to appear in every room) are a bit repetitive, but for anyone with a passing interest in the national dish the museum is worth a visit, if only for its novelty value. *No wheelchair access.*

Museo Storico dell'Arma dei Carabinieri

Via Cola di Rienzo, 294 (68 96 691). Metro Ottaviano/bus to Piazza del Risorgimento. **Open** 8.30am-1pm Tue-Sun. **Closed** Aug. **Admission** free.

Enter the *Boy's Own* world of the Carabinieri police force, carpeted in black with red stripes to match their uniform trousers. The force are proud of their semi-military status. When not at war, they were fighting malefactors at home, and somewhat idealised pictures show Carabinieri capturing Communists, bandits and *mafiosi*. The exhibition brings the history of the service right up to date with displays of forensic equipment. *Wheelchair access.*

Museo Storico Nazionale dell'Arte Sanitaria

Lungotevere in Sassia, 3 (68 35 23 53). Bus to Borgo Santo Spirito or Lungotevere in Sassia. **Open** 10am-noon Mon, Wed, Fri. **Admission** L3,000.

This gruesome collection of medical artefacts, from ancient times to the nineteenth century, is housed in a few rooms on one side of the hospital of Santo Spirito. As well as the usual collection of skeletons, organs, anatomical charts and surgi-

cal instruments, this museum has a collection of wax votive offerings, left at churches and shrines to encourage God to cure parts of the body conventional medicine could not reach. There are also reconstructions of a seventeenth-century pharmacy and an alchemist's laboratory.
No wheelchair access.

Private galleries

If you're planning to use your trip to Rome to catch up on the latest developments in the Italian art scene, prepare to be disappointed. Although in recent decades Italy has given the world such important movements as *Arte Povera* and the *Transavanguardia*, the evidence of burgeoning creativity at a national level is more likely to be found in Milan, Turin and, in the last two or three years, Naples. That said, many of Rome's 200-plus contemporary art galleries are hidden away in beautiful historic buildings and streets that have become works of art in their own right.

Admission to the galleries below is free unless otherwise stated. If you use a wheelchair, it pays to ring before setting out: many of the private galleries listed are on upper floors with no lifts.

Art Gallery Banchi Nuovi
Via Margutta, 28 (32 65 03 16). Metro Spagna or Flaminio. **Open** 10.30am-1pm, 4.30-7.30pm Tue-Fri. **Closed** July-Aug.
This gallery, which has recently moved from Via dei Banchi Nuovi, should be applauded for consistently showing new artists, although its often hectic programme reveals a predilection for metaphysically inspired magic realism that is not to everybody's taste.

Associazione Culturale L'Attico
Via del Paradiso, 41 (68 69 846). Bus to Corso Vittorio Emanuele. **Open** 5-8pm Mon-Sat. **Closed** Aug.
This gallery started off in an attic overlooking Piazza di Spagna but now occupies a beautiful apartment with frescoed ceilings near Campo de' Fiori. Since it opened in the late 1960s, it has been one of the most innovative galleries in Rome, a starting-point for new artists and a chance for well-known names to introduce new directions in their work.

Associazione Culturale Sala 1
Piazza di Porta San Giovanni, 10 (70 08 691). Metro San Giovanni/bus to Piazza San Giovanni in Laterano. **Open** 5-8pm Tue-Sat. **Closed** July-Sept.
Sala 1 occupies what was going to be the crypt of a church, started in the 1940s and left unfinished when the war intervened. The gallery opened in 1970 and specialises in the international avant-garde. In 1989 it presented the first exhibition of 'non-official' Soviet artists in Rome. American director Mary Angela Scroth is an adventurous art promoter, and exhibitions here are unusual and entertaining

Associazione Culturale Valentina Moncada
Via Margutta, 54 (32 07 956). Metro Spagna. **Open** 4-8pm Mon-Fri. **Closed** Aug.
This picturesque garden conceals a series of purpose-built nineteenth-century artists' studios. In their early years they were a hive of activity: Wagner, Liszt and Fortuny were among the famous visitors. A gallery was opened on the ground floor in 1990, specialising in the work of radical young artists. More established names like Tony Cragg and Ian Davenport are also represented.

Galleria Emanuela Oddi Baglioni
Via Gregoriana, 34 (67 97 906). Metro Spagna. **Open** 10am-1pm, 4-7.30pm Mon-Fri. **Closed** Aug.
The emphasis is on non-figurative Italian sculpture since 1960, and the owners act as agents for young sculptors. Biennale winner Marina Abramovic was recently featured, with fellow body-artists Orlan and Nan Goldin.

Galleria Gian Enzo Sperone
Via di Pallacorda, 15 (68 93 525). Bus to Piazza San Silvestro. **Open** 4-8pm Mon; 10am-1pm, 4-8pm Tue-Sat. **Closed** Aug.
Son of a well-known Turin art dealer, Gian Enzo Sperone is one of Rome's most prestigious art promoters. He has been based here since the mid-1970s and also runs a gallery in New York. Among the first to show the work of Warhol, Lichtenstein and other US pop artists in Italy, he now holds unusual, experimental shows.

Galleria Giulia
Via Giulia, 148 (68 80 20 61). Bus to Lungotevere dei Tebaldi. **Open** 4-8pm Mon; 10am-1pm, 4-8pm Tue-Sat. **Closed** July-mid-Sept.
This attractive gallery and bookshop opened in the early 1970s as a home for early twentieth-century work by famous artists. Since then it has carved out a niche for itself with a varied programme of shows by New Pop artists, German Expressionists and Italian contemporary artists from most schools. Graphic arts and sculpture are strong points.

Galleria Ugo Ferranti
Via dei Soldati, 251a (68 80 2146). Bus to Corso Vittorio Emanuele or Corso del Rinascimento. **Open** 11am-1pm, 5-8pm Tue-Sat. **Closed** Aug.
This has been one of the top galleries in Rome since it opened in 1974, concentrating on American and European conceptual artists such as LeWitt, Christo, Kounellis and Twombly. But owner Ugo Ferranti is constantly on the look-out for up-and-coming artists, including Andreas Serrano, with his recent controversial exhibition of morgue photographs.

Opera Paese Ex Lanificio Luciani
Via di Pietralata, 157 (45 03 797). Metro Pietralata/bus heading to Piazza Sempione. **Open** 10.30am-1pm, 4-6.30pm Tue-Sun. **Closed** July-Aug. **Admission** L3,000 annual membership card.
This recently converted industrial space on the outskirts of Rome is well worth a visit. As well as offering a cultural programme including concerts, seminars and book presentations, it plans major shows on German photography, in collaboration with the Goethe Institute.

Stefania Miscetti
Via delle Mantellate, 14 (68 80 58 80). Bus to Lungotevere della Farnesina. **Open** 4-8pm Tue-Fri. **Closed** usually July-Sept, but ring to check.
This is one of the most interesting galleries in the city, situated in a storehouse next to Regina Coeli prison. The gallery opened in 1990, with an exhibition of Hermann Nitsch, and holds unusual shows of sculpture and sculptural installations. It has been responsible for the first Italian shows by many foreign artists, among them Yoko Ono.

Studio d'Arte Contemporanea Pino Casagrande
Via degli Ausoni, 7a (44 63 480). Bus to San Lorenzo. **Open** 5-8pm Mon-Fri. **Closed** Aug.
In the increasingly hip area of San Lorenzo, Casagrande's loft-like exhibition space hosts some of Rome's most challenging exhibitions, with young British artists such as Mark Hopgood rubbing shoulders with the most interesting figures on the local and national scene.

The Vatican City

The history and treasures of the papal powerhouse.

Spiralling upwards to the **Vatican Museums**.

The Vatican State was given its current status in 1929 under a treaty with Mussolini known as *La Conciliazione*, or Lateran Pact. This was the papacy's consolation prize for having lost its temporal power in 1870, when Italy united and became a secular country. As consolation prizes go, it wasn't bad. Italy gave the Vatican 750 million lire and the income from a billion lire in state bonds, exempted it from taxes and duty on imported goods, and agreed to adopt canon law in marriage and make Catholic teaching compulsory in all schools.

Falling church attendance and the steady decline of Vatican influence over Italian politics have encouraged the Italian state to back-pedal. Divorce, contraception and abortion are legal, religious education is optional, and the Vatican is taxed on profits from the stock market, although its employees are still not taxed on their earnings.

The Vatican City occupies a hilly area west of the Tiber. Until Caligula, and then Nero, decided to build a circus there in the middle of the first century AD, the area was mainly used for the execution of religious troublemakers like the early Christians – the most famous being Saint Peter.

Several decades on, in 90 AD, the first monument was built over the supposed site of his martyrdom, and in the periods when the new faith was tolerated this became a popular spot for pilgrims.

In the mid-fourth century, Constantine built a basilica over Peter's tomb, but selected **San Giovanni in Laterano** as headquarters for the new official religion. Christians, however, preferred Peter's tomb, and dozens of buildings appeared in what became known as the Borgo (village).

After a series of invasions by Saracens and Lombards in the eighth and ninth centuries, Pope Leo IV encircled the area with a 12-metre-high defensive wall incorporating Hadrian's tomb, now **Castel Sant'Angelo**. In the Middle Ages, during the incessant battles for power between the popes, the aristocracy and the Holy Roman Emperors (*see chapter* **History**), popes often fled down the covered passageway connecting the Vatican to Castel Sant'Angelo.

After the sack of Rome by Charles V in 1527, the *Città Leonina* lost its strategic importance for ever. The papacy moved across the Tiber, first to the Lateran Palace, then to the Quirinal, where it stayed until ousted by the Piedmontese royals in

1870, at which point Pius IX scuttled back behind the safety of the Vatican walls. On the creation of the independent Vatican City, the Borgo remained part of the secular city of Rome.

Saint Peter's Basilica and the Vatican State

After 120 years as the world's most elegant building site, the current Saint Peter's was consecrated on 18 November 1626 by Urban VIII – exactly 1,300 years after the consecration of the first basilica. The earlier building was erected on the orders of the first Christian emperor, Constantine the Great. Records show that it was a five-aisled classical basilica, fronted by a large courtyard and four porticoes. It was steadily enlarged and enriched, becoming the finest church in Christendom. By the mid-fifteenth century, however, its south wall was on the point of collapse. Pope Nicholas V commissioned new designs and had 2,500 wagonloads of masonry from the **Colosseum** carted across the Tiber, but never got further than repair work. No-one wanted to demolish the most sacred church in Christendom. It took the arrogance of Pope Julius II and his pet architect Bramante to get things moving. In 1506 2,500 workers tore down the 1,000-year-old basilica and Julius laid the foundation stone.

Following Bramante's death in 1514, Raphael scrapped his plan for a basilica in the pattern of a Greek cross (*see* **Architectural Terms** *in chapter* **Directory**) and opted for an elongated Latin cross. In 1547, Michelangelo took command and reverted back to the Greek design. He died in 1564 aged 87, but not before coming up with the design for a massive dome and supporting drum. This was completed in 1590, the largest brick dome ever to have been constructed.

In 1607 Carlo Maderno won the consent of Pope Paul V to knock down the last fragments of the old basilica and put up a new façade, crowned by enormous statues of Christ and the Apostles. After his death, Bernini took over, and despite nearly destroying both the façade and his reputation by erecting towers on either end (one of which fell down), he became the hero of the hour with his sumptuous *baldacchino* and famous piazza. This was built between 1656 and 1667, its colonnaded arms reaching out towards the Catholic world in a symbolic embrace. The main oval measures 340m by 240m, and is punctuated by the central Egyptian obelisk (dragged from Nero's Circus in 1586), as well as two symmetrical fountains by Maderno and Bernini. The 284-columned, 88-pillared colonnade is topped by 140 statues of saints.

Inside, the basilica's size is emphasised on the marble floor, where a boastful series of brass line inscriptions measure the lengths of the 14 next-largest churches in the world. But it is Bernini's huge curlicued *baldacchino*, hovering over the high altar, that is the real focal point. This was cast from brass purloined from the **Pantheon**'s roof cladding, and is bathed in the light that floods in from the dome above.

Catholic pilgrims head straight for Arnolfo da Cambio's brass statue of Saint Peter (c.1296) to kiss its big toe, which has been worn down by centuries of pious smacking lips. Tourists group round the bullet-proof glass panel which now protects Michelangelo's *Pietà* (1499) from unwanted attentions. Bernini's *Throne of Saint Peter* (1665), flanked by papal tombs, dominates the far end of the nave behind the high altar, under an almost psychedelic stained-glass window. Dotted around the basilica are statues, tombs and monuments dedicated to popes, saints and religious figures.

The Vatican Grottoes – the Renaissance crypt beneath the basilica containing more papal tombs – are open to visitors. The Necropolis, where Saint Peter is believed to be buried, is beneath the Grottoes and can be visited by permission. The dome (reached via a cramped lift and hundreds of stairs) offers fabulous views of the Vatican Gardens, which can be toured.

Apart from the massive sprawl of the basilica, the papal apartments and the magnificent structure which houses the Vatican museums, the 44 hectares encompassed by the Vatican walls include smaller churches, foreign seminaries and minor papal residences. On a more mundane level, there are also post offices, a railway station, a heliport, a pharmacy, a supermarket and a petrol station.

Leading up to the Vatican is Via della Conciliazione, the perfect, austere foil to Bernini's elaborate curves. Although built by Mussolini in the 1930s, it had been on the papal agenda for centuries to clear out the labyrinthine Borgo streets and so create a monumental approach road to Saint Peter's Square.

For papal audiences, apply to the *Prefettura della Casa Pontificia* (69 88 30 17), by the *Portone di Bronzo* in Saint Peter's Square. For a private audience, your local bishop has to make a written request, which can take between three months and a year to be granted. If you're planning to visit Saint Peter's, dress demurely, or you may be turned away.

Saint Peter's (San Pietro)

Metro Ottaviano/bus to Piazza del Risorgimento.
Basilica *Nov-Mar* 7am-6pm daily; *Mar-Oct* 7am-7pm daily. **Admission** free.
Dome *Oct-Mar* 8am-5pm daily; *Mar-Sept* 8am-6pm daily. **Admission** L5,000 (without lift); L6,000 (with lift).
Necropolis apply at the *Uffizio degli Scavi* (open 9am-5pm Mon-Fri) to book an English-language tour several days in advance. **Admission** L10,000.
Vatican Gardens phone the Vatican Tourist Office (69 88 44 66) to book a tour three or four days in advance. **Admission** L18,000.

A saint's-eye view from the top of Bernini's colonnade.

Museums

It's a ten-minute walk from Saint Peter's to the entrance to the Vatican Museums, which contain one of the finest art collections in the world. Started in 1506 by Pope Julius II, the collection represents the accumulated fancies and obsessions of a long line of strong, often contradictory personalities. The popes' unique position allowed them to obtain treasures on favourable terms from other collectors, and their sheer power meant that artists had no choice as to whether they accepted papal commissions.

The collections are so vast that it is impossible to take in more than a quarter on one visit. The museum authorities have laid out four colour-coded routes, ranging from a race down to the Sistine Chapel to a conscientious five-hour plod round the lot. The following are selected highlights.

All the Vatican Museums are equipped for wheelchair users. There's a free morning opening on the last Sunday of each month. Opening times are liable to change at short notice; ring 69 88 33 33 to check.

The Vatican Museums

Metro Ottaviano/bus to Piazza del Risorgimento.
Open *Nov to mid-Mar and mid-June to end Aug* 8.45am-1pm Mon-Sat; *Mid-Mar to mid-June and Sept to end Oct* 8.45am-4pm Mon-Fri; 8.45am-1pm Sat. **Admission** L13,000; students L10,000.

Alternatively, head for the Sistine Chapel.

The Egyptian Museum

Founded by Gregory XVI in 1839 in rooms which are partly decorated in Egyptian style, this relatively small collection contains a representative selection of ancient Egyptian art from 3,000-600 BC. It includes statues of a baboon god, painted mummy cases and a white marble statue of Antinous, Emperor Hadrian's lover, who drowned in Egypt.

The Chiaramonte Gallery

Founded by Pius VII in the early nineteenth century and laid out by sculptor Canova, this is an eclectic collection of Roman statues, reliefs and busts. Don't miss the replica of a Greek statue by Polyeuctos of stuttering orator Demosthenes, and a much-reproduced copy of *Resting Satyr* by the Greek sculptor Praxiteles.

Pio-Clementino Museum

In the late eighteenth century Pope Clement XIV and his successor Pius VI began the world's largest collection of classical statues, which now occupies 16 separate rooms on two floors. Essential viewing are the first-century BC headless Belvedere Torso by Apollonius of Athens (*Sala delle Muse*); the Apollo Sauroctonos, a Roman copy of the bronze *Lizard Killer* by Praxiteles (*Galleria delle Statue*); and in the Octagonal Belvedere Courtyard, the exquisite *Belvedere Apollo* and *Laocoön*, who's being throttled by two serpents.

The Etruscan Museum

Founded in 1837 by Gregory XVI, and enlarged in this century, this collection contains Greek and Roman art as well as masterpieces from Etruria. Don't miss the Regolini-Galassi Tomb (*Room 2*), the Greek-inspired fourth-century BC Mars (*Room 3*), or the fifth-century BC young man and small slave (*Room 12*).

Galleria dei Candelabri and *Galleria degli Arazzi*

Roman marble statues in a long gallery studded with candelabra. In the next gallery are ten huge tapestries woven by Flemish master Pieter van Aelst from cartoons by Raphael (now in London's Victoria and Albert Museum).

Galleria delle Carte Geografiche

Gregory XIII (he of the Gregorian calendar, which we use today) had a craze for astronomy and was responsible for this 120-metre-long gallery, with its observation Tower of the Winds at the north end. Ignazio Danti of Perugia drew the maps on its walls, showing each Italian region, city and island with extraordinary precision for the time (1580-83).

The Raphael Rooms, Raphael's Loggia and the Chapel of Nicholas V

One of the masterpieces of the collection, these rooms were part of Nicholas V's palace, originally decorated by Piero della Francesca. Julius II then let Perugino, Lorenzo Lotto and others loose on them, until he discovered Raphael, whereupon he dispensed with his interior decorators and gave the young artist *carte blanche* to re-design four rooms of the Papal Suite.

The visiting order changes according to the time of year, but it makes sense to see the rooms in the order in which they were painted. The Study (*Stanza della Segnatura*) was Raphael's first bash (1508-11), and features philosophical and spiritual themes – the triumph of Truth, Good and Beauty. Best known is the celebrity-stuffed School of Athens fresco, with contemporary artists acting as classical figures (Leonardo is Plato). Raphael next turned his hand to the Waiting Room (*Stanza di Eliodoro*; 1512-14), frescoed with political themes such as *The Expulsion of Heliodorus*, a radical re-reading of a biblical episode designed to highlight Pope Julius II's supreme political savvy.

The Dining Room (*Stanza dell'Incendio*; 1514-17) is devoted to the feats of Popes Leo III and IV, among them *The Fire in the Borgo*, which Leo IV halted with the sign of the cross.

The Reception Room (*La Sala di Constantino*; 1523- 25) was completed by Giulio Romano after Raphael's death in 1520, but is based on Raphael's sketches on the Church's triumph over paganism.

This brings you to a long gallery, *La loggia di Raffaello*, with a beautiful view over Rome, started by Bramante in 1513 and finished by Raphael and his assistants. It features 52 little paintings on biblical themes, and leads into the *Sala* *dei Chiaroscuri* (Raphael's frescoes here were obliterated by Gregory XIII, but the magnificent ceiling remains) and the adjacent *Cappella di Niccolò V*, with outstanding religious frescoes by Fra Angelico (1448-50).

Borgia Rooms

A six-room suite adapted for the Borgia Pope Alexander VI (1492-1503) and decorated by Pinturicchio and his school

Swiss Role

They're the second-most photographed figures in the Vatican, but you're more likely to get a grin out of the Big Man himself. Standing stiffly to attention at the two main gates into the Vatican City, the stern-faced Swiss guards resent being treated as Disney characters in period costume by the camera-toting hordes. They are, after all, a force with a glorious 500-year history – and you don't opt for a job with a dress uniform of full sixteenth-century armour unless you take it pretty seriously.

The *Cohors Helvetica*, to use its Latin title, was founded by Pope Julius II at the beginning of the sixteenth century to defend the papal states against invading armies. In those days, before their country acquired its reputation for disinterested neutrality, Swiss soldiers were prized as the best mercenaries money could buy, and it wasn't long before they proved

their unwavering allegiance to their papal paymaster. In 1527 German and Spanish armies launched a ferocious attack on Rome, reaching the steps of Saint Peter's. They were held back by a troop of some 200 Swiss guards, most of whom lost their lives as Clement VII hightailed it to the nearby Castel Sant'Angelo.

Today, the risks facing Swiss guards come mainly from irate tourists unable to locate the Vatican Museums. But they're no pushovers. A few years ago, a knife-wielding would-be assassin found himself pinned to a wall by one of the formidable-looking halberds.

The Swiss Guard accepts candidates from any of the Swiss cantons. They must have done their military service back home, be unmarried, over 1.76m tall, prepared to stick it out for at least two years, and come highly recommended by a Catholic priest.

Net Surfers of the Holy See

The elderly clerics ambling through Bernini's Colonnade in front of Saint Peter's may still think of Michael, Gabriel and Raphael as archangels. Not so the bright young things of the Vatican Internet Office. For them, they're three 64-bit Alpha servers, and they're spreading the Word of God through cyberspace.

The tide of indifference and secularisation which has been sweeping the Catholic world for the past half-century has not escaped the notice of the higher echelons in the Holy See. Pope John Paul II has done his best to rally the troops, visiting some 40 countries since ascending the throne of Saint Peter's in 1978. Organisers of celebrations to mark the Jubilee Holy Year in 2000 hope to revive flagging enthusiasm and lure pilgrims by the million with the promise of a massive jamboree.

As the Millennium approaches, the Holy See has also been exploring the gospel-spreading potential of twenty-first-century communications technology. The result is satellite radio broadcasting across five continents, and an Internet site.

The satellite broadcasting system was inaugurated in January 1996. So incensed was one Vatican gardener at the two transmitter dishes marring his patch that he refused point-blank to prune back the branches of a tree which was interfering with transmission quality.

Launched on Easter Sunday 1997, the web site (at http://www.vatican.va) offers information and a wide range of papal encyclicals, epistles and other musings in English, Spanish, Italian, French, German and Portuguese, with Arabic and Chinese soon to be added to the list. Net-surfing Catholic couch potatoes will be disappointed, however, to find that the interactive options offered by the World Wide Web have been deliberately overlooked. Cyber confessions are still a long way off.

---

with a series of frescoes on biblical, classical and devotional themes. In 1973, some 50 rooms of the Borgia Apartment were renovated to house the *Collezione d'Arte Religiosa Moderna*, featuring modern religious works.

The Sistine Chapel

The world's most famous frescoes cover the ceiling and one wall of a chapel built by Sixtus IV in 1473-84. Over the centuries the chapel has been used for popes' private prayers and papal elections (conclaves). In the 1980s the 10,000 square feet of ceiling were subjected to the most controversial restoration job of all time, funded by the Japanese television company NHK in exchange for a period of exclusive broadcasting rights.

Moving from west to east, the scenes depict Separation of Light from Darkness, Creation of Sun, Moon and Planets, Separation of Land and Sea and the Creation of Fishes and Birds, Creation of Adam, Creation of Eve, Temptation and Expulsion from Paradise, Sacrifice of Noah, Flood, and Drunkenness of Noah.

These magnificent scenes are framed by monumental figures of Old Testament prophets and classical sibyls. Twenty-two years after completing this masterpiece, the aged and embittered artist rolled up his sleeves again and started work on The Last Judgement to fill the altar wall, which he finished in 1541. Hidden among the larger-than-life figures which stare, leer and cry out from their brilliant blue background, Michelangelo painted his own face on the wrinkled human skin held by Saint Bartholomew, below and to the right of the powerful figure of Christ the Judge. Pius IV wanted to destroy the fresco because it included a host of naked figures, but thankfully he was persuaded to settle for loincloths, most of which were removed in the recent restoration work.

Dwarfed by Michelangelo's work, the sorely-neglected paintings on the side walls of the chapel are a *Who's Who* of the Renaissance greats. On the right-hand wall you can see scenes from the life of Moses, frescoed between 1481 and 1483 by a team of artists including Perugino, Botticelli, Ghirlandaio, Roselli, Pinturicchio, Signorelli and Della Gatta. Botticelli and Ghirlandaio also painted the series of early popes who stand in the niches between the high windows.

Pinacoteca

Founded by Pius VI in the late eighteenth century, the *Pinacoteca* (Picture Gallery) includes many of the pictures the Vatican bosses managed to recover from Napoleon after their forced sojourn in France. The collection ranges from the Byzantine School and Italian primitives to eighteenth century Dutch and French masters, and includes Giotto's *Stefaneschi Triptych*, a *Pietà* by Lucas Cranach the Elder, Madonnas by Fra Filippo Lippi, Fra Angelico, Raphael and Titian, Raphael's last work *The Transfiguration*, Caravaggio's *Entombment* and a monochrome Saint Jerome by Leonardo.

Museum of Pagan Antiquities

This collection of Roman and neo-Attic sculpture has been housed since 1970 in the *Museo Paolino*, where it has benefited from modern techniques of lighting and layout. Highlights include the beautifully draped statue of Sophocles from Terracina, a *trompe l'œil* mosaic of an unswept floor and the wonderfully elaborate Altar of Vicomagistri.

Pio Cristiano Museum

The upper floor of the Museo Paolino is devoted to a collection of early Christian antiquities, mostly sarcophagi carved with reliefs of biblical scenes.

The Vatican Library

Founded by Pope Nicholas V in 1450, this is one of the world's most extraordinary libraries, with 100,000 medieval manuscripts and books and over a million other volumes. It is open to students and specialists on application to the *Prefettura* (69 88 30 17).

Rest and peace in the **Vatican Gardens**.

degli effetti

Alexander Mc Queen
Ann Demeulemesteer
Antonio Berardi
Carpe Diem
Comme des Garçons
Dries Van Noten
Helmut Lang
Issey Miyake
Jil Sander
John Galliano
Junya Watanabe
Martin Margiela
Prada
Raf Simons
Yohji Yamamoto

There wolf! + P. Bruno

Boutique Uomo Piazza Capranica, 79 00186 Roma tel. 06-6791650
Boutique Donna Piazza Capranica, 93 00186 Roma tel. 06-6790202

Consumer Rome

Accommodation

Live like a contessa or sleep like a monk.

Like any capital city, Rome is not a cheap place to stay, but unlike most cities in the rest of Europe and the US, it has resisted the encroachment of huge, impersonal chains. Most hotels are still privately run, and even those that aren't have generally retained their original charm.

Italian hotels are classified on a star system from one to five. This will give you some idea of the price and facilities to expect, but as many hotels choose to use a lower rating than they deserve in order to pay lower taxes, this is only a rough guideline.

The hotels listed below offer value for money. In the luxury category the emphasis is on opulence. Those in the mid- to upper-price range tend to be smaller in scale, often housed in old palazzi with pretty, if rather small, bedrooms and homely public rooms. A few have tranquil terraces or gardens tucked away from the riot of the city. *Pensioni* are fairly basic, but those picked out here are clean, friendly and usually family-run.

Few Roman hotels have even heard of non-smoking areas, and there aren't many places with access for the disabled. Although the staff are generally more than willing to help, most places have so many steep stairs there's not much they can do. We've indicated a few places that have special facilities. (*See also chapter* **Directory: Rome for the Disabled**.)

Most of the hotels listed here are around the city centre and fall roughly into one of the following areas: **Campo de' Fiori**, which is particularly strong on low- to medium-priced hotels with bundles of character; **Piazza di Spagna**, which has elegant, traditional and well-refurbished hotels in the upper-price brackets; **Termini**, which has hundreds of cheap *pensioni* and a scattering of decent mid-priced hotels (but the station and its environs can be an unpleasant place to walk about after dark); and **Piazza Navona**, with hotels in the mid- to-upper-price range. Some hotels are further out, in **Trastevere**, around the **Vatican** or on the **Aventine** hill. The cheaper places, especially around Termini or Campo de' Fiori, are popular with student and school parties, especially at the end of the summer term and in September, so don't always count on getting a room.

ADVANCE BOOKINGS

Always reserve a room well in advance, especially during peak times. For cheaper hotels this is usually summer (particularly July to September) and over Easter. Expensive hotels rely on business travellers nowadays; they are quiet in summer and busier in spring and autumn. In some cases you'll be asked for a deposit, which can be paid by credit card (even some of the hotels that don't accept credit cards for the final settlement will take a credit card deposit). Eurocheques or banker's drafts may also be accepted.

If you arrive in Rome with nowhere to stay, hunt out the **EPT** local tourist office or **Enjoy Rome** (*see* **Tourist Information** *in chapter* **Directory**). Either of these agencies can help you find a room. The **Hotel Reservations** agency (69 91 000) has details on room availability for 200 hotels of all price ranges in Rome and has desks at Termini and Fiumicino. Its phone line is open between 7am and 10pm, and staff speak English. It's best not to accept help from the touts that hang around Termini – you'll probably end up paying a lot more than you should for a pretty grotty hotel.

Prices quoted are those for peak rates in 1997 and are subject to change; while some hotels may actually reduce their prices, in popular areas (especially Campo de' Fiori) prices show no signs of doing anything but rising. Some hotels have special weekend rates sometimes, and it's always worth trying to get a discount for a longer stay or for groups.

If you're travelling with children, most hotels are more than happy to squeeze a cot or camp bed into your room, but will probably charge you anything between 30 and 50 per cent extra for the privilege.

Unless stated, prices are for a single or double room with its own bathroom, and include breakfast. This can be coffee and biscuits in a *pensione* or a massive buffet of fruit, cold meats, bread and cakes in a more up-market establishment. Services such as babysitting, laundry and car parking charged separately.

Several *pensioni* and most of the hostels listed have curfews of around 1am, so make sure you know how to get in if you're going to be later than that. Usually you can get a key from reception.

De Luxe

Aldovrandi Palace

Via Ulisse Aldovrandi,15 (32 23 993/fax 32 21 435/telex 61 61 41). Bus to Via B. Buozzi/tram to Via U. Aldovrandi. **Rates** *single* L550,000; *double* L650,000; *suite* L1,100,000. **Credit** AmEx, DC, EC, JCB, MC,V.
A haven of luxurious tranquillity on a busy road at the edge of the Villa Borghese Park, and one of the few central(ish) hotels to have a garden and swimming pool; but public transport to the *centro storico* is poor. The public areas are lavish. Two good restaurants, one overlooking the garden.

Hotel services *Air-conditioning. Bar. Car park.
Currency exchange. Fax. Garden. Gym. Laundry. Lifts.
Multi-lingual staff. Non-smoking rooms. Restaurant.
Wheelchair access.* Room services *Air conditioning.
Hair dryer. Mini-bar. Radio. Room service. Telephone.
TV (satellite).*

Ambasciatori Palace

*Via Vittorio Veneto, 62 (47 493/fax 47 43 601/telex 61
92 41 HOTAMB 1). Metro Barberini/bus to Via Veneto.*
Rates *(breakfast L25-35,000 extra) single* L380,000;
double L550,000. Credit *AmEx,DC, EC, JCB, MC, V.*
A *fin de siècle* hotel with an elegant entrance lounge and bar.
Upstairs are 100 large, comfortable rooms, several with two
bathrooms and a small balcony. The clientele is mainly business these days, but the staff are still very friendly.
Hotel services *Air-conditioning. Babysitting. Bar. Car
park (nearby garage, extra cost). Conference facilities (for
up to 200). Currency Exchange. Fax. Laundry. Lifts.
Multi-lingual staff. Non-smoking rooms. Restaurant.
Sauna. Wheelchair access.* Room services *Air-
conditioning. Hair dryer. Mini-bar. Radio. Room service
(24-hour). Safe. TV (satellite).*

Atlante Star

*Via Vitelleschi, 34 (68 73 233/fax 68 72 300/telex 62 23
55). Metro Ottaviano/bus to Piazza del Risorgimento or
Piazza Cavour.* Rates *single* L420,000; *double* L525,000.
Credit *AmEx, DC, EC, JCB, MC, V.*
This is a comfortable 70-room hotel, well-placed for the
Vatican and an easy bus ride from the *centro storico.* The
ultra-modern bedrooms are decorated in dark colours which
can either be soothing or claustrophobic, depending on the
size of the room – some are very small. The highlight of the
hotel is its upstairs restaurant and pretty roof garden (with
wonderful views of Saint Peter's). There's a free car pick-up
service from the airport, but outward journeys cost L60,000.
Hotel services *Air-conditioning. Babysitting. Bar.
Coffee garden. Conference facilities (for up to 70).
Currency exchange. Fax. Laundry. Lifts. Multi-lingual*

*staff. Non-smoking rooms. Restaurant. Safe. Solarium.
Tours arranged.* Room services *Air-conditioning. Hair-
dryer. Jacuzzi in suites. Mini-bar. Radio. Room service
(24-hour). Telephone. TV.*

Eden

*Via Ludovisi, 49 (47 81 21/toll-free reservations 16 78
20 088 from within Italy only/fax 48 21 584). Metro
Spagna/bus to Via Veneto.* Rates *(breakfast* L35,000-
L50,000 extra) *single* L495,000-L539,000; *double* L726,000-
L847,000; *suites* L1,595,000-L2,420,000; *royal suite*
L3,267,000. Credit *All major cards*
Situated just off the Via Veneto, the recently refurbished
Eden, part of the Forte group, has opulent reception rooms,
tastefully decorated bedrooms, and a roof terrace with a top-
rate restaurant and one of the most spectacular views over
Rome. A home-from-home for Tom Cruise and Nicole
Kidman (but so it was for Kenneth Branagh and Emma
Thompson as well... perhaps not a great omen for marital
bliss). Popular with business travellers.
Hotel services *Banqueting/conference facilities for up
to 120. Bars. Car rental. Currency exchange. Dry
cleaning. Garage nearby. Gym. Laundry. Reservations for
airlines, theatres. Restaurant. Secretarial
assistance.Wheelchair access.* Room services *Air-
conditioning. Fax and PC point. Hair dryer. Mini-bar.
Phone. Satellite TV. Radio. Safe.*

Excelsior

*Via Vittorio Veneto, 125 (47 081/fax 48 26 205/telex 61
02 32). Metro Barberini/bus to Via Vittorio Veneto.*
Rates *(breakfast* L33,000-L53,900 extra) *single* L357,500-
533,500; *double* L495,000-814,000; *suite* L1,210,000-
L1,925,000. Credit *AmEx, DC, EC, JCB, MC,V.*
Arguably the most splendid hotel in Rome. The entrance and
bar are decorated in luxurious turn-of-the-century blue and
gold, with thick carpets, chandeliers, swathing drapes and
antique clocks and furniture. Upstairs, the 377 bedrooms are
more Hollywood historic fantasy than genuine stately home;
they were redone for the 1990 World Cup in three colour

Feast of **Eden**: *something's cooking at Rome's celebrity hotel.*

schemes with matching, marble-rich bathrooms. Staff and management are appropriately attentive.

Hotel services *Air-conditioning. Babysitting. Bar. Beauty salon. Car park (nearby garage). Conference facilities (for up to 500). Currency exchange. Fax. Laundry. Lifts. Multi-lingual staff. Non-smoking rooms. Restaurant.* **Room services** *Air-conditioning. Hair dryer. Mini-bar. Radio. Room service (24-hour). Safe (in reception). Telephone. TV (satellite).*

Le Grand Hotel

Via Vittorio Emanuele Orlando, 3 (47 091/fax 47 47 307/telex 61 02 10). Metro Repubblica/bus to Piazza della Repubblica. **Rates** (breakfast L33,000 extra) *single* L418,000-L462,000; *double* L638,000-L704,000. **Credit** AmEx, DC, EC, JCB, MC,V.

Although somewhat overshadowed by its sister, the Excelsior on Via Veneto, the 170-room Grand is still one of the stateliest hotels in Rome, built in an era when public rooms and bedrooms were BIG. The ornate décor, with its columns and stucco relief, is fading, but the bedrooms have antique furniture and all is magnificently luxurious.

Hotel services *Air-conditioning. Babysitting. Car park (extra charge). Conference facilities (for up to 600). Currency exchange. Fax. Laundry. Lifts. Multi-lingual staff. Non-smoking rooms. Restaurant (with no-smoking section). Wheelchair access (contact manager).* **Room services** *Air-conditioning. Hair dryer. Mini-bar. Radio. Room service (24-hour). Safe for each room, in reception). Telephone. TV (satellite).*

Hassler Villa Medici

Piazza Trinità dei Monti, 6 (69 93 40/fax 67 89 991/telex 61 02 08). Metro Spagna. **Rates** (breakfast L34,000-L52,000 extra) *single* L650,000; *double* L980,000; *suite* L1,600,000-3,300,000. **Credit** AmEx, DC, EC, JCB, MC, V.

This hotel is marvellously located a few paces from the top of the Spanish Steps, and the views are tremendous. Opened in the late nineteenth century, the Hassler used to be *the* place to stay for visiting royalty and jet-setters; today it is more popular with business travellers and rich tourists. The 100 bedrooms are soothingly decorated with aged wood and marble. The rooftop terrace and restaurant have splendid views, and art exhibitions are sometimes held in the foyer.

Hotel services *Air-conditioning. Babysitting. Bars. Car park. Conference facilities. Currency exchange. Fax. Interpreters. Laundry. Lifts. Multi-lingual staff. Secretarial services. Tours arranged.* **Room services** *Air-conditioning. Hair dryer. Mini-bar. Radio. Room service (24-hour). Safe (in reception). Telephone. TV (satellite).*

Holiday Inn Crowne Plaza Minerva Roma

Piazza della Minerva, 69 (69 94 18 88/fax 67 94 165/telex 62 00 91 HINMIN). Bus to Largo di Torre Argentina. **Rates** (breakfast L33,000 extra) *single* L435,000; *double* L600,000; *suite* L990,000-L2,200,000 **Credit** AmEx, DC, EC, JCB, MC, V.

Not many hotels, even in Rome, have Bernini statues right outside their front doors. This one has an elephant (*see chapter* **Sightseeing**) and is within spitting distance of the Pantheon. The Holiday Inn chain took over this seventeenth-century *albergo* in the late 1980s and brought in Paolo Portoghesi to redesign the public rooms in post-modern style, with truckloads of marble, stained glass and neo-classical motifs. Most of the 133 bedrooms and suites are standard Holiday Inn fare. Not very atmospheric.

Hotel services *Air-conditioning. Babysitting. Bars. Conference facilities (for up to 120). Currency exchange.*

The best hotels for...

Sleeping like a monk

Head for the **Columbus** (*see* **Upper Range**), a one-time monastery next to Saint Peter's. The narrow beds are designed for the abstemious or the strictly missionary.

Sado-masochists

You'll need to bring your own whips and chains, but if rooms with padded walls and/or mirrored ceilings are your thing, the swish **Valadier** (*see* **De Luxe**) provides them at no extra charge.

Honeymooners (and other romantics)

Close to the house where Keats expired in 1821, the romantic setting, rambling staircases and intimate rooms of the **Scalinata di Spagna** (*see* **Upper Range**) provide a perfect setting for starry-eyed lovers.

Unrestrained opulence

At the **Excelsior** (*see* **De Luxe**), over-the-top views meet marble-clad bathrooms and glitz décor which owes more to Hollywood than ancient Rome.

A quick getaway

Right next to the station, the **Tony** (*see* **Budget**) will keep your bags locked up safe and sound while you dash off to Florence or Naples.

That Roman market experience

The **Manara** (*see* **Budget**) is a good no-frills cheap base but definitely not for light sleepers: it's right next to the market in Piazza San Cosimato.

Breakfasting in ruins

Caffè and *cornetti* are served up in a section of the first century BC Theatre of Pompey at the **Teatro di Pompeo** (*see* **Upper Range**).

...and Dining like an Emperor

The **Forum** (*see* **Upper Range**) rooftop restaurant gives you the opportunity to play Caesar, living it up while looking out over the Imperial Fora. All together now: 'Infamy! Infamy! They've all got it in for me!'

The **Excelsior** *shouts opulence.*

Take tea in the d'Inghilterra.

Fax. Fitness room. Laundry. Lifts. Multi-lingual staff. Non-smoking rooms. Restaurants. Wheelchair access. **Room services** *Air-conditioning. Hair dryer. Mini-bar. Radio. Room service. One room for disabled. Safe. Telephone. TV (satellite).*

d'Inghilterra

Via Bocca di Leone, 14 (69 981/fax 69 92 22 43/telex 61 45 52 HOTING). Metro Spagna. **Rates** (breakfast L30,000 extra) *single* L425,000; *double* L632,000; *suite* L1,093,000. **Credit** AmEx, DC, EC, JCB, MC, V.
Founded in the middle of the last century, this dignified hotel takes both itself and its illustrious past very seriously (Twain, Hemingway, Mendelssohn and Liszt all stayed here). It is indeed a splendid place, set in a quietish street near Piazza di Spagna and decorated in a colonial English style. The public rooms are particularly opulent, while the 105 bedrooms are relentlessly tasteful. Some have balconies but they can be rather cramped. **Hotel services** *Air-conditioning. Babysitting. Bars. Car park (nearby, pay extra). Currency exchange. Fax. Laundry. Lift. Multi-lingual staff. Restaurants. Wheelchair access.* **Room services** *Air-conditioning. Hair dryer. Mini-bar. Room service. Safe. Telephone. TV (satellite).*

Majestic

Via Vittorio Veneto, 50 (48 68 41/fax48 80 984). Metro Barberini/bus to Via Vittorio Veneto. **Rates** (breakfast L20,000 extra) *single* L480,000; *double* L640,000. **Credit** AmEx, DC, EC, JCB, MC, V.
A peaceful but rather formal atmosphere. The downstairs lounge is richly furnished in eighteenth-century style, with thick velvet curtains and grandiose flower arrangements. The 95 bedrooms (including the Madonna suite) are more modern, with striped wallpaper and big, glitzy bathrooms. **Hotel services** *Air-conditioning. Babysitting. Bar. Car park (extra charge). Currency exchange. Fax. Laundry. Lifts. Multi-lingual staff. Restaurant. Wheelchair access.* **Room services** *Air-conditioning. Hair dryer. Mini-bar. Radio. Room service. Safe. Telephone. TV.*

Plaza

Via del Corso, 126 (69 92 11 11/fax 69 94 15 75). Metro Spagna/bus to Piazzale Flaminio or Piazza San Silvestro. **Rates** (breakfast L23,000 extra) *single* L315,000-L370,000; *double* L490,000-L540,000. **Credit** AmEx, DC, MC, V.
The staircase that leads up from the rococo-style lounge is decorated with carved lions, and has probably been trodden by more famous feet than any other in Rome. There are 229

bedrooms and those on the upper storeys have little private terraces. The roof terrace is for the use of all the guests. **Hotel services** *Air-conditioning. Bar. Currency exchange. Fax. Lifts. Multi-lingual staff. Restaurant. Wheelchair access.* **Room services** *Air-conditioning. Hair dryer. Mini-bar. Radio. Room service. Telephone. TV.*

Valadier

Via della Fontanella, 15 (36 11 998/fax 32 01 558). Bus to Corso del Rinascimento. **Rates** *single* L390,000; *double* L490,000. **Credit** AmEx, DC, EC, MC, V.
This quiet, exclusive hotel, close to Augustus' tomb and the Ara Pacis, prides itself on being a romantic hideaway, and has an appropriately seductive atmosphere. The 40 bedrooms are slickly decorated and well-equipped. Narcissists and sado-masochists take note that some rooms have mirrors on the ceiling and padded walls. **Hotel services** *Air-conditioning. Babysitting. Bar. Lift. Multi-lingual staff. Restaurant.* **Room services** *Air-conditioning. Hair dryer. Mini-bar. Radio. Room service. Safe. Telephone. TV (satellite).*

Upper Range

Carriage

Via delle Carrozze, 36 (69 90 124/fax 67 88 279). Metro Spagna/bus to Via del Corso. **Rates** *single* L245,000; *double* L315,000; *triple* L395,000; *suite* L520,000. **Credit** AmEx, DC, EC, JCB, MC, V,
A pretty, comfortable hotel in the middle of the exclusive shopping area near Piazza di Spagna, situated in one of Rome's quieter streets. The 27 bedrooms are furnished with reproduction antiques and brass bedsteads, and there are several small suites for up to four people. As well as a breakfast room, there is a small terrace, and a few of the rooms have private patios. **Hotel services** *Air-conditioning. Babysitting. Fax (during office hours). Laundry. Lifts. Multi-lingual staff. Restaurant. Wheelchair access.* **Room services** *Air-conditioning. Hair dryer. Mini-bar. Radio. TV.*

Columbus

Via della Conciliazione, 33 (68 65 435/fax 68 64 874). Bus to Via della Conciliazione or Via dei Corridori. **Rates** *single* L230,000; *double* L320,000. **Credit** AmEx, DC, EC, MC, V.
Housed in an ivy-clad ex-monastery (the dining room occupies the former refectory) the Columbus is just in front of

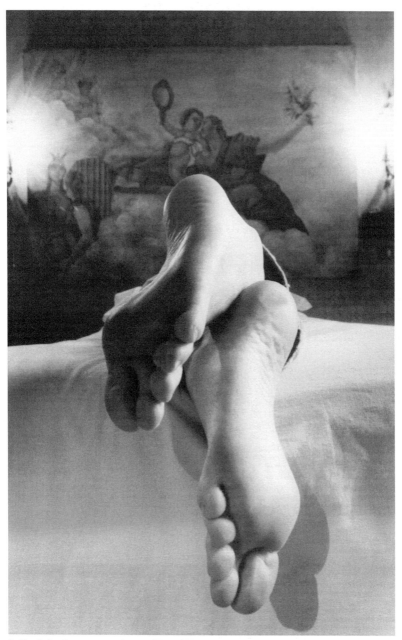

In the **Celio** *they come and go, talking of Michelangelo. See page 118.*

Saint Peter's Square and ideal for those who want to watch the continuous comings and goings of tourists and pilgrims to the Vatican. It has a quiet old-fashioned atmosphere.
Hotel services *Air-conditioning. Babysitting. Bar. Car park. Currency exchange. Fax. Laundry. Lifts. Multi-lingual staff. Restaurant. Wheelchair access.* **Room services** *Air-conditioning. Hair dryer. Mini-bar. Radio. TV.*

Due Torri

Vicolo del Leonetto, 23/25 (68 80 69 56/fax 68 65 442). Bus to Corso del Rinascimento. **Rates** *single* L190,000; *double* L295,000. **Credit** AmEx, DC, EC, JCB, MC, V.
Well-placed for those who want a peaceful central hotel in a quiet alley near Piazza Navona. The 26 bedrooms and bathrooms are pretty (if a little small), while the downstairs public rooms (including the breakfast room) are comfortable and gracious, having been redecorated in Italian-English country-house style. The staff are very friendly and helpful.
Hotel services *Air-conditioning. Babysitting. Bar. Car park (nearby garage, extra charge). Currency exchange. Fax. Laundry. Lifts. Multi-lingual staff.* **Room services** *Air-conditioning. Hair dryer. Mini-bar. Radio. Room service. Safe (for each room, in reception). Telephone. TV.*

Fontana

Piazza di Trevi, 96 (67 86 113/fax 67 90 024). Bus to Piazza San Silvestro. **Rates** *single* L260,000; *double* L300,000. **Credit** AmEx, DC, EC, MC, V.
A great place, unless you want peace and quiet – the Fontana is so close to the Trevi Fountain that you could almost dive in from some of the rooms. The noise of rushing water and shrieking tourists is overwhelming, but the rooms, all in shapes and sizes to fit into the rambling building, are bright and spacious.
Hotel services *Babysitting. Bar. Currency exchange. Fax. Laundry. Lift. Multi-lingual staff. Safe.* **Room services** *Hair dryer (from reception). Room service. Telephone. TV.*

Forum

Via Tor de' Conti, 25 (67 92 446/fax 67 86 479/telex 62 25 49). Metro Cavour/bus to Via Cavour and Via dei Fori Imperiali. **Rates** *(breakfast L25,000 extra) single* L350,000; *double* L510,000. **Credit** AmEx, DC, EC, MC, V.
A very civilised, calm hotel in the remains of a Renaissance palace just behind the Imperial Fora. The low-ceilinged downstairs lounge was refurbished recently and is particularly relaxing for a post sight-seeing drink, while the rooftop restaurant gives excellent views over the city. The 76 bedrooms are luxurious and comfortable.
Hotel services *Air-conditioning. Babysitting. Bar. Car park. Conference facilities (up to 150). Currency exchange. Fax. Laundry. Lifts. Multi-lingual staff. Restaurant.* **Room services** *Air-conditioning. Hair dryer. Radio. Room service. Safe. Telephone. TV.*

Raphael

Largo Febo, 2 (68 28 31/fax 68 78 993/telex 62 23 96 RHOTEL I). Bus to Corso Rinascimento. **Rates** *single* L385,000; *double* L555,000; *suite* L710,000. **Credit** AmEx, DC, MC, V.
The owner has filled the interior of his stately, ivy-draped building with antiques, and the 63 bedrooms are all individually decorated with pictures and well-chosen furniture. The Raphael is close to the Senate in Palazzo Madama and has long been popular with politicians.
Hotel services *Air-conditioning. Babysitting. Bars. Currency exchange. Fax. Lanundry. Lifts. Multi-lingual staff. Non-smoking rooms. Restaurants.* **Room services** *Air-conditioning. Hair dryer. Mini-bar. Room service. Safe (in reception). Telephone. TV (satellite).*

La Residenza

Via Emilia, 22-24 (48 80 789/fax 48 57 21) Metro Barberini/bus to Via Veneto. **Rates** *single* L140,000; *double* L295,000; *junior suite* L340,000. **Credit** AmEx, MC, V.

As its name suggests, this quiet 28-room hotel prides itself on being like a (rather grand) private home. The colour scheme is soothing and the furniture is there to be used, although the overall tone is hushed and formal. Some of the rooms have terraces, and all are well-equipped for this price range. There is also a roof garden. A good choice for those who want tranquillity near the city centre.
Hotel services *Air-conditioning. Bar. Car park (nearby garage). Currency exchange. Fax. Jacuzzi. Laundry. Lifts. Multi-lingual staff. Massage. Sunbed.* **Room services** *Air-conditioning. Hair dryer. Mini-bar. Radio. Room service (no food). Safe (in reception). Telephone. TV (satellite).*

Scalinata di Spagna

Piazza Trinità dei Monti, 17 (69 94 08 96/fax 69 94 05 98). Metro Spagna/bus to Piazza Barberini. **Rates** *single* L350,000; *double* L420,000; *triple* L480,000; *suite* L700,000. **Credit** AmEx, DC, MC, V.
One of the most romantic hotel settings in Rome, at the top of the Spanish Steps looking down over Keats' house to Piazza di Spagna. It's lovely inside, with lovely rambling staircases and antiques tucked away in corners. The 15 bedrooms are pleasantly old-fashioned, even though a few are rather small. There's a wonderfully secluded roof garden. A quiet, friendly, informal hotel, very popular with Americans.
Hotel services *Air-conditioning. Babysitting. Car park (nearby, extra charge). Currency exchange. Fax. Laundry. Multi-lingual staff.* **Room services** *Air-conditioning. Hair dryer. Mini bar. Room service (24-hour). Safe. Telephone. TV.*

Sole al Pantheon

Piazza della Rotonda, 63 (67 80 441/fax 69 94 0689). Bus to Largo di Torre Argentina. **Rates** *single* L350,000; *double* L490,000; *suite* L580,000. **Credit** AmEx, DC, EC, MC, V.
This attractive hotel traces its history back to 1467 and former guests range from the Renaissance poet Ludovico Ariosto to philosopher Jean-Paul Sartre. The hotel has been sensitively refurbished, with white walls, terracotta tiles and tasteful frescoes. Bedrooms are cool and fresh, with reproduction antique beds and soft colour schemes; some still have their original painted ceilings. Ten of the 27 rooms have spectacular views of the Pantheon.
Hotel services *Air-conditioning. Babysitting. Bar. Currency exchange. Fax. Laundry. Lifts. Multi-lingual staff.* **Room services** *Air-conditioning. Hair dryer. Jacuzzi in most rooms. Mini-bar. Radio. Room service (24-hour). Safe. Telephone. TV.*

Teatro di Pompeo

Largo del Pallaro, 8 (68 72 566/fax 68 80 55 31). Bus to Corso Vittorio Emanuele. **Rates** *single* L210,000; *double* L270,000. **Credit** AmEx, DC, EC, MC, V.
A Campo de' Fiori hotel that's a bit smarter than its neighbours and has kept it's prices stable. It can claim, at least in part, to be the oldest hotel in Rome: you can take breakfast in what was part of the Theatre of Pompey, from the first century BC. The décor of the bar and 12 bedrooms is pleasantly unfussy.
Hotel services *Air-conditioning. Bar. Conference facilities. Fax. Laundry. Lift. Multi-lingual staff.* **Room services** *Air-conditioning. Hair dryer (on request). Mini-bar. Radio. Room service. Safe. Telephone. TV (satellite).*

Moderate

Aventino

Via San Domenico, 10 (57 45 232/fax 57 83 604). Metro Circo Massimo/bus to Viale Aventino. **Rates** *single* L130,000; *double* L190,000; *triple* L210,000; *quad* L250,000. **Credit** AmEx, MC, V.
One of the cheaper hotels in the quiet, gorgeously green residential area of the Aventino. Like many of its neigh-

bours, it occupies a villa and is surrounded by a beautiful garden. Each of the 23 good-sized, comfortable bedrooms has its own bathroom. Although it's slightly off the beaten track, Trastevere and Testaccio are only a short distance away.
Hotel services *Babysitting. Bar. Car park (nearby, extra charge). Fax. Laundry. Multi-lingual staff.* **Room services** *Room service. Telephone.*

Campo de' Fiori

Via del Biscione, 6 (68 80 68 65/fax 68 76 003). Bus to Corso Vittorio Emanuele. **Rates** *single without bath* L90,000; *single* L160,000; *double without bath* L130,000; *double* L190,000; *triple* L240,000. **Credit** MC, V.
Housed in an ochre palazzo, this 27-room hotel has loads of character. Not only is there a roof terrace with good views of the *centro storico*, but the entrance is lined with mirrors and columns to create a kaleidoscopic *trompe l'œil* effect as you struggle in with your suitcases. The bedrooms are small and imaginatively decorated, some with ceiling paintings. Only a third of the rooms have their own bathrooms, but four more have box showers. There's no bar, but cold drinks are available from the reception.
Hotel services *Currency exchange. Fax. Multi-lingual staff.* **Room services** *Radio. Telephone.*

Celio

Via SS Quattro, 35c (70 49 53 33/fax 70 96 377). Metro Colosseo. **Rates** *single* L250,000; *double* L290,000. **Credit** MC, V
This small hotel, a stone's throw from the Colosseum, is a gem of tasteful decoration and comfort. Owned and run by a group of enthusiastic young people, the hotel's 10 rooms are beautifully frescoed with details inspired by Renaissance masters, and everything – from the soft furnishings to the bathroom fittings – is designed to please the eye. Breakfast is served in bedrooms.
Hotel services *Air-conditioning. Babysitting. Bar. Car park (nearby, extra cost). Currency exchange. Fax. Laundry. Multi-lingual staff. Non-smoking rooms. 24-hour room service.* **Room services** *Air conditioning. Hair dryer. Mini-bar. TV. Video.*

Domus Aventina

Via di Santa Prisca, 11b (57 46 135/fax 57 30 00 44). Metro Circo Massimo/bus to Viale Aventino. **Rates** *single* L200,000; *double* L300,000. **Credit** AmEx, DC, EC, MC, V.
Domus Aventina is right next to the church of Santa Prisca, and has lovely views of the cloisters from many of the the bedrooms and from its own roof terrace. Public rooms are frescoed with *trompe l'œil* views of Rome. The 25 spacious bedrooms (some with balcony) are painted soothing pinky colours and furnished with reproduction antiques. The owners and staff are friendly and attentive.
Hotel services *Air-conditioning. Bar. Car park (in public car park). Fax. Laundry.* **Room services** *Air-conditioning. Hair dryer. Mini-bar. Radio. Room service (24 hour). Telephone. TV (satellite).*

Hotel Locarno

Via della Penna, 22 (36 10 841/fax 32 15 249). Metro Flaminio. **Rates** *single* L195,000; *double* L290,000; *triple* L380,000; *suite* L360,000. **Credit** AmEx, DC, EC, MC, V.
The Locarno, on a noisy road between the Tiber and Piazza del Popolo, was founded in the 1920s and retains some original art nouveau details and accessories: a Tiffany lamp and grandfather clock in reception, and a wrought-iron cage lift. The lounge has a real fire in winter; there's also a lovely patio with a fountain. More than half of the 38 rooms and suites have been refurbished with parquet floors and green marble bathrooms, and the rest will be finished shortly. Regulars include film director Peter Greenaway.
Hotel services *Bar. Bicycles (free for guests). Garage (extra charge). Winter garden.* **Room services** *Air-conditioning. Mini-bar. Radio. Safe. Telephone. TV (satellite).*

Hotel Portoghesi

Via dei Portoghesi, 1 (68 64 231/fax 68 76 976). Bus to Corso Rinascimento. **Rates** *single* L170,000; *double* L250,000; *suite* L300,000. **Credit** MC, V.
A peaceful 27-room hotel in the heart of the *centro storico*, a couple of minutes away from Piazza Navona. Public rooms and bedrooms have quality reproduction and antique furniture, and now that the hotel has been restored all bedrooms have showers, and five have baths. There's a roof terrace and you can buy drinks from reception.
Hotel services *Air-conditioning. Currency exchange. Fax. Laundry. Lift. Multi-lingual staff.* **Room services** *Air-conditioning. Hair dryer. Room service. Telephone. TV.*

Marghera

Via Marghera, 29 (44 57 184/fax 44 62 539). Metro Termini/bus or tram to Termini. **Rates** (breakfast L25,000 extra) *single* L190,00; *double* L240,000. **Credit** MC, V.
This hotel opposite the main Italian tourist office has 20 spotlessly clean bedrooms, with white bedspreads and huge fat pillows. The atmosphere is calm and civilized; the owner and much of the clientele are musicians and you may occasionally hear gentle strumming from the other rooms.
Hotel services *Air-conditioning. Babysitting. Bar. Car park. Fax. Laundry. Lifts. Multi-lingual staff.* **Room services** *Air-conditioning. Hair dryer. Mini-bar. Radio. Room service (for breakfast). Telephone. Trouser press. TV. Video.*

Margutta

Via Laurina, 34 (32 23 674/fax 320 03 95). Metro Spagna/bus to Piazzale Flaminio. **Rates** *double* L147,000; *triple* L195,000. **Credit** AmEx, DC, EC, MC, V.
A very reasonable, quiet hotel in an expensive part of town. Don't be put off by the rather utilitarian reception and breakfast areas: all 24 rooms have been refurbished and are bright and sunny. A few rooms on the top floor open out onto a balcony. Three rooms on the ground floor can be adapted for wheelchair access.
Hotel services *Babysitting. Bar. Car park (on Piazza del Popolo). Currency exchange. Laundry. Lifts. Multi-lingual Staff. Wheelchair access.* **Room services** *Rooms for disabled. Telephone.*

Nerva

Via Tor de' Conti, 3 (67 81 835/fax 69 92 22 04). Metro Cavour/bus to Piazza Venezia. **Rates** *single* L220,000; *double* L325,000. **Credit** AmEx, DC, EC, MC, V.
Although the two proprietors don't speak very good English, they're kind and welcoming. The rooms have been beautifully refurbished without losing their original features, and every one is different: some look out onto Nerva's Forum, some onto pretty courtyards, and from others you can see the Palatine. Facilities for disabled travellers are excellent.
Hotel services *Bar. Multi-lingual staff.* **Room services** *Air-conditioning. Rooms for disabled (two). Safe.*

Ponte Sisto

Via dei Pettinari, 64 (68 68 843/fax 68 30 88 22/telex 63 00 54). Bus to Lungotevere dei Tebaldi, Via Arenula. **Rates** *single* L175,000; *double* L218,000; *triple* L278,000. **Credit** AmEx, DC, EC, MC, V.
With 130 rooms, this is the largest hotel in the Campo de' Fiori area. The public rooms have been restored, albeit not very tastefully – the hotel caters for tourist groups and feels like a waiting room. There is a huge, shady terrace in the pleasant courtyard where you can down a drink. The bedrooms, decorated with imitation French-style antiques are a reasonable size, although they have fewer facilities than other hotels in the same class. Bathrooms are also a good size and spotless. The hotel is very well-placed for restaurants and bars between Campo de' Fiori and Trastevere, just over the Ponte Sisto. Some of the rooms are adapted for wheelchair users.

Hotel services *Babysitting. Bar (open 24 hours). Car park. Conference facilities (up to 60). Fax. Laundry. Lifts. Multi-lingual staff. Restaurant. Safe. Wheelchair access.* Room services *Rooms for disabled. Telephone. TV.*

Rinascimento

Via del Pellegrino, 122 (68 74 814/fax 68 33 518). Bus to Corso Vittorio Emanuele. Rates *single* L130,000-L150,000; *double* L190,000-L230,000. Credit DC.

Housed in an appealing old palazzo in the heart of the Campo de' Fiori district, the Rinascimento has refurbished its 18 rooms, all of which (in spite of small bathrooms) are equipped well for the price range. As well as a small bar-cum-breakfast room, there is a fourth-floor terrace.

Hotel Services *Air-conditioning. Bar. Fax. Laundry. Lift.* Room services *Air-conditioning. Mini-bar. Radio. Telephone. TV (satellite).*

La Rovere

Vicolo Sant'Onofrio, 5 (68 80 67 39/fax 68 80 70 62). Bus to Lungotevere Gianicolense. Rates *single* L180,000; *double* L190,000-L240,000. Credit MC, V.

Tucked up a cutesy alley off the Lungotevere Gianicolense, this former *pensione*, which has been upgraded to a three-star hotel, is well-placed for Saint Peter's and the Vatican, although there aren't many places to eat in the immediate area (Trastevere is about a 20-minute walk away). There are 18 pretty rooms with flowered carpets, and new bathrooms equipped with hair dryers. Reception is open 24 hours. As we went to press, we received one complaint about rooms being left uncleaned, but hopefully it's just a blip.

Hotel services *Bar. Car park. Currency exchange. Multi-lingual staff. Non-smoking rooms. Safe.* Room services *Hair dryer.*

Sant'Anselmo

Piazza Sant'Anselmo, 2 (57 83 214/fax 57 83 604). Metro Circo Massimo. Rates *single* L170,000; *double* L250,000; *triple* L270,000; *quad* L310,000. Credit AmEx, DC, MC, V.

An exceptionally pretty hotel, housed in a villa with a garden, and owned by the same company as the **Aventino**. Some of the 46 bedrooms are furnished with antiques, and all but six have their own bathrooms. It is one of the few Roman hotels to have rooms adapted for wheelchair access.

Hotel services *Babysitting. Currency exchange. Fax. Laundry. Multi-lingual staff. Wheelchair access.* Room services *Room service. One room for disabled. Telephone. TV (on request).*

Villa Borghese

Via Pinciana, 31 (85 30 09 19/fax 84 14 100). Bus to Via Pinciana, Via Po. Rates *single* L170,000-L200,000; *double* L220,000-L260,000; *triple* L255,000-L295,000; *suite* L280,000-L335,000. Credit AmEx, DC, MC, V.

Once the family home of writer Alberto Moravia (who was born here), this cosy, friendly hotel overlooking the Villa Borghese park retains a country house feel. Recently refurbished, the public rooms are intimate and beautifully decorated with Persian rugs and chintzy soft furnishings the walls decked with original prints, paintings and drawings by the assistant manager. The 22 rooms of varying size and colour are similarly tasteful. There is an ivy-draped patio.

Hotel services *Air-conditioning. Bar. Lift. Multi-lingual staff.* Room services *Air-conditioning. Hair dryer (on request). Mini-bar. Radio. Room service. Telephone. TV.*

Villa del Parco

Via Nomentana, 110 (44 23 77 73/fax 44 23 75 72). Bus to Via Nomentana. Rates *single* L192,000; *double* L246,000. Credit AmEx, DC, EC, JCB, MC, V.

Rare decorative flourish at the **Casa Kolbe**.

Further from the *centro storico* (a short bus ride away) than most listed here, the hotel occupies an attractive nineteenth-century villa surrounded by gardens. Bedrooms are a good size and furnished with antique and near-antique furniture.

Hotel services *Air-conditioning. Bar. Car park. Conference facilities (meeting room). Currency exchange. Lift. Multi-lingual staff.* Room services *Air-conditioning. Mini-bar. Radio. Room service. Telephone. TV.*

Villa delle Rose

Via Vicenza, 5 (44 51 788/795/fax 44 51 639). Metro Termini/bus or tram to Termini. Rates *single* L190,000; *double* L260,000. Credit AmEx, DC, EC, JCB, MC, V.

A relaxed, family-run hotel, housed in a villa and with its own garden (a rarity so close to Termini). All 40 bedrooms have their own bathroom and some have air-conditioning. Although the décor is a bit stark, some of the rooms are split level, giving them a spacious feel and allowing for extra beds.

Hotel services *Babysitting. Bar. Fax. Laundry. Lifts. Multi-lingual staff. Non-smoking breakfast room.* Room services *Room service. Telephone. TV.*

Villa San Pio

Via San Anselmo, 19 (57 45 174/fax 57 83 604). Metro Circo Massimo. Rates *single* L170,000; *double* L250,000; *triple* L270,000; *quad* L310,000. Credit AmEx, MC, V.

A tranquil Aventine hotel with a country house feel set in a beautiful garden full of classical statuary. The ochre villa is well decorated and some of the 62 pretty bedrooms have floral stencils and embroidered soft furnishings.

Hotel services *Drinks in the garden. Lift.* Room services *Room service. Telephone.*

Budget

Abruzzi

Piazza della Rotonda, 69 (67 92 021). Bus to Largo di Torre Argentina. **Rates** *single without bath L68,000-87,000; double without bath L100,000-120,000.*
No credit cards.
The facilities in this 25-room hotel are basic (there are only eight bathrooms) but the rooms are a good size and several have a view of the Pantheon. It's an interesting old building, but ask for a room at the back if you want peace at night.
Hotel services *Multi-lingual staff.*

Casa Kolbe

Via San Teodoro, 44 (67 94 974/fax 69 94 15 50). Bus to Piazza Bocca della Verità. **Rates** *single L90,000; double L115,000.* **Credit** AmEx, MC, V.
A large hotel standing underneath the Palatine and providing excellent value for money. All 69 rooms have bathrooms and, although the interior is spartan, there is a large, pleasant garden and a dependable restaurant (special rates for full- and half-board). Helpful staff.
Hotel services *Bar. Conference room. Laundry. Restaurant.* **Room services** *Telephone.*

Fawlty Towers

Via Magenta, 39 (44 50 374). Metro Termini/bus to Termini. **Rates** *double without bath L75,000; double L100,000; dormitory L30,000-L35,000 per person.*
No credit cards.
A budget choice that is part *pensione* and part hostel. Guests can choose to share a room with up to two others or opt to have their own. The homely atmosphere makes it easy to forget you're only a stone's throw from Termini. There is a bright, friendly sitting room and terrace, a wide selection of English-language guides to Rome, paperbacks and satellite TV. It's a good base for anyone travelling alone and it has no curfew. Just don't mention the war.
Hotel services *Fridge. Microwave. Multi-lingual staff. Terrace. TV (satellite).*

Fiorella

Via del Babuino, 196 (36 10 597). Metro Spagna/bus 117. **Rates** *single without bath L59,000; double without bath L95,000.* **No credit cards.**
One of the very few cheap places to stay in this exclusive part of town, the Fiorella has eight bright, spacious bedrooms which share two bathrooms. All immaculately kept by the family owners, who have a parking permit which they lend to guests. The hotel shuts at 1am.
Hotel services *Multi-lingual staff.*

della Lunetta

Piazza del Paradiso, 68 (68 61 080/fax 68 92 028). Bus to Corso Vittorio Emanuele. **Rates** *single without bath L60,000; single L80,000; double without bath L100,000; double L140,000; triple without bath L135,000; triple L180,000.* **Credit** EC, MC, V.
A rambling, shabby old building, well-placed in the *centro-storico.* Almost half the 30 rooms have their own bathroom. There is a large lounge with TV downstairs, and several small sitting areas tucked away in the upstairs corridors. It's popular with student groups. No breakfast.
Hotel services *Multi-lingual staff.*
Room services *Telephone.*

Manara

Via Luciano Manara, 25 (58 14 713). Bus to Piazza Sonnino or Viale Trastevere. **Rates** *double without bath L65,000; triple without bath L85,000.* **Credit** AmEx, MC, V.
A very friendly, cheap *pensione,* well placed for the clubs and bars of Trastevere (all guests are supplied with a night key) and within walking distance of the *centro storico* on the other side of the river. The building retains an old-fashioned

ambience, although most of the furniture is recent. At the moment there is only one bathroom shared between the seven bright and breezy bedrooms – which are a pleasant surprise after the gloomy entrance.
Hotel services *Lifts. Multi-lingual staff.*

Mimosa

Via di Santa Chiara, 61 (68 80 17 53/fax 68 33 557). Bus to Largo di Torre Argentina. **Rates** *single without bath L70,000; double without bath L105,000; double L130,000; triple L150,000.* **No credit cards.**
It may not have the most beautiful interior in Rome, but the Mimosa is comfortable, clean, well-run, keen to have more British clientele and smack-bang in the *centro storico.* Four of the twelve rooms have *en suite* bathrooms, and the others share five between them. As well as a breakfast room, where you can get soft drinks, there are several sitting areas in the corridors. Smoking (and heavy drinking!) are not allowed in the bedrooms.
Hotel services *Currency exchange (US$ only). Non-smoking bedrooms.* **Room services** *Telephone (2 rooms).*

Navona

Via dei Sediari, 8 (68 64 203/fax 68 80 38 02). Bus to Corso del Rinascimento. **Rates** *single L80,000; double without bath L125,000; double L140,000.* **No credit cards.**
There's a friendly, communal atmosphere at this 30-room hotel, which makes it a good choice for lone travellers. Most bedrooms have their own shower. It's also a good place for people with young children: the owners, an Italian woman and her Australian husband, have a child of their own and are very happy to babysit. It's an attractive, romantic old building, close to Piazza Navona; the rooms are spacious and comfortable and the *pensione* is used by several universities during the academic year. There's no bar, but you can buy wine, beer and soft drinks from reception.
Hotel services *Babysitting. Currency exchange. Fax. Multi-lingual staff. Wheelchair access (with help).*

Perugia

Via del Colosseo, 7 (67 97 200/fax67 84 635). Metro Colosseo/bus to Via dei Fori Imperiali or Via Cavour. **Rates** *single without bath L65,000; single L90,000; double without bath L90,000; double L120,000.* **Credit** AmEx, DC, EC, JCB, MC, V.
Friendly without being fussy, conveniently placed between the Colosseum and the Forum and excellent value for its price. Bathrooms have recently been added to all eight of the double rooms, but the three singles don't have their own facilities. Some of the rooms have been refurbished, and everything is spotlessly clean. No breakfast.
Hotel services *Multi-lingual staff.*
Room services *Telephone.*

Piccolo

Via dei Chiavari, 32 (68 80 25 60). Bus to Corso Vittorio Emanuele. **Rates** (breakfast L7,000 extra) *single without bath L110,000; double without bath L120,000; double L150,000.* **Credit** AmEx, MC, V.
A family-run hotel near Campo de' Fiori. All 16 immaculately clean rooms have bidets and, although only three have their own bathroom, five more have shower cabinets in the room. There is a TV in the breakfast room and a 1am curfew.
Hotel services *Bar. Currency exchange.* **Room services** *Telephone.*

Pomezia

Via dei Chiavari, 12 (68 61 371/fax 68 61 371). Bus to Corso Vittorio Emanuele. **Rates** *single without bath L80,000; single L120,000; double without bath L120,000; double L170,000.* **Credit** AmEx, DC, MC, V.
One of a number of excellent cheap hotels near Campo de' Fiori. This one has a small terrace and 11 of its 22 rooms have *en suite* bathrooms. The bedrooms are clean but small.

Unusually for a hotel of this class, there is a small bar in the reception area. The Pomezia is run by a family of three brothers and their mother.
Hotel services *Bar.* **Room services** *Telephone.*

Suisse

Via Gregoriana, 56 (67 83 641/fax 67 81 258). Metro Barberini/bus to Piazza Barberini. **Rates** *(breakfast L15,000 extra) single without bath L80,000; single L95,000; double without bath L95,000; double L130,000.* **No credit cards.**
The Suisse is a reasonably priced hotel in an otherwise luxurious area. All 13 bedrooms are kept spotlessly clean and interestingly decorated; some have their original ceilings and old-fashioned, semi-antique furniture.
Hotel services *Lift.* **Room services** *Telephone.*

Tony-Contilia

Via Principe Amedeo, 79d (44 66 942/fax 44 66 904). Metro Termini or Vittorio Emanuele/bus or tram to Termini. **Rates** *(breakfast L10,000 extra) single L80,000-L120,000; double L100,000-L130,000; triple L120,000-180,000.* **Credit** AmEx, DC, EC, JCB, MC, V.
Not content with its recent upgrading to a two-star hotel, the quiet, fifth-floor Tony (and its cousin Contilia on the second floor) are aiming for three. August 1997 saw the opening of a smart new reception area and breakfast room, with the added facility of a left-luggage room for those using Rome as their base. It's clean, safe and friendly, with plenty of fresh flowers and pleasing prints of Rome. All rooms have bathrooms and guests are given keys to the front door.
Hotel services *Lift. Multi-lingual staff.* **Room services** *Air-conditioning (L20,000 extra). Telephone. TV.*

Hostels

Thanks to the YWCA, women are better served in Rome than men. Women under 27 also have the **Protezione delle Giovane**, which has an office at Termini and a hostel on Via Urbana, if they arrive in Rome with nowhere to stay. *See also chapter* **Women's Rome.**

Ostello della Gioventù Foro Italico

Via delle Olimpiadi, 61 (32 42 571/fax 32 42 613). Bus to Lungotevere Maresciallo Cadorna. **Rates** *bed and breakfast L23,000.* **No credit cards.**
There are 334 beds in dormitories at this neo-brutalist-style building near the Foro Italico, which is a fair distance – though well connected by public transport – from the centre. This is the International Youth Hostel Association's main Rome hostel (standard category), open to members only, although you can join on the spot. There's a garden, restaurant and bar.
Wheelchair access.

Pensione Ottaviano

Via Ottaviano, 6 (39 73 72 53/39 73 81 38). Metro Ottaviano/bus to Piazza Risorgimento. **Rates** L25,000 per bed; L20,000 in winter.
A good alternative for those who don't want to stay in the Termini area. Guests can use the *pensione*'s e-mail.

Pensione Sandy

Via Cavour, 136 (48 84 585). Metro Cavour/bus to Via Cavour. **Rates** L25,000-50,000.
Offers central accommodation in rooms with up to six beds each. Guests all have keys to the front door, so there are no problems with curfews.

Villa Santa Cecilia

Via Argelato, 54 (52 37 16 88/fax 52 37 08 80). Train from Porta San Paolo or Magliana to Vitinia.

Rates *bed and breakfast L40,000; half board L60,000; full board L80,000.* **No credit cards.**
This hostel is a long way from central Rome (at least 20 minutes by train) and there is a midnight curfew, but there's plenty of greenery and it's only a few train stops from the beach at Ostia. It's run by a Catholic organisation, but all the bedrooms (for one, two, three or four people) have their own bathroom, making it feel more like a *pensione*. You can take bed and breakfast and half- or full-board (there's a bar and restaurant). Large groups especially welcome.

YWCA

Via Cesare Balbo, 4 (48 80 460). Metro Termini/bus or tram to Termini. **Rates** *single without bath L50,000; single L70,000; double without bath L80,000; double L100,000; triple/quad L33,000 per person; meals L20,000.* **No credit cards.**
Bedrooms with between one and three beds and a curfew at midnight. It's too close to Termini for comfort, but women travelling alone may feel safer than in a mixed hostel or *pensione.* No breakfast served on Sundays or public holidays.

Self-Catering

If you're staying in Rome for longer than a couple of weeks, especially if there are more than two of you, it's worth considering renting a flat or staying in a residential hotel. They are cheaper than normal hotels and give you more freedom, while offering similar services (your room is cleaned, and there are usually restaurant or bar facilities). The **EPT** office (*see* **Tourist Information** *in chapter* **Tourist Directory**) has a full list, although many are rather far from the centre.

Aldovrandi

Via Aldovrandi, 15 (32 21 430/fax 32 22 181). Bus or tram to Piazza Pitagora. **Rates** *flat for one (monthly) L2,200,000-3,300,000; flat for two (monthly) L4,070,000-6,050,000; flat for three (monthly) L6,600,000.* **Credit** AmEx.
One of the best-equipped residential hotels in Rome is just north of Villa Borghese.
Air-conditioning. Bar. Car park (nearby). Garden. Lift. Radio. Restaurant. Telephone. TV.

Ripa

Via degli Orti di Trastevere, 1 (58 611/fax 58 14 550/telex 61 03 42). Bus to Viale Trastevere. **Rates** *flat for one (fortnightly) L2,400,000; flat for two (fortnightly) L2,850,000; flat for three (weekly) L2,100,000; flat for four (fortnightly) L3,500,000; (monthly) L3,600,000.* **Credit** AmEx, MC, V.
A cross between a standard hotel and residential hotel, Ripa is well-placed if you want to make the most of the nightlife in Testaccio and Trastevere. The facilties are good, and there's access for people in wheelchairs. You can also rent the flats on a daily basis.
Bar. Car park (extra charge). Lift. Restaurant. Telephone. TV. Wheelchair access.

di Ripetta

Via di Ripetta, 231 (32 31 144/fax 32 03 959). Bus to Ponte Cavour. **Rates** *studio flats for 1-2 (weekly) L1,760,000-L1,980,000; 1-2 (fortnightly) L3,080,000-3,520,000; 1-2 (monthly) L4,620,000-5,720,000; flats for 3 (weekly) L2 035,000-L2,200,000; for 3 (fortnightly) L3,410,000-L4,290,000; for 3 (monthly) L5,170,000-L6,600,000.* **Credit** AmEx, MC, V.
A good central location close to Via del Corso, Piazza del Popolo and the *centro storico*.
Air-conditioning. Car park (lock-up garage). Lift.

Restaurants
by Area

Shawerma – *full of Middle Eastern promise. See page 142.*

Central Rome

Centro storico
Acchiappafantasmi (p139); Da Baffetto (p140);
La Carbonara (p133); Il Convivio (p128); Corallo
(p140); Ditirambo (p133); L'Eau Vive (p142); Da
Giggetto (p134); Grappolo d'Oro (p137); L'Insalata
Ricca (p132); Lilli (p137); Monserrato (p134); Al
Pompiere (p136); Sangallo (p131); Il Sanpietrino
(p131); San Teodoro (p136); Settimio al Pellegrino
(p136); Sora Lella (p131); Sora Margherita (p138);
Taverna Giulia (p131); Thien Kim (p142); Tito e
Quirino Fazioli (p138); Trattoria Pizzeria della Pace
(p141); Vecchia Roma (p128).

Tridente
Al 34 (p131); Albistrò (p131); Il Bacaro (p133); Dal
Bolognese (p128); Edy (p133); Fiaschetteria
Beltramme (p133); Fortunato al Pantheon (p129);
Gino in Vicolo Rosini (p137); Margutta (p132); Otello
alla Concordia (p134); PizzaRé (p141); La Rosetta (p128);
Supernatural (p141).

Via Veneto & Quirinal
Papà Baccus (p129); Cantina Cantarini (p136).

Trastevere
Antico Arco (p133); Augusto (p136); La Gensola
(p134); Da Giovanni (p137); L'Isola Felice (p134); Ivo
(p140); Panattoni (p140); Paris (p129); Dar Poeta
(p140); Da Vittorio (p141).

Monti & Esquilino
Africa (p141); Agata e Romeo (p128); Alle Carrette (p140);
Charly's Saucerie (p142); La Cicala e la Formica (p136);
Est! Est! Est! (p140); Il Guru (p142); Hasekura (p142);
Maharajah (p142); Monte Caruso (p129); Il Quadrifoglio
(p131); Sahara (p142).

Testaccio, Celio & Aventino
Checchino dal 1887 (p128); Nel Regno di Re Ferdinando II
(p134); Da Oio a Casa Mia (p137); La Piramide da Maometto
(p142); Pizza Forum (p140); Remo (p141); Shawerma (p142);
Taverna Cestia (p138); La Torricella (p138).

Vatican
Taverna Angelica (p131); Osteria dell'Angelo (p137);
PizzaRé (p141); Ruyi (p141).

Other Areas

San Lorenzo
Arancia Blu (p132); Il Dito e la Luna (p133); Marcello
(p137); Ministero della Pizza (p140); Pommidoro (p136);
Tram Tram (p136).

Northern Suburbs
Al Ceppo (p129); Il Forno della Soffitta (p140); Osteria
del Rione (p138); La Pergola dell'Hotel Hilton (p128);
Sawasdee (p142).

Southern Suburbs
Alfredo a Via Gabi (p131); Betto e Mery (p136).

Restaurants

You can have anything you like – as long as it's Italian.

Eating out in Rome is better than ever before – if you know where to go. Quality, service and wine lists are all improving, but this is still not Bologna or Tuscany, where food culture is so ingrained that it's difficult to go wrong. In order to experience the best of what the Eternal City has to offer, up-to-date inside knowledge is indispensable.

Until six or seven years ago, the scene was dominated by a clique of restaurants with reputations formed in the *Dolce Vita* years, often patronised by expense-account politicians for whom conspicuous consumption was all. These were aided and abetted by the tourist-trap 'fixed menu' brigade, specialising in reheated pasta dishes that were mediocre in four languages. There were, of course, honourable top-of-the-range establishments and numerous family-run *trattorie* serving up honest Roman fare – though the latter were often way out in the suburbs.

Two things have changed. One is the puncturing of the 'expensive means good' myth. Bills the size of an average weekly wage are no longer fashionable, and many restaurants have been forced to choose between offering value for money or going out of business. The move has been encouraged by the Rome restaurateurs' association and by the food monthly *Gambero Rosso*, which has long campaigned against the 'eat what you're given and like it' school of catering. The campaign has already chalked up a major victory. In the spring of 1995, Rome City Council forced the city's restaurateurs to abolish the notorious *pane e coperto* charge, which allowed them to add up to L4,000 a head to your bill for the privilege of a clean tablecloth and a few pieces of stale bread. (Be warned, though: many get around the ban either by ignoring or crossing out *coperto* and leaving *pane*.)

The other force for change has been the emergence of an army of serious local chefs. Many of these were born into the trade – some have been around for years – but the growing demand for quality has forced them to invent new dishes and perfect old ones.

Italy in general and Rome in particular have never taken a *nouvelle* or post-modern approach to food. Cheap, honest *trattorie* are always packed with locals, who eat out at least once a week on average and tend to be discerning gourmands rather than finicky gourmets. When they're not trying to impress, even the capital's journalists, doctors and lawyers favour home cooking over dishes with long French names. The peasant tradition survives: you're just as likely to find a humble dish like *spaghetti cacio e pepe* (spaghetti with seasoned sheeps' cheese and black pepper) in a top-of-the-range restaurant as in a spit-and-sawdust neighbourhood *osteria*.

The regional nature of Italian society means that cuisine from another region is seen almost as foreign, even if the recipes or ingredients are very similar. *La cucina romana* sits heavily on the stomach, and is based on and around offal, a tradition that goes back to ancient times, when the common people were only allowed to eat the leftovers from the patricians' tables. Luckily for vegetarians, though, Roman cuisine also boasts a large selections of salad and vegetable ingredients.

If you're not into Italian food, you've come to the wrong place: Rome is not an international restaurant city. Though Indian, Chinese and Korean restaurants can be found, better can be had elsewhere. The exception to the rule – a consequence of Italy's murky colonial history – is the good range of Eritrean, Somalian and Ethiopian cuisine on offer (*see* **International** *page 141*).

THE MENU

Most meals consist of a *primo* – pasta course; *secondo* – meat or fish course; and *contorno* – cooked vegetables or salad, served separately. An *antipasto* – hors d'œuvre – is often an alternative to a *primo* but may merely precede it, while the *dolce* – dessert – is often missed out altogether. Italian cuisine has relatively few of them.

Unless you're in an upmarket establishment, you're under no pressure to order three or four courses. It's perfectly normal to order a first course followed by a simple salad or a *contorno* (often the only option for vegetarians – *see* **Vegetarian Rome** *page 132*). As a rule, special tourist menus, especially those written in several languages, should be avoided. *See also* **Translating the Menu** *page 126*.

DRINKS

While top-range restaurants generally have respectable wine lists, *trattorie* and *osterie* tend to have a very limited selection, and you will see the same five or six labels of mostly white table wine almost everywhere you go. (*See* **Choosing the Wine** *page 135*.) Most people ask for *il bianco della casa* – the watery, uneventful house white. When they have it at all, house red is usually *Rosso*

Translating the Menu

Meals (pasti)

Prima colazione breakfast; Pranzo lunch; Cena supper; Uno spuntino a snack.

Basics (materie prime)

Aceto vinegar; Latte milk; Limone lemon; Olio d'oliva olive oil; Pane bread; Pepe pepper; Sale salt; Zucchero sugar.

Cooking techniques (modi di cottura)

Al dente cooked, but still firm; Al forno baked; Al sangue rare (for steaks); Al vapore steamed; Alla griglia, Grigliato grilled; Bollito boiled; Cotto cooked; Crudo raw; Fritto fried; In bianco plain, only with oil (for rice, pasta), or with no tomato (*pizza bianca*); In brodo in clear meat broth; In padella literally, in the frying pan, usually fried with garlic and chilli; In umido poached; Stufato stewed.

Pasta sauces (sughi)

Al pesto pine nuts, pecorino and basil, puréed; Al pomodoro fresco fresh, raw tomatoes; Al ragù 'bolognese', with minced meat and tomatoes; Al sugo (di pomodoro) puréed cooked tomatoes; All'amatriciana tomato, chilli, onion and sausage; All'arrabbiata tomato with chilli; Alla carbonara bacon, egg, Parmesan; Alla puttanesca olives, capers, garlic in hot oil; Cacio e pepe sheep's cheese and black pepper.

Meat (carne)

Abbacchio, Agnello lamb; Capra, Capretto goat, kid; Coniglio rabbit; Maiale, Maialino pork, piglet; Manzo beef; Pancetta similar to bacon; Pollo chicken; Prosciutto cotto, Prosciutto crudo 'cooked' ham, Parma ham; Tacchino turkey; Vitello, Vitella, Vitellone veal.

Meat dishes (piatti a base di carne)

Bollito con salsa verde boiled meat with parsley in vinegar sauce; Carpaccio, bresaola very thinly sliced types of cured beef; Cervello fritto fried calves' brains; Coda alla vaccinara oxtail stew; Involtini wrapped up strips of veal; Lingua tongue; Ossobuco beef shins with marrow jelly inside; Pajata newborn veal's intestines with mother's milk still in them; Polpette, Polpettine meatballs; Porchetta cold roast piglet; Rognoni trifolati stir-fried chopped kidneys, usually with mushrooms; Salsicce sausages; Saltimbocca veal strips and ham; Spezzatino casseroled meat; Spiedini kebabbed, on the spit; Straccetti strips of prime beef or veal, stir-fried; Trippa alla romana tripe in tomato sauce.

Cheeses (formaggi)

Cacio, caciotta young, coarse-tasting local cheese; Gorgonzola strong blue cheese which comes in creamy (*dolce*) or crumbly (*piccante*) varieties; Parmigiano Parmesan; Pecorino hard, tangy Roman cheese used instead of Parmesan; Ricotta fresh crumbly white cheese, often used in desserts; Stracchino creamy, soft white cheese.

Fish (pesce)

Many of the more delicate (and expensive) 'white-meat' fish are only found in the Mediterranean and thus don't have familiar English names – for example, sarago, dentice, orata, fragolino.

Alici, Acciughe anchovies; Baccalà salt cod; Cernia grouper; Merluzzo cod; Pesce spada swordfish; Razza, Arzilla sting-ray or thornback ray; Rombo turbot; Salmone salmon; Sarde, sardine sardines; Sogliola sole; Tonno tuna; Trota trout.

Seafood (frutti di mare)

Aragosta, Astice lobster; Calamari, Calamaretti squid, baby squid; Cozze mussels; Crostacei shellfish; Gamberi, Gamberetti shrimps, prawns; Granchio crab; Mazzancolle king prawns; Ostriche oysters; Polipo octopus; Seppie, Seppiette, Seppioline cuttlefish; Vongole clams.

Vegetables (verdura/il contorno)

Aglio garlic; Asparagi asparagus; Basilico basil; Broccolo green cauliflower; Broccoletti tiny broccoli sprigs, cooked with leaves on; Carciofi artichokes; Carote carrots; Cavolfiore cauliflower; Cetriolo cucumber; Cicoria green leaf vegetable, resembling dandelion; Cipolle onions; Fagioli haricot or borlotti beans; Fagiolini green beans; Fave broad beans; Funghi mushrooms; Funghi porcini boletus mushrooms; Insalata salad; Lattuga lettuce; Melanzane aubergines; Peperoncino chilli peppers; Peperoni peppers; Piselli peas; Pomodori tomatoes; Porri leeks; Prezzemolo parsley; Puntarelle bitter Roman salad usually eaten with anchovies; Radicchio bitter purple lettuce; Rucola, Rughetta rocket salad; Sedano celery; Spinaci spinach; Verza cabbage; Zucchine courgettes.

Fruit (frutta)

Albicocche apricots; Ananas pineapple; Arance oranges; Cachi persimmons; Ciliege cherries; Fichi figs; Fragole strawberries; Frutti di bosco woodland berries; Mele apples; Nespole loquats; Pere pears; Pesche peaches; Prugne, Susine plums; Uva grapes; Uvetta raisins.

Desserts (dolci/il dessert)

Gelato ice cream; Montebianco cream, meringue and chestnut purée; Panna cotta 'cooked cream', like a creamier-tasting crème caramel; Sorbetto sorbet; Tiramisù sponge with mascarpone and coffee; Torta della nonna flan with patisserie cream and pine nuts; Torta di mele apple flan.

A warm welcome awaits you at **Il Convivio**. *See page 128.*

di Montepulciano degli Abruzzi. Mineral water – *acqua minerale* – is either *frizzante/gasata/con gas* (sparkling), or *naturale/senza gas* (still), and usually comes in litre bottles. If you have a full meal, and they take a shine to you, you may also be offered (though it is quite OK to demand) free *amaro* – a bitter liqueur – after your coffee.

THE BILL

By law, service is supposed to be included, but some places still add it as a separate entry. Romans themselves tend not to tip, especially in family-run establishments. However, if you are satisfied with the meal, there is no reason not to apply the ten per cent rule. If service has been slack or rude, don't feel ashamed to leave nothing – or to check the bill in detail, as some restaurateurs can be rendered unaccountably innumerate where tourists are concerned. Again, by law, when you pay your bill (*il conto*), you should be given a detailed receipt or *ricevuta fiscale*. Technically, leaving the restaurant without it could result in a fine for you, but the rule is chiefly aimed at forcing recalcitrant restaurateurs to pay their taxes.

Italy is still a cash society, so never assume that you can use cards, travellers' cheques or Eurocheques without asking first.

GENERAL ADVICE

Taking children into restaurants – even the smartest – is never a problem in Rome. Enthusiastic waiters will happily oblige with a high chair (*una sediolina*), and will bring *mezze*

porzioni – half portions – on request. Women dining alone, however, may attract unwelcome attention in cheaper restaurants, even from smirking waiters. Single men can also have trouble getting a table in cheaper places at busy times. Eating out is a communal experience here.

Very few places impose a specific dress code, although shorts and T-shirts go down very badly if the joint is at all 'respectable'. Some restaurants are now enlightened enough to ban the use of mobile phones, and though no-smoking areas should be provided, they generally aren't.

The relaxed nature of Roman life means that it's relatively unusual to book a table. Where 'Booking essential/advisable' is indicated below, it means the place is either very smart or very popular.

RESTAURANT CATEGORIES

The restaurants listed here are arranged on the basis of price. This is not always an indication of quality, so although inclusion is in itself a recommendation, we have singled out a few establishments in each section, marked ***. These are places which either represent exceptional value for money or where the food, wine and/or ambience is so good as to merit those extra lire.

In theory the words *ristorante, trattoria* and *osteria* (sometimes called *hostaria*) should correspond to descending levels of quality, but they are often interchangeable and relate more to atmosphere than quality of food or service. Don't be misled by appearances: a starkly furnished *trattoria* with paper tablecloths may serve much better food than a self-proclaimed *ristorante* with pretentious neo-classical décor – and at at far lower prices.

The average price listed below includes a *primo*, a *secondo*, a *contorno* and a *dolce*, but does not include *antipasto*, wine or water. Roman opening times are so arbitrary that they are not listed here; if you're travelling any distance, it's always a good idea to ring before setting out. As a rule of thumb, most restaurants are open for lunch from around 12.30 to 2 or 3pm, and for dinner from around 8pm on (though some pizzerias kick off around seven). Bear in mind that although a restaurant may stay open until quite late, the kitchen is liable to close down at 10.30 or 11pm.

Splashing out: over L80,000

***Agata e Romeo

Via Carlo Alberto, 45 (44 66 115). Metro Vittorio Emanuele/bus to Santa Maria Maggiore. **Closed** Sun; two weeks Aug; two weeks Dec-Jan. **Average** L110,000. **Credit** All major cards.
The seedy area between the station and Santa Maria Maggiore is not where you would expect to find one of Rome's top gourmet treats – which is probably why you have to ring the doorbell to get in. Inside, the keynote is personal service (at just seven tables) and homely elegance. The cooking – best described as *nouvelle Romana* – is overseen by Agata Caraccio, while husband Romeo hovers in the dining room. Roman specialities like *pasta con broccoli in brodo di arzilla* (pasta with broccoli and ray broth) rub shoulders with international dishes (such as the raw tuna entrée) and in-house creations, notably a superb duck on a bed of lettuce with potatoes and spring peas. The desserts are excellent (pick of the bunch is a dream-like *millefoglie* pastry) – but then at L20,000 a throw they'd want to be. For serious foodies – or serious romance.
Air-conditioning. Booking essential.

Checchino dal 1887

Via di Monte Testaccio, 30 (57 46 318). Metro Piramide/bus to Via Marmorata. **Closed** Mon; Sun pm; two weeks Aug; Christmas. **Average** L90,000. **Credit** All major cards.
Nestling among the trendy bars and clubs opposite the Mattatoio is Rome's leading temple of authentic *cucina romana*. Specialities include *insalata di zampetti* (hoof jelly salad), *animelle al vino bianco* (sweetbreads in white wine) and *coratella con i carciofi* (veal heart with artichokes). Not content with offering the definitive versions of dishes which have kept Romans going for over 2,000 years, Checchino also has what is generally considered Rome's finest wine cellar, dug out of the broken amphora mountain that has become Monte Testaccio (ask to have a look). There's also an outstanding selection of cheeses, with recommended wine combinations, and an excellent grilled vegetable platter.
Booking advisable. Tables outdoors.

***Il Convivio

Via dell'Orso, 44 (68 69 432). Bus to Corso del Rinascimento. **Closed** Sat lunch; Sun; one week Aug. **Average** L110,000. **Credit** All major cards.
The three Troiani brothers have been running this tiny temple of foodie excellence near Piazza Navona for five years now, during which time it has swept to top place in the leading Italian restaurant guides. Chef Angelo makes innovative use of freshly-hunted ingredients in dishes like salt-cod in batter with gooseberry sauce and potato skins, or pigeon breast with sweet garlic sauce, capers and bacon. It ain't strictly Roman, but neither is it out-and-out culinary eclec-

ticism. Add intimate surroundings, a fine wine list, impeccable service and outstanding desserts to make this the best place in Rome for a splash-out with guaranteed returns.
Air-conditioning. Booking essential.

La Pergola dell'Hotel Hilton

Via Cadiolo, 101 (35 09 22 11). Bus to Piazza Medaglie d'Oro. **Dinner only**. **Closed** Mon; Sun; Jan. **Average** L120,000. **Credit** All major cards.
Who wants to eat in a hotel restaurant miles from the centre? The management of the luxury Hilton bunker on Monte Mario must have asked themselves this very question when they brought in young German master chef Heinz Beck to revitalise their uninspiring rooftop restaurant. In the space of a year Herr Beck had food critics reaching for the superlatives. The cuisine is international, with almost no pasta: our host does things with turbot, and *foie gras*, and filo pastry, and pigeons (with mushrooms) that shouldn't be allowed. The desserts are exquisite, the wine list ample, and the views over Rome and Saint Peter's quite breathtaking. But save some breath for the bill.
Air-conditioning. Tables outdoors. Booking essential.

La Rosetta

Via della Rosetta, 8/9 (68 30 88 41). Bus to Largo Argentina or Via del Corso. **Closed** Sat lunch; Sun; three weeks Aug. **Average** L140,000. **Credit** All major cards.
Rome's best fish restaurant, just a few metres north of the Pantheon, is packed with crustaceans, politicians and media personalities. The tables are cheek by jowl, the décor bright and floral, the service courteous but brisk. Chef and owner Massimo Riccioli comes from Sicily, and that island's simple, sauceless approach to fish is here exalted: seafood *antipasti*, first courses such as *spaghetti con scampi, fiori di zucca e pecorino* (prawns and courgette flowers with pecorini cheese) and party pieces such as the red prawns cooked in Verduzzo wine (a rare indulgence) set the standard for others to follow. Some may find it all so effortlessly simple as to resent the final bill, which has a tendency to induce vertigo. Still, you get a chocolate to take home afterwards.
Air-conditioning. Booking essential.

Vecchia Roma

Piazza Campitelli, 18 (68 64 604). Bus to Via del Teatro di Marcello or Piazza Venezia. **Closed** Wed; two weeks Aug. **Average** L85,000. **Credit** AmEx, DC.
Let's be honest: without its setting, this restaurant probably wouldn't make the grade – but what a setting! Piazza Campitelli, on the edge of the Ghetto, has to be one of the best places in Rome to eat outdoors. Brothers Tonino and Giuseppe (the latter one of the pioneers of post-war Italian restaurants in London) do a series of tried, tested and occasionally tired versions of Italian classics. Among the *primi*, the *pandacce* (home-made pasta) with fresh pecorino cheese and broccoli stand out. The winter menu is dominated by exhaustive variations on polenta sauces, while the summer menu revolves round a vast selection of imaginative salads. The service is urbane, the wines are excellent, and it's the perfect place to bring your parents. If they're paying.
Air-conditioning. Booking advisable. Tables outdoors.

Aiming high: L60,000 - L80,000

Dal Bolognese

Piazza del Popolo, 1 (36 11 426). Metro Flaminio/bus to Piazzale Flaminio or Piazza del Popolo. **Closed** Mon Sept-June; Sat-Sun July-Aug; two weeks Aug. **Average** L75,000. **Credit** AmEx, DC, MC, V.
This beshrubbed enclave on the Piazza del Popolo is still one of the most beautiful places in the world to eat a meal *al fresco*, and its cooking is as solidly conservative as ever: lots of solid salami, *tortellini in brodo*, and *tagliatelle al ragù* – what the British call a Bolognese sauce. Don't miss the *bollito misto*

con salsa verde or the excellent vegetable *fritto misto* either. Afterwards, go for coffee next door at **Rosati** (*see chapter* **Cafés & Bars**).
Air-conditioning. Booking advisable. Tables outdoors.

***Al Ceppo

Via Panama, 2 (84 19 696). Bus/tram to Piazza Ungheria. **Closed** Mon; three weeks Aug. **Average** L70,000. **Credit** AmEx, DC, V.
This elegant restaurant run by the Milozzi sisters has become the culinary hub of the fur-coated and mobile-phoned Parioli district. Cristina and Marisella's reworking of *cucina marchigiana* – in which mushrooms and fresh vegetables feature prominently, together with seafood – is bold and original without being risky or, as yet, overpriced. Try their delicious home-made fettucine with broad beans, ham and pecorino cheese, or, if you're here on a Sunday, the *vincisgrassi* – a delightfully calorific mix of lasagna and innards. Seconds are dominated by fish and game: rabbit, cuttlefish, mixed grills. Don't miss the desserts – including some delicious home-made ices.
Air-conditioning. Booking advisable.

Fortunato al Pantheon

Via del Pantheon, 55 (67 92 788). Bus to Largo Argentina or Via del Corso. **Closed** Sun; three weeks Aug. **Average** L65,000. **Credit** All major cards.
One of the few central Roman restaurants to have survived its kiss-of-death popularity with politicians, who still make their way from the parliament buildings in nearby Piazza Montecitorio to wallow in the sober, moderately luxurious surroundings. Old hands say it's hardly changed since the 1950s, and classic offerings like *spaghetti con le vongole*, *saltimbocca alla romana* and standard fresh fish main courses are as reliable and well-presented as ever.
Air-conditioning. Booking advisable. Tables outdoors.

Monte Caruso (previously Cicilardone)

Via Farini, 12 (48 35 49). Metro Termini/bus to Santa Maria Maggiore. **Closed** Mon lunch; Sun; Aug. **Average** L70,000. **Credit** All major cards.
Nothing is remarkable about the address or the anonymous décor, but the food here is well worth a spin. Owner-waiter-sommelier Domenico Lucia and his chef wife are almost alone in Rome in offering a highly personal, and extremely successful, version of *cucina lucana* – from Basilicata in Italy's instep. There are plenty of *piccante* flavours in the pasta and vegetable dishes – ginger is a favourite spice – as well as unusual, herb-packed meat offerings and the quaintly-named *glu-glu* (chicken breast with orange). The offbeat desserts are also justly celebrated.
Air-conditioning.

Al Moro

Vicolo delle Bollette, 13 (67 83 495). Bus to Via del Corso. **Closed** Sun; Aug. **Average** L75,000.
No credit cards.
Just round the corner from Fontana di Trevi, this restaurant was Federico Fellini's favourite in the 1960s. Its reputation could easily stand on its excellent menu and wine list, but it also has oodles of old-fashioned atmosphere, with a charismatic host and a chic/louche clientele. The cuisine is pan-Italian, mixing Roman influences, as in the stupendous *fritti misti di mozzarella e fiore di zucca* and Milanese *risotti*, and there are hints of Naples, Venice and Genova in other dishes, particularly the fish. The *dolci* are well above the usual standard.
Air-conditioning.

Papà Baccus

Via Toscana, 36 (42 74 28 08). Metro Spagna/bus to Via Veneto. **Closed** Sat lunch; Sun; one week Aug; one week Christmas. **Average** L65,000. **Credit** All major cards.
As befits the name of the street, this is *cucina toscana* at its

best, as all the raw materials – meats, oils, wine and cheeses – are directly imported from owner Italo Cipriani's native valley. Try the *crostini alla cacciagione* (toast with game) or the *filetto al Brunello* (fillet steak cooked in Brunello di Montalcino wine). It's also one of the few places in Rome to serve *ribollita*, a delicious Tuscan peasant soup made from beans, fresh vegetables and bread. Late opening is another bonus, as is a wine list with honest mark-ups.
Air-conditioning. Booking advisable. Tables outdoors.

***Paris

Piazza San Calisto, 7a (58 15 378). Bus to Viale Trastevere. **Closed** Mon; Sun eve; Aug. **Average** L65,000. **Credit** AmEx, DC, EC, MC.
Simple, elegant Paris does Roman Jewish cooking, and it does it well. Despite its location in Trastevere – across the river from the Ghetto – this is the place to come to sample *cucina ebraica* at its finest. The magnificent *fritto misto con baccalà* (fried vegetables with cod – including a perfect *carciofo alla giudia*, or deep-fried artichoke) is the star of the

Restaurants For...

...a tête-à-tête
Agata e Romeo; Il Convivio; Sangallo; Il Dito e La Luna; Il Bacaro; Taverna Angelica; San Teodoro; Tito e Quirino Fazioli; Shawerma.

...taking your parents
Vecchia Roma; Dal Bolognese; Fortunato al Pantheon; Sora Lella; Taverna Giulia; Al Pompiere; Grappolo D'Oro.

...eating outside
La Pergola dell'Hotel Hilton; Checchino dal 1887; Vecchia Roma; Dal Bolognese; Il Bacaro; La Carbonara; Monserrato; Otello alla Concordia; San Teodoro; Augusto; La Torricella.

...carnivores
Checchino dal 1887; Papà Baccus; Sora Lella; Pommidoro; Betto e Mery; Da Oio a Casa Mia.

...pescivores
La Rosetta; Sangallo; Il Sanpietrino; La Gensola; Nel Regno di Re Ferdinando II; La Torricella.

...pastavores
Al Ceppo; Monte Caruso; Taverna Angelica; Al 34; Alfredo a Via Gabi; Antico Arco; Edy; La Gensola; L'Isola Felice; Cantina Cantarini; Gino in Vicolo Rosini; Sora Margherita.

...meeting politicians
Fortunato al Pantheon; Gino in Vicolo Rosini.

meeting film stars
Dal Bolognese; Fiaschetteria Beltramme; Trattoria Pizzeria della Pace.

...meeting your maker (1)
L'Eau Vive.

...meeting your maker (2)
Osteria dell'Angelo.

Hotel Eden
Restaurant "La Terazza dell'Eden"
Open Brekfast Lunch & Dinner

HOTEL EDEN

ROMA

VIA LUDOVISI, 49 • 00187 ROMA • ITALIA
TEL. (39) 06-47812551 • FAX (39) 06-4821584
www.hotel-eden.it.

show, but simple dishes like the classic *pasta e ceci* (a thick broth of pasta and chickpeas) and *minestra di arzilla* (ray soup) make a fine supporting cast. Good value for money, if you can get a table.
Air-conditioning. Booking essential.

Il Quadrifoglio

Via del Boschetto, 19 (48 26 096). Bus to Via Nazionale. **Dinner only. Closed** Sun; two weeks Aug. **Average** L65,000. **Credit** AmEx, MC, V.
The tasteful, relaxed, romantic surroundings and invisibly efficient service make this ideal for an intimate dinner, which will get better as it goes along. First courses such as the pasta-and-seafood *penne allo scarpariello* are in the best Neapolitan tradition – though there is a tendency to overcook the pasta. Cook Annamaria Coppola comes good with the main courses, such as the *totani ripieni* (stuffed baby octopus). As usual with southern Italian cuisine, vegetarians will find plenty to keep them going. The real treat, though, is the desserts – among the best in Rome. A lemon sorbet with mandarin sauce makes you feel you've died and gone to Heaven.
Air-conditioning.

***Sangallo

Vicolo della Vaccarella, 11 (68 65 549). Bus to Corso Rinascimento. **Closed** Mon lunch *July-Aug*; Sun; two weeks Aug. **Average** L70,000. **Credit** Am Ex, MC, V.
The walls are lime yellow, the artwork sub-Dali surreal, the music easy-listening. What marks out *maitre d'* Gianfranco Panattoni is his unbridled enthusiasm, his vicarious joy in his clients' gastronomic and oenological satisfaction. This can become overwhelming, especially when you realise, after the third party-piece seafood *antipasto*, that the pasta course has yet to arrive. Those who prefer to lead and not be led will need to put up a fight. But go with the flow and this can be one of Rome's great dining experiences, with few troughs, like a tad too much salt in the pasta with *mazzancolle* (king prawns) and *pecorino* cheese, and many peaks, including a perfect, delicate baby squid and artichoke fry-up, a succulent *polipo* (octopus) *in salsa verde*; and just about any of the desserts. The wine list is small but reasonably priced.
Air-conditioning. Booking advisable.

Il Sanpietrino

Piazza Costaguti, 15 (68 80 64 71). Bus to Largo Argentina. **Dinner only. Closed** Sun. **Average** L60,000. **Credit** All major cards.
The entrance – a glossy black door in the corner of a square in the Ghetto – has the air of a dodgy private club, but once inside, the cordial (but slow) service and delectable *nouvelle Romana* cuisine set the tone. Among the first courses, the *pasta e fagioli ai frutti di mare* are excellent; afterwards try the *orata alle zucchine* (sea-bass with courgettes). As for wine, the *Le Vignole* white or the *Vigna del Vassallo* red are recommended. Good value for money – and the kitchen stays open till after midnight.
Air-conditioning.

Sora Lella

Via Ponte Quattro Capi, 16, Isola Tiberina (68 61 601). Bus to Piazza Monte Savello. **Closed** Sun. **Average** L65,000. **Credit** Am Ex, EC, MC, V.
Sora Lella was the plump, homely sister of '50s Italian film star Aldo Fabbrizi. Coming on as a Roman version of Hattie Jacques crossed with the Queen Mother, she became a folk idol and a major TV star. Son Aldo Trabalza set up this authentic Roman trat in her honour after she died in 1993. The restaurant avoids the obvious trap of out-and-out folksy kitsch, and offers some excellent, serious Roman cooking, such as *pasta e patate* (pasta and potatoes) and *abbacchio brodettato* (lamb in broth); a recent foray into fish offers a lighter alternative. Good for recharging the batteries on cold winter's days.
Air-conditioning. Booking advisable.

Taverna Angelica

Piazza delle Vaschette, 14a (68 74 514). Bus to Via della Conciliazione. **Closed** Mon lunch *Aug-June*; Sat lunch *July*; three weeks Aug. **Average:** L60,000. **Credit** All major cards.
Until this stylishly cool restaurant opened in 1994, Borgo – that part of the warren of lanes in front of Saint Peter's which survived Mussolini's clean-up in the 1920s – was a bit of a food desert. The décor is minimalist-modern, the cuisine creative and fish-based. Dishes like *fettucine nere con polpa di granchio e cedro* (black fettucine with crabmeat and lime), and *petto di pollo all'aceto e nero di seppia* (vinegared chicken breast with squid ink) establish the joint's *nouvelle* credentials. Service is attentive, and a well-selected wine list also includes a *mescita* (by-the-glass) option.
Air-conditioning.

Taverna Giulia

Vicolo dell'Oro, 23, off Via Acciaioli (68 69 768). Bus to Corso Vittorio Emanuele. **Closed** Sun; Aug. **Average** L65,000. **Credit** All major cards.
A pleasant, old-fashioned Genoese restaurant, in a charming fifteenth century house, which now caters to a largely business/politico clientele (not surprising, as it's right opposite the apartment of deposed Christian Democrat leader Giulio Andreotti). Ligurian specialities such as *trenette al pesto* or *stoccafisso alla genovese* (Genoese dried cod) are what they do best; avoid more recent experiments such as the alarming *penne al vodka*. Other high points are the *crème brûlée* and a limited but well-balanced wine list.
Air-conditioning.

Affordable: L40,000 - L60,000

Al 34

Via Mario de' Fiori, 34 (67 95 091). Metro Spagna/bus to Via del Corso or Via del Tritone. **Closed** Mon; three weeks Aug. **Average** L50,000. **Credit** All major cards.
Extremely popular and always crowded, Al 34 is one of the safest bets for a good-value meal in the Spanish Steps area. The atmosphere is cosy, candelit and slightly rustic, rendered elegant by the distinctly fashionable clientele. The menu features standard *cucina romana* plus a few other regional Italian influences – chiefly Sicilian (*involtini di pesce spada*) and Neapolitan (*maccheroncelli alla Positano*) – with various combinations of *radicchio* and *pinoli* (pine nuts) featuring prominently. Good wine with an acceptable mark-up.
Air-conditioning. Booking advisable.

Albistrò

Via dei Banchi Vecchi, 140a (68 65 274). Bus to Corso Vittorio. **Closed** Wed; mid-July to mid-Aug. **Average** L40,000. **No credit cards.**
The Swiss owner and his Italian wife have carved a bistro ambience out of this narrow space in the *centro storico*. The cuisine is international and creative: if you've never tried nettle-stuffed ravioli, now's your chance – maybe (the menu is strictly seasonal). The salads are good too, and an intelligent wine list is offered at near-*enoteca* (off-licence) prices. At the time of writing the pretty courtyard out the back, with room for a handful of tables, was out of bounds due to irate neighbours. This is good value for money, and money is what you must bring, for Jean Kurt is that rarest of beasts, a Swiss restaurateur who doesn't accept credit cards.

Alfredo a Via Gabi

Via Gabi, 38 (77 20 67 92). Metro Re di Roma/bus to Piazza Tuscolo. **Closed** Tue; Aug. **Average** L45,000. **No credit cards.**
A no-nonsense family-run *trattoria* with old-fashioned wood and brass décor. Alfredo mixes various regional influences: there are strong hints of the Marches in dishes like the *tonnarelli ai sapori di bosco* (pasta with wild mushrooms and

Vegetarian Rome

Italians have no great awareness of vegetarianism. There *are* Italian vegetarians, but they tend to be of the hard-line macrobiotic variety, and their numbers decrease every year, together with the communes and co-operatives that fuelled them.

That said, it's a lot easier for vegetarians here than in other European cities. The reason is simple: while you can count Rome's specifically vegetarian restaurants on the fingers of one hand, Italian cuisine – especially the poorer, spicier Southern variety – includes innumerable combinations of pasta, pizza, cheese and vegetables.

As long as you avoid the seriously *cucina romana* offal-with-everything places, you should be able to assemble a perfectly satisfying meal by sticking to the following guidelines:
1. The declaration *sono vegetariano* (I'm a vegetarian) tends to frighten waiters. It's better to say *non mangio la carne* (I don't eat meat) or *non mangio né carne né pesce* (I don't eat meat or fish).
2. Scan the *antipasti* and the *primi* carefully, as that's where most of your options will lie. When you order the pasta course, unless the topping is spelt out, it's worth checking by asking *non c'è carne, vero?* (There's no meat, is there?). *Ragù* is best avoided, as it is tomato sauce with mincemeat; ask for a simple *pomodoro* topping instead. *Ravioli* is OK if filled with *ricotta e spinaci* (soft cheese and spinach) rather than meat – and served *con burro e salvia* (with butter and sage).
3. Don't be afraid to send anything back if it does turn out to contain meat. Roman waiters are good at the 'yes, but there's only a *tiny* bit' act.

If you stick to the following dishes, you will be 99 per cent safe:

First courses
Pasta al pesto pasta with basil purée; **Pasta e ceci** soup with pasta and chick-peas; **Pasta e fagioli** soup with pasta and borlotti beans; **Penne all'arrabbiata** pasta with tomato sauce and lots of chilli; **Spaghetti aglio, olio e peperoncino** with garlic, olive oil and chilli, delicious if the ingredients are first-rate; **Spaghetti cacio e pepe** with crumbled cheese and black pepper; **Orecchiette ai broccoletti/cima di rape** ear-shaped pasta with tiny broccoli sprigs/green turnip-tops; **Risotto ai quattro formaggi** risotto made from four types of cheese.

Any pasta **alla puttanesca** or **alla checca** (literally 'à la whore' and 'à la raging queen') – based on olives, capers and tomatoes, though anchovies *(alici)* are sometimes slipped into the former.

Second courses
Carciofi alla giudia deep-fried artichokes, Jewish-style. Usually served as an *antipasto*, though there's no reason why you shouldn't ask for it as a *secondo;* **Fagioli all'uccelletto** haricot beans with tomato, garlic and olive oil. This Tuscan speciality is, strictly speaking, a *contorno*, but it's sufficiently protein-filled to take the place of a main course. **Melanzane alla parmigiana** aubergine with Parmesan, though this occasionally has meat in the topping; **Scamorza** grilled cheese. Specify that you want it without ham (**senza prosciutto**) or anchovies (**senza alici**).

Vegetarian restaurants and salad bars

Antico Bottaro
Passeggiata di Ripetta, 15 (32 40 200). Bus to Piazza Augusto Imperatore. **Closed** Wed. **Average** L55,000. **Credit** All major cards.
This restaurant has the same management as **Margutta** (*see below*), but is somewhat more upmarket, with a classier ambience and service. Home-made organic wine and beer.
Air-conditioning.

★★★Arancia Blu
Via dei Latini, 6 (44 54 105). Bus to Via Tiburtina. **Dinner only. Average** L40,000. **No credit cards.**
In its short life, this trendy San Lorenzo *locale* has quickly established itself at the sharper end of the vegetarian scene. The clientele is mostly ex-protest generation, but there is a good student influx from the nearby University. Now in roomier premises, Fabio Bassan's 'Blue Orange' does a good vegetarian take on Italian *cucina povera*, with a range of filling soups, pasta dishes and quiches. Wine is a strong point (they even hold tasting courses). There are plans to open in the afternoon as a tea-room-cum-cultural centre.

L'Insalata Ricca
Largo dei Chiavari, 85 (68 80 36 56); also Piazza di Pasquino, 72 (68 30 78 81). Bus to Corso Vittorio. **Average** L20,000. **No credit cards**.
This chain (there are branches in the suburbs too) is the nearest Rome has to a fast-food salad bar. It's not exclusively vegetarian, but there's plenty of choice, making it a good, cheap alternative to obligatory pasta and/or veggie ghettoes (though you can order pasta too). The main branch is more geared towards fast outdoor eating; the one in Piazza di Pasquino is a shade more comfortable and intimate.
Tables outdoors.

Margutta
Via Margutta, 119 (67 86 033). Metro Spagna or Flaminio/bus to Piazzale Flaminio. **Average** L35,000. **Credit** All major cards.
Claudio Vannini and the two D'Anna brothers have been running Rome's premier vegetarian restaurant since the late 1970s. In a plant-filled hall which also houses modern art exhibits, a broad selection of Italian dishes is on offer, reworked in a strictly vegetarian, but nonetheless imaginative and personal fashion. During the day the restaurant becomes a tea-room. Desserts are traditionally a strong point.
Air-conditioning.

herbs) and a Roman Jewish component which comes out in the wonders they work with artichokes. Come on a Saturday for hard-line *cucina romana*, innards and all. Famous for *bruschetta con indivia, uvetta e pinoli* (toasted bread with endives, pine nuts and sultanas) and a good selection of home-made desserts.
Air-conditioning. Tables outdoors.

***Antico Arco

Piazzale Aurelio, 7 (58 15 274). Bus to Via Carini. **Dinner only except Sun lunch. Closed** Mon; Aug. **Average** L55,000. **Credit** AmEx, MC, V.
Domenico, Maurizio and Patrizia have moved up in the world, in every sense. In their new, more spacious premises up on the Gianicolo hill – providing an excellent excuse for an appetite-building hike from Trastevere – the trio that put **Il Bacaro** (*see below*) on the map are finally able to give full rein to their culinary flair. Down there, with no space to swing a halibut, Patrizia worked wonders with cold cuts and smoked fish; here she's finally getting her teeth into an exciting range of meat, fish and game *secondi*. But first courses are still her forte: the *risotto al castemagno* (risotto with Castelmagno cheese) will bring tears to your eyes. The décor is effortlessly retro-elegant, the service as affable as you could wish, and the sweets deserve an entry to themselves. Add the trio's militantly honest pricing policy (and the advantage of being able to turn up and eat at 11 or later) and you have one of the best-value gourmet experiences in Rome. So book ahead.
Air-conditioning. Booking advisable.

Il Bacaro

Via degli Spagnoli, 27 (68 64 110). Bus to Corso del Rinascimento or Via del Corso. **Dinner only. Closed** Three weeks Aug. **Average** L45,000. **Credit** AmEx, EC, MC, V.
Patrizia and the boys have moved to roomier premises at the Antico Arco (*see above*), leaving their launch-pad in the hands of a group of likeable hipsters who can't quite match their predecessors. None of the atmosphere has faded, though – just around the corner from the Pantheon, this five-table restaurant (with room for a few more outside in the ivy-covered *vicolo* in summer) is a delightful place for a *tête-à-tête*. It is also a good bet for vegetarians. Among a variable set of first courses, the *orecchiette al pesto* are clear winners; main courses are dominated by simple cuts of meat and smoked fish dishes. The desserts are sumptuous, if a little pricey. Value for money is no longer one of *Il Bacaro*'s chief selling-points, but it is still undeniably *simpatico*.
Air-conditioning. Booking advisable.

La Carbonara

Piazza Campo de' Fiori, 23 (68 64 783). Bus to Corso Vittorio. **Closed** Tue; Aug. **Average** L50,000. **Credit** AmEx, MC, V.
Looming at one end of Rome's most picturesquely *folkloristico* square, those tables look like they just *have* to be a tourist trap. In fact, this old trooper does a surprisingly honest take on *cucina romana*, with all the old favourites: *penne all'a-matriciana, fritto di cervella e carciofi* (fried brains and artichokes). The wine list is not exactly inspired and the desserts are not exactly *nouvelle*, but they'll do – it's the setting that counts. A word of warning: keep an eye on your bag if you're at an outside table. Vespa swoops have been known to occur.

Ditirambo

Piazza della Cancelleria, 74 (68 71 626). Bus to Corso Vittorio. **Closed** Mon lunch; Aug. **Average** L40,000. **Credit** AmEx, DC, MC, V.
New, central, tasty, and good value: but why do the waiters have to look so hassled? Maybe it's the fact that the air-conditioning packs up in summer (when you should book ahead for one of the few outside tables). Still, they're young and (presumably) keen, and all the pasta is home-made. The

You can call me **Al 34**. *(See page 131.)*

maltagliati con i fiori di zucca ('bad cut-outs' with courgette flowers) are great. A decent range of salads and vegetable dishes makes this a good option for vegetarians too.
Air-conditioning (sort of). Tables outdoors.

Il Dito e la Luna

Via dei Sabelli, 51 (49 40 726). Bus to Via Tiburtina. **Dinner only. Closed** Sun; Aug; Christmas. **Average** L50,000. **No credit cards.**
A good place to bring that special person without either of you fainting over the bill, its softly-lit ambience is quite a contrast with its workaday location. The Sicilian-based menu changes regularly according to the season – don't miss the *caponata*, a Sicilian ratatouille, if they have it, and the *flan di cipolle di Tropea e fonduta di parmigiano* (onion flan with Parmesan sauce). The desserts are good, especially the *cannoli*. A modest wine list offers bottles at near-cost price.
Booking advisable.

Edy

Vicolo del Babuino, 4 (36 00 17 38). Metro Spagna/bus to Via del Babuino. **Closed** Sun; one week Aug. **Average** L40,000. **Credit** All major cards.
A simple, vaguely arty *trattoria* offering creative Roman cooking at reasonable prices: not bad in an area where the whiff of serious money is all-pervasive. The menu changes according to what's in season; among the *primi*, the house speciality is *spaghetti al cartoccio* (with seafood), where it's cooked and served in its own silver-foil packet.

Fiaschetteria Beltramme

Via della Croce, 39 (no phone). Metro Spagna/bus to Piazza Augusto Imperatore. **Closed** Sun; two weeks Aug. **Average** L40,000. **No credit cards.**
Also known as 'Da Cesaretto', this historic *trattoria* in the Tritone shopping triangle is little more than a front-room

*O fruit of my lions ... lunchtime at **Otello alla Concordia**.*

with paintings in dubious taste. But the 'no credit cards – no
phone' ruse and the rustic atmosphere disguise Cesaretto's
high-chic appeal: Madonna fled a gala dinner to eat here with
her bodyguards. Recommended dishes include *tonnarelli
cacio e pepe* and *pollo con i peperoni* cooked over charcoal.

***La Gensola

*Piazza della Gensola, 15 (58 16 312). Bus to Viale
Trastevere.* **Closed** Sat lunch; Sun; two weeks Aug.
Average L45,000. **Credit** All major cards.
Looks like an unassuming trat, and it can get pretty stuffy
in summer, without air-conditioning or outside tables. But
La Gensola has an ace up its sleeve: the Sicilian owner serves
up classic, simple versions of his island's specialities, including a perfect *pasta con le sarde* or *con i broccoli*, and fish
grilled *al punto giusto*. During the meal, mein host choreo-
graphs waiters, clients and flower-sellers with unflappable
ease. The house white is rustic but drinkable, and there's a
genuine Sicilian *cassata* to round things off.

Da Giggetto

*Via Portico d'Ottavia, 21/22 (68 61 105) Bus to Monte
Savello or Via Arenula.* **Closed** Mon; two weeks July.
Average L40,000. **Credit** All major cards.
No self-respecting Italian restaurant guide would recommend it, but Giggetto continues to churn out perfectly
respectable Roman Jewish cooking for a predominantly
tourist market in a unique setting that makes what's on your
plate a secondary consideration. On the main thoroughfare
of the Ghetto, and hard by the ancient Gate of Ottavia,
Giggetto's pavement tables add a Roman flavour to *carciofi
alla giudia* (deep-fried artichokes) and other specialities.
Tables outdoors.

L'Isola Felice

*Vicolo del Leopardo, 39a (58 14 738). Bus to Viale
Trastevere or Ponte Sisto.* **Closed** Mon lunch; Sun.
Average L45,000. **Credit** All major cards.
A pretty Trastevere backstreet, a few tables outside, a warm
welcome from cousins Anna and Wilma. They do a creative

version of Roman and regional *cucina povera*, with good first
courses (including *culurgiones*, a kind of Sardinian ravioli)
and some interesting main courses, such as pork with chest-
nuts and mushrooms. The *dolci* are excellent, the atmosphere
of the amiable front-parlour variety.
Air-conditioning.

Monserrato

Via Monserrato, 96 (68 73 386). Bus to Corso Vittorio.
Closed Mon; three weeks Aug. **Average** L55,000.
Credit AmEx, EC, MC, V.
A reliable *trattoria* around the corner from Piazza Farnese,
with summer seating in the charming square of Santa
Caterina della Rota. This place could get by on the setting
alone, but the food is not at all bad, though it lacks a sense
of regional identity. Fish is a strong point, especially grilled,
while pasta specialities include *bombolotti all'astice* (pasta
with lobster and tomato sauce).

***Nel Regno di Re Ferdinando II

*Via di Monte Testaccio, 39 (57 83 725). Bus to Piazza
del Mattatoio or Metro Piramide.* **Closed** Sun. **Average**
L50,000. **Credit** AmEx, EC, MC, V.
A good place to sample Neapolitan specialities such as *sartù
di riso* (rice, mushroom, meat and cheese bake) in pleasant,
busy surroundings without goggling at the bill. The new
premises of this popular restaurant are built into the bowels
of Monte Testaccio, complete with picture-windows onto a
cross-section of broken pots (*see chapter* **Sightseeing:
Testaccio**). Seafood is a speciality, and there is the bonus
of good *pizza napolitana* in the evening. Good sweets and
wines from Campania (the area around Naples).
Air-conditioning.

Otello alla Concordia

*Via della Croce, 81 (67 91 178). Metro Spagna/bus to
Piazza Augusto Imperatore.* **Closed** Sun; two weeks Jan-
Feb. **Average** L45,000. **Credit** All major cards.
A celebrated haunt of journalists, writers and owners of the
nearby antique shops, who pour into this quiet courtyard

Choosing the Wine

In Paris, it's safe to assume that the house wine will at least be drinkable. In Rome, it's safe to assume the opposite. In all but the most high-class restaurants the house wine will be white Frascati, also known as Castelli Romani. No longer the sweet nectar praised by Roman dialect poet Trilussa at the turn of the century, the stuff that goes into the carafe these days is at best bland and at worst a cloudy yellow brew with a paint-stripper bouquet that's guaranteed to give you a splitting headache.

It's a good idea, therefore, to know your labels, as it may be essential to seek an alternative. Most neighbourhood *trattorie* and *osterie* will have only a limited choice of the most obvious, mass-produced wines (*see below*), but some of these are not at all bad, and if you scan the menu (or the shelves) carefully, there is usually at least one bottle worth drinking. Most Roman waiters haven't a clue about how wine should be served, so it's wise to check the year – the bottle may have been on the shelf for some time – and the temperature, and ask for an ice bucket (*un secchiello di ghiaccio*) if the wine merits it. In *pizzerie* it's probably best to give up the struggle and do what most Romans do: drink beer, mineral water or soft drinks.

BEST OF THE BIG NAMES

Chianti. Avoid anything that comes in a straw-covered flask. Reliable names include Rocca delle Macie, San Felice, Agricoltori del Chianti Geografico, Frescobaldi (Chianti Nipozzano), Fattoria di Felsina, Vignamaggio, Macchiavelli and Melini.

Corvo Bianco/Rosso. Originating in the Duca di Salaparuta's huge Sicilian estates (now owned by Sicily's regional government), this is Italy's most mass-produced wine, with four million bottles rattling off the line every year. Once rather boring, it has been improving steadily through the '90s. Makes up in consistency and balance what it lacks in character. If they have it, go for the Colomba Platino white, a more refined version of the standard Corvo Bianco.

Frascati Superiore. A notch above the standard house Frascati, but still rather bland unless you're lucky enough to find Fontana Candida's Santa Teresa *cru*. Drink as young as possible. Other good Frascatis are produced by Villa Simone, Casale Marchese and Conte Zandotti.

Greco di Tufo. Clever marketing has turned this extremely dry, fresh white wine from the hills around Avellino, inland from Naples, into one of Italy's most fashionable whites, and it's not uncommon for even the most unassuming *osteria* to have a bottle or two. Top producer is Mastroberardino; expect to pay up to L20,000 with the restaurant mark-up. Drink very young.

Montepulciano d'Abruzzo. Most of the red house plonk in Roman trats is Montepulciano d'Abruzzo, and no great advertisement for its qualities. But if you can find it, Cantina Tollo's Colle Secco should reconcile you to this warm, tannic wine, which goes well with red meat.

Regaleali Bianco. This Sicilian 'industrial' white wine is ever-reliable, and excellent value for money. It is smooth and fragrant, with a sweet aftertaste. Drink young (this year or last). *Villa Tasca* is a pricier (but still good value) big-brother version.

Vini Bianchi Leggeri. A new generation of slightly sparkling, fresh whites, designed for summer lunches. The best known is Galestro Capsula Viola, produced by Tuscan giants Antinori, with a characteristic purple top. Another good bet is Cala Viola, made by reliable Sardinian winery Sella & Mosca, and Glicine, by Corvo. All should be drunk as young as possible.

Genial **Gino** (right) presides in Vicolo Rosini.

close to the Via Condotti. The vine-covered pergola and fruit-encrusted fountain are such a relief after a hard day's shopping that they almost make up for the uninspiring food (pan-Italian) and catch-me-if-you-can service. *Tables outdoors.*

Pommidoro

Piazza dei Sanniti, 44 (44 52 692). Bus to Via Tiburtina. **Closed** Sun; Aug. **Average** L55,000. **Credit** AmEx, EC, MC, V.
Still one of the most fashionable *trattorie* in San Lorenzo, opposite the *Accademia del Biliardo*, Pommidoro attracts a young crowd, with plenty of intellectual input from the University round the corner. It offers Roman *trattoria* service (slack) and traditions (a menu reeled off *a voce*), but makes up for this with good-quality food. *Spaghetti alla carbonara* and grilled game (pheasant, wild boar, hare) is a speciality. Still, the final bill is a bit steep for what's on offer. *Booking advisable. Tables outdoors.*

Al Pompiere

Via Santa Maria dei Calderari, 38 (68 68 377). Bus to Via Arenula. **Closed** Sun; Aug. **Average** L40,000. **Credit** MC, V.
If you can't afford the prices at **Paris**, this Ghetto alternative offers a more economical (and less refined) version of authentic Roman Jewish dishes alongside more standard *cucina romana*. In a huge first-floor dining room with frescoed ceilings, attentive waiters serve *carciofi alla giudia* (Jewish fried artichokes, their heads splayed out like sunflowers) and *abbacchio al forno con patate* (roast lamb and potatoes); round it off with a slice of *torta di ricotta e visciole* (ricotta and damson pie), supplied by the Jewish bakery around the corner. *Air-conditioning.*

San Teodoro

Via dei Fienili, 49/50 (67 80 933). Bus to Via del Teatro di Marcello. **Average** L50,000. **Credit** All major cards.
In summer, this is one of the best places in Rome to eat outside: on a raised terrace amid the medieval houses of this small residential enclave in the shadow of the Palatine hill. A shame, then, that the cooking can be patchy – though all the pasta is home-made. For best results, opt for the *tonnarelli San Teodoro* (with courgettes, king prawns and tomatoes) and stick to fish as a main course. The fruit-flavoured ice-creams are good.
Air-conditioning. Booking advisable for tables outdoors.

Settimio al Pellegrino

Via del Pellegrino, 117 (68 80 19 78). Bus to Corso Vittorio Emanuele. **Closed** Wed; Easter; Aug. **Average** L40,000. **No credit cards.**
A celebrated haven for Roman gastronomes, attracted as much by the curious 'closed door' policy (you are only admitted with a reservation, which is very odd for a humble *trat-*

toria), as by the extremely limited but excellent menu. In the best Roman tradition, Thursday is *gnocchi* day, while Friday spotlights *baccalà* (salt cod). The home-made *fettucine* and *seppie con piselli* (cuttlefish with peas) are recommended, as are the meatballs (*polpette di manzo*). *Air-conditioning. Booking essential.*

Tram Tram

Via dei Reti, 44/46 (49 04 16). Bus to Piazzale Verano/tram to Via dei Reti. **Closed** Mon; Aug. **Average** L45,000. **Credit** MC, V.
Taking its name from its proximity to the tram tracks (the best way to arrive), this good-value San Lorenzo *trattoria* attracts a young crowd – there is even a bar where you can wait for a table, an unusual feature in Rome. The menu is mainly southern Italian, and is strong on fish and vegetables – as in the *orecchiette vongole e broccoli*. Unusually, vegetarians will even find the odd main course here. Dine accompanied by good house wine and the regular rumble of passing trams.
Tables outdoors.

Bargain fare: L20,000-40,000

Augusto

Piazza de' Renzi, 15 (58 03 798). Bus to Viale Trastevere or Lungotevere Sanzio. **Closed** Sun; two weeks Aug. **Average** L25,000. **No credit cards.**
One of the last really cheap *osterie* in Trastevere, serving all the classics of simple Roman cuisine, such as *rigatoni all' amatriciana* and *pollo arrosto con patate*. Set in a typical piazza with tables outside, it's populated by a mixture of locals, both traditional *trasteverini* and the latter-day gentrified set. *Tables outdoors.*

★★★Betto e Mery

Via Savorgnan, 99 (24 30 53 39). Bus to Via Casilina or Metro Arco di Travertino. **Closed** Thur; three weeks Jan. **Average** L35,000. **No credit cards.**
Way off the beaten tourist track, but definitely worth a detour. The fire burns merrily away, even in summer, in anticipation of the *grigliata mista* (mixed grill); alternatively, there's *coda alla vaccinara*, *trippa alla romana*, *pollo con peperoni* and the Tuscan *straccetti con rucola*, as well as memorable home-made *gnocchi* and house-bottled wine. *Padrone* Betto is a local legend, and is cordial to all. *Tables outdoors.*

★★★Cantina Cantarini

Piazza Sallustio, 12 (48 55 28). Bus to Via XX Settembre. **Closed** Sun; Aug. **Average** L35,000. **Credit** All major cards.
A very high-quality *trattoria*, in a smart neighbourhood, that nevertheless offers extraordinarily reasonable prices. The food is *romana/marchigiana*; meat-based for the first four days, then fish-based for Friday and Saturday. The atmosphere is as *allegro* as the seating is tight, and the *fritto misto di pesce* (fried mixed fish) and *spaghetti alle vongole* or *al nero di seppie* (squid ink) should silence any doubts about your physical comfort.
Booking advisable at weekends. Tables outdoors.

La Cicala e la Formica

Via Leonina, 17 (48 17 490). Metro Cavour/bus to Via Cavour. **Dinner only. Closed** Sun; three weeks Aug. **Average** L35,000. **Credit** All major cards.
Despite the '80s pink and black decor, this is a good stand-by in a difficult area. Tomatoes, basil, aubergines and capers are the main ingredients of Wanda Ratti's Southern Italian style of cooking, making it a good bet for vegetarians. An imaginative range of home-made desserts – not always easy to come by in this price range – is a bonus.
Tables outdoors.

Gino in Vicolo Rosini
Vicolo Rosini, 4, off Piazza del Parlamento (68 73 434).
Bus to Via del Corso. **Closed** Sun; Aug. **Average**
L40,000. **No credit cards**.
Situated right behind Parliament, and filled by political journalists, *deputati* and their bagmen, this unreconstructed *trattoria romana* is a monument unto itself. The cuisine is more varied than the usual fare, and the *coniglio al vino bianco* (rabbit in white wine) and *zucchine ripiene* (stuffed courgettes) are recommended, as is the home-made *tiramisù*. Come early, especially at lunchtime, or be prepared to wait around for a table.

Da Giovanni
Via della Lungara, 41a (68 61 514). Bus to Lungotevere
della Farnesina. **Closed** Sun; Aug. **Average** L25,000.
No credit cards.
Unkindly dubbed 'the poisoner' by regulars, Giovanni de Blasio is *padrone* of what is possibly the cheapest place to sit down and eat in central Rome, and a key figure in the local community along Via della Lungara, which skirts the Tiber. Many diners are relatives of inmates from the Regina Coeli prison, almost next door. The two tiny rooms are always crowded, a queue usually extends well outside the door, and the kitchen closes at 10pm, so you're strongly advised to get there early. Awaiting you is simple Roman fare – *carbonara, ammatriciana, abbacchio* and so on – offering no great culinary surprises, but no disappointments.

Grappolo d'Oro
Piazza della Cancelleria, 80 (68 64 118). Bus to Corso
Vittorio Emanuele. **Closed** Sun; Aug. **Average** L35,000.
Credit All major cards.
The excellent basic Roman cuisine served here by the helpful, professional staff is outstandingly good value. Book ahead for one of their attractive tables on the piazza, just off the Campo de' Fiori, and settle down to watch the world go by. The *trippa alla romana*, *bucatini all'amatriciana*, and speciality *tagliatelle con la trota* (with trout) are all delicious. Not to be confused with two other restaurants of the same name in Rome.
Booking advisable. Tables outdoors.

Lilli
Via Tor di Nona, 26 (68 61 916). Bus to Lungotevere
Tor di Nona or Corso Vittorio Emanuele. **Closed** Sun;
two weeks Christmas. **Average** L30,000. **Credit**
AmEx, MC, V.
This place gets crowded in the evenings, and they don't take bookings, so come early or join the queue. It stands in a lively cul-de-sac by the river bank, not far from Piazza Navona, so is a pleasant experience in summer. The Ceramicola family serve up classic Roman fare like *bucatini all'amatriciana* and *rigatoni alla pajata*, as well as their speciality *petto di vitella* (roast breast of veal). Service is on the gruff side, but they don't come much cheaper than this.
Tables outdoors.

Marcello
Via dei Campani, 12 (44 63 311). Tram to Viale di Scalo
San Lorenzo. **Dinner only. Closed** Sat-Sun; Aug.
Average L32,000. **No credit cards**.
This *trattoria di quartiere* in the heart of San Lorenzo is always packed with locals. Order the *ravioli di ricotta e spinaci* or the *coda alla vaccinara* and you'll understand why. A surprisingly well-furnished wine and *grappa* selection is another reason to pay host Isidoro a visit.

Da Oio a Casa Mia
Via Galvani, 43/45 (57 82 680). Metro Piramide/bus to
Via Marmorata. **Closed** Sun. **Average** L35,000. **Credit**
AmEx, MC, V.
On the edge of Testaccio, hard by the Protestant Cemetery and this trendy area's myriad bars and clubs, this honest *trattoria di quartiere* is low on pretentions and high on old-fashioned elbow-to-elbow atmosphere. The food and clientele are resolutely Roman; the *pasta e ceci, pajata in umido* and other culinary warhorses are done by the book, and the service is friendly. It's deservedly popular, so come early to avoid the rush.
Tables outdoors.

Osteria dell'Angelo
Via Giovanni Bettolo, 24 (37 29 470) Metro
Ottaviano/bus to Via Ottaviano. **Closed** Sat lunch; Sun;
three weeks Aug. **Average** L30,000. **No credit cards**.

Crimes Against Taste

A Corinthian bronze donkey, its saddlebags stuffed with olives; a silver platter of succulent dormice sprinkled with honey and poppy seeds; peahen eggs wrapped in pastry and stuffed with tiny birds marinated in peppered egg yolks ... such was the *antipasto* (*gustum* or *gustaio* in Latin) served to guests at the fictional feast of Trimalchio in Petronius' first-century AD satire.

To the Romans, presentation was all-important, and at Trimalchio's feast, main course (*mensae primi*) dishes included a hare dressed up with wings to look like Pegasus, fish 'swimming in' pepper sauce, an immense wild boar with baskets of dates hanging from its tusks, led in by a noisy pack of Spartan hunting dogs, and a pig stuffed with roast sausages and giblets.

Fiction was scarcely stranger than reality. Much of what we know about Roman food comes from a first-century AD cookery book written by

one Apicius, who poisoned himself after realising that he had spent a hundred million sesterces on food, had only ten million left and would thus be unable to continue eating in the style to which he had become accustomed. His recipes include roast flamingo with a sauce of pepper, caraway, asafoetida, mint and rue (the same sauce is recommended for roast parrot); grilled sow wombs and udders stuffed with pepper, caraway and sea urchin; and porpoise rissoles. Wisely, Apicius also includes cures for indigestion and constipation.

Scores of Apicius' dishes are flavoured with garum or liquamen, a sauce made from fermented fish, rather like Thai fish sauce. The demand was so great that the sauce was made in factories – a small jar was discovered at Pompeii (destroyed in 79 AD) bearing inscription 'Best strained liquamen. From the factory of Umbricus Agathopus'.

Osteria dell'Angelo – *a byword for relaxed conviviality.*

Decorated with photos of boxers and rugby players, no to mention some action-packed frescoes, this outwardly charming traditional eatery is actually a charm-free zone presided over by gentlemen who've been known to refuse to serve tourists 'because we don't like foreigners'. If you want to take your chances, feel free. The food is undeniably good, but of the take-what-you're-given-and-like-it variety (no menu): classic Roman with *tonnarelli cacio e pepe* to die for (possibly literally). You get all you can eat and drink for L30,000, including a glass of *Romanella* (sweet wine) and *ciambelline* (aniseed biscuits). Take Mike Tyson with you. *Booking resented but essential. Tables outdoors.*

Osteria del Rione

Via Basento, 20 (85 51 057). Bus/tram to Via Po or Viale Regina Margherita. **Closed** Sat lunch; Sun; Aug. **Average** L25,000. **No credit cards**.
Had a hard morning on your endless quest for culture? Can't face all those Berninis without a square meal? This is the place for you: a cheap and cheerful *osteria* within striking distance of the Villa Borghese. You'll find all those old Roman faves – *pasta e ceci, fiori di zucca* – plus some lubricative house wine, all for a risible outlay.

★★★Sora Margherita

Piazza delle Cinque Scole, 30 (68 64 002). Bus to Via Arenula or Lungotevere de' Cenci. **Lunch only**.
Closed Sat-Sun; Aug. **Average** L25,000.
No credit cards.
La padrona Margherita Tomassini and her husband have been running this wonderful *osteria* in the heart of the Ghetto for over 20 years, opening only at lunchtimes and without so much as a sign over the door. Not everyone's idea of a light lunch, but no-one argues with serious Roman Jewish cooking at these prices. Apart from the classic Roman pasta and meat dishes, including a superlative *pasta e fagioli*, the daily-changing menu also offers fishy treats such as *baccalà al sugo* and *aliciotti con l'indivia* (anchovies with endives).

Taverna Cestia

Via della Piramide Cestia, 65 (57 43 754). Metro Piramide/bus to Porta San Paolo. **Closed** Mon; last two weeks Aug. **Average** L38,000. **Credit** DC, MC, V.
The busy tree-lined avenue stretching between the Pyramid of Gaius Cestius and Circus Maximus is not the obvious setting for a cheap-and-cheerful *trattoria di quartiere*: it's a stone's throw from the United Nation's FAO headquarters and the Aventine hill, with its leafy diplomatic villas. Which explains the mix: tram drivers from the nearby terminus rub shoulders with slumming ambassadors. This Jekyll-and-Hyde act has rubbed off on the cuisine too: by day the Taverna Cestia operates as a *trattoria*; by night it is equally convincing as a *pizzeria* – though the daytime menu can still be ordered.
Air-conditioning. Tables outdoors.

Tito e Quirino Fazioli

Via Santa Maria dell'Anima, 8 (68 68 100). Bus to Corso Vittorio or Corso Rinascimento. **Closed** Sun lunch. **Average** L38,000. **No credit cards**.
The abstracted lads who serve at this tourist-zone trat move as if they've just woken up from an afternoon's sunbathing. But with prices like these, no-one's complaining. Kick off with a truly excellent *mozzarella di bufala* antipasto, and move on to pasta dishes of the good home-cooking variety and a series of meaty main courses at L16,000. The wine is house white, take it or leave it (and it's just about takeable); desserts are fresh fruit.
Tables outdoors.

La Torricella

Via E Torricelli, 2/4 (57 46 311). Metro Piramide/bus to Via Aldo Manuzio or Via Marmorata. **Closed** Mon.
Average L35,000. **Credit** AmEx, DC, MC, V.
For the full Sensurround experience, come here in summer and sit at one of the outside tables in this residential street. Babies cry, families fight, dreams are made and shattered, and on big match nights a hundred televisions provide a

wall-of-sound accompaniment to your meal. The food is Roman with a fishy twist (the *spaghetti ai frutti di mare* is spectacular); in the evening pizzas are also on offer. *Air-conditioning. Tables outdoors.*

Pizzerias

The Neapolitans are coming! Roman *pizzaioli* have always been fiercely proud of their thinner, flatter, crispier *pizza romana*, but just recently the fickle public has started defecting to a growing range of fatter, puffier, more richly-spread Neapolitan outlets. As if that were not enough, the slow-rising heresy has begun to take hold of the hearts and stomachs of ordinary citizens (*see* **Nouvelle Pizza** *in chapter* **Snacks**).

Whichever you choose, avoid those reheated surface-of-Mars discs that shrivel and congeal outside tourist bars. *Pizza rotonda* (round pizza, as opposed to the square, tray-baked takeaway *pizza rustica*) should be rolled on a marble slab and baked as you wait, preferably in a wood oven (*forno a legna*). Dough-spinning acrobatics are fun to watch but not strictly necessary.

Average prices in this section are based on one pizza and one extra (*bruschetta, filetto di bacalà*, and so on). Note that pizzerias are almost always open in the evenings only (exceptions in the list below are marked 'Also lunch'), and that you can sit down to eat earlier than in restaurants – generally from 7pm onwards. Very few pizzerias accept credit cards.

Acchiappafantasmi

Via dei Cappellari, 66 (68 73 462). Bus to Corso Vittorio. **Also lunch. Closed** Tue *winter;* one week Aug. **Average** L25,000. **Credit** DC, MC, V.
The tongue-twisting name translates as 'Ghostbusters', a moniker justified by the Calabrian owners' speciality: the award-winning *pizza del campionato*, a vaguely spook-shaped tomato, mozzarella and aubergine creation with

The Pizza Menu

So orthodox is the range of toppings on offer in Roman pizzerie, so eyebrow-raising any departure from the norm, that it's worth learning some of the main varieties off by heart:

Pizzas

Calzone a doubled-over pizza, usually with cheese, tomato and home filling; **Capricciosa** ham, hard-boiled or fried egg, artichokes and olives; **Funghi** mushrooms; **Marinara** plain tomato, sometimes with a few salted anchovies; **Margherita** tomato and mozzarella; **Napoli** or **Napoletana** tomato, mozzarella and anchovy; **Quattro formaggi** four cheeses (in theory); **Quattro stagioni** a Vivaldian quartet: winter is usually mozzarella; spring, artichoke; summer, a fried egg; autumn, mushrooms.

You don't need to specify *una pizza con...* Just ask for *una Napoli, una funghi*, etc. If you want it without tomato, ask for *una ... bianca*; for example, *una gorgonzola bianca*.

Unless you can't face more than a pizza, it's customary to order gap-fillers while you're waiting for yours to be baked. What you can have depends on how well-stocked the pizzeria is, but a few of the most common variations are listed below.

Often you'll be offered desserts as well. You can always order wine (invariably low-grade Castelli Romani white), but most people drink *birra alla spina* or *in bottiglia* (beer, on tap or bottled), or soft drinks.

Extras

Bruschetta coarse toast with raw garlic rubbed into it and oil on top, usually topped with a layer of diced raw tomatoes; **Crochette** potato croquettes, often with a cheesy centre; **Crostini** slices of toasted bread, usually with a grilled cheese and anchovy topping; **Fagioli stu-**

fati white cannellini beans cooked in their own sauce, often with raw onion; **Filetto di baccalà** deep-fried salt cod in batter; **Olive ascolane** deep-fried, battered olives stuffed with sausage meat; **Suppli** deep-fried rice balls held together by tomato sauce with a lump of fresh mozzarella inside. Vegetarians beware: some contain mincemeat.

olives for eyes. Southern Italian gourmet treats like *pomodori secchi* and *bocconcini golosi* (mozzarella wrapped in bacon) provide an alternative to the usual range of pizzeria extras. The service is a little uncertain, as is the décor.

Da Baffetto

Via del Governo Vecchio, 11 (68 61 617). Bus to Corso Vittorio. **Closed** Two weeks Aug. **Average** L20,000. **No credit cards.**
Perhaps the most famous place for pizza in Rome, Da Baffetto is an institution on one of the city's most idiosyncratic shopping streets, the Via del Governo Vecchio (*see chapter* **Shopping**). The restaurant extends over two floors and has lightning-quick, there's-a-queue-outside service. The pizza and other dishes are all first-rate, but come early (6.30-8pm) or late (you can order after midnight) or expect a very long wait.

Alle Carrette

Vicolo delle Carrette, 14 (67 92 770). Metro Colosseo/bus to Via Fori Imperiali or Via Cavour. **Average** L20,000. **No credit cards.**
A good pizzeria in a charming but almost invisible cul-de-sac opposite the main entrance to the Forum. But the word is out: unless you arrive by 8.30pm, be prepared to queue. The two Egyptian brothers who run the place offer the usual selection of *pizze, bruschette* and *supplì*, plus a wide range of extras, including interesting variations on *scamorza* (grilled cheese). The cordial service makes a change from the usual Roman plate-throwing act.
Tables outdoors.

Corallo

Via del Corallo, 10 (68 30 77 03). Bus to Corso Vittorio Emanuele. **Average** L25,000. **Credit** AmEx, DC, MC, V.
Open well past midnight, Corallo offers fish-based *trattoria* dishes (in another price bracket) alongside the Roman-style pizzas. Its popularity can mean long waits for tables, and service is not exactly a well-oiled machine. But it remains a a good place to hang out and be seen.
Tables outdoors.

***Dar Poeta

Vicolo del Bologna, 45 (58 80 516). Bus to Piazza Sonnino. **Closed** Mon. **Average** L25,000. **Credit** AmEx, MC, V.
Four lads on the make – making pizzas, that is. One is an ex-student of Angelo Iezzi (*see* **Nouvelle Pizza** *in chapter* **Snacks**), and the influence shows both in the fluffy base (this is the only sit-down pizzeria in Rome to use Iezzi's slow-rise dough method) and in the creative toppings, which include the *taglialegna* – mixed vegetables, mushrooms, sausage and mozzarella – and the sweet *bodrilla* – apples and Gran Marnier. The pizzas are delicious, the varied *bruschette* are first-rate, and you can eat till late. But its fame is spreading. No bookings are taken, so come early or wait.

Est! Est! Est!

Via Genova, 32 (48 81 107). Metro Repubblica/bus to Via Nazionale. **Closed** Mon; three weeks Aug. **Average** L23,000. **Credit** MC, V.
One of the oldest and most old-fashioned *pizzerie* in Rome, Est! Est! Est! was extensively renovated not long ago, but with lots of dark wood and the same starched, elderly waiters, it certainly hasn't lost any of its conservative allure. The pizzas and *calzoni ripieni* (folded-over pizzas) are still good.
Air-conditioning.

***Il Forno della Soffitta

Via dei Villini, 1e (44 04 642). Metro Policlinico/bus to Porta Pia. **Closed** Sun; two weeks Aug. **Average** L30,000. **No credit cards.**
This recently opened pizzeria just outside Porta Pia on the Via Nomentana does authentic Neapolitan pizzas – they have a certificate to prove it. Watch the exhibitionist *pizzaioli* spin

All mod cons at Est! Est! Est!

the dough-circles in the air to get the required shape, and tuck into some of the best pizza to be had in Rome. They come on what look like giant table-tennis bats, and one size fits all – a single, monstrous pizza is divided into segments according to what you ordered. Upstairs is a proper Neapolitan restaurant, whose extras (delicious *antipasti* and gobsmacking desserts, delivered fresh each day from Naples) and wines (mainly from Campania) can be ordered downstairs as well. But if you do stray beyond pizza, the bill will leap. No bookings are taken, and the place fills up early.

Ivo

Via di San Francesco a Ripa, 158 (58 17 082). Bus to Viale Trastevere. **Closed** one week Aug. **Average** L20,000. **Credit** AmEx, DC, MC, V.
A rival to **Da Baffetto** (*see above*) as the most famous pizzeria in Rome, as is evident from the throngs of eager clients in the narrow street outside. The seating is extremely squashed, with 200 hungry souls being jammed into a space that would be tight for half that number, but the atmosphere is electric (especially on match days), the pizzas acceptable and the service prompt if inelegant. A sizeable pasta menu is also available for those who dare to go for both icons of popular Italian cuisine at the same sitting.
Tables outdoors.

Ministero della Pizza

Via dei Campani, 65/67 (49 02 17). Bus/tram to Piazza di Porta Maggiore. **Closed** Mon; three weeks Aug. **Average** L25,000. **Credit** AmEx, MC, V.
This highly popular pizza joint claims to lay down the law on how to make the classic Roman pizza – hence the name. However, they had to take down their original wall plaque, since it illegally featured the Italian State emblem. It's in the heart of the trendiest part of San Lorenzo and has an exuberant, friendly atmosphere. The menu features bill-boosting extras like Calabrian salami and marinated salmon.

Panattoni

Viale Trastevere, 53 (58 00 919). Bus/tram to Viale Trastevere. **Closed** Wed; three weeks Aug. **Average** L18,000. **No credit cards.**
Better known to Romans as *l'Obitorio* (the morgue) on account of its ice-cold marble slab tables, but there's nothing deathly about Panattoni, one of the liveliest, most enjoyable pizzerias in Trastevere. Service is sharp to the point of being ruthless, but it's very good value, and stays open until the small hours.
Tables outdoors.

Pizza Forum

Via San Giovanni in Laterano, 34-38 (70 02 515). Metro Colosseo/bus to Piazza del Colosseo. **Also lunch.** **Closed** Sat; Sun lunch *July-Sept.* **Average** L20,000. **No credit cards.**

Conveniently situated for the Colosseum, Pizza Forum's McDonald's-style interior and service technique can be off-putting in the extreme. But for all the glaring lights and bored waitresses, it does a surprisingly acceptable *pizza napolitana* with around 30 different toppings, cooked in a *forno a legna*. Great for kids – who are unlikely to out-scream the ambient noise – and open for lunch, too.
Air-conditioning.

PizzaRé

Via di Ripetta, 14 (32 11 468). Metro Flaminia/bus to Piazza del Popolo. **Also lunch. Closed** Sun lunch; public holidays. **Average** L18,000. **Credit** AmEx, DC, MC, V.
Branch: *Via Osteria, 39 (37 21 173).*
Another leader of the Neapolitan invasion, just a few paces from Piazza del Popolo. This formulaic but still lively pizzeria offers 14 varieties of high-risers, including the PizzaRé itself (with *mozzarella di bufala* and cherry tomatoes). Various *antipasti, pagnottielli* (a kind of neapolitan *calzone*) and a range of salads complete the menu. You can even order a steak. Service is cheery and efficient, the surroundings pleasantly retro, and there are some acceptable bottles of wine on offer.
Air-conditioning.

***Remo

Piazza Santa Maria Liberatrice, 44 (57 46 270). Metro Piramide/bus or tram to Via Marmorata. **Closed** Sun; Aug. **Average** L18,000. **No credit cards.**
One of the oldest pizzerias in Testaccio, with a prime location on the district's main piazza. You can sit at wonky tables perilously balanced on the street corner, or in the cavernous, subterranean interior. Patrons compile the order themselves by checking off the 20 or so options on a list. The *bruschette al pomodoro* are the finest in Rome.
Tables outdoors.

Supernatural

Via del Leoncino, 38 (32 65 05 77). Bus to Piazza Augusto Imperatore or Via del Corso. **Lunch only.** **Average** L18,000. **No credit cards.**
Rome's first vegetarian pizzeria. Service is rather uncertain and the tables outside are too flimsy for serious pizza-sawing, but it's cheap and fills a gap in the market: the small but appetising pizzas come with just about any topping you like (even pesto) – as long as it isn't meat or fish. There's a vegan menu with a variety of soya-based dishes. Even the home-made beer and cola are organic.
Tables outdoors.

Trattoria Pizzeria della Pace

Via della Pace, 1 (68 64 802). Bus to Corso Vittorio. **Also lunch** Oct-Apr. **Average:** L25,000. **No credit cards.**
Owner Bartolo also runs the ever-trendy Bar della Pace next door, and the combination of his sharp PR instinct and this outlet's strategic watch-and-be-watched pavement tables decreed immediate success from day one. Most nights a couple of *paparazzi* or a camera crew will be hovering here on the off-chance. The food hardly matters: Neapolitan-style pizzas, decent, home-cookin' pasta dishes, one or two more adventurous fishy and meaty mains, and a severely limited though reasonably priced wine list. Keeping the prices down was a smart move, and should ensure a steady flow of hovering wannabes well into the next decade. It's open until 2am and doesn't accept bookings, so come late or early to be sure of a table.

***Da Vittorio

Via di San Cosimato, 14a (58 00 353). Bus to Viale Trastevere. **Closed** Mon. **Average** L20,000. **No credit cards.**
Vittorio is a Neapolitan, who makes what he would consider 'real pizzas' – the soft, thick variety of his home town. Apart from all the classics, he does a couple of remarkable

inventions of his own – including, the *Vittorio* itself (mozzarella, Parmesan, fresh tomato and basil). The place is minute, but bursts with exuberance.
Tables outdoors.

International

The great strength of Italian food is its cultural solidity, the way that it defines a sense of national identity. Such is the steamroller nationalism and regionalism of the city's gastronomes (even Ligurian, Calabrian or Friulian cooking can have a hard time making headway) that foreign cuisine has always been regarded with a raised eyebrow.

But things are slowly changing. This is partly due to a budding spirit of adventure, especially in younger Romans. But it's also because a number of Asian and African communities are finally starting to put down roots in the city – especially around the Piazza Vittorio area. Chinese restaurants are a case apart – there have long been over a hundred in the city, but it's a mystery how they survive, as the quality is generally low and the tables empty.

Another exception is the long-standing community from Ethiopia and the Horn of Africa – a legacy of Mussolini's unedifying African adventure. But even here most of the half-dozen or so restaurants on offer service the community itself – few Italians have ever ventured into an Ethiopian or Eritrean restaurant. This is a pity, since this hot, spicy food is full of memorable dishes.

There is also a growing number of Middle Eastern restaurants in Rome, some of which base their success on their 'exotic' floorshows. Geographical proximity and shared cultural values give them a certain authentic feel that would be lacking in, say, northern Europe.

The best of what there is appears below (*see also chapter* **Snacks** for some eat-and-run options). Remember, though, that Rome is not London or New York. The main reason for eating in any of these restaurants is that you simply can't face another pizza or pasta dish.

Chinese

Ruyi

Via Valadier, 14 (32 15 804). Metro Lepanto/bus to Piazza Cola di Rienzo. **Average** L35,000. **Credit** All major cards.
One of the few Chinese restaurants in Rome to rise above the monosodium glutamate herd. Ms Hua, the owner, is from Shanghai, as is the cuisine. The spicy beef and spring rolls are worth a try.

Ethiopian/Eritrean

Africa

Via Gaeta, 26 (49 41 077). Metro Castro Pretorio or Termini/bus to Via Volturno or Termini. **Closed** Mon. **Average** L22,000. **No credit cards.**
Long-established Ethiopian/Eritrean restaurant, popular

both with right-on Romans and the city's Horn of Africa community, offering specialities such as *sambussa*, a dish of cigar-shaped meat and vegetable rolls, and *taita* – a sour, spongy bread filled with spicy meat and vegetables (there's also a vegetarian version). It's open from nine in the morning until after midnight.

Sahara
Viale Ippocrate, 43 (44 24 2583). Metro Policlinico/bus to Viale Ippocrate. **Closed** Wed; one week Aug. **Average** L28,000. **Credit** AmEx, MC, V.
A good place to try out Eritrean delicacies while sitting on a delightful and somehow un-Roman (if equally un-African) patio. The dishes are mostly meat-based, and all very spicy. *Zighini* (beef and lamb), *derho* (chicken) and *zilzil tibsi* (veal) are served on thick layers of *injiira* or Eritrean bread. There's a vegetarian menu as well. A glass of honey wine or cardamom tea makes a good accompaniment.
Tables outdoors.

French

Charly's Saucerie
Via San Giovanni in Laterano, 270 (70 49 47 00). Metro Colosseo/bus to Piazza San Giovanni in Laterano. **Closed** Mon lunch; Sat lunch; Sun; one week Aug. **Average** L55,000. **Credit** All major cards.
This Franco-Swiss restaurant just off Piazza San Giovanni is stuck in a time-warp – but it's a very pleasant one. Candles and a vaguely art nouveau décor set off the house specialities: fondues, snails and goulash, plus a range of crêpes to round things off, all backed up by a reliable French wine list. Charly's was one of the first places in Rome to abolish the cover charge – well before the city council forced rivals to follow suit.

L'Eau Vive
Via Monterone, 85 (65 41 095/68 80 10 95). Bus to Largo di Torre Argentina. **Closed** Sun; three weeks Aug. **Average** L70,000. **Credit** All major cards.
Possibly the oddest culinary experience in Rome. If Fellini had ever directed a James Bond film, he would have set it here. Picture the scene: an obscure order of multi-ethnic Third World nuns runs a sophisticated French *haute cuisine*-inspired restaurant in a beautiful sixteenth-century palazzo, with breathtaking Renaissance frescoes dancing round the ceiling. Sitting round the elegantly laid triumphs of antique silver, starched white linen and flower arrangements are the extras: an assortment of representatives from the Vatican, the CIA and what's left of the KGB, along with the sleazier elements of the erstwhile Christian Democrat Party. At 9pm, the diners are interrupted by the tinkle of a silver bell and invited to join in the Ave Maria. The food is standard French, with a rotating weekly selection of more exotic dishes. They also do a bargain-price tourist lunch, minus the silver service and the international intrigue.

Indian

Il Guru
Via Cimarra, 4/6 (47 44 110). Bus to Via Nazionale or Via Cavour. **Evenings and Sun lunch only.** **Closed** Mon; two weeks Aug. **Average** L35,000. **Credit** All major cards.
Nothing spectacular by London standards, but if you're dying for an Indian, Il Guru is a reliable option. Like the Maharajah (*see below*), it has a tandoori oven; the cuisine is standard pan-Indian, with a vegetarian menu. Friendly staff.

***Maharajah
Via dei Serpenti, 124 (47 47 144). Bus to Via Nazionale or Via Cavour. **Closed** Sun lunch. **Average** L40,000. **Credit** All major cards.

A recent arrival, right next door to the Guru, the Maharajah has the culinary edge, though it's also a tad more expensive. Classic Punjab cooking with a *tandoori* oven and a vegetarian menu.
Air-conditioning.

Japanese

Hasekura
Via dei Serpenti, 27 (48 36 48). Bus to Via Nazionale or Via Cavour. **Closed** Sun; Aug. **Average** L50,000. **Credit** All major cards.
The best-value of Rome's five serious Japanese restaurants, Hasekura is an intimate little place, with good *sushi* and *sashimi*. You can opt for fixed-price menus or go *à la carte*. *Air-conditioning.*

Middle Eastern

La Piramide da Maometto
Viale di Porta Ardeatina, 114 (57 59 880). Metro Piramide/bus or tram to Porta San Paolo. **Dinner only.** **Closed** Wed; three weeks Aug. **Average** L35,000. **No credit cards.**
The best-known Arab restaurant in Rome, with a spectacular view of the city's own Pyramid. The quality of the food – mostly classic Egyptian dishes – and of the service varies wildly. Many clients book for Thursday or Friday night, when the presence of an Egyptian orchestra and belly-dancer swells the prices.
Tables outdoors.

***Shawerma
Via Ostilia, 24 (70 08 101). Metro Colosseo/bus or tram to Piazza del Colosseo. **Closed** Mon; one week Aug. **Average** L35,000. **Credit** AmEx, DC.
An extremely well-run Egyptian restaurant near the Colosseum. You can sit downstairs on seats, or cross-legged on cushions upstairs on a low balcony. The cuisine is first-rate, with excellent couscous, and features lots of unusual milk-based desserts; lubrication comes in the form of rose wine. During the day it's an Arab café, where you can drink such exotic beverages as *hansun*, *salhab* and *erfa*, as well as mint tea and Egyptian coffee. Shawerma Express (*see chapter* **Snacks**), near the station, is their fast-food outlet.
Air-conditioning. Tables outdoors.

Thai

Sawasdee
Viale XXI Aprile, 13c (86 11 036). Metro Bologna/bus to Viale XXI Aprile. **Average** L35,000. **Credit** All major cards.
It's a bit out of the way – next door to the Thai Embassy in the eastern suburbs – but it does authentic Thai food, with good fish dishes and fresh vegetables.
Air-conditioning.

Vietnamese

Thien Kim
Via Giulia, 201 (68 30 78 32). Bus to Lungotevere dei Tebaldi. **Closed** Sun; Aug. **Average** L35,000. **Credit** AmEx, MC, V.
When this Vietnamese restaurant opened in 1975, coming to eat here was more a political statement than a culinary choice, but Thien Kim has survived as one of the capital's few worthwhile oriental outlets. The sweet-and-sour soup is good; frogs' legs, prepared in a variety of styles, feature prominently.

Snacks

Hours to go before your next meal and feeling a bit peckish? Help is at hand.

At first sight, Rome can appear an oddly snackless city, and it's true that people are more likely to opt for a full, sit-down meal than to eat on the run. Roman snack culture does exist, but a bit of inside knowledge will help you make sense of it.

Few new arrivals, for example, would consider stepping into a humble *alimentari* (grocer) to have their picnic lunch prepared – and yet for fresh bread and high-quality fillings, this is invariably the best option. And while you'll find the same white, triangular sandwiches lurking behind every bar, some of these establishments are lunchtime Meccas, with full-scale *tavole calde* (buffets) that allow those in a hurry to eat fast and well.

What follows is a selective and centre-biased guide to how and where to snack in Rome. For further snacking options, *see also chapters* **Wine Bars** *and* **Cafés & Bars**.

Alimentari

From around noon until they close for lunch at 1.30, Roman *alimentari* play host to a tradition which, for some reason, appears to be largely masculine. The client enters the shop and asks for *un panino con...* (a roll with...), waits while the man with the apron cuts the roll, prepares the filling, and puts it all together, and wanders out again clutching the bundle, plus a can of something, usually beer. Hey presto: lunch. Favourite casing is the ubiquitous Roman roll, *la rosetta*, or a slice of *pizza bianca* (plain oiled and salted pizza, to be eaten as is or cut down the middle and filled); fillings are generally ham, salami or cheese. Since *alimentari* do not sell fruit and veg, you have to do without the tomato or lettuce. Any Roman *alimentari* will perform this service for you. For upmarket deli outlets serving a gourmet version of the above (especially **Volpetti** and **Franchi**), *see chapter* **Shopping**.

L'Antico Forno
Via delle Muratte, 8 (67 92 866). Bus to Via del Corso or Via del Tritone. **Open** *Sept-May* 7am-9pm Mon-Wed, Fri-Sun; 7am-1pm Thur. *June-Aug* 7am-9pm daily.
Right next to the Trevi fountain, this bakery/general store does ready-made (but fresh) filled rolls, plus the usual *gastronomia* fare – rice and seafood salad and so on. Service is grumpy but efficient.

Bars

Bars that offer something beyond the usual cardboard sandwiches include the following.

Bar Sogo
Via Ripetta, 242-5 (36 12 272). Metro Spagna/bus to Via Ripetta or Piazza Augusto Imperatore. **Open** 8am-7.30pm Tue-Sat.
At first glance there's nothing particularly Japanese about this convenient and pleasant lunchtime bar, which offers the usual range of *panini* and *gelati*. But it's next door to Rome's only Japanese food store, and a few tables out back provide a Japanese fast-food service, with good *tempura* and *tofu* (though *sushi* is currently not on the menu).

La Casa del Tramezzino
Viale Trastevere, 81 (no phone). Bus to Viale Trastevere. **Open** 7am-2am Wed-Mon.
During one of his periodic struggles against foreign influences, Mussolini banned certain foreign words and coined new ones to replace them. Sandwich, for example, became *tramezzino*. Unlike some of his other attempts to redesign the language, this word stuck. La Casa del Tramezzino has the widest choice of sandwiches anywhere in Rome. Apart from classics like mozzarella and tomato, try their fried aubergine, rocket and Gorgonzola, or cheese and caviar. You can take away or eat at outside tables.

Galeani
Via Arenula, 50 (68 80 60 42). Bus/tram to Via Arenula. **Open** 6am-10.30pm Mon-Sat.
A lively bar packed with customers from the Justice Ministry

Snacks by Area

Centro Storico
Fratelli Paladini; Galeani; Da Giovanni; McDonald's; Zi Fenizia.

Tridente
Antico Forno; Birreria Fratelli Tempera; Focacci; McDonald's; Bar Sogo.

Monti & Esquilino
La Diligenza Rossa; Gran Caffè Strega; Kabir Fastfood; Palazza delle Esposizioni; Pizzeria Leonina; McDonald's; Shawerma Express; Vino e Porchetta.

Trastevere
La Casa del Tramezzino; McDonald's.

Testaccio, Celio & Aventino
Il Seme e La Foglia; Volpetti; Volpetti II.

across the road. Barman Giancarlo makes up filled *rosette* or slices of *pizza bianca* on the spot. The edge-of-the-Ghetto location is reflected in fillings like *bottarga* (mullet roe) and *pastrami* (salt beef).

Gran Caffè Strega
Piazza Viminale, 27-31 (48 56 70). Metro Repubblica/bus to Via Nazionale. **Open** 6am-midnight Mon-Sat.
Down a narrow alley tucked under the imposing Interior Ministry (which supplies most of its lunchtime custom), this

is a good place for a fast and inexpensive lunch. Highlights are pizza cooked *a legna* (in a wood oven), copious salad bar and cold buffet, and copious cakes and ice cream for the sweet-toothed.

Il Seme e la Foglia
Via Galvani, 18 (57 43 008). **Open** 7am-1.30am Mon-Sat. **Closed** Last two weeks Aug.
Once a po-faced macrobiotic affair, populated and run by ageing *sessantottini* (the 1968 student protest generation),

Nouvelle Pizza

As if to compensate for the sacrilege of what passes for pizza abroad, Italian *pizzaioli* tend to have a fundamentalist streak. True, there have always been regional schisms, especially between supporters of the thicker, doughier *pizza napoletana* and advocates of the much thinner and crisper Roman version. But such differences were really just fine tuning. The basic method was always the same: make up an impasto out of water, flour and yeast, knead it, and leave it to rise briefly before tearing off fist-sized balls of dough, which are then rolled flat, covered in the appropriate topping, and put in a very hot oven.

Such was the Gospel according to just about every *pizzaiolo* you cared to ask – until Angelo Iezzi came along. At the tender age of 33, Iezzi has become the Luther of the pizza world. The height of most Italian pizza makers' ambition is to set up shop on their own, but for Iezzi this was just the beginning. The problem was that Iezzi, like many *pizzaioli*, was in the business of takeaway pizza – what Romans call *pizza rustica*. The standard dough was all very well for restaurant pizzas, designed to be consumed immediately they emerged from the oven; but takeaway pizza tends to sit around for a while before getting reheated. The result can be a hard, indigestible slab.

In the late '80s, from his takeaway pizza parlour in the suburb of Monte Sacro, Iezzi began to experiment with different ingredients, different rising times, different temperatures. With the help of supplier Corrado Di Marco, he finally arrived at a dough based on a mixture of flours – including soya – which is left to rise for as long as 48 hours at low temperatures before it's ready for the oven. The resulting pizza is thicker than your average Roman pizza, but not heavy on the stomach like the Neapolitan version, because the enzymes have had time to do their work. The nouvelle pizza is light and airy – Iezzi disciple Mauro de Maio even claims that 'you can eat a kilo of it after dinner without regretting it' – and, importantly for the takeaway brigade, it stays fresh for much longer.

Colleagues were sceptical, but Iezzi took them on at the National Pizza Championships and won two years running. He has since retired from what he calls an 'unfair contest' and set up a school in Rome, dedicated to passing on The Method to eager disciples, including representatives from Israel, Sweden and even Bosnia. Gradually, Iezzi is taking over the key outlets, placing his priests of nouvelle pizza in the pizza parlours of Rome, Italy and the world. And its not just takeaways: The Method, according to Iezzi, works just as well in the round.

You can sample nouvelle pizza – with a variety of adventurous toppings – at the following addresses. Most are out in the eastern suburbs, but they're definitely worth the journey.

Takeaway
Angelo Iezzi *Via Nomentana, 581*, 11.30am-midnight Mon-Sat.
Il Tempio del Buongustaio *Via Tiburtina, 385*, 9am-midnight daily.
L'Altra Pizza *Viale Somalia, 262*, 9am-midnight.
Italia *Corso d'Italia, 103*, 9am-9.30pm Mon-Sat.
Pizzeria Elio Fattori *Viale di Valli Pamphili, 46a*, 10am-10pm daily.

Eat in
Dar Poeta *Vicolo Bologna, 45*, evenings only Tue-Sun.

For aspiring evangelists, Angelo Iezzi runs five-week beginners' courses at the **Scuola Italiana Pizzaioli**, *Via Taro, 14* (85 40 451).

this has become a lively daytime snack bar and evening pre-club stop. At lunchtime there is always one pasta dish, plus a range of salads and exotic filled rolls to choose from. The food is predominantly, but no longer exclusively, vegetarian. Many of the habitués are musicians from the *Scuola Popolare di Musica* around the corner.

Pizza a Taglio

Pizza a taglio or *pizza rustica* is classic Roman fast food: a slab of variously-topped pizza making for the classic quick meal. But as it is sold by weight, takeaway pizza is not always in the best interests of the customer's wallet or stomach – and beware too of outlets with a slow turnover, where the pizza on display is likely to have been out of the oven for a good few hours. This warning does not apply to the outlets below, nor to the adepts of *nouvelle pizza*, with its lighter, longer-rising dough base (*see* **Nouvelle Pizza** *page 144*).

Fratelli Paladini
Via del Governo Vecchio, 29 (68 61 237). Bus to Corso Vittorio Emanule. **Open** *Oct-May* 8am-2pm, 5-8pm Fri-Wed. *June-Sept* 8am-2pm, 5-8pm Mon-Fri.
This ancient, family-run bread shop looks like nothing special, but the crowd that spills outside at peak hours knows

different. The wood-fired *pizza bianca* is outstanding, and the staff will slice it open and fill it to order with hams, cheeses, fresh figs, dried tomatoes and other delights. Help yourself to mineral water.

Da Giovanni
Piazza Campo de' Fiori, 39 (68 77 992). Bus to Corso Vittorio Emanuele. **Open** *Sept-May* 8am-3pm, 4-9pm; *June-July* 8am-midnight. **Closed** Aug.
As well as a series of cold dishes, Giovanni does the best takeaway sliced pizza in the Campo de' Fiori area. Particularly good is the *fiori di zucca* – courgette flower pizza.

Pizzeria Leonina
Via Leonina, 84 (48 27 744). Metro Cavour/bus to Via Cavour. **Open** 7am-8pm Mon-Fri. **Closed** Aug.
One of the best *pizzerie a taglio* in Rome. Avoid peak meal times, as the queue is endless (you have to take a number). Wait as the great metal trays are hauled out of the oven every ten minutes or so, and pick the one that smells best. Not as cheap as one might hope, but with toppings like spicy beans, tuna salad and even apple strudel, it's still worth it.

Zì Fenizia
Via Santa Maria del Pianto, 64 (68 96 976). Bus or tram to Via Arenula. **Open** 9am-8pm Mon-Thur; 9am-noon Fri; 9am-8pm Sun. **Closed** Jewish holidays.
Rome's only kosher pizza outlet, Auntie Fenizia does over 40 flavours, including the speciality *con aliciotti e indivia* (with anchovies and endives).

McDonald's *at the Spanish Steps provides sustenance for the undemanding (page 146).*

A *rosticceria* roasts things on spits – usually chicken. The concept to overlap with a *tavola calda*, which offers a range of hot (or reheated) pasta, meat and vegetable dishes.

Birreria Fratelli Tempera
Via di San Marcello, 19 (67 95 310). Bus to Piazza Venezia. **Open** 12.30-2.45pm, 7.30-11.30pm Mon-Fri. **Closed** Two weeks Aug.
Much better known by its traditional name, the Birreria Peroni, after the Roman brewery, this is the perfect place for a lunchtime snack. Service is canteen-style, and the food – which always includes a couple of pasta options – is good and cheap. If you're really in a rush, you can even stand up at the counter to eat your spaghetti. Beautiful, original art nouveau décor, with slogans like 'Beer is the fountain of youth'. Get there early to avoid the lunchtime rush.

La Diligenza Rossa
Via Merulana, 271 (48 81 216). Metro Vittorio/bus to Via Merulana. **Open** 10am-10pm Tue-Sun.
The ultimate *rosticceria* in Rome – witness the spectacular

log fire on which the chickens are roasted, either whole, half or *alla diavola* (crushed flat). You can smell the aroma of oak-roasted *pollo* as you step out of Santa Maria Maggiore, 300 metres away. They also have a wide selection of cold dishes, and wines for takeaways as well as sit-down service. The head waiter, Ricchi, is a well-known Rome personality.

Vino e Porchetta
Via del Viminale, 2 (48 83 031). Metro Repubblica or Termini/bus to Termini. **Open** 8.30am-3pm, 5-9pm Mon-Fri; 8.30am-3pm Sat.
A minute hole in the wall near the Opera which specialises in one of the great culinary triumphs of the Roman countryside: *porchetta* – strongly peppered cold roast baby piglet – between two slices of *casareccio* bread and a glass of Castelli white wine. Utterly delicious.

Volpetti Più
Via Alessandro Volta, 8/10 (57 44 306). Metro Piramide/bus or tram to Via Marmorata. **Open** 9.30am-3.30pm, 6pm-midnight daily.
Close to the upmarket deli of the same name, this snack bar does excellent high-rise *pizza a taglio* and a range of other hot and cold dishes. Unusually for a buffet, it also has a range of good bottles of wine at *enoteca* (off-licence) prices.

Eating In

Match about to start on your satellite TV, and the hotel food's too awful to contemplate? Take the Roman way out: a quick dash to the local pizzeria.

Companies who will deliver to your door are few and far between. Long-term residents with a pizzeria nearby make a point of building up a close enough rapport with the man at the oven to be able to phone though an order and get him to ring your doorbell when it's ready. If you haven't reached this degree of integration into Roman society, and you can't risk missing the kick-off, try one of the following outlets:

China Cena
(37 25 453) **Open** 7-11pm daily. **Closed** Two weeks Aug. **No credit cards.**
One of the Roman pioneers of meals-on-wheels, offering standard Chinese dishes. Minimum order of L40,000.

Mille Una Cena
(32 31 388/32 31 484) **Open** 7-10.30pm daily. **Credit** AmEx, V.
Pizza, Indian, Chinese or Arabic food delivered to your door within 90 minutes of your phone call. Delivery is free, but minimum orders of L35,000 for Chinese and Arabic and L40,000 for pizzas are required.

Pizzeria All'Angolo
(32 27 494) **Open** 7pm-midnight Tue-Sun. **No credit cards.**
Delivers throughout north and central Rome for an additional 30% on top of your bill. They also deliver videos for no extra charge if you're a member of **Filmania 4** (*see chapter* **Services**).

Kabir Fastfood
Via Mamiani, 11 (44 60 792). Metro Vittorio/bus or tram to Piazza Vittorio. **Open** 9.30am-10.30pm Mon-Sat.
.Rome's only Indian takeaway, just around the corner from Piazza Vittorio Emanuele. You can eat in, too, accompanied by gloriously kitsch Indian music videos.

McDonald's
Piazza della Repubblica, 40 (48 15 510). Metro Repubblica/bus to Piazza della Repubblica or Termini. **Open** 8am-midnight Thur-Tue. **Central branches**: *Piazza di Spagna, 46/7 (69 92 24 00); Piazza Sonnino (58 97 127); Galleria Stazione Termini (48 28 985); Corso Vittorio Emanuele, 135 (68 92 412); Via Cola Di Rienzo, 156 (68 74 225); Via Firenze, 58 (48 19 758).*
The Piazza della Repubblica outlet is the world's third-busiest branch after Moscow and Champs-Elysées, but it's the only one with an eighteenth-century crystal chandelier. Architecturally, it's a real gem, and the toilets come in very handy when you're caught short on or near the Spanish Steps. Between 8 and 11am this and the Piazza di Spagna outlet do a full American breakfast.

Ristorante Self-Service del Palazzo delle Esposizioni
Via Milano, 9 (48 28 001). Bus to Via Nazionale. **Open** *Bar* 10am-9pm Wed-Mon; *buffet* 12.30-3pm Wed-Mon.
Downstairs, the bar in this split-level arts centre complex does standard bar food, including some knockout Sicilian pastries (*see chapter* **Cafés & Bars**). Go up in the glass lift to find a reasonably priced buffet with a good salad bar – a rarity in Rome. Ideal for a quiet lunch in an arty atmosphere away from the hustle of the Roman streets. You don't need to pay to see an exhibition. The separate bar/buffet entrance is on the left of the Palazzo, halfway up the stairs. *See also chapters* **Shopping**, **Museums & Galleries** *and* **Film**.

Shawerma Express
Via Catalafimi, 7 (48 18 791). Metro Termini/bus to Termini or Via Goito. **Open** 11am-midnight daily.
Good-value Arab and Middle Eastern specialities such as *felafel, fuul* (spicy beans), couscous and kebabs, served with pitta bread, to take away or to eat in. There are tables outside in summer.

Wine Bars

Eat, drink and be merry – all under the same roof.

Neighbourhood *enoteche* (wine shops) and *vini e oli* outlets have been around since ancient times, complete with their huddle of old men drinking wine by the glass (*al bicchiere* or *alla mescita*). But recently a number of upmarket wine bars has sprung up, offering a range of hot or cold lunchtime and dinner snacks. Such is the Roman predilection for eating over drinking that some of these – *Il Simposio, Trimani Wine Bar, Il Brillo Parlante, Ferrara* – are best thought of as restaurants with great cellars. For mere bottle-buying, *see chapter* **Shopping**.

Centro storico

L'Angolo Divino
Via dei Balestrari, 12 (68 64 413). Bus to Largo Argentina. **Open** 10.30am-3pm Mon; 10.30am-3pm, 5.30-1am Tue-Sun. **Closed** One week Aug. **Credit** EC, MC, V.
This punningly named wine bar on a quiet street near Campo de' Fiori has come up in the world since it opened as a humble *vini e oli* 50 years ago. The décor is simple but pleasing: terracotta floor, beamed ceiling and government-surplus tables. Fifteen or so wines are available by the glass, and many more by the bottle or to take away. There's a good range of salads – a rarity in Rome – plus smoked salmon, cheeses and, outside the summer season, at least one hot dish.

Bevitoria
Piazza Navona, 72 (68 80 10 22). Bus to Corso del Rinascimento or Corso Vittorio Emanuele. **Open** 11am-1am Mon-Sat. **Credit** All major cards.
A surprisingly relaxed and friendly little bar with tables outside on the Piazza Navona, and a few more inside that you should grab by 6pm if you want to linger for the evening. When it's not too busy, the owner is happy to show customers the cellars, which occupy part of the remains of Domitian's stadium. Another great attraction is the winter speciality of mulled wine.
Tables outside.

Bottega del Vino da Bleve
Via Santa Maria del Pianto, 9a-11 (68 65 970). Bus to Largo Argentina. **Open** *Enoteca* 9.30am-1pm, 4.30-8pm Mon-Sat; *wine bar* 12.45-3pm Mon-Sat. **Closed** Three weeks Aug. **Credit** All major cards.
This well-stocked wine-shop in the Ghetto has recently started offering a lunch menu: a good selection of salads, smoked fish and cheeses, two or three pasta dishes. Tables are arranged among the shelves of bottles and whisked away again in time for afternoon opening.

Cul de Sac
Piazza Pasquino, 73 (68 80 10 94). Bus to Corso Vittorio Emanuele. **Open** 6.30pm-12.30am Mon; 12.30-3pm, 6.30pm-12.30 Tue-Sun. **No credit cards.**
Rome's original wine bar, founded in 1968. It's cramped inside and out – slide along to the end of a bench, and new

arrivals will gradually hem you in – but anywhere that offers bottles this good at prices this low, within spitting distance of Piazza Navona, has got to be worth a spin. The food is standard wine bar fare, mainly cold. The Greek salad and *crema di lenticchie* (lentil soup) stand out from the rest. *Air-conditioning. Tables outside.*

Il Goccetto
Via dei Banchi Vecchi, 14 (68 64 268). Bus to Corso Vittorio. **Open** 10.30am-1.30pm Mon-Sat. **Closed** Three weeks Aug. **Credit** AmEx, MC, V.
One of the more serious and reasonably priced of the *centro storico* wine bars, Il Goccetto occupies the ground floor of a medieval bishop's house, with original wooden ceilings and a cosy, private-club feel (most of owner Sergio's clients are regulars). Wine (to drink here or take away) is the main point, with a satisfying range of by-the-glass options, but there's also a good selection of cheeses, salami and summer salads.

Il Piccolo
Via del Governo Vecchio, 74/75 (68 80 17 46). Bus to Corso Vittorio Emanuele. **Open** 11am-2am Mon-Fri; 7pm-2am Sat-Sun. **Credit** All major cards.

La Vineria – *seriously hip (see page 148).*

A fashionable and, consequently, not-cheap *enoteca* on the Via del Governo Vecchio, with tables on the street and fresco-like decoration inside. There's a good selection of Italian wines to drink in the bar or take home, but the great speciality is the wonderful *fragolino di bosco*, wild strawberry wine, available during the autumn months.

La Vineria

Campo de' Fiori, 15 (68 80 32 68). Bus to Corso Vittorio Emanuele. **Open** 9.30am-2pm, 6pm-2am, Mon-Sat. **Credit** V.
Known also as Da Giorgio, this is an authentic local wine bar with a gutsy-looking elderly clientele. The place is evocatively portrayed in Michael Dibden's novel *Vendetta* as the favourite drinking haunt of his cop hero, Aurelio Zen. By night, it becomes a seriously hip hang-out for bright young things (as well as some slightly tarnished older ones) who crowd its pavement tables. Also a good place to pick up a bottle after hours.

Tridente

Antica Enoteca di Via della Croce

Via della Croce, 76b (67 90 896). Metro Spagna/bus to Pizza Augusto Imperatore or Piazza di Spagna.
Open *Enoteca* 11am-1am daily; *restaurant* 12.30-3pm, 7-10.30pm, daily. **Credit** AmEx, DC, MC, V.
A good selection of wines by the glass from L4,000-10,000, plus a cold buffet at the counter and a restaurant with tables in the long back room offering a full range of hot dishes at meal times. When this place first opened in 1842 it was the favourite haunt of Scandinavian painters who lived in nearby Via Margutta. A tasteful revamp has retained most of the original fittings, including the marble wine vats and a venerable wooden cash desk. There's also a range of fine wines to take away.

Il Brillo Parlante

Via della Fontanella, 12 (32 43 334). Bus to Pizza del Popolo. **Open** *Upstairs bar* 11am-2am Mon-Sat; 7.30pm-1am Sun. *Downstairs restaurant* 12.30-2.45pm, 7.30pm-1am, Mon-Sat; 7.30pm-1am Sun. **Credit** All major cards.
Upstairs you can drink wines by the glass and have the odd nibble sitting at the marble counter, or at two tiny outside tables. Downstairs, this new wine bar, just around the corner from picturesque Piazza del Popolo, opens out into a vaulted cellar with heraldic frescoes. Unusually for a wine bar, it also does pizzas – admittedly, not exactly the best in Rome – as well as a good variety of hot and cold dishes. Your best bet is to sit back and let the friendly waiters guide you through the daily-changing specials.
Air-conditioning.

Nando Severini

Via Bocca di Leone, 44a (67 86 031). Metro Spagna. **Open** 8am-1pm, 5-8pm, Mon-Sat. **Closed** Two weeks Aug. **No credit cards.**
Nando is a legend in the *Tridente* quarter. This may be Rome's smartest shopping area, but Nando was born here and his family have owned a *vino e olio* outlet in the area for over 40 years. Despite a forced move seven years ago from premises now occupied by the restaurant **Al 34** (where you can still see the original mosaic shop-sign), this replica just around the corner continues to attract an eclectic clientele. They come to drink Nando's superlative, own-label *prosecco* and his delicious *fragolino* – a sweet sparkling rosé made from *uva fragola*, or strawberry grapes. Food consists of a few *tartine* with olive or mushroom paste. Perch on a

crate next to Nando's dog and look at his curious collection of newspaper cuttings and cubist paintings. Unmissable.

Trastevere

Ferrara

Via del Moro, 1a (58 03 769). Bus or tram to Viale Trastevere. **Open** 8.30pm-1am Wed-Mon. **Credit** All major cards.
In what is a surprisingly big space for Trastevere, the Paolillo sisters have set up this tasteful imbibery, with its well-stocked cellar. The apartheid wine list (one book for whites, another for reds) provides a happy evening's reading, and Mary in the kitchen puts together some wonderful soups which, along with the desserts, are the highlight of a varied and variable menu. In summer, you can wine and dine in a quiet garden at the back.
Tables outside.

Monti & Esquilino

Cavour 313

Via Cavour, 313 (67 85 496). Metro Cavour/bus to Via Cavour. **Open** *Sept-May* 12.30-2.30pm, 7.30pm-12.30am, Mon-Sat; 7.30pm-12.30am Sun. *June-July* 12.30-2.30pm, 7.30pm-12.30am, daily. **Closed** Aug. **No credit cards.**
A friendly atmosphere (despite the gloomy mahogany décor), a serious cellar and good snacks explain the eternal popularity of this wine bar at the Forum end of Via Cavour. Prices are reasonable and there's a wide selection of hot and cold snacks; in winter, they're especially strong on soups. With over 500 bottles on the wine list, choice is the only problem.
Air-conditioning.

Trimani Wine Bar

Via Cernaia, 37b (44 69 661). Bus to Via XX Settembre. **Open** 11.30am-3pm, 5.30pm-midnight, Mon-Sat. **Closed** Aug. **Credit** All major cards.
This recently-opened wine bar offshoot of Rome's leading *enoteca* (*see chapter* **Shopping**) has an excellent choice of Italian regional wines together with an appropriate choice of pasta dishes, quiches, soups and *crostini*. The desserts are absolutely first-rate – especially the *mousse al cioccolato*.

Northern Suburbs

Il Simposio di Piero Costantini

Piazza Cavour, 16 (32 13 210). Bus to Piazza Cavour. **Open** *Enoteca* 4.30-8pm Mon; 9am-1pm, 4.30-8pm, Tue-Sun. *Wine bar* 11.30am-3pm, 6.30pm-1am, Mon-Fri, Sun; 6.30pm-1am Sat. **Credit** All major cards.
The magnificent *enoteca* in the basement deserves a visit of its own, but the street-level wine bar has to be seen to be believed. Everything – the door, windows, the indoor staircase – is covered with a wrought-iron vine and grapes motif. Behind velvet drapes lies the restaurant, which serves five or six hot dishes a day, not to mention a range of salads, smoked salmon, cured meat, an encyclopaedic cheese board and delicious desserts. Prices are decidedly upmarket – expect to spend around L45,000 a head for a full meal – but then so is the quality. The wine list includes 2,000 Italian wines by the bottle and a daily selection of around 20 by the glass.
Air-conditioning. Booking advisable.

Cafés & Bars

They may not be the last word in sophistication, but they're the best place to observe modern Romans at close quarters.

Authentic Roman bars (or cafés – the terms are interchangeable) in salt-of-the-earth suburbs have zinc counters, a shelf of lurid liqueurs, a steaming coffee machine, a tray of limp *cornetti* (the Italian variant on the croissant), photos of football teams and floors strewn with sawdust, cigarette stubs and screwed-up paper napkins. The vast majority of their counterparts in the city centre have undergone the post-modernisation treatment, trading the zinc counter for highly-polished wood, but the other elements remain largely intact.

Whatever the décor, the fascinating cross-section of humanity frequenting them means that a visit to a Roman bar is rarely dull. There are still a few survivors from more splendid eras, while others offer such fantastic vantage points over the city that the interior decoration is immaterial.

All bars sell hot beverages, soft drinks and alcohol, together with sweets, chocolates and chewing-gum. Some also serve as late-night off-licences. Then come the variations on the bar theme: *bar/latteria* (selling dairy products); *bar/drogheria* (corner store incorporated); or *bar/tabacchi* (selling cigarettes, stamps and a regular Aladdin's Cave of other merchandise; *see* **Tabacchi** *in chapter* **Directory**). Other classifications you may find tacked on after *bar* include *gelateria* (ice creams and ice cream-based puddings), *pasticceria* (fancy cakes) and *torrefazione* (coffee roasting and grinding). There are no licensing hours, so have no qualms about ordering a *grappa* for breakfast.

Centro storico

Antica Pasticceria Bella Napoli

Corso Vittorio Emanuele, 248/50 (68 77 048). Bus to Corso Vittorio Emanuele. **Open** 7.30am-9pm Mon-Thur, Sat-Sun. **Closed** Three weeks Aug.
Best known for its Neapolitan *dolci* such as *sfogliatelle ricce* (pastry with ricotta filling), and *babà* (rum-soaked cake) to take away or eat on the spot with a *cappuccino*. Ask for *cappuccino scuro* if you don't want a lukewarm milkshake, and have your *sfogliatella* heated for a real treat.

Bar Le Cinque Lune

Piazza Cinque Lune, 86/8 (no phone). Bus to Corso Rinascimento. **Open** 5.30am-1am Tue-Sun.
This excellent bar serves great lunchtime snacks – *pane alle olive*, the wafer-thin Sardinian bread *piadina sarda*, and the classic Sicilian *paste alle mandorle* (almond-paste tarts). There are loads of tables outside.

Caffè Farnese

Via dei Baullari, 106/7 (68 80 21 25). Bus to Corso Vittorio Emanuele. **Open** 7am-2am daily.
This *gelateria/pasticceria* is a popular meeting-place on the corner of Piazza Farnese, with good people-watching potential from tables on the street. The coffee, *cornetti* and *pizza romana* are excellent.

Ciampini

Piazza Navona, 94-100 (68 61 547). Bus to Largo di Torre Argentina. **Open** 9am-midnight Tue-Sun.
A classic *bar/gelateria/ristorante*, busy night and day, with an outstanding view: seated outside in Piazza Navona, you can admire Bernini's Fontana dei Quattro Fiume (though the mark-up on your bill may detract from the pleasure). From the back of the bar you can watch Italy's senators arriving for a day's politicking.

Da Vezio

Via dei Delfini, 23 (67 86 036). Bus to Largo di Torre Argentina. **Open** 7am-8.30pm Mon-Sat.
Vezio Bagazzini is a legendary figure in the Ghetto area, on account of his extraordinary *bar/latteria* behind the former Communist Party HQ in Via delle Botteghe Oscure. Every square centimetre is filled with Communist icons and trophies – Italian, Soviet and Cuban. A place of pilgrimage for many *compagni*.

Dolce Vita

Piazza Navona, 70a (68 80 62 21). Bus to Corso del Rinascimento or Corso Vittorio Emanuele. **Open** 7.30am-2am daily.
Tiny inside, but with plenty of tables on the square, Dolce Vita is a pleasant alternative to other more touristy bars on the piazza.

Latteria del Gallo

Vicolo del Gallo, 4 (68 65 091). Bus to Corso Vittorio Emanuele. **Open** 8.30am-2pm, 5pm-midnight, Thur-Tue. **Closed** Two weeks Aug.
With its old marble slab tables and authentic atmosphere, this café in a side road between Campo de' Fiori and Piazza Farnese has remained impervious to passing fashions. Something of a *centro storico* institution, it's still popular with Rome's hippy community and foreign residents.

Pascucci

Via di Torre Argentina, 20 (68 64 816). Bus to Largo Argentina. **Open** 6.30am-midnight Mon-Sat.
This very modest bar in the centre of town has earned itself a reputation as milkshake heaven. Milk isn't obligatory: no combination of fresh fruit froth (frullati) is too exotic here.

Sant'Eustachio

Piazza Sant'Eustachio, 82 (68 61 309). Bus to Corso del Rinascimento. **Open** 8.30am-1am Thur-Tue.
The most famous coffee bar in the city, its walls are plastered with testimonials from world leaders. The coffee is quite extraordinary – if very expensive. They specialise in frothing up their *espresso*: the *schiuma* (froth) can be slurped out afterwards with spoon or fingers. Unless you

Trattoria Pizzeria della Pace

Via della Pace, 1 - 00186 Roma ☎ **06/68.64.802**
Orario di apertura 12.00-15.00 / 19.00-01.00 - Chiusura settimanale lunedì mattina

*Soak up coffee and atmosphere at **Antico Caffè Greco**.*

specify *caffè amaro*, it comes heavily sugared. Asking for a *cappuccino* here is the equivalent of having 'tourist' tattooed across your forehead.

La Tazza d'Oro

Via degli Orfani, 84 (67 89 792). Bus to Largo di Torre Argentina. **Open** 7am-8.15pm Mon-Sat.
The powerful aroma wafting from this ancient *torrefazione* is a siren call to all coffee lovers. It's packed with coffee sacks, tourists and regulars who flock for *la monichella* (*see* **How to Handle the Roman Bar** *page 152), granita di caffè* (coffee sorbet), and *cioccolata calda con panna* (hot chocolate with whipped cream) in winter.

The *Tridente*

Alla Scrofa

Via della Scrofa, 104 (68 69 552). Bus to Corso Rinascimento. **Open** 6am-9.30pm Mon-Sat.
One of the area's most enjoyable neighbourhood bars, despite a large quotient of politicos, particularly from the far-right *Alleanza Nazionale* party that's based just down the road. The ice cream is made on the premises and the staff make better-than-average snacks, including imaginatively stuffed sandwiches.

Antico Caffè Greco

Via Condotti, 86 (67 85 474). Metro Spagna. **Open** 8am-9pm Mon-Sat. **Closed** Two weeks mid-Aug.
Founded in 1760, this venerable café was the one-time hangout of Casanova, Goethe, Hans Christian Andersen, Wagner, Liszt, Stendhal, Baudelaire, Shelley and Byron. During the French Occupation of 1849-70, the organised opposition was based here. Now its sofas are packed with tourists, while locals cram the foyer. The décor is elaborate: brocade walls lined with ancient gilded mirrors and oil portraits, and marble tables and sofas. The waiters look like royal ushers but move far more slowly.

Babington

Piazza di Spagna, 23 (67 86 027). Metro Spagna/bus to Piazza San Silvestro. **Open** *Winter* 9am-11.30pm Mon, Wed-Sun; *summer* 9am-11.30pm Mon, Wed-Sat; 9am-1pm Sun. **Credit** AmEx, DC, EC, MC, V.
Britons may not consider visiting tea-rooms abroad a priority, but will often be directed here by well-meaning Romans, convinced that they cannot survive without an overpriced pot of tea and plate of cakes. Founded by two British spinsters, Babington has occupied this prime location for over a century. Tables outside now make it a more appealing spot in the summer.

Café Notegen

Via del Babuino, 159 (32 00 855). Metro Spagna/bus to Piazza del Popolo or Piazza San Silvestro. **Open** 7am-midnight daily.
An historical gathering spot for theatre people, artists and intellectuals, this century-old café prides itself on being a 'café in the French sense', serving hot and cold dishes at any hour to sophisticated customers in its dusty, rose-coloured velvet booths. Cabaret and other entertainments are staged during the evening from Thursday to Sunday.

Canova

Piazza del Popolo, 16 (36 12 231). Metro Flaminio/bus to Piazzale Flaminio or Piazza del Popolo. **Open** 8am-1am Mon-Thur, Sun; 8am-2am Fri-Sat.
According to tradition, Canova's clientele has always been extremely right-wing, and at dagger's drawn with the left-wing rabble at Rosati (*see below*), across the square. There is little evidence of this now, although these mirror-image bars are still rivals for first place in the piazza. Good for catching the late afternoon sun in spring and autumn.

Ciampini al Café du Jardin

Viale Trinità dei Monti (67 85 678). Metro Spagna/bus to Piazza Barberini. **Open** *Mar-Apr, Oct* 8am-7pm; *June-Sept* 8am-1am. **Closed** Nov-mid-March.
An open-air café surrounded by creeper-curtained trellises,

How to Handle the Roman Bar

It's normal practice to pay at the *cassa* (cash desk) before ordering at the counter. If this seems daunting, don't worry: most bars serve more or less the same fare, so it won't be long before you know the range and are handling it like a veteran. If the bar isn't busy, you can usually pay afterwards. Slap your *scontrino* (receipt) down on the bar (many Romans add L50-200 to get the *barista*'s attention), and place your order.

With the exception of the odd local *bar/latteria*, higher prices are charged for sitting down inside or *all'aperto*. The price difference must be displayed on the wall behind the *cassa*. Be aware that in particularly picturesque or exclusive areas you may pay dearly for the privilege of taking the weight off your feet.

By law, all bars must have a *bagno* (lavatory) which can be used by anyone, regardless of whether they buy anything in the bar. The *bagno* may be locked; ask the cashier for the key (*la chiave per il bagno*). Bars must also provide gasping passers-by with a glass of tap water, again with no obligation to buy.

COFFEE

All Roman bars serve beer, wines, spirits, soft drinks, hot and iced tea, but coffee accounts for 80 per cent of their takings. There are many ways of drinking coffee here, the most basic being the *espresso* (called simply *un caffè*, though *baristi* may presume you're asking for something less concentrated if you sound foreign) and the *cappuccino*. Italians only drink *cappuccino* for breakfast and elevenses, and find it hilarious that foreigners drink it after meals. Romans have an odd habit of drinking their *cappuccino* tepid (they've got things to do, they don't like waiting around till it cools), so you may prefer yours *molto caldo* (very hot) or even *bollente* (boiling).

Variations on the *espresso*

Caffè americano with a lot more water than usual.
Caffè corretto with a dash of liqueur.
Caffè freddo iced *espresso*, sugared unless you ask for a **caffè freddo amaro**.
Caffè Hag *espresso* decaf.
Caffè lungo a bit more water than usual.
Caffè macchiato with a dash of milk.
Caffè monichella *espresso* with whipped cream.
Caffè ristretto tooth-enamel removing coffee essence lining the bottom of the cup.
Caffè al vetro in a glass.

Variations on the *cappuccino*

Caffè latte more hot milk and less coffee, without the froth on top.
Cappuccino freddo iced *cappuccino*, sugared unless you ask specifically for a **cappuccino freddo amaro**.
Latte macchiato hot milk with a dash of coffee.

DRINKS

Birra. Rome has no appreciable beer culture, and beer in bars is peculiarly expensive. Beer is either *alla spina* (on tap) or *in lattina/bottiglia* (canned/bottled). *Alla spina* is served as *una birra piccola/media/grande* (33cl, 50cl, 1l).

Vino. You can buy wine by the glass in most bars, but, except in *enoteche*, the quality of *un bicchiere di vino rosso/bianco* is generally poor. The selection of bottles to take away is also limited and twice the price of an *enoteca* or shop. *Un prosecco* (a glass of dry sparkling white) is a better bet.

with a pond in the centre. There's an excellent selection of tasty sandwiches, pastas, cocktails, ices, and snack lunches. Also serves a good breakfast. A stunning view at sunset.

Dolci e Doni

Via delle Carrozze, 85b (67 82 913). Metro Spagna/bus to Piazza San Silvestro. **Open** 9am-8pm Mon-Sat; noon-8pm Sun. **Closed** One week Aug. **Credit** AmEx, DC, EC, MC, V.

A tiny, genteel tea-room, renowned for its cakes and chocolates, which also specialises in breakfasts, brunches and quick quiche-and-salad lunches.

Rosati

Piazza del Popolo, 5 (32 25 859). Metro Flaminio/bus to Piazzale Flaminio or Piazza del Popolo. **Open** 7.30am-11.30pm daily.

Enjoying a stunning, albeit traffic-snarled, situation on Piazza del Popolo, Rosati is the traditional haunt of Rome's intellectual left – Calvino, Moravia and Pasolini were all regulars. The art nouveau interior remains unchanged since its opening in 1922. All the cakes are baked in the original oven in the kitchens. Head *barista* Marco Frapietro will make you a *Sogni Romani*: fresh orange juice with four kinds of liqueur to form a concoction of red and yellow – the colours of the city and also of Roma soccer club.

Taddei

Via del Babuino, 171 (no phone). Metro Spagna/bus to Piazza del Popolo or Piazza San Silvestro. **Open** 8am-11.30pm Mon-Sat.

A real find: a welcoming *bar di quartiere* in one of Rome's most elegant shopping streets, just a few doors along from Emporio Armani. What's more, Taddei is also a *pasticceria* making excellent *budini di riso* (cakes made from sweet rice) and *sfogliatelle romane* (pastry with ricotta filling). There's no extra charge to sit at the two tables inside.

Via Veneto & Quirinal

Bar del Palazzo delle Esposizioni

Via Milano, 9 (48 28 001/48 28 540). Bus to Via Nazionale. **Open** 10am-9pm Wed-Mon. **Credit** AmEx, DC, MC, V.

The excellent bar at this major arts centre has made it a mecca for local office staff, who also flock to eat at the buffet restaurant upstairs (*see chapter* **Snacks**). You don't need to pay to see an exhibition; the separate bar entrance is on the left of the *palazzo*, halfway up the stairs. Standard bar food, including some knockout fresh cakes.

Café Doney

Via Vittorio Veneto, 145 (48 21 788). Metro Barberini/bus to Via Vittorio Veneto. **Open** 8am-1am Thur-Tue.

A wonderful place at any time of day, either for stand-up coffee or to sit down and relax on Via Veneto, watching the neighbouring doormen entice clients into the local nightclubs. Doney's had its place in the sun during the '50s and '60s, when it was a key meeting point for the Cinecittà set (Ava Gardner, Marcello Mastroianni, Tyrone Power, Anita Ekberg) and the Rome intelligentsia – Eugenio Scalfari dreamed up the *La Repubblica* newspaper here.

Café de Paris

Via Vittorio Veneto, 90 (48 85 284). Metro Barberini/bus to Via Vittorio Veneto. **Open** 8am-1.20am Mon-Tue, Thur, Sun; 8am-2am Fri-Sat.

During Via Veneto's *Dolce Vita* heyday, Café Doney (*see above*) was definitely for the nobs, and Café de Paris on the other side of the road was for those with street-cred. Here you could be served in your jeans (quite something in those days), and listen to the paparazzi badmouth their prey. Almost inevitably, this café became Brando's hangout while

he was filming in Rome. These days it can seem a bit squalid inside, so it's best to find a seat outdoors.

Dagnino

Galleria Esedra, Via VE Orlando, 75 (48 18 660). Metro Repubblica/bus to Piazza della Repubblica or Termini. **Open** 7am-10pm daily.

The split-level interior, with its angular frescoes, coffee bar furniture and shining mirrors, makes this one of Rome's best-preserved monuments to '50s décor. Dagnino specialises in Sicilian *pasticceria* (try the *cassatina*) and ice creams – their *granita di limone* (lemon sorbet) is the best in Rome. Far from trendy, it is mostly frequented by little old ladies and better-off foreign immigrants. Don't miss it.

Trastevere

Bar Gianicolo

Piazzale Aurelio, 5 (58 06 275). Bus to Via Carini. **Open** 7am-2.30am Tue-Sun.

Up the hill from Trastevere, wooden panels and benches lend this tiny bar at the site of Garibaldi's doomed battle with the French an intimate, chatty feel that's hard to find in Rome. Fresh carrots and apples juiced on the spot, plus a large variety of exotic sandwiches, make it a good spot for lunch or a snack. Tables outside. A hangout for the chaps at the nearby American and Spanish Academies.

Bar San Calisto

Piazza San Calisto (no phone). Bus to Viale Trastevere. **Open** 6am-1.30am daily.

Green tourists get their coffee or beer on Piazza Santa Maria in Trastevere. Locals and resident foreigners who know better go to this bar, known in the neighbourhood as Marcello's. Unassuming and inexpensive, it has tables outside; in the company of chatty local matrons on their way to do the shopping, you can watch Trastevere wake up. At night the bar's filled with arty and fringe types, plus a few questionable characters, downing beers or spooning an *affogato* (ice cream swamped with a liqueur).

Cecere

Via San Francesco A Ripa, 152 (58 97 457). Bus to Viale Trastevere. **Open** 6am-2am daily.

A really good selection of fresh, hot and fragrant *cornetti* are turned out non-stop all morning, and again from 9pm on. There's nothing quite like a steaming *Danese* after a tough evening out, and tired late-nighters – including a colourful transvestite crowd – throng this place after midnight.

Sacchetti

Piazza San Cosimato, 61/2 (58 15 374). Bus to Viale Trastevere. **Open** 6am-midnight Thur-Tue.

The Sacchetti family runs one of the best, and least touristy, bars in Trastevere, with tables outside all year round and a large tea-room upstairs. Everything is home-made; the *cornetti* and ricotta-filled *sfogliatelle romane* are recommended.

Sala da Tè Trastè

Via della Lungaretta, 76 (58 94 430). Bus to Viale Trastevere. **Open** 5pm-1am daily. **Closed** Aug.

On the main walkway from Viale Trastevere to Piazza Santa Maria, Sala da Tè Trastè is particularly known for its gastronomic section, fashionable décor and atmosphere. One of the few local places serving tea as a speciality.

Monti and Esquilino

Antico Caffè del Brasile

Via dei Serpenti, 23 (48 82 319). Bus to Via Nazionale. **Open** 5.30am-9pm Mon-Sat.

Despite an ugly '80s makeover, this *torrefazione* on the char-

Rosati, *leading left-wing haunt since 1922 (see page 153).*

acterful main street of Monti still retains its traditional atmosphere. Among its distinguished clientele was the current Pope, while he was still humble Cardinal Wojtyla. A tempting array of chocolates and sweets makes it hard to go away empty-handed.

Bar Gran Caffè dell'Opera

Via Torino, 140 (48 72 221). Metro Termini/bus or tram to Termini. **Open** 7am-2am Tue-Sun.

It says 'kaffè' above the door, a throwback to the '70s when a K looked vaguely revolutionary. Founded in 1880, at the same time as the opera house opposite, this is more a theme park than a bar. The walls are covered with over 300 signed photos of each and every great opera star of the last 130 years. Ideal for inter-act or after-theatre snacks, when you can catch a glimpse of the singers relaxing after the show. There's a hefty 20 per cent price increase after midnight.

Caffè dell'Olmata

Via dell'Olmata, 22 (48 24 601). Metro Cavour/ bus to Via Merulana or Via Giovanni Lanza. **Open** 6am-2am Mon-Fri; 6am-3pm, 8pm-2am Sat-Sun.

A stone's throw from Santa Maria Maggiore, Caffè dell'Olmata offers good snacks, including interesting salads and other cold plates, in a beautiful inner room with a high, beamed ceiling. Becomes something of a pub in the evening. A good place to check out the Roman *giovani* (youth).

Panella

Largo Leopardi, 2-10 (48 72 344). Bus to Piazza Vittorio Emanuele. **Open** 8am-1.30pm, 5.30-8pm, Mon-Wed, Fri; 8am-1.30pm Thur, Sat-Sun.

A bar with a delicatessen selling both Italian and international specialities. The variety of sweets and brioches makes choosing breakfast on Sundays difficult, but it's ideal for a stand-up lunch of spicy tiny pizzas, courgette fritters or vegetable filled crêpes. Most famous for the regional breads, freshly-baked in ovens on the premises, and shaped into crusty sculptures.

Petrucci

Via Ettore Battisti, 129 (67 83 720). Bus to Piazza Venezia. **Open** *Oct-June* 6.30am-midnight Mon-Fri, Sun; *July-Sept* 6.30am-12.30am Mon-Fri, Sun.

Busy all day, thanks to its position just off Piazza Venezia and its *tabacchi* counters, Petrucci really comes alive after dark, when the street outside is crammed with cars parked four-deep, and night-owls head inside for cigarettes and a drink. The later it gets, the more *louche* the atmosphere becomes, as the *carabinieri* from next door rub shoulders with crooks, drug dealers and transvestites.

Testaccio

Bar del Mattatoio

Piazza Orazio Giustiniani, 3 (57 46 017). Metro Piramide/bus to Via Marmorata or Via Galvani. **Open** 6am-9pm Mon-Sat.

A charming brick doll's house bar, with Gothic recesses in the front. One of the earliest-opening bars in Rome, it once catered for the meatworkers from the municipal slaughterhouse (Mattatoio) opposite, but nowadays it happily serves the dawn revellers emerging from Testaccio clubland.

Café du Parc

Piazza di Porta San Paolo (57 43 363). Metro Piramide/ bus or tram to Piazza di Porta San Paolo. **Open** *winter* 4am-9pm daily; *summer* 4am-2am daily.

This kiosk bar is the best place from which to admire the Pyramid of Cestius. The *gelati* are good, especially the *cremolati* – a kind of creamy sorbet. If they have it, try the raspberry. Table service is friendly and efficient, but doesn't come cheap. Now enjoying a major revival thanks to its proximity to Testaccio's flourishing nightlife.

Caffè Tevere

Largo Giovanni Battista Marzi, 8 (57 46 100). Metro Piramide/bus to Ponte Testaccio. **Open** 4.30am-11pm Mon-Sat.

From the outside this former meatworkers' bar, built into the wall of the old slaughterhouse, looks as if it was painted by a Roman Edward Hopper. Now that the beasts are slaughtered elsewhere, the bar has largely been taken over by the uniformed occupants of the nearby *vigili urbani* (traffic police) and pre-dawn truck drivers on their way to the news-stands with the morning papers. A useful stopping-off point for the nearby Villaggio Globale (*see chapter* **Music: Rock Roots and Jazz**).

EUR

Palombini
Piazzale Adenauer, 12 (59 11 700). Metro Magliana/bus to Piazza Guglielmo Marconi. **Open** 7am-midnight daily. **Closed** Two weeks mid-Aug.
In the imposing shadow of the *Palazzo del Civiltà del Lavoro* (aka the Square Colosseum) stands this airy pavilion, surrounded by sweeping gardens. It features a huge patio area covered by a steel and plastic tent arrangement, and has become the favourite meeting point for young Romans, with an impromptu street-party of cars, bikes and Vespas. This is the nearest Rome gets to Beverly Hills, and it's a very good imitation. As a *gelateria, pasticceria* and snack supplier, it's also first-rate.

Other Areas

San Lorenzo

Bar Sanniti
Piazza dei Sanniti, 38/40 (49 58 260). Bus/tram to Piazzale del Verano. **Open** 7am-8pm Mon-Sat.
A good observation point for the oddly-named *Sala Palazzo Accademia Biliardo* – an enormous, beautiful, early twentieth-century palazzo dedicated to workers' leisure pursuits. The bar is frequented by rather dodgy-looking characters, among them aspiring pool hoods attracted by the serviceable *buffet freddo* and *latteria*, and artists from the loft community of San Lorenzo.

Caffè Negresco
Piazza dei Campani, 6/8 (49 17 79). Bus or tram to San Lorenzo. **Open** 5am-10pm daily.
A rather dishevelled-looking but hip *bar/latteria/drogheria* in one of San Lorenzo's prettiest squares, where you can have a game of pinball while you stock up on groceries. Also a useful late-night off-licence.

La Caffetteria
Via Tiburtina, 22-26 (no phone). Bus to Termini or Porta San Lorenzo. **Open** 6.30am-11.30pm Mon-Sat.
Despite the standard-issue '80s refurbishment (the pistachio-green mood lighting is truly weird), this is a friendly, family-run bar with a local clientele and prices cheaper than most. It has a good selection of lunchtime snacks and so-so *gelati*, but is essentially a breakfast haunt, chiefly for its honey-filled, wholemeal *cornetti*. Get there before 10.30am.

Northern Suburbs

Antonini
Via Sabotino, 21-9 (37 51 78 45). Bus to Piazza Mazzini. **Open** 7am-9pm daily.
In winter you can't move for fur coats. This high-class *pasticceria* is the place to come to buy cakes to take to that important lunch or dinner party. Eating them *in situ* is a less expensive option – one *monte bianco* (meringue, sugar spaghetti and cream) should be all you need. They also do a nice line in savoury *tartine* – little canapés filled with

seafood, pâté, caviar and other goodies. Sit outside and catch the flavour of this old, prestigious neighbourhood.

Arcioni
Piazza Crati, 21-25 (86 20 66 19). Bus to Piazza Istria. **Open** 7am-9.30pm Tue-Sun.
A crowded bar on an outdoor market square, this is a morning meeting place for this north Rome neighbourhood. Fresh *cornetti* baked on the premises and above-average sandwiches can be accompanied by an exceptional *cappuccino* served by the tireless Luigi DeSimona (rated in a newspaper survey as one of the city's best barmen, for his acumen at the *espresso* machine and pleasant chatter). The bar also sells a good selection of imported foods and has a well-stocked wine shop next door.

Bar Due 'G'
Piazza Verbano, 17/18 (85 48 245). Bus to Piazza Verbano or Piazza Istria. **Open** *Winter* 6am-10.30pm Tue, Thur-Mon; *summer* 6am-10.30pm daily.
They're proud of their *cornetti* here, especially the *bombe calde*, literally sugar-covered bombs of custard cream that will keep you going way past lunchtime. Seafood and chicken salad sandwiches on fluffy focaccia bread are good at lunch. Tables outside let you see Roman driving at its most frenzied, as cars careen toward each other from all directions on the circular piazza.

Bar lo Zodiaco
Via del Parco Mellini, 90 (35 49 67 44/35 49 66 40). Bus to Piazzale Maresciallo Giardino. **Open** 10am-2am Mon, Wed-Sun; 3pm-2am Tue. **Credit** All major cards.
Perhaps the best truly panoramic view to be had over the city – although it's quite a hike to get up the Monte Maria hill, even by car. Choose a clear day without too much smog or heat haze. The best views are at night. There's also a piano bar in the evening, and a restaurant for lunch and dinner.

Faggiani
Via Giuseppe Ferrari, 23/5 (39 73 97 42). Metro Lepanto/bus to Piazza Risorgimento. **Open** 6.30am-9pm Mon-Tue, Thur-Sun. **Closed** Two weeks Aug.
As pleasant for breakfast as for an evening *aperitivo*, this classic family bar with excellent coffee has one of Rome's finest *pasticcerie* attached. Worth coming to Prati to sample their *cornetti* and *budino di riso* (desserts made from rice), probably the best in Rome.

Il Brutto Anatrocolo
Viale Parioli, 20 (80 82 348). Bus to Piazza Ungheria. **Open** 7.30am-1am daily.
Run by the same folks as Il Cigno (*see below*), this newer-version bar gets to stay up late and serve pizza, pasta and other basic main fare, outside if you like.

Il Cigno
Viale Parioli, 16 (80 82 348). Bus to Piazza Ungheria. **Open** 7.30am-9pm Thur-Tue.
This used to be the Via Veneto of the posh Parioli district, where on summer evenings you might find Marcello Mastroianni or Vittorio Gassman. Now its claims are more modest, but they include great *cornetti*. There are dozens of finely made varieties: try *marron glacé*, almond-paste or ricotta-filled ones with your coffee.

Mondi
Via Flaminia, 468a (33 36 466). **Open** 7am-midnight Tue-Sun.
Those who live in the Cassia-Flaminia area swear that this is the best *bar/pasticceria* in town. The cakes and *semi-freddi* (frozen desserts) are true works of art, and you'll be sure to impress if you take one when you're invited to dinner.

Pubs

No warm beer or cricket on the green, but Rome's hostelries strive to create a home from home.

Until not so long ago, you could count the number of pubs in Rome on one hand. They were dark, smoky dives, attracting mainly maudlin ex-pats prepared to go to any lengths for their draught Guinness fix. Then came the '90s explosion and all of a sudden there was a Ye Olde Pub on every corner. So why the change?

Italian drinking habits have undergone a mini-revolution, with beer-swilling northern Europe making ground on the wine-sipping south. Although often diluted to fit into local drinking and table-service traditions, the flourishing pub scene is also a sign that more and more Italians are travelling to northern climes and finding that there are alternatives to stand-up pit-stops and sit-down rip-offs. In the evening, a pub providing live music – or at least an up-to-date CD collection – is a budget alternative to the astronomically priced clubs and discos.

Italians may have warmed to the institution, but they still have a long way to go to catch up with their northern European counterparts. One glass will often suffice for the evening – an abstemiousness that has caused some canny publicans to allow in groups of Italians only on the condition that they're accompanied by a certain number of thirstier foreign friends.

To Italophiles who like their Rome picturesque and unchanging, the new generation of Roman pub shocks with its distinctly un-Mediterranean interior design (*see* **Bar Humbug** *page 157*). They are, however, a break for tourists who don't want to give up their pint, and punters with a perverse appreciation of the ersatz.

There are no Draconian licensing laws in Italy. There's no such thing as an under-age drinker, and opening hours depend on the likelihood of custom and the stamina of the bar staff.

Prices for a pint oscillate between L5,000-L9,000 depending on the pub and the time of day.

Centro storico

The Drunken Ship
Campo dei Fiori, 20/21 (68 30 05 35). Bus to Corso Vittorio Emanuele. **Open** 5pm-2am daily.
Owned and run by friendly Americans, the Ship has become one of *the* places to go to if you're a trendy young Roman. Great, central location (with seating in the piazza) and a slick, imaginative interior design distinguish it from nearby rivals. Special student discounts and music with a DJ in the evening.

The John Bull
Corso Vittorio Emanuele, 107a (68 71 537). Bus to Corso Vittorio Emanuele. **Open** 8.30am-3am daily.
One of the most crowded pubs in the city centre, it must also hold the Rome opening times record. A good place to rest your feet while shopping, it becomes raucous in the evening. A reasonable selection of Italian and English food faves with draught ales courtesy of John Bull breweries.

Mad Jack's
Via Arenula, 20 (68 80 82 23). Bus to Via Arenula. **Open** 11am-2am Mon-Fri; 6pm-2am Sat-Sun.
The evening clientele of this very central pub is a typical mix of young out-on-the-town Italians and bemused middle-aged Brits. Heavy metal on the juke-box music silences all but the most loud-mouthed, though during the day the pace slackens and you can sip your Guinness to the sound of the Spice Girls.

O'Connor's
Via dei Cartari, 7 (68 30 71 61). Bus to Corso Vittorio Emanuele. **Open** 9pm-2.30am daily.
Run by two friendly Italo-Irish sisters, O'Connor's is a cosy corner which seems miles from the traffic of the nearby Corso Vittorio Emanuele. The football memorabilia on the walls are a reminder that the pub is heavily frequented by the satellite TV match-watching younger crowd. Prices are slightly lower than other city centre locals.

Saint Andrew's Pub
Vicolo della Cancelleria, 36 (68 32 638). Bus to Corso Vittorio Emanuele. **Open** 8pm-1am Tue-Thur, Sun; 8pm-2am Fri-Sat.
A pub which does its utmost to provide a Scottish atmosphere, Saint Andrew's serves a reasonable variety of ales and offers an impressive selection of whiskies. Haggis is served on Thursday evenings (L15,000), with platefuls of other Caledonian-inspired specialities at other times.

Tridente

The Trinity College
Via del Collegio Romano, 6 (67 86 472). Bus to Via del Corso. **Open** 11.30am-3am Mon-Fri; 4.30pm-3am Sat-Sun.
Much frequented by the hip students of the nearby Visconti *liceo* (high school), as well as the thirstier employees of the cultural heritage ministry opposite. If the music becomes too intrusive, you can sit outside and appreciate one of the city's few neo-Gothic façades.

The Victoria
Via Gesù e Maria, 18 (32 01 698). Bus to Piazza del Popolo. **Open** 6pm-1.15am Mon-Sat; 5pm-midnight Sun.
The long-established older sister (or wife?) of the Albert (*see opposite*), the Vic is distinguished by sofas in dire need of re-upholstering and Italian bucks hoping to make a foreign gal go all doe-eyed. Traditional Bass and Tennent's ales.

Via Veneto & Quirinal

The Albert
Via del Traforo, 132 (48 18 795). Bus to Via del Tritone.
Open 11am-3am Mon-Sat; 5pm-1am Sun.
Until 10pm, when the youngsters move in and the volume is turned up, the Albert is a peaceful oasis in the Trevi Fountain area. A friendly staff (the owner once had a local in Scotland) serves good, basic pub grub throughout the day, with a generous happy hour (L5,000 for a pint, spirits half price) from 11am-9pm.

Monti & Esquilino

The Druid's Den
Via San Martino ai Monti, 28 (48 80 258). Bus to Piazza San Maria Maggiore. **Open** 5pm-1am daily.
Like its rival the Fiddler's Elbow *(see below)*, this is one of the pubs that was already well established in the Santa Maria Maggiore district before the current craze for pubs and all things Irish. A decent pint of Liffey water at the usual rates.

The Fiddler's Elbow
Via dell'Olmata, 43 (48 72 110). Bus to Piazza San Maria Maggiore. **Open** 4.30pm-12.45am daily.
One of the oldest and best known pubs in Rome which has remained remarkably unchanged over the years. Its narrow, basic wood-and-bench interior is as smoky as ever, with the alternative feel that has long made it popular with students.

Testaccio, Celio & Aventino

The Shamrock
Via Capo d'Africa, 26d (70 02 583). Metro Colosseo.
Open 6pm-2am daily.
Four cosy rooms, darts and occasional live music make this

The Shamrock: *a taste of Ireland.*

pub the local for the Colosseum area. In the summer months the Shamrock metamorphoses into the mammoth open-air 'Green of Ireland in the Green of Rome' shindig at the Parco della Resistenza (*Piazza Albania*), with music, massive crowds and higher-priced beer in smaller-sized plastic glasses.

Other Areas
San Lorenzo

Rive Gauche 2
Via dei Sabelli, 43 (44 56 722). Bus to Via Tiburtina.
Open 8pm-2am Mon-Sat daily.
A large, smoky watering-hole serving Guinness, Harp and salads. Very popular with the student/San Lorenzo crowd, so it can be tough finding a free table.

Bar Humbug

Fancy retiring to the Roman sun and setting yourself up in your own pub? First you'll have to sort out the bureaucracy. As pubs don't legally exist in Italy, they have to be registered either as 'cultural associations' (which is why some places ask you to fill in a membership card) or as combined restaurants *and* bars, forcing would-be publicans to cough up for two licences.

Red tape sorted, you can get down to creating that all-important atmosphere. DIY jobs won't do: whole interiors must be ordered from Blighty. This is the easy part. For a mere £900 a square metre you'll get everything fitted within two weeks, from the hand-stained tobacco-tinted wallpaper and framed front page ('Nation Mourns Prince Albert'), down to the wide-grain wooden floorboards. 'Country', 'City' and 'Victorian' are currently the most popular packages.

With one of the two giants, Bass or Guinness, providing your booze, and hopefully giving you a low-interest loan on the initial outlay, you now have to set up the all-important refrigeration unit in the cellar. Naturally you already know all there is to know about pressures, tubes and temperatures. Majoresque warm beer is not wanted here, so make sure you know how to face the rigours of the Roman summer. Don't expect instant fortunes, either. Italians make half a pint go a very, very long way. Start lighting candles for coach-loads of thirsty pilgrims.

OK, so you're almost ready to open your stained-glass doors. The sound system's up and running and the satellite dish is discreetly in place. You just need a name. Something Irish is best, though these days you'll have to dig culturally deep. *The Flann O'Brien, The Seamus Heaney* and even *The Edge* are already taken. How about *The Father Ted*?

Ice Cream

Just one cornetto ... isn't nearly enough, in the ice cream capital of the world.

As long as the sun shines, you're never far from an ice cream stand.

Many bars in Rome boast a well-stocked freezer cabinet with a sign bearing the promise *produzione artigianale* (home-made ice creams). Generally speaking, this is a con. Although the contents may have been whipped up on the premises, the lurid colours and chemical flavours come straight out of a tin. And while this doesn't necessarily mean the ice cream is going to be bad – indeed, in some cases this not-so-genuine-article can be very good indeed – it doesn't hurt to be selective if you're seeking a truly unique *gelato* experience.

Ices to take away are served in a *cono* (cone) or cardboard *coppetta* (tub) of varying sizes, usually costing from L2,000-6,000. Besides the two main kinds, *frutta* or *crema*, there's also *granita* (a rougher version of the *sorbetto*), and *semifreddo*, usually a chilled sponge-and-cream pudding resembling *tiramisu*.

It is also worth sampling a *grattachecca*, the time-honoured Roman version of water-ice, consisting of hand-grated ice poured into a cup, with flavoured syrup or juice on top. Once Rome was full of kiosks selling this treat; now there are only a handful, all

maintaining their authentic character. They are almost always on street corners (hence *angolo* in the addresses below), and most are closed through the winter, opening only when their proprietors feel the weather is warm enough to warrant taking down the shutters. Opening hours tend to be erratic.

Centro storico

Alberto Pica
Via della Seggiola, 12 (68 75 990). Bus to Via Arenula and Largo Argentina. **Open** 8am-1.30am Mon-Sat.
Next to the regular bar and *tavola calda* sections is a small but excellent selection of some 20 flavours, among which the rice specialities stand out – imagine eating frozen, partially-cooked rice pudding and you're starting to get the picture. The *riso alla cannella* (cinnamon rice) is particularly fine.

I Tre Scalini
Piazza Navona, 28-32 (68 80 1996). Bus to Corso Rinascimento or Corso Vittorio Emanuele. **Open** 8am-1am Thur-Tue.
The most famous bar in Rome's most famous square is famous for its speciality ice cream, the *tartufo* – a calorie-bomb chocolate ice cream with big lumps of chocolate inside. There are some 50 tables from which to view the square, and

a tea room for tired English matrons on the first floor. Otherwise, opt for a takeaway and enjoy it at Bernini's fountain, or do as the Romans do and stand at the crowded bar.

Tridente

Giolitti
Via Uffici del Vicario, 40, off Piazza Montecitorio (69 91 243). Bus to Via del Corso. **Open** 7am-12.30am Tue-Fri; 7am-2am Sat.

Perhaps the best-known *gelateria* in Rome, although by no means the best. Still, their range of flavours is vast, and some of them– *marron glacé, frutti di bosco, gianduia* – remain unsurpassed. The main bar has been a compulsory stop-off point on an evening *passeggiata* for several generations.

Trastevere

Sora Mirella
Lungotevere degli Anguillara, angolo Ponte Cestio (no phone). Bus to Viale Trastevere or Ponte Cestio. **Open** *summer* 10am-3am daily.

Mirella styles herself *la regina della grattachecca* (the queen of ices), and there seems no reason to argue with her. Her sons still grate the ice by hand with an iron glove. Sit on the Tiber embankment wall as you tuck into the *speciale superfrutta* – a melon, kiwifruit and strawberry concoction served in a special glass.

Monti & Esquilino

Il Palazzo del Freddo di Giovanni Fassi
Via Principe Eugenio, 65/7 (44 64 740). Metro Vittorio/bus or tram to Piazza Vittorio. **Open** *Oct-May* noon-9pm Tue-Fri, 10am-9pm Sat-Sun; *June-Sept* noon-midnight Tue-Fri, 10am-midnight Sat-Sun.

From its pompous name and breathtakingly kitsch interior to

Won't you come into my ice cream parlour?

its splendid ices, Fassi is typically Roman. Founded in 1880 by Giovanni Fassi, the walls abound with Edwardian adverts and fascist-era posters extolling the virtues of its wares. Escape the appalling 1980s restoration and the laughable service and head into the '30s courtyard and loggia. The ices are sublime: best of all is *riso* – rice pudding – and their own invention, *la caterinetta*, a mysterious concoction of whipped honey and vanilla.

Testaccio, Celio & Aventino

Chiosco Testaccio
Via Giovanni Branca, angolo Via Beniamino Franklin (no phone). Bus to Via Marmorata or Via Zabaglia. **Open** *summer* 11am-2am daily.

Still going strong after over 70 years in this working class neighbourhood, though the ice is now cut by mechanical means. The kiosk is painted a different colour each year: 1997 was pink. Tamarind and *lemoncocco* (lemon and coconut, also available in liquid form) are the specialities.

Da Pietro
Via Marmorata, angolo Largo M Gelsomini, Testaccio (no phone). Metro Piramide/bus to Via Marmorata. **Open** 6.45pm-1am daily.

Pietro's family have been in the *grattachecca* business since 1903; his cast-iron American hand-held grater comes from that period, although his sales technique is more modern. He uses Fabbri brand syrups and juices exclusively, along with a few liqueurs. Try his vodka or amaretto di Saronno.

Northern Suburbs

Duse
Via Eleonora Duse, 1e (80 79 300). Bus or tram to Piazza Ungheria. **Open** 8am-1am Mon-Sat.

In this otherwise entirely residential neighbourhood, Duse attracts well-off young *pariolini* (for which read Islingtonites/Valley girls and boys) on their motorbikes and in their jeeps. Late at night, it looks like a street party. Inside, the metal drums of the 30-odd flavours are stacked three deep behind the counter. Try their *dattero* (date) or *cioccolato bianco* (white chocolate).

San Filippo
Via di Villa San Filippo, 8/10 (80 79 314). Bus or tram to Piazza Ungheria. **Open** 7.30am-midnight Tue-Sun.

From the outside, this seems just another modest local *bar/latteria*. But this is the home of some wicked ice creams, despite the limited selection. Sample the *nocciola* and the *cioccolato* – the *gelato* connoisseur's litmus-test flavours – or a range of seasonal fruits: watermelon (*anguria*), peach (*pesca*) or melon (*melone*).

Southern Suburbs

Il Gelato di San Crispino
Via Acaia, 56, San Giovanni (70 45 04 12). Bus to Piazza Tuscolo. **Open** 11am-midnight Mon, Wed-Sun. **Branch** *Via della Panetteria, 42 (67 93 924). Metro Barberini/bus to Via del Tritone.* **Open** 10am-1am Mon, Wed, Sun; 10am-2am Fri-Sat.

Far and away the best ice-cream in Rome – some would say the world. The secret of brothers Giuseppe and Pasquale Alongi is an obsessive control over the whole process, from the selection of ingredients through to method of preparation. Flavours change according to what's around at the markets – in summer the *lampone* (raspberry) and *susine* (yellow plum) are mouth-watering. There's even a *funghi* flavour in autumn. Don't even think of asking for a cone: only tubs are allowed, as they 'interfere less with the purity of the product'.

Shopping

When you're sick of the sites, you can always find solace in retail therapy.

Despite the designer boutiques, Rome's shops are in many ways old-fashioned. There are plenty of one-off shops, ranging from delicatessens to furniture restorers, but supermarkets and department stores are few and far between.

Nonetheless, shopping in Rome is a serious business. Devotees stalk their prey rigorously, taking price, style and quality into careful consideration. When it's time to move in for the kill, you can try your bargaining skills: asking for a *sconto* (discount) is not uncommon in smaller outlets, though some proprietors may react indignantly, protesting that theirs is a respectable establishment and not a kasbah. Finally comes the euphoria of the catch and the donning of the trophy.

For the less intrepid, shopping can be a somewhat daunting experience. Just looking is not the norm, and many assistants, especially in the trendier stores, appear to assume that their vocation in life is to intimidate.

That said, if you don't let the fascists of hip bother you, Rome can be a wonderful place to shop. Scattered throughout the *centro storico* are scores of little shops selling beautiful clothing, designer artefacts, art, antiques, jewellery and cosmetics, to say nothing of marvellous food.

The densest concentration of *haute couture* is in the network of streets at the foot of Piazza di Spagna. Mainstream clothes and leatherwear are sold on Via Nazionale, Via dei Giubbonari and Via del Corso, second-hand clothes on Via del Governo Vecchio or in San Giovanni's Via Sannio market. Jewellery, antiques and art shops are found in the streets between Piazza Navona and the Tiber, and there are craft shops near Piazza Navona and Campo de' Fiori.

OPENING HOURS

The larger and more upmarket stores tend to stay open all day, between 9am and 7.30pm. Most of the smaller shops keep roughly similar hours, but with a lunch break beginning around 1pm and lasting from 2pm or even 4.30pm. Most food shops close on Thursday afternoons in winter, while other shops are closed on Monday mornings. In summer (June-Sept), shops of all kinds tend to stay open later in the day (until 8pm), but close on Saturday afternoons. Bear in mind, though, that shops – particularly small ones – may well open or close at other times, according to the level of trade and personal whim. **Only opening hours which differ from the norm have been specified in the listings that follow**.

Note too that most shops close for at least two weeks each summer (generally August), with no guarantee that any one shop will opt for the same period every year. If you are planning to go out of your way to visit a particular shop in summer, it is worth ringing first to avoid being confronted by a *chiuso per ferie* (closed for holidays) sign.

If you are a non-EU citizen, keep your official receipt (*scontrino*), as you are entitled to a VAT rebate on purchases of personal goods over L300,000, providing they are exported unused and bought from a shop displaying the Europe Tax Free sticker. The shop will give you a form to show to customs when leaving Italy.

One-Stop Shopping

Department stores and shopping malls are not common in Rome, and those that do exist tend to offer unadventurous clothing, and standard household goods.

Centro Commerciale Cinecittà Due

Viale Palmiro Togliatti, 2, Tuscolana (72 20 902). Metro Cinecittà. **Open** 9.30am-8pm Mon-Sat, occasional Sundays. **Credit** Depends on individual shop.
Rome's foremost shopping mall, a great glass and steel structure that incorporates 100 shops and eateries, includes branches of many of the smartest city-centre fashion stores.

COIN

Piazzale Appio, 7, San Giovanni (70 80 020). Metro San Giovanni/bus or tram to Piazzale Appio. **Branch** *Via Mantova, 1b (84 15 875). Bus to Piazza Fiume or Via Nizza.* **Credit** AmEx, DC, EC, MC, V.
Middle-of-the-road store, with some bargains – particularly at the make-up counter. Romans use it when they need a sensible skirt, or a set of sheets that will last. You may find the clothes more stylish than those in equivalent stores at home.

Drugstore Rosati 2

Piazzale Clodio, Prati (39 73 62 53). Bus to Piazzale Clodio. **Open** 24 hours daily. **Credit** Depends on individual shop.
Somewhat inflated prices, but you'll find almost everything you need, from clothing and CDs to freshly-baked pizza and the inevitable McDonald's. Becoming a popular Sunday-brunch venue.

Museum Drugstore

Via Portuense, 313 (55 93 342). Bus to Via Portuense. **Open** 24 hours daily. **Credit** Depends on individual shop.
Rather far from the centre, the attraction of this place lies in

the fact that it incorporates a second-century necropolis. It also boasts the usual food shops, a pub, a restaurant and an all-night tobacconist.

La Rinascente
Piazza Colonna or Via del Corso (67 97 691). Bus to Piazza San Silvestro. **Open** *Summer* 9.30am-8pm Mon-Sat; *winter* 9.30am-8pm Mon-Sat, 11am-8pm Sun. **Branch** *Piazza Fiume (84 12 31). Bus to Piazza Fiume, Corso D'Italia* **Credit** AmEx, DC, EC, MC, V.
Big store-style shopping: classy jewellery and accessories, designer and off-the-peg clothing. English-language desks give advice on tax-free shopping and shipping home.

Standa
Viale Trastevere, 62/64 (58 95 342). Bus to Viale Trastevere. **Open** 9am-8pm Mon-Sat. **Branches** *Via Cola di Rienzo , 173 (32 43 319). Metro Ottaviano/bus to Via Cola da Rienzo. Viale Regina Margherita, 117 (85 57 427) Bus or tram to Piazza Buenos Aires.* **Credit** EC, MC, V.
Roman Woolworths, but with less choice. Renowned for cheap underwear and cheerful clothes. The branches listed above all have basement supermarkets, some with good fresh-fish counters. Owned by magnate-turned-politician Silvio Berlusconi.

Termini Drugstore
Below Termini Station. Metro Termini. **Open** 24 hours daily. **Credit** Depends on individual shop.
Useful for picking up last-minute snacks before journeys this mall is a regular hang-out for transsexuals, back-packers and the homeless.

UPIM
Piazza di Santa Maria Maggiore (44 65 579). Metro Termini or Piazza Vittorio/bus to Piazza Santa Maria Maggiore or Termini. **Open** Depends on individual shop. **Branches** *Via del Tritone, 172 (67 83 336) Metro Spagna/bus to Largo Chigi. Via Nazionale, 211 (48 45 02). Bus to Via Nazionale.* **Credit** AmEx, EC, MC, V.
Lower-end-of-the-line store, with fashion and toiletries.

Antiques
Good but pricey places to look for antiques include Via del Babuino, Via Giulia and around Via de' Coronari, where dealers organise antiques fairs in May and October (*see chapter* **Rome by Season**). Most antique dealers take four to six weeks off during the summer.

Animalier
Via dei Banchi Vecchi, 16 (68 76 508). Bus to Corso Vittorio Emanuele. **Credit** All major cards.
For lovers of animals and antiques, this shop offers your favourite pets in collectable form, with prints, brooches and other knick-knacks to suit all pockets.

Bateleur
Via di San Simeone, 71 (68 77 184). Bus to Lungotevere Tor di Nona. **Credit** AmEx, DC.
An eleventh-century sacristy full of bric-à-brac and quality antiques. Signora Cuneo, the *padrona*, speaks English and runs a cultural association in the bar at the back.

Claudio & Laura Moretti
Via de' Coronari, 233a (68 80 13 69). Bus to Lungotevere Tor di Nona or Corso del Rinascimento. **Credit** AmEx.
A long, narrow shop, ringing with classical music and filled with classical statues, whose impassive marble faces loom eerily under the subtle lighting.

Gea Arte Antica
Via dell'Orso, 82 (68 80 45 47). Bus to Corso del Rinascimento. **No credit cards**.
Take home an authenticated fragment of the glory that was Greece, Rome, Etruria and so on. This shop specialises in the smaller bits of the past that have escaped museums, such as bronze pins and terracotta shards.

Bibli *stimulates body and mind. See* **Bookshops** *page 163.*

Flea Markets

Most Italians have little interest in second-hand clothes and bric-à-brac. Objects which have long been considered design classics in the UK and US are regarded as rubbish here, so there are some good bargains to be had.

In the larger markets, like **Porta Portese** and **Via Sannio**, it's *de rigeur* to bargain. The starting prices for antiques are about double what most stall-holders expect. This doesn't necessarily require a great command of Italian. Broken English and/or gestures will suffice for most deals.

The sign of a good market.

Borghetto Flaminio
Piazza della Marina, 32 (58 80 517). Tram to Piazza della Marina. **Open** Sept-June 10am-7pm Sun.
A partly covered, partly open-air garage sale, held in a well-heeled part of the city, although one of the conditions of setting up a stall is that prices are kept relatively low. You can often find interesting trinkets and curios from the fascist period. There's a L2,000 entry fee.

Fontanella Borghese
Piazza Borghese (no phone). Bus to Piazza Augusto Imperatore. **Open** 9am-5.30pm Mon-Fri; 9am-7pm Sat-Sun.
First editions, ancient tomes, engravings, and yellowing opera scores.

Galleria delle Stimmate
Largo delle Stimmate, 1 (33 37 884). Bus to Largo di Torre Argentina. **Open** 10am-7.30pm Sun.
At the upper end of what can be considered a flea-market, the 40 or so stalls in the environs of the Church of the Stigmata offer antique lace and amber, silver cutlery, and jewellery galore.

Il Giardino d'Inverno
Parco dell'Assunzione, Via Panama, 25 (84 48 27 39). Bus to Via Panama. **Open** 10am-7pm alternate Sundays.
Winter Garden is an enjoyable, strictly non-professional affair, selling everything from discarded designer clobber to small pieces of furniture.

Porta Portese
Viale Trastevere/Porta Portese (no phone). Bus or tram to Piazza Ippolito Nievo or Ponte Sublicio. **Open** 5am-2pm Sun.
Although it feels long-established, the famous Sunday market held in the streets between Porta Portese, Ponte Testaccio and Viale Trastevere has only been held since the late 1940s. If you enter the market from Piazza Ippolito Nievo, you'll find dealers in antique furniture, Asian carpets, canework and mirrors. Carry on southwards down Via Ettore Rolli to look at clothes, glass and ceramics, more antiques or African sculpture. Via Porta Portese is the market's main thoroughfare: at the Ponte Sublicio end, stalls sell mostly new items – CDs and tapes, kitchenware, jeans and leather goods. Towards Ponte Testaccio, you'll find second-hand clothes, as well as itinerant vendors of sunglasses, cigarette lighters and sad-eyed puppies. It's commonly said in Rome that if your camera or *motorino* is stolen, it's a good idea to look for it in Porta Portese. The trouble is, somebody may well try and pick your bag or pocket while you're there, so be extra careful.

Porta Portese 2
Corner of Via Palmiro Togliatti and Via Prenestina, Tor Sapienza (no phone). Bus to Via Prenestina. **Open** 6am-2pm Sun.
Suburban offspring of the original, selling virtually all the same goods, though lacking the Trastevere atmosphere.

Via Sannio
Via Sannio (no phone). Metro San Giovanni/bus, tram to Piazzale Appio. **Open** 10am-1.30pm Mon-Fri; 10am-6pm Sat.
Rather less frenetic that Porta Portese, it is easier to find good second-hand clothes here. The main section of the market consists of three covered corridors, rather like an Arab bazaar, offering new clothing at fairly reasonable prices. Behind this is a used and retro clothing section. Many dealers have a one-price policy, going as low as L2,000 on some stalls. At others you'll have to haggle. Dig deep among the mounds of junk: there are some real bargains to be found.

Mario Prili
Via Banchi Nuovi, 42 (68 68 816). Bus to Corso Vittorio Emanuele. **Credit** AmEx, V.
A tiny but fascinating shop, crammed with antiques of all ages, descriptions and pedigrees. It's the kind of enchanting place where you pause for just a moment and end up staying for an hour.

M Simotti-Rocchi
Largo Fontanella Borghese, 76 (68 76 656). Bus to Piazza Augusto Imperatore or Lungotevere Marzio. **No credit cards.**
Simotti-Rocchi is a specialist in Greek, Etruscan and Roman antiquities, including vases, *amphorae* and statues. The majority of the stock is far too large to take home, unless you've got exclusive access to an airliner hold, but the rings, bronze figurines and coins make unusual presents.

Le Troc
Via dei Greci, 38 (67 96 091). Metro Spagna/bus to Piazza Augusto Imperatore. **No credit cards.**
Turn-of-the-century Italian furniture, paintings, lamps and antique wine glasses in a cluttered but invariably friendly showroom conveniently close to Via Condotti.

Bookshops

See also **Libraries** *page 249.*

Amore e Psiche
Via Santa Caterina da Siena, 61 (67 83 908). Bus to Via del Corso. **Open** 2.30-8pm Mon; 9am-2pm, 4-8pm, Tue-Fri; 10am-8pm Sat-Sun; *July-Aug* 2.30-8pm Mon; 9am-2pm Tue-Fri; 10am-10pm Sat-Sun. **Credit** AmEx, MC, V.
This centrally located store has a good selection of books on psychology, poetry and the arts, in addition to some English and French classics. Beautifully renovated in 1995.

Bibli
Via dei Fienaroli, 27/8, Trastevere (58 84 097/58 14 534). Bus to Piazza Sonnino. **Open** 5pm-midnight Mon; 11am-midnight Tue-Sun. *Aug* 5pm-midnight daily.
Credit All major cards.
This bookshop is unique in Rome because it also functions as a cinema, music venue and tea room. There are over 30,000 books on sale, and computers allow browsers to play in cyberspace. The tea room menu includes salads, sandwiches and desserts.

Feltrinelli
Largo di Torre Argentina, 5a (68 80 32 48). Bus to Largo di Torre Argentina. **Open** 9am-8pm Mon-Sat; 10am-1pm, 4-7.30pm, Sun. **Branches** *Via del Babuino, 39/40 (67 97 058). Metro Spagna/bus to Piazza San Silvestro. Via Emanuele Orlando, 84/6 (48 44 30). Metro Repubblica/bus to Piazza della Repubblica.***Credit** AmEx, DC, MC, V.
Excellent, modern, well-organised bookshops, notable for a wide selection of art, photography, history and Italian comic books, and a choice of books in English and other languages. Also stocks magazines, maps, postcards, art posters, arty T-shirts and creative wooden toys.

Giuseppe Casetti
Via della Reginella, 28 (68 80 77 25). Bus to Largo di Torre Argentina. **No credit cards.**
This small but well-stocked antiquarian bookshop is a treasure trove for those interested in reasonably priced first editions dealing with Italian history, literature and the applied arts. It also hosts frequent exhibitions.

Libreria Monte Cicerone
Largo Chigi (69 94 15 54). Bus to Via del Corso. **Open** 9.30am-8pm Mon-Sat; 9.30am-1pm, 4-8pm, Sun. **Credit** EC, MC, V.
A subterranean complex selling cut-price prints, antique and rare books, and comics. If you want to trace the history of the Italian media, look out for the wartime newspapers with articles written by Mussolini.

Libreria del Viaggiatore
Via del Pellegrino, 78 (68 80 10 48). Bus to Corso Vittorio Emanuele. **Credit** AmEx, DC, EC, MC, V.
Specialises in travel literature, with books on Italy written by Stendhal, Twain, Dickens, Goethe, Strindberg and Ruskin. Mostly in Italian, with some English selections.

MEL Libreria
Via Nazionale, 254/5 (48 85 405). Metro Repubblica/bus to Via Nazionale. **Open** 9am-8pm Mon-Sat; 10am-1pm, 4.30-8pm, Sun. **Credit** All major cards.
A massive selection of volumes on all subjects, a new and used CD department and an attractive café. Don't miss the shelves of English-language books near the door.

Rinascita
Via delle Botteghe Oscure, 1/2 (69 92 24 36) Bus to Piazza Venezia. **Open** 10am-8pm, Mon-Sat; 10am-2pm, 4-8pm, Sun **Credit** AmEx, MC, V.
Traditionally a temple to left-wing culture, Rinascita now

You'll be spoilt for choice at **MEL Libreria.**

offers a good selection of modern literature, art and comic books, with one whole floor devoted to videos, many of them in the original language.

Roma e Lazio
Via della Croce, 74a (67 90 325). Metro Spagna/bus to Piazza San Silvestro or Piazza Augusto Imperatore. **No credit cards.**
A specialist bookshop selling new and old books, prints, maps and magazines on aspects of Rome and Lazio. The staff are well-informed and helpful, and browsers are welcome.

English-Language Bookshops

Anglo American Book Co
Via della Vite, 102 (67 95 222). Bus to Piazza San Silvestro. **Credit** AmEx, MC, V.
A good selection of books in English, with an emphasis on scientific and technical texts aimed at university students.

The Corner Bookshop
Via del Moro, 48, Trastevere (58 36 942). Bus to Viale Trastevere. **Open** 3.30-7.30pm Mon; 10am-1.30pm, 3.30-8pm, Tue-Sat; 11am-1.30pm, 3.30-8pm, Sun. **Credit** AmEx, DC, EC, MC, V.
A hole-in-the-wall store, covering fiction, non-fiction and general interest – in all, 25,000 titles at non-rip-off prices.

Economy Book & Video Center
Via Torino, 136 (47 46 877). Metro Termini/bus to Via Nazionale. **Open** 3-8pm Mon; 9am-8pm Tue-Sat. **Credit** (over L25,000) AmEx, DC, EC, MC, V.
Although anything but economical, this bookshop imports the latest from London and New York, as well as dealing in second-hand books, so check before buying anything new. There's also a good noticeboard for those seeking work, shelter or Italian lessons.

The English Bookshop

Via di Ripetta, 248 (32 03 301). Metro Flaminio/bus to Piazzale Flaminia. **Open** 10am-7.30pm Tue-Fri; 10am-1pm Sat. **Credit** All major cards.

A general bookshop, handily situated in the *centro storico*.

Feltrinelli International

Via Emanuele Orlando, 84 (48 27 873). Metro Repubblica/bus to Piazza della Repubblica. **Open** 9am-8pm Mon-Sat; 10am-1.30pm, 4-7.30pm, Sun. *Aug* 9am-8pm Mon-Sat.

Try here for your reading matter before subsidising other over-priced English language bookshops. This attractive new store offers fiction, poetry, drama, magazines, guide books and a surprisingly wide range of glossy erotica.

The Lion Bookshop

Via dei Greci, 33 (32 65 40 07). Metro Flaminio. **Open** 10am-7.30pm Mon-Fri; 10am-1pm Sat. **Credit** AmEx, EC, MC, V.

The Lion has always been one of the reference points for English-speaking ex-pats. Now at its new address, it also offers a reading room where you can browse over the reading matter over a free tea or coffee.

Cosmetics & Perfumes

Perfume and cosmetic stores abound throughout the city, but the real forte of Rome's chemists is the making of traditional soothing unguents and herbal products, ranging from toothpaste and soaps to aromatherapy oils. For more mundane items, don't automatically shop at department stores. Many neighbourhood *profumerie* offer sizeable discounts.

Antica Erboristeria Romana

Via di Torre Argentina, 15 (68 79 493). Bus to Largo di Torre Argentina. **Open** 9am-1pm, 4-7.30pm, Mon-Fri; 9am-1pm Sat. **Credit** AmEx, DC, MC, V.

A curiosity shop, founded in the eighteenth century, selling herbal health products, scented paper from Eritrea, liquorice and hellbane.

Body Shop

Via del Corso, 168 (67 98 887). Metro Spagna/bus to Piazza San Silvestro. **Open** 4-8pm Mon; 10am-8pm Tue-Sat. **Credit** AmEx, DC, EC, MC, V.

The famous UK line of beauty-without-cruelty products, but beware – the prices are considerably higher than in Britain.

Erboristeria M Messegué

Galleria Ras, Piazza San Silvestro, 8 (67 97 294). Bus to Piazza San Silvestro. **Credit** MC,V.

Tucked into the cool marble courtyard of the elegant Galleria Ras, a selection of natural health and beauty products from the celebrated French herbalist.

La Taste

Via M Dionigi, 49 (32 04 675). Bus to Piazza Cavour. **Open** 9.30am-8pm. **Credit** AmEx, DC, EC, MC, V.

A Provence-style boutique with hand-made soaps, teas, herbal creams, and enough dried flowers to make your head ache.

Design & Household

Bagagli

Via di Campo Marzio, 42 (68 71 406/68 65 680). Bus to Largo Chigi. **Open** 3.30-7.30pm Mon; 9am-7.30pm Tue-Sat. **Credit** AmEx, DC, EC, MC, V.

A temple to design in a wonderful, airy shop with a cobblestone floor. All the best names are here: Villeroy and Boch crystal, Domus cookware, Alessi cafetières and Denby pottery.

Ceramiche Musa

Via Campo Marzio, 39 (68 71 242/12 04). Bus to Largo Chigi. **No credit cards**.

Modern showroom selling reproductions of traditional ceramic tiles with those gorgeous blues and greens that brighten bathrooms and kitchens all over Italy.

Ceramiche Nicola Fasano

Via Monte della Farina, 61 (68 67 550). Bus to Largo di Torre Argentina. **Credit** AmEx.

An array of terracotta heads, painted angels and fruit festoons, set alongside the traditional blue, yellow and green pottery of Puglia's Nicola Fasano.

Coas Tradizione Casa

Piazza Cardelli, 5a (68 67 579). Bus to Piazza Augusto Imperatore. **Open** 3.30-7pm Mon; 10am-7pm Tue-Sat. **No credit cards**.

Romans long for a kitchen rigged out by Coas Casa, which offers all the most up-to-date Italian designs.

CUCINA

Via del Babuino, 118a (67 91 275). Metro Spagna/bus to Piazza San Silvestro. **Open** 3.30-7.30pm Mon; 9am-7.30pm Tue-Sat. **Credit** AmEx, DC, EC, MC, V.

A kasbah for cooks, this subterranean warehouse contains everything you will need to make – and present – Italian coffee, ice cream, pasta, flans, pizza or roasts. Perfect for the hurried shopper looking for a fistful of espresso cups or a funny baking mould.

Dolmen

Via de' Cestari, 43 (68 80 19 01). Bus to Largo di Torre Argentina **Credit** All major cards.

The owners of Dolmen are interior decorators who redo homes and offices in simple, beautiful styles. They sell Venini, Kosta and Boda glassware, as well as ceramics and porcelains of their own making.

Habitat

Via Cola di Rienzo, 197 (32 43 233). Bus to Via Cola di Rienzo. **Open** 4-8pm Mon; 10am-8pm Tue-Sat. **Branches** *Viale Marconi, 259 (55 82 701). Bus to Piazzale della Radio. Viale Regina Margherita, 18/20 (85 58 641). Bus or tram to Viale Regina Margherita.* **Credit** AmEx, EC, MC, V.

As you might expect, the Italian version of Habitat tends to offer slicker goods at steeper prices. The range is also more limited than in its British counterparts, but the shop's position in busy shopping street Via Cola di Rienzo makes it worth a look.

Home

Largo di Torre Argentina, 8 (68 68 450). Bus to Largo di Torre Argentina. **Open** 10am-7pm Mon-Sat. **Credit** AmEx, DC, EC, MC, V.

An outlet for kitchen equipment, ornaments and furniture. A good central place for present-buying, but the real bargains are in the ethnic carpet department at the back, with everything from kelims to cross-stitch.

Magazzini Forma e Memoria

Vicolo Sant'Onofrio, 24 (68 80 10 88). Bus to Lungotevere Gianicolense. **Open** 10am-7.30pm Mon-Sat. **Branch** *Passeggiata di Ripetta, 19 (32 14 768). Bus to Piazza Augusto Imperatore.* **Credit** AmEx, EC, MC, V.

Forma e Memoria is one of Italy's most imaginative design studios, and the furniture, clothes, toys and accessories produced by the group are sold in their multi-purpose building, occupying all four storeys of an old printworks. In the basement you can browse through design magazines, including the studio's own.

Myricae

Via Frattina, 36 (67 95 335). Metro Spagna/bus to Piazza San Silvestro. **Open** *Sept-June* 9.30am-8pm Mon-Sat; regular times in summer. **Branch** *Piazza del Parlamento, 38/39. Bus to Largo Chigi.* **Credit** AmEx, DC, V.
Painted furniture from Bassano, Sicilian ceramics and diverting wrought-iron furniture from Tuscany, in strong Mediterranean colours. Nice prices.

Palazzo delle Esposizioni

Via Milano, 9a (48 28 540). Bus to Via Nazionale. **Open** 10am-9pm Wed-Mon. **Credit** All major cards.
Down one side of this giant exhibition centre (*see chapter* **Museums & Galleries**) and up a flight of steps, is a showcase for design. As well as a good art and crafts bookshop, there is a display of cookware, stationery, watches, games, lamps and other objects by top-name designers, all for sale.

Paola Agostara

Via dei Chiavari, 8 (68 93 777). Bus to Corso Vittorio Emanuele. **Credit** AmEx, EC, MC, V.
A stylish collection of *trompe l'œil* mirrors, hand-painted furniture, Pugliese pottery and lovely, inexpensive glassware from Poland, the Czech Republic and Mexico. Ms Agostara's own furniture and fabric designs are tempting.

Spazio Sette

Via dei Barbieri ,7 (68 69 708). Bus to Largo di Torre Argentina. **Credit** AmEx, DC, EC, MC, V.
Rome's slickest furniture and *objet* store occupies all three storeys of a Renaissance palazzo. Admire the latest in interior design, Italian and otherwise, beneath frescoed ceilings, with glimpses of a lush garden courtyard from the windows and the shop cat purring in the kitchen department.

Stock Market

Via dei Banchi Vecchi, 51 (68 64 238). Bus to Corso Vittorio Emanuele. **Open** 3pm-8pm Mon; 10am-8pm Tue-Sat. **Credit** AmEx, DC, EC, MC, V.
Rather like an exotic Reject Shop, this outlet shifts end-of-line kitchen goods, quirky light fittings and odd articles of Indian furniture that no one else manages – or wants – to sell. Prices are often low and rapid turnover makes it worth visiting, particularly if you're looking for gifts. Where Bertolucci picked up props for his film *Stealing Beauty*.

Storage

Via del Babuino, 65 (32 30 943). Metro Spagna/bus to Piazza San Silvestro. **Credit** AmEx, DC, EC, MC, V.
Sister to CUCINA (*see above*), offering an eclectic collection of trendy designer objects, from mailboxes and rubbish bins to hat racks and picnic hampers. They are all made from purely natural materials.

TAD

Via di San Giacomo, 5 (36 00 16 79). Metro Spagna/bus to Piazza del Popolo. **Open** 3.30-7pm Mon; 10am-7pm Tue-Sat. **Credit** AmEx, DC, EC, MC, V.
An interesting interiors shop on three colourfully painted floors – linens, furniture, screens, cloth dyes, stencils, candlesticks and vases imported from all over the world.

Fashion

Accessories

Bottega Artigiana

Via di Sant'Ignazio, 38 (67 95 119). Bus to Via del Corso. **Credit** AmEx, DC, EC, MC, V.

Simple, breezy handbags hand-stitched by Antonio Ferretti at the rear of the shop. His partner, Rita Tegolini, makes sophisticated but casual suits and tops.

Cravatteria Nazionale

Via Vittoria, 62 (32 17 085). Metro Spagna/bus to Piazza Augusto Imperatore. **Open** 3.30-7.30pm Mon; 9.30am-7.30pm Tue-Sat. **Credit** AmEx, DC, EC, MC, V.
Rome's best-stocked tie shop, with designs by Dior, Zegna, Moschino, Valentino, I Lumi, Krizia, Missoni and Liberty. Prices start at L45,000.

Valextra

Via del Babuino, 94 (67 92 323). Metro Spagna/bus to Piazza San Silvestro. **Credit** AmEx, DC, EC, MC, V.
Milan-designed handbags and purses at prices that would keep most families for a week.

Designers

Byblos

Via Frattina, 34a (67 94 55 56). Metro Spagna/bus to Piazza San Silvestro. **Open** 1-7.30pm Mon; 10am-7.30pm Tue-Sat. **Credit** AmEx, DC, EC, MC, V.
Fun, young styles by English designers, featuring reckless checks and cool white suits. Even the mannequins have designer stubble.

Davide Cenci

Via Campo Marzio, 1-7 (69 90 681). Bus to Via del Corso. **Open** *Oct-Mar* 10am-7.30pm; regular opening in other months **Credit** AmEx, DC, EC, MC, V.
The place where Italians come to dress their classical best. Cenci has catered to Rome's wealthy since 1926, offering a 'made in Italy' treatment of classic suits, shirts and shoes.

Degli Effetti

Piazza Capranica, 93-4 (67 90 202). Bus to Largo di Torre Argentina. **Men's wear branch** *Piazza Capranica, 75-9 (67 91 650).* **Credit** AmEx, DC, EC, MC, V.
Stunning – and often OTT – clothes by Vivienne Westwood, John Galliano, Issey Miyake, Comme des Garçons, and Romeo Gigli. Be prepared to pay horrendous prices.

Il Discount dell'Alta Moda

Via Gesù e Maria, 14-16a (36 13 796). Metro Spagna/bus to Piazza Augusto Imperatore. **No credit cards**.
Cut-price, but still budget-bashing, end-of-line designer fashion, in a more-laid back atmosphere than is normal in snooty *couture* outlets.

Dolce e Gabbana

Piazza di Spagna, 82/3 (67 92 294). Metro Spagna/bus to Piazza San Silvestro. **Open** 3.30-7.30pm Mon; 10am-7pm Tue-Sat. **Credit** AmEx, DC, EC, MC, V.
The first D&G shop to open in Rome, selling the weird and wonderful (and occasionally over-exposed) creations of the famous duo.

Emporio Armani

Via del Babuino, 140 (36 00 21 97). Metro Spagna. **Open** 3.30-7.30pm Mon; 10am-7.30pm Tue-Sat. **Casual wear branch**: **Armani Jeans** *Via del Babuino, 70a (36 00 18 48).* **Credit** AmEx, DC, EC, MC, V.
Lower-priced clothes by the master of understated chic. Don't be put off by the fascist-style statue in the foyer or the take-it-or-leave-it attitude of some of the assistants.

Ex Nihil

Corso Vittorio Emanuele, 339 (68 33 853). Bus to Corso Vittorio Emanuele or Ponte Vittorio Emanuele. **Open** 10am-1.30pm, 3.30-8pm Mon-Sat. **Credit** AmEx, V, MC.
Small outlet selling selected slick numbers by the likes of Gigli and Paul Smith.

Gianni Versace: *the legend lives on.*

Fendi

Via Borgognona 4e, 4l, 36a-38b, 39-40 (67 97 641/2/3/4). Metro Spagna/bus to Piazza San Silvestro. **Open** *Leather shop* 10am-7.30pm Mon-Sat; *furrier* 10am-8pm Mon-Sat. **Credit** AmEx, DC, EC, MC, V.
The Fendi sisters have colonised much of the street. Rome's most successful *couture* house sells high-fashion furs, shoes and leather accessories, a ready-to-wear collection, and gifts.

Galassia

Via Frattina, 20/21 (67 97 896). Metro Spagna/bus to Piazza San Silvestro. **Open** 9.30am-7.30pm Mon-Sat. **Credit** AmEx, DC, EC, MC, V.
Fashions for all by Gigli, Gaultier, Sibilla, Ozbek, Yamamoto, Matsuda and Smith, with hefty reductions in the July sales.

Gianfranco Ferrè

Via Borgognona, 42b (67 90 050). Metro Spagna//bus to Piazza San Silvestro. **Credit** AmEx, DC, EC, MC, V.
A space-age boutique of steel and black mosaics filled with the creations of the ex-Dior stylist.

Gianni Versace

Via Borgognona, 29 (67 95 292). Metro Spagna/bus to Piazza San Silvestro. **Open** 3.30-7.30pm Mon; 7.30pm Tue-Sat. **Branches**: **Versus** *Via Borgognona, 33/4 (67 83 977). Bus to Piazza San Silvestro.* **Women's wear** *Via Bocca di Leone, 26 (67 80 521). Bus to Piazza San Silvestro.* **Credit** AmEx, DC, EC, MC, V.
The late, great Calabrian designer gave *haute couture* a high-camp twist. Startlingly rich combinations of colours, fabrics and pattern are offset by the understated décor of these shops. The street-cred Versus range gives youthful lines to glaring colours.

Giorgio Armani

Via Condotti, 77 (69 91 460). Metro Spagna/bus to Piazza Augusto Imperatore. **Open** 3.30-7pm Mon; 10am-7pm Tue-Sat. **Credit** AmEx, DC, EC, MC, V.
The Roman outlet of the king of Milanese fashion sells men's suits and jackets with elegant, clean lines, plus women's accessories and bags.

Laura Biagiotti

Via Borgognona, 43-44 (67 91 205). Metro Spagna/bus to Piazza San Silvestro. **Credit** AmEx, DC, EC, MC, V.
A vast, white, glass-roofed showroom sets off the bright colours of Biagiotti's easy-to-wear clothes and accessories.

Max Mara

Via Condotti, 46 (67 87 946). Metro Spagna/bus to Piazza San Silvestro. **Credit** AmEx, DC, EC, MC, V.
Simple, well-cut dresses, plus understated suits, shirts and skirts at moderate prices (for Via Condotti). Also good for bags and other accessories.

Mimmo Siviglia

Via della Vite, 63 (67 97 474). Bus to Piazza San Silvestro. **No credit cards**.
A tiny store tucked out of the way from Via Condotti, where rows of cottons and silks are waiting to be hand sewn into stylish shirts for fashion-conscious executives.

Oliver

Via del Babuino, 61 (36 00 19 06). Metro Spagna/bus to Piazza San Silvestro. **Credit** AmEx, DC, V.
The youth-oriented part of the Valentino empire, featuring off-the-shoulder cocktail dresses and evening wear in a perfumed atmosphere of utter leisure.

Roccobarocco

Via Bocca di Leone, 65a (67 97 914). Bus to Piazza San Silvestro. **Credit** All major cards.
Crest-of-the-wave Neapolitan stylist who specialises in ultra-feminine diaphanous creations.

Valentino

Via Bocca di Leone, 15 (67 95 862). Metro Spagna/bus to Piazza San Silvestro. **Open** 3.30-7.30pm Mon; 10am-7.30pm Tue-Sat. **Credit** AmEx, DC, EC, MC, V.
Top quality, ready-to-wear lines for women. Very chic, very conservative and very, very conscious of its role at the top of Rome's fashion pole.

High-Street Fashion

Bacillario

Via Laurina, 41/3 (67 89 627). Metro Spagna/bus to Piazza Augusto Imperatore. **Open** 9.30am-7.30pm Mon-Sat. **Credit** AmEx, V.
Avant-garde shop styled along British punk lines. Leather jeans and jackets, see-through shirts and scrappy bikinis.

Diesel

Via del Corso, 185 (67 83 933). Bus to Piazza San Silvestro. **Open** 10.30am-8pm Mon-Sat. **Credit** AmEx, DC, EC, MC, V.
Retro-look for the masses in a slickly attractive setting, with whimsical window displays. Relatively little stock is spread out over two floors in this showpiece outlet.

Energie

Via del Corso, 486 (32 27 044). Bus to Largo Chigi. **Credit** All major cards.
Trend-setter and follower, Energie is one of *the* shops for Roman youth, particularly those from the outskirts. Stocking the hippest labels, including its own, it also charges higher-than-average prices.

Eventi

Via della Fontanella, 8 (36 00 25 33). Bus to Via del Corso or Piazza del Popolo. **Credit** All major cards.
The '70s revisited, with '90s street-chic. One of the few places in Rome where you can find lurid synthetic tops that clash superbly with tulip-embellished five-inch platforms. Worth visiting for the shop's bathroom-style décor: you change in shower units, and try on shoes sitting on the loo.

Invicta

Via del Babuino, 27/8 (36 00 17 37). Metro Spagna/bus to Piazza del Popolo. **Credit** AmEx, DC, EC, MC, V.
Purveyors of classic travelwear since 1906, Invicta specialises in casual and sportswear and a wide range of bags. Responsible for the stripy rucksacks without which Italian teenagers feel incomplete.

Planet

Via dei Baullari, 132 (68 80 13 96). Bus to Corso Vittorio Emanuele. **Credit** AmEx, MC, V.
Streetwear and rave gear: Stussy hats and Oshkosh trousers, and Pumas for your feet. Second-hand Oshkosh overalls for kids, at an average price of L30,000.

Replay Country Store

Salita dei Crescenzi, 1/2 (68 33 073). Bus to Corso del Rinascimento. **Open** 3.30-7.30pm Mon; 10am-7.30pm Tue-Sat. **Credit** AmEx, MC, V.
Expensive but durable clothes for men, women and children. Western gear, leather jackets, dresses and sweatshirts are displayed in an old-time country store.

Strada Studio

Via del Corso, 94 (67 93 011). Bus to Via del Corso. **Open** 2-8pm Mon; 9.30am-8pm Tue-Sat. **Credit** AmEx, DC, EC, MC, V.
Well-tailored casual clothes for women. They also sell Pinko and Romeo Gigli's G line.

Le Tartarughe & Co

Via Pie' di Marmo, 17 (67 92 240). Bus to Largo di Torre Argentina or Piazza Venezia. **Credit** AmEx, DC, EC, MC, V.
Simple, stark designs that give a sophisticated, alternative look from top to toe. Accessories can be bought at their annex across the road at number 29.

Timberland

Via del Babuino, 75 (67 90 836). Metro Spagna/bus to Piazza del Popolo. **Credit** AmEx, DC, EC, MC, V.
'English-style' rain- and sportswear with an Italian cut. Also stocks its own lines of jeans.

Independent designers

Romans are known for their finely tailored and conservative clothing rather than their wacky or eclectic dress sense. Here it's not considered cool to stand out – looking beautiful, well groomed and exactly like all your friends is what matters. Consequently, clothes sold in one store look frighteningly similar to those in the shop next door. But fear not: Rome does have its fair share of designers who are chipping away at the monolith in an attempt to introduce some diversity into the world of fashion.

Maga Morgana

Via del Governo Vecchio, 27 (68 79 995). Bus to Corso Vittorio Emanuele. **Open** 10am-8pm Mon-Sat. **Credit** All major cards.
One of the first in Rome to stray away from the pack, designer Luciana Iannace has acquired a devoted clientele of artists,

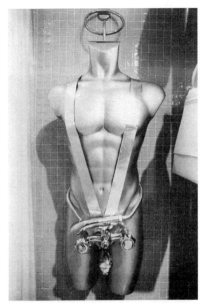

Eventi *re-lives the decade that taste forgot.*

actors and theatre people. She began designing jumpers 20 years ago and, with the help of her designer son and a fabrics specialist, now makes original clothes for women – velvet, linen and silk dresses, woollen coats and long, low-slung skirts. Wedding dresses embroidered with antique lace are made to order.

Pane e Pasta

Via dei Campani, 17 (49 41 207). Bus to Via Tiburtina. **No credit cards**.
Here, New Yorker Glenda Cohen and partner Ruth Valiant house their two clothing lines: the simple and elegant Glenda Cohen Concept, and the lower-priced, younger 2Funky line. The clothes are hand-made, only three or so pieces are made in each design, and natural fabrics are used throughout. What's more, they're surprisingly affordable. Cohen also tailors made-to-order designs for individual customers.

Peter Langner

Via Pietro da Cortona, 1 (32 00 525). Bus to Piazzale Manila. **Open** *appointment only.* **No credit cards**.
Trained by Dior and Ungaro before working with Norman Hartnell, Peter Langner has descended on Rome to supply the city with exquisite, custom-tailored bridal gowns and evening dresses. His designs are sophisticated and sombre – no frills and flounces here – and are all hand-made.

Lingerie

Lingerie stores are found all over town, particularly in the maze of streets around Via Condotti. Most markets have at least one *bancarella* selling inexpensive underwear, and the Rinascente department store (*see above*) is a good bet for middle-range items.

Food Markets

Fancy a peach? Avoid the expensive fruit stalls lurking beside famous monuments and head for one of Rome's many local markets. Every area has one (open from approximately 7.30am-1pm), selling everything from canteloupe melons to courgettes, not to mention flowers, cold cuts, cheeses and basic household items.

The best markets on the sightseeing trail are those in **Campo de' Fiori**, **Piazza San Cosimato** in Trastevere and **Piazza Testaccio**. Hungry pilgrims emerging from the Vatican should head for the covered market in **Piazza dell'Unità** (on Via Cola di Rienzo) or the much cheaper stalls of **Via Trionfale** just up the road. If you're staying in a hotel north of the station, try the reasonably priced stalls at the far end of **Via Milazzo**. Those on the southern side should join the thousands of shoppers at Rome's largest and most cosmopolitan market, currently in **Piazza Vittorio Emanuele** but soon to be moved to the nearby Via Giolitti area, which offers halal meat and exotic spices, vegetables and pulses alongside local fare. Kitchen equipment also abounds, and this is an excellent place to get your new espresso coffee pot, or to find one of those frustratingly unobtainable rubber rings that fit inside.

Bruscoli
Via del Corso, 113 (67 95 715/67 85 797). Bus to Piazza San Silvestro. **Open** 3.30-7.30pm Mon; 9.30am-7.30pm Tue-Sat. **Credit** AmEx, D, MC, V.
A large selection of stockings, bathing suits, undergarments and dance wear.

Treppiedi
Via del Teatro Valle, 54d (68 80 62 68). Bus to Corso Vittorio Emanuele or Corso del Rinascimento. **Credit** AmEx, DC, EC, MC, V.
Skin-tingling silk lingerie edged with lace, made-to-measure negligées and exotic bathing costumes.

YL Bodywear
Via del Nazareno, 1c (67 84 514). Metro Spagna/ bus to Piazza San Silvestro. **Open** 3.30-7.30pm Mon; 10am-7.30pm Tue-Sat. **Credit** AmEx, DC, EC, MC, V.
Heaven for underwear addicts, with lingerie from every designer imaginable.

Second-hand Clothes

Traditionally, there has been little demand in Rome for second-hand clothes, which were seen as cast-offs and hand-me-downs rather than recherché fashion items. More used-clothes shops are springing up, however, as Italian fashion slowly begins to take a rebellious turn. Via del Governo Vecchio is a good place to look.

Bianco e Nero
Via Marrucini, 34, San Lorenzo (44 50 286). Bus to Via Tiburtina. **Credit** V.
Ignore the ostentatious sign outside – there are some real bargains within. Both new and second-hand clothes, plus a load of accessories, for very low prices.

Rags Utd
Piazza Campo de' Fiori, 11/12 (68 79 344). Bus to Corso Vittorio Emanuele. **Open** regular times, plus 10pm-midnight May-Sept. **No credit cards.**
Bright Hawaiian shirts, long, flowing dresses from the 1920s to the '50s and classic American denims. Unfortunately, the prices are a bit higher than in the UK and the US.

Shoes & Leather Goods

Like clothes shops, most of Rome's shoe stores are pretty interchangeable. But be persistent in your search: small shops come and go with amazing styles and the occasional bargain. For the budget shopper, try Testaccio market (*see* **Food Markets** *above*), where a whole row of stalls sells shoe manufacturers' samples at a fraction of retailers' prices.

Beltrami
Via Condotti, 84 (67 91 330). Metro Spagna/bus to Piazza Augusto Imperatore. **Open** 10am-7.30pm Mon-Sat. **Credit** AmEx, DC, EC, MC, V.
A snooty showroom which has its very own fountain and an intimidating décor to remind you that you're in the presence of a leatherwork legend. Awesomely elegant shoes and custom-made bags.

Carlotta Rio
Via dell'Arco della Ciambella, 8 (68 72 308). Bus to Largo di Torre Argentina. **Credit** AmEx, EC, MC, V.
A stylish showroom, with easy chairs to sink into. Handmade bags, shoes and sandals. Good, simple quality.

Fausto Santini
Via Frattina, 120 (67 84 114). Metro Spagna/bus to Piazza San Silvestro. **Open** 3.30-7.30pm Mon; 10am-7.30pm Tue-Sat. **Credit** AmEx, DC, EC, MC, V.

Santini is the city's most famous shoe designer, and rightly so. The designs are sleek, sophisticated and original, yet surprisingly durable. Alternatively, pick up a pair of last year's model at the Santini shop on Via Santa Maria Maggiore, 165 (48 80 934). The price difference is astounding.

Gucci

Via Condotti, 8 (67 89 340). Metro Spagna/bus to Piazza Augusto Imperatore. **Open** 3-7pm Mon; 10am-7pm Tue-Sat. **Branch** *Via Condotti, 77 (67 96 147).* **Credit** AmEx, DC, EC, MC, V.
Gucci produces the very finest designer luggage, shoes and handbags, as well as watches, scarves and other accessories. All items are displayed without price tags, presumably to stop customers passing out.

H30

Via Frattina, 96/96a (67 90 168). Metro Spagna/bus to Piazza San Silvestro. **Open** 3.30-7.30pm Mon; 10am-7.30pm Tue-Sat. **Credit** AmEx, DC, EC, MC, V.
Suede knee-length boots, plastic rain boots, and mules in orange and lime green as well as the more customary blacks and browns. Plus a wide selection of boots and thick-soled shoes for men.

Leoni Cuoio

Via del Vantaggio, 21e/f (32 19 296). Metro Flaminio/bus to Piazzale Flaminio. **Credit** AmEx, DC, V.
This family-owned leather business resuscitated the carpet-bagger style in shoes and suitcases 15 years ago and still makes excellent boots, purses and briefcases at reasonable prices. Friendly and relaxed.

Rocco Shoes

Via Gioberti, 22-6 (44 67 299). Metro Termini. **Credit** EC, MC, V.
Mock croc, hoods' spats, business brogues and woven slip-ons for men, as well as a wide selection of children's loafers and Italian-made sandals. Great prices.

Food & Drink

Food-buying in Rome is generally done at individual shops, and fruit and vegetables are bought at the markets (*see* **Food Markets** *page 169*). Stores like *Catena* and *Volpetti* (*see below*) and humbler local grocery shops *(alimentari)* stock an assortment of cured meats, cheeses, and wines. The best coffee is found at the *torrefazioni* (*see* chapter **Cafés & Bars**).

Prosciutto (ham) comes *crudo* (raw; the best is from Parma) or *cotto* (cooked). Other things to ask for at the cold cuts counter are *bresaola* (air-dried beef) and salami (*piccante* if you like it spicy). Extra-virgin olive oil (the best is from Tuscany and Liguria), *parmigiano* (Parmesan) and *pecorino* (hard, salty cheese made from sheep's milk) are found in most food shops. *Parmigiano*, *pecorino* and other dry cheeses such as Asiago, Taleggio and *provola* (smoked buffalo cheese) all travel well. Mozzarella and ricotta do not. Most deli products are sold by the *etto* (100g) rather than the kilo. When ordering, ask for *un'etto*, *due etti*, and so on. (*See* **Using the Lingo** *page 262*.)

Look out, too, for fruit mustards (*mostarda di Cremona*), the extraordinary range of Italian vinegars, and, if you're feeling extravagant, truffles, mushrooms and *bottarga* (smoked tuna roe).

For advice on buying wine, *see* **Choosing the Wine** *in chapter* **Restaurants**. However, some of the best Italian wines are simply labelled *vino da tavola* (table wine). Many *enotecas* sell wine from large barrels by the litre (bring your own container); cheap it may be, but unless you're very lucky, the resemblance to paint-stripper may be more than passing.

Ai Monasteri

Piazza delle Cinque Lune, 76 (68 80 27 83). Bus to Corso Rinascimento. **No credit cards**.
Founded in 1892, this dark and cavernous store sells wines, liqueurs, honey, herbs, preserves and other natural products, all grown or gathered at seven Italian monasteries. Some, like flavoured *grappas*, *sambuca*, Vermouth and Marsala, will be familiar to you, but fennel cordial and other elixirs will intrigue.

Castroni

Via Cola di Rienzo, 196, Prati (68 74 383). Metro Ottaviano/bus to Piazza del Risorgimento. **Open** 8am-8pm Mon-Sat. **Branch** *Piazza Balduina, 1 (35 49 68 06).* **No credit cards**.
A wonderful shop that stocks Italian regional specialities. Castroni is also Rome's largest importer of international food products. Expect to find anything from Chinese food and kidney beans to pancake mix and Worcestershire sauce. Prices are reasonable, and they also gift-wrap or pack goods carefully for you to get them home.

Catena

Via Appia Nuova, 9, San Giovanni (70 49 16 64). Metro San Giovanni/bus to Piazzale Appio. **No credit cards**.
This luxury grocery store, opened in 1928, is the nearest thing that Rome has to London's Fortnum & Mason. A bewildering variety of sweets can be bought by the *etto*, and there's a huge range of regional preserves, biscuits, coffees, hams, cheeses, vintage wines and liqueurs. They will also make up delicious hampers to order.

La Corte

Via della Gatta, 1 (67 83 842). Bus to Piazza Venezia. **Credit** V.
Englishman John Fort smokes fish in a village south of Rome for his tiny shop off Piazza del Collegio Romano. It's the place to go if you need smoked swordfish or salmon. Other delicacies include Italian caviar.

Delucchi

Via della Croce, 74. (67 91 630). Bus to Via del Corso. **No credit cards**.
The appeal of Delucchi is the superb display of candied fruit in the shop window. It's a good basic grocery, which also sells fruit and veg, but it's not cheap.

Franchi

Via Cola di Rienzo, 204, Prati (68 64 576). Metro Ottaviano/bus to Piazza del Risorgimento. **Open** 8am-8pm Mon-Sat. **Credit** AmEx, EC, MC, V.
A rival to its close neighbour Castroni (*see above*), this traditional food store contains an encyclopaedic selection of cheeses and hams from every part of Italy and an equally comprehensive stock of wines. Also on offer are an assortment of prepared dishes to be taken away, including mouth-watering *antipasti* and roast meats.

Pasta all'Uova

Via della Croce, 8 (67 93 102). Bus to Via del Corso. **No credit cards**.

Diesel: *slick and smooth (see page 166).*

Reflected glory at **Valentino** *(page 166).*

This unassuming shop sells both fresh and dry pasta. Amaze and delight your dinner guests back home with *favette* (penis-shaped pasta) or harlequin tagliatelle in fetching post-modern shades of turquoise and lilac.

Rossi
Piazza della Rotonda, 4 (68 75 989). Bus to Largo di Torre Argentina. **Credit** AmEx.
Rossi is proud of his salamis, *prosciutto* and *mortadella*, but don't neglect his fruit preserves, balsamic and flavoured vinegars, black and white truffles and *funghi porcini*.

Salumeria Focacci
Via della Croce, 43 (67 91 228). Metro Spagna/bus to Piazza Augusto Imperatore. **Credit** AmEx, EC, MC, V.
A corner store, close to Via Condotti, offering a fine array of gourmet products, from Italian game pâtés, truffles and juniper-flavoured olive oil to *bottarga* (mullet roe).

Vincenzo Tascioni
Via Cola di Rienzo, 211, Prati (32 43 152). Metro Ottaviano/bus to Piazza del Risorgimento. **No credit cards.**
Thirty different kinds of pasta, including varieties flavoured with octopus ink and chilli pepper, all prepared in the back room. You can watch the entire process in action while you buy.

Volpetti
Via Marmorata, 47 (57 46 986). Metro Piramide/bus to Via Marmorata. **Credit** All major cards.
A Testaccio tradition, Volpetti is one of the best delis in Rome, with exceptional hand-made pasta (try their pumpkin-filled tortelloni), cheeses, wines and mouth-watering antipasti. Once in, it's hard to get away without one of the jolly assistants filling you up with samples of their wares – and persuading you to buy twice as much as you want. Volpetti Più, just around the corner in Via Volta, is their self-service diner.

Ethnic foods

The area around Piazza Vittorio Emanuele, slowly becoming home to Rome's immigrant population, is the best place to go in search of Indian, Korean, Chinese and African foodstuffs.

Oriental Store
Via Filippo Turati, 130 (44 55 631). Metro Piazza Vittorio Emanuele. **No credit cards.**
Mexican and American as well as Oriental items.

Pacific Trading Co
Viale Principe Eugenio, 17-20 (44 67 934/44 68 406). Metro Vittorio Emanuele. **No credit cards.**
A huge range of imported foodstuffs from the Far East.

Chocolates

Confetteria Moriondo e Gariglio
Via del Pie' di Marmo, 21/2 (69 90 856). Bus to Piazza Venezia. **Open** 9.30am-7.30pm Mon-Sat. **No credit cards.**
Rome's only family-run chocolate confectioners moulds and sells dark, liqueur-filled confections on the premises. At Easter and Valentine's Day, Romans queue to have their special gifts sealed inside beautifully-packaged chocolate eggs and hearts. Home deliveries anywhere within Italy.

Health Foods

Albero del Pane
Via Santa Maria del Pianto, 19/20 (68 65 016). Bus to Largo di Torre Argentina. **Open** 9am-8pm Mon-Wed, Fri, Sat; 9am-1pm Thur. **Credit** AmEx, MC, V.
Honey, grains and Italian-blended herbal teas, and a collection of wines and olive oils, all free of artificial additives.

Tack along the Tiber

Papal litter at Saint Peter's.

As any serious collector of kitsch is aware, nothing brings out bad taste as effectively as the presence of organised religion. The area around the Vatican will not disappoint you. Although the vendors round Saint Peter's sell an uninspiring assortment of statuettes, guidebooks, T-shirts and plastic rosaries, Borgo Pio, to the east of Vatican City, offers a wealth of tacky souvenirs.

Comandini (Borgo Pio, 151) has one of the best selections in Rome – a cornucopia of memorabilia ranging from plug-in Virgin Mary lamps to Vatican pens with benignly floating bishops, to hologram Pope John Paul II keyrings.

Alternatively, explore the underbelly of Italian obsessions with sex, mobile phones and football, as well as some of the weirder imports in an increasingly cosmopolitan capital. And keep your eyes open for that ultimate collector's item: a **Hard Rock Café – Rome T-shirt**, celebrating a venue that doesn't yet exist.

TASTELESS TOP TEN

1. Scar your friends with a **dragon cigarette lighter**-cum-blowtorch. Tug on his paw and see him do untold mischief. (Chinese street vendors.)
2. Seduce that special dinner guest with **penis and vagina-shaped pasta** (sold separately) in a disturbing range of colours and sizes. (Marco Roscioli, Via dei Chiavari, 34.)
3. Light up your living room with a plastic **Saint Peter's Basilica lamp** in papal gold. (Shops in Termini Station)
4. The Rev. Ian Paisley would probably appreciate a **Vatican brass ashtray** to flick his ash into. (Street souvenir stands.)
5. If music be the food of love, get a **musical condom** and whistle while you work. (Condomania, *see page 176*).
6. Send the nipper to bed in a red and yellow infant-size pair of **Roma football club pyjamas**. (Roma Shop, *see chapter* **Sport & Fitness**.)
7. Pope your cork with a **papal bottle opener**-cum-John Paul II medallion. (Souvenir stands.)
8. Don't look uncool. Ring up your imaginary friends on your plastic **imitation mobile phone**. (Street vendors.)
9. Forget those tired old views of the Forum and the Trevi fountain. Instead, send your loved ones slushy, soft-focus **postcards** of flare-clad couples or mournful pups. (Most postcard stands.)
10. Take a short-cut to Paradise. Buy a **papal indulgence** with a dotted line for your name. (Souvenir shops on Via della Conciliazione.)

Il Canestro

Via Luca della Robbia, 47, Testaccio (57 46 287). Metro Piramide/bus or tram to Via Marmorata. **Open** 12.30-8pm Mon; 9am-8pm Tue-Sat. **Branch** *Via San Francesco a Ripa, 106 (58 12 621). Bus to Viale Trastevere.* **No credit cards**.

Il Canestro offers a full range of natural health foods, cosmetics and medicines, mostly from within Italy, including some organic versions of regional specialities. Also to be found in the building are a centre for alternative medicine and a vegetarian restaurant.

Maya

Via degli Equi, 35 (44 51 834). Bus to Via Tiburtina. **No credit cards**.

Tofu, *tempeh* and a wide selection of macrobiotic foods are sold alongside natural health and cleaning products in this shop in San Lorenzo. Herbal tea cocktails are custom-made on the spot to help all kinds of ailments, including stress, menstrual cramps and kidney problems.

Drink

See also chapter **Eating & Drinking**.

Buccone

Via di Ripetta, 19/20 (36 12 154). Bus to Piazza Augusto Imperatore. **Open** 9am-1.30pm, 4-8.30pm, Mon-Sun. **Credit** AmEx, EC, MC, V.

Inside a seventeenth-century palazzo, this *enoteca* is filled from floor to arched ceiling with wines and spirits, all clearly sub-divided into region. Prices range from a cheap Valpolicella to a Brunello Riserva at over one million lire. The atmosphere is friendly, and the son of the house speaks English. Buy to take home or sample their stock over the bar.

Costantini

Piazza Cavour, 16 (32 13 210). Bus to Piazza Cavour. **Open** 9am-1pm, 4.30-8pm, Mon-Sat. **Credit** All major cards.

A vast, cavernous cellar containing just about any Italian

*Try plunging yours in boiling water ... phallic pasta at **Marco Roscioli** (see page 173).*

wine you want, divided by region. Not the cheapest place to buy wine in Rome, but certainly one of the city's most extensive selections.

Enoteca Carso

Viale Carso, 37/39 (37 25 866). Bus to Piazza Mazzini. **Open** 9am-10pm Mon-Sat. **No credit cards**.
A unique Roman pleasure: the shelves buckle under the weight of wines and liqueurs, while film and TV people drown their sorrows in jugs of *verdicchio* at the tables outside. Prices are among the cheapest in town.

Enoteca M Vinicolo Angelini

Via Viminale, 62, Esquilino (48 81 028). Metro Termini/bus to Termini. **Open** 9am-1pm, 4-8pm, Mon-Sat. **Credit** AmEx.
Angelini's sells wines and spirits from all over Italy and the world. A 1964 Barolo or Chianti Classico runs from L50,000 up, while there's real Frascati (not the bleached stuff they put in bottles) from the barrel at L4,000 per litre.

Trimani

Via Goito, 20 (44 69 661). Metro Termini/bus to Piazza Indipendenza. **Open** Usual times, plus 10am-1.30pm, 4-7.30pm, Sun. **Credit** All major cards.
The oldest and best wine shop in Rome was founded in 1821 by Francesco Trimani, whose descendent Marco still presides. Delivery anywhere in the world.

Gifts

General

La Chiave

Largo delle Stimmate, 28, Largo di Torre Argentina (68 30 88 48). Bus to Largo di Torre Argentina. **Open** 10am-7.30pm Mon-Sat. **Credit** AmEx, DC, MC, V.
Well-priced silver jewellery from India and South America, Indonesian clothing, children's toys and knick-nacks, baskets and wooden furniture. There is also a well-stocked stationery section with a range of goods made out of recycled paper.

Guaytamelli

Via del Moro, 59 (58 80 704). Bus to Viale Trastevere. **Credit** AmEx, MC, V.
Old-fashioned timepieces: silver and bronze sundials to wear on a chain around your neck, hour-glasses and free-standing sundials – all beautifully hand made by the watchmaker at the back of the shop.

Mappamundo

Via dei Baullari, 21 (68 80 69 87). Bus to Corso Vittorio Emanuele. **Open** 4-8pm Mon; 9am-1.30pm, 4-7pm, Tue-Sun. **Credit** EC, MC, V.
A mishmash of wonderful, colourful mobiles, giant wooden flowers, silver jewellery and bright, painted animals and dolls, imported from all over the world.

Roberto e Roberta Betti

Via Monterone, 10-13 (68 77 097). Bus to Largo di Torre Argentina. **Open** 3.30-7.30pm Mon; 9am-7.30pm Tue-Sat. **No credit cards**.
Wickerwork and raffia spill out onto the narrow cobbled road where the Bettis keep alive one of Rome's traditional crafts. There are baskets, chairs and more unusual gifts to be found amid the clutter.

Single

Via Francesco Crispi, 47 (67 90 713). Metro Barberini/bus to Piazza Barberini. **Credit** All major cards.
Head straight to this bastion of one-upmanship in the kitchen for the very latest Alessi toasters and fruit juicers, stainless steel thermoses, sleek silver flasks, marble book-ends, glass butter dishes, and hundreds of other beautifully-designed but ultimately pretty useless objects.

Jewellery

As well as the grand international empires like Bulgari (*see below*) there are plenty of tiny jewellery shops where artisans create filigree ear-rings and set ancient stones. An increasing number of shops now sell ethnic and outlandish contemporary pieces, and there are still shops where you can take a stone and design the setting yourself with the help of the jeweller – try Oddi e Seghetti at Via del Cancello, 18. Look out as well for designs based on Etruscan and Ancient Roman originals.

Biagini/Stop & Swatch

Via Frattina, 59 (67 97 001). Metro Spagna/bus to Piazza San Silvestro. **Open** 9.30am-8pm Mon-Sat. **Branch** *Via Frattina, 103a (67 96 702).* **Credit** AmEx, DC, EC, MC, V.
Italians have turned limited edition Swatches into a cult. Otherwise law-abiding citizens smuggle them in from the US – where they're cheaper – to make a killing on a market that's tightly controlled by a few dealers. Biagini's is one of them.

Bulgari

Via Condotti, 10 (67 93 876). Metro Spagna/bus to Piazza San Silvestro. **Credit** AmEx, DC, EC, MC, V.
Dodge the tourists lining up to be photographed with this grand store as a backdrop. Then sweep past the tight, unfriendly security to drool over the fantastically expensive creations. The glittering watches are arranged in splendid isolation, while clients admire them from upright antique chairs. The cheapest watches start at a cool L8,000,000.

Carlo Eleuteri

Via Condotti, 69 (67 81 078). Metro Spagna/bus to Piazza Augusto Imperatore. **Credit** AmEx, DC, EC, MC, V.
A mecca for watch collectors, with Baume, Mercier, Tiffany and Cartier on display. Small and unfriendly, but a superb collection of art deco and mid-century jewellery.

Manasse

Via di Campo Marzio, 44 (68 71 007). Bus to Via del Corso. **Credit** AmEx, DC, EC, MC, V.
An exquisite, museum-like shop, justly famous for its collection of Russian antique jewellery and icons, as well as for the extreme cordiality of its staff.

Ouroboros

Via di Sant'Eustachio, 15 (68 80 45 84). Bus to Corso Rinascimento. **Open** 11am-8pm Mon-Sat. **Credit** AmEx, V, MC.
A wonderful selection of exquisite, hand-made silver jewellery in funky, modern designs.

Peppino Capuano

Via Condotti, 61 (67 95 996). Metro Spagna/bus to Piazza san Silvestro. **Credit** AmEx, DC, EC, MC, V.
Don't be intimidated by the heavy security. The walk across the courtyard of Palazzo Caffarelli alone is worth your while. Inside you'll discover some of Italy's finest silver in a dark panelled room.

Siragusa

Via delle Carrozze, 64 (67 97 085). Metro Spagna/bus to Piazza Augusto Imperatore. **Credit** AmEx, DC.
Original stones from Magna Grecia (as southern Italy was known under ancient-Greek control), in modern gold settings with amulets, seals, medallions and chains based on models from antiquity. Part jewellery museum, part gallery.

Odds & Ends

Condomania

Via de' Prefetti, 25 (no phone). Bus to Corso del Rinascimento. **No credit cards.**
Wacky condoms and other sexual sundries. Youngsters under 18 are not allowed in.

Records & Music

Cassettes, records and CDs are more expensive in Italy than in the UK and US, and there are no huge cut-price chains like Virgin and Our Price. Some world music and indie releases are difficult to track down, and even the range of classical – especially contemporary classical – music on offer is more limited than you'll find in London or New York.

CD Best by Remix

Via Vodice, 15 (37 51 73 97). Metro Lepanto. **Open** 9am-8pm Mon-Sat. **Credit** All major cards.
Vast selection of imported and Italian underground mixes.

Disfunzioni Musicali

Via degli Etruschi, 4-14, San Lorenzo (44 61 984). Bus to Via Tiburtina. **Open** 10.30am-7.30pm Mon-Sat. **Credit** AmEx, DC, MC, V.
Just a few steps away from the university, this is one of the best places in Rome to buy underground and rare records, both new and second-hand, including recent US and British indie releases. Check the notice board for musical events, for goings-on at the *centri sociali* (*see chapter* **Music: Rock, Roots and Jazz**) or if you have aspirations to join a band.

Goody Music

Via Cesare Beccaria, 2 (36 10 959). Metro/bus to Piazzale Flaminio. **Credit** AmEx.
Tons and tons of dance, house, underground and rap vinyl mixes, plus equipment. DJs from all over Italy come here to find the latest tracks. There's also a good selection of tapes and CDs.

MozArt's

Via del Pellegrino, 10 (68 75 488). Bus to Corso Vittorio Emanuele. **No credit cards.**
Traditional lute-maker Enrico Baldi has turned his shop into something like a small private museum. He re-strings old instruments and re-tunes pianos, but is also happy to spend time discussing his work.

Ricordi

Via Cesare Battisti, 120c (67 98 022). Bus to Piazza Venezia. **Open** 3.30-7.30pm Mon, Sun; 9am-7.30pm Tue-Sat.
Branches *Via del Corso, 506 (36 12 331); Viale Giulio Cesare, 88, Prati (37 35 15 89).* **Credit** AmEx, DC, EC, MC, V.
Rome's best-known music shop, now divided into two adjacent stores: classical and pop. Ricordi stocks cassettes, CDs, videos, books and scores and also offers sound equipment for sale or hire.

Rinascita

Via delle Botteghe Oscure (69 92 24 36). Bus to Piazza Venezia. **Open** 10am-8pm Mon-Sat; 10am-2pm Sun. **Credit** All major cards.
Conveniently central music store with all the basics plus a good collection of CD singles and the latest trends, from new age to techno.

Services

Locked out? Need a haircut? Want to send a fax? All three? Look no further.

On arriving in Rome, throw away all your pre-conceptions about how things should work. Here, services function according to their own special rhythm, and the more Taoist your attitude, the better off you're likely to be. You'll find that certain services creak like rusty machinery, while others unexpectedly require no prodding or patience whatsoever.

For more information on additional services, the best place to start looking is in the city's English-language press, in the twice-weekly *Porta Portese* (*see chapter* **Media**). As anywhere, the best information is spread by word of mouth, so don't hesitate to milk every contact you have.

Clothing Repairs

F Pratesi (Clinica della Borsa)
Piazza Firenze, 22 (68 80 37 20). Bus to Via del Corso or Piazza San Silvestro. **Open** 9.30am-1pm, 4-8pm, Mon-Fri; 9.30am-1pm Sat. **Credit** AmEx, DC, MC, V.
A small leatherware shop that specialises in repairing bags slit open by thieves. Repairs take up to three days and cost from L10,000. Credit cards are accepted for purchases only.

Vecchia Sartoria
Via dei Banchi Vecchi, 19 (68 30 71 80). Bus to Corso Vittorio Emanuele. **Open** 9am-7pm Mon-Fri; 9am-1pm Sat. **No credit cards.**
Run by a skilled traditional tailor and a seamstress, who undertake clothing repair quickly and at reasonable prices.

Dry Cleaners & Launderettes

Dry cleaners (*tintorie*) are fairly expensive in Rome. Most laundries are not self-service, but will do your washing by the kilo. Self-service launderettes are listed in the Yellow Pages as *lavanderie a gettone*.

Greensec & Lavasecco Ecologico
Via Napoleone III, 97 (49 17 22). Metro Vittorio Emanuele. **Open** 9am-1pm, 3-7pm, Mon-Fri.
An environmentally-aware dry cleaners offering a 24-hour dry-cleaning service at a fixed price of L3,500 per item.

Onda Blu
Via Lamarmora, 12 (44 64 172). Metro Vittorio Emanuele. **Open** 8am-10pm daily.
Wash six kilos of dirty clothes for L10,000. There is no dry cleaning service, but they will iron clothes for L1,500-2,000. Bright and friendly place.

Tintoria Rita
Campo de' Fiori, 38 (68 79 096). Bus to Corso Vittorio Emanuele. **Open** 8.30am-8pm Mon-Fri; 8.30am-2pm Sat.
Central dry cleaners with same-day cleaning. They will wash your laundry – the price is L25,000 for five kilos.

Faxing & Photocopying

Faxes can be sent from specialised shops and *tabacchi*, and some stationers (*cartolerie*) also have photocopiers. Prices vary, but in the San Lorenzo area there's a concentration of photo-copying centres, offering discounts to students. For information on the post, telephones and courier services, *see chapter* **Directory**.

Tecnoroma
Corso Vittorio Emanuele, 337a (phone/fax 68 64 354). Bus to Via Corso Vittorio Emanuele. **Open** 8.30am-1pm, 3.30-7pm, Mon-Fri. **No credit cards.**
A fax to Britain costs L4,500 for the first page, L2,500 for any additional pages. To receive is L1,000 per page.

World Translation Service
Via del Viminale 76/78 (48 81 039/48 25 986; fax 47 46 665). Metro Termini/bus to Via Cavour. **Open** 9am-7pm Mon-Fri. **No credit cards.**
In the heart of hotel-land for the past 25 years, WTC offers a translation service, cut-price international calls and a remarkably cheap fax service at around L.1,000 per page, plus the phone units used.

Xeromania
Via San Francesco a Ripa, 109 (58 14 433/fax 58 17 506). Bus to Viale Trastevere. **Open** 9am-1pm, 3.30-7.30pm, Mon-Fri; 9am-1pm Sat. **No credit cards.**
A good general photocopying shop in Trastevere, with a reliable fax sending and receiving service.

Hairdressers

Most hairdressers in Rome are closed on Monday. Appointments are not usually necessary, but you must be prepared to wait if you don't book.

Franco
Via Alessandro Volta, 18 (57 47 817). **Open** 8am-6.30pm Tue-Sat. **No credit cards.**
Franco spent many years in the US, picking up some basic English without losing his Italian knack for effortless, elegant cuts. Clientele ranges from diplomatic blue-rinses to models. L45,000 for a wash, cut and blow-dry.

Hair Tech Academy
Via Carlo Caneva, 64/66 (43 94 512). Metro Tiburtina. **Open** 9am-7pm Tue-Sat. **No credit cards.**
A slick, trendy salon, recently transplanted from London with English-speaking staff. On Mondays it's a school of hairdressing, from Tuesday to Saturday a full-time salon. Haircuts start at L50,000.

Marisa
Corso Vittorio Emanuele, 291 (68 61 217). Bus to Corso Vittorio Emanuele. **Open** 8.30am-6pm Tue-Sat. **Credit** AmEx.

One of the best deals in the city centre. Prices start from L22,000 for a simple cut, but any other service, such as washing and blow-drying, can add up to 50 per cent to your bill.

Internet Points

These are springing up all over Rome. The points listed here charge around L5,000 for 30 minutes.

Bibli
Via dei Fienaroli, 27/8 (58 84 097/58 14 534). Bus to Piazza Sonnino. **Open** 11am-midnight Tue-Sun; 5pm-midnight Mon. **Credit** AmEx, DC, MC, V.

Centro Turistico Studentesco (CTS)
Via Genova, 16 (46 79 271). Bus to Via Nazionale. **Open** 9am-1pm, 3-7pm, Mon-Fri; 9am-1pm Sat. **No credit cards**.

Locksmiths

Avoid the 24-hour emergency locksmiths listed under *Fabbro* in the local Yellow Pages, as their charges are little short of robbery. Instead, go to a local hardware shop (*ferramenta*) and ask if they can suggest anybody. If you're locked out of a house or flat at night, call the fire brigade; to get into a locked car, call the **ACI**, the Automobile Club d'Italia (*see chapter* **Directory**).

Opticians

Capaldo Ottica
Via delle Coppelle, 24 (68 77 364). Bus to Corso Vittorio Emanuele or Corso Rinascimento. **Open** 9.30am-1pm, 3.30-7.30pm, Mon-Fri; 9.30am-1pm Sat. **Credit** AmEx, DC, MC, V.
Eye tests, designer specs and contact lens specialists.

Ottica Scientifica Tonel
Via delle Convertite, 19/20 (67 92 579). Bus to Via del Corso or Piazza San Silvestro. **Open** 4-8pm Mon; 9.30am-1pm, 4-8pm, Tue-Sat. **Credit** AmEx, DC, MC, V.
Eye-tests, repairs, contact lenses and a range of glasses are on offer at Ottica. Credit cards are not accepted for contact lens purchases.

Ticket Agencies

Box Office
Via Giulio Cesare, 88 (37 35 15 89). Metro Lepanto. **Open** 3.30-7pm Mon; 10am-7pm Tue-Sat. **Branch** Via del Corso, 506 (36 12 682).
No credit cards.
Tickets for most concerts, theatres and sporting events in Italy. There is a Prenoticket service (52 20 03 42) which allows you to reserve tickets and pay by credit card. The reservation fee is 12 per cent of the ticket price.

Orbis
Piazza Esquilino, 37 (48 27 403). Metro Termini/bus to Piazza Esquilino. **Open** 9.30am-1pm, 4-7.30pm, Mon-Fri. **No credit cards**.
A well-established agency that can find tickets for most concerts, theatre and sporting events.

Travel Agencies

Centro Turistico Studentesco (CTS Student Travel Centre)
Corso Vittorio Emanuele, 297 (68 72 672/3/4). Bus to Corso Vittorio Emanuele. **Open** 9.30am-1pm, 3.30-7pm, Mon-Fri; 9.30am-1pm Sat. **No credit cards**. **Branches** *Via Genova, 16 (46 79 271). Bus to Via Nazionale.* **Open** 9am-1pm, 3-7pm Mon-Fri; 9am-1pm Sat. *Via degli Ausoni, 5 (44 50 141). Bus or tram to Via Tiburtina.* **Open** 9.30am-6.30pm Mon-Fri.
The official student travel service offers discounts on air, rail and coach tickets for all destinations. To use CTS's services you must have membership (L15,000). They issue International Student cards and have a bureau de change.
See also **Students** *in chapter* **Directory**.

Elsy Viaggi
Via di Torre Argentina, 80 (68 80 13 72/68 96 460). Bus to Largo di Torre Argentina. **Open** 9am-1pm, 3.30-6.30pm, Mon-Fri; 9am-1pm Sat. **No credit cards**.
This professional and very busy shop has some of the cheapest European and long-haul flights in Rome.

Lazzi Express
Via Tagliamento, 27b (88 40 840). Bus to Via Tagliamento. **Open** 9am-1pm, 3-6.30pm, Mon-Fri. **Credit** AmEx, MC, V.
Lazzi has information and tickets for the Euroline coach services to European cities.

Transalpino
Piazza Esquilino, 8a (48 70 870). Metro Termini/bus to Piazza Esquilino. **Open** 9am-6.30pm Mon-Fri; 9am-1pm Sat. **Branch** Stazione Termini (48 80 536). **Open** 8am-9pm Mon-Sat; 9am-8pm Sun. **Credit** AmEx, EC, MC.
Discount prices on rail tickets for the entire European network, and some air tickets.

Viaggiare
Via S. Nicola in Tolentino, 18 (47 46 751). Metro Barberini. **Open** 9.30am-7.30pm Mon-Fri; 9.30am-12.30pm Sat. **Credit** AmEx, DC, EC, MC, V.
Friendly and always busy. One of the best places for flights to the US and scheduled flights to Britain, and one of the few agencies to accept all credit card payments.

Video Rental

To become a member of the video clubs listed below, you will need some form of ID. *See also chapter* **Shopping**: **Bookshops**.

Filmania 4
Viale Donatello, 37 (32 24 992). Bus or tram to Via Flaminia. **Open** 10am-midnight daily. **Credit** AmEx, MC, V.
There are over 300 English-language films in stock, and membership is free. A one-day rental costs L4,000, and if you order a delivery from the **Pizzeria All'Angolo** (32 27 494) they will also bring you the video of your choice (*see* **Eating In** *in chapter* **Snacks**). This service is available throughout north and central Rome.

Videoteca Navona
Piazza Navona, 103/105 (68 69 823). Bus to Corso del Rinascimento. **Open** 9am-9pm Mon-Thur; 9am-midnight Fri-Sat. **Credit** AmEx, MC, V.
A huge selection of Italian and English language films, with new arrivals each month, plus a decent collection of French and Spanish films. Membership costs L50,000 (or leave a L50,000 deposit). A two-day rental will set you back L5,000.

Arts & Entertainment

Children

How to keep the bambini amused in the land of the family.

Paradox number one: Italy has the world's lowest birth rate – but you'll see kids everywhere you go, dressed up to the nines, running around restaurants, helping Daddy drive his Vespa. Paradox number two: Italy lets you take kids just about anywhere – and yet lays on almost no facilities for them.

A visit to Rome with kids in tow will bring you right up against these contradictions. Your children – especially if they are very small – will be cooed over from the moment you get off the plane, and yet you are likely to have to trek miles to find a decent set of swings. Nobody will mind if you take your five-year-old to the opera, but you won't be able to barter good behaviour against a trip to a children's farm or an adventure playground, because there aren't any. As for museums, Rome's are definitely of the hands-off variety.

For all that, there is no reason why your children should not have the time of their life in Rome. The key to their enjoyment is careful preparation. If you tell little Clara that the Basilica Aemilia in the **Forum** was built by the censors Marcus Aemilius Lepidus and Marcus Fulvius Nobilior in 179 BC, she'll be chasing pigeons before the end of the sentence; but point out the marks left by the coins which melted in the great fire which destroyed the building in AD 410 and you might grab her attention. If this all sounds like too much homework, try buying a children's guide to Ancient Rome, or to the myths and legends it generated (*see below*).

And if all else fails, there are many beautiful parks, not to mention glorious ice cream (*see chapter* **Ice Cream**). In the summer, whole entertainment villages mushroom in public parks, many of which have a section dedicated to youngsters. In June and July, check out the Citta in Tasca children's fair. Information on current events for children can be found in *Time Out Roma* under Bambini; *Roma C'e* under Children's Corner in the English section, or in *Trovaroma*, the supplement that comes with Thursday's *La Repubblica* newspaper, under *Città dei Ragazzi*.

THE FAMILY

If your image of the Italian family includes a buxom *mamma* clucking over her extensive brood, think again: the children of the *boom economico* of the '60s have now come of age, and though the clichéd, over-protective relationship between a mother and her children – especially the males – is still alive and kicking, an ever-growing

Unruly kids? Take them to the **Colosseum**.

percentage of *mamme* have to divide their time and attention between offspring and careers.

Mothers being out of the house all day has done little to change household roles, however, and few Italian men ever expect to be called upon to iron a shirt, much less make a meal. And although most of the 33 per cent of Italian 25-34 year-olds still living at home will cite the difficulties of finding rented accommodation as the biggest hurdle to leaving the nest, the attractions of independence can look bland beside great home-cooked pasta and a never-ending supply of clean laundry.

Given this, it should come as no surprise that Italy boasts the world's lowest birth rate: the wonder is, that large families were ever the norm. But that boom of the 1960s put paid to more than just full-time, constantly-breeding housewives: in wiping out the immense poverty of this country, it gave Italians an out-sized attachment to material comforts, and a burgeoning unwillingness to share limited dwelling space with small, screaming, time-consuming bundles.

The relatively few kids who squeeze through the net seem to have it made: they get great clothes and all the adoration which used to be shared out amongst much larger broods. Close contact with family members of all ages makes even the smallest children able socialites, and you will see a six-year-old respond to an elderly friend or uncle just as naturally as he would to his peers. This kind of relationship breeds mutual respect. If your kids are a little too rambunctious, don't worry; '*meglio vivaci*' (they're meant to be lively), long-suffering grannies will tell you.

SCHOOL

In Italy, compulsory schooling starts at six and finishes at 14, although planned reforms will change that to 5 and 16. There is a three-stage system of *scuola elementare, scuola media* and *scuola superiore*, followed by the alternatives of university-oriented *licei* or get-a-job-oriented *istituti tecnici* and *istituti professionali*. The number of hours spent on each subject is fixed by the Education Ministry, but otherwise teachers are relatively free to design their own curriculum. There is a sprinkling of go-ahead *scuole sperimentale*, but in general, despite Montessori's influence, most schooling in Italy is fairly traditional.

There is no special kudos attached to private schools: indeed, they are often looked on as havens for kids unable to make it at state ones. Standards in the state system vary from school to school and even from class to class, but on the whole they are considered to be the natural place to send your child, whoever you are: it would not be anything out of the ordinary for the son of a building worker to share a desk with the daughter of a government minister.

LEGALITIES

The voting age in Italy is 18, which is also the legal age of consent – though in the 14-17 age group, cases of sex involving consenting minors lead to prosecution only if the adolescent concerned is judged too immature to exercise a free choice. There are no restrictions on the sale of alcohol or cigarettes.

Telefono Azzurro

(*19 696*). **Open** 24 hours daily.
A freephone helpline for children and young people with child abuse problems (normally Italian-speaking only).

Transport

Most of the *centro storico* is walkable, even with kids (as long as you try it in reasonable doses) which is just as well, as other transport options are all tricky. Buses are often very crowded, so moving any group involving more kids than adults and/or a pushchair can be a major hassle. The 30 or 30b tram route, which runs from **Piramide** to the **Villa Borghese**, can be made into quite an adventure, if trams are a novelty. The hot, stuffy metro is limited in scope and best avoided during the morning and evening rush hours, but in between it's the fastest way to go if it goes where you want to go.

On all city transport, kids up to a metre tall go free. Above that, and you have to get a full-price ticket for them.

Sightseeing with Kids

Unire l'utile con il dilettevole (mix business with pleasure), Italians will tell you, and with kids in tow in Rome, this advice goes a long way. No kid wants his holiday ruined by being dragged to every museum and church, but there's no reason for adults to feel frustrated because they presume their kids won't want to see what they do. It's worth taking half an hour to plan ahead, so you can combine sightseeing with a trip to a park or gelateria.

You can't really expect a seven-year-old to last two hours as you look at 14th century religious art in **Palazzo Barberini**. But you may win an hour of patience out of her if you promise to stop in the nearby 'bone church', officially **S. Maria della Concezione** at the foot of Via Veneto, where five subterranean chapels are decorated top to bottom in elaborate patterns with the bones of some 4,000 Cappucin monks, with a number of full skeletons of shrunken brothers on guard like so many grim reapers. Or promise them a picnic in the grand **Villa Borghese** park 10 minutes away, with some bike riding thrown in, and you may buy yourself an hour or so at the newly-restored **Galleria Borghese**, one of the greatest art collections in the world.

The Roman **Forum** may look to youngsters like little more than a heap of rocks, but with the help of a book with transparencies (easily found at nearby stands) that show the 'then and now', you might spark their imagination. Finish your visit with a picnic snack on the **Palatine** in the cool of the **Farnese Gardens** and maybe a game of hide and seek among the remains of walls and aqueducts on the south side, where there's plenty of shade and long grass.

Children will love the **Colosseum** if you play up the Christians and lions for all they're worth. They'll never forget their visit if you snap them with one of the many self-styled centurions dressed in full regalia – leather tunics, thonged sandals, bronze breastplates and Roman headgear – who now wander the vicinity happy to pose for a couple of thousand lire. The nearby church of **San Clemente** provides a touch of mystery as dark stairs take you down through several layers of civilization, until you get to what the kids really like: a glimpse of a section of the Cloaca Maximus, Rome's first great sewer system, where the water still rushes noisily down to the Tiber.

Up the hill from San Clemente is the church of **Quattro Coronati**, a convent for cloistered nuns, where access to the frescoes of the life of San Silvestro in the chapel to the right of the entrance depends on your being privy to a dark secret: impress the kids by knocking on the wooden panel, knowingly putting down a L1,000 bill, and remaining unmoved as an invisible hand takes the money, replacing it with the key to the chapel. Inside the church, ringing a bell will summon a smiling nun who will let you into the charming cloister where kids can examine flowers, a fountain, a mysterious chapel and ancient Latin epigraphs on the wall.

If it's gore your children like, the frescoes in **Santo Stefano Rotondo** depict martyrs being boiled in oil, stretched, devoured by dogs and other occupational hazards of the early Church.

In the Vatican, a trip up to the dome of **Saint Peter's**, from where you can peer down into the basilica below or take in the sweeping views over the city outside, is another great children's favourite. If you have a pushchair, it can be left in the cloakroom to the right of the steps for no charge – although carrying a toddler up into the dome is only recommended for the very fit. In the

Rainy Day Ideas

It doesn't rain all that frequently in Rome, but when it does, it tends to be torrential. The city has no child-friendly museums where kids' minds can be kept occupied – and feet kept dry – for hours on end. The following ideas offer brief shelter from the storm.

• The **Biblioteca Centrale per i Ragazzi** has books in English, plus a large selection of board games and a few CD-ROMs.

• If the detailed scale models of ancient Rome in the **Museo della Civiltà del Lavoro** don't fascinate your kids, they can at least get some exercise in the long, empty echoing corridors.

• Well-loved children's classic films are shown regularly at the **Cinema dei Piccoli** in the **Villa Borghese**. Check out what's on in the local press: your children may know the film so well that it loses none of its appeal in a foreign language.

• Pick up the 30 or 30b tram on Viale Trastevere, and wend your way past the pyramid, the **Circus Maximus**, the **Colosseum** and innumerable suburbs until you reach the far side of the **Villa Borghese**: handy for the zoo if the sun's come out in the meantime.

• Escape the rain and go underground: Rome's catacombs are great fun for children, in particular those at **Sant'Agnese fuori le Mura**.

Vatican Museums, children may not be interested in the Raphael Rooms but they should like the huge painted 16th century maps and globes you pass on the way there. The crowds in the Sistine Chapel may overwhelm them, but the less crowded Egyptian Museum is full of sarcofagi, mummies and sundry curiosities.

Any touring that brings you through the city's Medieval and Renaissance sections between the Tiber and Via del Corso can be rewarded by a *gelato* and some pigeon-chasing at **Piazza Navona**, the **Pantheon**, or **Campo de' Fiori**.

Try to include a couple of surprises in every itinerary: the giant marble hands and feet in the courtyard of the **Capitoline Museums**, the single marble foot at the beginning of Via Santo Stefano di Cacco, just off Piazza del Collegio Romano; the obelisk-bearing elephant outside the church of **Santa Maria Sopra Minerva**; and the charming **Fontana delle Tartarughe** (turtle fountain) in the Ghetto. And of course there's the **Fontana di Trevi**: if you're there on a Monday, you might just catch the council employees in thigh-length waders raking in the coins.

A children's museum is still a dream on Roman drawing boards, but in the meantime there are a few that have enticing bits for kids. **Castel Sant'Angelo** is a historic pope-bunker full of passageways, turrets and dungeons that kids love to explore, and the **Museo del Folklore** has fun waxwork tableaux and other exhibits depicting ordinary life in Rome in the last century. When children are beginning to get bored with looking round ruins, take them to the **Museo della Civiltà Romana** in the EUR district to see its huge, painstakingly detailed scale models of ancient Rome. The museum is also conveniently close to the **LUNEUR Park** funfair and the **Piscina delle Rose** swimming pool.

Palazzo degli Exposizioni has an eclectic variety of shows, many of which are unusual enough to interest kids. The **Museo della Mura** sets you off on a walk along a good bit of the Roman wall that surrounds the city and gives an interesting vantage point. If air traffic controllers turn your homewards trip into a nightmare, take a ten-minute walk from Fiumicino airport to the **Museo delle Navi Romane**, where kids can see what Roman ships were really like.

Out of Town

The best child-oriented sights within reasonable distance of Rome are the bizarre Renaissance Parco dei Mostri – Monster Park – at **Bomarzo**, huge scary sculptures that kids can climb in and on, and the fountains and cascades of Tivoli's **Villa D'Este**, and nearby Hadrian's Villa for picnics. In **Bracciano**, about 40 kilometers north of Rome, the 15th century Castello Orsini-Odescalchi is an interesting tour, with its many suits of armour and 16th century loos. On weekends it's transformed into an amusement park with games, plays, costumed jesters, contests and refreshments, all harking back to the castle's Renaissance past.

Lago di Bracciano, or in its smaller neighbour **Lago di Martignano**, both have decent beaches and fairly clean water. The water on the coast near Rome is not the cleanest, but is actually improving each year, and there are many beach clubs at **Ostia** or **Fregene**, and miles of sand at **Castelporziano**.

Walking tours

If you are in a group, or are willing to pay for a personalised tour, there are now many cultural associations in Rome which offer in-depth information about a given area or museum, often complete with historical anecdotes that make the dry facts more palatable for children. You can find an English-speaking guide through **Gente e Paesi** (85 30 17 55), **Palladio** (686 78 97), or **La Serliana** (39 72 02 52), which specialises in children's tours.

Parks and Entertainment

Villa Borghese is the park with the most to offer children: bike rental, train and donkey rides, pedal boats, bumper cars and merry go round, Rome's only children's cinema, **Cinema dei Piccoli**, and the city zoo.

For the best playground equipment, try **Villa Celimontana**, **Villa Sciarra**, the **Parco Nemorense**, **Villa Pamphili** and **Villa Ada**. They are all lovely in their own way, and offer plenty of shade, fountains, ponds and picnic spots. On the **Gianicolo**, you can see puppet shows as well.

On Sunday, the **Via dei Fori Imperiali**, which stretches from Piazza Venezia to the Colosseum, is closed to traffic. You'll find the street lined with performers of varying degrees of sophistication. The stiltwalkers, small theatre ensembles, one-person shows, dance performances, musical groups and clowns seem to fascinate kids no matter how bad they are. And it's all free... though the hat gets passed after every show.

Biblioteca Centrale per i Ragazzi (Central Children's Library)

Via San Paolo alla Regola, 16 (68 65 116). Bus to Largo di Torre Argentina, via Arenula. **Open** *Oct-June* 9am-6.30pm Tue-Fri, 9am-1pm Sat; *July-Oct* 9am-6.30pm Tue-Thur; **closed** three weeks in August.

Right in the centre of the old city, just around the corner from Largo Argentina and Campo de' Fiori, this well-run library has a small selection of English, French, German and Spanish books to while away a rainy day. The building is also worth a look in its own right, a 16th-century structure built on Roman foundations. Non-residents are welcome to use the library, but may not take books out on loan.

Tarantino for teenies: the **Gianicolo** *puppets.*

Giardino Zoologico (Zoo)

Viale del Giardino Zoologico, Villa Borghese (32 16 564). Bus to Piazza Ungheria/tram lines 19, 19b, 30. **Open** 8.30am-5pm Mon-Sat; 8.30am-6pm Sun; **closed** 1 May. **Admission** L10,000; free for children under 1.3m tall, over-60s. **No credit cards.**

Rome's small zoo has lush landscaping and impressive early 20th century architecture – just don't look too closely at the animals in their tiny cages, which are definitely not up to modern zoo standards. An ambitious plan has been drawn up which will replace bars with more open spaces and natural barriers. Many animals will be gradually phased out to leave only endangered species, animals native to Italy or those with a natural habitat similar to that of the Italian peninsula. Also due for refurbishment is the truly surreal and little-visited **Museo Zoologico**. Row upon row of every kind of stuffed bird, reptile and mammal are accompanied by handwritten labels that haven't been changed since the '50s. Very un-PC, it's worth a visit before the collection is relegated to the back rooms for scholars' use only. Make a beeline for the insects.

Luna Park (LUNEUR)

Via delle Tre Fontane, EUR (59 25 933). Metro Magliana/bus to Via delle Tre Fontane, EUR. **Open** 4pm-midnight Mon-Fri; 4pm-1am Sat; 10am-1pm, 3pm-midnight, Sun. **Admission** free; rides L1,000-5,000 each. **No credit cards.**

Rome's funfair is 30 years old and it shows, but is saved by the sheer theatricality of its rides and exhibits decorated in an era when amusement parks were meant not only to whirl you around, but also to transport you to a fantasy world. There is a very respectable roller coaster, two haunted houses, a hall of mirrors, and boat, car and pony rides for smaller children. Best of all is the ferris wheel, an enormous white construction that calls to the adventurous on their way to the nearby Mussolini-designed EUR district.

See **Piazza del Popolo** from the back of a lion.

Acquapiper

Via Maremmana Inferiore, km 29, Guidonia (0774 32 65 38). Metro to Rebibbia then COTRAL bus to Palombara/by car SS 5 (Tivoli road) then SS5ter to Guidonia. **Open** *mid May-mid Sept* 9am-6pm Mon-Fri; 9am-7pm Sat, Sun. **Admission** L25,000 adults entering before 2pm Sat, Sun; L20,000 adults entering after 2pm Mon-Fri; L17,500 adults entering after 2pm Sat, Sun; L15,000 adults entering after 2pm Mon-Fri; L15,000 4-10s; free under-4s. **Credit** AmEx, DC, MC, V.

This aquatic park is off the road to Tivoli, and so can be combined with a trip to **Villa Adriana** or the **Villa D'Este**. It boasts a small children's pool with a tortoise waterslide, plus kamikaze slides for older children, an enormous pool with a wave machine, and pony and camel rides. There is also a shady picnic area, a bar/restaurant and the inevitable electronic games room.

Hydromania

Grande Raccordo Anulare, exit 33-Casale Lumbroso Pescaccio (66 92 844-66 92 851). **Open** *mid-May to mid-Sept* 9.30am-6.30pm Mon-Fri; 9.30am-7pm Sat, Sun. **Admission** (Mon-Fri) L22,000 adults, L15,000 under-12s; (Sat) L25,000 adults, L18,000 under-12s, free under-6s; (Half-day) L15,000 adults.

Plenty of shady trees, umbrellas and space, this water park has a pool with a wave machine, a Twister tube, kamikaze water slide, a huge multi-lane slide, kiddie pool, hydromassage and self-service restaurant.

Piscina delle Rose

Viale America 20, EUR (59 26 71 7). Metro EUR Palasport/bus to Viale Europa. **Open** *mid June-end Sept* 9am-7pm daily. **Admission** L18,000; L13,000 9am-2pm or 2-7pm only; L7,000 1-4pm only; children under 1 metre free.

A child-friendly pool and so apt to get a bit crowded, especially in the afternoon. Prices and hours are reviewed every year.

Puppeteers and theatre

Italy's long and glorious puppet tradition centres on Sicily and Naples, but Rome also offers decent shows. Theatres open and close all the time, but two stalwarts remain and claim to be the only real *burattinai* (puppeteers) left. One is on the **Gianicolo**, run by Mr. Piantandosi and identifiable by the sign *Non Tirate Sassi!* (Don't throw Stones!). The other is in Largo K. Ataturk, EUR, in an open-air booth near a Giolitti ice cream emporium. Both serve up Pulcinella, just as violent and mysogynistic as his English descendant Mr Punch, and deliver it in a Neapolitan accent

so thick that most local kids don't understand either: it's the whacks on the head that really count anyway.

English Puppet Theatre

Via Grottapinta (68 61 311). Bus to Corso Vittorio Emanuele. **Open** about 5pm, Sat, Sun; by appointment weekdays; **closed** July, Aug.

It's literally a hole in the wall but this tiny puppet theatre manages to pack in about 25 kids on benches at weekends, offering Punch and Judy and well-known tales like Pinocchio and Puss in Boots. English productions can be arranged in advance. The snacks passed around during the interval should mollify children who've been frightened by ogres or witches.

Teatro Verde

Circonvallazione Gianicolense, 10 (58 82 034). Bus/tram to Stazione Trastevere. **Shows** 5pm Sat, Sun.

The best-known children's theatre in Rome, Teatro Verde offers both puppets and acted plays (usually musical) in Italian. A visit to the costume and prop workshop before the curtain goes up, plus the energy of most productions, should allow most English speakers to enjoy the show. Booking advisable.

Babyminders and Kindergartens

United Babies

Piazza Nicoloso da Recco, 9 (58 99 481/57 59 543). Bus/tram to Viale Aventino. **Rates** differ depending on attendance. **No credit cards.**

American Lucy Gardner runs this bilingual playgroup, offering creative play, healthy snacks and romps in the courtyard for kids from about one year-old to four. Most children are regulars, but short-term stays can be arranged. A hot lunch is also provided. The playgroup is closed during most of August.

Buonidea

Via C. Fracassini, 4 (32 01 380). **Rates** *before midnight* L12,000 an hour; *after midnight* L14,000.

Screened, referenced baby-sitters, usually Italian speakers only.

Books

If you're on an outing at the Forum and you can't quite make the Temple of the Vestal Virgins come alive for your 10-year-old, get some printed help. Those tacky technicolour guidebooks on sale at every strategic tourist crossroads may not appeal to you, but your offspring could draw unlimited inspiration from them. On a more up-market note, the English-language *Ancient Rome for Kids*, on sale at **Feltrinelli** book stores (*see chapter* **Shopping**), gives succinct explanations for major sites, illustrated by drawings of Roman kids doing what kids did in ancient Rome. Or before you set out, pick up any of the following: Usborne's *Who Were the Romans?* for kids of six and up; *The Usborne Pocket Guide to Ancient Rome* for slightly older children; and, for an end of holiday treat, *Make this Model Roman Amphitheatre*. The Dorling Kindersley pocket guide, *Ancient Rome*, though aimed rather loosely at 'enthusiasts of all ages', is clearly laid out and visually enticing.

Finally, if your child fancies practising his language skills, *The Usborne Guide to Italian* is a fun cartoon-format phrase book for eight to 11 year-olds.

Film

From 'Bicycle Thieves' to 'Dear Diary', Rome is a city that loves to bear its soul for the camera.

Rome has been the centre of the Italian film industry since the **Cinecittà** studios were opened by Mussolini in 1937. With 15 sound stages, immense grounds for exterior shooting, complete production and processing facilities, and costume and design departments, Cinecittà's facilities were unrivalled outside Hollywood. The fascination Cinecittà held for Italians can be seen in Visconti's *Bellissima* (1951), in which Anna Magnani moves heaven and earth to get her plain little daughter to the fore in a studio-run competition to find 'the most beautiful little girl in Rome'. But American film-makers were also attracted there in the '50s, when the studios were used for widescreen epics such as *Ben Hur*, *Helen of Troy* and *Sodom and Gomorrah*. Relations were soured, though, by the disastrously protracted shoot and escalating budget on *Cleopatra* in 1961-3, one of the most spectacular flops ever made. It almost destroyed Twentieth Century-Fox, ruined the producer Walter Wanger and discouraged further influx from Hollywood.

Today Cinecittà works at only half the capacity it did at its peak 30 years ago. But it's been saved from terminal decline by popular comedies like Roberto Benigni's *Il Mostro* and the occasional US action blockbuster, such as the dire Stallone vehicle *Cliffhanger*. More recently, parts of Anthony Minghella's *The English Patient* and Jane Campion's *Portrait of Lady* were filmed here.

The Italian government still owns the studio, but has begun a long, slow move towards privatisation. Once a year, usually in early autumn, the whole complex is thrown open for evening tours and sideshows. Outside this period it's best to phone first for an appointment. Attractions on view include the remains of the sets for *Cleopatra*, including the pool where Burton and Taylor first met.

Cinecittà
Via Tuscolana, 1,055 (72 29 31). Metro Cinecittà/bus to Via Tuscolana.

MOVIEGOING IN ROME

As a place to go to the cinema, Rome is booming. Since 1995, new screens have been opening at the rate of around 15 a year; the city currently has around 70 first-run cinemas – only a handful of which are multiplexes – and a galaxy of smaller clubs or seasonal outlets. Deputy Premier Walter

Veltroni has cut the red tape surrounding the granting of cinema licences, allowing merchandising in cinema foyers and, above all, reducing the price of tickets for early midweek screenings by 40 per cent.

Another recent development is the end of the city's exhibition duopoly. Most of Rome's screens have long been controlled by Italy's two big private media empires, the Cecchi Gori Group and Silvio Berlusconi's Fininvest. But recently a group of independents, led by state distributor Istituto Luce, has formed Circuito Cinema. This now controls six first-run arthouse outlets around the city: the Archimede, the **Greenwich**, the **Intrastevere**, the Mignon, the Nuovo Olimpia and the **Quattro Fontane**, as well as the **Pasquino** and the **Labirinto** cine-club.

The downside of Italian cinema is the dubbing. Italian dubbers are widely recognised as the best in the world, but that's no consolation for those who like their films in the original language (*versione originale* – VO). There is one dedicated English-language cinema – the old faithful **Pasquino** – plus a handful of venues which screen original-language films (generally English) on a Monday or Tuesday (*see* **VO Round-up** *p188*). In addition, since autumn 1997, Circuito Cinema has been offering occasional Thursday screenings of English- and French-language films in its six first-run cinemas.

Italian films account for around 30 per cent of the home market, with the US taking around 50 per cent. Most of the *prima visione* (first-run) cin-

Festivals & Summer Programmes

Around the beginning of July, as cinemas close for the summer and box-office figures nosedive, Rome becomes a great place to take in a film. A plethora of second-run or arthouse open-air cinesplurges spring up, under the auspices of the Estate Romana (*see chapter* **Rome by Season**) and often in breathtaking settings. In addition, various *arene* (fixed open-air screens) provide the chance to catch up with that blockbuster you missed last season, or to take in that obscure underground classic.

Recent years have seen a huge boom in open-air summer screens, and an exponential increase in the number of English-language offerings. In 1997, the **Pasquino** organised the Independent Picture Show in a space on the Gianicolo, while the That's Cinema festival in Piazza Vittorio offered two English-language films each evening. Best of the lot was the *Passeggiate Romane* festival, a series of films shown in their original settings or against appropriate backdrops: Vittorio De Sica's *Bicycle Thieves* in the 1940s suburb of Val Melaina; Marco Ferreri's *La Grande Abbuffata* in Rome's central fruit and vegetable market; and Fellini's *Satyricon* on the Via Appia Antica. There is a good chance that this and the other initiatives will be repeated.

Away from July and August, entirely new titles can be found at the Fantafestival, held each June, which features horror, fantasy and science fiction films from around the world, including previews of major new releases. There are also two regular mini-festivals, *Cannes a Roma* and *Venezia a Roma*, which offer the chance to see a selection of original-language films from these major European festivals about a fortnight after they close, in May and September respectively. Venues change annually: check local papers for details.

Though festivals and *arene* come and go, the following three are regular summer fixtures:

Arena Esedra
Via del Viminale, 9 (48 37 54). Metro Termini/bus or tram to Termini. **Shows** 9pm and 10.45pm daily. **Tickets** L8,000.
Rome's last big, arena-style open-air cinema is impressively situated near one of the surviving fragments of the city's fourth-century BC Servian Wall, and now hosts a festival each year from mid-June to September. Two films are screened every evening, and one ticket will get you into both. The programmes feature retrospectives of classic directors, together with children's films, reruns of the previous season's biggest titles, and a few previews of forthcoming releases. All foreign-language films are dubbed. *Wheelchair access.*

Cineporto
Parco della Farnesina (32 12 430). Bus to Lungotevere Maresciallo Diaz. **Information** 90 08 01 52.
The park just in front of the Foreign Ministry, facing the Tiber by the Olympic Stadium, is the venue for one of the most successful and popular summer festivals. During July and August separate screens show two films a night, with a high proportion of major recent releases. Concerts are often mounted between the shows, and ample food and drink helps to create a sense of occasion. *Wheelchair access*

Massenzio
Parco del Celio (44 23 93 80) Bus or tram to Colosseum. **Shows** Three per evening at big screen (2,000 seats) and small screen (400 seats), starting 9.15pm daily. **Tickets** L10,000. **No credit cards.**
The biggest and most politically correct of Rome's open-air film festivals features some 200 films between mid-July and the end of August. The venue has changed several times over the years: most recent was the Parco del Celio, the little ruin-strewn, tram-traversed rise opposite the Colosseum. The imaginative programmes are organised around directors, actors, countries, genres or themes. There are three films a night, usually dubbed, though sometimes in VO. There's also a jazz space, a couple of bars, and even an all-night supermarket. *Wheelchair access.*

emas concentrate on fairly mainstream material; more varied and adventurous programmes can be found at the *cinema d'essai* (roughly, art cinemas) and cine clubs (*see below*). For a standard 90-minute film, the four daily screenings will almost invariably be at 4.30, 6.30, 8.30 and 10.30; the box-office generally opens half an hour before the first showing. Credit card payment is still rare.

Summer is the time when all Rome closes, and cinemas are no exception. More of the mainstream cinemas now stay open through the year, but many cinemas and most of the cine clubs still close completely in July and August. Compensation can be found, though, in the open-air cinemas and festivals that open up around the city for the summer months (*see* **Festivals & Summer Programmes**).

The best source for information on what's on at any of the cinemas in Rome, including the summer venues, is the local section of the daily newspaper *La Repubblica*. Other useful sources are the weekly listings magazine *Roma C'è*, which comes out on Thursdays and has a *Film in lingua originale* section, and *Time Out Roma* – though as a monthly this carries only festival and cine-club listings rather than the first-run schedule.

First-run Cinemas

All first-run cinemas now offer cut-price admission for the first two screenings between Monday and Friday – usually at 4.30pm and 6.30pm. In 1997 this was pegged at L7,000.

Alcazar

Via Cardinal Merry del Val, 14 (58 80 099). Bus to Viale Trastevere. **Tickets** L12,000. 200 seats.
A red-plush jewel, and one of the first major Rome cinemas to screen original-language films. They're now shown on Mondays only; for the last two showings it is wise to book ahead (tickets must be picked up 30 mins beforehand). *Air-conditioning. Wheelchair access.*

Augustus

Corso Vittorio Emanuele, 203 (68 75 455). Bus to Corso Vittorio. **Tickets** L12,000. Sala 1: 400 seats. Sala 2: 800 seats.
A central fleapit which has been turned into a simple but comfortable two-screener, the Augustus shows English-language films on Tuesdays, repeating the billing screened at the Majestic (*see below*) the day before. *Air-conditioning. Wheelchair access.*

Dei Piccoli

Viale della Pineta, 15, Villa Borghese (85 53 485). Metro Spagna/bus to Porta Pinciana. **Tickets** L10,000. 63 seats.
Built in 1934 as a children's theatre in the Villa Borghese park, the tiny Dei Piccoli now presents children's film shows (mainly dubbed cartoons) each afternoon. The interior has recently been restored. In the evening the cinema serves as a showcase for films from the Italian Film Archives. It also presents some first-run films, often in the original language. *Air-conditioning. Wheelchair access.*

Greenwich 1, 2 & 3

Via Giovanni Battista Bodoni, 59 (57 45 825). Metro Piramide/bus to Via Marmorata or Via Zabaglia. **Tickets** L12,000. Sala 1: 230 seats. Sala 2: 150 seats. Sala 3: 60 seats.

A three-screen house that was built in 1992 from the remains of a parish cinema. Situated in an anonymous residential street in trendy Testaccio, the 'Gren-witch' as the locals call it is extremely popular with younger Romans. It is strong on Italian and international arthouse films, and has occasional VO films on Thursdays. Ther's a small bar. *Air-conditioning. Wheelchair access.*

Intrastevere

Vicolo Moroni, 3a (58 84 230). Bus to Ponte Sisto. **Tickets** L12,000. Sala 1: 220 seats. Sala 2: 120 seats. Sala 3: 40 seats.
In one of the unlikeliest settings in Rome – a seventeenth-century *palazzo* in a Trastevere back street – this arthouse specialises in European and American independents. There are occasional original-language screenings on Thursdays. *Air-conditioning. Wheelchair access.*

Majestic

Via Santi Apostoli, 20 (67 94 908). Bus to Piazza Venezia. **Tickets** L12,000. 450 seats.
Built as a theatre in the 1920s, used by Pirandello and his company, and then transformed into a cinema after World War II. Under the same management as the Augustus (*see above*) but unrepentantly single-screened, the Majestic shows English-language films on Monday nights. *Air-conditioning. Wheelchair access.*

Nuovo Sacher

Largo Ascianghi ,1 (58 18 116). Bus or tram to Viale Trastevere. **Tickets** L10,000. 500 seats.
The Nuovo Sacher is owned and run by film director Nanni Moretti, who bought it out of irritation at the poor state of film distribution in Rome. Films are always shown in their original language on Mondays, and occasionally the rest of

VO Round-up

The following is a weekly breakdown of *versione originale* viewing opportunities in Rome.
Daily: Pasquino (English only).
When the mood takes them: Arsenale, Modernetta, Azzurro Scipioni, Grauco, Palazzo delle Esposizioni.
Monday: Alcazar, Majestic, Nuovo Sacher.
Tuesday: Augustus.
Thursday (occasional): Circuito Cinema chain (Archimede, Greenwich, Intrastevere, Mignon, Nuovo Olimpia, Quattro Fontane).

the week as well. During the summer, they are screened in the open-air arena alongside the cinema. Nuovo Sacher has become a meeting place for local cinematic talent, and makes an effort to support independent Italian filmmakers, with initiatives such as a short-film festival every July. In addition, it presents strong arthouse titles from abroad (Ken Loach and Iranian director Abbas Kiarostami are favourites). This is also one of the few Rome cinemas with a decent bar and bookshop.
Air-conditioning. Wheelchair access.

Pasquino
Vicolo del Piede ,19 (58 03 622). Bus to Viale Trastevere. **Tickets** L10,000. 200 seats.
This venerable and slightly threadbare insitution is the only cinema in Rome to show English-language films every day. The programmes change every few days, with nearly-new offerings at weekends, and classics or more recherché titles midweek. The cinema has the added attraction of a sliding roof, opened in summer. The cinema is currently undergoing a major refurbishment.
Wheelchair access.

Quattro Fontane
Via Quattro Fontane, 23 (47 41 515). Bus to Via Nazionale. **Tickets** L12,000. Sala 1: 350 seats. Sala 2: 200 seats. Sala 3: 150 seats. Sala 4: opening soon.
The showcase miniplex of new indie distribution cartel Circuito Cinema (*see above*), the Quattro Fontane is a designer cinema with a state-of-the-art sound system and a small bar in the foyer. Thursday is VO day.
Air-conditioning. Wheelchair access

Cinema d'Essai & Cineclubs

Cinema d'essai are generally small and cheap, and feature mainly classics or prestige contemporary cinema, often in VO. It is in these cinemas and the still smaller cine clubs that the full range of international cinema and the best of the Italian cinema heritage can be seen. All are private ventures except the **Palazzo delle Esposizioni**, the municipal arts centre whose single screen provides Rome's only answer to London's National Film Theatre. Some clubs also re-screen films that suffered from truncated first releases. Many of the *centri sociali* (*see chapter* **Music**: **Rock, Roots and Jazz**) offer screenings of alternative films: among

the most active is Forte Prenestina, which organises the OFF underground cinema festival in June.

A membership card (*tessera*) is required by many clubs, but this can be bought at the door for a minimal extra charge.

L'Arsenale
Via Giano della Bella, 45 (44 70 00 84). Metro Piazza Bologna/bus to Piazza delle Province. **Tickets** L7,000 or L5,000 with annual membership card (L10,000). 70 seats.
A student-run film club near the University, which organises regular original-language screenings.
No wheelchair access.

Azzurro Scipioni
Via degli Scipioni, 82 (39 73 71 61). Metro Lepanto/bus to Via Marcantonio Colonna. **Tickets** Sala Chaplin L7,000 Mon-Fri; L,10,000 Sat-Sun. Sala Lumière L15,000 for monthly *tessera*. Sala Chaplin: 140 seats. Sala Lumière: 50 seats.
Best-known of the *D'essai* cinemas, with two screens: the *Sala Chaplin*, showing recent arthouse successes, and the *Sala Lumière*, with a video projector, devoted to cinema classics, some in the original language. If you want to see Fellini's *Roma* in situ – an unforgettable experience – you'll find it here most weeks. Streetsweepers get in free!
Wheelchair access with assistance.

Grauco
Via Perugia, 34 (78 24 167). Bus or tram to Piazzale Prenestino. **Membership** L10,000 per year (includes one ticket). **Tickets** L5,000-L8,000. 35 seats.
One of the most interesting of the film clubs, with an extensive, browsable library, the Grauco concentrates on powerful independent (and sometimes marginal) cinema from around the world, with a particular day of the week often devoted to one country. On Saturday and Sunday afternoons children's classics are screened in Italian. Films are usually shown at 9pm.
No wheelchair access.

Labirinto
Via Pompeo Magno, 27 (32 16 283). Metro Lepanto/bus to Via Giulio Cesare. **Membership** L3,000 per year. **Tickets** L9,000. Sala A: 100 seats. Sala B: 60 seats. Sala C: 45 seats.
A three-screen complex, old but comfortable, which usually shows re-runs of the best of the previous season's releases. Films are seldom in VO.
Air-conditioning. No wheelchair access.

Modernetta
Piazza della Repubblica (48 80 285). Metro Repubblica/bus to Piazza della Repubblica. **Tickets** L7,000. 280 seats.
Formerly one of the grubbiest of Rome's porn cinemas, the Modernetta has been fumigated and refitted as a second-run cinema, offering occasional seasons of English-language films, especially in summer.
Wheelchair access.

Palazzo delle Esposizioni
Via Nazionale, 194 (48 85 465). Metro Repubblica/bus to Via Nazionale. **Open** 10am-9pm Mon, Wed-Sun. **Admission** (per day, to whole of centre) L12,000; students and OAPs L6,000; L20,000 joint ticket for four admissions. 200 seats.
The Palazzo was reopened in 1990 as a multi-media venue, mainly for large-scale exhibitions. With its rooftop terrace bar, it has also become a popular meeting-place for filmgoers. A different cycle of films is presented in the *Sala Rossellini*, almost every week: it could be a Fellini retrospective, a season of modern Dutch films, or a special on Woody Allen. *See also chapters* **Museums & Galleries** *and* **Shopping**.
Air-conditioning. Wheelchair access.

Is Italian Film Dead?

They don't make 'em like they used to: Fellini's 1972 film, Roma.

No, but it's in bed with a temperature. The domestic success of romantic comedies such as Roberto Benigni's *Il Mostro* and Leonardo Pieraccioni's *Il Ciclone* (at $40m Italy's highest-grossing film ever) has done little to make up for the low profile of the country's celluloid exports since the glory days of the '50s and '60s.

Most of us associate post-war Italian cinema with a cohort of *auteurs* whose most stimulating work was achieved before 1975: Fellini, Pasolini, Antonioni, Bertolucci, the Taviani brothers. Of the big-name survivors, some have drifted off into a sentimental mist (the Tavianis), while others have specialised in commercially successful widescreen epics (Bertolucci). The search for heirs has been intense, but the various candidates, such as Giuseppe Tornatore or Gabriele Salvatores, seem to lack the necessary staying power.

Then there are the mavericks. Chief among these is actor/director Nanni Moretti – a bizarre hybrid of Woody Allen, Jacques Tati and Sergei Eisenstein. Moretti's films have become increasingly autobiographical over the years, as witness the title of his 1994 outing, *Caro Diario* (Dear Diary). The Italian left wing, modern Italy and human stupidity are Moretti's preferred themes; he has the knack of making satisfying cinema out of a few very basic ingredients (and very little money), as anyone who has seen the marvellous Vespa-ride-through-Rome sequence of *Caro Diario* will recognise.

However, one Titian does not make a Renaissance. In the '80s, a rigidly low-budget, government-subsidised mentality was encapsulated in the notorious Articolo 28, a state funding mechanism that handed out money for many films that were never made or never seen. Since the centre-left alliance came to power in April 1996, government policy – helmed by film buff Deputy PM Walter Veltroni – has been oriented more towards opening cinemas and getting bums on seats.

Gay Rome

The lowdown, whether you're cruising, boozing or just musing.

Despite the odd bout of finger-wagging from the Vatican, Italy has been notably free of anti-gay legislation. During the first half of this century, life was cheap, attitudes were relaxed, and boys were both. In the last 40 years, however, Italy's economic boom has broken the traditional link between poverty and sexual availability, and juvenile male prostitution is no longer a popular alternative to a paper-round, although off-duty national servicemen have been known to turn wrist-engineers for a small fee.

Politically, the situation is confused. In 1994, the electoral success of media mogul Silvio Berlusconi opened governmental gates to the newly-blooded remnants of Italian fascism with its cultural baggage of ferocious anti-gay sentiment. So it was only natural that after the 1996 electoral victory of the centre-left Olive Tree coalition, Italian lesbians and gay men should have expected a new gay-friendly agenda. Dream on. Even before the election, it was clear that the New Left's efforts to transform Italy into a 'normal' country would leave little room for gays.

The national scene has been reflected in the capital. After a full term as mayor, Francesco Rutelli's earlier and much-publicised courtship of Rome's gays has left a post-honeymoon bitter taste in many mouths. Apart from his appointment of Vanni Piccolo as token gay councillor and a brief presence on one Pride march, Rutelli has been more concerned with currying Vatican favour than with meeting gay needs. There has been a largely unremarked-on suppression of the traditional outdoor scene, and the slash-and-burn deforestation of the city's cruising spots continues. Downtown Monte Caprino – the wooded enclave on the southern slopes of the Capitoline – is threatened by enclosure, with the unofficial promise of a tiny unfenced 'gay reserve'. The Buco, Rome's nudist beach, situated along the Ostia-Torvaianica road, is also under attack, with the council fencing off the offending strip of dunes and bushes along the coast and privatising the whole length of the previously free beach. The only consolation is that no fence can long resist determined queens bearing wire-cutters.

Outdoors, Indoors

Visitors who expect to find some kind of gay village in Rome will be disappointed. For some, however, Rome has always proved a Pandora's box of sexual opportunity. Until recently, having an active sex life in Rome meant varding someone in the street or going to one of the cruising areas dotted around the city. Older Romans talk about the hedonistic delights once available along the banks of the Tiber, at the Circus Maximus (before the bushes were uprooted) or inside the Colosseum (before the railings were put up). In recent years, popular outdoor sites, apart from the Monte Caprino side of the Capitoline *(see above)*, include Piazzale Gramsci, opposite the British Academy, and the park behind the Square Colosseum at EUR. Even in these hallowed places, however, street lighting has been improved, pissoirs demolished and, above all, the most concealing shrubs severely pruned.

This won't be a problem for those who are less at ease with street cruising, particularly as gay life is moving resolutely indoors. Bars, clubs and saunas now provide the chance to meet without the risk of encountering the pickpockets, neo-fascists or police raids that sometimes threaten outdoor trysts. Nevertheless, most gay places continue to hide behind anonymous doors and windowless walls; the city still has no bars or cafés where gays can meet during the day or where couples feel at ease. Gay coffee-bar culture has yet to hit the Eternal City.

PERSONAL SAFETY
Discretion is the keyword. Although Romans pride themselves on their worldly acceptance of human variety, public effusions are best avoided. The police are as likely to protect you as they are to harass, although investigations into a seemingly endless chain of recent gay murders have been noticeably unsuccessful.

AIDS
In many ways the AIDS issue in Italy has been absorbed into the larger question of drug use. Unlike many other countries, most Italians with AIDS are victims of infected needles than unsafe sex, although the high percentage of addicts involved in prostitution has led to a spill-over into traditionally 'low risk' groups. Government policy tends to be based on the personal vagaries of whoever happens to be health minister at the time.

TRANSVESTITES AND TRANSSEXUALS
When gay pioneer Mario Mieli published *Homosexuality and Liberation* in 1977 (English edition: Gay Men's Press, 1980), transvestites were seen as the cutting edge of gay politics. These days in Rome the vast army of South American *viados*, and some home-grown transvestites, do little more than satisfy the needs of the Italian sex industry. Whether their customers are heterosexual, gay or confused is a moot point, although the men who frequent

transvestite and transsexual venues would certainly never consider themselves homosexual. Rome's **Circolo Mario Mieli** has given increasing space to transsexual issues, while its cultural programmer and ringmaster/mistress Vladimir Luxuria is a constant presence on Italian TV, though not always to the delight of more traditional gay campaigners.

TERMINOLOGY

The queer/gay quandary currently enlivening gender linguistics in the Anglo-Saxon world would baffle most Italians, who are used to even quality newspapers using such euphemisms as *ambiguo* (ambiguous) and *diverso* (different). The most widely-used term is *gay*, while more colourful alternatives like *frocio* (homosexual) and *finocchio* (literally, fennel – don't ask) change their politics according to who's using them.

Bars

Rome's gay venues open and close at an alarming rate, so a phone call to check that the bar still exists might not be a bad idea before you slip into something sexy. Some bars charge no entrance fees but oblige you to buy a drink. Others require you to show an **Arcigay** annual membership card (L20,000, available at most venues that request it and valid nationwide).

In most bars you are given a small printed slip, on which the barman ticks off what you consume; you pay the total on leaving. Don't lose your slip, as there's a stiff penalty.

L'Apeiron

Via dei Quattro Cantoni, 5 (48 28 820). Metro Cavour/ bus to Via Cavour. **Open** 10.30pm-3.30am Mon-Sat. **Admission** free with membership card. Compulsory first drink. **Membership** L5,000 per year.

A relaxed club on two floors with several distinct ambiences and often whimsical interior design. The bar and lounge area are dominated by a fuzzy maxiscreen showing music videos; a dank stand-up cellar shows porno videos next door to Rome's first darkroom. Conveniently located for bar-hopping with **Hangar** (*below*); frequented by a mixture of timid suburbanites and hardened darkroom devotees.

Frutta e Verdura

Via Principe Umberto, 36 (44 64 862). Metro Vittorio Emanuele. **Open** 10.30pm-2am Tue, Thur, Sun; 10.30pm-3.30am Fri-Sat. **Admission** free with Arcigay card. Compulsory first drink.

*Rome, too, has its Pride, usually held in June. Phone **Arcigay** for details. See page 193.*

One of the city's newest and largest gay spots, Fruit & Veg boasts Keith Haring-inspired décor and two floors given over to 'homosexual happenings'. These include The Cage disco (Thur-Sun after midnight) and the 11pm performances of the club's resident men-in-frocks: slick and honey-voiced Kim (is his Madonna better than his Mick Hucknall?) and trash-bag Papaya who organises anything-but-PC game shows before getting down to the serious business of taking off Mina and Shirley Temple.

Hangar

Via in Selci, 69 (48 81 397). Metro Cavour/bus to Via Merulana. **Open** 10.30pm-2am Mon, Wed-Sun. **Admission** free.

Rome's oldest gay bar was opened in 1983 by American John Moss, who still mans the ticket window by the entrance, and his partner Gianni. It maintains its friendly but sexy atmosphere whether it's half full (occasionally midweek) or packed (weekends and Mondays). Two bars are linked by a long, dark passage, although the pissoir is reputed to be livelier. There are porn video shows on Monday nights. The clientele consists of younger Romans, plus foreign residents and tourists of all ages.

K

Via Amato Amati, 6-8 (0347 622 0462). Bus to Via Casilina. **Open** 10pm-2am Mon-Thur, Sun; 11pm-5am Fri, Sat. **Admission** L10,000 (with free membership card).

One of gay Rome's newest and furthest-flung additions, K has been billed as the city's first SM/leather venue. Its main attraction, however, appears to be its variety of well-equipped dark areas. Fairy lights at the entrance detract from the otherwise butch atmosphere.

Max's Bar

Via Achille Grandi, 3a (70 30 15 99). Metro Manzoni/ bus to Piazza di Porta Maggiore. **Open** 10.30pm-2.30am Tue-Sun. **Admission** compulsory first drink, L15,000 Tue-Thur, Sun; L20,000 Fri, Sat.

A stone's throw from one of the city's liveliest transvestite prostitution areas. The dance floor and crowded bar are rumoured to be popular with bus drivers, which may explain its bluff, chummy charm and also why it attracts a fair share of Rome's over-fifties.

Officina

Via Ignazio Danti, 20 (27 53 508). Bus to Via Casilina. **Open** 10pm-3am Mon-Sun. **Admission** L10,000 (includes first drink).

The enterprising Mimmo D'Antuono, who also runs oMo Publications, was the first to give uptown Rome its first taste of gay night life. Apart from the main drinking area (with requisite maxiscreen), curtained-off areas satisfy aficionados of porn videos and dark rooms. Officina offers a friendlier atmosphere than similarly equipped venues, but not all foreign visitors might be up to participating in the midweek karaoke and board game sessions.

Skyline

Via degli Aurunci, 26/28 (44 00 817). Bus to Via Tiburtina. **Open** 10.30pm-2am Tue-Fri, Sun; 10.30pm-3am Sat. **Admission** with Arcigay card.

A compact club in the predominantly student, cheap-eats San Lorenzo district. The décor, however, is strictly New York, from the reproduction Manhattan skyline (geddit?) to the stainless steel tables and chairs. A relaxed, mixed crowd with constant to-ing and fro-ing between the bar and the cruisy balcony and porn flicks above. Straights allowed in on Thursdays.

Expect to pay L15-20,000 at weekends, less during the week – and occasionally nothing at all. This may be at the doorman's discretion: it's considered a big deal in Rome to get in free.

L'Alibi

Via di Monte Testaccio, 44-57 (57 43 448). Metro Piramide/bus to Via Marmorata. **Open** 11pm-4am Wed-Sun. **Admission** L15,000 Wed, Fri, Sun (includes first drink); free Thur; L20,000 Sat (includes first drink).

Arguably Rome's leading gay disco, this paved the way for Testaccio's boom as a quarter with an alternative feel (*see chapter* **Nightlife**). There are two floors in winter, three in summer; the roof garden is the club's best feature, attracting a regular gay-disco crowd. There's a good sound system (disco favourites on one level, gay pounding rhythms below), occasional floor-shows and a noticeably competitive atmosphere throughout.

L'Angelo Azzurro

Via Merry del Val, 13, (58 00 472). Bus to Viale Trastevere. **Open** 11pm-4am Fri-Sun. **Admission** L15,000 Fri, Sun; L20,000 Sat.

Rome's other leading gay disco has a varied clientele, including a transvestite contingent, in its series of column-adorned cellar rooms. Popular as a venue to visit with friends, the atmosphere encourages fun as well as cruising. Friday is mixed night.

Residencies/one-nighters

Mucca Assassina (Killer Cow), the DJ crew based at the **Mario Mieli** gay centre runs the largest and best one-nighters around Rome. On Fridays from October to May they're at Qube (*Via Portonaccio, 212*), usually transferring to the Alpheus (*Via del Commercio, 36*) for the summer months, though it's worth calling the Mario Mieli centre to check. The crew mixes a standard disco diet with novelty theme evenings (uniform night is popular) and celebrations of legendary 1960s stars. Local listings have news of other, sporadic one-nighters.

Europa Multiclub

Via Aureliana, 40 (48 23 650). Metro Repubblica/bus to Via XX Settembre. **Open** 3pm-midnight Mon-Thur; 1pm-6am Fri; 3pm-2am Sat; 1pm-midnight Sun. **Admission** L25,000 with Arcigay card (L20,000 for students; L15,000 after 11pm Fri). Special rates for out-of-towners.

Rome's newest, largest and smartest sauna with a friendly, imaginative staff and mixed clientele. Leave your togs in the multi-coloured lockers and cruise on down to the steam, sweat and romantically star-lit booths. The only place in Rome to do all night sessions (Fri), it is set to add a gym and an Internet point to its many other facilities.

Mediterraneo Sauna

Via Villari, 3 (77 20 59 34). Metro Manzoni/bus to Via Merulana. **Open** 2-11pm daily. **Admission** L20,000, plus annual membership card L20,000.

Tasteful décor and an emphasis on hygiene distinguish this sauna from many of its rivals. The steam room, sauna and jacuzzi provide repose prior to the exertions which take place in the so-called 'relax rooms' on the upper level. All ages and body types.

Terme di Roma/Body Center

Via Persio, 4, Quarto Miglio (71 84 378). Bus to Via Appia Nuova. **Open** 3pm-midnight Thur, Sun; 3pm-2am Fri-Sat. **Admission** L20,000-L25,000.

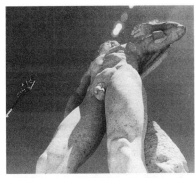

*Full-on fascist art at the **Foro Italico**.*

system, and better-run, the Gemelli is the largest Catholic hospital in Rome but is somewhat out-of-centre. The Spallanzani is a state hospital with a STD clinic.

Books, Videos & Magazines

Edicole (open-air news-stands) are often good for gay material. Around Termini station there are several with a fair amount of material on display by day and masses by night.

Edicola Antrilli *Corner of Via Giolitti/Via Gioberti.*
Edicola Di Fabrizio *Corner of Piazza dei Cinquecento/ Via Gaeta.*
Edicola Lazzari *Corner of Piazza dei Cinquecento/Via Volturno.*
Edicola Camponeschi *Corner of Piazza Colonna/Largo Chigi.*

Adam

Tattilo Editrice, Via del Casale Piombino, 30 (30 52 641/fax 30 52 506).
A lightweight fashion, style and pin-ups mag (L10,000), with a bias towards the boy band school of tease-eroticism. Unjustifiably filed under porn at news-stands.

A friendly place but a bit far from the centre, this venue boasts mega-jacuzzi and gym facilities, and offers a full range of sauna services with reduced prices after 9.30pm.

Babele

Via Paola, 44 (68 76 628). Bus to Corso Vittorio Emanuele. **Open** *9.30am-7.30pm Mon-Sat.*
The only exclusively gay and lesbian bookshop in Rome. A small space contains a surprisingly large selection of books (with a well-stocked English section), videos, guides, post-cards and magazines. The small noticeboard near the door is useful for keeping track of local events and openings.

Information

There are about 30 gay activist organisations in Italy, mostly in the north. Foremost are the Bologna-based **Arcigay** network run by Franco Grillini; and the Turin-based FUORI, headed by charismatic bookseller/politician Angelo Pezzana.

Babilonia

Babilonia Edizioni, Casella Postale (PO Box) 11224, 20110 Milano (02 56 96 468/57 40 788/fax 02 55 21 34 19).
Italy's principal gay publishing house, responsible for a fairly lively monthly magazine, *Babilonia* (L8,000, at selected news-stands) and the annual Italian/English *Guida Gay* (L20,000), which gives the most comprehensive and accurate information on gay life in Italy and other European cities.

Arcigay Pegaso

Via Primo Acciaresi, 7 (41 73 07 52). Metro Tiburtina. **Open** *4-7pm Mon-Sat.*
National HQ: Piazza di Porta Saragozza, 2, 40123 Bologna (051 580 563).
Rome branch of the Bologna-based group, closely linked to the PDS (ex-Communist party). Responsible for political, social and welfare activities; also runs a helpline.

Cobra Videofilms

Via Barletta, 23 (37 51 73 50). Metro Ottaviano/bus to Viale delle Milizie. **Open** *9am-7.45pm Mon-Sat.*
Via Giolitti, 307/313 (44 70 06 36). Metro Vittorio Emanuele. **Open** *9am-7.45pm Mon-Sat.*
A well-stocked (for Rome) small chain of gay/hetero video shops, with monthly arrivals from abroad. Specialises in 'trans' material. Over-18s only.

Circolo Mario Mieli di Cultura Omosessuale

Via Corinto, 5 (54 13 985/fax 54 13 971). Metro Basilica San Paolo/bus to Via Ostiense. **Open** *9am-9pm Mon-Fri.*
A cultural and political organisation run by and for gays, with an AIDS/HIV testing and care centre, a general helpline and a counselling service (*see* **Health & Helplines** *below*). The most important gay and lesbian centre in Rome, a base for debates, cultural events and the one-nighters run by the highly popular **Mucca Assassina** DJ crew, Mario Mieli also offers courses in Italian (phone for details).

Europa 92

Via Boezio, 96 (68 71 210). Metro Ottaviano. **Open** *3-7.45pm Mon; 9.15am-1.30pm, 3-7.45 pm, Tue-Sat.*
A predominantly gay video shop which also sells magazines and a variety of toys and gadgets. The heavier stuff is kept in the basement.

Marco

Edizioni Moderne, Casella Postale (PO Box) 17182, 20170 Milano (02 29 51 74 90).
Contact mag with ads and amateurish photographs, sometimes sexy, occasionally depressing and often hilarious. Also provides up-to-date info on venues and meeting-places.

Health & Helplines

AIDS Hotline

Assistenza Aids, Circolo Mario Mieli (see above).
Counselling, help at home and psychological support.

Pianta Gay di Roma (Rome Gay Map)

(oMo Edizioni)
Available from some *edicole* and bookshops; a comprehensive list of all the gay activities in Rome. Particularly detailed on the main cruising spots, which are helpfully highlighted on the map. Quadrilingual. Updated annually.

Sexually Transmitted Diseases

Policlinico Gemelli Largo Agostino Gemelli, 8 (30 152). Train/bus to Pineta Sacchetti.
Ospedale Spallanzani Via Portuense, 292 (55 38 91 21). Bus to Via Portuense.
For the treatment of sexually transmitted diseases, go to the *Clinica Dermosifilopatica* in main hospitals. Outside the state

Lesbian Rome

You may not be able to see it, but it's out there.

Although Rome has yet to host a permanent lesbian club or disco, there are enough one-nighters and special events to offer the occasional good night out.

There are two distinct factions in *Roma lesbica*. The older lesbian groups have their roots in the feminist movement of the seventies, and continue to claim separate identity from men, gay or straight. They tend to meet primarily for ideological or political purposes, but also to chill in the café, at the **Buon Pastore Centre** (Via della Lungara, 19; 68 64 201). Then there are the younger lesbians who meet at the **Circolo Mario Mieli** (*see chapter* **Gay Rome**) or are part of the Arci-Lesbica association (*see below*). They have joined forces with their male counterparts to form the basis of a homosexual community. Joint ventures like the **Mucca Assassina** (*see chapter* **Gay Rome**) get good turn-outs from both gays and lesbians.

So whether you're up for a debate on feminism or a dance into the 'oui' hours, do your homework first. Check the bulletin board at the **Babele** bookshop (*see chapter* **Gay Rome**), stop by the Buon Pastore, or ring up the Arci-Lesbica or Circolo Mario Mieli for the latest happenings. Some predominantly male venues also run occasional women-only nights, notably **Frutta e Verdura** and **Skyline** (*see chapter* **Gay Rome**).

The soothing café at **Buon Pastore Centre**. *See introduction.*

as the Masquerade Ball at **Carnevale** (*see chapter* **Rome by Season**) and visits to Immaginaria, the Bologna lesbian film festival held in February.

Coordinamento Lesbiche Romane

Via San Francesco di Sales, 1a, Trastevere (68 64 201). Bus to Lungotevere della Farnesina. **Open** *phone for details.*
The little sister of the lesbian associations, the CLR was set up in 1995 to facilitate contacts among lesbians throughout Italy, regardless of ideology. Still separatist at heart, it strives to make lesbians more visible in the media.

Information

Libreria delle Donne: Al Tempo Ritrovato

Via dei Fienaroli, 31d, Trastevere (58 17 724). Bus to Viale Trastevere. **Open** *3-8pm Mon; 10am-8pm Tue-Sat.* **No credit cards.**
A well-stocked lesbian section with some books in English, and an information-packed noticeboard.

Organisations and Events

Arci-Lesbica

Via Primo Acciaresi, 7 (41 73 07 52). Metro Tiburtina. **Open** *4-7pm Thur; 4-8pm Sat.*
A spin-off from **Arcigay** (*see chapter* **Gay Rome**), Arci-Lesbica offers a helpline, and organises get-togethers twice a week, as well as special events through the year.

Collegamento fra le lesbiche italiane

Via S. Francesco di Sales, 1a (68 64 201). Bus to Lungotevere della Farnesina. **Open** *7-9pm Tue.*
Formed in 1981, this separatist lesbian group meets in the Buon Pastore once a week to discuss politics. It's strictly women-only, but you don't need to be a member to take part. Completely self-financing, the CLI publishes a monthly newsletter, *La Bollettina del CLI.* As well as holding conferences and literary evenings, it organises concerts, dances, holidays and other events, such

Discos, Clubs and One-nighters

L'Angelo Azzurro

Via Cardinale Merry del Val, 13 (58 00 472). Bus to Viale Trastevere. **Open** *11pm-4am Fri.* **Admission** *L10,000 (includes first drink).*
This male club offers a women-only disco every Friday.

Jolie Cœur

Via Sirte, 5 (86 21 58 27). Bus to Viale Eritrea. **Open** *10pm-5am Sat.* **Admission** *L12,000.*
Saturday is women's night at Rome's long-established club, which now includes a karaoke room and a billiard table. On the dance floor, it's strictly techno, while the youthful atmosphere is more pyjama-party than disco. No men allowed.

La Stanza dei Frutti Rubini

Via Corinto, 5 (54 13 985). Metro San Paolo/bus to Via Ostiense. **Open** *8-11pm Wed.* **Admission** *free.*
Laid-back, women-only event in the **Mario Mieli Centre**.

Travel information

Zipper Travel Association

Via Castelfidardo, 18 (48 82 730). Metro Castro Pretorio/bus to Piazza Indipendenza **Open** *9.30am-6.30pm Mon-Fri.* **Credit** *AmEx, MC, V.*
The only travel agency in Italy offering customised travel for gay women. It guarantees lesbian or lesbian-friendly addresses for accommodation and entertainment.

Media

If you're looking for brain fodder, the Roman diet is unvarying – tits with everything.

The Italian are like a distorting mirror, reflecting all the tawdry intrigues and incomprehensible waffle of the ruling classes. In a country where gossip has more substance than fact, and where the virtual reality of the small screen exercises more fascination than the real world, one can be forgiven for thinking that the media *are* Italy, and Italy merely a bad daytime-soap travesty of itself. A few years ago, much was made of the entry of Silvio Berlusconi, television mogul extraordinaire, into the political arena and of the grotesque conflicts of interest that he represented. Oh, for those heady days of public outrage and political controversy. Now, with Berlusconi firmly ensconced in the political firmament, nobody even seems to care. Berlusconi also has considerable leverage in the print media, controlling one national daily, *Il Giornale* of Milan, and two influential weeklies, *Panorama* and *Epoca*. His biggest competitors are also big-league industrialists. *La Repubblica* belongs to Carlo de Benedetti's Olivetti group, while *La Stampa* and *Corriere della Sera* come within Fiat chairman Gianni Agnelli's sphere of influence. In general, newspapers have taken their cue from television and moved relentlessly downmarket, relying more and more on glossy supplements and cheap videos to buoy up circulation.

Newspapers

Italian newspapers can be a frustrating read. Stories, particularly on politics, tend to be long and indigestible, so you have to wade through reams and reams of copy to find out what the point is. Often there isn't one. There is little background explanation; not only do you not get told what position any given public figure holds, you're lucky if they're given a first name. Italian journalists are so terrified of missing anything that they hang out together in packs. As a result, their stories often look suspiciously similar. Likewise, editors tend to be unadventurous and almost always follow the news agenda set by the television news the night before. Even Italians complain that their newspapers look like photocopies of each other.

On the plus side, Italian papers are delightfully unsnobbish and happily blend serious news with well-written, often surreal, crime and human-interest stories. If politics bore you or leave you reeling with incomprehension, turn to the *cronaca* (a catch-all term meaning anything which isn't politics, economics or sport) pages where, even with rudimentary reading Italian, you will be transfixed by tales of weird suicide pacts, grotesquely overprotective parents and chilling murders.

Corriere della Sera

Milan's, and at the moment the country's, leading daily. It has plenty of talented reporters, notably those specialising in judicial issues and foreign news, but also a regrettable tendency towards rubbish.

Il Giornale

Quite apart from its pro-Berlusconi politics, this is an unlikeable newspaper whose stories are often malicious or wide of the mark. Worth reading, however, to know what the centre-right camp is thinking, and for the occasional good human-interest piece.

Il Messaggero

Rome's favourite popular newspaper, with the best *cronaca* pages around. Politically a bit iffy following a recent management takeover (it has become the mouthpiece for various city political interests). The Sunday edition carries an insert on property sales and lettings, while Thursday is the main day for small ads.

L'Osservatore Romano

An immovable feature of the Roman scene, this is the Vatican's official newspaper. It was an organ for liberal Catholic thought during the 1960s and '70s, but under the present Pope it has been brought to heel and now reflects the conservative orthodoxies issuing from the top. There are weekly editions in English and other languages.

La Repubblica

Italy's youngest major newspaper (founded 1976) has to some extent been a victim of its own success, as growth has led to sensationalism and sloppy reporting. The political coverage is often incoherent, and the paper has a weakness for waffling, pseudo-intellectual front-page commentaries. Despite this, it's excellent on the Vatican, the Mafia and the media.

La Stampa

The organ of the Agnelli family is traditionally strong on business news. Despite some great leaps forward in the early 1990s, it has recently proved disappointing in other areas. New editor Carlo Rossella wants to make it more accessible, but asking *La Stampa* to be populist is like asking a Turinese countess to turn up at a society ball in bondage gear – the result is unconvincing and faintly ridiculous.

L'Unità

These days, the party organ of the left-wing PDS is as confused and abstruse as the centre-left coalition it champions. For a while, as an opposition broadsheet, it built up a reputation for clear, remarkably objective reporting and vibrant cultural coverage, but it has not recovered from the elevation of its talented editor, Walter Veltroni, to the upper echelons of government. Neither has he, but that's another story.

Foreign Titles

Rome has two listings magazines wholly in English: *Metropolitan* and *Wanted in Rome*. *Roma C'è* has a section printed in English, while a Roman version of *Time Out*, in Italian, appears once a month. British dailies appear by mid-afternoon on the day of publication, while the *International Herald Tribune*, the *Financial Times* and the *Wall Street Journal* are out in the morning.

The big news-stands in the centre (in the Piazza Colonna, Largo Argentina, Piazza Navona, Pantheon, and, above all, on the Via Veneto) are the best places to buy foreign papers.

Magazines

Magazines in Italy are one big parade of tits, tits and more tits, whether they're serious current affairs publications such as *Panorama* or *L'Espresso* (which at least usually restrict the naked flesh to the front cover), or harbingers of celebrity sleaze like *Novella 2000*, *Eva Tre Mila* and their imitators. *Panorama* is currently the best of the bunch, thanks to some robust editing; two weekly supplements, *Sette* (with *Corriere della Sera* on Thursdays) and *Il Venerdì* (with *Repubblica* on Fridays) aren't bad either. For sheer trash value, don't miss *Cronaca Vera*, Italy's home-grown version of *National Enquirer*, which does not even pretend that its stories – a hilarious mixture of sex, religion and weird family values – are true. One other publication worth mentioning is *Internazionale*, an excellent digest of world news translated from the best foreign newspapers.

Listings Magazines

Metropolitan

An English-language fortnightly with some occasionally interesting features on local life. It has listings and a small-ads service. Free.

Porta Portese

Not really a listings magazine, but this twice-weekly small-ads paper (published on Tuesdays and Fridays) is essential reading for anyone looking for a place to live in Rome (along with the weekly *Solo Case*). Small ads are free, and sections include household goods and cars, as well as houses and flats to rent or buy. To take real advantage of it, you should get your copy and start ringing as soon as possible after 8.30am on publication days.

Roma C'è

A weekly cultural guide with comprehensive listings for theatre, music venues, dance, film and nightlife. The magazine comes out every Thursday and is available on news-stands. English-language section.

Time Out Roma

Same format as the London version, except that this one is in Italian and comes out once a month. Usually goes a step further than other local listings mags, sifting through the events and highlighting the most interesting ones.

Wanted in Rome

This unassuming fortnightly bulletin started life as a photocopied freesheet in the mid-eighties. It's a good source of essential information and up-market housing ads.

Television

Italy has six main networks (Berlusconi's three, plus the state-owned Radio Televisione Italiana, or RAI), one minor one (Telemontecarlo) and any number of local stations to provide hours of channel-zapping fun. Most of the fare on offer is compulsively awful (*see opposite* **The Good, the Bad and the Ugly**). If you watch nothing else, look out for a programme on RAI-3 called *Blob*, which goes out on most weeknights. *Blob*

The good, the bad & the ugly

It's not *quite* true to say there's nothing worth watching on Italian TV. News programmes are frequent, and the amount of attention dedicated to world events can make British equivalents look like parish magazines. The range of films shown – especially of the old *commedia all'italiana* variety – is also impressive.

But the salient (and most-watched) feature of Italian television is the array of endless quiz/variety shows. These are staged on glitzy sets, adorned by pouting babes barely contained by plunging, clinging dresses, and feature games that are incomprehensible, inconsequential and, like as not, designed to place the participants in excruciatingly embarrassing situations.

Italian television shows are the *ne plus ultra* of the national tendency towards doing-as-you-hate-to-be-done-by. An extension of the obsession with

bella figura (saving face), this involves a morbid fascination with any situation in which others are held up to ridicule. Hence programmes where warring couples are invited to air their differences, egged noisily on by an army of relatives, or where the audience is invited to award points to the 'best couple', the criteria for best-ness being obscure but the humiliation for not-best being ensured. The whole farrago is normally conducted by the sort of middle-aged men whose cologne strips paint at 50 paces, or women with that permanently surprised expression that bespeaks multiple visits to the plastic surgeon.

It's the nadir of broadcasting, but audience figures show that it's what the public wants. And as television everywhere gets trashier, you can't help feeling it may be the shape of things to come.

---

is a collage of the most excruciating, embarrassing and extraordinary moments of the previous 24 hours' television, pieced together with great skill and wit and recalling Karl Marx's observation that history is played out first as tragedy, then as farce. Politicians are so scared of the programme that they periodically try to have it taken off the air.

RAI-3 is generally the most intelligent channel, with more talk and fewer low-budget South American soaps than the others. Check the newspapers for films, although unless they are on at two in the morning they are going to be dubbed into Italian. Some of the minor stations sometimes surprise with a Hitchcock or Fritz Lang; just as often, though, they advertise telephone sex lines, tacky furniture and anti-cellulite treatments.

Radio

Italian culture is so obsessed with image that radio doesn't get much of a look-in. The three state-owned stations (RAI-1 on 89.7 MHz FM and 1332 KHz AM; RAI-2 on 91.7 MHz FM stereo and 846 KHz AM; RAI-3 on 93.7 MHz FM) are almost indistinguishable from each other. They mostly play classical and light music, with thorough news bulletins every couple of hours and the odd discussion programme or phone-in. Commercial stations offer a touch more variety.

Radio Centro Suono
101.3 MHz FM.
Dance and soul, hip-hop, reggae and ragga, on the air 24 hours a day.

Radio Città Futura
97.7 FM.
Italy's most PC 24-hour station has been established for over 20 years and broadcasts *Radiofax* at 10am daily, listing the day's events in Rome. A rather more controversial news programme goes out at 1.30pm daily, dealing specifically with aspects of racism and immigration. On Monday evenings there's an English-language music programme.

Radio Kiss Kiss Network
97.250 MHz FM.
Based in Naples and networked to other cities, this 24-hour music and talk station is considered a real alternative in Italian radio. DJs are given complete liberty to sound off on heated topics, and zany competitions have included one where listeners were asked to steal their partners' underpants and send them in. In another, people sent in photos of their least-favourite parts of their bodies – the winner won free plastic surgery.

Radio Radicale
88.6 MHz FM; 102.4 MHz FM.
Italy wouldn't be the same without this quirky station, a platform for the Radical party. Dubbed 'Radio Bestemmia' (radio swear-word) because of its heated phone-ins.

Vatican Radio
93.3 MHz FM; 1530 KHz AM.
Rome wouldn't be the same without this station either. Announcers, who must be good Catholics, read the world news, which tends to shy away from ticklish subjects like contraception and divorce. Broadcast in some 35 languages, including English.

Music: Classical & Opera

After a decade of neglect, Rome's classical music scene is starting to find its feet again.

Though local talent is a bit thin on the ground, Rome plays host to some of the world's top musical names, especially in the two world-class international chamber music seasons at the **Accademia Nazionale di Santa Cecilia** and the **Accademia Filarmonica**.

Named after the patron saint of music, the Accademia Nazionale di Santa Cecilia is Rome's main musical establishment and most prestigious music academy. It has had many homes and functions since it was founded by the sixteenth-century composer Palestrina, but for the time being it's based at the **Auditorio Pio**. Bruno Cagli, the academy's current president, first raised the level of guest conductors to include names like Carlo Maria Giulini, Wolfgang Sawallisch, Valery Gergiev, Georges Pretre and Pierre Boulez, and then secured the appointment of Myung-Whung

String 'em up – it's the only answer.

Chung as principal conductor. Famous for having revamped Paris's Bastille opera, Chung is expected to provide the orchestra with a much-needed overhaul and a longed-for recording contract with Deutsche Grammophon.

Cagli has also brought the venerable old institution up to date, with world-class programmes, autumn festivals dedicated to single composers, and a pioneering commitment to classical/popular cross-overs with artists such as Keith Jarret and Michael Nyman. Programming of the summer season at the remarkable outdoor venue in Villa Giulia is always thoughtful and imaginative. (*See* **Open Air Festivals** *page 201*.)

The Accademia Filarmonica was founded in 1821, and included among its early members Rossini, Donizetti, Paganini and Verdi. Traditionally it combines the activities of a choir school (with a repertoire which reflects the dubious musical taste of its director, Father Pablo Colino) with a season of mainly chamber music. Revitalised by its previous artistic director, Paolo Arcà, the concert programme now extends to multi-media events (among them the popular Momix Dance Theatre), chamber opera performances, and some contemporary music. The appointment of veteran Massimo Bogianckino, who has held every job worth having in the Italian music world, as artistic director will probably mean less experimentation but no decline in quality. The concert season runs from mid-October to mid-May in one of the Accademia's own venues, **Teatro Olimpico** (*see below* **Auditoriums**).

A third institution, the **Istituzione Universitaria dei Concerti (IUC)**, was founded after the last war in the hope of bringing a bit of life to Rome's culturally-dead campus. Today the IUC offers a varied season built around a standard programme of international and Italian recitals and chamber music, usually mounted at its main auditorium, the **Aula Magna**. There's a refreshing emphasis on ancient music, classical/popular cross-overs, and music with distinct sound textures. The IUC serves a mixed audience, with numerous elderly subscribers drawn by the

Time to face the music at **Santa Cecilia**.

afternoon concerts, and students and university staff on cut-rate subscriptions. It is also a forum for Rome débuts for young international competition winners and composers.

As for the once glorious **Teatro dell'Opera**, it hit rock bottom in the first half of the 1990s, but the appointment of the dynamic Sergio Escobar has brought it back from the brink. Standards are still variable and seats are not cheap, but the good productions can be very good indeed.

Work is finally under way on Renzo Piano's new world-class auditorium, a vast three-hall complex in the northern suburbs which is scheduled to be in service for the 1999-2000 season. And none too soon either: Rome has been without a real concert hall since 1936, when Mussolini demolished the famed *Augusteo* to expose what was left of the emperor's family mausoleum.

TICKETS

Getting hold of tickets is not always easy. Most good inexpensive seats are already taken by subscribers, so keep an eye out for concerts which are *fuori abbonamento* (non-subscription). **Santa Cecilia** pre-sells single tickets for concerts after subs close, but if your time is limited try an agency (*see chapter* **Services**); these charge a booking fee. If your time is limited, a trip to the box office can make things easier. Get there early with cash (plastic can be touch and go). Tickets usually become available six days before performances. Prices at main auditoriums start at around L30,000.

Auditoriums

Auditorio Pio
Via della Conciliazione, 4 (68 80 10 44). Bus to Lungotevere Vaticano. **Concerts** Oct-June.
Since it was first rented from the Vatican in 1958, this has

been 'temporary' home to the **Accademia Nazionale di Santa Cecilia** concert series. More like an oversized school hall than a real auditorium, its acoustics have been greatly improved over the years, but few will be sorry to leave it when Rome's new auditorium is ready.

Aula Magna dell'Università la Sapienza
Piazzale Aldo Moro (36 10 052). Metro Policlinico/bus or tram to Viale Regina Elena. **Concerts** Oct-May.
Comfortable seating, kitsch fascist décor, reasonable acoustics and ample parking; the Aula Magna is now the principal auditorium for the **IUC** season. Tickets can also be bought from the IUC's headquarters at Lungotevere Flaminio, 50 (10am-1pm, 2-6pm, Mon-Fri).

Sala Casella
Via Flaminia, 118 (32 01 752). Bus to Piazza Mancini/bus or tram to Via Flaminia. **Tickets** Teatro Olimpico (*see below*).
The in-house concert hall of the **Accademia Filarmonica**, restored and equipped to the highest level in terms of acoustics, comfort and safety. Seats an intimate 180, and its atmospheric interior is ideal for offbeat programmes.

Teatro Brancaccio
Via Merulana, 244 (48 74 563). Metro Vittorio Emanuele/bus to Via Merulana. **Box office** 10.45am-5pm Tue-Sat; 10.45am-8.30pm on concert days.
A huge former cinema that is the second home of the **Teatro dell'Opera**, used for ballet performances and non-classical concerts. Not much atmosphere and a boomy acoustic.

Teatro Olimpico
Piazza Gentile da Fabriano, Flaminio (32 34 890). Bus to Piazza Mancini/bus or tram to Via Flaminia. **Box office** 10am-1pm, 2-7pm, daily. **Concerts** Sept-May.
A highly successful cinema conversion has resulted in one of the most attractive venues in Rome for all types of performances: comfortable seats and good acoustics, even in the cheapest seats. Owned by the **Accademia Filarmonica**, it's used for their Thursday concerts. (*See also chapter* **Theatre & Dance**.)

Teatro dell'Opera di Roma
Via Firenze, 72 (48 16 01). Metro Termini/bus to Via Nazionale or Termini. **Box office** 10.45am-5pm Tue-Sat; 10.45am-8.30pm on concert days.

Concerti Telecom Italia

This unusual series of mainly Sunday morning concerts was known as the *concerti del Italcable* until the sponsor, Italy's state telecommunications company, changed its name to Telecom. There seems to be no shortage of money under the new administration and the series is branching out from chamber music into opera and concerts by visiting orchestras, like the Orchestre de Paris. Consequently, performances are now held at the **Teatro dell'Opera** and **Auditorio di Via della Conciliazione**, as well as the traditional venue of **Teatro Sistina** (*see chapter* **Theatre & Dance**).

These world-class radio concerts (broadcast on RAI Radiotre, *see chapter* **Media**) are hosted by the indefatigable organiser of the series, Stefano Mazzonis, who gives a chatty intro to each piece for the benefit of the radio audience. The tickets are free, but you have to queue for them on the morning before the concert. Although not a nation of queuers, Italian music-lovers are an exception. Turn up any time from 4am to 7am to get your numerino, then go away until the 9am roll call and ticket distribution. Around 500 to 700 tickets are usually given away.
Administration Via Gianturco, 2. **Information** 9am-1pm Mon-Fri (36 88 27 13/36 88 24 25).
Box office opens the day before the concert in the concert venue until all seats taken.

Never in the La Scala or San Carlo class, the late nineteenth-century Teatro Costanzi, as it was then called, built a reputation which lasted until the late 1950s. But it fell hostage to the Italian political favours system, and was subsequently paralysed by the hyper-unionised orchestra and stagehands. During the early 1990s the place was run by Giampaolo Cresci, a self-proclaimed musical ignoramus, whose circus stunts and glitzy décor attracted largely undeserved and often counter-productive publicity. Apart from the struggling potted palms, Cresci's only legacy was a massive increase in the company's already astronomical debts.

The current director, Sergio Escobar, has managed to put the theatre's finances back in order (thanks to massive injection of funds by Rome's centre-left council), and his appointment of experienced Israeli conductor Gary Bertini reflects the urgent need to raise orchestral standards. The explosive Escobar has even managed to win jaded Roman audiences back to the opera with his *Turandot at the Stadium* spectacular. Not content with this nightly audience of 10,000, he has vowed that the Baths of Caracalla will once again play host to opera. As a taste of things to come, he persuaded the archaeologists to agree to a series of concerts among the ruins in the summer of 1997.

As for the building itself, the austere 1930s exterior is not to everybody's liking, to say nothing of the tacky entry canopy. The lavish traditional *teatro all'italiana* interior comes as quite a surprise after Mussolini's angular façade: you'll find towering rows of boxes, loads of stucco, nineteenth-century frescoes and gold paint everywhere. Acoustics vary greatly – the higher (and cheaper) seats are distinctly unsatisfactory.

San Giovanni, kitsch amplification completely destroys the effect of the singing. The only really outstanding choir in the city is that of the Russicum, the Eastern Rite church in front of Santa Maria Maggiore.

To make matters worse the Church hierarchy won't allow the use of churches for paying concerts. They do allow some free concerts by visiting choirs, so it is worth keeping an eye on the wall posters at church entrances. Sadly, the preferred venue, **Sant'Ignazio**, is a massive barn of a church with an acoustic wholly unsuited to polyphonic music. Get there and grab a seat in the front row – anywhere else is a waste of time.

Organ buffs should make a bee-line for the splendidly restored 1670s instrument in San Giovanni de' Fiorentini (played for organ mass at noon on Sunday; the church is in Via Giulia) and the organ of **Santa Maria Sopra Minerva** (*see chapter* **Churches**).

Rome's theatres also put on occasional concerts. The small **Teatro Ghione** (63 72 294) hosts a modest but interesting musical programme, and the **Teatro Sistina** (48 26 841) has a regular series of free Sunday morning dates. You have to book beforehand, however. (*See chapter* **Theatre & Dance**.)

Churches and Other Venues

There is nothing in Rome to compare with the church music tradition of cities like Vienna and London. Of the great city basilicas, only **San Giovanni** and **Santa Maria Maggiore** still bother to maintain a choir and a weekly sung mass. **Saint Peter's** has a football stadium acoustic and choirs to match, and among the city's monasteries and convents, only **Sant'Anselmo** manages some rather turgid plainchant. Here, like

Minor Musical Associations

During the eighties and early nineties, while the city's major cultural institutions were languishing in a torpor of mediocrity, these smaller associations took up much of the slack. Some are mere vehicles for ego-tripping founders, but others offer fine music. Many amateur associations, particularly choirs, advertise at the start of each season (September or October) for new members. Concert programmes and musical workshops usually run from November to May.

Accademia Barocca

Via Vicenzo Arangio Ruiz, 7 (66 41 17 49).
Italy's relatively recent interest in Baroque music has produced small groups like this one. The Accademia Barocca organises concerts (no fixed date) in the Episcopal church of San Paolo entro le Mura in Via Nazionale, and at the Palazzo della Cancelleria.

Associazione Il Tempietto

Piazza Campitelli, 9 (48 14 800).
An energetic organisation which gives young and relatively inexperienced performers a public forum. Concerts are held at the Sala Baldini in Piazza Campitelli and the Basilica of San Nicola in Carcere in winter, and the Teatro di Marcello in summer (nightly). *See* **Open Air Festivals: Concerti del Tempietto**.

Associazione Musicale Romana

Via dei Banchi Vecchi, 61 (68 68 441/fax 68 30 86 80).
Organises good varied concerts, often in the Oratorio di Caravita, and a varied summer season which includes Gershwin and Piazzola as well as mainstream chamber music. Don't miss the short but sweet annual organ festival in September (a wonderful opportunity to hear the superb instrument in **San Giovanni de' Fiorentini** being played by the big names), or the harpsichord festival, held in spring.

Associazione Nuova Consonanza

Via S. di Saint Bon, 61 (37 00 323).
The Associazione organises the prestigious Festival di Nuova Consonanza, often in collaboration with the Goethe Istitut, and representing the very best in European contemporary music.

Associazione Nuovi Spazi Musicali

Via Divisione Torino, 139 (50 21 208).
One of the most energetic promoters of contemporary music.

Il Gonfalone

Oratorio del Gonfalone, Via del Gonfalone, 32a (68 75 952). **Concerts** Oct-June. **Information** Vicolo della Scimmia, 1b (68 75 952). **Open** 9am-1pm Mon-Fri; 9am-9pm day of concert.
The Gonfalone has its own Oratorio del Gonfalone where it specialises in chamber music and solo concerts, with some excellent visiting groups.

Open Air Festivals

Teatro dell'Opera

Via Firenze, 72 (48 16 02 55). Metro Termini/bus to Via Nazionale or Termini. **Box office** 10.45am-5pm Tue-Sun.
For the 1997 season, the Stadio Olimpico soccer stadium hosted summer operas, while the spectacular Baths of Caracalla, declared off-limits for opera performances, was used for concerts only. Whether Romans will ever again hear opera in the old Roman baths is anyone's guess. Check July newspapers for latest developments in the running battle between the opera and the archaeologists.

Accademia of Santa Cecilia at Villa Giulia

Piazzale di Villa Giulia, 9 (67 86 428/67 80 742/3/4/5; also Associazone Amici di Santa Cecilia: 68 33 242). Bus or tram to Via Flaminia or Viale delle Belle Arti. **Concerts** July.
Probably the best way to listen to symphonic music anywhere in Rome, in this exquisite Renaissance courtyard. The programme also includes symphonic, early and chamber music, with classical/popular cross-overs, ballet and even gospel choirs.

Concerti del Tempietto

Via del Teatro di Marcello, 44 (48 14 800). Bus to Via del Teatro di Marcello. **Concerts** Nov-June. **Tickets** from box office two hours before concert, or from bar opposite, Piazza Campitelli, 42.
Rather low-level musically, but a pleasant outdoor setting. Occasionally features well-known performers, but generally students and recent graduates presenting varied and accessible programmes.

Rome Festival

Auditorio Papa Sisto V, Piazza S. Salvatore in Lauro (39 37 86 63). Bus to Corso Rinascimento or Lungotevere Tor di Nona. **Concerts** June-mid Aug.
A well-balanced, low-budget summer festival organised and directed by maestro Fritz Maraffi. The venue varies from year to year.

Out of Town Festivals

Estate Tuscolana

Various villas and churches in the Frascati area (94 47 471/94 47 271). June-Aug.
Interesting programme in a small town just outside Rome, making use of some stunning local villas.

Festival dei Due Mondi, Spoleto

Rome office *Via Beccaria, 18 (32 10 288). Bus to Piazzale Flaminio.* June-July.
Possibly Italy's most famous performing arts festival. After 40 years, the beauty of this Umbrian hill town 200km north of Rome still draws a predominantly Roman audience. While much of the dynamism of earlier years has gone, the more innovative performances are often excellent and are surprisingly underbooked.

Festival Pontino

Castello Caetani/Abbazia di Fossanova, Sermoneta (07 73 60 55 51). June-July.
Good-quality orchestras and duos in two outstandingly beautiful venues 70km south of Rome. The medieval Castello Caetani stands above the pretty hill town, and the perfectly restored abbey is close by.

Choirs

One of the healthiest areas of Rome's musical life is the amateur choral scene. In September and October many of these groups place advertisements for new members.

Agimus

Via dei Greci, 18 (36 00 18 24). **Concerts** mid-Oct to mid-June.
The Associazione Giovanile Musicale is the principal choral organisation in Rome. In addition to major performances, it organises concerts in venues like the small church of San Teodoro al Palatino.

Coro Romani Cantores

Corso Trieste, 165 (44 24 05 61).
This specialises in early music, usually accompanied by period instruments.

Coro da Camera Italiano

Via R. Fauro, 62 (77 20 41 43).
This outstanding amateur choir is the only Roman group to research and perform less well known choral works of the Baroque period. Unfortunately, it only gives a couple of concerts a year, at the Chiesa Valdese in Piazza Cavour or at Saint Paul's Episcopal Church.

Music: Rock, Roots and Jazz

Despite first impressions, Rome's music scene is alive and kicking – but you may have to go to an abattoir to find it.

London, Paris or even Melbourne may attract more big names, but Rome's live scene has plenty to offer. Forget the international stars, and explore the home-grown variety: if it's simply a musical night out you want, there's something here to suit all tastes.

Winter months are dominated by local rock and Latin, with the occasional visit from foreign and big-name Italian rock stars such as Pino Daniele or homegrown rapper Lorenzo Cherubini, alias Jovanotti. Rome lacks a good large-scale venue, however, and this, combined with slack professional promotion and organisation, tends to deter many of the acts which play other Italian cities.

Smaller bands have fewer troubles. The *Centri Sociali* (*see* **Social Services** *page 204*) and organisations such as *Cervello a sonagli* (*see* **Shake, Rattle and Roll** *page 206*) do a great job of providing cheap, alternative facilities.

Some of the local names which you may not know but might find interesting include: **Almamagretti**, an Adrian Sherwood/African Headcharge-inspired dub band; **Mau Mau** and **Daniele Sepe** – the former a Négresses Vertes soundalike, the latter offering jazz-folk-rock, both with a political bent; and the popular rap group **Sud Sound System**. There's a string of Italian World Beat bands such as **Novalia** and **Agricantus** which are well worth checking out. And if Sardinian **Elena Ledda** happens to be in town, go along for some real Italian roots music.

As for local jazz, piano and accordion player **Antonello Salis** is always good, as is **Roberto Gatto**. For R&B and soul fans, Rome has long been home to American ex-pat **Herbie Goins**, who was one of the singers to pass through Alexis Korner's many bands in the late 1960s (Mick Jagger was another). He still does a great Wilson Pickett-type gig that's worth catching.

If you're after something more unusual, look out for **Giovanna Marini** and her all-woman a cappella group, which does a mixture of Italian folk and roots, contemporary music and improvisation, and **Alvin Curran**, the American contemporary piano player, composer and improviser, who lives and sometimes performs in Rome between tours and teaching. Then there's Englishman **Mike Cooper**, a folk/jazz improviser who cuts across all genres with his steel guitar playing.

During the summer months, the clubs close and outdoor venues move to the fore. This is the time when international acts are most likely to make an appearance in Rome. Whatever's on offer, the joy of sitting under the stars, often in beautiful, historic surroundings, can turn an ordinary night out into something special.

Concert listings can be found in the monthly Rome edition of *Time Out* magazine, in newspapers such as *Il Manifesto* and *La Repubblica* (which on Thursday produces a what's-on supplement called *Trovaroma*), and in the weekly listings magazine **Rome C'è**, which has a token English section. Radio Città Futura (97.7 FM) lists the day's events on *Radiofax* at 10am. (*See chapter* **Media**.) Whatever your source of information, bear in mind that times and events should be read as vague suggestions rather than definitive indications.

One peculiarity of Roman clubs is the *tessera* (membership card) which you will have to buy at the door. You're not being ripped off: this is the law. *Tesserae* are usually valid for the season and will often entitle you to free entry on subsequent visits. Sometimes there is an entrance as fee on top of the price of the *tessera*, which may or may not entitle you to a free drink.

Venues

Akab
Via Monte Testaccio, 69 (57 40 44 85). Metro Piramide/bus to Via Marmorata. **Open** 10.30pm-4am Mon-Sat. **Admission** L15,000-L20,000 depending on event. Includes free drink.
Situated near the **Mattatoio** (*see chapter* **Cafés & Bars**), Akab presents a mix of musical styles, as well as some cabaret and theatre nights. DJ after the gigs.

Alpheus
Via del Commercio, 36 (Ostiense). (57 47 826). Metro Piramide/bus to Via Ostiense. **Open** 10pm-3am Tue-Sun. **Admission** from L10,000.

*Fun Lovin' Criminals and Courtney Pine have headlined at the **Horus Club**.*

A former cheese factory located near a huge gasworks, with three big halls featuring live rock, Latin, world music and jazz, followed by a disco. There's a pizzeria and an ice-cream parlour in the garden. Plenty of street parking but be sure to pay the self styled 'parking attendant' or you might find a vital piece of your car missing.

Circolo degli Artisti
Via Lamarmora, 28 (44 64 968). Metro Vittorio Emanuele/bus to Piazza Vittorio. **Open** 9pm-4am Tue-Sun. **Admission** membership L5,000 plus L5,000-15,000.
One of Rome's best venues, catering for a diverse range of tastes with its wild and often eclectic programme. The place includes a concert hall, bar and video room where foreign and Italian bands play rap, reggae, ragga, cyberpunk, grunge and whatever else happens to be in. There's usually a disco after the gigs.

Folkstudio
Via Frangipani, 42 (48 71 06 30). Metro Colosseo/bus to Via dei Fori Imperiali or Via Cavour. **Open** Oct-June 9pm-midnight daily. **Admission** membership L5,000 plus L10,000-20,000.
An historic Roman venue which has hosted most of the world's acoustic and folk acts in its time. Opened in the 1960s (albeit in a different location), it has a weekly open-stage session for brave new acts, and presents theatre, classical, jazz, world music and folk in a refreshingly no-smoking atmosphere. No bar, but feel free to bring your own drinks.

Fonclea
Via Crescenzio, 82a, Prati (68 96 302). Metro Ottaviano or Lepanto/bus to Piazza Cavour or Piazza Risorgimento. **Open** end Sept-June 8.30pm-2am daily. **Admission** L10,000 for special events.
Restaurant pub and cellar featuring soul, Latin, and funk.

Frontiera
Via Aurelia, 1,051 (66 92 878). Drive west along the Via Aurelia, beyond Grande Raccordo. **Open** 9pm; closing times vary. **Admission** depends on event.
This is one of the biggest venues in Rome and the one where you're most likely to find a name band. The tricky part is it's a long way from the centre of town and you really need a car to get there. If you don't know where it is, it's easy to miss the turn-off, so take someone who knows it. Huge disco when there's no concert.

Horus Club
Corso Sempione, 21, Montesacro (86 89 91 81). Bus to Piazza Sempione. **Open** Sept-June 9pm-3am daily. **Admission** L 20,000.
One of the few music venues in the north of the city and a good place to avoid other tourists, the Horus is a former cinema with billiard tables, seats and a bar. Presents visiting acts such as Fun Loving Criminals, Courtney Pine and Steve Earle. An eclectic programming policy with a disco after the concert.

Jake & Elwood
Via Giovanni Carlo Odino, 45/47, Isola Sacro, Fiumicino (65 83 566). Train from Piramide to Lido Centro, then bus to Isola Sacra. **Open** 10pm-3am Tue-Sun. **Admission** from L10,000.
A cottage surrounded by rusty ships on the banks of the Tiber. Twenty kilometres from Rome but worth the trek, J&E is at its best in summer, when local R&B and cover bands play outside. Disco after every concert, with a strict no-house policy.

Jive
Via Giuseppe Libetta, 7, Garbatella (57 45 989). Metro Garbatella/bus to Via Ostiense. **Open** 9.30pm-3.30am daily. **Admission** membership L10,000; remainder depends on event.

Social Services

Get slaughtered at **Villagio Globale**.

If a visit to a giant squat in a tumbledown municipal white elephant doesn't rank high on your list of holiday priorities, think again. As any local musician will tell you, the best place to feel the pulse of Rome's music scene is in the *Centri Sociali* – semi-legal social centres, tolerated until noise-plagued neighbours call the police in, organising concerts, film screenings, theatre and dance events, evening classes, language courses and a host of other activities.

Though standards vary, and sound systems often buzz so loudly that the music is inaudible, many of the *Centri* have established themselves

as important indie venues. Some acts – Linton Kwesi Johnson, for example – will opt to play there rather than in plusher surroundings.

The daily paper *Il Manifesto*, the weekly *Roma C'è* listings magazine and the monthly *Time Out Roma* give the fullest details of *Centri* events. Also look out for posters, especially in the San Lorenzo district near the university, and in Disfunzioni record shop (Via degli Etruschi, 4/14; 44 61 984). Otherwise, try calling Radio Onda Rossa (87.9 FM; 49 17 50), Radio Città Aperta (88.875 FM; 43 93 383) or Radio Città Futura (97.7 FM; 49 11 437) for news of activities.

Besides allowing you a glimpse of where Roman music is heading, some of the *Centri* are fascinating architectural monuments in their own right. Try these for size:

Villaggio Globale

Lungotevere Testaccio (57 30 03 29). Bus to Lungotevere Testaccio or Piazza dell'Emporio/tram to Piazza dell'Emporio. **Open** daily; concert times vary. **Admission** depends on event.
Situated in a gloriously pompous but now sadly crumbling former slaughterhouse, the **Mattatoio** (*see chapter* **Sightseeing**: **Testaccio**), the Villaggio Globale was set up in 1990 by and for Rome's immigrant community. Its immense central courtyard plays host to summer concerts (Papa Wemba, African Headcharge, Lee Perry and Willy de Ville have appeared in the recent past) while a huge range of courses – from Basque language to Mexican mural painting – is on offer in the lofty rooms. Currently being eyed by the city council for potential development, in view of the Millennium Holy Year celebrations, when millions of Catholics are expected to descend on Rome and its inadequate infrastructure.

Forte Prenestino

Via F. Delpino (21 80 78 55). Bus/tram to Via Prenestina. **Open** 24 hrs daily.
A nineteenth-century explosives depot houses this long-established *Centro*, where a labyrinth of tunnels and small chambers is occupied by bars, a cinema, a disco and other attractions. Two larger areas are used for concerts. The Forte holds an international arts festival each spring and a *Festa del Non-Lavoro* (Non-Labour Day) celebration each May 1.

Once known as the Classico, this stylish club features local African, Latin and funk groups and special DJ nights. There are regular outdoor gigs in summer, which come highly recommended.

Il Locale

Vicolo del Fico, 3 (68 79 075). Bus to Corso Vittorio Emanuele or Corso Rinascimento. **Open** 10pm-3am; closing day varies. **Admission** L10,000.
A long-standing popular hangout for local musicians and theatre people, Il Locale features mostly Italian bands playing their own compositions, with occasional theatre, cabaret and films.

Palaeur

Piazzale Dello Sport, EUR (59 25 205). Metro EUR Palasport/bus to Palazzo dello Sport.
See press for times, programme and admission. The saucer-shaped Palaeur is the only megastar-sized venue in town. This doesn't stop smaller acts playing it, often with disastrous results – the acoustics are appalling. Somewhat less atmospheric than an empty aircraft hangar.

Saint Louis Music City

Via del Cardello, 13 (47 45 076). Metro Cavour or Colosseo/bus to Via Cavour. **Open** 8.30pm-2am Mon-Sat. **Admission** membership L10,000.
Décor: urban street furniture. Music: local R&B and Latin.

Non-stop festivals keep Rome swinging during the dog days of summer.

Shake, Rattle and Roll

Rome has never had much time for avant-garde music, dismissed by the promotion establishment as 'difficult' and 'not commercial'. But the runaway success of *Cervello a Sonagli* (Brain Rattlers), an independent cultural association promoting alternative and experimental music, shows just how badly the establishment has miscalculated.

Formed in 1991, *Cervello a Sonagli* has 12 members, no headquarters, no office, and no outside funding. *Centri Sociali* (*see* **Social Services** *page 204*) provide the venues for most of their

events, which range from workshops to concerts and the annual Linguafonia improvisation festival, held in late spring. But as audiences continue to expand, the organisation has been forced to break out into theatres and larger clubs.

Always interesting, always challenging, *Cervello a Sonagli*'s events are well advertised in distinctive black and white wall posters, especially in the Trastevere and San Lorenzo districts. Details can also be obtained from the press, and the Disfunzioni record shop at Via degli Etruschi, 4/14 (44 61 984).

Teatro degli Artisti
Via San Francesco di Sales (68 80 84 38). Bus to Piazza Sonnino, Viale Trastevere or Lungotevere della Farnesina. **Open** 9.30-11.30pm daily. **Admission** membership L15,000 plus L15,000-L18,000.
Frequented by an arty audience; presents a wide range of musical activity, some theatre and performance art.

Jazz

Alexanderplatz
Via Ostia, 9 (39 74 21 71). Metro Ottaviano/bus to Piazza Risorgimento. **Open** Oct-June 9pm-1.30am Mon-Sat. **Admission** membership L10,000; tourists free with passport.
A club and restaurant where cocktails, Creole and Roman dishes are served up with live jazz, which is usually played by visiting American stars. Dinner reservations are taken.

Big Mama
Vicolo San Francesco a Ripa, 18 (58 12 551). Bus to Viale Trastevere. **Open** Oct-June 9.30pm-1.30am daily. **Admission** membership L20,000 plus charge for big names; includes one drink.
Deep in the heart of Trastevere, this is the home of blues in Rome, but Big Mama also presents visiting and local jazz, American singer-songwriters, and local and out-of-town blues. No smoking.

Latin American

Rome's thriving Latin American and Caribbean community, with resident musicians and a constant stream of visiting bands, has created a healthy Latin music scene. One of the longest-established of local groups is **Yemaya Orchestra**, formed in 1975 by the Flores brothers Cairo and Henry. Others include **Caribe**, **Sabor Cubano**, **Trio Berimbau**, **Connexion Sonora** and **Diapson**.

As for visitors, **Tito Puente**, **Oscar D'Leon**, **Celia Cruz** and **Los Van Van** make frequent appearances in Rome. Many summer festivals feature Latin events, but the focal point is the **Fiesta Capannelle** (*see below*) at the race track of the same name, down the Via Appia

Nuova. The festival runs from the end of June through August and features bands from Cuba and the Caribbean.

Berimbau
Via dei Fienaroli, 30 (58 13 249). Bus to Viale Trastevere or Piazza Sonnino. **Open** Oct-June 10.30pm-3am Wed-Sun. **Admission** free Mon-Thur, Sun; L20,000 (includes one drink) Fri-Sat.
Colours and sounds of Brazil in this cocktail bar featuring live music, a disco, and Rome's most cosmopolitan clientele.

Bossanova
Via degli Orti di Trastevere, 23 (58 16 121). Bus to Viale Trastevere. **Open** 10pm-3am Tue-Sun. **Closed** Aug. **Admission** L 7,000-10,000; includes one free drink.
A friendly club with Brazilian music every night. Great for uninhibited dancing.

Caffè Caruso
Via Monte Testaccio, 36 (57 45 019). Metro Piramide/bus or tram to Via Marmorata or Porta San Paolo. **Open** 9pm-2am Tue-Sun. **Admission** membership L20,000.
A typical Testaccio club specialising in live Latin sounds from Rome-based Caribbean and Brazilian musicians. Also mounts rock gigs. Packed on the Sunday disco night, which features rock, hip hop, rap and salsa.

African

Stazione Ouagadougou
Via della Lungaretta, 75 (58 12 510). Bus to Viale Trastevere. **Open** 10.30pm-3am Tue-Sun. **Admission** membership L5,000.
The only place in Rome which features live African music. This small bar has superb African décor, an art gallery, and African food and beer.

Festivals

When clubs close down for the summer, outdoor festivals abound. **L'Estate Romana** (Roman Summer) is the mother of all festivals, running from mid-June through August (*see chapter* **Rome by Season**) and attracting many foreign acts to the stunning venues that are set aside for the occasion.

Big names do play Rome, but your best bet is to seek out local talent.

Smaller festivals occur during the rest of the year, and a free outdoor May Day concert in Piazza San Giovanni, organised by trade unions, usually attracts a star or two, plus crowds which can number hundreds of thousands.

Along Came Jazz
Various venues in Tivoli (07 74 33 15 97). Bus from Rebibbia. **Dates** early July. **Admission** free.
This jazz festival runs for two or three days at the beginning of July in Tivoli, just outside Rome, and features mainly Italian musicians, such as Antonello Salis, Pino Minafra, Mauro Orselli, together with international guests such as Evan Parker.

Fiesta Capannelle
Via Appia Nuova, 1,245 (78 34 65 87/71 82 139). Bus to Via Appia Nuova. **Dates** mid-June to Aug.
Admission L10,000.
Top international names in Latin American music perform here at Rome's major racecourse, where Latin American food and atmosphere abound.

Jazz and Image Festival
Villa Celimontana (70 49 50 05). Bus to Piazza della Navicella or Colosseum. **Dates** June-Aug. **Admission** L8,000.
Organised by the **Alexanderplatz** Jazz Club (*see above* **Jazz**), this is the best outside venue in which to hear jazz in summer. In the glorious Villa Celimontana, a formal garden dotted with ancient remains, international and local bands play under the spreading branches. There are also film and video projections.

RomaEuropa Festival
Various venues in Rome (47 42 286). **Dates** mid-June to Sept. **Box office** at individual venues. **Admission** depends on event.

This eclectic performing-arts festival now ranks as one of the top international events of its kind (*see also chapter* **Theatre & Dance**). Though it's the classical offerings that predominate, RomaEuropa has hosted the likes of Manu Dibango, Cesaria Evora and gypsy groups from Andalusia and Pakistan.

Roma Incontra il Mondo
Villa Ada, Via di Ponte Salaria (41 80 370). Bus to Via Salaria. **Dates** end June to September. **Admission** L5,000-L10,000.
One of the most beautiful sites in Rome: the banks of a small lake in the forested grounds of the Villa Ada. Roma Incontra il Monda (Rome Against the World) is a festival of world music, jazz and roots groups. There's food, a bar and a small market on site.

Roma Live Festival
Viale Olimpiadi, Largo de Bosis (44 23 32 26). Bus to Lungotevere Maresciallo Cadorna. **Dates** mid-June to end July. **Admission** L10,000.
The sports facilities around the Olimpico football stadium area provide a huge festival site during the summer months, with outdoor concerts, cinema, discos, restaurants and bars. It's one of the few venues that manages to get the big international names to play in Rome during the summer months.

Testaccio Village
Viale del Campo Boario (57 28 76 61). Bus to Piazza dell'Emporio or Via Galvani. **Dates** June-Sept.
Admission L10,000.
Many of Testaccio's clubs (*see chapter* **Nightlife**) move outside for the summer season, to this quiet area behind Rome's former slaughterhouse, the Mattatoio (*see chapter* **Sightseeing** *and* **Social Services** *page 204*). Concerts, which begin at 10pm, include international and Italian rock, jazz, Latin and funk. But come earlier for food, markets, stalls and bars, and stay later for the disco.

Nightlife

The night has a thousand dives.

The ancient Romans, who debauched and partied their Empire into the ground, would have had little time for their sedate, conformist descendants. For modern Romans, an exciting night out is a long lazy dinner and a stroll through the city centre with an ice cream. That said, there are a few good clubs, loads of flashy seventies-style discos, some interesting late bars, and the weird and wonderful world of the *Centri Sociali* (*see chapter* **Music**: **Rock Roots & Jazz**). Ibiza it isn't, but then Ibiza doesn't offer the stunning beauty of night-time Rome.

Party night is Saturday, when dedicated party animals hop in Daddy's car and head for the clubs of Rimini and RicciFone on the Adriatic coast – or even across the border into Slovenia, where raves are wild, with no regulations to check extremes.

The effect of this migration on Italian drink-related road deaths is dramatic.

The less adventurous – and less foolhardy – remain in in the capital. If you're a fan of commercial hip hop, Rome might be your idea of paradise. If not, one week's clubbing in the Eternal City and you'll never be able to listen to the Fugees again (assuming you could stand the omnipresent cover artists in the first place). What is known locally as 'black music' is what most clubs are playing. Failing this, the music tends to be garage or house. For something out of the ordinary, seek out alternative scenes. The *Centri Sociali* play host to most of Rome's independent and experimental music, not to mention after-hours bars, parties and raves (*see* **Social Services** *in chapter* **Music**: **Rock, Roots & Jazz**).

Gilda: *you've been warned (see page 212).*

Eat up – chefs here finish early (page 212).

American Bar - Piano Bar

An exclusive meeting place for a cocktail to listen some good music after dinner. From 11.00 a.m. to 02.00 p.m.

Ristorante - Piano Bar

An elegant restaurant with Italian and international cuisine and Grande Parte with selection of wines. Sale Privèe for reservation dinner. From 12.30 a.m. to 15.00 p.m. and from 19.30 p.m. to 01.00 p.m.

Bistrot

Straight on Via Veneto with a wonderful view of Porta Pinciana. From 12.00 a.m. to 24.00

Closed on Sunday and a week in mid Agoust
All credit cards accepted
For information and reservation: Harry's Bar Roma
Via Vittorio Veneto, 150
00187 Roma Tel. 06/484643 fax. 06/488311

PLACES

Discobars are popular in Rome, and there's no shortage of lively Irish pubs (*see chapter* **Pubs**). There is no central clubbing zone, although Testaccio (*see* **Dancing in the Dump** *page 214*) is emerging as one of the liveliest quarters in this respect. The area around Via della Pace has long been Rome's most fashionable night-time hangout, with a selection of late-opening bars. Trastevere and San Lorenzo also offer happy hunting grounds for bar-hopping, as does the well-heeled northern suburb of Parioli – though you'll feel out of place if you forget your husky, Timberland boots and four-wheel drive.

PRICES

Romans love not having to pay for things, and will exploit even the most tenuous connection with the owner/bouncer/DJ to avoid coughing up. In some places being female is enough simply to get past the man at the door. Entry prices for clubs are generally higher than in the UK or US – owners need to subsidise the freeloaders *and* compensate for Italians' very low levels of alcohol consumption. For what it's worth, your ticket usually includes a 'free' first drink.

Discobars and Clubs

Akab

Via Monte Testaccio, 69 (57 44 485). Metro Piramide/bus to Via Marmorata or Via Galvani. **Open** 10pm-4am Mon-Sat. **Admission** L15,000-25,000 depending on event.

This '80s-style designer-vibe venue hosts live acts followed by funk, soul and R&B. You might have to endure long queues, so try to make friends with the bouncers.

Alibi

Via Monte Testaccio, 39 (57 43 448). Metro Piramide/bus to Via Marmorata or Via Galvani. **Open** 11pm-4am Wed-Sun. **Admission** free Wed, Sun; L15,000 Thur, Fri; L20,000 Sat.

Rome's answer to Heaven. This gay club becomes more hetero-tolerant during summer months, when the glorious roof terrace is opened up. The basement disco has a great sound system, thumping out house hits and classics from the '70s and '80s.

Alien

Via Velletri, 13-19 (84 12 212). Bus to Piazza Fiume. **Open** 11pm-4am Tue-Sun. **Admission** L30,000-35,000 depending on event.

This big, flashy disco – one of Rome's most famous – comes with all the trimmings: strobes, scantily-clad dancers on the bar, two rooms with different DJs ... but the music tends to be a pretty uninspired mix of house, trance and garage. There are sometimes experimental evenings in the small room, with musicians playing along with the DJ. The crowd are mainly under-25s. The cringeworthy 'VIP room' is a serious turn-off.

Alpheus

Via del Commercio, 36 (57 47 826). Metro Piramide/bus to Via Ostiense. **Open** 10pm-4.30am Tue-Sun. **Admission** L10,000 Tue, Wed, Sun; L15,000 Thur-Sat.

A spacious multi-room venue in old industrial building, catering for a variety of live bands, theatre and cabaret, followed by DJs every night. The central pink bar, with its kitsch fountain and sculpture, demands to be seen. Students get in free on Wednesdays.

Anima

Via Santa Maria dell'Anima, 57 (68 64 021). Bus to Corso Vittorio Emanuele or Corso Rinascimento. **Open** 10.30pm-4am Tue-Sun. **Admission** L10,000 Mon, Wed-Sat; free Sun.

Wacky décor and central location by Piazza Navona make Anima worth a pitstop on your night out. It's more bar than disco, but the music can be good, varying from hip hop to house and jungle.

Summer Grooves

As temperatures rise, usually about mid-June, most clubs shut up shop. It's time to head for the water – either on the beach or along the river.

On the coast, **Fregene** and **Ostia** (*see chapter* **Trips out of Town**) come alive with clubs and bars, but they're a pale imitation of the scene at the Adriatic resort of Rimini, and have a nasty tendency to attract pushy teenyboppers and aging hipsters of the **Gilda** (*see* **Discobars and Clubs**) variety. If this appeals, try the slightly more acceptable **Gilda on the Beach** (see listing below) or take pot luck with the dozens of back-to-back discos on offer. Heaven Beach and La Playa in Ostia are old favourites, as are the Miraggio Club, Ciak 2 Mare and Tattou in Fregene. But remember, if you're not independently mobile, plan for long-term partying: public transport to Fregene and Ostia dries up around 10pm, and the first train back is after 5am.

Alternatively, stay in Rome and head north along the river, where the banks from Ponte Duca D'Aosta to Ponte Tor di Quinto hum with after-dark activity. A mishmash of bars, market stalls, live concerts and night clubs lurks below road level in atmospheric riverside locations which make up for the fake-tropical cheesiness of much of the décor. Organisers and precise locations change from year to year: check the local press for details (*see chapter* **Media**).

Gilda on the Beach, *Lungomare del Ponente, 11, Fregene (66 56 06 49).* **Open** *June-Oct.* 11pm-4am Tue-Sun. **Admission** L30,000 Tue, Wed; L35,000 Thur, Sun; L40,000 Sat.

B-Side

Via dei Funari, 21a (68 83 32 32). Bus to Piazza Venezia or Via del Teatro di Marcello. **Open** 11pm-4am Wed-Sun; 11pm-6am Fri-Sat. **Admission** free Wed; L10,000 Thur, Sun; L50,000 Fri, Sat.

Formerly very trendy, this small, smoky, sweaty late-night discobar plays mainly funk and 'black'.

Black Out

Via Saturnia, 18 (70 49 67 91). Metro Re di Roma/bus to Piazza Tuscolo. **Open** 10pm-4am Thur-Sat; 4.30-7.30pm, 10pm-4am Sun. **Admission** L15,000-20,000 depending on event.

Spooky gothic nights and Indie music are the speciality in this stalwart of the Rome club scene.

Bombastic Café

Corso Rinascimento, 70 (68 80 61 48). Bus to Corso Rinascimento. **Open** 9pm-3am Wed-Sun. **Admission** free Wed, Sun; L10,000 Thur-Sat.

Discobar playing 'black' to a funky mixed crowd.

Caffè Latino

Via di Monte Testaccio, 96 (57 44 020). Metro Piramide/bus to Via Marmorato or Via Galvani. **Open** 10.30pm-2.30am Wed-Fri; 10.30pm-4am Sat, Sun. **Admission** L10,000-20,000 depending on event.

Multi-room venue mixing live acts and DJs.

Cave

Via di Monte Testaccio, 68 (57 44 485). Metro Piramide/bus to Via Marmorata or Via Galvani. **Open** 10pm-3am Mon-Sat. **Admission** L15,000 Mon-Wed, Fri-Sat; L10,000 Thur.

A cool cave downstairs, a big bar upstairs and interesting music ranging from hip hop to ethno-jazz. A new venue that's worth a visit.

Circolo degli Artisti

Via Lamarmora, 28 (44 64 968). Metro Vittorio Emanuele/bus to Piazza Vittorio Emanuele. **Open** 9pm-3am Tue-Sun. **Admission** free Tue-Fri, Sun; L10,000 Sat.

Big, grungy venue which mixes live acts with DJs. Fridays are reggae, hip hop and jungle; Saturdays tend towards rock, thrash and heavy metal.

DDT

Via dei Sabelli, 2 (49 58 338) Bus or tram to Piazzale Verano. **Open** 10.30pm-3am Tue-Sun. **Admission** free.

One of the few late-night venues in the San Lorenzo district. A long underground bar and disco, playing anything from rock to Latin.

Gilda

Via Mario de' Fiori, 97 (67 84 838). Metro Spagna or Limousine/bus to Piazza San Silvestro. **Open** 11pm-4am Tue-Sun. **Admission** L40,000.

Don't even think about it unless you are (1) an aging film star, (2) a politician of the slimy variety, or (3) very rich/drunk/stupid. All silicone and no soul, Gilda is a dame you shouldn't touch with a pair of sterilized tongs.

Goa

Via Libetta, 13 (57 48 277). Metro Garbatella/bus to Via Ostiense. **Open** 11pm-4am Tue-Sat. **Admission** L20,000 Thur, Fri, Sat; L15,000 Tue, Wed.

New, ethnically-inspired club – incense, exotic artefacts, slide projections and those things you plug yourself into to chill out. Currently among Rome's trendiest. Music is hip hop via tribal to house, courtesy of Rome's DJ star Giancarlino.

Groove

Vicolo Savelli, 10 (68 72 427). Bus to Corso Vittorio Emanuele. **Open** 9pm-3am Tue-Sun. **Admission** free.

Discobar offering vast selection of cocktails and strictly 'black' music in its medieval-style basement.

Hang-out

Via Ostiense, 131 (57 83 146). Metro Garbatella/bus to Via Ostiense. **Open** 9pm-2am Tue-Sun. **Admission** Tue-Fri, Sun; L10,000 Sat.

Old-fashioned American-style discobar which serves food early in the evening and gets funky later with some of the best hip hop DJs in Rome.

Jazz Café

Via Zanardelli, 12 (68 61 990). Bus to Corso Rinascimento or Lungotevere Tor di Nona. **Open** noon-2am Mon-Sat; 11pm-3am Sun. **Admission** free.

Jazz, funk, and soul on two floors: spacious bar upstairs, sweaty disco downstairs.

MCA

Via di Villa Aquari, 4-6 (78 25 405). Bus to Piazza Zama. **Open** 11pm-4am Tue-Sat. **Admission** free.

Small, dark subterranean house/techno club with 'smart' bar. Great potential.

Piper

Via Tagliamento, 9 (84 14 459). Bus to Via Tagliamento or Corso Trieste. **Open** 11pm-4am Tue-Sun. **Admission** L25,000 Tue-Fri, Sun; L35,000 Sat.

A classic among Roman discos, this huge subterranean *Saturday Night Fever*-style venue launched many Italian pop stars of the '60s, many of whom are still about and have an alarming tendency to return to their roots (now heavily dyed) at the Piper. Saturday and Sunday Afternoon Fever sessions for teenagers.

Qube

Via di Portonaccio, 212 (43 81 005). Metro Tiburtina/bus to Via Tiburtina or Via di Portonaccio. **Open** 11pm-3am Fri-Sun. **Admission** L15,000.

Hugely successful club with classic disco lights and three bars, plus second-floor chill-out room with sofas and pool tables. Plays mainly underground, progressive and 'happy music'. Expect queues.

Radio Londra

Via di Monte Testaccio, 67 (57 50 04). Metro Piramide/bus to Via Marmorata or Via Galvani. **Open** 10.30pm-5am Wed-Mon. **Admission** L10,000-20,000 depending on event.

Small but very loud, plays only house and underground.

The Saint

Via Galvani, 46 (57 47 945). Metro Piramide/bus to Via Galvani or Via Marmorata. **Open** 11.30-4am Tue-Sat. **Admission** L15,000 Tue-Thur; L20,000 Fri, Sat.

New club with roof terrace in summer. Naff fake ancient Roman décor, the two floors symbolising heaven and hell. Incomprehensible music policy embracing live acts and DJs of all kinds – plus poetry readings.

Velvet

Via Cairoli, 29 (22 83 511). Metro Vittorio Emanuele/bus to Piazza Vittorio Emanuele. **Open** 10pm-4am Tue-Sat. **Admission** free Tue-Fri, Sun; L10,000 Sat.

Dark, gothic disco specialising in indie, industrial and post-punk weirdness on its pitch-dark dance floor. Great for self-conscious dancers or for trying out that new dance routine un-noticed. (Wear black.)

Eating late can be a problem in Rome. Turn up to the majority of restaurants at midnight and, even

Bright lights, big city: **Ponte Duca D'Aosta** *comes alive after dark (see page 211).*

if tables are still crowded, you're likely to be told *la cucina è chiusa* – the kitchen's closed and the cook's gone home. Pubs (*see chapter* **Pubs**) can be a good bet for late snacky dining, and some wine bars serve cold cuts and salads until well into the small hours.

The following restaurants and *pizzerie*, listed in *chapter* **Restaurants**, keep their kitchens open until late: Africa, Antico Arco, Da Baffetto, Ivo, Panattoni, Papà Baccus, Pizzeria della Pace, and Dar Poeta.

Bars in the centre, especially around **Campo de' Fiori** and **Via della Pace**, tend to stay open well into the morning.

Bar della Pace

Via della Pace, 4 ,5, 7 (68 61 216). Bus to Corso Rinascimento or Corso Vittorio Emanuele. **Open** 9am-2am daily.
For many years this has been Rome's prime posing spot. The ivy-clad location is as beautiful as the prices are horrific. A

must for first-time visitors to the Eternal City looking for a taste of old-style Roman glamour.

Bar del Fico

Piazza del Fico, 26-28 (68 65 205). Bus to Corso Rinascimento or Corso Vittorio Emanuele. **Open** 8am-2am daily.
Round the corner from the Bar della Pace, the Fico has come into its own in recent years, hiking prices accordingly and attracting a very cool crowd. Nice fig tree.

La Base

Via Cavour, 274 (47 40 659). Metro Cavour/bus to Via Cavour. **Open** 8pm-5am daily.
Combined bar and pizzeria which stays open all night, frequented into the wee hours by hungry clubbers and transvestites. Also open for lunch from noon to 4.30 every day except Tuesday.

The Drunken Ship

Piazza Campo de' Fiori, 20-21 (68 30 05 35). Bus to Largo di Torre Argentina or Via Arenula. **Open** 4pm-2am daily.
Big noisy bar, usually chock-full of American teeny-boppers.

Hemingway

Piazza delle Coppelle, 10 (68 64 490). Bus to Via del Corso or Corso Rinascimento. **Open** 8.30pm-2am daily.
Classy, decadent hole, with comfy sofas. Sunday brunch (11am-4pm) is highly recommended. A great winter bar.

Jonathan's Angels

Via della Fossa, 16 (68 93 426). Bus to Corso Rinascimento or Corso Vittorio Emanuele. **Open** 4pm-2am daily.
Spectacular in summer, with its abundant candles inside and out. The interior's decked out with kitsch religious-style paintings of Jonathan and his Harley. Great *fragolino* strawberry-flavoured wine, and far and away the best loo in Rome.

Selarum

Via dei Fienaroli, 12 (58 19 130). Bus to Piazza Sonnino. **Open** 9pm-2am daily June-Sept.
Bamboo seats and blue lighting create a laid-back garden atmosphere in Selarum's leafy courtyard. Serves cocktails and food (lunch 11am-3pm daily) and often has live music. Prices on the high side.

Stazione Ouagadougou

Via della Lungaretta, 75 (58 12 510). Bus to Piazza Sonnino. **Open** 10pm-2am Tue-Sun. **Admission** membership L5,000.
Gorgeous new African bar, awash with African art. Worth a visit just for the décor. Hosts art and photography exhibitions and live music every evening. Serves African food from a range of countries from Thursday to Sunday. Unpretentious and overwhelmingly friendly.

Vineria

Piazza Campo de' Fiori, 15 (68 80 32 68). Bus to Corso Vittorio Emanuele or Via Arenula. **Open** 10am-4pm, 6pm-2am, Mon-Sat.
Known to the *cognoscenti* as Giorgio's, the Vineria now runs a close second to the Colosseum as Rome's trademark monument. On summer evenings, the crowd spills out and takes over the Campo; in winter, it becomes more demure and cosy, so you can take your time browsing through the impressive wine selection or simply get your frozen lips around a Vecchia Romagna.

Zwinin-go

Via della Meloria, 78 (39 73 53 05). Bus to Piazza degli Eroi. **Open** 4pm-2am daily. **Admission** free.
One of the most congenial Internet cafés in Rome, with pristine décor, background music, beer on tap and home made cakes.

Newspapers

Late-night news-stands are a great Roman tradition, though if you want English-language papers you'll have to settle for the *International Herald Tribune*. Many vendors swap their innocuous daytime fare for an amazing display of porn after the sun goes down. Here are some options for party animals (*see also chapter* **Media**):
Via Veneto two stands in different places; **Via del Corso** right across from Piazza Colonna; **Piazza Cola di Rienzo** in Prati; **Piazza Ungheria** in Prati; **Piazza Sonnino** in Trastevere; **San Giovanni in Laterano** at the beginning of Via Appia Nuova; **Piazza del Cinquecento** in front of Termini station.

The Morning After...

There's only one way to finish your night on the town, and that's with a hot *cornetto* munched on a street corner. By the time most daytime bars open, party animals are well on their way to bed. So aim to swing through Trastevere on your way home, and stop off at the anonymous, unwelcoming *forno* (baker's) on Vicolo del Cinque. You'll be scowled at and ignored by the grumpy bakers there, but the *cornetti* are great, and you can draw comfort from the fact that even if you were Roman born and bred, you'd be treated in the same disrespectful fashion ... and you'd keep going back for more.

Dancing in the Dump

Just south of the Aventine hill, rising incongruously amid the apartment blocks of Testaccio, lies **Monte Testaccio**. Though it looks convincingly like a hill today, it is, in fact, a heap of some 53 million broken amphorae, flung there in the first and second centuries AD by environmentally-challenged dock workers. Buried into its flanks are cellar after cellar, and, as the evening gets going, those cellars are packed with happy clubbers.

In a city which has long lacked a night time mecca, Monte Testaccio (also known as *Monte dei Cocci* – Shard Mountain) has filled a massive gap. Rome's veteran gay club **L'Alibi** paved the way, causing many raised eyebrows when it took up position just a couple of doors down

from the exclusive **Checchino dal 1887** restaurant (*see chapters* **Gay Rome** *and* **Restaurants**). Very gradually, the idea began to catch on. Here, after all, was a unique space at low rents with ample parking, just minutes from the centre of town. And, with ancient pots protruding every which way, it was an interior designer's dream.

A quick glance at the listings says it all. Where once a club-hopping evening in Rome cost a fortune in taxi fares, today it can be one-stop shopping. In summer, it's even simpler: many of the clubs move outdoors and join together to present live bands, discos, bars in the collective **Testaccio Village** in the shadow of the hill.

Sport & Fitness

Romans would rather talk about it than do it.

Romans are passionate about sport, although considerably more passion goes into spectating than participating. Which is perhaps just as well, because the city provides far more and far better facilities for professionals than it does for amateurs.

The 1960 Olympic Games and the 1990 soccer World Cup left Rome with a legacy of high-class professional facilities, although much of the money allocated to the World Cup was frittered away on meaningless prestige projects. Most sports centres, especially in accessible central areas, are private, and require a hefty annual membership fee. If, on the other hand, you want to experience sport the traditionally Roman way, you could do worse than catching a soccer game at the Stadio Olimpico.

Soccer

Rome has two clubs, AS Roma and Lazio, which share the Stadio Olimpico on the north bank of the Tiber. City derbies are hotly contested affairs, but violence is rare. As with almost everything else in Italy, Roman soccer is highly politicised: Roma's supporters traditionally hail from the working-class left, while Lazio is the team of the right, drawing support from the wealthy Parioli district and the surrounding countryside.

The Italian Cup is a second-rate affair, with most attention focused on the League Championship. League games are played on Sunday, with Cup and European games played during the week, usually on Wednesdays. Tickets can be bought directly from the Olimpico box office (32 37 333), from the merchandising outlets listed below, and from Orbis (*Piazza Esquilino, 37; 48 27 403; Metro Termini/bus to Piazza Esquilino*). The most devoted fans opt for the *Curva Nord* and *Curva Sud* (north stand and south stand), where tickets are cheapest (*see* **Sunday Sport** *page 218*).

The following shops stock official strips and merchandise:

Lazio Point

Via Farini, 34 (48 26 768). Metro Vittorio Emanuele/bus to Piazza Vittorio Emanuele or Via Principe Amedeo. **Open** 3.30-7.30pm Mon; 9.30am-1pm, 3.30-7.30pm, Tue-Sat. **Credit** AmEx, MC, V.

The **Stadio Olimpico** was built for the 1960 Olympics and later hosted Italia 90.

La Piscina delle Rose, *part of Mussolini's abortive Universal Expo.*

Roma Shop

Via Paolina, 8 (48 21 664). Bus to Piazza Esquilino or Via Merulana. **Open** 9am-1pm, 3.30-7.30pm, Mon-Sat. **Credit** AmEx, MC, V.

Golf

Golf is an exclusive game in Italy. In most clubs, including those listed below, you have to produce a membership card of a club at home, together with your handicap, before you're allowed to play. It is not normally necessary to be introduced by a member. Fees, including those quoted below, are normally charged per day rather than per round.

Circolo del Golf di Roma

Via Appia Nuova, 717a (78 03 407). Metro Colli Albani, then taxi. **Open** 8am-sunset Tue-Sun. **Rates** L80,000 Tue-Fri; L110,000 Sat, Sun. Clubs L35,000. Driving range L18,000 Tue-Fri; L35,000 Sat, Sun (use of range included in green fees).
You can take part in competitions on Sundays.

Country Club Castelgandolfo

Via Santa Spirito, 13 (91 23 01). Metro Anagnina, then taxi. **Open** 8.30-8pm Tue-Sun. **Closed** two weeks Aug. **Rates** L60,000 Tue-Fri; L100,000 Sat, Sun. Electric cart L70,000. Trolley L10,000. Clubs L30,000. Driving range L10,000 (included in green fees).
This club outside Rome was designed by American architect Robert Trent Jones inside a volcanic crater, and is overlooked by a sixteenth-century club house.

Gyms

Many of Rome's gyms are as snooty as they are expensive, and unless you're wearing all the latest gear and have a perfect figure you may feel a mite self-conscious. Although public gyms exist, they are few and far between and hard to find. Some of the more luxurious hotels have their own. The following facilities are private.

Body Image
Via Enrico Fermi, 142 (55 73 356). Bus to Via Gugliemo Marconi. **Open** 9.30am-9pm. **Closed** Aug. **Rate** L80,000 per month.
This women-only centre offers all kinds of health treatment. No sign-up fee required. The facilities include weight room, aerobics and a sauna.

Navona Health Centre
Via dei Banchi Nuovi, 39 (68 96 104). Bus to Corso Rinascimento or Corso Vittorio Emanuele. **Open** 9am-9pm Mon-Fri; Sat 11am-8pm. **Closed** Aug. **Rates** daily L15,000; monthly L100,000.
Small gym where you don't need to be introduced by a member or pay a sign-up fee. Includes sauna, two fitness rooms, weights and changing rooms.

Roman Sports Center
Villa Borghese, Via del Galoppatoio, 33 (32 01 667/32 18 096/32 23 665). Bus to Via Veneto. **Open** *Sept-May* 9am-10pm Mon-Sat; Sun 9am-3pm. **Rates** L2,000,000 per year; L25,000 per day.
Strictly speaking, you should be introduced by a member, but the rules are often bent. Rome's largest health centre includes two aerobic rooms, sun beds, saunas, hydromassage pools, two gyms, squash courts and two Olympic-size swimming pools. There is a second centre (the original one) at Largo Somalia, 60 (*86 21 24 11/86 21 24 81; bus to end of Viale Libia*).

Jogging

Crowds of people and omnipresent cars make a jog through central Rome a memorably unpleasant experience. The best bet is to make for one of the parks.

The leafy avenues of **Villa Borghese** are popular with locals at weekends, when you can hire rollerblades and bikes when your feet get tired. Roman joggers opt for **Villa Doria Pamphili**, which has work-out stations along the trail. Other options are **Villa Ada**, with paths running between ponds and lakes, **Parco di Monte Mario** for a stiff, uphill workout, and **Parco della Caffarella**, between the Via Appia Nuova and Via Appia Antica. For a feel of Ancient Rome, try working out in the **Circo Massimo**, but go early or late as it gets crowded with tourists during the day. Serious runners congregate on the stretch of lawn running along **Via delle Terme di Caracalla**, opposite the ancient Roman baths of the same name.

The Rome City marathon, held each spring, is slowly making a name for itself in international running circles, though it remains an essentially Roman event. A city-to-sea race is also held during the spring (*see chapter* **Rome by Season**).

Swimming

Despite Rome's torrid summer temperatures, pools are not numerous and, apart from a few far-flung exceptions, those that do exist are privately run. The beaches near Rome are not particularly inviting; you're better off making a day of it and exploring some of the nearby coast (*see chapter* **Trips out of Town**).

Alternatively, head for one of the following private pools:

Oasi della Pace
Via degli Eugenii, 2, Via Appia Antica (71 84 550). Accessible by taxi. **Open** *June-mid-Sept*, 9.30am-6pm daily. **Rates** L15,000 Mon-Fri; L18,000 Sat, Sun.
A pleasant open-air pool surrounded by high hedges and cypresses. Simple facilities.

La Piscina delle Rose
Viale America, 20, EUR (59 26 717). Bus to Palasport. **Open** *June-Sept* 9am-7pm daily. **Rates** L18,000 full day, L13,000 half day (9am-2pm; 2pm-7pm), L7,000 1pm-4pm. Ten-day ticket L120,000.
Open-air pool in the centre of Mussolini's purpose-built Rome business suburb, constructed in the 1930s for the Universal Expo which never took place.

Hotel Pools

Most international chains have pools that can be used by non-residents.

Cavalieri Hilton
Via Cadlolo, 101, Monte Mario (35 09 29 50). Bus to Piazzale Medaglie D'Oro. **Open** *May-Sept* 9am-7pm daily. **Rates** L70,000 Mon-Fri; L80,000 Sat, Sun (children under 12 half price).
Luxurious hotel pool with fabulous views down Monte Mario hill across Rome. Prices include towel and use of showers. A covered pool is currently being built.

Holiday Inn
Via Aurelia Antica, 415 (66 42). Bus from Largo Fiorentini to Aurelia Antica/infrequent Holiday Inn shuttle bus service from Pantheon. **Open** *June-Sept* 9am-7pm daily. **Rates** L40,000 Mon-Fri; L50,000 Sat, Sun.
Located along one of ancient Rome's consular roads, beyond the Villa Pamphili park. The hotel also offers a rather complicated system of monthly, two-weekly and seasonal swimming passes.

Parco dei Principi
Via M Mercadante, 15 (85 44 21). Bus to Via Mercadante/tram to Viale Rossini. **Open** *May-Sept*, 10am-6pm daily. **Rates** L45,000 Mon-Fri; L60,000 Sat, Sun.
An outside pool, set in its own gardens, and much favoured by local swimmers (especially at weekends). There's a 20 per cent discount for children.

Tennis

Circolo della Stampa
Piazza Mancini (32 32 452). Bus to Piazza Mancini. **Open** 8am-11pm Mon-Fri; 8am-8pm Sat, Sun. **Court hire** L16,000 for 50 minutes. Floodlights L6,000.
Owned by the Italian journalists' association, but friendly

and open to non-members, the *Circolo* offers both clay and synthetic grass courts. No dress code but studded trainers are not allowed.

SC Ostiense

Via del Mare, 128 (59 15 540). **Open** 9am-6.30pm daily. **Closed** Aug. **Rates** L16,000 (singles/hour); L24,000 (doubles/hour). Floodlights: L10,000.
Friendly club with no membership conditions. Book at least two days before, as it can get crowded.

Riding

I due Laghi

Localita' La Quercia (99 60 70 59).Train to Anguillara from Ostiense or Trastevere, then a long walk. **Open** 9am-1pm, 3pm-sunset, Tue-Sun. **Rates** Trekking (in groups with a guide) L30,000/hour; L50,000/two hours. Lessons L30,000/hour; L250,000/eight lessons.
Best reached by car, this riding school is lodged between Lakes Bracciano and Martignano. There is a restaurant for lunch and evening meals.

Il Galoppatoio

Villa Borghese, Via del Galoppatoio, 25 (32 26 797). Metro Spagna/bus to Via Veneto. **Open** 8.30-6pm Tue-Sat; 8.30-2pm Sun. **Closed** Aug. **Rates** Sign-up fee L400,000 per year. Lessons L300,000 (minimum 10 lessons, plus L.35,000 insurance). Under 18s: sign-up fee L100,000 per year. Lessons L200,000 per month.
Rome's most exclusive riding club, deep in the Villa Borghese, has a predictably snooty atmosphere and prices to go with it. You must take a doctor's certificate with you. Lessons last one hour and can be booked between 8-10am or 3-6pm.

Enjoy the ride of your life at **Il Gallopatoio**.

Sunday Sport

Standing among the raucous Roma supporters who throng the *Curva Sud* (South Stand) of the Stadio Olimpico at any Sunday home game, you might assume that one of Italy's premier soccer clubs was on show. Not true. Roma has failed to make top form for more than a decade, and its undying appeal owes more to a combination of myth and wishful thinking than it does to goal-scoring.

The tone is set for the pre-match build-up with banner headlines in the city's *Corriere dello Sport* newspaper: 'Roma, make our dreams come true!' In cafés, young men discuss form and old ones harp fondly back to *la magica*, the Roma team which won the championship in 1982-3, as they gamely predict overwhelming victory for the home side on their *schedina* (pools coupon).

Come Monday morning, Roma's inevitable heavy defeat is being put down to sheer bad luck. Two weeks later, the team's supporters unfailingly return to the 85,000-capacity stadium, host to the 1990 World Cup final, to go through the whole process again.

Not even the hardest evidence will persuade a Roma fan to concede that any other team is superior. Turin's Juventus may have won the League 24 times in its history, against Roma's meagre two post-war victories, but what's a trophy more or less compared to the collective pride from supporting the capital's 'original' team?

Particular scorn is reserved for the city's other team Lazio, Roma's arch-enemy – especially since it began buying up foreign stars and beating Roma in the League table. The *giallorossi* (red and yellow) army will tell you Lazio are false pretenders to the Roman football crown, despite the fact that Lazio was founded 27 years before Roma, in 1900. And if history goes against them, they'll happily resort to myth: Roma's wolf is cited by die-hards as proof that their side is just as legendary as Romulus and Remus.

Armed with this information, the exuberance of the *Curva Sud* may not seem quite so over-the-top. And at the end of each season, bar-stool oracles gather to predict a great year for Roma ... next year.

Theatre & Dance

Rome has some spectacular venues and great summer festivals, but you have to search very hard to find any innovative or cutting-edge performances.

Rome can seem a sleepy backwater to drama and dance enthusiasts familiar with the scene in other European capitals, but a night out at the theatre here has a flavour of its own.

First, there is the pleasure of watching theatre-going Romans: theatres are the city's see-and-be-seen venues *par excellence*. Then there are Rome's 80-plus theatres themselves, many of which are truly beautiful: the **Teatro dell'Opera** with its frescos, plush red and gold seats and boxes and enormous glittering central chandelier, the **Teatro Argentina** with its glamorous interiors and perfect proportions, the smaller **Teatro Valle** which resembles a miniature Opera House, and the modern **Teatro Vascello** with its wooden amphitheatre structure contrasting with stark black walls.

The main season runs from October to May, with different theatres sticking firmly to their own specialities. Costly productions directed by star stage-directors such as Luca Ronconi, Giorgio Strehler and Gabriele Lavia are to be found on the programme of the publicly-funded **Teatro Argentina** (also known as the Teatro di Roma). The Teatro Argentina occasionally hosts dance performances as well, but because they're so rare, the city's entire dance-related population turns up, along with the *glitterati*, so tickets are hard to get.

The **Teatro Nazionale** favours popular Italian comedies along the lines of the Neapolitan School of Edoardo De Filippo; the **Teatro Valle**'s programme usually includes productions of reworked Greek Classical theatre, Russian repertoire and works by modern British and American playwrights translated into Italian; while the **Teatro Quirino** features a rather traditional programme of classic Italian works, *Commedia dell'Arte, Comedie Française* and the odd contemporary piece. The fashionable **Teatro Sistina** is the place to go for musicals and light Italian musical comedies, while the **Teatro Vittoria** specialises in international box office hits translated into Italian.

The best venue for viewing fringe theatre – of which there is much of vastly differing quality –

is the **Vascello**, which also hosts dance and theatre conferences, lectures and workshops.

Foreign Academies occasionally organise arts festivals in the city and they tend to favour the **Palazzo delle Esposizioni** (*see chapter* **Museums & Galleries**) as the venue for what are often excellent avant-garde productions.

The **Teatro Agorà** holds a brief season of international theatre in English, French and Spanish, while the **Colosseo Ridotto** presents English language shows every Monday.

DANCE

Dance enthusiasts should head for the **Teatro Olimpico**, which has Rome's best dance stage and excellent acoustics. The Olimpico is home to the Accademia Filarmonica Romana and always carries at least five or six dance events in its very varied and usually high-class annual music season. The Filarmonica tries hard to please everyone with a programme that takes in the popular (Momix, Joaquin Cortés), the beautiful (Les Ballets de Montecarlo, the Balletto di Toscana), the ethnic (Flamenco y Kata), the contemporary and high-brow (Susanne Linke, Michael Clarke) and a dance theatre production (Moni Ovadia, Lindsay Kemp).

Rome's opera house, the magnificently plush late 19th century **Teatro dell'Opera**, always includes a few classical ballets in its season, but administrative and political problems have resulted in a disrupted artistic management and the *corps de ballet* is in a sorry state, although international *etoiles* often lend their glittering presence on the first few nights.

Finding dance outside these mainstream venues is not easy: watch out for posters announcing alternative events which, though often hastily arranged, can prove rewarding. It is during summer that Rome comes into its own, with festival organisers taking advantage of dramatic city backdrops to stage both dance and drama events (*see box:* **Under the Stars**).

Rome-based dailies such as *La Repubblica* and *Il Messaggero* carry theatre and dance listings, as do the monthly *Time Out Roma* magazine and the weekly *Roma C'e'* – which has a token English section at the back. Tickets can be bought at theatres themselves or at box office agencies (*see chapter* **Services**).

Theatres

Palazzo delle Esposizioni
Via Nazionale, 194 (47 45 903). Bus to Via Nazionale/Metro Repubblica. **Open** 10am-9pm Mon, Wed-Sun. **Closed** Tue.
Mainly an exhibition venue, Rome's only multi-cultural arts centre has a cinema, lecture hall and a dance space. It also has a bar and roof-garden restaurant.

Teatro Argentina
Largo di Torre Argentina, 52 (68 80 4601/2). Bus to Largo di Torre Argentina. **Box office** 10am-2pm, 3-7pm, Mon-Sat. **Shows** *Oct-June* 9pm Mon-Wed, Fri, Sat; 5pm Thur, Sun.
Beautiful official seat of the Teatro di Roma, with a range of exchange programmes and productions in conjunction with other state-subsidised theatres.

Teatro Belli
Piazza Sant'Apollonia, 11a (58 94 875). Bus to Lungotevere Sanzio, Piazza Sonnino. **Box office** 4.30-9pm Tue-Sat. **Shows** *Sept-May* 9pm Tue-Sat; 5.30pm Sun.
Small, private theatre with an emphasis on Italian plays. Named after Rome's great dialect poet, Giuseppe Gioachino Belli (*see chapter* **Sightseeing: Trastevere**), it was set up as a showcase for dialect theatre.

Teatro Colosseo
Via Capo d'Africa, 5 (70 04 932). Bus to Colosseum/Metro Colosseo. **Box office** 8-10pm Tue-Sat. **Shows** *Sala Grande* 9pm Tue-Sa, 5.30pm Sun; *Ridotto Sala A* 8.45pm Tue-Sat, 5pm Sun; *Ridotto Sala B* 10.30pm Tue-Sat, 7pm Sun.
Run by the *associazione culturale* Beat 72, the Colosseo provides a showcase for young Italian directors and actors outside the state-subsidised theatres. Original, avant-garde productions are held in the theatre's three different spaces.

Teatro degli Artisti
Via S. Francesco di Sales, 14 (68808438). Bus to Trastevere. **Box office** from 7.30pm until beginning of show.
Mainly a contemporary dance stage, it also makes space for young experimental theatre groups.

Teatro della Cometa
Via del Teatro Marcello, 4 (67 84 380). Bus to Piazza Venezia. **Box office** 9am-7pm Tue-Sat; 10am-1pm Sun. **Shows** 9.15pm Tue-Sat; 5pm Sun.
A fringe theatre staging farces and social commentaries by the 'new generation' of Italian playwrights, directors and actors.

Teatro Eliseo
Via Nazionale, 183 (48 82 114). Bus to Via Nazionale. **Box office** 10am-1pm, 4-7pm, Tue-Sun. **Shows** 8.45pm Tue, Thur-Sat; 5pm Wed, Sat, Sun.
A huge, rather dreary theatre, which nevertheless is an important venue for mainstream productions.

Teatro Ghione
Via delle Fornaci, 37 (63 72 294). Bus to Piazza di Porta Cavalleggeri. **Box office** 10.30am-1pm, 4-8pm, Tue-Sun. **Shows** 9pm Tue, Wed, Fri, Sat; 5pm Thur, Sun.

A velvet-swathed Victorian theatre holding theatrical and musical productions and run by formidable Italian actress Ileana Ghione.

Teatro Greco
Via Ruggero Leoncavallo, 16 (8607513). Bus to Largo Somalia. **Shows** 9pm.
New dance venue connected to one of the city's most important dance schools.

Teatro Nazionale
Via del Viminale, 51 (48 54 98/48 70 614). Metro Termini. **Box office** 10am-7pm daily, Sept-May. **Shows** 9pm Tue, Thur, Fri; 4.30pm Mon; 4.30pm, 9pm Sat; 5.30pm Sun.
The flagship of the ETI – the Italian Theatre Board, the powerful state-run body which is responsible for distributing funds amongst theatres – reopened a few years back, specialising in light comedy and musical classics, including the works of Edoardo de Filippo.

Teatro Olimpico
Piazza Gentile da Fabriano, 17 (32 34 936). Bus to Piazza Mancini. **Box office** 11am-7pm daily. **Shows** 9pm daily, Oct-May.
Vast theatre with excellent acoustics and a programme divided between music, dance and theatre.

Teatro Orione
Via Tortona, 9 (77 20 6960). Metro Furio Camillo. **Box office** opens one hour before performance.
A modest parish theatre putting on the occasional dance production.

Teatro dell'Opera
Via Firenze, 72 (48 16 02 55/48 17 003). Metro Termini, Repubblica/bus to Via Nazionale. **Box office** 10.45am-5pm; closed Mon.
Rome's official venue for opera, dance and symphonic concerts is a beautiful opera house with excellent acoustics. Since losing permission to use the Roman Baths of Caracalla as their summer season venue, the artists have become nomads in the city during July and August, changing abode depending on the whims of (very whimsical) city administrators.

Teatro dell'Orologio
Via de' Filippini, 17a (68 30 8735/68 30 8330). Bus to Corso Vittorio Emanuele. **Box office** 4-8pm Tue-Sat; 4-6pm Sun, Sept-June. **Shows** *Sala Grande* 9pm Tue-Sat, 5.30pm Sun; *Sala Caffèteatro* 9pm Tue-Sat, 6pm Sun; *Sala Orfeo* 9pm Tue-Sat, 5pm Sun.
Leading fringe theatre with texts by contemporary authors.

Teatro Quirino
Via Marco Minghetti, 1 (67 94 585). Bus to Via del Corso, Piazza Venezia. **Box office** 10am-1pm, 3-9pm, Tue-Sat; 10am-1pm, 3.30-5pm, Sun. **Shows** 9pm Tue, Fri, Sat; 5pm Wed, Thur, Sun.
ETI-owned venue used for productions of serious classics and tragedies by big name directors and major Italian casts.

Salone Margherita Bagaglino
Via Due Macelli (67 91 439/67 98 269). Metro Spagna. **Box office** 9am-1pm Mon-Sat. **Shows** 9.30pm Mon-Fri; 10.30pm Sat.
Rome's nearest equivalent to a Parisian dinner-theatre, frequented by the city's upper crust.

The innovative **Teatro Valle**. *See page 222.*

Teatro Sistina
*Via Sistina, 129 (48 26 841). Bus to Piazza Barberini/
Metro Barberini.* **Box office** 10am-1pm, 3.30-7pm, daily.
Shows 9pm Tue-Sat; 5pm Sun.
Glitzy Italian musicals and even glitzier international musical box office hits alternate here with concerts and prize-giving ceremonies.

Teatro Valle
*Via del Teatro Valle, 23a (68 80 37 94). Bus to Corso
Vittorio Emanuele, Corso Rinascimento.* **Box office**
10am-7pm Tue-Sun; 10am-1pm Sun. **Shows** 9pm Tue,
Fri, Sat; 5pm Wed, Thur, Sun.
A beautiful little theatre, with one of the city's most interesting repertoires, including some very good reworkings of old classics.

Teatro Vascello
*Via Giacinto Carini, 72, Monteverde (58 81 021). Bus to
Via Carini.* **Box office** 8.30pm Tue-Sat; 4.30pm Sun.
Shows 9pm Tue-Sat; 5pm Sun.
The Teatro Vascello is mostly known for some fairly decent experimental theatre and dance productions, but it is also used as a venue for conferences and workshops. Usually something going on.

Teatro Vittoria
*Piazza Santa Maria Liberatrice, 8 (57 40 170/57 40
598). Bus to Via Marmorata.* **Box office** 10am-1pm, 4-7pm, Mon; 10am-7pm Tue-Sat; 10am-1pm Sun. **Shows**
9pm Tue-Sat; 5pm Sun.
Cavernous venue in Testaccio's main square, specialising in translated texts and international variety.

Under the Stars

There are few things lovelier than sitting on the old stone tiers of the Roman Anfiteatro del Tasso on the Gianicolo hill on a mellow summer's night with the hum of crickets in one ear and Plautus in the other. Better still, grab a cushion and head for Ostia Antica where top international theatre events take place in the breathtaking amphitheatre at the heart of the ancient ruined city.

For if Rome's theatre and dance offerings can appear tame during the winter, the summer season offers not only high-class productions but settings which no other city in the world can beat.

Many of the best shows come under the aegis of the RomaEuropa festival, once a small but impressive summer happening organised by the French Academy, but now a major date in the international performing arts calendar, stretching for months and taking place in a host of atmospheric venues scattered around the city.

Also responsible for a stunning annual under-the-stars season of dance and opera is the **Teatro dell'Opera** (*see* **Theatres**) which, however, has a nasty habit of running into bureaucratic obstacles, and has therefore been forced to change venues several times in recent years. The spectacular towering ruins of the Baths of Caracalla provided a backdrop for dancers and opera singers for many years until the cultural heritage ministry decided that the vibrations were putting too much strain on the monument. Piazza di Siena, deep in the Borghese Gardens, has also done service as the Teatro's summer home. For the 1997 season, the outdoor theatre of the Accademia Nazionale di Danza on the leafy Aventine Hill hosted the Teatro dell'Opera's dance programme.

But summer offerings do not stop at these high-profile events. Courtyards and gardens are alive with performances; the problem is finding them. Keep your eyes on the wall posters all over the city, and consult the local press for listings.

Anfiteatro della Quercia del Tasso
*Passeggiata del Gianicolo (57 50 827). Bus to Piazza
Sonnino, 100 Trastevere night service.* **Box office**
from 7pm each evening at the Anfiteatro; 9am-2pm
daily at Teatro Anfitrione, Via San Saba, 24. **Shows**
9.15pm Mon-Sat, July-Sept; occasional afternoon
matinees.
An ancient amphitheatre with a spectacular view over Rome, specialising in classic Greek and Latin, and 18th-century Venetian comedy. Matinee performances of special productions for children.

Fondazione RomaEuropa
*Via XX Settembre, 3 (47 42 286, 47 42 308). Bus to
Piazza Venezia.* **Box office** varies from venue to
venue, tickets sold at major booking agencies (*see*
chapter **Services**) or at individual venues.
The brainchild of Rome's highly active French Academy, this world-class performing arts festival has expanded exponentially year by year. It now involves many other foreign academies, and receives some funding from the city council.

Giardino degli Aranci
*Via di Santa Sabina, Aventino (39 73 9700). Metro
Circo Massimo.* **Box office** from 8.30pm Tue-Sun.
Shows 9pm Tue-Sun.
This beautiful park on the Aventine hill is transformed into a theatre for the summer, with spectators seated at tables among the orange trees. One play per season, often classic comedies and tragedies.

Teatro Romano di Ostia Antica
*Ostia Antica (68 75 445). Metro Magliana and train
to Ostia Antica.* **Box office** from 6pm daily; also at
Teatro Argentina (*see above*). **Shows** 8.30pm daily,
July.
This wonderfully-preserved Roman amphitheatre, set amid the ruins of ancient Rome's main port, hosts prestigious productions of Roman and Greek classics (*see*
chapter **Trips out of Town**).

Trips Out of Town

Trips Out of Town

Can't stand the heat? Then escape into the mountains, villages and beaches of the Roman countryside.

Getting There

By Bus

The Lazio transport authority **COTRAL** (*see* chapter **Directory**) has bus services to nearly all destinations within the region. Buses leave from several termini within Rome, each serving a different direction and following roads that roughly correspond to the ancient Roman highways, now modified as state roads (*strade statali* or SS). Places further afield are served by private lines from Rome, or other regional companies. Many have offices in or near Piazza dei Cinquecento or Piazza della Repubblica. For schedules and fares, visit the *capolinea* (terminus) you need, or phone for information – even though staff are usually Italian-speaking only and getting through can be well-nigh impossible.

COTRAL Information
Via Volturno, 65 (59 15 551/2/3/4). Bus to Piazza dei Cinquecento. **Open** 8am-1.40pm, 2.10-4.40pm, Mon-Fri; 8am-1.40pm Sat.

COTRAL Termini
Anagnina (*Metro Anagnina*).
For Ciampino, Castelli Romani and Frosinone (Via Appia/Casalina, SS7/SS6).
Lepanto (*Metro Lepanto/bus to Viale Giulio Cesare*).
For the coastal route north (Cerveteri, Civitavecchia, Tarquinia) and Lake Bracciano (Via Aurelia, SS1).
EUR Fermi (*Metro EUR Fermi/bus to Viale America*).
For the coastal route south: Latina, Anzio, Terracina (Via Pontina, SS148).
Rebibbia (*Metro Rebibbia/bus to Via Tiburtina/Rebibbia.*)
For Tivoli and the east (Via Tiburtina, SS5).
Saxa Rubra (*Train from Piazzale Flaminio.*)
For Viterbo and the north (Via Cassia/Flaminia, SS2/SS3).

By Road

Rome is surrounded by a ring road, the *Grande Raccordo Anulare* (GRA), which links up with the motorways (*autostrade*) and *strade statali* (SS). It is currently having a third lane added around its whole length, a project due for completion by the year 2000, but meanwhile tending to cause chronic hold-ups. No doubt they'll then start on the fourth lane.

From Rome, *autostrada* A1 leads to Florence and the north, A24 to the Adriatic coast, A2 to Naples and the south, and A12 to Civitavecchia and then by state road to Livorno. Motorways are

quick, but tolls are fairly steep. You can save on time (but not costs) at toll stations by using a motorway card (Viacard), available from *tabacchi* shops (*see chapter* **Directory**). The ring road also links the *statali*. Be aware that these are commonly known by their ancient names – Aurelia, Salaria, Tiburtina and so on – rather than their numbers, even on road signs. Most state roads leading from Rome follow the line of ancient roads, and although they often have spectacular views they can be quite slow. Signposting can be very efficient, non-existent, or an infuriating combination of the two.

Before setting off on longer journeys it is advisable to check whether there may be delays due to road works. Ring the ACI automobile club's 24-hour travel information number, 44 77 (English-speaking staff). For details of the ACI and further information on driving in Italy and on car hire companies, *see* chapter **Directory**: **Getting Around**.

By Train

Train tickets can be bought at stations or travel agents with the FS (Ferrovie dello Stato – State Railways) sign. At Termini and other main stations there are automatic ticket machines with instructions in most western European languages. There is a 20 per cent discount on FS services for those aged under 26 with the Carta Verde card (L40,000 for one year), and occasional family discounts. The faster Intercity (IC) and Eurocity (EC) trains require supplements, and bookings are often obligatory (an R inside a square on train timetables indicates this). The supplements are paid for and bookings made at special ticket windows marked *prenotazioni* (bookings), which should issue tickets as well. Windows marked *biglietti*, on the other hand, cannot handle supplements or bookings – bear this in mind if you've arrived at the station with seconds to spare. When travelling on IC or ES trains you can apply for a refund if the train is delayed for over an hour.

You must stamp your ticket – and any supplement you may have – in the yellow machines at the head of each platform before boarding the train: failure to do this can result in a hefty fine. (However, being foreign, looking forlorn, and not understanding the

Ostia Antica: *take a step back in time ...*

... and see some flawless remains.

Car-free Jaunts

If you're dying to get out of Rome, but can't face risking tenuous public transport connections in Lazio's far-flung villages, try one of the following simple jaunts:

Castel Gandolfo – summer residence of the popes, this pretty town above Lago Albano is reached by a wonderfully picturesque train ride from the *stazione laziale* section of Termini station (40 mins).

Cerveteri – there is a coach service from Lepanto (1hr 20mins), but why not follow in the footsteps of DH Lawrence, who opted for the train to Cerveteri station (50 mins)... then panted dramatically through the 6km hike up to the necropolis. You can read all about his ordeal in *Etruscan Places* (see **Further Reading** *page 266*).

Ostia Antica – a beautifully-preserved Roman port just half an hour's train ride from the Roma-Lido station next to Metro Piramide. Five minutes' walk to the site at the other end.

Sabaudia – this surprisingly pleasant fascist-era beach resort has some of the cleanest water near Rome. Take the coach from EUR Fermi Metro station (2 hrs).

Tivoli – the coach from Rebibbia to the main square in Tivoli takes little over half an hour (make sure you take the one with a sign saying *autostrada* on its windscreen, or you'll find yourself held up in traffic along the old *strada statale*) and leaves you within strolling distance of the Villa D'Este and the Villa Gregoriana. Ask to be set down below the town if you want the Villa Adriana.

Trevignano – for a refreshing plunge in the clean waters of Lake Bracciano, take the coach from Lepanto to the walled town of Trevignano (40 mins). Alternatively, trains from Trastevere or Ostiense (near Piramide Metro) station will take you to the town of Bracciano (1 hr 10mins): a leafy flight of steps leads down to the water.

And further afield

Orvieto – just over the border into Umbria, Orvieto and its dramatic *duomo*, complete with newly-restored Signorelli frescoes, can be reached by train in just over an hour from Termini or Orvieto.

Spoleto – another Umbrian town and setting for the annual Two Worlds performing art festival (see chapter **Music: Classical and Opera**), but worth a visit in its own right, for its spectacular Roman viaduct and its cathedral. Train from Termini (1 hr 30 mins).

---

language should get you off with all but the nastiest ticket collector if you forget.) Booking seats on regular services is sometimes advisable, especially if you're travelling at peak times (Friday evening/Saturday morning/Sunday evening). There is a standard booking fee of L4,500. Though ticket windows at major stations display credit card symbols, their policy in this area was rather haphazard at time of writing. After years of only accepting cards issued in Italy, a seemingly indiscriminate selection of foreign-issue cards are now accepted at any given station or window. Most travel agents persist in accepting cash only for train tickets.

Ostia Antica

If it weren't for the lack of the dramatic backdrop of Vesuvius, Ostia Antica would be as famous as Pompeii: it certainly conveys what contemporary life was like in a working Roman town. It was Rome's main port for over 600 years, until its decline in the fourth century AD. Thereafter, river mud and sand gradually buried the town, which had the effect of preserving most buildings from the second storey down. Visit on a sunny weekday, and bring a picnic to eat under the pines, or on the steps of the amphitheatre, as it's a place which needs to be taken leisurely.

The main street, the **Decumanus Maximus**, runs from the **Porta Romana** for almost a kilometre, past the **amphitheatre** and the **forum**, before forking to the left to reach what used to be the sea (it's now about 3km away at **Lido di Ostia**, *see below*). The right fork, the **Via delle Foce**, leads towards the Tiber. On either side of these main arteries is a network of parallel and intersecting lanes, and it's here that many of the more interesting discoveries can be made, by scrambling over the truncated walls and half-hidden mosaics.

Behind the **amphitheatre** is the **Forum of the Corporations**, ringed by offices and shops with mosaics referring to the trades practised by each of the ancient guilds: the **Thermopilium**, an ancient Roman bar, complete with marble counter, a fresco advertising the day's fare and a garden with fountain out the back; the elegant fourth century **House of Cupid and Psyche**; and the fine polychrome mosaics in the **House of the Dioscuri**. The **museum** has a good collection of artefacts from the site, including a series of bas-reliefs showing scenes of everyday life and two rooms documenting the eastern and Mithraic cults which proliferated at Ostia.

The medieval fortified village of Ostia, five minutes walk from the entrance to the excavations, has a brick castle (built 1483-86 for the future Pope Julius II) and some picturesque cottages that were originally set aside for the workers in the nearby salt pans.

Transport & Information

Getting there *by train* from the Ferrovia Roma-Lido station (next to Piramide Metro station: every 15 mins); Ostia Antica is the sixth station along.
Opening times *Excavations Apr-Oct* 9am-6pm, *Nov-Mar* 9am-4pm winter; *museum* 9am-2pm Tue-Sun.
Admission L8,000.

The Coast
South of Rome

The sea near Rome is not the clear blue you might have hoped. The local riviera for Romans is the Lido in **Ostia**, with dark sandy beaches occupied by private bathing establishments that fill to bursting every summer, and a somewhat murky sea. Bathers are advised to head towards **Torvaianica**, 11km south of Ostia, where the sea is a bit cleaner. The nudist beach about 9km south from Ostia is also very good. Cheap food and drink stalls are set up there in summer for snacks (*see also chapter* **Gay Rome**).

Further down are the ports of **Anzio** and **Nettuno**, the site of Allied landings in 1944, and now surrounded by giant war cemeteries. The towns are not particularly interesting, but good for fish restaurants. Ferries to the Pontine Islands leave from Anzio. The two main islands, **Ponza** and **Ventotene**, are popular tourist venues which have managed to retain most of their Mediterranean charm. The mixture of pastel-painted local architecture, rocky coves and curious Roman remains makes them more than worth a stopover. They can also be reached from **Gaeta**, **Terracina** and **San Felice Circeo**.

The cleanest sea near Rome is probably at **Sabaudia**, a surprisingly pleasant town built from scratch in the 1930s, and the fascist answer to Bournemouth. It stands in the **Parco Nazionale del Circeo**, next to a large artificial lake with sailing and canoeing course available. The beaches (1km from town) are clean and sandy, and the sea is good for children. Looming to the left is the Rock of Circeo, said to be where Odysseus was waylaid by beautiful Circe while his men were changed into pigs.

On the other side of Circeo a road leads up to **San Felice Circeo**, a pretty little town which becomes a poseurs' paradise in the summer. The resort suburbs of Circeo spread a long way down the coast road: a string of holiday homes, bars, restaurants and endless traffic jams makes the place seem like any other seaside resort. The sea is quite clean, but the beaches are small and crowded.

From **Terracina** to **Gaeta** there are sandy beaches and a clear blue sea. You have to pay for the privately-run beaches (with deckchairs, a bar, toilets and showers) in and around the towns, but along **Salto di Fondi** and near the grotto of Tiberius at Sperlonga there are *spiaggie libere*, which means you can stick your towel where you want to. Near Gaeta you will often have to pay to park your car on the road (L3,000-5,000) and to use the steps down to beaches, even if they themselves are *spiaggie libere*.

Terracina is a port-town with two centres. The pleasant modern part is mainly down by the sea and along the Via Flacca. Up in the historic centre, the medieval town lies on top of the ancient forum of the major Roman port of Anxur. The cathedral was built out of the main hall of a Roman temple dedicated to Augustus. Above the portico is a 12th-century mosaic frieze, while below it is a big basin reputedly used for boiling Christians. The paving slabs in the piazza are those of the old forum, and just beyond is a gate and stretch of the ancient Via Appia. Bombing during World War II uncovered these ancient remains and made space for the modern town hall and the archaeological museum (*07 73 70 22 20*; **open** *Oct-Apr* 9am-2pm Mon-Sat. *May-Sept* 9am-1pm, 5-7pm, Tue-Sat; 8am-1pm Sun. **Admission** free).

Up above the town, and spectacularly lit at night, is the first-century BC Temple of Jupiter (follow the signs to the hospital and carry on up), which offers views from Circeo to Gaeta.

Sperlonga is a very pretty seaside resort with some of the cleanest sea in Italy. The whitewashed medieval town on the spur overlooking the town's two beaches fills up with wealthy Romans during the summer months. The car-free, narrow alleyways of the historic centre are filled with potted geraniums, boutiques, bars and restaurants. The archaeological museum, at the end of the fine sandy beach to the south of the town, contains some important 2nd century BC sculptures depicting scenes from the story of Odysseus. The visit includes a tour of Tiberius' Villa and Grotto (**Open** 9am-one hour before sunset daily. **Admission** L4,000).

If you get tired of the beach, consider hopping inland to **Fondi**. This thriving market town contains two fine medieval churches, a chunk of megalithic wall, a splendidly intact castle and one of the biggest open-air markets in the entire region, good for second-hand clothes and delicious local produce (every Sunday morning).

The last resort along this stretch of coast is **Gaeta**. Three towns in one, Gaeta has an important commercial and pleasure-boat harbour, a medieval quarter with more tackily-adorned Madonnas in wall-niches than Naples, and an impressive cathedral and castle. The Serapo beach to the north is long, wide and, not surprisingly, very crowded in summer.

Transport & Information

Getting there: **Ostia** from the Ferrovia Roma-Lido station beside Piramide Metro station: trains leave every 10-15 minutes throughout the day. **Other destinations**: by COTRAL bus from EUR Fermi; by car via Appia (SS7) or Via Pontina (SS148) to Sabaudia (93km), Terracina (105km), or Sperlonga (123km); by train from Termini, Tiburtina or Ostiense to Priverno (for Sabaudia and local buses/trains to Terracina), Fondi (for Sperlonga), and Formia (for Gaeta); by train from Termini for Anzio and Nettuno.

Where to eat & drink: If you want to spend a bit more on a fine fish and seafood meal in **Ostia**, go to Villa Irma, Corso Regina Maria Pia, 647 (56 03 877). **Terracina** has many places to eat, but try the fun and cheap Il Vesuvio, Via San Domenico, 29 (07 73 70 11 96; open Thur-Tue). It serves excellent, fresh seafood, great antipasti and pizza cooked in a wood oven. It's also worth making a small gastronomic detour inland to **Fondi**, where you'll find Taverna Gonzaga in the courtyard of the historic Palazzo del Principe (Corso Appio Claudio, 11 (07 71 53 14 98; open Tue-Sun) for reasonably priced fresh fish and local delicacies and excellent antipasti, and La Cantina di Galba (Via Filza, 11-13 (07 71 50 00 58; closed Tue). In **Sperlonga** there's good fresh food at the family-run La Bisaccia, Via Romita, 25 (07 71 54 576; open daily). In **Gaeta** there's the inexpensive Da Tanino, Lungomare Caboto Vico, 10 (open Tue-Sun). Not to be missed in this area are the *mozzarella di bufala* and olives from Gaeta sold in stalls along the road. All along the coast there are plenty of beach discos, an Italian summer institution. Two in **San Felice Circeo** are La Stiva on Lungomare Circe (no phone) and Valentino Notte at Lungomare Circe, 41 (07 73 78 43 10), a romantic disco/piano bar that could be a Barry Manilow fan's idea of heaven. Aenea's Landing (07 71 74 17 13) on Via Flacca in **Gaeta** is a very popular club with a funky atmosphere.

The Coast
North of Rome

If you're looking for discos, grilled fish and *racchettone* (beach tennis), resorts along the Lazio coast like **Fregene**, **Ladispoli** and **Santa Marinella** will not disappoint. Romans flock here every summer by day and night (*see chapter* **Nightlife**). But if you want a nice clean sea to go swimming, forget it. Away from the high season, the beach at **Santa Severa** is just about acceptable but, further north, the power stations, Sardinian ferries and industrial waste of **Civitavecchia** soon scupper the theory that the further you travel from Rome, the cleaner it gets. In general, it's not until you reach the border with Tuscany that things start to improve again. The sandy beaches around **Capalbio** are the best you'll find in this part of the world, and the gently shelving shoreline makes them ideal for kids.

In Santa Severa, 54km north-west of Rome, the four-square **Castello Orsini** squats like an outsized sandcastle on the beach. It's in almost as much danger of being washed away, according to

a recent report. Inside (you are free to wander around) is a proper little village, complete with church, a chapel with 14th-century frescoes, and a fountain. The castle is now owned by the local town council, which organises concerts there in summer, and lets out some of the tiny 17th-century cottages as holiday homes. Next to the castle are the remains of the once-busy Etruscan port of **Pyrgi**, the main sea outlet of Cervéteri (*see below* **Etruscan Lazio**) and also the site of an important sanctuary dedicated to the Etruscan goddess Uni (Roman Juno). There's a small museum of finds from the excavations, the **Antiquarium** (open 9am-1pm Tue, Thur, Sat). The beach to the right of the castle is fine for a swim if you don't look too closely at the colour of the water.

Continuing northward, past the port of Civitavecchia, it's remarkable how quickly things change once you cross into Tuscany. **Chiarone** is a tiny place – a dainty railway station, a shop, a couple of bars and a few houses – but it has the first really clean sea and sandy beach this side of Rome (1km from the village). Behind the dunes is a good campsite, the **Chiarone** (05 64 89 01 01; open May-Sept).

You can walk along the beach from here all the way (12km) to the hill at **Ansedonia**. This is the site of the Etruscan town of Cosa, and now bristling with upmarket holiday villas. Halfway along, just beyond the **Lago di Burano**, an important bird sanctuary under the protection of the World Wide Fund for Nature, is the **Marina di Capalbio**, marked by the incongruous bulk of the **Casale di Macchiatonda**, a former hunting lodge. For many years this has been the beach resort for Rome's monied Left, though according to recent reports they are now forsaking their villas in the hills behind here for houses in the beautiful walled village of **Capalbio** itself (7km inland). Without a car, the only way to get here directly from Rome is to take the train to Capalbio station, and walk the 3km to the beach.

This Sporting Life

Lazio has several ski resorts which also offer trekking and rock climbing in summer. Skiing holidays are best organised at travel agencies back home, but some resorts are close enough for day or weekend trips from Rome: **Terminillo** is above Rieti, **Campo Felice** on the edges of Abruzzo, and **Monte Livata** to the east of Subiaco. Lazio is also good for walking, climbing and cycling. The best maps are the military IGM series, available from large bookshops (*see chapter* **Shopping**). For excursions, contact the following groups:

CAI (Club Alpino Italiano)
Piazza Sant'Andrea della Valle, 3 (68 61 01 11). Bus to Corso Vittorio Emanuele. **Open** Mon-Fri. **Rates** L70,000 a year.
Weekend excursions in the mountains for around L25,000-30,000.

LIPU
Piazzale Clodio, 13/14 (39 73 09 03). Bus to Piazzale Clodio. **Open** 9am-7pm Mon-Fri. **Rates** around L20,000 an excursion.
Sunday walking trips to various sites in Lazio with specialist guides who are wildlife experts.

Beyond Ansedonia the mountainous promontory of **Monte Argentario** rises out of the sea. It's joined to the mainland by three narrow isthmuses. On the central one the town of **Orbetello** bulges out like a swollen knuckle; the nearest one, the **Tombolo della Feniglia**, is a nature reserve with a healthy colony of deer and numerous species of aquatic birds, visible from the shore facing the lagoon. A path (walkers and cyclists only) under shady umbrella pines runs the whole length of the *Tombolo* (to get here, take the Porto Ercole bus from Orbetello Scalo station and ask to be put off at *il bivio per la Feniglia*). From here you can cut across to the beach which – because it's inaccessible by car – is among the emptiest you'll find in mainland Italy (though in the high season 'empty' is a relative concept). One piece of advice: the mosquitoes which frequent the lagoons are monsters. Come prepared.

Transport & Information

Getting there: Santa Severa *by bus* COTRAL from Lepanto; *by car* 54km, by A12 or Via Aurelia (SS1); *by train* (infrequent) from Termini, Ostiense, or Trastevere to Santa Severa, then 1km walk to beach. **Chiarone**, **Capalbio**, **Monte Argentario** *by car* A12 or Via Aurelia (SS1) to Chiarone (124km); *by train* from Termini, Ostiense or Trastevere to Chiarone and Capalbio (infrequent: 4/5 per day in summer; you may need to change at Civitavecchia) and Orbetello Scalo (around 10 per day in summer).

Where to eat: In Santa Severa there's a good beach trattoria right next to the castle, **L'Isola del Pescatore** (07 66 74 01 45), which is open for lunch and dinner every day from Easter until the end of September. On the beach in Chiarone is the bar/trattoria **L'Ultima Spiaggia** (05 64 89 02 95, open 1 June-20 Sept 8am-8pm, later on Sat). The station bar in Capalbio is also a front for an excellent, cheap trattoria (05 64 89 84 24, closed Tue in low season). Otherwise, you can eat on Capalbio beach at the pricey but atmospheric **Carmen Bay** (05 64 89 31 96; open Sat, Sun Easter-end May, Oct; daily June-Sept).

Tivoli & Palestrina

The town of Tivoli, founded by an Italic tribe, was conquered by the Romans in 338 BC. The surrounding area soon became a popular location for country villas, and Tivoli itself was littered with temples. Long a favourite destination for day trips from Rome, its greatest attractions are the largest of the Roman Imperial villas, the **Villa Adriana**, and the Renaissance **Villa d'Este**.

Also worth looking at are the **Villa Gregoriana**, a wild park descending a rocky gorge next to two waterfalls (open Sept-May 9.30am-one hour before sunset, June-Aug 10am-7.30pm, Tue-Sun; admission L2,500); the cathedral of **San Lorenzo**, which contains a famous 13th-century wood-carving of the Descent from the Cross; and a very well preserved circular Roman **Temple of Sybil**. Up at the top of the town is a 15th-century castle built by Pope Pius II: the **Rocca Pia**.

Nearby is **Palestrina**, a medieval town built on the remains of a temple to an ancient oracle. A few kilometres east of Tivoli is the small town of **Castelmadama**, where a Palio (traditional horse race) is held every July (*see chapter* **Rome by Season**). Also, if you have children to entertain, take note that not far from the road between Tivoli and Rome is the AcquaPiper aquatic park (*see chapter* **Children**).

Villa Adriana (Hadrian's Villa)

(07 74 53 02 03). **Open** 9am-6.30pm daily; last ticket one hour before closing. **Admission** L8,000.

Hadrian started work on this huge and grandiose country retreat in the mountains near Tibur (ancient Tivoli) in 118 AD. It was completed in 134, and later used by several other emperors. In the centuries following the fall of the Empire, it became a luxury quarry for later builders, but the years of decay failed to destroy it completely; the restored remains, lying between olive groves and cypresses, are still extensive and impressive (you can look at a model in the pavilion, to get an idea of its original size). Hadrian was a great traveller, and in his old age built himself replicas of some of his favourite buildings. After dinner he could stroll in the shade of the once arcaded Stoà Poikile, with its huge pool, and feel he was back in Athens. Or he could recline around the pool in the Canopo, surrounded by Egyptian statues, a reminder of his adored favourite, a Greek boy called Antinous, who had drowned in Egypt. If he was feeling particularly miserable, he could take a trip to his reconstruction of Hades, the underworld. The huge main palace is *Palazzo Imperiale*. The complex included extensive guest and staff apartments, dining rooms, assembly halls and libraries. Occupying the central area of the site are the large and small baths complexes and the stadium.

It is thought that between military campaigns Hadrian spent his time painting and studying. His private study was probably on the little island in the middle of the beautiful and well-preserved *Teatro Marittimo*, a small artificial pool with a bridge that could be retracted. The whole villa complex was connected up by a series of underground passages (*cryptoporticus*), which provided a welcome relief from the beating sun. Parts of the *cryptoporticus* are still visitable.

Villa d'Este

(07 74 31 20 70). **Open** 9am-6pm; closed Mon. **Admission** L8,000.

This lavish villa was built over a Benedictine monastery in 1550 for Cardinal Ippolito d'Este, the son of Lucrezia Borgia, purely as a pleasure palace. Inside are frescoes and paintings by Correggio, da Volterra and Perrin del Vaga. Its greatest attraction is the garden, beautifully cool and refreshing, with huge, elaborate and ingenious fountains. The *Fontana dell'Organo Idraulico* used water pressure to compress air and play tunes like an organ; another, the Owl Fountain, imitated an owl's song.

The villa has become sadly decayed over the centuries, and restoration is an uphill struggle – the musical fountains have not made a sound for years, though others have now been returned to their original splendour. They're probably best seen illuminated at night; the EPT in Rome (48 89 91) has details of late-night openings.

Palestrina

Museo Nazionale Archeologico Prenestino. **Open** 9am-7pm Tue-Sun. **Admission** L4,000 including excavations. This attractive small town was built over a huge temple, first built in the 6th century BC, dedicated to the oracle Fortuna Primigenia. The ancient Etruscan town, known as Praeneste, fought many wars with the Romans before being defeated by Sulla in 87BC. The temple was rebuilt on a grander scale, and Praeneste subsequently became a favourite holiday resort – Pliny the Younger had a villa here. After the oracle ceased to be consulted in the 4th century AD, the medieval town was built on top, though bits of the ancient ruins can be seen at many different points. Bombing during World War II further exposed the remains.

A round temple with a statue of the goddess Palestrina originally topped the oracle, where the 17th-century **Palazzo Colonna-Barberini** now stands. Today this houses the town museum. Its star exhibit is the Nile Mosaic (2nd century BC) – a work, admired by Pliny, which came from the most sacred part of the temple, where the cathedral now stands. It is an intricately detailed, brightly-coloured representation of the Nile in flood from Ethiopia to Alexandria, including warriors hunting exotic animals, people wining and dining, goddesses preaching and hundreds of birds of all types. Palestrina's other claim to fame is as the birthplace of Giovanni da Palestrina, the great 16th century composer of polyphonic choral music.

Transport & Information

Getting there: **Tivoli** *by bus* COTRAL from Rebibbia; *by car* 32km, by A24 or Via Tiburtina (SS5); *by train* from Termini or Tiburtina to Avezzano, stops at Tivoli (very slow). **Palestrina** *by bus* COTRAL from Rebibbia; *by car* 39km, by Via Prenestina (SS155).

Where to eat: The best way to see the Temple of Sybil in Tivoli is to eat at the restaurant Sibilla, Via della Sibilla, 50 (0774 20 281; open Tue-Sat). It has a great location overlooking the waterfalls and a square Temple of Vesta in its garden.

The Castelli Romani

The tame volcanoes which make up the Alban Hills have long provided refuge for Romans on Sunday outings or *scampagnate*, with numerous *trattorie* and abundant local wine to soothe urban angst. The 16 small towns which make up the

Tivoli – *founded by Italics.*

Villa Adriana *is home to some outsized pond life.*

Castelli Romani, dotted here and there around the Alban Hills, are not all equally worth a visit; but there is plenty of good eating and walking, and wonderful sights such as Frascati's **Villa Aldobrandini**, the **Abbazia di San Nilo** at Grottaferrata and beautiful **Lake Nemi**.

Most of the modern-day Castelli are creations of the struggle for power and influence between Rome's noble families (the Savelli, Colonna, della Rovere), who took turns to put their scions on the papal throne throughout the Middle Ages and the Renaissance (*see chapter* **History**). In pre-Classical times this area was the centre of the Latin League, whose capital, Alba Longa, on the ridge above **Lake Albano**, has now made way for **Castel Gandolfo**, summer residence of the Pope. Subjugated by Rome, the area became a favourite summer haunt of Roman patricians – no fewer than 43 villas are known to have existed on the hills around now-deserted **Tuscolo**, where there are the remains of a Roman amphitheatre. Their Renaissance successors also built themselves a number of villas.

Frascati is the closest of the Castelli, and offers perhaps the most satisfying balance of food, wine and culture. Of the numerous Renaissance villas sprinkled over the hillside behind the town, the only one open to the public (garden only) is the **Villa Aldobrandini** (aka Villa Belvedere), which dominates the main Piazzale Marconi – where the Tourist Office will provide you with a visitor's permit (free) and a map of the town. The villa was built in 1598-1603 by Giacomo della Porta for Cardinal Pietro Aldobrandini, whose uncle had just become Pope Clement VIII. The grand fountain, the **Teatro delle Acque** by Carlo Maderno, is still impressive, although now rather decrepit, and there is also an elegant smaller fountain designed by Bernini.

The name 'Frascati' is synonymous with uninspiring Italian table wine, but you'd do well to give it another try. Local topers claim that it has to be drunk *sul posto* – on site – and, quaffing it fresh from the barrel in a cool cellar, you may well agree. There is a number of wine shops around town: cavernous rooms in which jugs of wine and hearty snacks are served. Particularly characteristic is the den run by Carlo Taglienti at Via Sepolcro di Lucullo, 8 (on the left of Corso d'Italia, just before the turn for the Villa Aldobrandini).

Grottaferrata is a small, lively town whose main street leads down to the 10th-century **Abbazia di San Nilo** (open 5.30am-7.30pm daily), a mainly Romanesque monastery fortified in the 15th century by Michelangelo's patron Pope Julius II. The abbey church of Santa Maria has a fine 12th-century campanile, and an even finer carved marble portal. Inside, the Cappella di San Nilo contains frescoes by Domenichino. The museum (**open** 8.30am-noon, 4.30-6pm, Tue-Sun) contains pieces of Classical sculpture and frescoes moved from the nave of the church.

Among the other Castelli, **Nemi** is definitely the most picturesque – so try to avoid visiting on a Sunday, when it fills up with Roman strollers. Perched on the edge of Lake Nemi's tree-covered crater is a site once used for worship by the primitive cult of Diana. The tiny medieval village nearby, beneath the Ruspoli family castle, is mad on strawberries. They're grown in greenhouses by the lake shore, and heavily promoted, particularly through the Strawberry Festival in June.

On the other side of the lake is **Genzano**, which holds the annual Corpus Christi Flower Festival (early June). The main streets of the town are decorated with elaborate carpets of flowers (*see chapter* **Rome by Season**).

Transport & Information

Getting there: *by bus* COTRAL from Anagnina; *by car* A2 or Via Tuscolana (SS5) to Grottaferrata (18km), Frascati (20km); Via Appia (SS7) to Genzano (29km), Nemi (33km); *by train* from Termini-Laziali, lines run to Frascati and Castel Gandolfo/Albano. The latter is especially picturesque.

Where to eat: In **Frascati**, you're spoilt for choice. Among the crowd, Cacciani, Via Armando Diaz, 13 (94 20 378; closed Mon and 10 days in mid-Aug) stands out as one of the best restaurants in the Castelli (with prices to match). For something simpler, try Zarazà in Via Regina Margherita, 2 (94 22 053; closed Mon and Aug). In **Grottaferrata** don't miss Al Fico Nuovo, Via Anagnina, 134 (94 59 276; closed Wed and second half of August). It's well worth the 15-minute uphill trek out of town (on the Rocca Priora road) for the home-made fettuccine, cool garden terrace and delicious house wine. The best place to eat in **Nemi** is Lo Specchio di Diana, Corso Vittorio Emanuele, 13 (93 68 016; open daily). There's a terrace overlooking the lake, and pizzas so huge they arrive on two plates.

Lakes North of Rome

A group of Lazian shepherds once asked Hercules to demonstrate his great power. Ever ready to show off, he picked up his club, thrust it deep into the ground and challenged the shepherds to extract it. Sure enough, they were too weak and Hercules had his moment of glory, whereupon fresh water gushed forth, filled the hole and created **Vico**, a beautiful lake surrounded by forests, and now a nature reserve.

The other lakes in northern Lazio are **Bracciano**, **Martignano** and **Bolsena** – the most northerly, and the largest, volcanic lake in Europe.

Lago Bracciano

This large, sparklingly clean lake about 40km north of Rome is surrounded by picturesque villages and sailing, windsurfing and canoeing clubs. Swimming is possible all around the lake, but the best places are around **Bracciano** and south of **Trevignano**. Trevignano is a medieval town with a pleasant *lungolago*, with bars and several restaurants. **Anguillara** possibly takes its name from the eels (*anguille*) that populate the lake, or else from a Roman villa built on this corner (*angolo*) of the lake's coast. In ancient times this was a popular site for holiday homes. The medieval town is perched on a rocky promontory, and is especially beautiful at sunset. There are great views from the belvedere overlooking the lake.

Bracciano is the main town on the lake and is dominated by the **Orsini Castle** (*see also chapter* **Children**), built in 1470, with fine apartments decorated by Antoniazzo Romano and the Zuccari brothers (open 9am-12.30pm, 3-6.30pm, Tue-Sat; admission L7,000). Close by is the **Lago di Martignano**, a quieter, smaller, offshoot of the Bracciano crater. There's a small beach, and you can rent sailing boats, pedaloes and canoes. To get there, turn sharp right at the little chapel before Anguillara; follow the road past a drinking trough and go left on a track for 3km. Parking your car will set you back L5,000.

Lago di Bolsena

In the heart of Etruscan Lazio, this vast lake is great for sailing, windsurfing, boating and swimming. There are good beaches all around it, but especially on the road from **Gradoli** to **Capodimonte**. In mid-lake, there are also two privately-owned islands. The **Isola Bisentina** was a papal summer residence, and has a *Via Crucis* with seven Renaissance churches and chapels designed by Antonio da Sangallo. The **Isola Martana** was where the daughter of Ostrogothic king Theodoric (*see chapter* **History: A New Religion**) was imprisoned and killed by her husband Teodato in the fifth century. Boats to Isola Bisentina leave from Capodimonte (07 61 87 07 60) and Bolsena (07 61 79 80 33) in the summer.

On the eastern shore of the lake is **Bolsena**, a charming medieval town with a castle housing an **archaeological museum** (open Oct-Mar 9am-1pm, 4-8pm, Sat, Sun. Apr-Sept 9am-1pm, 4-8pm, Wed-Sun; admission L3,000). There's also a fifteenth-century church, **Santa Caterina**, and the remains of a Roman city with an amphitheatre, walls and houses (open 9am-1pm Tue-Sun). Heading south to **Capodimonte**, with a little harbour and a Farnese castle built by Sangallo the Younger. **Marta** is a pretty medieval and Renaissance town situated on the river Marta where it joins the lake.

To the south-east is **Montefiascone**, a hilltop town dominated by the huge dome of **Santa Margherita** – the third largest in Italy. At the bottom of the town is **San Flaviano**, a 12th-century church containing the tomb of the German monk who named the local wine; the church is built on top of an earlier one facing the opposite way. On his travels, the monk was accompanied by an assistant who went ahead marking the places where the wine was good with an 'Est!' (here). At Montefiascone it merited an 'Est! Est!! Est!!!' Uncharitable souls have suggested that without the story, this ordinary little wine would have sunk without trace; but now a local producer, **Poggio dei Gelsi**, has set about salvaging its reputation, with some degree of success.

Transport & Information

Getting there: Bracciano *by bus* COTRAL from Lepanto; *by car* Via Braccianense (SS493) to Anguillara (32km), Bracciano (40km); Via Cassia (SS2) to Trevignano (43km); *by train* from Termini, Tiburtina to Anguillara or Bracciano.
Bolsena *by bus* COTRAL from Saxa Rubra (summer only; in winter change at Viterbo); *by car* Via Cassia (SS2) to Montefiascone (100km), Marta (106km), Capodimonte (108km), Bolsena (116km).
Where to eat: Bracciano Vino e Camino, Via delle Cantine 11 (06 99 80 34 33, closed Mon) is an excellent new wine bar just around the corner from the Castello Orsini.
Bolsena There is a good number of restaurants in Marta, serving fish from sea and lake. Try **Gino al Miralago**, Lungolago Guglielmo Marconi, 58 (0761 87 09 10; closed Tue except in Aug).

Villas

The villas in northern Lazio were built in competition with Villa d'Este in Tivoli and those in Castelli Romani. They were not just country retreats, but personal and political statements. The impressive **Villa Farnese**, the refined **Villa Lante** and the mysterious **Bosco Sacro** at Bomarzo were all commissioned in the 16th century by patrons related to one other. They also used the same architects, artists and craftsmen (*see also* **Tivoli & Palestrina** *page 229* and the **Castelli Romani** *page 230*).

Bomarzo

(07 61 92 40 29). **Open** *May-Sept* 8am-7.30pm daily; *Oct-Apr* 8am-4.30pm daily. **Admission** L15,000 adults; L13,000 3-8 year olds; L13,000 groups.
Important in the Roman Empire, much of this town was owned by the powerful Orsini family from the beginning of the 14th century onwards. The park, **Il Sacro Bosco**, also known as the **Parco dei Mostri** or 'Monster Park', is situated just below the town, and was built by Duke Vicino Orsini (1523-84) shortly after his wife died. But this is no dignified retreat for a bereaved husband, more of a bizarre Renaissance theme park. Orsini spent years filling the park with surreal, sometimes grotesque sculptures, which were completely at odds with the conventional tastes of his day. Lurking in the undergrowth are enormous, absurd beasts, which children (and adults) are free to clamber on. A huge elephant mauls a Roman soldier and giants brawl – the park was much appreciated by Salvador Dalí, who played a part in publicising it and making it one of Lazio's most popular tourist attractions.

Villa Farnese

Caprarola (07 61 64 60 52). **Open** *Nov-Feb* 9am-4pm, Tue-Sun; *Mar, Apr, Sept-Oct* 9am-5pm Tue-Sun; *May-Aug* 9am-7pm Tue-Sun. **Tours** of the park at 10am, 11.30am, 3pm (and 5pm, *Apr-Sept*), daily. **Admission** L4,000, under-18s and over-60s free.
The little town of **Caprarola** is dwarfed by the imposing Villa Farnese. It started as a castle designed by da Sangallo the Younger and Peruzzi, but was taken over by Vignola, who kept the pentagon design. As you approach the villa, it appears to be only two storeys high, but climb the semi-circular ramps and the ground floor appears. Vignola raised and extended the approach road, burying the lower storeys of the existing houses in order to provide as many views as possible of the villa. Inside, a wide spiral staircase, which Alessandro Farnese climbed on horseback, leads up to the **Piano Nobile**, the only part open to the public. In the **Salone dei Fasti Farnese** are frescoes depicting the heroic deeds of the Farnese family: note the Farnese Pope Paul III in the act of excommunicating Henry VIII of England. There is also a room with a frescoed map of the world from 1500, and another in which whispers rebound from wall to wall. The gardens are beautiful.

Villa Lante

Bagnaia (0 761 28 80 08). **Open** *park* 9am-one hour before sunset Tue-Sun; *garden* and *villa* guided visits every half hour, 9.30am-half an hour before sunset daily. **Admission** L4,000, under-18s and over-60s free.
Near **Viterbo**, the town of **Bagnaia** lies beneath the gardens and park of **Villa Lante**. The villa was built for

*The grounds of **Villa Farnese** are full of hidden surprises.*

Cardinal de Gambera (perhaps to a design by Vignola) and is a superb example of Renaissance landscape gardening. The two identical palaces are surrounded by a geometrically perfect formal Italian garden, punctuated with fountains and pools. Fed by a spring at the top of the garden, water cascades down over the five terraces, performing spectacular water-games to impress and surprise guests. Inside the villa are frescoes by the Zuccheri brothers and a series of paintings of the Lazian villas.

Transport & Information

Getting there: Bomarzo *by bus* COTRAL from Saxa Rubra, change at Viterbo; *by car* A1 to Attigliano exit, then SS204 (90km); *by train* from Termini or Tiburtina to Attigliano-Bomarzo on Orte line (5km from park). **Caprarola** *by bus* COTRAL from Lepanto; *by car* Via Cassia (SS2), then road to Ronciglione/Caprarola (60km). **Bagnaia** *by bus* COTRAL from Saxa Rubra, change at Viterbo; *by car* A1 to Attigliano or Orte exit, then SS204 (90km); *by train* from Roma-Nord/Piazzale Flaminio to Bagnaia, change at Viterbo.

Into the Mountains

When the city gets too hot and the sea too crowded, smart Romans head for the hills. There are some serious mountains (2,000m+) within an hour and a half of the capital, but you don't need to go that far to find clean air, good walks and some unspoilt villages.

The nearest range is the **Monti Lucretili**, 40km north-east of Rome (you can see them on a clear day from the Gianicolo). Despite its proximity to Rome, this Regional Park has remained relatively untouched by the metropolis. A good base is the pretty hill-town of **Licenza**, with the remains of Horace's country retreat, **Sabine Farm**, close by. From **Civitella di Licenza**, a tiny satellite-hamlet a couple of kilometres beyond Licenza, it's possible to climb **Monte Pellecchia** (1,368m), the highest peak in the Lucretili, in about two and a half hours.

On the other side of the A24 motorway, beyond the tree-covered slopes of the **Monti Ruffi**, the long, bare crest of the **Monti Simbruini** stretches away to the south-east, marking the border between Lazio and Abruzzo. Since 1982, the whole of the Lazio side has been a Regional Park, which at least means that further development of dire ski-resorts like those at Monte Livata and Campo Staffi has been curbed. The big tourist draw of the area is the town of **Subiaco**, in the eastern foothills, with its twin monasteries of **Santa Scolastica** and **San Benedetto**. From here you can go by car or ski-lift to Monte Livata and the plain of Campo dell'Osso, starting-point for the easy ascent of **Monte Autore** (1,855m; one hour), from which there is a magnificent view. Other good launching-pads for long, solitary hikes are the hamlets of **Camerata Nuova** and **Vallepietra**, both served by buses (infrequent) from Rome's Rebibbia terminus.

Across the border and some distance to the south-east is one of Italy's oldest national parks,

the **Parco Nazionale di Abruzzo**. It contains some breathtaking mountain scenery, and a range of fauna that includes the rare Apennine brown bear (the park's symbol), chamois, wolves and golden eagles. The park's administrative centre and only town of any size is **Pescassèroli**, which fills up with second-homers in summer. Information on hostels, refuges and campsites and detailed maps of the area can also be obtained from information offices in the more attractive villages of **Opi** or **Civitella Alfadena** further up the valley. From the latter, one of the best of the many walks in the park (all clearly marked and colour-coded – this one is itinerary I1) leads up through the beech woods of the Val di Rosa to the Passo Cavuto. From here you can traverse (chamois sightings possible) to the refuge of **Forca Resuni** (1,952m). You start your descent here (itinerary I4), via the Valle Jannanghera, to the starting-point. In all the trek should take about six hours.

For something less strenuous, wander up the beautiful valley of the **Camosciara** (itinerary G6) or alongside the torrent of the **Valle Fondillo** (itinerary F2 – the best route for would-be bear-spotters).

Transport & Information

Getting there: *by bus* COTRAL from Rebibbia to all destinations in Lazio; **Abruzzo National Park**, ARPA runs a service to Pescassèroli; buses depart from Tiburtina; *by car* A24 or Via Tiburtina (SS5) to Licenza (54km) or Subiaco (72km); A24 then A25 to Abbruzzo National Park; *by train* very slow, very infrequent services from Termini or Tiburtina to Avezzano will take you through selected mountain destinations in Lazio and Abruzzo.

Abbeys

The Cistercian order built several abbeys in Southern Lazio, and these offer a refreshing blast of simplicity after the overwhelming Baroque of Rome. The abbeys of **Valvisciolo**, **Trisulti**, **Casamari** and **Fossanova**, south of Rome, are all fairly near one another. In northern Lazio, **San Martino al Cimino** is worth a visit if you're passing Lake Vico; and the abbey of **Farfa**, about 50km north of Rome, has a reasonable hotel run by nuns, and is a good base from which to explore the area.

The **Abbey of Valvisciolo** (open 8am-noon, 3.30-6pm, daily), set in stunning countryside near Sermoneta and Ninfa, was founded in the 8th century, rebuilt in the 13th, and handed over to the Cistercians in the 14th. Don't miss the cloister, or the honey made by the resident monks. From here follow the Via Appia south and then take the local road to Priverno, which passes the **Abbazia di Fossanova** (open Oct-Mar 8am-noon, 3.30-5.30pm, Apr-Sept 8am-noon, 4-7.30pm, daily). Recent restoration has exposed the elegance of its Gothic architecture, with a gorgeous rose window

Abandoned Villages

In and around Rome you soon get used to leaning against, sitting on and passing by venerable remains. The area around Rome is dotted with ruined villages and by no means all of them are ancient: some were abandoned in comparatively recent times. Frequently it was the mal'aria (malaria, literally bad air) which forced villagers to leave their homes in search of healthier locations. North of Rome are **Galeria** and **Monterano**; 90km to the south is **Ninfa**, now engulfed in the Caetani Botanical Gardens.

Along the Via Boccea, which runs due east from Rome from near the Villa Pamphili, a flimsy sign reading *Città Morta* (dead city) on the bend before **Santa Maria in Galeria**, points towards **Galeria**, now sadly over-exposed and prone to looking like a rubbish tip after the weekend. Follow the track to the end, where a narrow footpath leads up along the old walls, through the entrance gate and into the devastated town. The 16th- and 17th-century buildings are overgrown, trees break through walls and ceilings, and a 16th-century bell tower rises intact over the shell of the church. After exploring the village, walk down to the river Arrone in the valley, where there are the remains of a bridge and an old mill.

Much further north, **Monterano** lies abandoned in a valley under the newer town of **Canale di Monterano**. A three-tier Roman aqueduct leads into the village, which was already almost deserted because of malaria before being sacked by the French in 1799. As well as the remains of medieval houses, there is the large baronial palace and a Bernini-designed church, now an elegant ruin of crumbling stucco with a fig tree growing inside, forming a sub-

stitute dome. Film directors love it. Once here you can trek around the surrounding nature reserve: follow the yellow striped posts.

In comparison to the wild, rambling villages in the north, **Ninfa**, in the Caetani Botanical Garden, is more ordered (68 80 32 31, open Apr-June, Sept-Nov 9am-noon, 2.30-6pm, July-Aug 9am-noon, 3-6pm, first Sat, Sun of the month. Admission L10,000; free under-10s. Tickets on site or in advance from Palazzo Caetani, Via delle Botteghe Oscure, 32, Rome; open 8am-7pm Mon-Fri; 8am-11pm Sat). The medieval lakeside village still has its towers, ancient walls, palaces, a castle, streets and houses. In spring the place blossoms with thousands of flowers. Ninfa was abandoned in the 17th century. If you look up high into the surrounding mountains you'll just make out the massive cyclopean walls of the ancient Volscian city **Norba**, itself abandoned in 87 BC.

Transport & Information

Getting there: Galeria *by car* Via Boccea, then left about 2km before Santa Maria in Galeria. **Monterano** *by bus* COTRAL from Lepanto to Canale di Monterano; *by car* Via Cassia (SS2), then Via Braccianense (SS493) to Manziana, local road to Tolfa and then Canale; *by train* from Roma-Nord/Piazzale Flaminio to Canale. Follow yellow signs in village (just before bus stop) down hill, turn right (signed), continue past derelict houses and at top of concrete slope turn left, continue for 2km. **Ninfa** *by bus* COTRAL from EUR Fermi, change at Latina; *by car* Via Appia (SS7), then follow the yellow signs to Ninfa (turn left about 6km after Cisterna); there's an unmarked entrance just before the lake. For **Norba** take the mountain road to Norma (signed). Just before entering the town, turn left and then take the track on the left on the second bend. **Where to eat:** In *Norma*, close to Ninfa and Norba, the restaurant Il Fraginale, Via Fraginale, 7 (0773 34 991; open Wed-Mon) has fresh local produce, and a terrace perched on the edge of a 400m ridge.

and Cosmati mosaics on the unfinished facade. Saint Thomas Aquinas died here, and his room can be visited.

Further on, past Priverno and Frosinone, is the **Abbazia di Casamari** (open *Oct-Mar* 3-6pm, *Apr-Sept* 9am-noon, 4-6.30pm, daily). It's a beautiful example of Cistercian architecture, elegantly proportioned with finely-detailed carving, especially around the door. This is a functioning monastery, with a cloister, meeting room and gardens. If it is shut, ring on the bell near the pharmacy for guided tours (in Italian). The cemetery is also worth a visit.

A mountain road (signed Collepardo) leads up to the **Certosa di Trisulti** (open 9.30am-noon, 4-

6pm, Mon-Sat; 9.30am-noon Sun). It was built in the 13th century for the Carthusian order over an abandoned Benedictine abbey. It looks wonderful, perched on the edge of a steep gorge surrounded by 2,000m-high mountains, though the buildings, restored in the 18th century, are disappointing. There is a fascinating 18th-century pharmacy, complete with little bottles and flasks stacked on shelves, and in the afternoon the Cistercian monks, who took over the place in 1947, will talk you through your visit (in Italian). There's also a shop selling monastic herbal products and liqueurs.

Directly north of Rome, the **Abbazia di Farfa** was, in medieval times, one of the most famous monastic centres in Italy, and its large library holds 12th-century manuscripts (07 65 27 70 65; open *Oct-Mar* 9.30am-noon, 3.30-5pm; *Apr-Sept* 9.30am-noon, 3.30-6.30pm, Tue-Sun. Guided tours only, every hour Mon-Fri; every 30 mins Sat, Sun. Library open (for study) 9am-1pm Mon, Tue, Fri . Admission L5,000). A religious centre was established here as early as the 6th century, but the buildings were destroyed and rebuilt many times, the last time in the 15th century by the Orsini family when the earlier church was incorporated as the transept. Remains of the earlier churches on the site can be seen in part of the paving, the crypt and the relief carving on the pulpit.

The abbey is now occupied by nuns, who provide reasonably-priced food and board, making it a good place to stay if you want to explore the surrounding areas. In the valley of Farfa is the nature reserve surrounding the Tiber. Also close by is the provincial capital, **Rieti**, with a cathedral and well-preserved medieval walls. There are many isolated medieval villages, two large artificial lakes, **Turano** and Salto, a castle in the form of an eagle at **Rocca Sinibalda**, and a church called **San Vittorino** (just past **Città Ducale**), which is half buried in the ground, with a fresh spring gushing from its door.

Transport & Information

Getting there: Valvisciolo, Fossanova, Casamari, Certosa di Trisulti *by bus* COTRAL from EUR Fermi or Anagnina, change at Latina or Frosinone; *by car* Via Appia (SS7) or Via Pontina (SS148) to Latina, then left on road to Norma (77km), after 13km turn right to Valvisciolo; Via Appia to Priverno and Fossanova (99km); A2 or Via Casilina (SS6) to Frosinone, then SS214 to Casamari and Trisulti (95km); *by train* from Termini or Tiburtina to Priverno and Frosinone. **Farfa** *by bus* COTRAL from Tiburtina; *by car* Via Salaria (SS4) then road to Poggio Mirteto (55km).

Where to stay and eat: In an outbuilding of the abbey at **Fossanova** is the restaurant/pizzeria La Grancia (open Wed-Mon) where you can eat *ceccapreti* (priest blinders) and *bufaletta* (baby buffalo cow) outside in the gardens. In **Farfa** the *Centro Internazionale Ecumenico*, Via del Monastero, 12 (07 65 27 70 72) has 30 rooms and provides meals. Bed and full board is L70,000 per person, lunch Sun, L28,000 (book in advance).

Viterbo

Originally an important Etruscan town and then an insignificant Roman one, Viterbo was fortified in the 8th century by the Lombard King Desiderius as a launching pad for sacking Rome. As well as enduring many bloody internal battles, Viterbo also managed to get caught up in the medieval quarrels between the Empire and the Church. Depending on which way the wind blew, the town played host to both Popes and anti-Popes, several of whom relocated here when things in Rome got too hot to handle. Gregory X was elected Pope in Viterbo and lasted a month; Hadrian V died on arriving in town; and John XXI was killed a year after his election when his bedroom floor in the Papal Palace collapsed.

Viterbo was badly bombed in World War II, but has been meticulously restored and retains its medieval appearance. Wandering around the narrow streets you will stumble across medieval laundries, ancient porticos, imposing towers and crenellated buildings. You will also notice that there are lions (the symbol of Viterbo) and fountains everywhere.

The medieval quarter of **San Pellegrino** lies at the southern edge of the city, flanked to the east by Piazza della Morte. Across the bridge is the cathedral of **San Lorenzo**, a large and elegant twelfth-century building, although much altered and restored since. Next door is the **Palazzo Papale**, built for the popes in the thirteenth century and restored in the nineteenth. From the Loggia outside, the newly elected popes would bless the people of Viterbo. Close by is the Piazza delle Morte, perhaps named in tribute to all the popes who passed away here.

Nearby, off the Via San Lorenzo, is the pretty church of **Santa Maria Nuova**, dating from the twelfth century. There is an ancient head of Jupiter on the facade, and a pulpit on the left, from where Saint Thomas Aquinas preached. At the back of the church there remains about half of a small Lombard cloister (always open).

Piazza del Plebiscito is dominated by the **Palazzo Comunale** (1500); its arched doorway opens onto a lovely courtyard with a seventeenth-century fountain and a view across the Faul valley. A staircase on the left leads to the Senate rooms, which are usually open in the morning. At the top of the stairs, the Chapel of the Commune is sealed off by glass, displaying, as if in a shop window, two huge canvasses by Sebastiano del Piombo and a *Visitation* by Bartolomeo Cavarozzi. In the largest room, the **Sala Regia**, there are comical frescoes by Baldassare Croce, relating mythical and historical local events. From the piazza, Via Roma leads past the **Lion Fountain** into **Corso d'Italia**, where at number 11 there is the famous **Caffè Schenardi**, a fifteenth century hotel that has been a café since 1818. Mussolini had breakfast here in 1938; he eased his commodious form behind the third table on the right.

North of the city is the **Museo Archeologico**, housed in the impressive **Rocca Albanorez** (1354). Here the emphasis is on living Etruscans, with reconstructions of their domestic life.

Outside the walls, opposite Porta della Verità, is **Santa Maria della Verità**. This 12th-century church was badly damaged during World War II, but has a Gothic chapel (**Cappella Mazzatosta**) with frescoes by Lorenzo di Viterbo, dated 1469. The chapel pavement has some remains of the *maiolica* decoration; other fragments are exhibited at the V&A in London. In the old convent is the **Museo Civico**, which is presently being restored.

If you are in Viterbo on September 3, you can attend the *festa* of Santa Rosa. At 9pm the citizens parade a 30m-high illuminated tower (*la macchina*) around the town. A new tower is built every five years – on one occasion it was so high that it swayed out of control, and in the panic 21 people were trampled to death. In the **Museo della Macchina di Santa Rosa** (Via San Pellegrino, 60) models and photos document the festival's history. Santa Rosa herself lies shrivelled in a glass tomb in the church of her name.

Near the Porta Romana, there is the church of **San Sisto**, now rebuilt but dating originally from the ninth century, with an impressive raised chancel and two curious twisting columns inside.

Transport & Information

Getting there: *by bus* COTRAL from Lepanto or Saxa Rubra; *by car* A1 or Via Cassia (SS2) to Viterbo (85km); *by train* from Ostiense (by Piramide Metro) or Trastevere to Viterbo. There are also very infrequently trains from the Roma Nord station in Piazzale Flaminio. Both train routes are ludicrously slow (2 hours minimum).
Tourist Information: Piazza dei Caduti, 16 (07 61 30 47 95). **Open** 8am-2pm Mon-Sat; Piazza della Morte (07 61 34 52 29). **Open** *Apr-Sept* 9am-7pm Mon-Sat.
Opening times: *Palazzo Papale* open only for concerts and conferences. Information 0 761 32 11 24. *Museo Archeologico* (*Oct-Mar*) 9am-1pm, (*Apr-Sept*) 9am-7pm, Tue-Sat. **Admission** L4,000. *Museo della Macchina di Santa Rosa* 10am-noon, 4-7pm, Sat, Sun.
Where to eat: A reasonably-priced restaurant serving good food in a friendly, family atmosphere is the **Porta Romana**, Via della Bontà, 12 (07 61 30 11 18; open Mon-Sat), near the church of San Sisto.

Etruscan Lazio

Over the centuries, people have projected their own obsessions onto the Etruscans. Herodotus was so impressed by their art that he decided they must have come from Greece. For DH Lawrence, they were creative souls trampled underfoot by the jackboots of the Roman Empire. He particularly admired the apparent sexual equality of Etruscan society, suggested by countless scenes, in wall-paintings and on terracotta sarcophagi, in which couples recline in attitudes of intimate enjoyment.

However, comparatively little is really known about the Etruscans and their language still has not been deciphered. It has been suggested that they had migrated from Asia, although more recently the theory has gained ground that they had lived in the Tuscany area since at least the Iron Age. It is known that they were more sophisticated than the early Romans and passed on to them many of their engineering techniques. Their houses were built of wood, so the only parts of the towns that have survived are the tombs, dug down into the volcanic rock. This can create a false impression, and has led some observers to suggest that the Etruscans were obsessed with death.

The territory occupied by the Etruscan League covered a wide area, but for practical purposes

Etruscan Lazio can be considered as the wide strip stretching from just north of Rome to the Tuscan border, with most of the important towns (**Cerveteri**, **Tarquinia** and **Vulci**) set on hills a few kilometres back from the coast. The best-preserved tombs are at Cerveteri and Tarquinia, and it's here you should come if you are short of time. If you have a car and a decent map, it's worth considering a trip to **Norchia**, a spectacular cliff-face necropolis between Tarquinia and Viterbo.

For an overview of the Etruscans' talents as potters, goldsmiths and engineers, have a look round the **Etruscan Museum** in the Villa Giulia in Rome (*see chapter* **Museums & Galleries**) before setting out for the Etruscan sites. The contents of most of the excavated tombs have ended up either here or in the Vatican's **Museo Gregoriano** (*see chapter* **The Vatican City**). The only on-site museum which contains exhibits of the same quality is at Tarquinia.

Cerveteri

Cerveteri has atmosphere. Underneath the pines, this town of the dead – complete with streets, piazzas and tidy little houses – is one of the most touching archaeological sites in Italy. There's a feeling of good humour about the place, despite the fact that, like most Etruscan sites, it consists almost solely of tombs.

In the drab modern town, the 16th-century Orsini castle is home to the small **Museo Nazionale di Cerveteri**, with finds from Cerveteri and the nearby port of Pyrgi (modern Santa Severa; *see above* **The Coast: North of Rome**). Most of the best discoveries are in the museums in Rome. It's a better idea to head straight for the **Banditaccia Necropolis** (signposted from the main piazza; 1km).

Etruscan Kysry, romanised as Caere, was a vast, prosperous town with three ports, one of the great trading centres of the Mediterranean between the 7th and 5th centuries BC. It was situated further along the same volcanic spur occupied by the modern town, but covered an area some twenty times greater. Similarly, the visitable area of the necropolis represents only a small part of its total extent.

The earliest tombs date from the 7th century BC; the latest are from the 3rd, by which time there had been a progressive impoverishment of tomb size and decoration. Don't miss the well preserved 6th-century BC **Tomba dei Capitelli**, the 4th-century BC **Tomba dei Rilievi**, with its bas-reliefs of weapons and domestic utensils, and the three parallel streets of fifth- and sixth-century BC cube-shaped tombs between the main **Via degli Inferni** and the **Via delle Serpi**. Sadly, this is as close as we'll ever come to seeing what a row of Etruscan upper middle-class terraced houses looked like. Ask a guardian to accompany you to the **Tomba degli Scudi e delle Sedie** outside the main gate, with its chairs carved out of the tufa rock and bas reliefs of shields adorning the walls. The guardians will also take you to see other outlying tombs; some can be explored independently (bring a torch).

Transport & Information

Getting there: *by bus* COTRAL from Lepanto; *by car* 44km, by A12 or Via Aurelia (SS1); *by train* from Termini, Tuscolana, Ostiense, or Trastevere to Cerveteri-Ladispoli station (6km out of town).
Opening times: Museo Nazionale di Cerveteri (99 41 354) 9am-7pm Tue-Sun; **Banditaccia Necropolis** *Oct-Apr* 9am-4pm, *May-Sept* 9am-7pm, Tue-Sun.
Admission: *museum* free; *necropolis* L8,000.

Tarquinia

There's not the same feel of a living city here as there is at Cerveteri: the tombs are hidden underground beneath a grassy hill, peppered with modern entrances like a crazy fallout shelter. Tarquinia, though, has the art that Cerveteri lacks: over a hundred painted tombs, many of them masterpieces for their vivacity of colouring and composition and for the insight they give into Etruscan life. Cerveteri promotes a cosy, domestic view of the Etruscans, Tarquinia scenes of work and social life, athletic contests, mysterious religious rituals, and some that are vaguely pornographic.

There is a snag: on any given day, only about a dozen tombs are open to the public. Start off in the **museum**, which has one of the best Etruscan collections outside Rome or Florence. Its chief exhibit is a pair of fourth-century terracotta winged horses from a temple frieze, proof that the Etruscans could model with as much finesse and naturalism as the Greeks. There are also some good sarcophagi, several imported Greek vases, and some tomb paintings that have been moved here for protection.

To see the best paintings in situ, head for the **necropolis**, about 2km out of town (signposted from the museum). A list of tombs currently open is posted inside the museum. If at all possible, try to see the 6th-century **Tomba della Caccia e della Pesca**, with its delightful fishing and hunting scene; and the **Tomba dei Leopardi**, in which couples recline in a banqueting scene (note the man passing his partner an egg – a recurrent symbol, though experts disagree as to what of). There is a similar scene with dancers in the elegant **Tomba delle Leonesse**.

Finally, the **Tomba dei Tori**, one of the oldest tombs so far discovered, offers a stylised mythological scene of Achilles lying in wait to ambush Troilus, and another scene containing *un po' di pornografico*, as DH Lawrence's guide gleefully described it. Today's guides tend, sadly, to be rather more discreet. The modern town bristles

with medieval defensive towers and the 12th-century church of **Santa Maria di Castello** dominates the plain below.

Transport & Information

Getting there: *by bus* COTRAL from Lepanto; *by car* 91km, by A12 and Via Aurelia (SS1); *by train* (irregular) from Termini or Ostiense to Tarquinia.
Opening times: **Museo Nazionale Tarquinia** and Necropolis (07 66 85 60 36) 9am-7pm Tue-Sun.
Admission: L8,000, ticket valid for museum and necropolis.
Where to eat: Le Due Orfanelle in Via di Porta Tarquinia 11a (07 66 85 62 76). Follow signs to the church of San Francesco to find this excellent, reasonably-priced trattoria. Closed Tue.

Tuscania

In Tuscania it's the post-Etruscan bits which stand out – even though the town itself, already depopulated in the post-war years, was dealt a devastating blow by a major earthquake in 1971. Signs of earthquake damage are still visible in the fabric of the two Romanesque-Lombard churches on the adjacent hillock, **San Pietro** and **Santa Maria Maggiore**; but much was preserved.

The Colle San Pietro, on which they stand, was the site of an Etruscan and then a Roman settlement; fragments of the pre-Christian acropolis are incorporated into the apse of **San Pietro**. This church was started in the 8th century, and reworked between the 11th and the 13th, when the adjacent bishop's palace and defensive towers were added. Close to, the façade is startling: animals and vegetation are densely interwoven with three-faced *trifrons*, snakes and dancers which seem to owe more to pagan culture than to Christian iconography. The interior is rather less startling, with squat pillars, a pretty Cosmatesque pavement and damaged 12th-century frescoes. **Santa Maria Maggiore**, just down the hill from San Pietro, was built at the same time, with tamer beasts carved in the marble façade, and a more harmonious interior.

The main Etruscan find in the town is in the small **archaeological museum**, housed in the cloisters of the **Santa Maria del Riposo** convent. Inside, four generations of the same Etrusco-Roman family, discovered in one of the rare unopened tombs in the area, gaze placidly from the lids of their sarcophagi.

Transport & Information

Getting there: *by bus* COTRAL from Saxa Rubra (summer only; in winter bus to Viterbo, then change); *by car* 85km, Via Cassia (SS2) to Vetralla, then local road.
Museum (07 61 43 62 09) *winter* 9am-5pm; *summer* 9am-7pm. **Closed** Mon.
Where to eat: Despite its isolation, Tuscania has one of northern Lazio's best restaurants: **Al Gallo**, Via del Gallo, 22 (07 61 44 33 88) – it's signposted from Via Cavour. Its gourmet dishes and extensive wine list raise it a notch or two above the usual *trattoria di campagna*. **Closed** Mon.

Directory

Essential Information

Directory (sidebar)

Arriving in Rome

Visas

EU nationals and citizens of the USA, Canada, Australia and New Zealand do not need visas for stays of up to three months. For EU citizens, a passport or national identity card valid for travel abroad is sufficient, but all non-EU citizens must have full passports. In theory, all visitors have to declare their presence to the local police within eight days of arrival. If you're staying in a hotel, this will be done for you. If not, contact the *Questura Centrale*, the main police station, for advice.

Customs

EU citizens do not have to declare goods imported into or exported from Italy for their personal use, as long as they arrive from another EU country. They can still take advantage of duty free shops to buy small quantities of tobacco, alcohol and other goods. Random checks are made for drugs.

For non-EU citizens, the following limits apply:
• 400 cigarettes **or** 200 small cigars **or** 100 cigars **or** 500 grams (17.64oz) of tobacco.
• One litre of spirits (over 22 per cent alcohol) **or** 2 litres of fortified wine (under 22 per cent alcohol); 50 grams (1.76oz) of perfume.

There are no restrictions on the import of cameras, watches or electrical goods. Visitors are also allowed to carry up to L20 million in cash.

Insurance

EU nationals are entitled to reciprocal medical care in Italy, provided they have an E111 form. This will cover you for emergences, but using an E111 naturally involves having to deal with the intricacies of the Italian state health system, and for short-term visitors it's better to take out health cover under private travel insurance. Non-EU citizens should take out private medical insurance for all eventualities before setting out from home.

Visitors should also take out adequate property insurance before setting off for Italy. If you rent a vehicle, motorcycle or moped, make sure you pay the extra charge for full insurance cover, and sign the collision damage waiver when hiring a car. *See* **Car & Bike Hire** *page 257.*

Business

If you're doing business in Rome, a stopover at your embassy's commercial sector is always a good move for gathering information. There you will find trade publications, marketing reports and databases of fairs, buyers, sellers and distributors. (*See* **Embassies & Consulates** *page 243.*)

As ever, any personal recommendations will smooth your way immensely. Use them shamelessly and mercilessly.

Auditors & Accountants

Arthur Andersen & Co
Via Campania, 47 (48 29 71/fax 48 23 684).

Coopers & Lybrand
Via delle Quattro Fontane, 15 (44 62 00 71/fax 48 85 318).

Deloitte Touche
Via Flaminia Vecchia, 495 (33 22 841/fax 33 22 82 82).

KPMG Peat Marwick Consultants
Via Petrolini, 2 (80 97 11/fax 80 77 475).

Price Waterhouse & Associates
Via Giovanni Battista de Rossi, 32b (44 19 22/fax 44 24 48 90)

Banks

Foreign and main offices of major Italian banks only are listed below. Consult the phone book under *banca* for listings of branches.

Abbey National Bank
Via Cicerone, 58 (32 14 910/fax 32 21 536).

Banca Commerciale Italiana
Via del Corso, 226 (67 121/fax 67 12 49 23).

Banca Nazionale del Lavoro
Via Vittorio Veneto, 119 (47 021/fax 47 63 25 08).

Banca di Roma
Via Marco Minghetti, 17 (67 071/fax 67 00 54 35).

Barclays Bank
Via Mercadante, 32 (84 12 753/fax 85 49 656).

Chase Manhattan
Via Bertoloni, 26 (80 85 655/fax 80 85 766).

Deutsche Bank
Largo del Tritone, 161 (67 181/fax 67 92 090).

Istituto Bancario San Paolo di Torino
Via della Stamperia, 64 (85 751/fax 85 75 27 53).

Istituto Mobiliare Italiano (IMI)
Viale dell'Arte, 25 (59 591/fax 59 59 38 88).

Merrill Lynch
Largo della Fontanella Borghese, 19 (68 39 31/fax 68 39 32 31).

Morgan Stanley
Piazza dell'Aracoeli, 1 (69 94 00 02/fax 69 94 09 74).

Ufficio Italiano Cambi
Via Quattro Fontane, 123 (46 631/fax 48 25 591).
The official Italian foreign exchange office.

Woolwich Bank
Via di San Martino della Battaglia, 22-30 (44 61 332/ fax 44 56 674).

Business Centres

Finding temporary office space and services can be difficult in Rome, and the little that's on offer is nothing special. The following provide basic facilities, including conference and secretarial services.

Centro Uffici Parioli
Via Lima, 41 (85 30 13 50/fax 85 30 13 29).

Pick Center
Via Attilio Regolo, 19 (32 43 087/fax 32 24 637).

Conference Organisers

Rome offers superb facilities for conferences in magnificent *palazzi* and castles. Most of the major hotels, especially the Grand on Via Emanuele Orlando and the Excelsior on Via Veneto, can cater for events of all sizes (*see chapter* **Accommodation**). If you don't wish to handle the details yourself, a number of agencies will smooth the way for you.

Studio Ega
Viale Tiziano, 19 (32 21 806/fax 32 22 006).

Tecnoconference
Via Udine, 30 (44 04 271/fax 44 04 272).

Triumph Congressi
Via Proba Petronia, 3 (39 72 77 07/fax 39 73 51 95).

Couriers (local delivery)

Speedy Boys *(39 888).*

Presto *(39 890).*

Boy Express *(48 90 01 05).*

Line Service *(77 297/Toll Free 16 70 13 601).*
Linked with UPS for international deliveries.

Couriers (international delivery)

DHL *(Toll Free 16 73 45 345).*

Federal Express *(Toll Free 16 78 33 040).*

UPS *(Toll Free 16 78 22 054).*

Interpreters

CRIC *Via dei Fienili, 65 (67 87 950/fax 67 91 208).*

Law Firms

These companies specialise in international corporate and finance law.

Tonon & Associates
Via Toscana, 30 (42 87 10 33/fax 42 74 47 08).
Offices in Milan, New York and Los Angeles.

Frere, Cholmeley, Bischoff
Via Bruno Buozzi, 47 (80 80 133/fax 80 80 134).
London firm specialising in acquisitions and joint ventures.

Communications
Post

In ancient times a letter from Rome to Bari took three days. Times have changed and today the same journey can take three weeks or more. The

Directory

Who to Ring in an Emergency

The *carabinieri* take their public-protection role seriously, and even if your Italian's not up to much, their freephone general emergency helpline (112) should be your first port of call in any emergency.

The phone will be answered in Italian but you'll be put straight through to a *carabiniere* who is a fluent speaker of English, French, German or Spanish, depending on your needs, and can give you advice, support and information on what to do. You should dial this number if you need an ambulance, are the victim of any sort of crime, have an accident (road or other), are taken ill

suddenly or lose anything or anyone. The *carabinieri* patrol the city 24 hours a day, so they can be with you in a few minutes or will be able to tell you where to go to find the help you require.

Alternatively, you can phone any of the following numbers, all of which operate round the clock:
Police/Fire/Ambulance (*Polizia/Vigili del Fuoco/Ambulanza*) 113.
Medical Emergencies (*Emergence sanitarie*) 118.
Fire Service (*Vigili del Fuoco*) 115.
Central Police Station (*Questura Centrale*) 46 861.
Municipal Police (*Vigili urbani*) 67 691.
ACI Auto Assistance (*Automobile Club d'Italia*) 116.

Italian postal system is notoriously unpredictable. Letters can and do arrive in reasonable time, but this is never something that you can rely on.

A good alternative is to use the Vatican post office, at least for anything you're sending abroad. It is run in association with the Swiss postal service and is considerably more reliable than the Italian system. See **Business** page 240.

Post Offices

There are local post offices (*ufficio postale*) in each district, and these are open from 8.25am to 6pm, Monday to Friday (8.25am-2pm in August), and from 8.25am to 1.30pm on Saturday. They close two hours earlier than normal on the last day of each month. The four main post offices in the centre of town have longer opening hours and a range of additional services, including fax facilities.

Centro Pacchi (Parcels Office)

Piazza dei Caprettari (Information 160). Bus to Corso del Rinascimento. **Open** 8.25am-3.20pm Mon-Fri.
Parcels can be sent from any post office, but this is the only branch where they can be sent insured. Given the unreliability of the postal system, it is advisable to send any package worth more than L100,000 from here.

Posta Centrale (Main Post Office)

Piazza San Silvestro, 18/20 (67 71; Information 160). Bus to Piazza San Silvestro. **Open** 9am-6pm Mon-Fri; 9am-2pm Sat (closes at noon last Sat of month); 9am-6pm Sun.
This is the hub of Rome's postal system, although the other main post offices have many of the same services. Letters sent *Poste Restante* (*Fermo Posta* in Italian) to Rome should be addressed to *Roma Centro Corrispondenza, Posta Centrale, Piazza San Silvestro, 00186 Roma.*
You will need your passport to collect letters, and you have to pay a small charge. At the San Silvestro office, there is a 24-hour fax service, but it cannot transmit or receive from certain other countries.

Other Main Offices

Via Taranto (70 04 350). Metro San Giovanni.
Stazione Termini (47 45 671). Metro Termini/bus or tram to Termini.
Via Federico Galeotti, 49 (62 23 006). Bus to Ciconvallazione Aurelia.

Poste Vaticane (Vatican Post Office)

Piazza San Pietro; Vatican Museums complex (69 82). Bus to Piazza del Risorgimento. **Open** 8.30am-7pm Mon-Fri; 8.30am-6pm Sat.
Charges are a little higher than the Italian system (L850 for letters within the EU, for example). You must use Vatican stamps, and mail must be posted in special Vatican post boxes.
Letters to the UK usually arrive in three or four days, and those to the US in a week. Staff are used to dealing with foreigners and speak several languages between them.

Stamps & Charges

Stamps can be bought at *tabacchi (see page 249)* or from post offices. A letter of up to 20 grams costs L800 to any destination in the EU, L1,300 to the USA or Canada, and L1,400 to Australia or New Zealand.

Most post boxes are red and have two slots, *Per la Città* (for Rome) and *Tutte le Altre Destinazioni* (for everywhere else). New blue post boxes decorated with the EU star symbol have also started to appear throughout the city: these are for international mail only. All going well, a letter will take about five days to the UK and eight to the US. To speed things up, mail can also be sent *Raccomandata* (registered; L4,000 extra) or *Espresso* (express, supposedly the quickest; L3,600 extra).

Telegrams & Telexes

These can be sent from the main post offices. The telegraph office at the Posta Centrale on Piazza San Silvetro (entrance 18) is open 24 hours a day. Alternatively, you can dictate telegrams over the phone by dialling 186 from a private phone.

Faxes

These can be sent from most large post offices, which will charge you for the units used, plus a surcharge per sheet. They can also be sent from some photocopying outlets. In all cases, the surcharge will be hefty. Occasional fax/phones can be found in main stations and at Fiumicino airport.

Telephones

Although the pressures of competition have led to some price cuts, the Italian telephone company (*Telecom Italia*) still operates one of the most expensive systems in Europe, particularly for international calls. The minimum charge for a local call from a private phone is about L150 (L200 from a public one) but the normal rate for a minute to the UK is L1,081; to the rest of northern Europe L1,245; to the US L1,395; and to Australia and New Zealand L3,048. In all cases it's more if you're using a public phone. One way to keep costs down is to phone off-peak (10pm to 8am Monday to Saturday, and all day Sunday). Another is to avoid using phones in hotels, which may carry extortionate surcharges. Phoning from a telephone centre (*see below*) costs the same as from a phone box, but it's more convenient for long-distance calls because you avoid the need for large amounts of change or several phone cards. Additional services are listed in the local phone book, the *elenco telefonico*.

Phone Numbers

To call Rome from outside the city, dial 06 before the number. All numbers beginning with 1678 are freephone lines. Rome is currently changing its phone numbers from seven to eight digits, so any seven-digit number should be treated with caution. If you try a number and cannot get through, an extra digit may already have been added. For the first two months after the change, there will normally be a recorded message stating the new number, but if you have difficulties, ring the operator (12) to check.

Public Phones

Rome has no shortage of public phone boxes (although they tend to be clustered in areas where the traffic makes it almost impossible to hear) and many bars have payphones. Many public phones only accept phone cards (*carte telefoniche*); a few also accept major credit cards. Telephone cards cost L5,000, L10,000 and L15,000, and are available from *tabacchi* (*see page 249*), some newspaper stands and a few bars. When you use a new card, break off one corner as marked and insert the card into the slot in the phone. The available credit is shown on a digital display. Beware: phone cards have expiry dates (usually 31 December or 30 June) after which, no matter how much credit you think you've got, you won't be able to use them. Irritatingly, the Vatican City has its own special phone cards, obtainable from the Vatican post offices for the same prices and usable only within the City State. To use public phones you will need L100, L200 and L500 coins. The minimum charge for a local call is L200.

International Calls

To make an international call from Rome, dial 00, and the appropriate country code: Australia 61; Canada 1; Irish Republic 353; New Zealand 64; United Kingdom 44; United States 1. Then dial the area code (for calls to the UK, omit the initial zero of the area code) and the individual number.

To phone Rome from abroad, dial the international code (00 in the UK), then 39 for Italy and 6 for Rome, followed by the individual number. To make a reverse charge (collect) call, dial 170 for the international operator in Italy. Alternatively, to be connected to the operator in the country you want to call, dial 172 followed by a four-digit code for the country and telephone company you want to use (for the UK and Ireland this is the same as the country code above; for other countries see the front of the phone directory). In a phone box you will need to insert a L200 coin, which will be refunded after your call.

Phone Centre

At the phone centre in the main hall at Termini station you are allotted a booth, and pay at the desk when you have finished.

Operator Services

All these services are open 24 hours daily.
Operator and Italian Directory Enquiries (12).
International Operator (170).
International Directory Enquiries (176).
Communication problems on national calls (182).
Communication problems on international calls (17 23 535).
Alarm calls (114). (An automatic message will ask you to dial in the time you want your call, with four figures on a 24-hour clock, followed by your phone number.)
Tourist information (110).

All but the most antiquated wiring systems work on 220v, which is compatible with British and US bought appliances. Buy two-pin adaptor plugs before leaving for Italy, as they will almost certainly cost more here. Otherwise, they can be bought at any electrical shop (look for *Casalinghi* or *Electricità*). See **Emergency Repairs** *page 244.*

Embassies can be an invaluable source of information if you're in the city for commercial reasons (*see* **Business** *page 240*). It's always a good idea to phone and make an appointment before visiting, since opening hours vary depending on what you want to do or who you want to see. In general, if you phone an embassy or consulate between about 9am and 1pm, or from about 2 to 4.30pm Monday to Friday, you'll get a reply; the rest of the time there's usually only an answering machine, which may or may not give you information about what to do in an emergency.

Listed below are the embassies of some of the English-speaking countries, but a full list is found under *Ambasciate* in the telephone directory. Except where indicated, consular offices, which provide most services of use to tourists and the general public, share the same address as the embassies.

American Embassy
Via Vittorio Veneto, 119 (46 741).
Metro Barberini/bus to Piazza Barberini or Via Veneto.
Emergency duty officer 24 hours daily.

Australian Embassy
Via Alessandria, 215
(85 27 21). Bus to Via Nomentana.

British Embassy
Via XX Settembre, 80a
(48 25 551). Bus to Piazzale Porta Pia.

Canadian Embassy
Embassy Via G B de Rossi, 27
(44 59 81).
Consulate: Via Zara, 30
(44 59 81). Bus to Viale Regina Margherita.

Irish Embassy
Piazza Campitelli, 3
(69 79 121). Bus to Piazza Venezia.

New Zealand Embassy
Via Zara, 28 (44 02 928).
Bus to Viale Regina Margherita.

South African Embassy

Via Tanaro, 14 (85 25 41). Bus to Piazza Buenos Aires, Via Tagliamento.

Emergency Repairs

If you need to report a malfunction in any of the main services, the following emergency lines are open 24 hours a day. Which of the two Rome electricity companies (ACEA or ENEL) you should call will be indicated on your electricity meter.

Electricity (ACEA) (57 51 61; emergency number 167 22 88 33).
Electricity (ENEL) (answering machine 16 441; operator 32 12 200).
Gas (Italgas) (16 78 03 020).
Telephone (Telecom Italia) 182).
Water (ACEA) (57 51 71; emergency number 167 22 99 88).

Health

Emergency health care is available for all travellers through the Italian national health system and, by law, doctors must treat emergency cases who present themselves at the casualty department of any hospital. However, if you're only visiting for a short time, it's worth taking out private health insurance (*see* **Insurance** *page 240*).

Hospitals

If you need urgent medical care (but not an ambulance) it is best to go to the *Pronto Soccorso* (casualty department) of the nearest hospital. The hospitals listed below are open 24 hours a day.

Ospedale Fatenbenefratelli
Isola Tiberina (58 731). Bus to Piazza di Monte Savello or Lungotevere degli Anguillara or Piazza Sonnino.

Opsedale San Giacomo
Via Canova, 29 (36 261). Metro Spagna/bus to Via del Corso.

Ospedale San Giovanni
Via Ambra Aradam, 8 (77 051). Metro San Giovanni/bus to Piazza San Giovanni.

Bicycle Thieves

Murders and serious assaults are compararively rare in Rome. Bag-snatching, traditionally committed by *motorini*-riding *scippatori* who sometimes pull their victims to the ground as they wrestle for bags and cameras draped insecurely over shoulders, poses the biggest physical threat to most visitors. The highest-risk areas are the *centro storico*, around the Vatican, the Forum, the Colosseum and Trastevere, where a few years ago a woman died as a result of injuries from a passing *motorino*.

Child pickpockets operate by swarming around their victims and disorienting them while they get to work. A few still patrol the main approach roads to the Vatican and the Colosseum, but most pickpocketing takes place in crowded shopping areas or on buses – especially those frequented by tourists, such as the 64 from Termini to the Vatican. If you are the victim of any crime, call 112.

Policlinico Umberto I
Viale Policlinico (44 62 341). Metro Policlinico/bus or tram to Viale Regina Elena.

Pharmacies

Pharmacies (*farmacia*, identified by a large red or green cross) function semi-officially as mini-clinics, with staff giving informal medical advice for straightforward ailments, as well as making up prescriptions from your doctor (for which you have to pay).

If you're staying in Rome any length of time, it's worth checking out where your nearest pharmacy is. Normal opening hours are from 8.30am to 1pm and from 4pm to 8pm, Monday to Saturday.The best-stocked pharmacy in Rome is the one in the Vatican, which has a range of medicines not normally found in pharmacies.

During closing times, a duty rota system is in operation. A list by the door of any pharmacy indicates the nearest ones which are open outside normal hours. The daily rota is also published in the local papers, and there are phone lines for information on which chemists are open in each

district (1921 is the number for the central zone and 1922 to 1925 for other areas; operators do not usually speak English).

At duty pharmacies there is a surcharge of L5,000 per client (but not per item) when the main shop is shut and only the special duty counter is open, which in most cases is between midnight and 8.30am.

The following pharmacies are open outside normal times:

Farmacia della Stazione
Piazza dei Cinquecento (corner of Via Cavour; 48 80 019). Metro Termini/bus to Termini. **Open** 24 hours daily. **Credit** Amex, DC, EC, MC, V.

Farmacia del Vaticano
Porta Sant'Anna entrance, Città del Vaticano (69 88 34 22). Metro Ottaviano/bus to Piazza del Risorgimento. **Open** 7.30am-1pm, 3.30-6.30pm, Mon-Fri; 7.30am-1pm Sat. **Credit** No credit cards. Many staff here speak English.

Internazionale
Piazza Barberini, 49 (48 25 456). Metro Barberini/bus to Piazza Barberini. **Open** 24 hours daily. **Credit** EC, MC, V.

Piram
Via Nazionale, 228 (48 80 754). Metro Repubblica/bus to Via Nazionale. **Open** 24 hours daily. **Credit** MC,V.

Help Lines & Agencies

For information on additional counselling services, *see also chapters* **Gay Rome, Lesbian Rome** and **Women's Rome**.

Alcoholics Anonymous

Via Torre Rossa, 35 (66 36 620/66 36 629). Bus to Piazza San Giovanni Battista de la Salle.
This is the address of the Italian branch. An active English-speaking support group holds meetings at the church of Saint Paul's-within-the-Walls (Via Napoli, 56) on Monday, Wednesday and Friday at 8pm, and on Saturday and Sunday at 7pm, and at Saint Andrew's Presbyterian Church (Via XX Settembre, 7) on Tuesday and Thursday at 7pm.

Drug Hotline

Via Ramazzini, 31 (65 74 11 88). Train to Stazione Trastevere/bus to Circonvallazione Gianicolense. **Open** 9am-9pm daily.
This centre provides medical and psychiatric assistance for all drug-related problems, and also has an emergency service and a 24-hour phone helpline. Staff do not usually speak English.

Narcotics Anonymous

(86 04 788)
Meetings are held (usually in Italian) at various places across the city. A recorded message on the above number gives the current timetable and addresses.

Samaritans

(70 45 44 44/70 45 44 45). **Open** *Sept-Jun* 1-10pm daily; *July-Aug* Listen to answering machine message for timetable.
Staffed by native English speakers, this confidential help and counselling line was set up for the diplomatic and expatriate community. Most of the volunteers also speak Italian.

Dentists

George Eastman Clinic

Viale Regina Elena, 287 (41 60 95 06/24-hour emergency number 84 48 31). Metro Policlinico. **Open** 7.30-1.30pm Mon-Sat.

Veterinary Care

Centro Veterinario Gregorio VII

Via Gregorio VII, 518 (68 21 686). Train to Stazione San Pietro/bus to Via Gregorio VII. **Open** 24 hours daily.

Left Luggage

The left luggage offices by platforms 1 and 22 of Termini station are open from 5.20am to 12.20am daily, and Rome's Fiumicino airport has left luggage offices in its international (24 hours a day) and domestic (7.15am-11.15pm) terminals. If you're staying in a hotel, staff are generally willing to look after your luggage for you during the day, even after you have checked out.

Lost Property

Anything mislaid on public transport, or stolen and subsequently discarded, may turn up at one of the lost propery offices (*ufficio oggetti rinvenuti*) listed below.

For the emergency numbers to call if you lose (or have stolen) a credit or charge card or travellers' cheques, *see* **Banks & Foreign Exchange** *below.*

ATAC

Via Nicolò Bettoni, 1 (58 16 040). Train to Stazione Trastevere/bus to Circonvallazione Gianicolense. **Open** 8.30am-1pm Mon, Fri; 8.30am-1pm, 2.30-6pm, Tue-Thur.
Anything found on the city bus and tram network may turn up here.

COTRAL

For property lost on the Metro A line, phone 48 74 309; on the Metro B line phone 57 54 295; and on COTRAL buses phone 57 531 or 59 15 551.

FS/Stazione Termini

Via Giovanni Giolitti, 24 (47 30 66 82). Metro Termini/bus or tram to Termini. **Open** 7am-10pm daily.
Articles found on the state railway anywhere in the Rome area are sent here – the office is near platform 22. If you're in luck, you may find one or more members of staff who speak rudimentary English.

Money

The Italian currency is the *lira* (plural *lire*). Coins for L50 and L100 come in a variety of sizes. An attempt to replace the traditional large coins with minute ones met with such public dismay that a new in-between size has recently been introduced; all three sizes continue to circulate. There are also coins for L200 and L500. Each of the six denominations of bank notes carries a picture of a famous Italian, from Maria Montessori on the L1,000, L2,000, L5,000, L10,000 and L50,000 note, to the L100,000 note with its portrait of Caravaggio. A L500,000 note will soon be issued. In many shops and businesses, assistants will throw up their hands in horror if asked to change L50,000 or L100,000 notes when you're buying something inexpensive.

Prices are rounded up to the nearest L50. By law, after any transaction you must be given a full receipt (*scontrino fiscale*). Some places will insist you take it, but others may try to avoid giving you a receipt for tax reasons, in which case it is your right and according to the *guardia di finanza*, or financial police, also your duty) to ask for one. In the unlikely event of your being accosted by the *guardia di finanza* as you exit a shop, you, as well as the shopkeeper, are liable for a fine if you do not have proof of payment for any goods you have purchased.

Banks & Foreign Exchange

Banks usually have better exchange rates than the private bureaux de change (*cambio*). The main Rome offices of most of the banks are along or near Via del Corso. It's a good idea to take a passport or other identity document whenever you're dealing with money, and you will definitely need one if you want to change travellers' cheques or withdraw money on a credit card. Commission rates vary considerably: you can pay from nothing to L10,000 for each transaction. Watch out for

'No Commission' signs, as the rate of exchange will almost certainly be terrible.

Many bank cash machines (*Bancomat*) can also be used with major credit cards or banking cards bearing the Eurocard symbol (up to L300,000 per day). Most banks will also give cash advances against a credit card, but this varies according to the bank, and increasing numbers refuse to do so if you do not have a PIN number.

There are several automatic cash exchange machines around the city, which accept notes in most currencies. Notes need to be in good condition for the machine to take them. If you need to have money sent over from home, the best method is via American Express, Thomas Cook or Western Union.

Most banks are open from 8.30am to 1.45pm and from 2.45pm to 4.30pm. Some branches now have extended hours, opening until 6pm on Thursdays and 12.30pm on Saturdays. Banks participating in this scheme display signs in their windows and on their counters. All banks are closed on public holidays, and staff work reduced hours the day before a holiday, usually closing around 11am.

American Express

Piazza di Spagna, 38 (67 641).
Metro Spagna/bus to Piazza San Silvestro. **Open** *Apr-Sept* 9am-5.30pm Mon-Fri, 9am-3pm Sat; *Oct-Mar* 9am-5.30pm Mon-Fri, 9am-12.30pm Sat.
All the standard AmEx services are available, such as travellers' cheque refund service, card replacement, *Poste Restante*, and a cash machine which can be used with AmEx cards. Money can be transferred from any American Express office in the world within 24 hours.

Main Post Offices

Piazza San Silvestro (Information 160). Bus to Piazza San Silvestro.
Open 9am-6pm Mon-Fri, Sun; 9am-2pm Sat.
Via della Mercede (Information 160). Bus to Piazza San Silvestro. **Open**

8.30am-1.50pm Mon-Fri; 8.30am-12.50pm Sat.
Via Terme Diocleziano, 30 (Information 160). Metro Repubblica/bus to Piazza della Repubblica. **Open** 8.30am-6.30pm Mon-Fri; 8.30am-2pm Sat.
Main post offices have exchange bureaux. Commission is L1,000 for all cash transactions, L2,000 for travellers' cheques up to the value of L100,000, and L5,000 for any greater amount. Only American Express travellers' cheques are accepted. *See* **Post Offices** *page 242.*

Thomas Cook

Piazza Barberini, 21 (48 20 082). Metro Barberini/bus to Piazza Barberini. **Open** 8.30am-7.30pm Mon-Sat; 9am-1.30pm Sun.
Branches *Via della Conciliazione, 23/25 (68 30 04 35).* **Open** 8.30am-7.30pm Mon-Sat; 9am-5.30pm Sun. *Via del Corso, 23 (32 00 224).* **Open** 9am-8pm Mon-Sat; 9.30am-1.30pm Sun.
The three branches of Thomas Cook are among the very few exchange offices open on Sunday. A 2.5 per cent commission is charged on all transactions apart from Thomas Cook, MasterCard and Swiss Bankers' travellers' cheques, which are cashed free of charge. MasterCard holders can also withdraw money here. Money can be transferred to the Rome offices from any Thomas Cook branch in the UK. Commission is charged to the sender, and the transfer should take around 48 hours.

Western Union Money Transfer

Agenzia Tartaglia, Piazza di Spagna, 12 (Toll Free 16 70 16 840). Metro Piazza di Spagna. **Open** 9am-6pm Mon-Fri.
The quickest, though certainly not the cheapest, way to send money, which should arrive within the hour. Western Union has hundreds of agents in the US and the UK, but only two in Rome. The commission is paid by the sender, on a sliding scale.

Credit Cards

Italians still have an enduring fondness for cash, though persuading them to take plastic has become considerably easier over the past few years. Nearly all hotels of two stars and above now accept at least some of the major credit cards, and Eurocheques are also accepted – albeit grudgingly – with the necessary guarantee card.

If you lose a credit or charge card, phone one of the

emergency numbers listed below. All lines are freephone numbers, have English-speaking staff and are open 24 hours a day.
American Express *(16 78 64 046).*
Diner's Club *(16 78 64 064).*
Eurocard/Carta Si (including Mastercard and Visa) *(16 78 68 086).*
Mastercard *(16 78 74 299).*
Visa *(16 78 77 232).*

On public holidays (*giorni festivi*) virtually all shops, banks and businesses are closed, although (with the exception of May Day, *ferragosto* and Christmas Day) bars and restaurants tend to stay open.

The public holidays are as follows: New Year's Day (*Capo d'anno*), 1 January; Epiphany (*La Befana*), 6 January; Easter Monday (*Pasquetta*); Liberation Day, 25 April; May Day, 1 May; Patron Saints' Day (*San Pietro e San Paolo*), 29 June; Feast of the Assumption (*ferragosto*), 15 August; All Saints' (*Tutti santi*), 1 November; Immaculate Conception (*Festa dell'Immacolata*), 8 December; Christmas Day (*Natale*); Boxing Day (*Santo Stefano*).

There is very limited public transport on 1 May and Christmas afternoon. Holidays falling on a Saturday or Sunday are not celebrated the following Monday. However, if a holiday falls on a Thursday or a Tuesday, many people will take the Friday and Monday off as well. *See chapter* **Rome by Season**.

Public Lavatories

If you need a loo, the easiest thing is usually to go to a bar (which won't necessarily provide toilet paper). There are modern lavatories at or near most of the major tourist sites; the majority of these have attendants and you must pay to use them. Fast food joints, and some of the larger department stores, can also come in handy.

Queuing

Lining up one behind the other doesn't always come easy to the Italians, although despite the apparent chaos, queue-jumpers are usually given short shrift. Hanging back deferentially, on the other hand, is taken as a clear sign of stupidity and if you're not careful the tide will sweep contemptuously past you. In busy shops and bars, be aware of who is in front of you and behind you and, when it's your turn, assert your rights emphatically. Queues at ticket offices are generally more orderly.

Religion

There are over 400 Catholic churches throughout the city (*see chapter* **Churches** for details of the most historically and artistically interesting). Several hold mass in English. The main British Catholic church is San Silvestro at Piazza San Silvestro, 1 (67 97 775). San Patrizio, which is at Via Boncompagni, 31 (48 85 716), is the principal Irish church in Rome, and the American Catholic community church is Santa Susanna, at Via XX Settembre, 14 (48 27 510). For information on papal audiences *see chapter* **The Vatican City**.

Some of the non-Catholic denominations and religions represented in Rome are listed below, with the times of their main services or prayer times.

American Episcopal Church

Saint Paul's-within-the Walls, Via Napoli, 58 (48 83 339). Metro Repubblica/bus to Via Nazionale or Piazza della Repubblica. **Services** 8.30am, 10.30am Sun.
This socially active church also has services in Spanish for its large Filipino congregation. The crypt is used for, among other things, English meetings of Alcoholics Anonymous.

Anglican

All Saints, Via del Babuino, 153b (36 00 18 81). Metro Spagna/bus to Via del Corso. **Services** 6pm Tue-Thur; 10.30am Sun.
The church was opened in 1887 but the chaplaincy dates from 1816 when services were held in the chaplain's rooms in Piazza di Spagna. Today it hosts an active programme of cultural events, including regular, high-quality concerts. Times are liable to change, so ring ahead.

Jewish

Comunità Israelitica di Roma Lungotevere Cenci (68 40 061). Bus to Piazza di Monte Savello.
There are services every day but the times vary throughout the year. Guided tours of the synagogue are offered from the museum, the Museo di Arte Ebraica (*see chapter* **Museums & Galleries**).

Methodist

Ponte Sant'Angelo Church, Via del Banco di Santa Spirito (68 68 341). Bus to Corso Vittorio Emanuele. **Services** 10.30am Sun.

Muslim

La Moschea di Roma, Viale della Moschea (80 82 167). Train to Campi Sportivi.
Paolo Portoghesi's masterpiece is always open to Muslims for prayer. It can also be visited by non-Muslims, but phone first to find out when (no admission is allowed during special prayer hours).

Presbyterian (Church of Scotland)

Saint Andrew's, Via XX Settembre, 7 (48 27 627). Bus to Via XX Settembre. **Services** 11am Sun.
The church is also used by Korean Presbyterians during the week and on Sundays.

Safety

Muggings are fairly rare in Rome, but pickpockets and bag snatchers (including children operating singly or in gangs) are particularly active in the main tourist areas (*see* **Bicycle Thieves** *page 244*). You will find that a few basic precautions will greatly reduce a street thief's chances:
• Don't carry wallets in back pockets, particularly on buses. If you have a bag or camera with a carrying strap, wear it across the chest and not dangling from one shoulder.
• Keep bags closed, with your hand on them. If you stop at a pavement café or restaurant, do not leave bags or coats on the ground or the back of a chair where you cannot keep an eye on them.
• Avoid attracting unwanted attention by pulling out large wads of notes to pay for things at street stalls or in busy bars.
• When walking down a street, hold cameras and bags on the side of you towards the wall, so you're less likely to become the prey of a motorcycle thief or *scippatore*.
• If you see groups of children brandishing pieces of cardboard, avoid them or walk past as quickly as possible, keeping a tight hold on your valuables. They'll use the cardboard to distract your attention while accomplices pick your pockets or bags.

If you are the victim of crime go immediately to the nearest police station and say you want to report a *furto* (*see* **Who to Ring in an Emergency** *page 241*). A *denuncia* (written statement) of the incident will be made by or for you.

It is unlikely that your things will be found, but you will need the *denuncia* for making an insurance claim. A lost or stolen passport should be reported to your embassy or consulate immediately.

It's also a good idea to phone the emergency credit card lines (*see* **Banks & Foreign Exchange** *page 245*) to report any missing traveller's cheques, or credit or charge cards.

Students

Some Italian is useful before embarking on any study programme, but it's not essential: English is spoken in many of the universities and institutes. If notified in advance,

Directory

Tabacchi

The only places in Italy where you can legally buy cigarettes are *tabacchi* (tobacconists), identified by distinctive white 'T's on black or dark blue signs. Some bars have a *tabacchi* counter, which is fine if you just want to buy cigarettes, but to get the full range of goods and services that these eclectic institutions offer (and bear in mind that the most basic supplies can suddenly run out in an entire area), head for your nearest *tabacchi* shop.

It will usually have at least some of the following: salt (which, like tobacco, is a state monopoly, although you can buy it in most food shops now); postage stamps; the official stamps and stationery you need when dealing with Italian bureaucracy; bus, Metro and local train tickets; phone cards; and lottery tickets, including the ubiquitous *gratti e vinci* (scratch and win) cards. Some *tabacchi* also offer fax and photocopying services, though the specialised agencies tend to be cheaper.

What's more, you're likely to find an Aladdin's cave of sweets, toiletries, postcards, souvenirs and the sort of luxurious-looking 'gifts' that scream 'I didn't know what else to buy you' to their unlucky recipients.

many schools make special arrangements for groups of foreigners, offering discounts and providing facilities in their own language.

The three state universities, **La Sapienza**, **Tor Vergata** and **Roma Tre**, and the private LUISS (*Libera Università Internazionale degli Studi Sociali*) offer exchanges with European universities through the Erasmus programme. Some American universities, such as the Rhode Island School of Design, have campuses in Rome, which students attend on exchange programmes.

There are also many private Catholic universities which run some of the most highly respected Faculties of Medicine in the country. The student scene, however, is dominated by La Sapienza, and specialist bookshops are to be found in the neighbouring San Lorenzo district and along Viale Ippocrate. *See also* **Voluntary Work & Study Groups** *page 252.*

Bureaucracy & Services

Foreigners studying on any type of course in Italy must obtain a student's permit from the police (for regulations *see* **Living & Working in Rome** *page 261*).

Apart from student offices in the universities themselves, there are private agencies that deal with the business of applications and enrolments.

Centro Turistico Studentesco (CTS)

Via Genova, 16 (46 79 271). **Open** 9am-1pm, 3-7pm, Mon-Fri; 9am-1pm Sat.

The CTS student travel centre issues student cards guaranteeing lower rates on travel tickets, hostels and language courses.

Nuovo Centro Servizi Universitari

Viale Ippocrate, 160 (44 55 741). Metro Policlinico. **Open** 8.30am-7pm Mon-Fri.

This private agency takes charge of enrolment, registration for exams and all other time-consuming details. Staff are well informed about the procedures and courses of the

university and can quickly tell you what you need. Along with the L10,000 membership fee, there are travel offers and discounts to concerts and cinemas.

Libraries

There are libraries all over Rome, but if you're intending to carry out any research, be prepared for red tape, restricted hours and patchy organisation. Most libraries do not have computer catalogues, so finding a book – even if you know it's there – can be a deeply frustrating experience.

All the libraries listed below are open to the public. Other specialist libraries can be found under *Biblioteche* in the phone book. It is always useful to take an identity document, with you; in some cases, a letter from your professor stating the purpose of your research will be required. *See* **Bookshops** *in chapter* **Shopping**.

Biblioteca Alessandrina

Piazzale Aldo Moro, 5, Centre of Città Universitaria (44 56 820). Metro Policlinico. **Open** 8.30am-7.30 pm Mon-Fri; 8.30am-1pm Sat.

La Sapienza's main library is grossly inefficient for the needs of a huge university. There are no computers available for student use, and to take books out, students need to fill out a form and attach two photographs.

Biblioteca Nazionale

Viale Castro Pretorio, 105 (49 89). Metro Castro Pretorio. **Open** Sept-mid July 8.30am-7pm Mon-Fri; 8.30am-1.30pm Sat; mid July-Sept 8.30am-1.30pm Mon-Sat. **Closed** Two weeks mid-Aug.

The Biblioteca Nazionale holds 80 per cent of everything that is in print in Italy, as well as books in other languages. The system is not computerised, however, so finding what you need may be challenging, to say the least. To take books out, students need to fill out a form and then have it signed by both their professor and their university secretary.

Biblioteca dell'Università Gregoriana

Piazza della Pilotta, 4 (32 22 155). Bus to Piazza Venezia. **Open** 8am-6.30pm Mon-Fri; 8am-12pm Sat.

Much better organised than La Sapienza's library, but books are not allowed off the premises.

Biblioteca Vaticana

Via di Porta Angelica (69 88 50 51). Metro Ottaviano/bus to Saint Peter's. **Open** 8am-1.30pm, mid-Sept to mid-July.

To consult the invaluable papal tomes, students need a letter signed by a professor stating the purpose of their research.

The British School at Rome

Piazzale Winston Churchill, 5 (32 22 155). Bus to Via Bruno Buozzi/tram to Piazza Thorwaldsen. **Open** 9.30am-1pm, 2-7.30pm, Mon-Fri. The wood-panelled reading room of the British School contains a large collection of English and Italian books on every aspect of Rome, especially archaeology, classical art history and topography. To be admitted, students need two passport-sized photos and a letter of presentation from a university or museum. No borrowing.

Time & Weather

Italy is one hour ahead of British time. Rome can sizzle at over 40°C in high summer. Spring and autumn are usually warm and pleasant, although there may be occasional heavy showers, particularly in March, April and early May. Between November and February you cannot rely on good weather, and might either come across a week of rain, or crisp, bright (sometimes even warm) sunshine. The compensation is the comparative scarcity of fellow tourists.

Tipping

Foreigners are expected to tip more than Italians, but the 10 per cent customary in many countries would be considered generous even for the richest-looking tourist. Most locals leave L100 or L200 on the counter when buying drinks at the bar and, depending on the standard of the restaurant, L2,000 to L10,000 for the waiter after a meal. Many of the larger restaurants now include a 10 or 15 per cent service charge. Tips are not expected in family-run restaurants, although even here a couple of thousand is always

appreciated and may get you an extra-warm welcome when you return. It is not usual to tip taxi drivers.

Tourist Information

The offices of Rome's provincial tourist board, **EPT**, and also the state tourist board, **ENIT**, have English-speaking staff, but they seem to have a surprisingly limited amount of information, and what they can tell you you can be unreliable or out of date.

For a more personal service, the private agency **Enjoy Rome** comes recommended: their staff are friendly and well-informed. For more specific information on city tours *see chapter* **Sightseeing**. The local English-language press is another useful source of information; for details *see chapter* **Media**).

The international English Yellow Pages is based in Rome and lists English-speaking services and useful numbers. It is found in international bookshops, and most hotels will also have copies that you can borrow. For a list of English-language bookshops, *see chapter* **Shopping**.

Enjoy Rome

Via Varese, 39 (44 51 843; fax 44 50 734). Metro Termini/bus or tram to Termini. **Open** 8.30am-1pm, 3.30-6pm, Mon-Fri; 8.30am-1pm Sat. This friendly English-speaking company is a very handy place for information and advice on everything you might need to know about Rome.

The office is near the main railway station, Termini, and provides an accommodation-booking service and left luggage facilities, both for free. They also arrange walking tours (three-hour tours in Rome: L25,000 under-26, L30,000 over-26) and trips to Pompeii (L55,000 each). The phone is manned until 10pm Monday to Friday for booking hotels.

Ente Provinciale per il Turismo di Roma (EPT)

Head office: Via Parigi, 11 (48 99 91). Metro Repubblica/bus or tram to Piazza della Repubblica. **Open** 8.15am-7.15pm Mon-Fri; 8.15am-1.45pm Sat. *Information from: Via*

Parigi, 5 (48 89 92 53/48 89 92 55). Metro Repubblica/bus or tram to Piazza della Repubblica. **Open** 8.15am-7.15pm Mon-Fri; 8.15am-1.45pm Sat. **Offices** *Stazione Termini (48 71 270/48 24 078). Metro Termini/bus or tram to Termini.* **Open** 8.15am-7.15pm daily. *Fiumicino Airport (65 95 6074/65 95 4471).* **Open** 8.15am-7.15pm daily.

The EPT, the official tourist board, provides free brochures on the various attractions and events in Rome and Lazio, as well as a rather basic map. It is better to go along to one of the branches in person than to attempt to get through on the phone, as the lines appear to be constantly engaged. At the time of writing, their free hotel booking service had been suspended indefinitely.

Ente Nazionale Italiana per il Turismo (ENIT)

Via Marghera, 2-6 (49 711/49 71 282). Metro Termini/bus or tram to Termini. **Open** 9am-5.30pm. While EPT concerns itself with Rome and Lazio, ENIT provides information about the rest of the country, and neither of them will tell you anything about the other's domain. ENIT has offices in most major cities worldwide (these do have information about Rome and Lazio). They also produce an annual calendar of events throughout the country, and a useful booklet, the *Traveller's Handbook to Italy*. These are both written in English, as is the literature suggesting the best tours and itineraries.

Ufficio Informazioni Pellegrini e Turisti

Piazza San Pietro (69 88 44 66). Bus to Piazza della Risorgimento. **Open** 8.30am-7pm Mon-Sat. The Vatican's own tourist office. Its English-speaking staff will give you all the information you need on the Holy See, plus a free pamphlet.

Maps

A very basic street map is available free from EPT offices (and also from McDonald's) but better ones can be bought at newspaper stands and in bookshops. The official Metro and bus map has detailed street plans, with the transport systems clearly marked. It also includes a booklet listing ticket prices and bus routes. The phone company, Telecom, supplies subscribers with a free street atlas, *TuttaCittà*. If you need to look up a street too

Rome for the Disabled

There's no denying that Rome is a difficult city for disabled travellers, especially for anybody who uses a wheelchair. You'll almost certainly have to depend on other people more than you would at home, and you need to be prepared for a certain amount of patronising admiration for your incredible guts and determination.

The narrow streets and parked cars make life difficult for those who can't flatten themselves against a wall to let passing vehicles by, while the picturesque cobblestones turn even wheelchairs with excellent suspension into bone-rattlers. Once off the streets, you're faced with the problems of old buildings with narrow corridors, lifts that, if they're there at all, are too small for a wheelchair, and toilets at the top or bottom of impossibly steep staircases.

Things are beginning to improve. Whereas in the past disabled people relied exclusively on their extended family for help, there is now great enthusiasm for improving access and facilities in museums, restaurants, stations and public offices.

Information

CO.IN

Via Enrico Giglioli, 54a (23 26 75 04). **Open** 9am-5pm Mon-Fri. CO.IN (short for *Consorzio Cooperativa Integrate*) are publishers of a multilingual guide, *Roma Accessible*, which is sometimes available at the EPT and lists the disabled facilities at museums, restaurants, department stores, theatres, stations (including the Metro), hotels and so on. It also supplies a map of Rome showing disabled parking places. There's one big drawback: the guide is only updated when the last batch of copies has

been sold, and the current edition dates from 1991. At the time of writing, there were no immediate plans to produce another.

Transport

Only two bus routes are equipped for disabled passengers: the **157**, which serves the eastern suburbs and finishes at Termini, via Porta Maggiore; and the **590**, which follows the more useful (to tourists) route of the Metro A from Cinecittà to Prati, via the *centro storico*. The Metro itself is something of a no-go area, as only some of the further-flung stations on Line B have lifts. Most taxi drivers will carry wheelchairs (although they have to be folded to fit in the boot); it's better to ring and book in advance if you can (*see* **Getting Around** *page 252*).

The state railway company is beginning to introduce special easy-access carriages, particularly on trains from Fiumicino airport. In the meantime, anybody travelling from Termini station should telephone 48 81 726 to arrange for assistance (there is usually somebody who speaks English). If you're flying into Fiumicino, speak to your airline before you leave home. On your way back, phone the airport on 65 631 (ask for the Salamica) to arrange for assistance there.

Hotels, Restaurants & Bars

The **Accommodation** chapter gives some indication of which hotels are accessible for disabled travellers but it's still rare to find specially designed rooms in even the most luxurious places. Cheaper

hotels and *pensioni*, which are often on the first or second floors of old *palazzi*, are difficult to get in to. If you have special needs, make them known when you book. Hotels in all price categories are usually only too happy to lend a hand, though, again, the downside is the loss of personal freedom.

Most restaurants and bars can accommodate wheelchairs, though you may need help at the door. If you can, it's a good idea to phone in advance to reserve an appropriate table. In summer, the multiplicity of outdoor restaurants and bars means you'll usually be able to eat and drink in comfort. Things may get a bit complicated if you want to visit the toilets, though, so it's useful to find out where they are and whether you'll be able to get to them.

Sites

Well designed ramps, lifts and toilets are being installed in many of the main museums. Among these are the Vatican Museums; the re-opened Galleria Borghese; the Gallery of Modern Art; and the Palazzo delle Esposizioni (*see chapter* **Museums & Galleries**).

A group called **Museum** organises gallery tours for the blind. One or two blind people are accompanied by an English-, Italian- or French-speaking guide armed with braille notes about the exhibits, copies of some of the main paintings in relief, and permission to touch sculptures and other artefacts. Fax Museum in advance (54 02 762) or ring 51 39 855 or 57 30 05 51. Museum does not operate in August.

Directory

small to be marked on the usual maps, most bars and hotels will have a copy.

Voluntary Work & Study Groups

Volunteer work/study programmes are organised by various national and international groups. An initial fee should normally include tuition, food and (basic) lodgings for the duration of the project. While you're working, you will be under the guidance of experts, and with luck you should be involved in genuinely

significant research. Get on mailing lists, and book as early as possible, as places tend to fill up quickly.

Centro Turistico Studentesco (CTS)

Via Nazionale, 66 (46 791). Bus to Via Nazionale. **Open** 9.30am-1pm, 3.30-7pm, Mon-Fri; 9.30am-1pm Sat.
The CTS travel group has study and research camps all over Italy. These include everything from archaeological digs to calculating the number of wolves and bears left in the Abruzzo region (north-east of Rome). Nearer the city there are stretches of the ancient Via Amerina to restore. Fees range from approximately L500,000-750,000 for seven- to 12-day projects.

Gruppi Archeologici d'Italia

Via degli Scipioni, 30a (39 73 36 37). Metro Ottaviano. **Open** 9.30am-2pm, 3-6.30pm, Mon-Fri.
Recent excavations have included an Etruscan necropolis near Tolfa, and Roman villas near Allumiere. Expect to pay about L700,000 a month, which includes full-board, a six-hour day and expert archaeologists who are available on site.

Legambiente

Via Salaria, 403 (86 26 81). Bus to Via Salaria. **Open** 9.30pm-2pm, 3-6.30pm, Mon-Fri.
The Legambiente organises study/work courses throughout the country. Near Rome, these include archaeological digs at Monterano. Fees start at L300,000 for a fortnight-long stint.

Getting Around

The two and half million vehicles jostling for space on Rome's roads are daunting even for the most valiant driver, so it's just as well that the best way to get around the city is on foot. Terrifying first impressions can be deceptive, though. By local convention, the pedestrian nearly always has priority, and cars will often wait for you to meander out of the way.

Even on busy main roads you should find that if you edge your way into the road, making eye-contact with oncoming drivers, vehicles will slow down or part around you. Follow someone who knows the ropes until you get the hang of it. If you simply stand and wait for the traffic to stop, you may be there a long time, even at a zebra crossing or at traffic lights.

When your feet give out, buses, the Metro (underground) and taxis are all at hand to help you around the city. Otherwise, one of the quickest ways of getting about Rome is on a hired scooter, once you put fear aside and get used to the hectic pace. For information on scooter, cycle and car hire *see* **Car & Bike Hire** *page 257.*

See also **Rome for the Disabled** *page 251.*

Arriving in Rome
By Air

From Fiumicino Airport

Fiumicino Airport Information (65 951). **Open** 24 hours daily.
Rome's main airport, also known as Leonardo da Vinci, is about 30 kilometres (18 miles) from the city, and handles all scheduled flights. There is an **express rail service** direct to Termini, which takes about 30 minutes and runs hourly between 7.38am and 10.08pm. The service from Termini to the airport runs between 6.52am and 9.22pm. Tickets in either direction cost L15,000.

The normal rail service from Fiumicino stops at Trastevere, Ostiense, Tuscolana and Tiburtina stations in Rome, and takes 25-40 minutes. Trains leave about every 15 minutes (though service can be erratic on Sundays) and run between 6.25am-12.15am (5am-11pm to Fiumicino). The journey costs L7,000. You can buy tickets for both these services from automatic machines in the main airport lobby, or from the ticket office (open 7am-9pm), the *tabacchi (see page 249)* and the automatic machines in the railway station. Some of the carriages have access for wheelchair users.

Ostiense is close to Piramide Metro station, for trains to the city centre, but depending on your final destination in Rome, you may find it more convenient to get off at one of

the other stations instead, particularly when the Metro is closed.

During the night an invaluable **bus service** leaves Fiumicino from outside the arrivals hall. Tickets cost L7,000 from automatic machines, and buses run roughly once an hour through the night from Fiumicino to Tiburtina and vice-versa. Tiburtina station is most definitely not the most attractive place to be at night, and it's advisable to get a taxi directly from there to your final destination. The Metro line B closes at 11.30pm (12.30am Sat). After that it is sensible to change on to the 42N nightbus at Tiburtina, which runs as far as Termini.

A **taxi** ride into Rome from Fiumicino will cost about L70,000, including the special surcharge (L11,500 from Fiumicino, L14,000 from Rome) for the airport trip. Use only the yellow or white officially licensed cabs lined up at ranks (ignore all touts), and make sure you check the meter before paying. Any surcharges should be clearly displayed in several languages inside the vehicle. (*See* **Taxis** *page 256.*)

From Ciampino Airport

Ciampino Airport Information (79 49 41). **Open** 24 hours daily.
Ciampino, about 15 kilometres (nine miles) to the south-east of the city, is primarily a military airbase but is also used by most charter flights to Rome. If you are using public transport, getting to and from Ciampino can be much more of a hassle than using Fiumicino. The best way into town is by the COTRAL bus to Anagnina Metro station on Line A, which links with

Termini. Buses for Anagnina leave from the front of the arrivals hall every 30-60 minutes from 7.05am to 11.55 pm (6.10am-11pm from Anagnina to Ciampino), and the fare is L1,500. Tickets can be bought from an automatic machine in the arrivals hall and from the newspaper stand in the departures hall. A taxi to the centre, on the other hand, will set you back about L60,000.

Airport Information & Services

For general enquiries, ring the airport information numbers given above. Some staff can answer queries in English. At Fiumicino there is an office of the Rome tourist board, the **EPT** (*see* **Tourist Information** *page 250*), banks and cash machines. Exchange facilities at Ciampino are inadequate, so it's advisable to have some Italian money with you.

The major airlines can be reached on the following numbers.

Alitalia

Via Leonida Bissolati, 11 (domestic flights 65 641; international flights 65 642). Metro Barberini/bus to Via Bissolati. **Open** 9am-6pm Mon-Fri. **Credit** AmEx, DC, EC, MC, V. *Fiumicino Airport (65 643).* **Open** 24 hours daily.

British Airways

Via Leonida Bissolati, 54 (14 78 12 266). Metro Barberini/bus to Via Bissolati. **Open** 9am-5pm Mon-Fri. **Credit** AmEx, DC, EC, MC, V. *Fiumicino Airport (65 01 15 13).* **Open** 7am-6.30pm daily.

Qantas

Via Leonida Bissolati, 35 (48 88 101). Metro Barberini/bus to Via Bissolati. **Open** 9am-5pm Mon-Fri. **Credit** AmEx, DC, MC, V. *Fiumicino Airport (65 01 04 68).* **Open** 9am-5pm Tue-Sat.

TWA

Via Barberini, 59 (47 211/47 212). Metro Barberini/bus to Piazza Barberini. **Open** 9am-5pm Mon-Fri. **Credit** AmEx, DC, EC, MC, V. *Fiumicino Airport (65 95 49 01).* **Open** 7.30am-2.30pm daily.

By Bus

There is no central long-distance bus station in Rome. Most international and national coach services terminate outside the following underground stations: Lepanto, Rebibbia and Tiburtina (routes north); Anagnina and EUR Fermi (routes south). For more

information, *see chapter* **Trips Out of Town**.

By Train

Most long-distance trains arrive at Termini station, which is also the centre of the Metro and city bus networks. It is open from 5am to midnight daily. The station is a pickpocket's haven, so watch your luggage. Trains arriving by night stop at Tiburtina or Ostiense, both some way from the centre of Rome. Bus routes **9** and **492**, or night bus **42N**, run from Tiburtina into the city. If you arrive at Ostiense after the Piramide Metro closes at 11.30pm, take night buses **20N** or **29N**. Alternatively, take a taxi to the city centre.

Some trains also bypass Termini during the day. The Napoli Express to and from Paris, for example, only stops at Ostiense. Many trains also stop at more than one station in Rome, and it may be more convenient to get off at one of the smaller stations rather than go into Termini.

Train tickets can be bought at stations, or travel agents with the FS (Ferrovie dello Stato – State Railways) sign. At Termini and other main stations there are automatic ticket machines, with instructions in most western European languages. The faster Intercity (IC) and Eurostar (ES) trains require supplements, and booking is often obligatory (an R inside a square on train timetables indicates this). The supplements are paid for and bookings made at special ticket windows marked *prenotazioni* (bookings), which should issue tickets as well. Windows marked *biglietti* cannot handle supplements or bookings – bear this in mind when you've arrived at the station with seconds to spare. You can apply for a reimbursement on IC or ES services if the train is delayed for over an hour.

Remember that you must stamp your ticket –and any supplement – in the yellow machines at the head of each platform before boarding the train. Failure to do this can result in a hefty fine, though being foreign, looking forlorn and not understanding the language should bring out the better nature in all but the crustiest ticket inspector.

Booking seats on regular services is sometimes advisable, especially if you're travelling at peak times (Friday evening, Saturday morning, Sunday evening). There's a standard booking fee of L4,500. Although ticket windows at main stations display most major credit card symbols, an apparently indiscriminate selection of cards is usually accepted. Most travel agents persist in accepting cash only for railway tickets.

The principal stations in Rome, and some of the suburban ones, are listed below. All Italian stations now have the same information-service number. As it is notoriously difficult to get through – and find someone who speaks English – probably your best bet is to enquire at a travel agent.

Stazione Ostiense

Piazzale dei Partigiani (14 78 88 088). Metro Piramide/bus to Piazzale Porta San Paolo.

Stazione di Piazzale Flaminio (Roma Nord)

Piazzale Flaminio (36 10 441). Metro Flaminio/bus to Piazzale Flaminio.

Stazione Termini

Piazza dei Cinquecento (14 78 88 088). Metro Termini/bus or tram to Termini.

Stazione Tiburtina

Circonvallazione Nomentana (14 78 88 088). Metro Tiburtina/bus to Piazza Stazione Tiburtina.

Stazione Trastevere

Piazzale Biondo, Trastevere (14 78 88 088). Bus or tram to Circonvallazione Gianicolense.

Directory

Public Transport

The Rome transport system is made up of three companies. The city transport authority, **ATAC**, runs the orange buses and trams that operate within the city. The regional transport body **COTRAL** (formerly ACOTRAL, and many signs still show the old name) is responsible for the blue buses operating within the Lazio region and for Rome's two Metro lines. The company also operates three special suburban railway lines in the Rome area from Termini, Porta San Paolo and Roma Nord stations. Local lines of the **FS**, the state railway, are now integrated into the city transport network.

Travelling on public transport is pretty safe, even at night, though you should be wary of pickpockets on crowded buses such as the 64 route between Termini station and the Vatican.

Buses & Trams

ATAC buses and trams are the mainstay of Rome's transport network. There are eight tram routes, mainly serving suburban areas, and a new express tram service will link Largo di Torre Argentina and Trastevere with the suburbs to the south-west of the city. Trams and buses form an integrated network and have exactly the same tickets and pricing system. Owing to continual changes in the network, however, routes and numbers are subject to change: if you plan to use public transport, it's a good idea to pick up a copy of the latest city bus map, available free of charge from the ATAC kiosk outside Termini station, or fork out L8,000 for one at most news-stands.

Passengers must have a ticket *before* getting on a bus or tram, as they are not sold on board (*see below* **Tickets**).

ATAC

Information *Piazza dei Cinquecento (46 95 44 44). Metro Termini/ bus to Termini station.* **Open** 7.30am-7pm daily.
The main ATAC information desk has English-speaking staff, although its phone line (8am to 8pm Monday to Saturday) is Italian-speaking only. ATAC offers tickets for the entire transport network. Automatic ticket machines (*see below* **Tickets**) are scattered throughout the city centre.

Daytime Services

All ATAC routes, except the special night services, run between about 5.30am and midnight every day, with a frequency of from 10 to 45 minutes depending on the route. The chaotic Rome traffic, however, often causes severe delays on central lines. You are expected to board buses and trams by the rear or front doors, and get off by the middle doors. When buses are crowded, it can be impossible to work your way through to the central doors, and so it's acceptable to use the nearest exit you can find.

Each bus stop (*fermata*) lists the stops on each route in the direction to be followed. Because of the many one-way systems, buses do not necessarily follow the same route on return journeys, and it's often useful to consult a transport map. If you're not sure of where to get off, mention the name of your destination to your fellow passengers, who will usually be happy to help.

Useful Routes

The following daytime routes are particularly useful for visitors: **23**, from Prati and Piazza del Risorgimento, along the Tiber to the Piramide and down to San Paolo fuori le Mura; **46**, from Piazza Venezia to the Vatican and the Via Aurelia; **64**, from Termini station to the Vatican; **85**, from the southern suburbs to Piazza San Silvestro via San Giovanni and the Colosseum; **218**, from Piazza San Giovanni to the Via Appia Antica and the Catacombs; **492**, from Tiburtina station to Piazza del Risorgimento via Termini station and Largo Argentina. The **119** is a handy minibus that runs on a circular route around the *centro storico*; the **170** goes from Termini to San Paolo, through Largo Argentina and Viale Trastevere. The **590**, which follows the route of the Metro's Line A, has special facilities for disabled passengers. Bear in mind that the bus service is under constant review, and both routes and numbers can change without warning.

Night Buses

There are currently 27 night routes, which run from about 12.10am to 5.30am daily. They run every 30 minutes to an hour, and the schedule for each route (identified by an N after the number) is written on bus stops. The following routes are particularly useful: **20N**, from Piazzale Flaminio to Piramide and back via Termini station and Santa Maria Maggiore; **29N**, from Piramide to Piazza del Risorgimento and the Villa Borghese via San Giovanni; and **42N**, from Tiburtina station to Termini. The **78N** runs between the Vatican and Termini.

Metro

The building of an underground railway system for Rome has been a long-drawn out saga. At every inch the tunnel diggers have unearthed some archaeological wonder, causing continual stoppages and delays. The two Metro lines are still being extended, although dreams of constructing a third, to link San Giovanni in Laterano with Saint Peter's in time for Holy Year 2000, are unfortunately fading fast.

Metro Times

The two Metro lines form a rough cross on the map, meeting at Stazione Termini. Line A runs from the south-east to the north-west, and Line B from EUR in the south to the north-eastern suburbs. Both are open from 5.30am to 11.30pm daily (12.30 am on Saturday). On Sundays it is possible to travel with bicycles on Line B of the Metro and on the connecting Ostia line from Porta San Paolo; just stamp an extra ticket at the barrier before the start of your journey and use the front carriage only.

COTRAL Information

Via Ostiense, 131l (56 30 41 10). **Open** 8am-1.40pm, 2.10-4.40pm, Mon-Fri; 8am-1.40pm Sat.
Fiumicino airport bus information 65 95 45 52.

Tickets

There are various bus, tram and Metro tickets, which all must be bought before boarding. They are available from ATAC's automatic ticket machines, *tabacchi*, some bars and news-stands. When you get on a bus, you must stamp single tickets in the small orange machines by the rear

Directory

doors. Some people do not pay, but there are inspectors on the system, and the on-the-spot fine for non-payment has increased from an inoffensive L10,000 to a more painful L50,000.

Timed Ticket (Biglietto Integrato a Tempo – BIT)

Valid for 75 minutes of travel on all ATAC buses and for one trip on the Metro, this ticket costs L1,500.

Integrated Ticket (Biglietto Integrato Giornaliero – BIG)

At a cost of L6,000, this ticket is valid for one day and covers all the systems (except Fiumicino airport) in the urban network, whether ATAC, COTRAL or the FS suburban trains.

Weekly Ticket (Carta Integrata Settimanale – CIS)

Costs L24,000 and covers all the bus routes and the Metro system, including the lines out to Ostia.

Monthly Ticket (Abbonamento Mensile)

Monthly tickets cost L50,000 for unlimited travel on the entire transport system. For people over 65 years of age, the ticket is discounted to L30,000. Note that monthly tickets are valid for a specified calendar month, not one month from the day you buy them.

Regional Ticket (Biglietto Integrato Regionale Giornaliero – BIRG)

This is a one-day ticket covering rail travel within the Lazio region. The price varies according to the zone of your destination. For example, a ticket to Frascati and back costs L8,500, while for Sperlonga the price is L17,000. The BIRG is valid on the Metro, buses and the FS (second class only) but not on routes to and from Fiumicino airport.

Because of the rapidity with which bus numbers change, this guide gives nearest major bus stops (and Metro stations) for all the places listed, rather than route numbers.

Taxis

Licensed taxis are painted yellow or white, and have a meter. If anyone comes up to you at Termini or any of the other major tourist magnets, muttering 'Taxi?' always refuse, as they are likely to charge you up to 400 per cent

more than the normal rate. Real taxis are normally found waiting at a rank.

Taxi Fares & Surcharges

If you pick up a taxi at a rank, make sure the meter reads zero. As you set off, it will begin to indicate the minimum fare, currently L4,500 for the first 200 metres, after which the charge will go up fairly rapidly. There are surcharges on Sundays, public holidays, trips to and from the airport, and L2,000 for each item of luggage placed in the boot. L5,000 is added to the fare between 10pm and 7am. Most of Rome's taxi drivers are honest workers; if, however, you suspect you are being ripped off, make a note of the driver's name and number, from the metal plaque attached to the inside of the vehicle's back door. The more ostentatiously you do this, the more likely you are to find the fare returning to its proper level. Complaints can be lodged with the drivers' co-operative (the phone number of which is clearly visible on the outside of the car) or, in serious cases, with the police.

Taxi Ranks

Ranks are indicated by a blue sign with Taxi written in white, but are often identifiable by the number of people in the queue rather than the presence of taxis. In the central area there are ranks at Largo di Torre Argentina, the Pantheon, Piazza Venezia, Piazza San Silvestro, Piazza Sonnino (Trastevere) and Piazza di Spagna.

Phone Cabs

You can phone for a taxi from any of the following companies. Some of the operators speak sufficient English for you to make yourself understood. When your call is answered, name the street and number, or the name and location of a bar, club or restaurant where you wish to be picked up. You will then be given the taxi code-name (always a geographic location followed by a number) and a time, as in 'Bahama, 69 in tre minuti' (Bahama, 69 arriving in three minutes). A radio taxi will start the meter from the moment your call is answered.

Cooperativa Samarcanda (55 51). Credit card facilities.
Cosmos Radio Taxi (88 177).
Società Cooperativa Autoradio Taxi Roma (35 70).
Società la Capitale Radio Taxi (49 94).

Driving

Having a car in Rome can be great fun, or a huge liability. At first glance, Roman driving

resembles the chariot race in *Ben Hur*, until you realise that it's like a high-speed conversation, with its own language of glances, light flashing and ostentatious acceleration, all carried out with panache.

If you do use a car in the city, some tips to be borne in mind are listed below. Short-term visitors should have no trouble driving on their home licences, though if they happen to be written in different scripts or less common languages, an international licence may come in handy. If you are an EU citizen, you are obliged to change your licence to an Italian after your first year in Rome (*see* **Living and Working in Rome** *page 261*). Remember:

• You are required by law to wear a seat belt at all times and to carry a warning triangle in your car.
• Keep your driving licence, Green Card, vehicle registration and personal ID documents on you at all times.
• Do not leave anything of value (including a car radio) in your car, and never leave bags or jackets visible on the seats. Take all your luggage into your hotel when you park.
• Flashing your lights in Italy means that you will *not* slow down (contrary to British practice).
• If traffic lights flash amber, you should STOP and give way to the right.
• Watch out for death-defying mopeds and pedestrians. By local convention, pedestrians usually assume they have the right of way in the older, quieter streets without clearly-designated pavements.

Restricted Areas

Large sections of the centre are closed to non-resident traffic during business hours, and sometimes in the evening, too. The municipal police stand guard over these areas, and they may fine you if you are caught trying to get in. If you are in a hired car or have foreign plates and are stopped, you can sometimes get through by unscrupulous means. Just mention the name of a hotel in the area you want to enter, and you will often be waved on.

Breakdown Services

It is advisable to join a national motoring organisation, like the AA or RAC in Britain or the AAA in the US, before taking a car to Italy. They have reciprocal arrangements with the **Automobile Club d'Italia** (**ACI**), who will tell you what to do in the case of a breakdown, and provide useful general information on driving in Europe. Even for non-members, the ACI is the best number to call if you have any kind of breakdown.

If you require extensive repairs and do not know a mechanic, pay a bit more and go to a manufacturer's official dealer, as reliable garages are hard to find in Rome. Dealers are listed in the Yellow Pages under *auto*, along with specialist repairers under classifications such as *gommista* (tyre repairs), *marmitte* (exhaust repairs) and *carrozzerie* (bodywork and windscreen repairs). The English Yellow Pages has a list of garages where English is spoken.

Automobile Club d'Italia (ACI)

Via Marsala, 8 (49 981/24-hour emergency phone line 116/24-hour information phone line 44 77). Metro Termini/bus or tram to Termini. **Open** 8.30am-2pm Mon-Sat (Mon-Fri in July and Aug). The ACI has English-speaking staff and provides a range of services for all foreign drivers, free or at low prices. Members of associated organisations are entitled to basic repairs free, and to other services at preferential rates. Non-members will be charged, but prices are generally reasonable. Phone 44 77 for information on ACI services, driving regulations and customs formalities in Italy, and traffic and weather information. It is not necessary to have membership in order to use the phone lines.

Parking

A system in which residents park free and visitors pay has recently been introduced to many areas of the city, and is fairly efficiently policed: watch out for the tell-tale blue lines. Parking fees are paid at the pay-and-display ticket dispensers at the rate of L2,000 per hour. In some areas you can park free after a certain time in the evening, or at weekends, so look carefully at the instructions on the ticket machine before feeding it with coins. For longer stays, a L50,000 parking card, available from *tabacchi*, allows you to deduct parking fees gradually, and saves you having to search your pockets for small change.

Elsewhere, anything resembling a parking place is up for grabs, with some exceptions: watch out for signs next to entrances saying *Passo Carrabile* (access at all times), *Sosta Vietata* (no parking), and disabled parking spaces marked by yellow stripes on the road. The sign *Zona Rimozione* (tow-away area) means no parking, and is valid for the length of the street, or until the next tow-away sign, with a red line through it denoting the end of the restricted area. If a street or square has no cars parked in it, you can safely assume it's a seriously-enforced no-parking zone.

Although your car is fairly safe in most central areas, you may prefer to pay the hefty rates charged by underground car parks to ensure the vehicle is not tampered with. The three listed below are centrally located and open daily. **Trastevere Parking** *Via dei Marescotti, 6 (58 03 884). Bus to Viale Trastevere.* **Open** 6.15am-12.30am daily. **Rates** L5,000-L8,000 for first hour; L3,000-L4,000 for each additional hour. **Villa Borghese** *Metro Spagna/bus to Via Veneto.* **Open** 24 hours daily. **Rates** L1,800 per hour for up to 4

hours; L1,500 per hour for 4-24 hours; L23,000 for 24 hours. **Valentino** *Via Sistina, 75e (67 82 597). Metro Spagna.* **Open** 7am-1am Mon-Sat; 7am-12.30am, 6pm-1am, Sun. **Rates** L10,000 for 3 hours.

Car Pounds

If you do not find your car where you left it, it has probably been towed away. Phone the municipal police on 67 69 28 38/67 69 28 37 and quote your number plate to find out which of the various car pounds it has been taken to. Cars can be retrieved from 8am to 8.30pm daily. **Via T. de Coubertin**, 24 (80 83 108). *Bus to Viale Tiziano.* **Via del Cocchieri**, 1 (54 11 639). *Train from Ostiense or Trastevere to Stazione Magliana, then taxi.* **Via Giglioli**, 20 (26 74 720). *Bus to Via Casilina.* **Via di Casale Rocchi** (45 01 206). *Metro Pietralata, then bus 211 to Via Casale Rocchi.* **Via Ostiense** (23km from Rome; 56 50 972). *Train from Piramide to Ostia Antica, then walk 800m back towards Rome.*

Petrol

Most petrol stations sell unleaded petrol (*senza piombo*) and regular (*super*). Diesel fuel is *gasolio*. All petrol stations have full service during weekdays. Pump attendants do not expect tips. At night and on Sundays many stations have automatic self-service pumps that accept L10,000 or L50,000 notes, in good condition. Unofficial 'assistants' will do the job for you for a small tip (L500-L1,000). Italy's petrol is the most expensive in the EU.

Car & Bike Hire

Car Hire

To hire a car you must be over 21 – in some cases 23 – and have held a licence for at least a year. You will be required to leave a credit card number or a substantial cash deposit. It is advisable to take out collision damage waiver (CDW) and personal accident insurance (PAI) on top of basic third party insurance. Companies which do not offer a CDW are best avoided.

Avis

Via Sardegna, 38a (42 82 47 28). Metro Spagna/bus to Via Vittorio Veneto. **Open** 8am-8pm Mon-Fri; 8am-1pm, 3-6pm, Sat; 8am-1pm Sun. **Credit** AmEx, DC, EC, MC, V. **Branches** *Fiumicino Airport (65 01 15 31).* **Open** 7am-midnight daily. *Ciampino Airport (79 34 01 95).* **Open** 8.45am-12.30pm, 2.15-8pm, Mon-Fri; 10am-3.30pm Sat; noon-8pm Sun.

Maggiore Budget

Fiumicino Airport (65 01 0678/Toll Free 14 78 67 07). **Open** 7am-11.30pm daily. **Credit** AmEx, DC, MC, V. **Branches** *Stazione Termini (48 80 049).* **Open** 7am-7.30pm Mon-Sat. *Ciampino Airport (79 34 03 68).* **Open** 7.30am-8.30pm Mon-Fri; 8.30am-12.30pm, 5pm-8pm, Sat-Sun.

Thrifty

Via Ludovisi, 60 (48 20 966/7). Metro Barberini/bus to Piazza Barberini. **Open** 8am-7pm Mon-Fri; 8am-noon, 2-6pm Sat; 8am-noon Sun. **Credit** AmEx, DC, MC, V. **Branches** *Fiumicino Airport (65 29 134).* **Open** 7am-

11.30pm daily. *Ciampino Airport (79 34 01 37).* **Open** 9am-1pm, 3-6pm, Mon-Sat.

Moped, Scooter and Bicycle Hire

To hire a scooter or moped (*motorino*) you need a credit card, an identity document and/or a cash deposit for the hire company. Helmets are required on motorbikes and on all *motorini* for people under the age of 18. For bicycles, it is normally sufficient to leave an identity document rather than pay a deposit.

Apart from the companies listed below, there are useful pay-and-ride bike hire stands with similar rates outside Spagna Metro station, in Piazza del Popolo (near Rosati's bar), and at the tiny bar in Piazza di Ponte Milvio, at the start of the pleasant cycle path which takes you out of central Rome along the banks of the river Tiber .

Happy Rent

Via Farini, 3 (48 18 185). Bus to Via Cavour. **Open** 9am-7pm Mon-Sun. **Credit** AmEx, EC, MC, V.

Friendly outlet with lots of special offers and ideas for the tourist. Daily rates: bikes L15,000; mopeds L44,000; scooters L60,000; 600cc bikes L120,000.

I Bike Rome

Villa Borghese car park, level 3 (32 25 240). Metro Flaminio or Spagna. **Open** 8.30am-7.30pm daily. **Credit** EC, MC, V.
A selection of bicycles can be rented hourly (from L4,000), by the day (L10-15,000), for a week (L38,000) or a month (L63,000). Alternatives include mopeds, which cost L45,000 per day, or scooters (L70,000).

Scoot a Long

Via Cavour, 302 (67 80 206). Metro Cavour. **Open** 9am-8pm daily. **Credit** AmEx, MC, V.
Based near the Colosseum, this company offers special student discounts. The daily and weekend rates for mopeds are L50,000 and L80,000 (scooters L80,000 and L140,000). Motorbikes are also available. A deposit of L200,000, plus a passport, is required.

Scooters for Rent

Via della Purificazione, 84 (48 85 485). Metro Barberini. **Open** 9am-7pm daily. **Credit** AmEx, EC, MC, V.
Daily rentals of *motorini* cost L50,000, smaller Vespas L60,000 and scooters L80,000. For a week's rental, you pay five days instead of seven. A deposit of L300,000 is required.

Women's Rome

As you're walking down the street being whistled at, pinched, pursued by squadrons of Vespa-riders and generally hassled, take comfort in the fact that most Italian men are all mouth and no trousers. Compared with many of its European counterparts, Rome is a relatively safe city, and as long as you stick to central areas it is one of the few cities where you can still walk alone late at night without wishing you'd brought your mace.

For women on their own, common sense will usually be enough to keep potential harassers at bay. If you're not interested, ignore them and they'll probably go away. Alternatively, duck into the

nearest bar: they'll give you up as a lost cause and look for a new victim.

Young Roman blades head for **Piazza di Spagna** and **Fontana di Trevi** to pick up foreign talent, especially after dark. If you prefer to enjoy Rome's nocturnal charm in peace, you're better off in the areas around Campo dei Fiori, **Testaccio** and **Trastevere**, which are teeming with people out to have a drink, partake in a pizza or just enjoy the night air. The area around **Termini** station gets seriously seedy after sundown.

Accommodation

The vast majority of Rome's hotels and *pensioni* are perfectly suitable for women travellers,

but if you're uneasy about walking the streets at night, avoid those near Termini station and around Via Nazionale, a major shopping artery which becomes pretty deserted once the shops are shut. Stick to the more populated areas in the *centro storico* where you can still get good prices and enjoy the night-life without too much fret. The *pensioni* to the east of Piazza di Spagna are conveniently situated and cater to a healthy variety of travellers. Otherwise, many convents offer a bulwark against the city's perceived threats, as well as a bed. Some come complete with curfews and holy water; others are more like simple *pensioni*. If you don't feel like getting thee to a nunnery, Rome also has several hostels for women travellers. The hotels listed below are known to be particularly female-friendly.

Casa Tra Noi
Via Monte del Gallo, 113 (39 38 73 55; fax 39 38 74 46). Bus to Via Monte del Gallo. **Rates** single L82,000; double L142,000; mini-apartments for 4 L276,000.
No credit cards.
The management is religious but fairly low-profile. Inside a safe but somewhat anonymous complex, the rooms are comfortable and clean, and breakfast is included. Situated close to the Vatican.

Hotel Cisterna
Via della Cisterna, 7/9 (58 17 212/58 81 852; fax 58 10 091). Bus to Trastevere. **Rates** single L130,000; double L160,000. **Credit** AmEx, MC, V.
Prices include bath and phone. Family-run, friendly atmosphere, but very few rooms, so book several weeks ahead.

Protezione della Giovane
Via Urbana, 158 (48 81 489). Metro Cavour/bus to Piazza Esquilino. **Rates** L24,000-27,000 per person.
No credit cards.
This is a Catholic organisation for the protection of young women, offering cheap accommodation to under-25s. There is a 10pm curfew. The hostel runs an information office at Termini station (*48 27 594*).

Santa Francesca Romana Convent
Via dei Vascellari, 61 (58 35 797). Bus to Viale Trastevere. **Rates** single L80,000; double L116,000.
No credit cards.
Prices include baths. Doors are locked 1-7 am.

Suore Pie Operaie
Via di Torre Argentina, 76 (68 61 254). Bus to Largo di Torre Argentina. **Rates** L20,000 per person. **No credit cards**.
Right in the centre of Rome, this hostel has ten rooms with two or three beds in each. Women only; 10.30pm curfew. Book ahead: the cheap rates make the hostel exceptionally popular.

YWCA
Via Cesare Balbo, 4 (48 80 460; fax 48 71 028). Metro Termini. **Rates** *per person with shared bath* single L50,000; double L40,000; triple L33,000; *per person with private bath* single L70,000; double L50,000. **Open** 7am to midnight. **No credit cards**.

It's a bit close to Termini, but you may prefer this to a convent. Men are allowed as part of a couple or group, in which case they can share a room. Reservations are recommended. Fax ahead to confirm.

Health

Condoms are on sale near the check-out in supermarkets, or over the counter at chemists. They're expensive. Tampons (*assorbenti interni*) and sanitary towels (*assorbenti esterni*) are cheaper in supermarkets or drugstores, but you can also get them in pharmacies.

Health Centres

Consultori Familiari (Family Planning Centres)
Each district has a *Consultorio Familiare*, run by the local health authority, and EU citizens with an E111 form are entitled to use them, paying the same low charges for services and prescription drugs as locals. Queues can be interminable, but you will eventually get any advice and help you need on contraception, abortion and gynaecological problems. Some of the clinics also offer ante-natal courses.

The pill is freely available on prescription. Abortions are legal, but performed only in state-run hospitals. For gynaecological emergencies, head for the *Pronto soccorso* at your nearest hospital (*see* **Health** *page 244*).

The most centrally located *consultori* are:
Via Arco del Monte, 99a (68 80 35 45). Bus to Largo di Torre Argentina. **Open** 11.30am-5pm Mon; 9-11am Tue; 9am-6pm Wed; 9am-2pm Thur, Fri.
Via San Martino della Battaglia, 16 (44 41 393). Bus to Termini. **Open** 8.30am-12.30pm Mon-Sat.

AIED
Via Toscana, 30/31 (42 82 53 14). Metro Barberini. **Open** 9am-7pm Mon-Fri; 9am-1pm Sat.
Viale Gorizia, 14 (85 57 731). Bus to Corso Trieste. **Open** 9am-1pm, 2-7pm, Mon-Fri; 9am-1pm Sat.

These private family-planning clinics offer medical care, check-ups, contraceptive advice, menopause counselling and smear tests. Once you buy a membership card (*tessera*) for L10,000, check-ups cost L65,000. Smear tests cost L25,000 and follow-up visits are free.

ARIS
Viale Trastevere, 60b (58 11 069/58 10 267). Bus to Viale Trastevere. **Open** 10am-noon, 3-7pm, Mon-Fri.
A private surgery of predominantly female gynaecologists, paediatricians, and homeopaths. Offers scans, counselling, ante-natal courses and occasional seminars on women's health and parenting topics. Check-ups cost from L100,000, smear tests are L50,000.

Artemide
Via Sannio, 61 (70 47 62 20). Metro San Giovanni. **Open** 10am-7pm Mon-Fri.
This private clinic offers gynaecological check-ups (L90,000) and smear tests (L30,000), together with a wide range of other tests and services. Appointments can be made at 24 hours' notice, and emergencies are invariably taken on immediately.

Helplines & Crisis Centres

Dial 112 or 113 in case of emergency. For more specific help or counselling, try one or more of the following:

Centro d'Accoglienza per Le Donne Che Non Vogliono Subire Violenza
Viale di Villa Pamphili, 100 (58 10 926/58 11 473). Bus to Piazza Ottavilla. **Open** 24 hours daily.
A short-stay hostel for female victims of domestic violence, and their children, plus a 24-hour emergency line.

Centro Anti-Violenza
Via delle Tre Canelle, 15 (67 80 537/67 80 563). **Open** 24 hours daily.
A helpline for victims of sexual violence. The women-only volunteers at the Centro Anti-Violenza offer legal assistance and psychological support, and some are English-speaking.

Telefono Rosa
68 32 690/68 32 820/68 32 675. **Open** 10am-1pm, 4-7pm, daily.
An excellent helpline, Telefono Rosa provides sympathetic counselling and sound legal advice to women who have been victims of either sexual abuse or sexual harassment.

Directory

Living & Working in Rome

Rome has over 200,000 registered foreign residents who are here (temporarily or permanently) for a wide variety of reasons, be they work, study, political asylum, religion or love. What they have in common is the vast gamut of emotions that living in Rome puts them through, from fizzing excitement about being in one of the most beautiful cities in the world, to uncontainable frustration when confronted by so-called public services or forced to contend with the most advanced red tape ever developed by mankind.

To get newcomers off to a flying start, **Welcome Neighbor** is a group of English-speaking ex-pats which organises talks on various aspects of living in Rome. Phone 30 36 69 36 for information on events.

Everybody living in Italy is armed with an impressive array of permits, cards and other documents proving who they are, what they do and where they live. Foreigners intending to stay in Italy for longer than a few weeks need to acquire many of these, and more besides.

EU citizens shouldn't have any difficulty getting hold of all the essential documentation once they arrive in Italy, but non-EU citizens are advised to enquire at the Italian embassy or consulate in their own country to find out about these formalities. There have been cases of people having to return to their home countries in order to go through complicated and apparently pointless procedures there before they can return to live in Italy.

Further information on how to obtain all the documents listed here is given in the useful *Roma per te* booklet issued by the *comune* (city council) with the telephone directory. There is also an automatic information line (in Italian only) on 67 03 03. The computerized system, through which you can – in theory – apply for certificates from computer terminals at main post offices and other strategic sites around town, is still being installed. There are private agencies which specialise in getting all kinds of documents if you can't face going through all the procedures yourself (see under *Pratiche e certificati – agenzie* in the Yellow Pages).

Carta d'Identita (Identity Card)

This isn't essential for foreigners living in Rome, who can use their passports as identification. However, if you feel your life is incomplete without an ID card, you'll need three passport photographs, a *permesso di soggiorno*, and a special form which will be given to you at your *circoscrizione* – the local branch of the central records office, which will issue the card once requisite paperwork has gone through. To find the office in your area, look in the telephone directory under *Comune di Roma: Circoscrizioni*.

Codice Fiscale (Tax Code)

Anybody working in Italy needs one of these plastic cards, and you're often asked to give your number when doing anything official, such as opening a bank account, arranging a new telephone line or receiving certain types of medical care. Take your passport and *permesso di soggiorno* to the tax office, *Ufficio Imposte Dirette*, in Via della Conciliazione, 5 (68 82 41), which is open from 8.30am to noon Monday to Saturday, fill in a form and return a few days later to pick up the card. You can also ask to have it posted on to you.

Partita IVA (VAT Number)

The self-employed or anybody doing business in Italy may also need a VAT number. These cost L250,000 and most people pay an accountant to get one for them. Make sure you cancel it when you no longer need it: failure to do so may result in an unpleasant visit from tax inspectors years later.

Permesso di Soggiorno (Permit to Stay)

EU citizens need one of these if they're staying in Italy for more than three months; non-EU citizens should (but usually don't) apply for one within eight days of their arrival in Italy. Take three passport photographs and your passport to the *Commissariato* (police station) nearest your home (see the phone directory under *Polizia di Stato* for addresses), or to the Questura Centrale (the main police station) in Via Genova, 2 (468 61) between 9am (though people start queueing much earlier) and 12.30pm. EU citizens usually get their permit on the spot; non-EU citizens have to return a few

The Paper Chase

The documents described in this section are only the most common of a dazzling array that you can collect. Among the more obscure are the *certificato di stato libero* which proves that you're *not* married; *stato di famiglia*, which proves that you live with who you live with; and *carichi pendenti*, which states whether or not you have any legal charges against you.

The prize for the most bizarre item of paperwork must go to the *certificato di esistenza in vita* (the certificate of existence) which proves that you're real and not just a figment of your own imagination. Bureaucracy aficionados are distraught at a threat to do away with this gem in the near future. All these documents are available at the *anagrafe* offices.

Using the Lingo

Any attempt at spoken Italian – no matter how incompetent – will be appreciated.

Italian is spelt as it is pronounced, and vice versa. Though traditional grammars will tell you that the stress usually falls on the penultimate syllable, this is a very dodgy rule: accents must be learnt by trial and error.

There are two forms of address in the second person singular: 'Lei', which is formal and should be used with strangers and older people; and tu, which is informal. The personal pronoun is usually omitted.

PRONUNCIATION

Vowels

a – as in ask.
e – like a in age (closed e) or e in sell (open e).
i – like ea in east.
o – as in hotel (closed o) or in hot (open o).
u – as in boot.

Consonants

Romans have a lot of trouble with their consonants, and take much stick for it from Italians from other regions. **C** often comes out nearer **g**; **n**, if in close proximity to an **r**, disappears.

Remember that **c** and **g** both go soft in front of **e** and **i** (becoming like the initial sounds of check and giraffe respectively).

An **h** after any consonant makes it hard. Before a vowel, it is silent.

c before **a**, **i** and **u**: as in cat.
g before **a**, **i** and **u**: as in get.
gl: like lli in million.
gn: like ny in canyon.
qu: as in quick.
r: always rolled.
s: has two sounds, as in soap or rose.
sc: like the sh in shame.
sch: like the sc in scout.
z: can be sounded ts or dz.

USEFUL PHRASES

hello and goodbye (informal) – ciao, salve.
good morning – buon giorno.
good evening – buona sera.
good night – buona notte.
please – per favore, per piacere.
thank you – grazie.
you're welcome – prego.
excuse me, sorry – mi scusi (formal), scusa (informal).
I'm sorry, but… – mi dispiace…
I don't speak Italian (very well) – non parlo (molto bene) l'italiano.
I don't/didn't understand (anything at all) – non capisco/ho capito (niente).
how much is (it)? – quanto costa? or quanto viene?
is there a discount? – c'è uno sconto?
open – aperto.
closed – chiuso.
entrance – entrata.
exit – uscita.

TIMES AND TIMETABLES

could you tell me the time? – mi sa dire l'ora?
I don't have a watch – non ho l'orologio.
it's – o'clock – sono le (number).
it's half past – sono le (number) e mezza.
when does it (re-)open? – a che ora (ri)apre?
does it close for lunch? – chiude per pranzo?

DIRECTIONS

(turn) left – (giri a) sinistra.
(it's on the) right – (è a/sulla destra.
straight on – sempre diritto
where is…? – dov'è…?
could me show me the way to the Pantheon? – mi potrebbe indicare la strada per il Pantheon? (Note: it's always best to ask several people, and take the most-frequently-proffered directions. Romans would rather make something up than disappoint the visitor by saying they don't know.)
is it near/far? – è vicino/lontano?
would you like to go with me? – mi vorrebbe accompagnare?
would it be better to take the bus or can I walk? – sarebbe meglio prendere l'autobus, o posso andare a piedi? (Bear in mind that Romans consider walking uncool and will tell you it's miles away if it's more than a couple of hundred metres.)

TRANSPORT

car – macchina.
bus – autobus.
coach – pullman.
taxi – tassi, taxi.
train – treno.
tram – tram.
plane – aereo.
ferry – traghetto.
bus stop – fermata (d'autobus).
station – stazione.
platform – binario.
ticket/s – biglietto/biglietti.
one way – solo andata.
return – andata e ritorno.
(I'd like) a ticket for – (vorrei) un biglietto per…
where can I buy tickets? – dove si comprono i biglietti?
fine – multa.
are you getting off at the next stop? (i.e. get out of my way if you're not) – che, scende alla prossima?
I'm sorry, I didn't know I had to stamp it (the lament of foreigners alarmed at the threat of a heavy fine for not having stamped their tickets before getting on the train or bus) – mi dispiace, non sapevo che lo dovevo timbrare.

COMMUNICATIONS

phone – telefono.
fax – fax.
stamp – francobollo.
how much is a stamp for England/ Australia/the United States? – quanto viene un francobollo per l'Inghilterra/ l'Australia/ gli Stati Uniti?
how much does it cost per minute/page? – quanto viene al minuto/alla pagina?

can I send a fax? – posso mandare un fax?
can I make a phone call? – posso telefonare/posso fare un colpo di telefono?
can I borrow the telephone directory? – mi può prestare l'elenco telefonico?
letter – lettera.
postcard – cartolina.
e-mail – posta elettronica, e-mail.
net-surfer – navigatore.
courier – corriere, pony.

SHOPPING

I'd like to try the blue sandals/black shoes/brown boots – vorrei provare i sandali blu/le scarpe nere/gli stivali marroni.
do you have it/them in other colours? – ce l'ha in altri colori?
I take (shoe) size … – porto il numero …
I take (dress) size… – porto la taglia …
it's too loose/too tight/just right – mi sta largo/stretto/bene.
100 grams of … – un etto di …
300 grams of … – tre etti di …
can you give me a little more/less? – mi dia un po' di più/meno?
one kilo of … – un kilo (chilo) di …
five kilos of … – cinque chili di …
a litre/two litres of … – un litro/due litri di …

ACCOMMODATION

a reservation – una prenotazione.
I'd like to book a single/twin/double room – vorrei prenotare una camera singola/doppia/matrimoniale.
you must have a room for me; I booked weeks ago – è impossibile che non ci sia una camera per me; ho prenotato settimane fa.
I'd prefer a room with a bath/shower/window over the courtyard – preferirei una camera con vasca da bagno/doccia/finestra sul cortile.
can you bring me breakfast in bed? – mi porti la colazione al letto?

EATING & DRINKING

I'd like to book a table for four at eight – vorrei prenotare una tavola per quattro alle otto.
this is lukewarm; can you heat it up, please? – è tiepido; me lo può riscaldare, per favore?
this wine is corked; can you bring me another bottle, please? – questo vino sa di tappo; mi può portare un'altra bottiglia per favore?
can I have an ice bucket? – mi può portare un secchiello (di ghiaccio)?
that was poor/good/(really) delicious – era mediocre/buono/(davvero) ottimo.
if it's not a family secret, could you give me the recipe? – se non è un secreto della famiglia, mi potrebbe dare la ricetta?
the bill – il conto.
is service included? – è incluso il servizio?
I think there's a mistake in this bill – credo che il conto è sbagliato.
there's a fly in my soup – c'è una mosca nella mia zuppa.

(*See also* **Translating the Menu** *in chapter* **Restaurants**.)

FEMALE SELF-DEFENCE

no thank you, I can find my way by myself – no grazie, non ho bisogna di una guida.
I'm not interested – non mi interessa.
can you leave me alone – i vuole (or vuoi – informal – if you want to make it clear you feel very superior) lasciare in pace?
my boyfriend/my husband/my girlfriend is a boxing champion – mio ragazzo/mio marito/mia ragazza è un campione (una campionessa) di boxe (strangely, the final E is not pronounced).
if you don't leave me alone, I'll call the police – se non mi lascia (or lasci – informal) in pace, chiamerò la polizia.
fuck off – vaffanculo.

OR ALTERNATIVELY …

thank you, I'd been hoping someone like you would come along – grazie, speravo di trovare qualcuno come Lei.
I'd love to go for a spin on your Vespa – mi piacerebbe tanto fare un giro con Lei in Vespa.
I'd love to see your etchings – mi piacerebbe molto vedere le Sue incisioni.
you are the man/woman of my dreams – Lei è l'uomo/la donna dei miei sogni.

DAYS & NIGHTS

Monday – lunedì.
Tuesday – martedì.
Wednesday – mercoledì.
Thursday – giovedì.
Friday – venerdì.
Saturday – sabàto.
Sunday – domenica.
yesterday – ieri.
today – oggi.
tomorrow – domani.
morning – mattina.
afternoon – pomeriggio.
evening – sera.
night – notte.
weekend – fine settimana or, more usually, weekend.
have a good weekend! – buona domenica!
see you tomorrow/on Monday! – a domani!/a lunedì!

NUMBERS

0 zero; 1 uno; 2 due; 3 tre; 4 quattro; 5 cinque; 6 sei; 7 sette; 8 otto; 9 nove; 10 dieci; 11 undici; 12 dodici; 13 tredici; 14 quattordici; 15 quindici; 16 sedici; 17 diciasette; 18 diciotto; 19 dicianove; 20 venti; 30 trenta; 40 quaranta; 50 cinquanta; 60 sessanta; 70 settanta; 80 ottanta; 90 novanta; 100 cento; 200 duecento; 1,000 mille; 2,000 duemila; 1,000,000 un milione; 2,000,000 due milioni; 1,000,000,000 un miliardo; 2,000,000,000 due miliardi;
5,347,293,751 cinquemiliarditrecentoquaranta-settemilioniduecento-novantatremilasettecentocinquantuno.

Architectural Terms

Apse – large recess at the end of a church.
Baldacchino – stone canopy over an altar.
Basilica – rectangular public building, often used as a church by the early Christians.
Campanile – bell tower.
Caryatid – pillar carved in the shape of a woman.
Entablature – section above a column including the frieze and cornice.
Greek cross – cross with arms of equal length, adopted as the floor plan for churches.
Loggia – gallery, open on one side.
Palazzo – important building (not necessarily a palace).
Peristyle – temple or court surrounded by columns.
Piazza – town or city square.
Rococo – highly decorative style, popular in the eighteenth century.
Trompe l'œil – deceptive stylistic effect (often to make a surface appear three-dimensional).

Directory

days later. There is an information line: 46 86 29 28 (8am to noon, 5pm-7pm, Monday to Friday).

Permesso di Lavoro (Work Permit)

In theory, all non-Italian citizens who are employed in Italy need a work permit. Application forms can be obtained from the *Ispettorato del Lavoro* (Works Inspectorate) in Via Cesare de Lollis, 6 (44 49 31). The form has to be signed by your employer and you'll also need to take your *permesso di soggiorno* and a photocopy back to the *Ispettorato* when you apply. The office is open from 9am to 12.30pm and from 2.45pm to 4.30pm, Monday to Thursday, and from 9am to noon on Friday and Saturday. It takes about 60 days to get your *permesso di lavoro*. Don't rush to get one: in many cases the requirement is waived, or your employer organises everything for you.

Residenza (Residency)

This is your registered address in Italy, and you'll need it for such transactions as buying a car or getting customs clearance on goods brought from abroad. Take your *permesso di soggiorno* (which must be valid for at least another year) and your passport to your local *circoscrizione* office (*see* **Carta d'Identita** above). They will check that the rubbish collection tax (*nettezza urbana*) for your address has been paid (ask your landlord about this) before issuing the certificate, which can take several weeks.

Work

Casual employment can be hard to come by in Rome, so unless you're prepared for babysitting or your Italian is

good enough for you to be employed in the few bars not manned exclusively by the owners' relations, try to sort out work before you arrive. Most of the lower-paid jobs available are not declared to the authorities, and so do not require documentation.

If you have a Teaching English as a Foreign Language qualification, you may be able to pick up some work (but probably not a full-time contract) from the plethora of language schools. These and the equally numerous translation agencies are mobbed with applicants, so it helps if you've got more to offer than a raw qualification. The Food and Agriculture Organization of the United Nations is now very difficult to get into unless you're well qualified in the specific skills they are looking for.

The classified ads paper *Porta Portese* (published on Tuesday and Friday) has a daunting number of job advertisements and sometimes has offers worth following up. Other good places to look are *Wanted in Rome* and the noticeboards in the English-language bookshops (*see chapters* **Media** *and* **Shopping**: **Bookshops**). You could also place an ad yourself

in any of the media above. For serious jobs look in *Il Messaggero*, the *Herald Tribune*, the *Guardian* and *La Repubblica*.

Outside the PDS (ex-Communist Party) centre in Via dei Giubbonari, just off Campo de'Fiori, there's a noticeboard where you can advertise for free and may find anything from private English classes to cleaning jobs.

Accommodation

Whether you want to live alone or find a flat share, the best places to look for accommodation are, again, *Porta Portese* (but you'll have to move pretty quickly), *Wanted in Rome*, the English-language bookshops and the PDS centre. It's also worth looking out for *Affittasi* (for rent) notices on buildings, and thumbing through the classified ads in *Il Messaggero* on Thursday and Sunday.

When you move into an apartment in Rome, it's normal to pay a month's rent in advance plus two months' deposit, which should be refunded when you move out, although some landlords create problems and delays over this. You'll probably get a year's contract, which is normally renewable. If you rent through an agency, expect to pay the equivalent of two months' rent in commission.

EuroCenter

Via della Grande Muraglia, 336-342 (52 20 53 91/fax 52 20 53 89). **Open** 9am-7.30pm Mon-Fri. As well as having a range of furnished and unfurnished apartments for rent, this agency helps with relocation, bureaucracy and shipping problems.

Gondrand

Via Idrovore della Magliana, 163 (65 74 63 40/fax 65 74 63 55). **Open** 9am-1pm, 2-6pm, Mon-Fri. This excellent international and local shipping company can organise the shipping of your goods to Italy. It also provides storage facilities and free estimates. English spoken.

International Services USA

Via del Babuino, 79 (36 00 00 18/9/fax 36 00 00 37). **Open** 9am-7.30pm Mon-Fri.
An English-speaking office offering short- and long-term rentals of villas and apartments.

Property International

Viale Aventino, 79 (574 31 70/fax 574 31 82). **Open** 9.30am-1pm, 3-5.30pm, Mon-Fri.
This agency, staffed by native English speakers, offers weekly and monthy villas and apartments in Tuscany, as well as short- and long-term rentals in Rome. Staff are often available outside official hours.

Health

EU citizens are entitled to state health care in Italy. Get an E111 form before your leave for Rome, then take it to your nearest health centre (USL – see the phone book under *Azienda Unita Sanita Locale*). If you don't have an E111, take your passport, *permesso di soggiorno, residenza* and *codice fiscale*. Non-EC citizens should take their documents to the local INPS (national insurance board) and will have to pay an annual fee (currently L1.2 million).

You have to contribute to the costs of visits to specialists, lab tests, X-rays, scans and so on, and prescription drugs. This contribution is called a *ticket* and is payable immediately before or after the goods or services are received. Family planning advice is available through the state system but dentistry (other than emergency) is not.

Driving

If you're staying in Italy for more than a year and intend to drive, you'll need an Italian driving licence and for this you'll have to present, at the very least, a *certificato di residenza*. For holders of the new-style EU driving licences this involves a relatively simple trip to the nearest *Motorizzazione civile* (see the

phone book) with your current licence, passport and *certificato di residenza*. You will be issued with a slip of paper which you have to attach to your licence. If you haven't got it after about six months, try ringing 16 72 32 323. In all probability, however, you'll never get through and will have to return to the *Motorizzazione* office.

For everybody else, including EU citizens with old-style licences, the procedure becomes more complicated. As well as your passport and *certificato di residenza*, you'll need a health certificate from your (Italian) doctor, three passport photos, your original licence (plus photocopy and a certified translation into Italian), and a declaration (signed by you) that the licence is valid. The citizens of nearly all non-EU countries still have to take a driving test, which includes written road safety and basic car maintenance.

The licence is valid for ten years, but you'll need to buy a stamp every year (current price L70,000) to prove you've paid the licence tax. You can get these in *tabacchi*.

Opening a Bank Account

A lot depends on the bank you choose, but in general Italian banks are less customer-friendly than in other parts of the world. Ask around among the other non-Italians you know because not all banks offer the full range of facilities (such as automatic banking cards, called *bancomat*) to foreign clients and some can take weeks to credit your account with cheques. You should, in any case, be prepared to provide the bank of your choice (and choose one that's easy to get to because it'll make your life a lot easier if you do all your transactions at your own branch) with a valid *permesso di soggiorno* or *certificato di*

residenza, your *codice fiscale*, proof of regular income from your employer (or a fairly substantial sum to deposit — Italian banks aren't interested in dealing with pocket money) and, of course, your passport. You won't necessarily be granted immediate access to the money you've deposited and, although some interest is paid even on current accounts, you'll be charged more than you are in most other European countries for every transaction you make.

Schools

There are several international, British, American and other foreign schools in Rome, but these tend to be extremely expensive (see the schools supplement published annually in *Wanted in Rome*). To get your child into the Italian state system, you'll need the birth certificate, vaccination certificates, a *certificato di stato di famiglia*, your child's *permesso di soggiorno*. You'll also need to produce a certificate proving the level your child had reached at his or her last school which must have been translated into Italian at the Italian consulate of the country you are coming from. These must all be taken to the school of your choice, where you'll be given a form to fill in. Schools are listed in the phone directory under *Scuole pubbliche*.

Telephones

To get a new phone line put in, contact your nearest Telecom centre (see the phone directory or ring freephone 187). It costs about L250,000 and takes a couple of days.

Voting

Only Italian citizens can vote in national elections. However, EU citizens who are living permanently in Rome can vote in EU and local elections.

Further Reading

Ancient Rome

Catullus *The Poems*
Catullus' poems are well worth a read: sometimes malicious, sometimes pornographic, and occasionally exquisite.
Dudley, Donald *Roman Society*
A concise account of the history of Rome from the ninth century BC until the fourth century AD: recommended if you want a broad overview which includes culture, politics and economics.
Gibbon, Edward *The Decline and Fall of the Roman Empire*
The definitive account; to be dipped into.
Grant, Michael *History of Rome*
This, like all Grant's books on the ancient world, is highly readable and full of useful factual information.
Graves, Robert *I, Claudius; Claudius the God*
Damning portraits of the imperial family – especially the women – which help flesh out the historical facts.
Juvenal *Satires*
A contemporary view of ancient Rome's seedy underbelly.
Lawrence, DH *Etruscan Places*
Lawrence frolics empathetically through countryside formerly inhabited by sensual Etruscans.
Lefkovitch, Mary and Fant, Maureen *Women's Life in Greece and Rome*
A riveting collection of extracts, covering everything from ancient gynaecology to how to select a wet-nurse.
Massie, Allen *Augustus; Tiberius; Caesar*
Popular rewrites of history, in biographical or autobiographical form. Strong on ancient history, while bringing emperors and their families to life.
Ovid *The Erotic Poems*
Includes raunchy, ironic love poems, a manual on cosmetics, and the *Ars Amores*, a handbook for cynical lovers, which got the poet banished from Rome. Ted Hughes' 1997 translation of *Metamorphoses*, called *After Ovid*, is compelling.
Pomeroy, Sarah *Goddesses, Whores, Slaves and Wives*
A readable, meticulously researched account of the lives of women in ancient Rome and Greece.
Sear, Frank *Roman Architecture*
An accessible overview of ancient Roman architecture and building techniques, with plenty of illustrations.
Shakespeare, William *Julius Caesar*
Get into the mood for a visit to the Forum with a re-reading of this classic.
Suetonius, Gaius *The Twelve Caesars*
Salacious, scandal-packed biographies of Roman rulers from Julius Caesar to Domitian. A great read.
Virgil *The Aeneid*
The founding myth of Rome, written as propaganda for Augustus. A great yarn.

History, Art, Religion & Culture

Cellini, Benvenuto *Autobiography*
Bitchy, slanderous and egotistical tales of the Renaissance goldsmith's street brawls, sexual conquests and art.
Ginsborg, Paul *A History of Contemporary Italy*
Excellent introduction to the ups and downs of post-war Italy.
Hebblethwaite, Peter *In the Vatican*
Opinionated insights into the inner workings of the Vatican.
Hibbard, Howard *Bernini*
An accessible interpretation of Bernini's work, with pictures.

Hibbert, Christopher *Biography of a City*
An engaging, effortlessly readable account of Rome's history, from the Etruscans to Mussolini. Great illustrations too.
Levey, Michael *The High Renaissance*
A readable, well-illustrated guide to the era of Raphael, Michelangelo *et al.*
Masson, Georgina *Courtesans of the Italian Renaissance*
A revealing, entertaining study of the most famous courtesans of the fifteenth and sixteenth centuries. Like all books by this indomitable American traveller, contains fascinating anecdotal insights into Roman life.
Morton, HV *A Traveller in Rome*
Classic Roman guide book. Written in the 1950s and still highly readable.
Ranke-Heinemann, Uta *Eunuchs for the Kingdom of Heaven*
An engagingly witty critique of the Catholic church's attitude to sex, from Saint Jerome to JPII.
Stille, Alexander *Excellent Cadavers*
The story of the rise, successes, failure and ultimate assassinations of anti-Mafia prosecutors Giovanni Falcone and Paolo Borsellino.
Vasari, Giorgio *Lives of the Artists*
This sixteenth century biography of great masters was the first art history book but is purely Florentine in outlook: chiefly responsible for consigning the artists and craftsmen of Rome to the dustbin of history.
Warner, Marina *Alone of all her Sex*
An impressive, stimulating and beautifully written account of the cult of the Virgin Mary.
Wittkower, Rudolf *Art and Architecture in Italy 1600-1750*
Everything you ever wanted to know about the Baroque. Loads of illustrations and photos.
Yallop, David *In God's Name*
A sensational but fun tale of Vatican intrigue and the death of Pope John Paul I.

Fiction

Davis, Lindsay *Venus in Copper (etc)*
Series of lightweight comic crime thrillers set in ancient Rome.
Dibdin, Michael *Vendetta (etc)*
Thriller set in deftly-evoked contemporary Rome, where cop-hero Aurelio Zen hangs out in the *Vineria* on Campo de' Fiori. Other Zen adventures continue the theme.
Hawthorne, Nathaniel *The Marble Faun*
A quaint, moralising novel about two female artists in Rome. Stilted characters, but a page-turner nonetheless.
James, Henry *The Portrait of a Lady (etc)*
James' adoration of Rome is legendary, and some of his greatest works are set here. Try *Portrait, Daisy Miller*, and a couple of gushing essays in *Italian Hours*.
Morante, Elsa *History*
A brilliant evocation of everday life for a Roman woman during and after World War II.
Moravia, Alberto *Roman Tales; Two Women (etc)*
Grandfather of post-war Italian literature, Moravia was a keen observer of Roman life, though his literary clout sometimes outstripped the quality of his work.
Wharton, Edith *Roman Fever*
Stinging short story from 1911 about two old American ladies in Rome reminiscing about the past.
Yourcenar, Marguerite *The Memoirs of Hadrian*
A sombre novel, told by Hadrian as he approaches death.

Index

Advertisers' Index

Please refer to the relevant sections for
addresses/telephone numbers

Maps

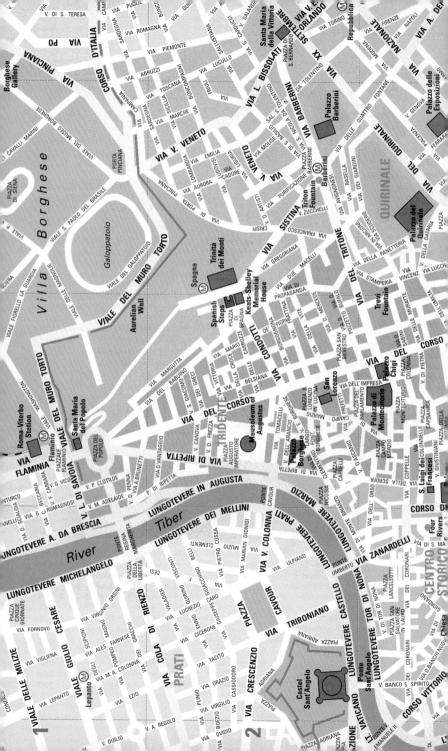

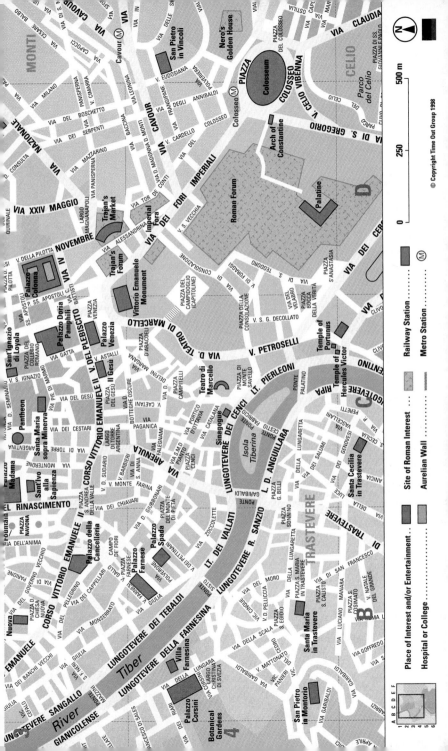

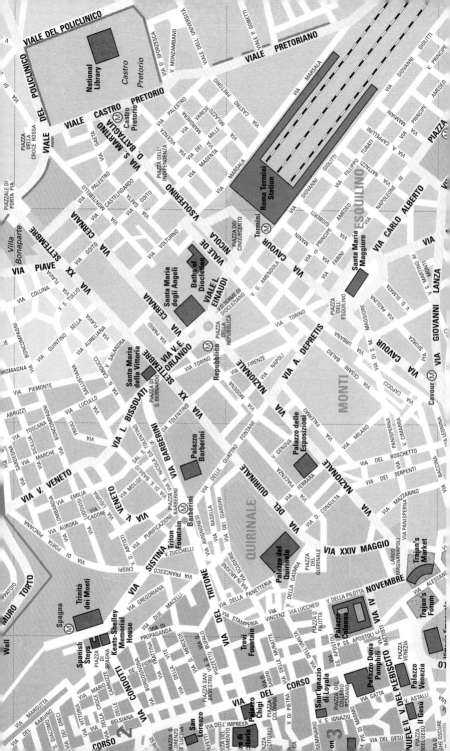

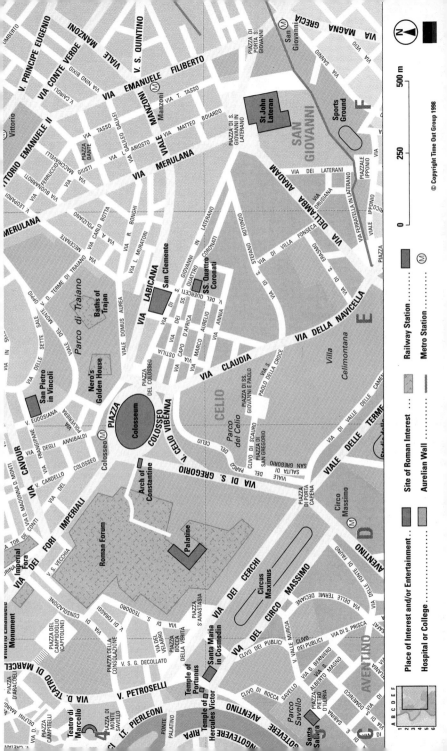

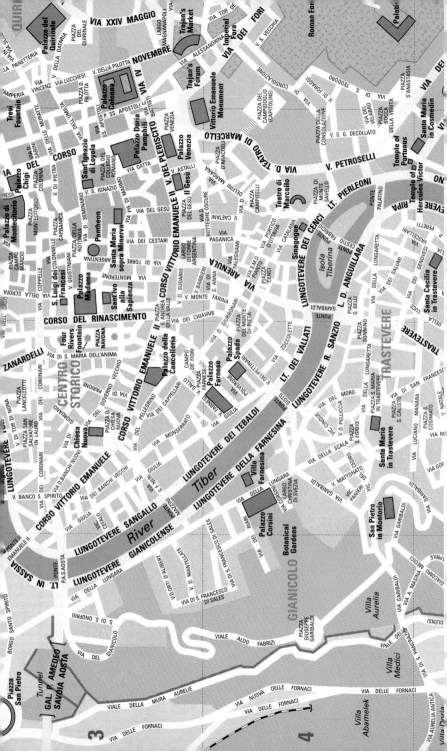

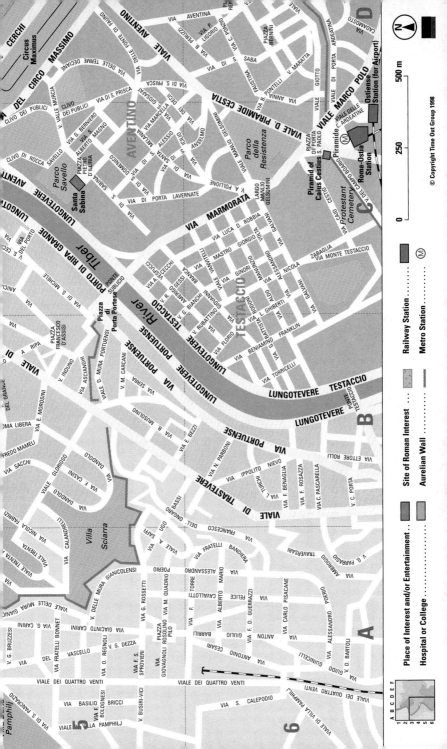

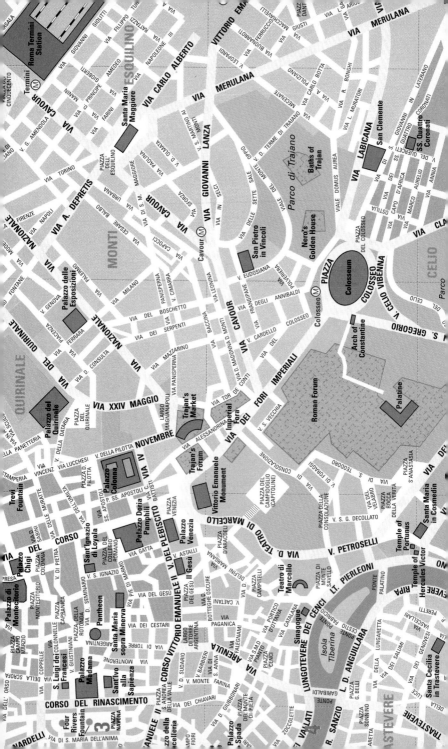

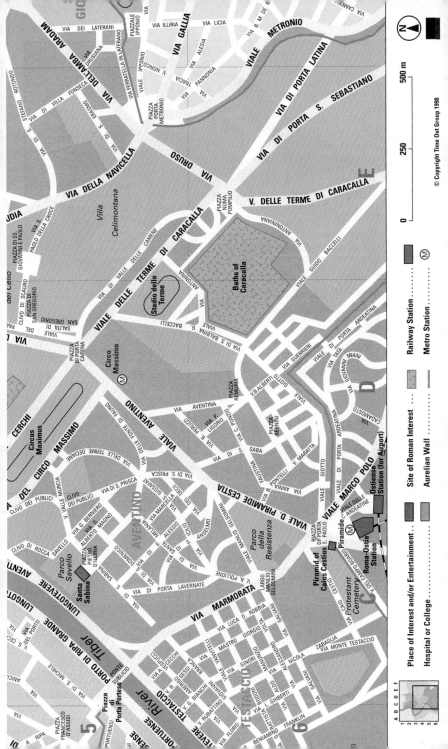

Open every day between 6.30 pm and 2.00 am

♦ *Salad bar from monday to friday*
  from 12.30 am to 3.00 pm

♦ *International ambience*

♦ *Music and sports events*
  every day live from satellite

Credit Cards: MASTERCARD, VISA, EUROCARD,
EDC, AMERICAN EXPRESS, MAESTRO, ELECTRON

Via delle Coppelle, 13 (Pantheon)
ROMA - Tel. 06 - 683.22.20

Street Index

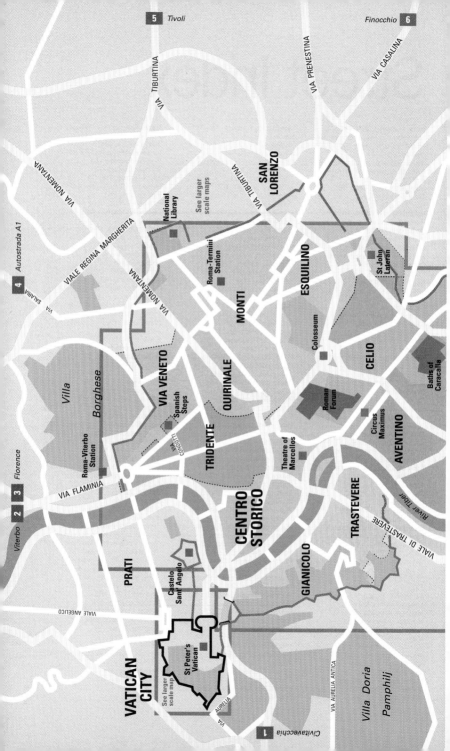

Around Rome

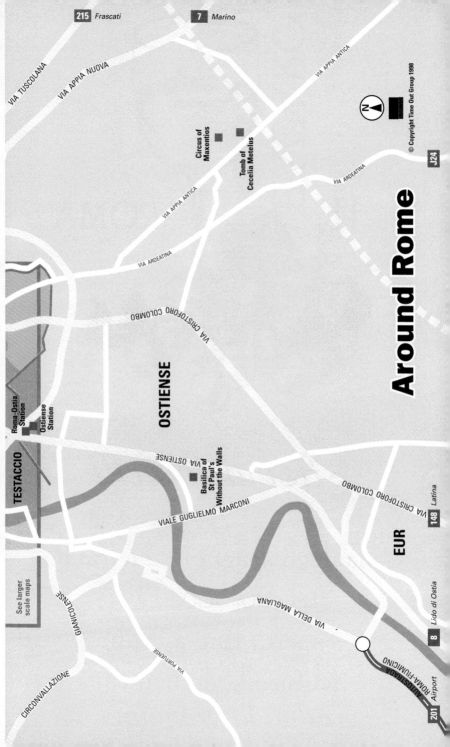

215 Frascati
7 Marino

VIA TUSCOLANA
VIA APPIA NUOVA

VIA APPIA ANTICA

Circus of Maxentios

Tomb of Cecelia Metelus

VIA APPIA ANTICA

VIA ARDEATINA

© Copyright Time Out Group 1998

J24

N

VIA APPIA ANTICA

VIA ARDEATINA

VIA CRISTOFORO COLOMBO

OSTIENSE

Roma-Ostia Station

Ostiense Station

TESTACCIO

VIA OSTIENSE

Basilica of St Paul's Without the Walls

VIALE GUGLIELMO MARCONI

VIA CRISTOFORO COLOMBO

148 Latina

EUR

See larger scale maps

GIANICOLENSE

VIA PORTUENSE

CIRCONVALLAZIONE

VIA DELLA MAGLIANA

8 Lido di Ostia

AUTOSTRADA ROMA-FIUMICINO

201 Airport

IL **BACARO** ROMA

sfizi ai fornelli

via degli spagnoli, 27 roma
tel. 06/6864110
aperto fino a tardi
(chiuso la domenica)
é gradita la prenotazione

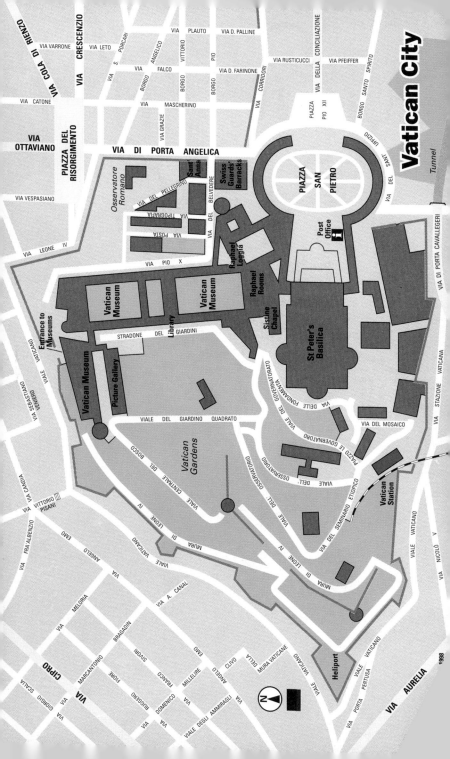

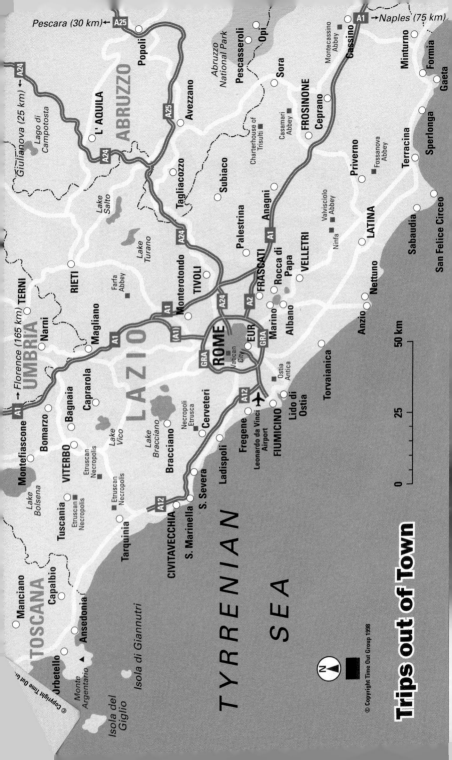

Trips out of Town

© Copyright Time Out Group 1998